Wissenschaftliche Untersuchungen
zum Neuen Testament · 2. Reihe

Herausgeber / Editor
Jörg Frey (Zürich)

Mitherausgeber/Associate Editors
Markus Bockmuehl (Oxford) · James A. Kelhoffer (Uppsala)
Tobias Nicklas (Regensburg) · Janet Spittler (Charlottesville, VA)
J. Ross Wagner (Durham, NC)

584

Sajan George Perepparambil

Jesus as the Way to the Father in the Gospel of John

A Study of the Way Motif and John 14,6 in Its Context

Mohr Siebeck

Sajan George Perepparambil, Catholic priest, Manjummel Province of the Order of the Discalced Carmelites (OCD); 2012 Mag. Theol. and 2018 Doctorate in Biblical Studies, University of Vienna, Austria; currently professor of Bible at Jyotir Bhavan, Institute of Theology and Spirituality, Kalamassery, Kerala.
orcid.org/0000-0003-1088-5781

ISBN 978-3-16-161925-0 / eISBN 978-3-16-161926-7
DOI 10.1628/978-3-16-161926-7

ISSN 0340-9570 / eISSN 2568-7484
(Wissenschaftliche Untersuchungen zum Neuen Testament, 2. Reihe)

The Deutsche Nationalbibliothek lists this publication in the Deutsche Nationalbibliographie; detailed bibliographic data are available at *http://dnb.dnb.de*.

© 2023 Mohr Siebeck Tübingen, Germany. www.mohrsiebeck.com

This book may not be reproduced, in whole or in part, in any form (beyond that permitted by copyright law) without the publisher's written permission. This applies particularly to reproductions, translations and storage and processing in electronic systems.

The book was printed on non-aging paper by Laupp & Göbel in Gomaringen, and bound by Buchbinderei Nädele in Nehren.

Printed in Germany.

In Loving Memory of My Parents
Perepparambil George and Annamkutty

Acknowledgements

The Gospel of John is like a magic pool in which an infant can paddle and an elephant can swim. In my effort to understand the mysteries of this deeply spiritual Gospel by means of a monograph, first and foremost, I thank God for his providence and guidance in writing this work (cf. John 16,13). I gratefully remember my parents, Perepparambil George and Annamkutty, my brother Xavier, my sister Sheena and family relatives. I cherish the memory of my late but living mother who was an ardent lover and propagator of the word of God. While I was writing this work, she advised me to ask God to understand the hidden mysteries behind the word of God, citing Jer 33,3: "Call to me and I will answer you, and will tell you great and hidden things that you have not known". She taught me that with intellectual gymnastics alone one cannot understand the mysteries of the word of God. To the honour and loving memory of my parents, I dedicate this monograph.

This work is a slightly revised version of my doctoral dissertation, which I defended successfully on 27th September 2018 at the Faculty of Catholic Theology of the University of Vienna, Austria, obtaining a doctorate in the field of Biblical Studies (Bibelwissenschaft) with Summa cum Laude. I am greatly indebted to the supervisors (Doktorväter) of this dissertation, namely o. Univ.-Prof. Dr. Roman Kühschelm (University of Vienna) and em. Univ.-Prof. Dr. Martin Hasitschka SJ (University of Innsbruck). I thank sincerely Prof. Roman Kühschelm for his painstaking efforts to read this dissertation meticulously in order to give scholarly and critical corrections. In my attempt to choose a topic, it was Prof. Martin Hasitschka SJ who encouraged me to study John 14,6. I am heartily grateful to him for his goodwill to supervise this dissertation, for reading it and for giving scholarly suggestions and corrections. I am thankful to the examiners (Beurteiler) of this dissertation, namely Univ.-Prof. Dr. Christoph Niemand (Linz) and ao. Univ.-Prof. Dr. Martin Stowasser (Vienna) for their critical remarks and valuable suggestions. I am also bound to thank Prof. Johannes Beutler SJ (Sankt Georgen, Frankfurt), who provided me with a comfortable stay in Frankfurt for discussions with him and is ever available to me to give his scholarly opinion. I remember with gratitude Prof. Georg Fischer SJ (Innsbruck), Prof. Gerald O'Collins SJ (Melbourne), late Prof. Larry W. Hurtado (Edinburgh) and late Prof. Don Giancarlo Biguzzi (Urbanianum, Rome) for their suggestions and encouragement. I extend sincere thanks to my Old Testament professors of the University of Vienna, namely Prof. Georg Braulik OSB, Prof. Ludger Schwienhorst-Schönberger the Joseph-Ratzinger Prize laureate of 2021 and Prof. Agnethe Siquans. I am grateful to Mr. Robert Szczypiorkovski, the librarian of the theological faculty in Vienna for his support and friendship and also to the librarians of Pontifical Biblical Institute (Biblicum), Rome. It was the Austrian province of my Order (Order of Discalced Carmelites, OCD) who provided me with all facilities and financial support for my stay and study in Vienna. I thank sincerely the present Austrian provincial Fr. Alexander Schellerer OCD, the former provincials, Fr. Roberto Maria Pirastu OCD and Fr. Paul Weingartner OCD, all members of the Austrian province, especially the Vienna community in which I lived, for their generosity, brotherly fraternity and support.

I extend my heartfelt gratitude to the French OCD community in Paris and the Italian OCD community in Rome for providing me with the accommodation in my effort to learn French and Italian languages respectively. I owe a debt of thanks to the late provincial of Manjummel Province, Fr. Datius Kanjiramukkil OCD who sent me to Austria for higher studies in Sacred Scripture, my present provincial, Fr. Thomas Marottikkaparambil OCD, the OCD communities in Dilldorf and Siegburg and to the parishioners of St. Josef, Essen-Ruhrhalbinsel, where I worked as assistant parish priest for four years, for their support and encouragement. I am also grateful to my present superior Fr. Wilson Srampickal OCD and all the members of Jyotir Bhavan (Institute of Theology and Spirituality), where I currently stay and teach Bible, for their brotherly concern and support.

I thank the chief editor Prof. Dr. Jörg Frey (University of Zürich) and the associate editors of WUNT II for accepting my dissertation into this prestigious series. I would also like to thank the Mohr Siebeck team in Tübingen, especially Katharina Gutekunst, Elena Müller, Tobias Stäbler, Markus Kirchner, Jana Trispel and Josephine Krönke for their pleasant cooperation at the various stages of preparing this manuscript for publication. I express my gratitude to Gerd Frömgen (Essen) and Benedict Whyte (London) for checking the English language. Finally, I remember with thanks Franz Kampmann (Essen) and all those who have encouraged and helped me in various ways.

Sajan George (Paul) Perepparambil OCD
Jyotir Bhavan,
Institute of Theology and Spirituality,
Kalamassery, Kerala, INDIA.
01.03.2023

Table of Contents

Acknowledgements VII
Abbreviations XVIII

General Introduction 1

Part One: A Study of Way Motif

Chapter I: Way Motif in Greek-Jewish Literature 33

1. "Way" in Classical Greek Literature 33
  1.1 Various Terminologies 33
  1.2 Meaning and Usage of ὁδός 34
    1.2.1 Literal Meaning and Usage of ὁδός 34
    1.2.2 Metaphorical Meaning and Usage of ὁδός 35
  1.3 Conclusion 39

2. "Way" in the Hebrew Bible 40
  2.1 Important Nouns and Their Significance 41
    2.1.1 דֶּרֶךְ 41
      2.1.1.1 A Survey 41
      2.1.1.2 Theological Usage 44
    2.1.2 אֹרַח 56
    2.1.3 נָתִיב and נְתִיבָה 57
    2.1.4 מְסִלָּה and מַסְלוּל 57
  2.2 Important Verbs and Their Significance 58
    2.2.1 הָלַךְ 58
      2.2.1.1 Secular Usage 59
      2.2.1.2 Theological Usage 59
    2.2.2 יָצָא 64
    2.2.3 יָרַד and עָלָה 65

	2.2.4 נהל 66
	2.2.5 נָחָה 66
	2.2.6 נָהַג I 67
	2.2.7 דֶּרֶךְ 67
	2.2.8 בוֹא 68
	2.2.8.1 Promise-Fulfilment 68
	2.2.8.2 Coming of God/Saviour to His People 69
	2.2.8.3 Coming of the People to God 69
2.3 Conclusion 70

3. "Way" in the Septuagint 72

3.1 Important Way-Lexemes 73
    3.1.1 Ὁδός … 73
        3.1.1.1 In General 73
        3.1.1.2 In the Deutero-Canonical Books 74
    3.1.2 Other Way-Lexemes 75
3.2 Some Important Verbs of Journey 75
    3.2.1 Verbs for "to and fro Movement" 76
        3.2.1.1 Πορεύομαι and ἔρχομαι 76
        3.2.1.2 Ἀναβαίνω and καταβαίνω 77
    3.2.2 Verbs for "Leading" 78
        3.2.2.1 Ἄγω … 78
        3.2.2.2 Ἐξάγω … 79
        3.2.2.3 Ὁδηγέω … 79
3.3 Conclusion 79

4. "Way" in the Dead Sea Scrolls 80

5. "Way" in the Works of Philo and Josephus 85

5.1 Philo of Alexandria 85
5.2 Josephus Flavius 88

6. "Way" in the New Testament 88

6.1 Synoptic Gospels 89
6.2 Acts 90
6.3 Letters 92
6.4 Revelation 93
6.5 Conclusion 94

7. Journey Motif in the Gospel of John 94

7.1 Jesus' Journeys in General 95

    7.1.1 Cosmic Journey 95
        7.1.1.1 Journey from the Father into this World........................96
        7.1.1.2 Departure from this World to the Father.....................101
        7.1.1.3 Return to the Believers..103
    7.1.2 Jesus' Geographical Journey..105
  7.2 Jesus' Cosmic Journey in John 13–14..107
  7.3 Believers' Journey to Jesus...111
  7.4 Conclusion..114

8. Contribution to the Study of Way in John 14,6..115

  8.1 Prophetic Fulfilment of Future Salvation in Jesus as the Way............116
  8.2 The Literary Background of Johannine Journey Language 118

Part Two: A Study of John 14,6 in Its Context

Chapter II: John 14,6 in Its Literary Context............................ 123

1. Preliminary Observations..123

  1.1 Genre of the Farewell Discourse..123
  1.2 Unity of the Farewell Discourse 127
  1.3 Structure and Organization of John 13–14 129

2. Analysis of the Near and Immediate Context (John 13–14)....................138

  2.1 The Preceding Near Context (John 13) 139
    2.1.1 The Backdrop of the Farewell Discourse (13,1–30) 139
        2.1.1.1 The Setting: The Cosmic Journey
                and the Cosmic Conflict (vv. 1–3) 139
        2.1.1.2 "The Way to Go" Prefigured (vv. 4–5)........................141
        2.1.1.3 Meaning of "the Way to Go" Explained (vv. 6–20)......141
        2.1.1.4 Judas' Journey into Darkness (vv. 21–30)....................143
    2.1.2 Announcement of Jesus' Glorification (vv. 31–38)..................144
        2.1.2.1 Glorification (vv. 31–32) 145
        2.1.2.2 Departure (v. 33)..146
        2.1.2.3 Commandment of Love (vv. 34–35)............................146
        2.1.2.4 Prediction of Peter's Denial (vv. 36–38) 147
  2.2 The Immediate Context: Exegesis of John 14,1–14.............................147
    2.2.1 Textual Criticism 147
    2.2.2 Structure 151
    2.2.3 Syntactical Analysis..153

       2.2.4 Translation 155
       2.2.5 Interpretation: The Command to Believe
            and Jesus' Journey to the Father 156
            2.2.5.1 Command to Believe (v. 1) 156
            2.2.5.2 Jesus' Going and Coming Again (vv. 2–3) 158
            2.2.5.3 Jesus as the Way to the Father (vv. 4–6) 163
            2.2.5.4 Jesus' Oneness with the Father (vv. 7–11) 165
            2.2.5.5 Fruits of Belief in Jesus (vv. 12–14) 168
   2.3 The Following Near Context (vv. 15–31) 171
       2.3.1 The Command to Love and the Trinitarian God's Journey
            to the Believers (vv. 15–24) 171
            2.3.1.1 The Command to Love (v. 15) 172
            2.3.1.2 The Coming of the Paraclete/the Spirit of Truth
                  (vv. 16–17) 172
            2.3.1.3 Coming of the Son (vv. 18–21) 173
            2.3.1.4 The Coming of the Father with the Son (vv. 22–24) 174
       2.3.2 Recapitulation/Conclusion (vv. 25–31) 175
            2.3.2.1 The Eschatological Gifts of Jesus (vv. 25–29) 176
            2.3.2.2 Cosmic Conflict and Cosmic Journey (vv. 30–31) 178
   2.4 Conclusion 180

Chapter III: The Unity and Integrity of John 14,6 185

1. Vocabulary in v. 6b 186

2. Relation between v. 6a and v. 6b 187

3. Relation between v. 6 and v. 7 189

4. Thrust of John 14,4–7 190

5. John 14,6 as an ἐγώ εἰμι-Saying 192

6. Conclusion 192

Chapter IV: Possible Background of John 14,6
and Its Context 194

1. Introductory Views 194

2. *Background of "Way" (14,4–6) and Its Context (14,2–3)*.......................197

3. *Background of "the Way and the Truth and the Life"*............................206

4. *Background of John 14,6b*..209

5. *Parallels Between the Contexts of Isa 40,3 and John 14,6*....................213

6. *Influence of Isaiah Quotations in John 12,38–41 upon John 14,7–14*.....216

   6.1 A Brief Examination of John 12,38–41..216
   6.2 Influence of John 12,38–41 upon John 14,7–14 and Its Context........220

7. *Conclusion* 223

Chapter V: Important Motifs of John 14,6 in the Gospel Context..226

1. "Truth" (ἀλήθεια) in the Gospel of John 226

   1.1 Grace and Truth in Jesus Christ (1,14.17)..229
   1.2 Doing the Truth (3,21)..229
   1.3 Worship in Spirit and Truth (4,23.24)..230
   1.4 Witness to the Truth (5,33)..230
   1.5 Knowing and Saying the Truth (8,32.40.45.46; 16,7) 231
   1.6 Truth and Life (8,44) 231
   1.7 Jesus as the Truth (14,6) 232
   1.8 The Spirit of Truth (14,17; 15,26; 16,13)...232
   1.9 Sanctification in the Truth (17,17.19) 233
   1.10 Truth on Trial (18,37.38) 234
   1.11 Conclusion..235

2. "Life" (ζωή) in the Gospel of John 237

   2.1 Light and Life (1,4; 8,12)...239
   2.2 Belief and Life (3,15–16.36)..240
   2.3 The Living Water and the Life (4,14) 241
   2.4 Reaping for Eternal Life (4,36)..242
   2.5 Jesus' Authority over Life (5,24.26.29) 243
   2.6 Witnesses to Jesus and Life (5,39.40)...244
   2.7 The Bread of Life (6,27.33.35.40.47.48.51.53.54.63.68) 245
   2.8 Jesus' Words and Life (6,63.68) 248
   2.9 Gate/Shepherd and Life (10,10.28) 249

2.10 Resurrection and Life (11,25) 250
2.11 Earthly Life (ψυχή) and Eternal Life (12,25)...........................251
2.12 Commandment and Eternal Life (12,50) 251
2.13 Jesus as the Life (14,6) 252
2.14 Knowledge of God and Jesus and Eternal Life (17,2.3) 252
2.15 Purpose of the Gospel and Life (20,31)..................................253
2.16 Conclusion..254

3. Relation of Way with Truth and Life 255

4. "Father" in the Gospel of John 260

4.1 Jesus' Relationship with the Father/God 262
  4.1.1 Jesus' Exclusive Relationship with the Father.........................263
    4.1.1.1 Jesus as the Only Son of the Father (1,14)....................263
    4.1.1.2 Jesus as the Exegete of the Father (1,18)......................263
    4.1.1.3 Jesus' Authority from the Father over Everything
          (3,35; 13,3a; 17,2)..264
    4.1.1.4 God as Jesus' Own Father and Jesus' Equality
          with God (John 5) 265
    4.1.1.5 Jesus as the Son of Man with the Father's Seal (6,27)..268
    4.1.1.6 Jesus as the Only One Who Has Seen the Father (6,46)268
    4.1.1.7 Jesus' Relationship with "the Living Father" (6,57).....269
    4.1.1.8 Jesus' Origin and Identity under Question (8,12–59) ...269
    4.1.1.9 Jesus' Oneness with the Father as the Messiah
          and the Son of God (John 10)...270
    4.1.1.10 Jesus' Prayer to the Father
           (11,41–42; 12,27–28; 17,1–26) 271
    4.1.1.11 The Father as the Provenance and Destination
           of Jesus' Journey 273
    4.1.1.12 Jesus' Relationship with the Father in Various Ways 273
  4.1.2 Jesus' Relationship with "God" (θεός) 274
4.2 Believers' Relationship with the Father/God 274
  4.2.1 In Terms of πατήρ... 275
  4.2.2 In Terms of θεός... 275
  4.2.3 Significance of "No One Comes to the Father
      Except through Me"..276
    4.2.3.1 Significance of "No One" (οὐδείς) 276
    4.2.3.2 Significance of "Come to" (ἔρχομαι πρός) 278
    4.2.3.3 Significance of "the Father" (ὁ πατήρ) 279
    4.2.3.4 Significance of "Except through Me" (εἰ μὴ δι' ἐμοῦ).289
4.3 Conclusion..290

Chapter VI: John 14,6 in the Context of "I Am"-Sayings 293

1. Introductory Remarks 293

2. Classification 295

3. Possible Sources and Background of ἐγώ εἰμι-Sayings 296
    3.1 Exodus 3,14 297
    3.2 אֲנִי יְהוָה and אֲנִי הוּא 298
    3.3 "I"-Style Speeches in Wisdom Literature 302
    3.4 Synoptic Tradition and Johannine ἐγώ εἰμι 303

4. Ἐγώ εἰμι without Images 304
    4.1 Ἐγώ εἰμι Addressed to the Samaritan Woman (4,26) 305
    4.2 Ἐγώ εἰμι Addressed to the Disciples on the Waters (6,20) ... 306
    4.3 Ἐγώ εἰμι Addressed to the Jews (8,18.24.28.58) 308
    4.4 Ἐγώ εἰμι before the Betrayal (13,19) 311
    4.5 Ἐγώ εἰμι Addressed to Jesus' Enemies (18,5.6.8) 312

5. Ἐγώ εἰμι with Images 314
    5.1 Jesus as the Bread of Life (6,35.41.48.51) 315
    5.2 Jesus as the Light of the World (8,12) 317
    5.3 Jesus as the Gate and the Good Shepherd (10,7.9.11.14) 319
        5.3.1 Context of the Shepherd Discourse 320
            5.3.1.1 Macro Context 320
            5.3.1.2 Micro Context 321
        5.3.2 Structure 322
        5.3.3 Interpretation 324
            5.3.3.1 The παροιμία (vv. 1–6) 325
            5.3.3.2 Jesus as the Gate (vv. 7–10) 328
            5.3.3.3 Jesus as the Good Shepherd (vv. 11–18) 334
        5.3.4 Conclusion 335
    5.4 Jesus as the Resurrection and the Life (11,25–26) 336
    5.5 Jesus as the Vine (15,1.5) 338

6. John 14,6 in Relation to other ἐγώ εἰμι-Sayings 340
    6.1 In Relation to Absolute ἐγώ εἰμι-Sayings 340
        6.1.1 John 14,6 as a Revelatory Statement 340
        6.1.2 Ἐγώ εἰμι as Expression of Jesus' Oneness with the Father 341
    6.2 In Relation to ἐγώ εἰμι-Sayings with Images 342
        6.2.1 Relation with the Context 342

6.2.2 Significance of Soteriology 342
6.2.3 Relation between Gate and Way 343
6.2.4 Significance of Truth 345
6.2.5 Significance of Life 345
6.2.6 Significance of Exclusivism and Uniqueness 347
6.2.7 Significance of Inclusivism and Universality 348
6.2.8 Images and Their/Jesus' Relationship with the Father 349

7. *Conclusion* 349

Chapter VII: John 14,6 in Its Historical Context 352

1. Is Exclusivism of John 14,6 Caused by Expulsion from the Synagogue? . 352

2. Is John 14,6 an Anti-Judaistic and a Sectarian View? 357

3. Possible Historical Context for the Exclusive Claim in John 14,6 363

3.1 An Appeal to the Context of Acts 4,12 363
3.2 Relation between Worship and Exclusivism 366
3.3 Worship in the Gospel of John 369
3.4 Possibility for an Early High Christology 374

4. Conclusion 377

Chapter VIII: John 14,6 in the Context of Today's Religious Pluralism 379

1. Universal Salvation in John 381

1.1 Universalism in John 14,6 and in Its Immediate Context ... 381
1.2 Universalism in the Broad Context 381
  1.2.1 Significance of "the World" (κόσμος) 382
  1.2.2 One Flock and One Shepherd (10,16) 384
  1.2.3 Gathering God's Children (11,51–52) 385
  1.2.4 Salvation for the Gentiles (12,20–23.32; 19,19–20) ... 385

2. Juxtaposition of Exclusivism and Universalism

in Acts 4,12; 1 Tim 2,3–5 386

3. The Catholic Church's Approach to Other Religions 388

4. Conclusion 394

General Conclusion 396

Bibliography 421

Index of References 447

Index of Modern Authors 460

Index of Subjects 467

Abbreviations

AB	Anchor Bible
ABD	D. N. Freedman et al. (ed.), *The Anchor Bible Dictionary* (New York 1992) I–VI.
ACJD	Abhandlungen zum christlich-jüdischen Dialog
AnBib	Analecta Biblica
ATR	*Anglican Theological Review*
AYB	Anchor Yale Bible
BBB	Bonner Biblische Beiträge
BBR	*Bulletin for Biblical Research*
BDAG	W. Bauer et al. (ed.), *A Greek-English Lexicon of the New Testament and Other Early Christian Literature* (Chicago ³2000).
BDB	F. Brown et al., *The Brown-Driver-Briggs Hebrew and English Lexicon. With an Appendix Containing the Biblical Aramaic* (Boston 1906, Peabody 2005).
BDF	F. Blass et al., *A Greek Grammar of the New Testament and Other Early Christian Literature* (Chicago 1961).
BDS	La Bible du Semeur
BECNT	Baker Exegetical Commentary on the New Testament
BETL	Bibliotheca Ephemeridum Theologicarum Lovaniensium
BFC	Bible en français courant
Bib	*Biblica*
BInterp	*Biblical Interpretation*
BIS	Biblical Interpretation Series
BLit	*Bibel und Liturgie*
BTB	*Biblical Theology Bulletin*
BThZ	*Berliner Theologische Zeitschrift*
BWANT	Beiträge zur Wissenschaft vom Alten und Neuen Testament
BZ	*Biblische Zeitschrift*
BZAW	Beihefte zur Zeitschrift für die alttestamentliche Wissenschaft
BZNW	Beihefte zur Zeitschrift für die neutestamentliche Wissenschaft
CBQ	*Catholic Biblical Quarterly*
CIET	Collection Institut d'Études Théologiques
CNT	Commentaire du Nouveau Testament
CTQ	*Concordia Theological Quarterly*
DCH	*Dictionary of Classical Hebrew*
DSS	Dead Sea Scrolls
DTh	*Deutsche Theologie*
EDNT	H. Balz and G. Schneider (ed.), *Exegetical Dictionary of the New Testament* (Grand Rapids 1990–1992) I–III.
EThL	*Ephemerides Theologicae Lovaniensis*
EÜ	Einheitsübersetzung
EvQ	*Evangelical Quarterly*
ExAud	*Ex Auditu*

ExpTim	*Expository Times*
FOTL	Forms of the Old Testament Literature
FRLANT	Forschungen zur Religion und Literatur des Alten und Neuen Testaments
FzB	*Forschung zur Bibel*
GNT[5]	B. Aland et al. (ed.), *The Greek New Testament* (Stuttgart [5]2014).
HALOT W.	Baumgartner et al. (ed.), *The Hebrew and Aramaic Lexicon of the Old Testament* (tr. M. E. J. Richardson) (Leiden 1994–2000) I–V; trans. *Hebräisches und aramäisches Lexikon zum Alten Testament* (Leiden 1967–1996) I–V.
HBS	Herders Biblische Studien
Hfa	Hoffnung für Alle
HNT	Handbuch zum Neuen Testament
HThKAT	Herders Theologischer Kommentar zum Alten Testament
HThKNT	Herders Theologischer Kommentar zum Neuen Testament
HUCA	*Hebrew Union College Annual*
HUT	Hermeneutische Untersuchungen zur Theologie
ICC	International Critical Commentary
ITQ	*Irish Theological Quarterly*
JAOS	*Journal of the American Oriental Society*
JBL	*Journal of Biblical Literature*
JES	*Journal of Ecumenical Studies*
JETS	*Journal of the Evangelical Theological Society*
JQR	*Jewish Quarterly Review*
JSHJ	*Journal for the Study of the Historical Jesus*
JSNT	*Journal for the Study of the New Testament*
JSNTSS	Journal for the Study of the New Testament, Supplement Series
JSOTSS	Journal for the Study of the Old Testament, Supplement Series
JTI	*Journal of Theological Interpretation*
JTISup	Journal of Theological Interpretation Supplementary
LCL	Loeb Classical Library
LNTS	Library of New Testament Studies
LS	*Louvain Studies*
LSJ	H. G. Liddel and R. Scott, *A Greek-English Lexicon. Revised and Augmented throughout by H. S. Jones. With New Supplement* (Oxford 1996).
m.Sukk	*Mishnah Sukkah*
MNT	Münchener Neues Testament
MThS	Münchener Theologische Studien
N-A[28]	Nestle-Aland, *Novum Testamentum Graece* (Stuttgart [28]2012).
NAB	New American Bible
NCBC	The New Centuary Bible Commentary
Neot	*Neotestamentica*
NGÜ	Neue Genfer Übersetzung
NIB	New Interpreter's Bible
NICNT	New International Commentary on the New Testament
NICOT	New International Commentary on the Old Testament
NIDNTT	C. Brown (ed.), *The New International Dictionary of New Testament Theology* (Grand Rapids 1975–1978) I–III; trans. L. Coenen et al. (ed.), *Theologisches Begriffslexikon zum Neuen Testament* (Wuppertal 1967, 1969, 1971) I–III.
NIDOTTE	W. A. VanGemeren (ed.), *New International Dictionary of Old Testament Theology and Exegesis* (Grand Rapids 1997) I–IV.

NIV	New International Version
NJB	New Jerusalem Bible
NKJ	New King James Version
NLT	New Living Translation
NovT	*Novum Testamentum*
NovTSup	Novum Testamentum, Supplements
NRSV	New Revised Standard Version
NRT	*La Nouvelle Revue théologique*
NSK.AT	Neuer Stuttgarter Kommentar. Altes Testament
NTA.NF	Neutestamentliche Abhandlungen. Neue Folge
NTS	*New Testament Studies*
OBO	Orbis Biblicus et Orientalis
ÖBS	Österreichische Biblische Studien
OBT	Overtures in Biblical Theology
OCT	Oxford Classical Texts
ÖTK	Ökumenischer Taschenbuchkommentar
OTL	Old Testament Library
PHeid	Heidelberg Coptic Papyrus
PzB	*Protokolle zur Bibel*
RB	*Revue Biblique*
RBL	*Review of Biblical Literature*
ResQ	*Restoration Quarterly*
RivBib	*Rivista Biblica*
RSR	*Recherches de science religieuse*
SBAB	Stuttgarter Biblische Aufsatzbände
SBB	Stuttgarter Biblische Beiträge
SBL	Society of Biblical Literature
SBLDS	Society of Biblical Literature, Dissertation Series
SBLMS	Society of Biblical Literature, Monograph Series
SBS	Stuttgarter Bibelstudien
SJT	*Scottish Journal of Theology*
SNTS	Society for New Testament Studies
SNTSMS	Society for New Testament Studies. Monograph Series
SNTU	*Studien zum Neuen Testament und seiner Umwelt*
SPIB	Scripta Pontificii Instituti Biblici
ST	*Studia Theologica*
StAns	Studia Anselmiana
StANT	Studien zum Alten und Neuen Testament
Str-B	H. L. Strack and P. Billerbeck, *Kommentar zum Neuen Testament aus Talmud und Midrasch* (Munich ²1956) II.
SUNT	Studien zur Umwelt des Neuen Testaments
TANZ	Texte und Arbeiten zum neutestamentlichen Zeitalter
TB	Theologische Bücherei
TBT	Theologische Bibliothek Töpelmann
TDNT	G. Kittel and G. Friedrich (ed.), *Theological Dictionary of the New Testament* (tr. G. Bromiley) (Grand Rapids 1964–1976) I–IX; trans. *Theologisches Wörterbuch zum Neuen Testament* (Stuttgart 1933–1979) I–IX.
TDOT	J. Botterweck et al. (ed.), *Theological Dictionary of the Old Testament* (tr. D. E. Green and D. W. Stott) (Grand Rapids 1975–2015) I–XV; trans. *Theologisches Wörterbuch zum Alten Testament* (Stuttgart 1973–2015) I–X.
TENT	Texts and Editions for New Testament Study

ThHKNT	Theologischer Handkommentar zum Neuen Testament
ThKNT	Theologischer Kommentar zum Neuen Testament
ThPh	*Theologie und Philosophie*
ThR	*Theologische Rundschau*
TLNT	C. Spicq, *Theological Lexicon of the New Testament* (tr. J. D. Ernest) (Peabody 1994) I–III; trans. *Notes de lexicographie néo-testamentaire* (OBO 22.1–3; Fribourg 1978, 1982) I–III.
TLOT	E. Jenni and C. Westermann (ed.), *Theological Lexicon of the Old Testament* (tr. M. E. Biddle) (PEABODY 1997) I–III; trans. *Theologisches Handwörterbuch zum Alten Testament* (Munich/Zurich 1971, 1976) I–II.
tr.	translator(s)
trans.	translation of
TWNT	G. Kittel and G. Friedrich (ed.), *Theologisches Wörterbuch zum Neuen Testament* (Stuttgart 1933–1979) I–IX.
TWOT	R. L. Harris et al. (ed.), *Theological Wordbook of the Old Testament* (Chicago 1980) I–II.
TynB	*Tyndale Bulletin*
VT	*Vetus Testamentum*
WBC	Word Biblical Commentary
WMANT	Wissenschaftliche Monographien zum Alten und Neuen Testament
WUNT	Wissenschaftliche Untersuchungen zum Neuen Testament
ZAW	*Zeitschrift für die alttestamentliche Wissenschaft*
ZNT	*Zeitschrift für Neues Testament*
ZNW	*Zeitschrift für die neutestamentliche Wissenschaft*
ZTK	*Zeitschrift für Theologie und Kirche*

General Introduction

1. Relevance of the Subject

This monograph is an attempt to study John 14,6 in its context with a special focus on the way motif. John 14,6 is one of the most impressive statements in the Bible and one of the most important claims of Christianity.[1] This claim is among the most memorable and the most disputed texts of the New Testament. Hence, it is always "a hot potato" in scholarly and academic circles as well as in theological discussions. In the context of today's religiously pluralistic culture and inter-religious dialogue, the exclusive claim in John 14,6 is for many exegetes a "hard nut to crack" and for many theologians "a stumbling block" to dialogue.[2] A proper interpretation of the text is, therefore, a desideratum today.

---

[1] J. Zumstein, *L'Evangile selon Saint Jean 13–21* (CNT 4b; Geneva 2007), 68, considers John 14,6 as "la quintessence de la théologie joh" and says, "Dans cette declaration se trouvent concéntres les fondements de la théologie, de la christologie et de la sotériologie joh". In the words of H. Gollwitzer, "Außer Christus kein Heil? (Johannes 14,6)", *Anti-Judaismus im Neuen Testament. Exegetische und Systematische Beiträge*, ed. W. P. Eckert et al. (ACJD 2; München 1967), 171, "Der Vers stellt die konzentrierteste Formel und damit zugleich den Höhepunkt aller christologischen Formulierung des Johannes-Evangeliums dar, ja darüber hinaus: in seiner Position und seiner Negation gibt er die zugespitzteste Formel für die ganze Christusbotschaft des Neuen Testaments". According to D. A. Carson, *The Farewell Discourse and Final Prayer of Jesus. An Exposition of John 14–17* (Grand Rapids 1980), 27, John 14,6 is "one of the greatest utterances in Holy Scripture". H. Ridderbos, *The Gospel of John. A Theological Commentary* (Grand Rapids 1997), 493, calls John 14,6 "the core statement of this entire Gospel". R. Schnackenburg, *The Gospel According to St. John* (New York 1982) III, 65, regards John 14,6b as "a culminating point in Johannine theology" and "a classical summary of the Johannine doctrine of salvation that is based entirely on Jesus Christ".

[2] For interpreters like James H. Charlesworth and Laura Tack, John 14,6b is an insurmountable problem. The seriousness of the problem is deducible from Charlesworth's provoking and rash comment, "John 14,6b is a relic of the past. It is not the Word of God for our time". See J. H. Charlesworth, "The Gospel of John: Exclusivism Caused by a Social Setting Different from that of Jesus (John 11,54 and 14,6)", *Anti-Judaism and the Fourth Gospel. Papers of the Leuven Colloquium, 2000*, ed. R. Bieringer et al. (Assen 2001), 510. For Laura Tack, John 14,6 is a stumbling block to her project of Jewish-Christian dialogue. Laura's interpretation sounds even childish when she accuses Jesus of

2. Status Quaestionis

The following survey of scholarship on John 14,6 will present the important available literature on John 14,6 (from 1920 onwards) and discuss their relevant contents.[3] In his article on ὁδός in *TDNT* (originally in *TWNT*, V), Wilhelm Michaelis has paid some attention to the meaning of ὁδός in John 14,6.[4] In his view, the πρὸς τὸν πατέρα of 14,6b corresponds to the πρὸς ἐμαυτόν of 14,3.[5] Michaelis does not consider the exclusivism of 14,6b as a polemic directed against outsiders. He states, "If the saying polemically excludes other attempts to reach God, it is primarily directed, not against the attempts of others, but against other attempts by the disciples".[6] He believes that the negative side of the statement (v. 6b) is less important than the positive side (v. 6a), and that v. 6b is simply designed to support the claim of v. 6a.[7] "Coming to the Father", which could be understood as attaining fellowship with God, is equivalent to knowing and seeing the Father (cf. 14,7–9).[8] He admits that ὁδός takes precedence over ἀλήθεια and ζωή, which are explanatory concepts.[9] Both terms, ἀλήθεια and ζωή, carry an eschatological reference and might be regarded here as descriptions of the goal of salvation.[10] He suggests that in 14,6 there is an antithesis to the Torah since the Torah is called way, truth and life, and the statements about the Torah are transferred to Jesus elsewhere in the Gospel, but he does not think that 14,6 is as a whole

---

his forgetfulness, "*For a moment he seems to have forgotten* that the way, the truth and the life to which he refers are given to him from his relationship with the Father". The emphasis is mine. Tack also finds problems with the text and even accuses the evangelist of his shortcomings: "In John 14,6, the balance is out of balance. Perhaps under the influence of a perceived external threat, the evangelist has overemphasized the person of Christ. In this respect, John allowed himself to be more guided by the human shortcomings associated with his own socio-historical situation, rather than opening the way to divine revelation". See L. Tack, *John 14,6 in Light of Jewish-Christian Dialogue: Sharing Truth on the Way to Life* (WUNT II 557; Tübingen 2021) 355, 423. But my work will show that the problem and the shortcomings are not with Jesus or the text or the evangelist but with the interpreter.

[3] Only the important and original contributions to the study of John 14,6 will be mentioned here. The views of various commentators are not exposed here but will be dealt with in the course of this study. The literature is presented here in chronological order.

[4] W. Michaelis, "ὁδός", *TDNT*, V, 78–84.

[5] Michaelis, "ὁδός", 80.

[6] Michaelis, "ὁδός", 80. But it is diificult to accept Michaelis' view. See my criticism of such views on p. 13, n. 126.

[7] Michaelis, "ὁδός", 80.

[8] Michaelis, "ὁδός", 80.

[9] Michaelis, "ὁδός", 81–82.

[10] Michaelis, "ὁδός", 81.

directed against the Torah.[11] Furthermore, he rejects the gnostic conception of the heavenly journey of the soul as the background behind 14,2–6, since the context does not support this view and the term ὁδός is not used elsewhere in the Gospel in a gnostic sense (cf. 1,23; Isa 40,3).[12] Neither does he believe that the ἐγώ εἰμι of 14,6 is a conscious anti-thesis to the corresponding claims of other entities in the world around the evangelist.[13]

In his book *Je suis la route. Le thème de la route dans la Bible*, André Gros comprehensively discusses the theology and spirituality of the way in the Bible.[14] However, he does not pay considerable attention to the study of John 14,6. He believes that in the Gospel of John Christ is truly the new Moses who leads the new exodus of the people of God.[15] About John 14,6 Gros remarks, "C'est là une affirmation lapidaire qui enserre tout le mystère pascal du Christ".[16] He believes that among the three concepts of way, truth and life, the concept of way takes precedence over the other two, which explicate and qualify the way.[17] He considers the nouns "truth" and "life" in accordance with Hebrew grammar as adjectives, which qualify the noun "way".[18] Hence, he translates 14,6a as "I am the true and the living way".[19]

Most of the commentators and interpreters today rely on the work of Ignace de la Potterie in their interpretation of John 14,6.[20] At the very outset, it should be noted that the focus of Potterie's work is on truth, even though he examines John 14,6 in its context. In the status quaestionis, he examines the relationship among the concepts of way, truth and life in the past studies. In this regard, he pays special attention to the interpretation by the church fa-

---

[11] Michaelis, "ὁδός", 82.

[12] Michaelis, "ὁδός", 82–84.

[13] Michaelis, "ὁδός", 84.

[14] A. Gros, *Je suis la route. Le thème de la route dans la Bible* (Bruges 1961). This work includes five chapters. In the first chapter, Gros presents the important vocabularies for way and their various usages. The second chapter is concerned with the historical road of the people of God, including the route and journey of the patriarchs and the exodus. In the third chapter, the focus is on the progressive spiritualization of the way by paying attention to the prophetical literature (Hosea, Isaiah and Jeremiah) and Psalms and on the ritualization of the way by considering the feasts of Israel. The attention of the fourth chapter is on the completion of the way in the person of Christ. Gros sees in Christ the new Moses and the new Israel. According to him, the paschal mystery of Christ is the exodus of Christ, and in the exodus of Christ our exodus is realized. The final chapter discusses the new way of the Church in the light of the New Testament.

[15] Gros, *Je suis la route*, 99.

[16] Gros, *Je suis la route*, 103.

[17] Gros, *Je suis la route*, 103–104.

[18] Gros, *Je suis la route*, 104.

[19] Gros, *Je suis la route*, 104.

[20] I. De la Potterie, "Je suis la voie, la vérité et la vie (Jn 14,6)", *NRTh* 88 (1966), 907–942. This study can be found as a part of his monumental work *La vérité dans Saint Jean. Le Christ et la vérité, L'Esprit et la vérité* (AnBib 73; Rome 1977) I, 241–278.

thers, who are often influenced by Greek philosophy. Potterie thinks that John 14,2–3 is inspired by the exodus event, where God goes ahead to seek a place for his people for camping (Deut 1,29–33).[21] He believes that the focus in 14,6 is on the metaphor of way and that the other two terms (truth and life) explain the way and, therefore, he regards the first καί as epexegetical.[22] He rejects gnostic or Greek parallels as the literary background of John 14,6 and insists that this verse should be understood in the sense present in the Jewish tradition.[23] For him, 14,6 is an instance of the originality and novelty of Johannine formulation.[24] Truth and life are not considered as the goal of the way.[25] Jesus is the way because he is the truth and the life.[26] Jesus is the way to the Father because he gives the life of the Father by means of truth or in the truth revealed by him and gives access to the knowledge of and communion with the Father.[27]

According to Helmut Gollwitzer, the three concepts of way, truth and life refer to the direction, meaning and purpose of human life respectively.[28] Christ is the way because he is one with the Father (10,30).[29] Our "coming" to God is made possible because of God's coming to us.[30] Gollwitzer beautifully explains how Jesus becomes the way to the Father as follows:

> die Wahrheit Gottes und das Leben Gottes gehören in den geschlossenen Kreis des Lebens zwischen dem Vater und dem Sohn; hier gibt es keinen Zugang von außen für einen in diesen Kreis einbrechen wollenden Menschen. Die Öffnung dieses Kreises geht nicht von außen nach innen, sondern nur von innen nach außen. Nur dadurch, daß der geschlossene Kreis des göttlichen Lebens zwischen Vater und Sohn sich nach außen öffnet und ein Ausbruch nach außen geschieht, gibt es dann auch den 'Weg' zu dem Vater.[31]

For John, the coming to the Father is identical with the coming of the Father to us in Jesus Christ.[32] Gollwitzer holds that the exclusivism of the New Testament is inherited from Judaism.[33]

Frank Charles Fensham points out that there are two problems with regard to the interpretation of John 14,6: a semantic problem in which we have to discover the precise sphere of the meaning of way, truth and life and a gram-

---

[21] De la Potterie, "Je suis la voie", 915.
[22] De la Potterie, "Je suis la voie", 915–917.
[23] De la Potterie, "Je suis la voie", 917–926.
[24] De la Potterie, "Je suis la voie", 926.
[25] De la Potterie, "Je suis la voie", 927.
[26] De la Potterie, "Je suis la voie", 929.
[27] De la Potterie, "Je suis la voie", 929, 933, 937.
[28] Gollwitzer, "Außer Christus", 172.
[29] Gollwitzer, "Außer Christus", 172.
[30] Gollwitzer, "Außer Christus", 180.
[31] Gollwitzer, "Außer Christus", 180.
[32] Gollwitzer, "Außer Christus", 180.
[33] Gollwitzer, "Außer Christus", 181–182.

matical problem in which we have to ascertain the precise function of the three words and their relation to each other.[34] When Jesus says, "I am the way", he implies, "I am the way of God, I am the way which leads to God; I am not a human way, but a way which is not understood by mankind".[35] Fensham remarks, "The three concepts appear as predicate independently, but are also connected as a unity. They are bound into a close unity by the subject ἐγώ εἰμι without either sacrificing their sphere of meaning or giving up their unity. It is thus impossible to fix the meaning of one concept, say way, without considering truth and life".[36] The saying in 14,6 implies that in Jesus Christ there is "a way of life, a genuineness and truthfulness as well as real life, everlasting life, which gives all Christians an eschatological hope".[37]

Margaret Pamment tries to examine the apparently contradictory metaphors of path and residence in the Gospel and shows how they are related to each other, nevertheless.[38] Since the sheep follow the shepherd through the door to find the pasture, Jesus' way of life makes him both a door and a shepherd.[39] The daily experience of walking along a path makes the metaphor, "Jesus' life is the way" readily comprehensible.[40] Since Jesus' life is the way, his disciples are those who follow his way of life (1,37–44; 8,12; 12,19.26; 18,15; 21,20.22) or draw back from it (6,66; 16,32).[41] "I am the way" can imply, "My life shows the way to God".[42] In the light of 14,2–3, it is possible to suppose that the way in which Jesus directs his disciples leads to a permanent dwelling with God.[43]

In the article "The Gospel of John as a Document of Faith in a Pluralistic Culture", one of the three concerns of Alan Culpepper is the issue of interpreting the exclusive claims of the Gospel like 14,6 in a pluralistic culture.[44] He finds in John 1,9 the basis for the notion of "cosmic Christ" and believes that John's Logos allows Christians to affirm that the adherents of other religious traditions may come to know God through the work of the cosmic

---

[34] F. C. Fensham, "I am the Way, the Truth and the Life", *Neot* 2 (1968), 81.

[35] Fensham, "I am the Way", 84.

[36] Fensham, "I am the Way", 86.

[37] Fensham, "I am the Way", 87.

[38] M. Pamment, "Path and Residence Metaphors in the Fourth Gospel", *Theology* 88 (1985), 118–124. Pamment misses the point when she thinks that path and residence are contradictory metaphors because John uses a lot of metaphors and it is not his concern to maintain the logical consistency between various elements of different metaphors.

[39] Pamment, "Path and Residence", 120.

[40] Pamment, "Path and Residence", 120.

[41] Pamment, "Path and Residence", 119.

[42] Pamment, "Path and Residence", 120.

[43] Pamment, "Path and Residence", 123.

[44] R. A. Culpepper, "The Gospel of John as a Document of Faith in a Pluralistic Culture", *"What is John?" Readers and Readings of the Fourth Gospel*, ed. F. F. Segovia (Atlanta 1996), 121–127.

Christ.[45] However, Culpepper goes beyond the boundaries of the Gospel when he thinks that its exclusivist claims must be understood "in the context of the opening claim that the revelation that came through Jesus Christ is the same as that which is universally present in the Logos".[46] The Gospel may allow us to think that the Logos can enlighten anyone at any time without boundaries. But it does not hold a perspective that the revelation that came through the historical Jesus is "the same" as that which is universally present in the Logos. Moreover, it is difficult to explain in what respects the cosmic Christ and the historical Jesus are both the same and different. But later, in the article "Inclusivism and Exclusivism in the Fourth Gospel", Culpepper becomes aware of the inclusivism of the Gospel of John.[47] He categorizes both the inclusivism and the exclusivism of the Gospel into social and theological. Theological exclusivism is further divided into soteriological determinism, Christological exclusivism and fideistic exclusivism. Theological inclusivism is further divided into universal election and Logos Christology. He considers 14,6 as the clearest expression of John's Christological exclusivism. He points out that the exclusivism of the Gospel should be balanced by its inclusivism.

In the monograph *'I Am' in John's Gospel*, David Mark Ball examines systematically all forms of ἐγώ εἰμι-sayings in the Gospel and discusses their literary function, background and theological implications.[48] He analyses the immediate literary context of 14,6 and follows Ignace de la Potterie in his understanding of the relationship among the three concepts in 14,6.[49] Jesus' declaration to be the way, the truth and the life should be understood in the light of where he is going and the way to get there.[50] Truth and life are to be regarded as another explanation of how Jesus is the way.[51] Ball suggests that the meaning of the phrase "the way of the Lord" in 1,23 may have a bearing on the meaning of ὁδός in John 14.[52] He detects various links between the context of Isa 40,3 and that of John 1,23 and 14,6 and also makes allusions to many way passages from Isa 42,16; 43,19; 48,17; 57,15; 62,10; Mal 2,8; 3,1.[53] He believes that the uses of the term "way" in Isaiah provide a sufficient basis to think that Jesus' claim to be the way to the Father at least al-

---

[45] Culpepper, "The Gospel of John as a Document of Faith", 124.
[46] Culpepper, "The Gospel of John as a Document of Faith", 123.
[47] A. Culpepper, "Inclusivism and Exclusivism in the Fourth Gospel", *Word, Theology and Community in John*, ed. J. Painter et al. (St. Louis 2002), 85–108.
[48] D. M. Ball, *'I Am' in John's Gospel. Literary Function, Background and Theological Implications* (JSNTSS 124; Sheffield 1996).
[49] Ball, *I Am*, 119–126.
[50] Ball, *I Am*, 126.
[51] Ball, *I Am*, 126.
[52] Ball, *I Am*, 232, n. 4.
[53] Ball, *I Am*, 233–240.

ludes in part to Isaianic usage.[54] According to Ball, the possibility of basing Jesus' self-identification as the way on Isaiah's concept of "the way of the Lord" is strengthened by the fact that the Qumran community was called "the Way".[55] Finally, Ball also considers the possibility that the way, the truth and the life may refer to the Torah in the Old Testament (cf. Deut 8,6; Ps 119,15.30.37).[56] The weakness of Ball's positions is that he points out too many texts as the background for the designation of Jesus as the way in 14,6a. It seems that the addition, "the truth and the life" confounds him and he is not able to stick to one view. Moreover, he keeps silent about the background of 14,6b.

In his article, Reinhold Mayer considers the expulsion from the synagogue as the historical context for the Gospel of John as a whole.[57] He does not examine 14,6 in its context but notices that the concepts of way, truth and life in the Old Testament are identified with the Torah.[58] He believes that the Johannine Jesus can claim to be the way, the truth and the life because he is the personified Word of God.[59]

In the monograph *Ich bin es*, Christian Cebulj examines John 14,6 in the immediate context of 14,1–11, which he divides into three units, vv. 1–4, vv. 5–7, vv. 7–11.[60] It is not made clear whether he regards v. 7 as a transition. He considers vv. 4–11 as "eine Art Kompendium johanneischer Theologie".[61] He thinks that the concepts of truth and life explain the way metaphor and believes that vv. 7–11 form an exposition of v. 6.[62] In his view, the troubling of the hearts of the disciples should be understood as the troubling of the faith identity of the Johannine circle.[63] Cebulj considers 14,6 as an expression that originated in the context of "the stigmatized situation" of the Johannine circle as a result of their conflict with the Jews and their expulsion from the synagogue.[64] He writes, "Mit dem ἐγώ εἰμι-Wort vom Weg zeigt E, daß der joh

---

[54] Ball, *I Am*, 237.
[55] Ball, *I Am*, 237.
[56] Ball, *I Am*, 240.
[57] R. Mayer, "'Ich bin der Weg, die Wahrheit und das Leben'. Ein Versuch über das Johannes-Evangelium aus Anlass der neu erwachten Debatte zur Judenmission", *Johannes Aenigmaticus. Studien zum Johannesevangelium für Herbert Leroy*, ed. S. Schreiber and A. Stimpfle (Regensburg 2000), 184–185.
[58] Mayer, "Ich bin der Weg", 190–192.
[59] Mayer, "Ich bin der Weg", 192–194.
[60] C. Cebulj, *Ich bin es. Studien zur Identitätsbildung im Johannesevangelium* (SBB 44; Stuttgart 2000), 219–234.
[61] Cebulj, *Ich bin es*, 221.
[62] Cebulj, *Ich bin es*, 221.
[63] Cebulj, *Ich bin es*, 227.
[64] Cebulj, *Ich bin es*, 229.

Kreis nicht in seiner stigmatisierten Lage verharren muß, sondern in Jesus einen Weg hat, auf dem ἀλήθεια und ζωή zu finden sind".[65]

For James Hamilton Charlesworth, John 14,6 is an embarrassment.[66] As his introductory words suggest, this is due to his intense desire to please the persons of other religions, especially the Jews. He thinks that the exclusive claim in 14,6 is to initiate or to inflame hatred against Jews and misrepresentative of the fundamental message of Jesus.[67] He thinks that 14,6a is directed to those in the community and 14,6b to those outside the community.[68] He believes that 14,6b is an anti-Jewish and sectarian statement and argues that 14,6b is a redactional expansion to 14,6a.[69] Therefore, for him, John 14,6b is a relic of the past and not the Word of God for our time.[70] It is, in fact, his desires that dictate to him what is to be found in the text. I will later critically evaluate Charlesworth's arguments and make a response to them.[71]

The main concern of John Ashton in his article "Riddles and Mysteries. The Way, the Truth and the Life" is to examine the riddles in the Gospel in the light of Jesus' return to the Father, exposed in John 8,21–24 and 13,31–14,6.[72] Ashton believes that the Johannine motif of the way originates in the Jewish wisdom tradition.[73]

Michael Theobald thinks that the saying in John 14,6 originally had an independent existence of its own.[74] He notices that it is shaped by an *inclusio* and has a chiastic structure.[75] In his view, the semantic emphasis in 14,6a is on the term ὁδός and in 14,6b on "through me".[76] He believes that the saying in 14,6 in "the original form" (Urgestalt) was like this, "I am the way. No one comes to the Father except through me".[77] If Jesus were only the way and not the truth and the life, i.e., the destination, he would become "superfluous" (überflüssig) when the destination (the Father) was reached.[78] Since this original form did not satisfactorily represent the evangelist's Christological per-

---

[65] Cebulj, *Ich bin es*, 233.
[66] Charlesworth, "The Gospel of John: Exclusivism", 493–513.
[67] Charlesworth, "The Gospel of John: Exclusivism", 493.
[68] Charlesworth, "The Gospel of John: Exclusivism", 494.
[69] Charlesworth, "The Gospel of John: Exclusivism", 494–513.
[70] Charlesworth, "The Gospel of John: Exclusivism", 510.
[71] See pp. 185–193, 352–353.
[72] J. Ashton, "Riddles and Mysteries. The Way, the Truth and the Life", *Jesus in Johannine Tradition*, ed. R. T. Fortna and T. Thatcher (Louisville 2001), 333–342.
[73] Ashton, "Riddles and Mysteries", 340. For a critical review of Ashton's positions, see Tack, *John 14,6 in Light of Jewish-Christian Dialogue*, 109–110.
[74] M. Theobald, *Herrenworte im Johannesevangelium* (HBS 34; Freiburg 2002), 305.
[75] Theobald, *Herrenworte*, 307.
[76] Theobald, *Herrenworte*, 308.
[77] Theobald, *Herrenworte*, 311–312.
[78] Theobald, *Herrenworte*, 311.

spective, he had to add "truth and life".[79] Theobald also examines the background of the way motif in the Old Testament, the writings of Philo and in the New Testament and its reception by the evangelist.[80] He writes, "Jesus und der Weg sind derart *identisch*, dass die Begegnung mit dem gegenwärtigen Christus im Glauben jetzt schon die Begehung jenes mit ihm eröffneten Weges bedeutet".[81] In his view, the conception of Jesus as the way cannot be understood in the future-oriented eschatological sense apart from the concepts of truth and life.[82]

Reginald Ernest Oscar White believes that Jesus' claim in 14,6 should be interpreted in the light of Christ's universal and eternal mediation in creation (1,1–5) and in revelation (1,18; 5,19; 7,16; 8,28; 9,4; 12,49; 14,10.24.31, etc.).[83] Behind 14,6 there lies John's dominant thought that Jesus stands between God and the human being (1,18).[84] He believes that the universal Christ may mediate divine light and power wherever people seek in sincerity and truth (cf. 4,23–24).[85] He thinks that John understood Jesus' words in 14,6 "not as denying there could be any valid religious experience outside the Christian creed, church and commitment, but as affirming the far larger, more wonderful truth that all glimpses of divine reality come only through Christ, the way to God, the truth of God, and the life of God, the light that lighteneth every soul that is willing to learn".[86]

Angelo Colacrai notices the antecedents of "the way and the truth and the life" in the Old Testament usage, especially in "the way of truth" and "the way of life".[87] According to him, "Gv 14,6 è un insieme descrittivo di Gesù come salvatore del mondo in quanto Maestro e Signore".[88] Jesus is true because he is the image and the resemblance of the Father in his words and works.[89] Being God-man, Jesus presents himself as a synthesis of heaven and earth.[90] In John 14,6b, Jesus draws attention to the Father as an eschatological point of arrival but contemporarily presents himself as a unique way for the disciples to reach God.[91]

---

[79] Theobald, *Herrenworte*, 311–312.
[80] Theobald, *Herrenworte*, 312–322.
[81] Theobald, *Herrenworte*, 321.
[82] Theobald, *Herrenworte*, 321.
[83] R. E. O. White, "No One Comes to the Father but by Me", *ExpTim* 113 (2002), 117.
[84] White, "No One Comes to the Father", 117.
[85] White, "No One Comes to the Father", 117.
[86] White, "No One Comes to the Father", 117.
[87] A. Colacrai, "Gesù Cristo Salvatore e Signore Via Verità e Vita, Secondo Gv 14,6", *Studia Missionalia* 52 (2003), 117–168.
[88] Colacrai, "Gesù Cristo Salvatore e Signore", 137.
[89] Colacrai, "Gesù Cristo Salvatore e Signore", 157.
[90] Colacrai, "Gesù Cristo Salvatore e Signore", 164.
[91] Colacrai, "Gesù Cristo Salvatore e Signore", 165.

Craig R. Koester has made a good attempt to deal with the problem of exclusivism associated with 14,6.[92] He presupposes humanity's separation from God and thinks that the primary concern of the evangelist is to show how people can come to know God.[93] The purpose of Jesus' coming into the world is that people come to God, know him and believe in him.[94] The claim "No one comes to the Father" assumes humanity's estrangement from God through sin.[95] Since this is a fundamental human problem, not only the Jews who oppose him, but also his inner circle of disciples are unable to go where Jesus goes (7,34; 13,33).[96] The phrase "except through me" introduces the possibility of relationship with God in spite of human estrangement from God.[97] Before Jesus speaks of being the way, he speaks of going the way through his death and resurrection.[98]

Koester says, "To call Jesus 'the way' is to call him 'the Crucified and Risen One'".[99] He believes that "the promise of the way, which is mentioned in Isaiah, finds its realization in Jesus' death for the sake of others".[100] The statement "I am the way" implies that Jesus reveals God through his death and resurrection.[101] Jesus is the way because he went the way of the cross and resurrection to reveal God's love for a world that was separated from him.[102] Therefore, "it would be exclusivistic to say that Jesus is the way for some but not all, for it would mean that Jesus reveals God's love only for some but not for all".[103] He rejects the view of some scholars that Johannine Christianity is a kind of introverted sect on the basis of the Gospel's persistent emphasis on sending (cf. 17,18; 20,21–22) and the community's openness to include the Jews, the Samaritans and the Greeks alike.[104]

---

[92] C. R. Koester, "Jesus as the Way to the Father in Johannine Theology (John 14,6)", *Theology and Christology in the Fourth Gospel. Essays by the Members of the SNTS Johannine Writings Seminar*, ed. G. Van Belle et al. (BETL 184; Leuven 2005), 117–133. Cf. idem, "Jesus the Way, the Cross and the World According to the Gospel of John", *Word & World* 21 (2001), 360–369; idem, *Symbolism in the Fourth Gospel. Meaning, Mystery, Community* (Minneapolis ²2003), 287–299; idem, *The Word of Life. A Theology of John's Gospel* (Grand Rapids 2008), 209–214.
[93] Koester, "Jesus as the Way", 117.
[94] Koester, "Jesus as the Way", 120.
[95] Koester, "Jesus as the Way", 122–123.
[96] Koester, "Jesus as the Way", 123–125.
[97] Koester, "Jesus as the Way", 125.
[98] Koester, "Jesus as the Way", 127.
[99] Koester, "Jesus as the Way", 128.
[100] Koester, "Jesus as the Way", 129.
[101] Koester, "Jesus as the Way", 130.
[102] Koester, "Jesus as the Way", 133.
[103] Koester, "Jesus as the Way", 133.
[104] Koester, "Jesus as the Way", 118–119.

Under the title "Joh 14,6 und ein Absolutheitsanspruch des Christentums?", Hartwig Thyen, in his *Studien zum Corpus Iohanneum*, briefly examines the reactions of a few authors towards the absolute claim of 14,6 in the context of the Jewish-Christian dialogue.[105] Thyen admits that the claim of 14,6 is regarded not only as the absolute claim of Jesus or the Johannine community but also as that of the whole Christianity.[106] He views, "Das Johannesevangelium ist jener Wirt, ohne den der christlich-jüdische Dialog bisher seine Rechnung gemacht hat".[107]

In his theological approach to 14,6, John R. Franke evaluates the uniqueness of Jesus in the context of the contemporary religiously pluralistic culture. He explains the uniqueness of Jesus on the basis of the fact that we learn about love by looking at Jesus.[108] He says, "Jesus Christ is the living embodiment of God's gracious character as the One who loves. This love is not an abstract notion or a set of feelings, but is rather characterized by the action of God in the person of Jesus Christ".[109] Hence, commitment to Jesus as the way implies that we do not presume to know the nature of divine love ahead of time.[110] "Our understanding of true love, the love of God, is shaped by the particular way in which God loves in and through Jesus Christ".[111] Consequently, the affirmation of Jesus as the way means to acknowledge that he shows us who God is and how God acts in the world, and the unique nature and character of the divine mission.[112] Denial of the uniqueness of Jesus would compromise the redemption accomplished through his life and death as well as the way of life he models for us to follow.[113]

In his monograph *Nur Ich bin die Wahrheit*, Peter G. Kirchschläger tries to interpret 14,6 in the immediate literary context of vv. 5–11 in dialogue with modern commentators and interpreters.[114] As a working hypothesis of his thesis, he suggests that the cult and the temple of Artemis in Ephesus at the end of the first centuary, emperor worship and the Jewish community in diaspora constitute the socio-historical context of the Gospel.[115] But he does not

---

[105] H. Thyen, *Studien zum Corpus Iohanneum* (WUNT 214; Tübingen 2007), 635–637.

[106] Thyen, *Studien zum Corpus Iohanneum*, 635.

[107] Thyen, *Studien zum Corpus Iohanneum*, 635.

[108] J. R. Franke, "Still the Way, the Truth and the Life", *Christianity Today* 53 (2009), 28, 27–31.

[109] Franke "Still the Way", 28.

[110] Franke "Still the Way", 28.

[111] Franke "Still the Way", 28.

[112] Franke "Still the Way", 28.

[113] Franke "Still the Way", 28.

[114] P. G. Kirchschläger, *Nur Ich bin die Wahrheit. Der Absolutheitsanspruch des johanneischen Christus und das Gespräch zwischen den Religionen* (HBS 63; Freiburg 2010), 199–228.

[115] See Kirchschläger, *Nur Ich bin die Wahrheit*, 39–45.

make use of this socio-historical context to interpret 14,6. Jesus is the truth and the life because the way of God is the way of truth and life.[116]

According to the tradition-critical study of Johannes Beutler, the tradition behind 14,6 is Ps 43,3, where God's light and truth "lead" (ὁδηγέω) the worshipper to the sanctuary.[117] He also refers to the midrash on Ps 43,3 in which the light and truth of God are interpreted as Elijah and the Messiah. The theme of life appears in Ps 42,3.9, where the worshipper thirsts for the living God (42,3) and prays to the God of life (42,9).[118]

Ma. Lucia C. Natividad, in her theological and pastoral approach to 14,6, follows basically the interpretations of Ignace de la Potterie, Raymond Brown and Rudolf Schnackenburg.[119] Jesus' claim that he is "the way, the truth and the life" reflects and defines his relationship with humanity.[120] She thinks that way should be understood in a strictly eschatological sense.[121] John presents Jesus as the revelation of the Father and as such he is "the way".[122] She tries to understand 14,6 in the light of John's prologue (1,14.18) and views that Jesus is the only way to the Father because he alone is at the same time flesh among all people and the Word with the Father.[123]

In 2017, Laura Tack published in an article the important findings of her doctoral dissertation, which was completed at the Faculty of Theology and Religious Studies of the Katholieke Universiteit Leuven in 2015.[124] Her work is centred on the interpretation of John 14,6. Tack sees John's high Christology at the heart of the anti-Judaism of the Gospel and consequently regards John 14,6 as an anti-Judaistic text.[125] Her view, "Niet de hele wereld, maar enkel de christenen zijn de geadresseerden van Joh 14,6" ("Not the whole world, but only the Christians are the addressees of John 14,6"), is

---

[116] Kirchschläger, *Nur Ich bin die Wahrheit*, 211–212.

[117] J. Beutler, *Do not Be Afraid. The First Farewell Discourse in John's Gospel* (Frankfurt am Main 2011), 41. This work is the English translation of Beutler's *Habt keine Angst. Die erste johanneische Abschiedsrede (Joh 14)* (SBS 116; Stuttgat 1984). The English translation is preferred in this work since it is an updated version.

[118] For a critical evaluation of Beutler's views, see pp. 194–195.

[119] Ma. L. C. Natividad, "I am the Way, the Truth and the Life (John 14,6)", *Asian Perspectives in the Arts and Humanities* 2 (2012), 75–92.

[120] Natividad, "I am the Way", 78.

[121] Natividad, "I am the Way", 81.

[122] Natividad, "I am the Way", 79.

[123] Natividad, "I am the Way", 88.

[124] Her findings in this article were evaluated in my dissertation before I submitted it in 2018. See L. Tack, "Onderweg met de dialogerende Jezus. Enkele hermeneutische richtlijnen bij het Jezuswoord in Joh 14,6", *Tijdschrift voor Theologie* 57 (2017), 116–133. Cf. L. Tack, *Weg van de Waarheid? Een historisch-kritisch en hermeneutisch onderzoek van Joh 14,6 in het licht van de joods-christelijke dialoog* (Dissertation, Katholieke Universiteit Leuven 2015).

[125] Tack, "Onderweg", 119.

problematic and contradicts very clearly the universal scope of salvation highlighted in the Gospel.[126]

Very recently, Laura Tack has published her monograph *John 14,6 in Light of Jewish-Christian Dialogue: Sharing Truth on the Way to Life*.[127] It is the English translation of the revised version of her doctoral dissertation.[128] In the introduction, Tack discusses the relevance of the topic, research questions, methodology and the structure of the monograph. The main part of the work is divided into five chapters.[129] While the first three chapters deal with the exegesis of John 14,6, the last two chapters are hermeneutical in nature. The first chapter examines John 14,6 in the literary context of John 13,31–14,31. Here the author examines the relation of John 14,6 with the main motives of the text unit, namely the complementarity of the future-oriented and realized eschatology and the theme of the mutual indwelling of the Father and the Son. In her view, John 14,6 signifies a turning point from a realized eschatology towards a future-oriented eschatology and from a mutual indwelling limited to the unity of the Father and the Son towards a concept of mutual indwelling that also includes the believing community.

In the second chapter, she examines the background of John 14,6 and shows how the concepts of way, truth and life connect this verse to the rest of John's Gospel. She finds in Philo's *Quod Deus immutabilis sit* 142–143.159–161 and *De posteritate Caini* 102 the best parallels to explain how John uses the term way. In these passages, Philo presents wisdom and the Logos respectively as the equivalent of the way to God and also emphasizes the uniqueness of these mediators. As a working hypothesis, Tack proposes that the ὁδός in John 14,6 stands for the way to the Father and is as such an expression of the relationship between the Father and the Son. According to Tack, John 14,6b manifests an incomplete soteriology since the role of the Father does not come to the fore in the salvation process. She thinks that ἀλήθεια and ζωή do not belong exclusively to Jesus. She understands truth on a conceptual level as the loving unity of being between the Father and the Son.

---

[126] Tack, "Onderweg", 130. The English translation is mine. It should be specially noted that Jesus does not say οὐδεὶς ἐξ ὑμῶν but rather οὐδείς referring to everyone. For a discussion on the meaning of οὐδείς in John 14,6 and the universal scope of salvation in John, see pp. 276–278 and pp. 381–386 respectively.

[127] See p. 2, n. 2. Laura Tack and I began our dissertations almost simultaneously and worked independently. To my surprise, we had absolutely different approaches and consequently varying conclusions. In many respects, our monographs may complement each other and the readers may profit from both.

[128] This dissertation was translated from Dutch. Unfortunately, the translation has several English grammar mistakes and, in some instances, the language looks wooden and stiff.

[129] The following presentation of her work is primarily based on the introductions and conclusions of each chapter and the general conclusion.

Truth is totally a relational concept, one which forms the pre-requisite for salvation. Life stands for the life that the Johannine Jesus shares with the Father and vice versa. The gift of life originates from the loving unity of the Father and the Son.

In the third chapter, she explains the relation between the concepts of the way, the truth and the life. She understands the conjunction καί, which connects the three concepts, in an epexegetical way. Jesus is the way in the sense that he is the truth, i.e., a part of the Father's and the Son's loving unity of being, and he is the way in the sense that he is the life, i.e., that which constitutes the Father's and the Son's loving unity of being. She interprets the "I am"-saying in John 14,6 as a metaphorical expression. As a metaphorical expression, John 14,6a carries within it two semantic tensions. On the one hand, there is a mutual tension between the three central concepts of the verse (way, truth, life) and, on the other hand, also between the "I am" and these concepts. According to Tack, the way *is* and *is not* like the truth, and the way *is* and *is not* like the life. In other words, the way *is* like the truth and the life because it expresses the relational component of these two Johannine concepts. The metaphorical tension reveals that Jesus' identity is largely determined by relationship, not only to a human being, but above all, to the Father and, in the future, to the Spirit.

The fourth chapter is divided into three sections. The first section deals with the case study on the reception of John 14,6 in *Nostra Aetate* (1965) and *Dominus Iesus* (2000). The second section describes the stumbling blocks encountered in the interpretation of John 14,6 from the perspective of the Jewish-Christian dialogue. These stumbling blocks are caused either by the prejudices of the interpreter or by the formulation of the evangelist. Tack accuses the evangelist that he has explicitly neglected the role of the Father and the Spirit in the formulation of "I am"-sayings. In her view, the evangelist is responsible for the anti-Jewish potential in the ambiguous wording of John 14,6. The third section focuses on the solutions that have been proposed since the second half of the twentieth century for the problems posed by John 14,6 in the inter-religious and the Jewish-Christian dialogue. As important parameters for interpretation, she suggests that an adequate hermeneutical approach must simultaneously be aware of the historical situatedness of the Gospel and focus on the content of the literary text and the context of the Fourth Gospel itself.

In the fifth and last chapter, Tack adopts the approach of the normativity of the future as a hermeneutical framework. This approach was developed by Reimund Bieringer in the mid-1990s. As a revelatory text, the biblical text has three temporal dimensions of the past, the present, and the future. These dimensions are based on the three facets of the text: "the world behind the text", "the world of the text" and "the world before the text". These facets can be represented by three images of window, mirror and icon respectively. Tack studies John 13,31–14,31 under "three worlds" of the text as window, mirror and icon. According to her, reading the text as a window reveals that 14,6a is aimed at strengthening the identity *ad intra*, and v. 6b is meant to demarcate the community's identity *ad extra*. As a mirror, the text bears witness firstly to what it means to be Jesus' disciple and secondly to Jesus, the Father and the Spirit, each of whom is focused on the disciples' future. As an icon, the text gives a future vision. According to this vision, the house of the Father is the destination; Jesus is the way that leads to this house, and the Spirit is the guide that leads the faithful to this destination. The many dwellings highlight the inclusive vision of the future, which calls upon readers to love one another already in the present. The general conclusion brings together the main results of her research.

The greatest merit of the work of Laura Tack is that she has made an excellent research on secondary literature and has presented very systematically the status quaestionis with regard to the interpretation of John 14,6. Moreover, she has ventured to make new avenues for the interpretation of John 14,6 by relying on a theory of metaphor and an approach of the normativity of the future, even though their legitimacy and utility are questionable. At the same time, the work has many limitations.

The greatest weakness of Tack's work is that she has approached the text with a very explicit and specific agenda. This is clear from the very title of her work: *John 14,6 in Light of Jewish-Christian Dialogue*. Certainly, no interpretation is absolutely objective. However, the interpreter should try to approach the text neutrally or with minimum agenda as far as possible. Tack has already decided how the text should speak in favour of her agenda, namely the demands of Jewish-Christian dialogue. Tack's work is written as a part of a project which sees John 14,6 as a stumbling block to Jewish-Christian dialogue and aims at removing such blocks to dialogue. The lens of her agenda is discernible throughout her work. E.g., she states, "This exclusive connection between Jesus and the terms belonging to the predicate of the 'I am'-saying becomes a stumbling block in Jewish-Christian dialogue if one explains the historical background of the terms in the predicate exclusively from the Old Testament or the Jewish tradition in a broad sense".[130] In fact, nobody can challenge the indebtedness of the Fourth Evangelist to the Old Testament, which is his first and primary reference book. But Tack cannot accept the Old Testament background of "I am"-sayings mainly because that can cause stumbling blocks to her project and will not suit her agenda of

---

[130] Another example is: "For Origen, the 'I am'-sayings clearly express the divinity of the Johannine Christ in a prototypical way. This observation is not problematic in itself, but it certainly is when it is thrown into the debate with Judaism". It implies that for Tack the divinity of Christ is not problematic in itself, but it is certainly problematic in Jewish-Christian dialogue. See Tack, *John 14,6 in Light of Jewish-Christian Dialogue*, 343, 347.

Jewish-Christian dialogue. Any attempt to understand John in the light of the Old Testament is likely to be a better option available to us than to understand him in the light of modern theoretical constructs. Her interpretation of John 14,6 *in the light of* Jewish-Christian dialogue has become, in fact, an interpretation *for the sake of* pleasing her counterparts (in dialogue) at the expense of the intended meaning of the the author or the meaning understood by the original readers. Hence, some of her findings are conditioned and coloured by her subjectivity.

On account of her subjectivity (agenda), Tack has made serious but unnecessary and unacceptable accusations against Johannine Jesus, the evangelist and the revelation of the Gospel itself. She accuses Johannine Jesus of his forgetfulness and regards John 14,6 as his pretentious and harsh claim.[131] She blames the evangelist for the anti-Judaistic potential of John 14,6: "The evangelist can thus be held responsible for this anti-Jewish potential which is expressed by the ambiguous wording of John 14,6 and which brings the reader on the wrong track".[132] She thinks that in John 14,6 the evangelist has unbalanced the delicate balance between unity and diversity in the relationship between the Son and the Father and focused one-sidedly on the Son.[133] Therefore, according to Tack, the Father and the Spirit are sidelined in 14,6, and Christology in this verse is problematic.[134] In short, she finds "the problems situated on the level of the Gospel text itself".[135] But as far as John 14,6 is concerned, the shortcomings are not with the evangelist but with Tack's limited way of understanding and interpretation. By making a series of accusations against the Gospel of John, she does not allow the text to be itself and to speak in its own voice. The words of Sandra M. Schneiders are worth mentioning here: "Allowing the text to be itself, to speak in its own voice, is the primary purpose of biblical scholarship, that is, of exegesis and criticism".[136] It is better to let John speak for himself than to accuse him. Had Tack approached the text without any agenda, she would not have made these accusations against the Gospel of John.[137]

---

[131] Tack, *John 14,6 in Light of Jewish-Christian Dialogue*, 355–356, 411.

[132] Tack, *John 14,6 in Light of Jewish-Christian Dialogue*, 364, 440.

[133] Tack finds fault with the evangelist thus, "In this respect, John allowed himself to be more guided by the human shortcomings associated with his own socio-historical situation, rather than opening the way to divine revelation". See Tack, *John 14,6 in Light of Jewish-Christian Dialogue*, 364, 423–424.

[134] Tack affirms, "Indeed, the one-sided emphasis on the actions of the 'Son of God' in this verse disregards the role of the Father. This blind spot is the heart of christological anti-Judaism". See Tack, *John 14,6 in Light of Jewish-Christian Dialogue*, 342, 380.

[135] Tack, *John 14,6 in Light of Jewish-Christian Dialogue*, 380.

[136] S. M. Schneiders, "Biblical Spirituality", *Int* 56 (2002), 136.

[137] There is a saying, "Do not cut the person to fit the coat, but rather cut the coat to fit the person". In a way, Tack's accusations against the Gospel appear to be attempts to cut the Gospel to fit her agenda.

2. Status Quaestionis

The Gospel of John was not written in the light of the demands of Jewish-Christian dialogue (cf. John 20,31). "Jewish-Christian dialogue" was not a concern of the evangelist. It is a later development. Therefore, we may question whether it is appropriate to interpret John 14,6 in order to meet the (modern) demands of Jewish-Christian dialogue since it is more likely to bring out prejudiced and biased results. By *bringing into the text* the problems and demands of Jewish-Christian dialogue, Tack has not allowed the text to be itself. She has dictated how the text should be and thus turned her interpretation of John 14,6 into an *eisegesis* rather than into an *exegesis*.

Another related defect of Tack's work is that she has tried to solve the problem of Jewish-Christian dialogue at the level of the text itself. It is worth questioning whether we can settle the problems of Jewish-Christian dialogue at the level of the text, i.e., exegetically. In academic circles, usually, the modern discipline of inter-religious dialogue comes under the area of systematic and practical theology. The appalling spectre of emerging anti-Semitism in Europe today is a modern problem. It is to be confronted and solved at the level of systematic and pastoral theology. Therefore, Andreas Dettwiler makes a distinction between historical exegetical analysis of John 14,6 and systematic theological responsibility: "eine Unterscheidung zwischen einer historisch-exegetischen Analyse des Satzes 14,6 und seiner systematisch-theologischen Verantwortung".[138] He proposes that the problem of exclusivism in 14,6 must be handled from a systematic theological perspective.[139] It seems that Tack has blurred the line between the exegetical view and the systematic-pastoral theological perspective. The Catholic Church has taken many measures to deal with the Christological exclusivism of the Christian faith. Tack has paid attention only to the reception-history of John 14,6 in *Nostra Aetate* and *Dominus Iesus*. She has failed to take into account comprehensively the Church's current approach to the salvation of other religious believers.[140]

Tack has devoted more than forty pages of her dissertation to purely theoretical discussions.[141] She has heavily as well as very confidently relied on external (non-biblical) and even modern philosophical theories of metaphor in order to interpret the "I am"-saying in John 14,6. We may question wheth-

---

[138] A. Dettwiler, *Die Gegenwart des Erhöhten. Eine exegetische Studie zu den johanneischen Abschiedsreden (Joh 13,31–16,33) unter Berücksichtigung ihres Relecture-Charakters* (FRLANT 169; Göttingen 1995), 166.

[139] "Damit ist zum Problem des Exklusivitätsanspruchs allerdings noch nicht alles gesagt, was vor allem in theologisch-systematischer Hinsicht gesagt werden muss". See Dettwiler, *Die Gegenwart des Erhöhten*, 166.

[140] My monograph will pay special attention to the Church's approach to other religions in the light of the Christological exclusivism of the Christian faith.

[141] See Tack, *John 14,6 in Light of Jewish-Christian Dialogue*, 286–305, 314–315, 381–403.

er these theory-clad discussions have satisfactorily shed more light upon the understanding of John 14,6 and whether their results can convince the reader. "I am"-sayings with predicative nominatives are very often called "metaphorical 'I am'-sayings", and they are usually interpreted metaphorically without resorting to modern theories of metaphor.[142] Modern philosophical theories of metaphors are not so necessary for interpreting the metaphors in the Gospel of John. An observation of the literal context of the text and adequate information about the historical, cultural and social context of the evangelist are sufficient keys to interpret the metaphors in John's Gospel. One may question whether Paul Ricoeur's philosophical theory of metaphor is in keeping with the theological spirit of the Fourth Gospel. For instance, when Johannine Jesus utters predicateless "I am" (e.g., 8,58), it is difficult to think that the author and the reader have sensed a semantic tension between "I am" and "I am not". If the evangelist and his readers had understood the "I am" in 8,58 in the sense of Paul Ricoeur's theory of metaphor, then the evangelist would not have recorded the sentence "So they picked up stones to throw at him" (8,59).

It is very unlikely that the "I am"-sayings in the Gospel are expected by the evangelist to be read through the lens of modern philosophical theory of metaphor, namely Paul Ricoeur's theory of metaphor. Moreover, theories of metaphor vary from time to time and person to person. It is, therefore, inappropriate to apply the modern philosophical theories of metaphor to an ancient text like John's Gospel. J. van der Watt himself, who made a deductive approach to the study of metaphor in the Gospel of John,[143] is aware of the danger of applying modern philosophical theories of metaphor to the Gospel of John when he gives this warning:

Although one may contemplate the use of a specific theory of metaphor to analyze the relevant sections of the Gospel, it has been found that the use of modern theories of metaphor would be unsuitable for the interpretation of the dynamics of metaphor in the Gospel, not only on account the multiplicity of theories about metaphors, but also because of the

---

[142] Tack, *John 14,6 in Light of Jewish-Christian Dialogue*, 423, states, "It is mainly the literal reading of the 'I am' as a literal identification, as opposed to a reading of the 'I am' saying as a metaphorical expression, which is problematic". But Tack's fear and rigidity are unwarranted. In reality, it is very unlikely that any interpreter has identified Jesus literally with the way in the sense of a road, whether he notices metaphorical meaning at the level of a sentence or a word. That Jesus *is like* the way is already understood when one identifies Jesus with the way metaphorically and states, "Jesus *is* the way". That Jesus *is not* or *is not like* the way does not say anything more than that Jesus is not literally the way.

[143] Tack has followed an inductive approach to the study of the metaphorical expression in John 14,6. Perhaps, a deductive approach that pays attention to the metaphor (imagery) of the journey in the Gospel would have brought out better results.

methodological problem of applying modern theories to an ancient text, such as the Gospel.[144]

Tack divides the relationship of the "I am" to the predicate into three categories: as an identification formula, as a relational formula, or as a metaphor.[145] Tack's categorization into these three water-tight compartments is misleading and unacceptable. In fact, these three categories are not mutually exclusive. The metaphorical character of the saying is not lost even if one explains the relationship as an identification formula or as a relational formula. Moreover, Johannine scholars like Ruben Zimmermann, Hartwig Thyen, J. Van der Watt and Silke Petersen, who have studied in detail the "I am"-sayings and metaphors in John's Gospel, never maintain such categorical classification as Tack does.[146] It is doubtful whether she has succeeded in maintaining these distinctions. When she states in the conclusion of her study on "I am"-sayings, "Jesus is the way in the relational sense", she is affirming the relationship of the "I am" to the predicate as a relational formula. Again, when she says, "we can see Jesus' *identity as a way*", she is pointing out the identification between Jesus and the way and thus affirming the relationship of the "I am" to the predicate as an identification formula.[147] When she states without any reservation, "Jesus Christ is the way, the truth and the life and is the access to salvation", she is understanding "I am" as identification.[148] Again, since she considers 14,6b as an explanation of 14,6a, then obviously she has to identify Jesus with the way, truth and life.[149]

---

[144] Van der Watt, *Family of the King*, xx.

[145] Tack, *John 14,6 in Light of Jewish-Christian Dialogue*, 268.

[146] See Zimmermann, *Christologie der Bilder*, 121–133; Thyen, "Ich bin das Licht der Welt", 19–46; Van der Watt, *Family of the King*; Petersen, *Brot, Licht und Weinstock*.

[147] To identify" means "to perceive or to state or to ascertain the identity of someone or something". See https://www.merriam-webster.com/dictionary/identify (*Merriam-Webster Dictionary*). Therefore, identification means "making a statement about one's identity". But Tack seems to take contradicting positions in the following sentences: "By establishing a *connection* between himself and the way, the Johannine Jesus makes a statement about his *identity*, which indirectly also has soteriological implications for the disciples"; "The fixed form of the 'I am' saying with predicate establishes a *connection* between the subject ('I') and the predicate (e.g., the bread) via the copula ('am'). I proposed to consider this *connection not as an identification*, but as a metaphor" (the emphasis is mine). On the one hand, Tack considers the connection between Jesus and the way as identification. On the other hand, she regards this connection not as an identification but as a metaphor. See Tack, *John 14,6 in Light of Jewish-Christian Dialogue*, 259, 285, 310.

[148] See Tack, *John 14,6 in Light of Jewish-Christian Dialogue*, 364.

[149] Tack has to understand "I am" as identification when she states, "In this verse the Johannine Jesus describes himself – and only himself – not only as the way, the truth and the life, but also as the only means of access to the Father". See Tack, *John 14,6 in Light of Jewish-Christian Dialogue*, 361, 364.

Tack has failed to notice that Jesus' claim to be the way in John 14,6 is intimately related to the motif of journey portrayed in John 13–14. She has situated her study of John 14,6 within the limited context of 13,31–14,31. The farewell speech of Jesus cannot be read separately from the entire setting provided in chapter 13. John 13,1–30 forms an inseparable backdrop of the farewell discourse. The motifs of Jesus' journey and conflict with the devil control John 13–14 and provide the fitting context to understand Jesus' claim to be the way in 14,6. Hence, my monograph will approach John 14,6 within the literary context of John 13–14. Tack understands "way" as an expression of the relationship between the Father and the Son.[150] But in 14,6 "way" is, more importantly, an expression of Jesus' relationship with the believers. In Jesus' answer to Thomas' question, the focus is more on Jesus' relationship with the disciples. The relationship between Jesus and the Father is explained later in the following verses (vv. 7–11).

After investigating the historical background of the term way and showing how the concept of way connects John 14,6 to the rest of John's Gospel, Tack makes the following conclusion: "The study of the pictorial language of 'the way' in John 14,6b has confirmed the following working hypothesis. The way in John 14,6b refers to the way to the Father and is as such an expression of the relationship between the Father and the Son".[151] It is explicitly that John presents Jesus as *the way to the Father* in 14,6 and any sensible reader can recognize this. The noun "way" and the corresponding verb of movement (journey) "come" along with the prepositional phrase "to the Father" clearly demonstrate it.[152] But it looks strange to find that John's presentation of Jesus as the way to the Father in 14,6 is for Tack *still only a working hypothesis.*[153]

According to Tack, the passages from Philo's *Quod Deus immutabilis sit* 142–143, 159–161 and *De posteritate Caini* 102 explain best how John uses the term way in 14,6. But the exact relationship between Philo and the Gospel of John is still a subject of debate. "There is no evidence whatsoever of a genetic relationship between Philo and John, or even evidence for a mediated Philonic influence upon the evangelist".[154] Philo's concept of the Logos is

---

[150] Tack, *John 14,6 in Light of Jewish-Christian Dialogue*, 95.

[151] Tack, *John 14,6 in Light of Jewish-Christian* Dialogue, 159.

[152] Apart from the movements of "coming" and "going" (journey), the way has no meaning.

[153] Tack is not sure about this. Therefore, she has to say, "In this passage, the way *probably* stands for the way to the Father"; "This in turn means that v. 6cd offers support for *the working hypothesis* that Jesus is presented in v. 6 as the way to the Father". The emphasis is mine. See Tack, *John 14,6 in Light of Jewish-Christian Dialogue*,127, 158.

[154] J. S. Sturdevant, *The Adaptable Jesus of the Fourth Gospel: The Pedagogy of the Logos* (Supplements To Novum Testamentum 162; Leiden 2015), 48, n. 4. According to J. Frey, "Between Torah and Stoa: How Could Readers Have Understood the Johannine Logos?", *The Prologue of the Gospel of John. Its Literary, Theological, and Philosophical*

rooted in the metaphysics of Middle Platonism in a way that the concept of the Logos in John's Gospel is not.[155] Despite some terminological affinities, it is clear that "in Philo, the Logos is never fully personal, certainly never incarnate, and never the object of faith and love".[156] It is as the object of faith and love that John presents Jesus in the immediate context of 14,6. John's presentation of Jesus as the way in 14,6 is placed between the command to believe in Jesus (14,1) and the command to love him (14,15). In Philo, the concept of way is inseparable from the concept of two ways of virtue/philosophy and vice. The Gospel of John does not develop the notion of two ways and does not regard the way in an ethical sense. As Tack claims, the theme of the two ways does not lie at the basis of John 14,6.[157] For John, there is only one way to the Father, not because other ways are false and Jesus' way is true, but because the Father has only one Son who is Jesus (3,16). Above all, the only body of writings upon which John definitively depends is the Old Testament.[158] This is especially true in the case of the use of way metaphor (see John 1,23, where he cites Isa 40,3). Hence, seeking antecedent for the Johannine notion of way outside of the Old Testament cannot be satisfactorily supported.[159]

In the Gospel of John, truth and life belong ultimately to the Godhead wherein Jesus as the Son shares. Tack's view that truth and life do not exclu-

---

Contexts. Papers read at the Colloquium Ioanneum 2013, ed. J. G. van der Watt (WUNT 359; Tübingen 2016), 215, it is doubtful whether John had direct access to Philo's thought or works.

[155] T. H. Tobin, "Logos", *ABD*, IV, 354. Frey, "Between Torah and Stoa", 213, says, "Philo's Logos primarily fits into the pattern of the intermediate figure found in most Middle Platonic systems".

[156] Frey, "Between Torah and Stoa", 215. Dodd, *Interpretation of the Fourth Gospel*, 73, distinguishes between the Logos of John and that of Philo as follows: "The evangelist conceives of the Logos as incarnate, and of the ἀληθινὸς ἄνθρωπος as not merely dwelling as νοῦς in all men, but as actually living and dying on earth as a man. This means that the Logos, which in Philo is never personal, except in a fluctuating series of metaphors, is in the Gospel fully personal, standing in personal relations both with God and with men, and having a place in history. As a result, those elements of personal piety, faith and love, which are present in Philo's religion but not fully integrated into his philosophy, come to their own in the Gospel. The Logos of Philo is not the object of faith and love. The incarnate Logos of the Fourth Gospel is both lover and beloved; to love Him and to have faith in Him is of the essence of that knowledge of God which is eternal life". Cf. P. Borgen, *The Gospel of John: More Light from Philo, Paul and Archaeology. The Scriptures, Tradition, Exposition, Settings, Meaning* (Supplements To Novum Testamentum 154; Leiden 2014), 80.

[157] See Tack, *John 14,6 in Light of Jewish-Christian* Dialogue, 107.

[158] Borgen, *The Gospel of John: More Light from Philo*, 81.

[159] This monograph will seek the antecedent for the Johannine notion of way within the Old Testament itself in accordance with the intra and inter-textual connections which the evangelist himself provides in the Gospel.

sively and completely coincide with Jesus is irrelevant and meaningless as far as Johannine soteriology is concerned because the Gospel does not claim that anybody can have access to the truth and the life of God except through his Son.[160] The evangelist does not draw boundaries between the Father, the Son and the Spirit in this regard. In the view of Tack, in John 14,6 "the concept of life does not so much represent the eternal life that qualifies the salvation of the faithful, but refers to the life that Jesus himself shares with the Father".[161] This is a problematic view. There is no evidence in the Gospel of John to show that the evangelist makes a distinction between the eternal life that qualifies the salvation of the faithful and the life that Jesus himself shares with the Father, even if such a distinction really exists. Moreover, such a distinction is usually not supported by Johannine scholars.[162] On the other hand, the evangelist has tried to relate the life, which the Father and Jesus share, to the life to which the disciples have access through Jesus (5,26; 6,57; 14,19). John 5,26, 6,57 and 14,19 indicate a chain of relationships between the life of the Father and the life of the disciples in and through Jesus (cf. 1 John 4,9). The Son has a share in the life of the Father so that the Son can give the same life to whomever he wishes (5,21). It is because of the Father that Jesus is the life, and the life that he gives is the life of the Father. There is a clear-cut contradiction between Tack's positions in the major part of her monograph and in its sub-title. She understands the conjunction καί in 14,6 epexegetically and does not hold that the way leads to life.[163] But in the sub-

---

[160] A. J. Köstenberger, "What is Truth? Pilate's Question in its Johannine and Larger Biblical Context", *JETS* 48 (2005), 35, states, "Jesus, then, is the truth because he is sent from God and has come to reveal the Father and to carry out his salvation-historical purposes. For this reason, the only way for us to know the truth is to know God through Jesus Christ (8,31; 14,6; 17,3)". Cf. Tack, *John 14,6 in Light of Jewish-Christian Dialogue*, 219, 438–439.

[161] Tack, *John 14,6 in Light of Jewish-Christian Dialogue*, 258, 278, 355. But Tack seems to make no distinction between life in 14,6 and eternal life when she states: "The post-paschal community was probably fully aware of the promise of eternal life. It must have firmly believed that this life is obtained through participation in the life-giving relationship between the Father and the Son through the mediation of the Spirit. For this community, Jesus is at the centre of this gift of life. He is the one who can bestow on the disciples the life he received from the Father" (see p. 410).

[162] E.g., Brown, *John*, II, 630; Zumstein, *Saint Jean 13–21*, 66; U. Wilckens, *Das Evangelium nach Johannes* (Das Neue Testament deutsch; Teilband 4; Göttingen 2000), 224; M. M. Thompson, "The Living Father", *God the Father in the Gospel of John*, ed. A. Reinhartz (Semeia 85; Atlanta 1999), 23. Schnackenburg, *John*, II, 355, says, "The life man receives through Christ is not material improvement or magic power but divine reality, a share in the life of God, the living Father and source of all life (cf. 5,26; I Jn I,2)". Y. Simoens, *Selon Jean. 3. Une interprétation* (CIET 17; Brussels 1997), 621, remarks, "Celle-ci est à comprendre comme la vie même de Dieu, communiquée à l'homme. Elle dit la vie de Dieu dans la vie de l'homme, la vie de Dieu en tant qu'elle donne vie à l'homme".

[163] Tack, *John 14,6 in Light of Jewish-Christian Dialogue*, 286.

title of her monograph (*Sharing Truth on the Way to Life*), she holds the view that the way leads to life.

In her approach to "I am"-sayings, Tack has totally neglected the Old Testament background with which the Fourth Evangelist is in constant touch. The majority of scholars have recognized the revelatory character of "I am"-sayings. It is self-evident that Tack has neglected it mainly because it is a threat to her agenda of Jewish-Christian dialogue.[164] The fact that authors do not supply the exact same list of absolute "I am"-sayings is not a sufficient reason to deny the revelatory nature of "I am"-sayings.[165] On the other hand, Tack has maintained a wavering position, "John, however, *consciously chooses* to express his Christology by means of the 'I am' saying, which explicitly emphasises Jesus".[166] If John *consciously chooses* "I am"-saying, where does he *choose it from*? and is it not then a divine formula? Moreover, Tack has also missed to interpret John 14,6 in the light of the network of other metaphorical "I am"-sayings in the Gospel.

Very frequently, Tack has lamented and accused that in John 14,6 the evangelist has ignored and sidelined the role of the Father and the Spirit due to his one-sided focus on the unique mediation of Jesus Christ.[167] According to her, John 14,6b expresses Christomonism and an incomplete soteriology. In fact, Tack's accusation against the evangelist is baseless and meaningless and is a natural outcome of her agenda and prejudiced interpretation. Her accusations show that she has not properly understood the spirit and the purpose of the Gospel of John. The Gospel is written very clearly with an exclusive purpose. Its purpose is exclusively to show who Jesus is and what his role is. The Father and the Holy Spirit are not the protagonists of the Gospel of John. There is only one protagonist. That is Jesus and he alone.[168] In the Gospel story, the Father and the Spirit have their significance only in relation to Jesus. This does not mean that the Father and the Spirit are sidelined. There is no knowledge of the Father and the Spirit apart from the Son (cf. 1,18; 10,30; 14,7–14.26; 15,26; 16,7.14–15). It is in terms of the relationship with Jesus that all relationships of believers with the Father and the Spirit are and should be defined. Hence, Tack's complaint itself that the evangelist is out of balance is imbalanced.

---

[164] Hence, Tack, *John 14,6 in Light of Jewish-Christian Dialogue*, 379, admits plainly, "The understanding of the 'I am' as divine speech can, in the first place, give rise to anti-Jewish interpretations".

[165] Cf. Tack, *John 14,6 in Light of Jewish-Christian Dialogue*, 265, n. 12. Also see my criticism against Tack on p. 294, n. 5.

[166] Tack, *John 14,6 in Light of Jewish-Christian Dialogue*, 364. The emphasis is mine.

[167] Tack, *John 14,6 in Light of Jewish-Christian Dialogue*, 341–342, 356, 363, 423, 438.

[168] This is true in the case of the Synoptic Gospels as well. It is enough to look at how Matthew (1,1), Mark (1,1) and Luke (1,1–4) begin their Gospels.

Now, some questions naturally arise. Why is Tack so much concerned with the evangelist's exclusive focus on Jesus only in the "I am"-sayings? Why does not she make such accusations against the evangelist for his neglect of the role of the Father and the Spirit and his exclusive focus on Jesus Christ in many other soteriological statements in the Gospel? For instance, in the very purpose statement of the Gospel in 20,31, which is also soteriological in nature, the evangelist has totally ignored the role of the Father and the Spirit and exclusively focused on the role of Jesus. In that case, Tack will have to accuse that the purpose of the whole Fourth Gospel is one-sided and deviated. Similarly, there are many soteriological statements in the Gospel where the role of the Father and the Spirit is not expressed (e.g., 3,15; 5,40; 10,10; cf. 6,51; 8,12; 10,9; 11,25–26). According to Tack's outlook, they are all incomplete and one-sided soteriological statements. Her view that John 14,6 is an expression of Christomonism is misleading and a misrepresentation of Johannine Christology. The unity of Jesus as the Son with the Father and the Spirit is beyond Tack's calculation and so intimate in the work of salvation that Tack's all accusations against the evangelist become groundless. Her accusations are clear signs of her inadequate and biased exegesis which is motivated by her agenda of Jewish-Christian dialogue. Even though Tack has argued much for the role of the Father, she has failed to pay special attention to the role of the Father and to his relationship with his Son in her study of John 14,6.[169]

Tack has maintained a negative approach to the theology of fulfilment in the New Testament. But that Jesus is the fulfilment of the Old Testament is the perspective of the entire New Testament which Tack can never overturn. The Gospel of John is very emphatic in the view that Jesus is the fulfilment of Old Testament Scripture as such.[170]

The basic theological framework of the entire New Testament is eschatological. John 14,6 is situated already within an eschatological framework. For the evangelist, Jesus' death, resurrection, preparation of the dwelling place in the Father's house, his return, giving of the Spirit, indwelling and the giving of peace and joy (cf. John 13–14) are eschatological events. In other words, John 13–14 has already a normativity of the future within it, and a sensible reader can find it out without the external help of large-scale theoretical discussions. The reader may doubt whether those conclusions which Tack has made as a result of the application of "normativity of future approach" shed much light on the understanding of John 14,6. Tack has recognized in mono-

---

[169] My monograph will attempt to give special attention to the role of the Father and to show how the Father and the Spirit play their role implicitly in 14,6.

[170] See F. J. Moloney, "The Gospel of John as Scripture", *CBQ*, 67 (2005), 459; J. Beutler, "The Use of 'Scripture' in the Gospel of John", *Exploring the Gospel of John*, ed. R. A. Culpepper and C. C. Black (Louisville 1996), 147.

theism the solution to the problem of exclusivism but has failed to explore that possibility. My monograph will try to pay some attention to it.

Besides these published works, which are, except the work of Tack, either articles or sections in books,[171] there are some unpublished works on themes related to 14,6. Two master's degree dissertations by R. W. Gilbert[172] and Sebastian Vattapparambil[173] were accessible. The scope of Gilbert's work is very limited. Its purpose is basically concerned with the meaning of ὁδός in 14,4–6. He views that the meaning of ὁδός in 14,4 is the means of Jesus' getting to heaven and in 14,6 the means of the disciples' getting to heaven.[174] In many respects, the work of Gilbert is insufficient. He does not satisfactorily take into account the background of "way" in 14,6. He does not even consider the only other occurrence of ὁδός in 1,23. In his study, Vattaparambil examines the context of 13,31–14,31, various concepts like ἐγώ εἰμι-sayings, way, truth, life, Father and finally the positions of the Second Vatican Council toward non-Christian religions. As the subtitle indicates, Vattaparambil's approach to 14,6 is basically biblical-theological and does not pay due attention to the role and significance of the way motif. He does not confront various issues like the background of John 14,6, the relationship of way with truth and life and the historical setting for the emergence of the exclusivism in 14,6. Moreover, his analysis of various concepts of 14,6 does not satisfactorily and synthetically contribute to the interpretation of 14,6.

3. Reasons for the Present Study

The above survey shows that except the monograph of Tack all the published works on John 14,6 are either in the form of articles or in the form of sections of books which deal with some other themes. The only comprehensive pub-

---

[171] There are also other minor published articles on 14,6. E.g., M. L. Gubler, "Ich bin der Weg und die Wahrheit und das Leben (Joh 14,6)", *Diakonia* 24 (1993), 373–382, exclusively focuses on the notion of truth in John's Gospel and does not pay attention to the study of 14,6. G. Parrinder, "Only One Way? John 14,6", *ExpTim* 107 (1995), 78–79, notices the difficulty in interpreting 14,6 and encourages the readers to follow the teaching of the Second Vatican Council in their approach to non-Christian religions. R. B. George, "Jesus the Way to the Father in John 14,1–14 and African Situation", *Hekima Review* 35 (2006), 33–45, makes basically a theological approach to 14,6. The author follows commentators like R. E. Brown, G. O'Day, F. Moloney to understand the text and Jacques Dupuis to understand the universal salvation. For a homily on 14,6, see H. Vogel, "Predigt über Johannes 14,6", *BThZ* 3 (1986), 127–131.

[172] R. W. Gilbert, *The Meaning of Hodos in John 14,4-6* (Master's Degree Dissertation, Grace Theological Seminary; Winona Lake 1985).

[173] S. Vattapparambil, *Ist Jesus der wahre Weg zum Heil? Eine Bibeltheologische Analyse von Joh 14,6* (Diplomarbeit, Universität Innsbruck; Innsbruck 1988).

[174] Gilbert, *The Meaning of Hodos*, 51.

lished study on John 14,6 is the work of Tack. But Tack's work has many weaknesses, which have been exposed above in detail.[175] Those weaknesses will give much impetus to my work. My study does not regard John 14,6 as an anti-Judaistic text, and it will pay more attention to the biblical context than to external theories in the interpretation of John 14,6. My monograph will challenge many of Tack's positions and will provide the reader with a very different perspective on John 14,6. In that sense, my work will serve as a corrective to Tack's work.

Even a comprehensive study of the way motif in Greek-Jewish literature in a single work is rare.[176] Moreover, the present study intends to highlight certain aspects which are lacking in the past studies. This work will question some established conclusions and positions regarding John 14,6 and will impart a new outlook on the text. This will be evident in discussing the following topics: the possible background for the designation of Jesus as the way and for the addition of "the truth and the life", the interrelation between way, truth and life, the meaning and significance of the statement, "No one comes to the Father except through me" and the historical setting for the emergence of exclusivism. In the past, none of the authors mentioned above has adequately demonstrated how an understanding of the network of ἐγώ εἰμι-sayings in the Gospel can illuminate the interpretation of 14,6. However, this monograph will also make use of certain views of some authors mentioned above in the course of this study, and some of their views will be emphasized.

4. Methodology

This work is not written to demonstrate the application of a new theory or to test the utility of a new method or approach. It does not believe in engaging with theories and abstract approaches whose outcome is often very little or insignificant.[177] But it believes that the best method to interpret John 14,6 is

---

[175] For a review of Tack's work and a detailed discussion on the weaknesses of Tack's monograph, see pp. 12–25.

[176] Even though the literature on "way" is numerous, none of them singly and comprehensively deals with the theme of way in classical Greek literature, Hebrew Bible, Septuagint, New Testament, Dead Sea Scrolls, Philo and Josephus. Even though Tack discusses the background of the term way, she is very selective. From her work, it is difficult for the reader to get a rather comprehensive view of the theme of way in classical Greek literature, the Old Testament (Hebrew Bible, Septuagint), Dead Sea Scrolls and Philo.

[177] J. H. Hayes and C. R. Holladay, *Biblical Exegesis. A Beginner's Handbook* (Louisville ³2007), 179–180, rightly say, "Doing exegesis is less about applying methods and more about seeking meaning. As you engage in the latter, you will do the former". As mentioned above, Tack's work contains a lot of abstract theoretical discussions to interpret

to interpret it with John himself. Therefore, the best way to understand John 14,6 is to think it through in the context of John's Gospel itself.[178] Hence, the text is interpreted in its literary and historical contexts. Various literary contexts within the Gospel and the entire Bible are sought out to illuminate the text. This study assumes that the Gospel of John is characterized by interactions, on the one hand, with the Gospel itself, and, on the other hand, with other biblical literature.[179] Therefore, intra-textual connections are used to pinpoint the inter-textual relationship of the text. Thus, this monograph will "allow the text to be itself and to speak in its own voice"[180] without accusing the text and resorting to external abstract theories, which are modern and even unknown to the evangelist and to his original readers.

The dominant literary and conceptual context of the Gospel of John is the Old Testament. Therefore, the observation of Saeed Hamid-Khani seems to be very important advice to the interpreters of this Gospel: "If we are to interpret the Fourth Gospel correctly, John's absolute dependence upon the Old Testament must be one of our exegetical assumptions".[181] John's hermeneutical strategy is "Scriptural hermeneutics". John reads the whole Old Testament as a web of symbols that must be understood as figural signifiers for Jesus and the life that he offers.[182] Since John engages Israel's Scripture chiefly as a source of symbols, he often references the biblical stories not through direct quotation of texts but through allusions and echoes.[183] This work will attempt to interpret the text in the light of the echoes and the thematic allusions to John's Scriptures.

John 14,6. It is even possible to attain some of her conclusions without resorting to large-scale theoretical discussions.

[178] Cf. Koester, *The Word of Life*, 210.

[179] The views of literary critics that no text can be formulated independently of what has already been written in other texts and that every text is a new construction of past quotations are worth mentioning here. See J. Zumstein, "Intratextuality and Intertextuality in the Gospel of John", *Anatomies of Narrative Criticism. The Past, Present and Futures of the Fourth Gospel as Literature*, ed. T. Thatcher and S. D. Moore (Atlanta 2008), 121.

[180] Cf. Schneiders, "Biblical Spirituality", 136. See the full quotation of Schneiders on p. 16.

[181] See S. Hamid-Khani, *Revelation and Concealment of Christ: A Theological Inquiry into the Elusive Language of the Fourth Gospel* (WUNT II 120; Tübingen 2000), 408, 410.

[182] John makes extraordinary claims about Jesus not by rejecting Israel's Scripture but by rereading it to show how it points to Jesus. See R. B. Hays, *Echoes of Scripture in the Gospels* (Waco 2016), 405.

[183] Hays, *Echoes of Scripture*, 405. Hamid-Khani, *Revelation and Concealment of Christ*, 326, points out, "Any meaningful explication of John's Gospel and the function of its language must reckon with the author's systematic allusions to the Scriptures".

5. Plan and Procedure

As it is indicated in the subtitle "A Study of the Way Motif and John 14,6 in its Context", the scope of this study can be broadly divided into two parts: a study of the way motif and a study of John 14,6. Part one consists of a comprehensive and independent examination of the way motif in Greek-Jewish literature. There are various reasons for doing this. The ἐγώ εἰμι-saying in John 14,6a contains three theologically loaded predicates, namely ὁδός (way), ἀλήθεια (truth) and ζωή (life). The concepts of truth[184] and life[185] occur more frequently in the Gospel and, naturally, they have attracted more attention in the scholarly world. The word ὁδός is used only 4 times in John, 3 times in 14,4–6 and once in 1,23 in order to cite Isa 40,3. Consequently, it has not received as much attention as the concepts of truth and life. Nevertheless, an observation of the context of John 14,6 will make clear that among the three concepts the way is the prominent one in its literary context. It should be noted that ὁδός has already occurred in 14,4–5 before its occurrence in 14,6 along with ἀλήθεια and ζωή, which both appear in the context like intruders. Jesus' entire statement and his self-designation as the way in 14,6 are placed in the near context of Jesus' imminent journey (John 13–14) and in the immediate context of a discussion on way (John 14,4–5). Hence, a study of John 14,6 should give special attention to the meaning and significance of the way and the journey motif.

A study of the way motif in Greek-Jewish literature will provide the conceptual background to understand the way/journey motif in John. It will also enable the reader to grasp the conceptual milieu of the author in which the concept of way was found. This conceptual world is divided into two: Greek and Jewish. Since the author has written the Gospel in the Greek language, it is necessary to comprehend the concept of way in Greek literature. An understanding of way in secular Greek language helps to compare it with an understanding of way in the Hebrew Bible and the Septuagint. Today, a majority of scholars agree that John's Gospel owes much more to the Old Testament than to any other literature. This work is written with this assumption. John employs many Old Testament salvific images whose fulfilment he finds in Jesus. The image of the way is one among them. It is likely that John has the whole Old Testament picture of the way in his mind when he calls Jesus "the way"

---

[184] The word ἀλήθεια occurs 25 times in John whereas it is used only once in Matthew and only 3 times in Mark and Luke. Monographs on truth in the Gospel of John are numerous. For various literature, see p. 227, n. 13.

[185] The word ζωή occurs 36 times in John whereas it is found only 7 times in Matthew, 4 times in Mark and 5 times in Luke. Monographs on life in the Gospel of John are plenty. For various literature, see p. 237, n. 59.

5. Plan and Procedure

in 14,6. Hence, a complete understanding of John's use of way is difficult without a comprehensive study of the way motif in the Old Testament.

Moreover, since the evangelist cites Isa 40,3 in John 1,23, "Make straight the way of the Lord, as the prophet Isaiah said",[186] a study of the way concept in the Old Testament is indispensable. Since in the Old Testament and other Jewish literature the concept of way is closely associated with one's movement or journey, important verbs of journey are also examined. This is also in view of the Johannine style, according to which the evangelist is more interested in the verbs of journey than in the nouns for way. He frequently uses the verbs "go", "come", "come down", "go up", "depart", etc. Since he uses the noun "way" very rarely but uses the verbs of journey frequently, special attention is paid to study the journey motif in the Gospel of John separately. At the end of this section, Jesus' journey in chapters 13–14 is also specially examined. This opens the door to enter into the specific study of John 14,6 because it is in the context of the journey motif in the Gospel, particularly in chapters 13–14, that Jesus' claim as the way is to be interpreted. Part one ends with a concluding evaluation, which will examine how the study of the way/journey motif in the Old Testament contributes to the understanding of the way/journey motif in John. It is in the light of this general evaluation that the particular literary background of John 14,6 is discussed in the second part.

Part two is exclusively a study on John 14,6 in its context. After the preliminary observations on genre, unity and structure of the farewell discourse, the near and immediate context of John 14,6, i.e., John 13–14, is examined. This will help us to understand more vividly the literary setting in which 14,6 is placed and the verse's relationship with the events and themes narrated in chapters 13–14. After examining the unity and integrity of 14,6, the next step will be to explore the possible influences on the formulation in 14,6. In this regard, we do not analyse this verse in isolation, its neighbouring context is also taken into account. Then, the important motifs of 14,6 other than way, namely truth, life and Father in the Gospel context are examined. Special attention is paid to clarify the interrelation between way, truth and life. The motif of the Father is explained in terms of the exclusive relationship of Jesus with the Father and the believers' relationship with the Father, which will be attained through Jesus. Since 14,6 is an ἐγώ εἰμι-saying, its meaning and significance are discussed in the light of other ἐγώ εἰμι-sayings in the Gospel. An attempt is also made to find out the cause of exclusivism in 14,6 in its historical context. Finally, the verse is placed in the context of today's religious pluralism. To handle the issue of exclusivism in 14,6, solutions are drawn out from the Gospel itself, and it is shown how the Gospel's solutions are incorporated in the approach of the Catholic Church to the believers of

---

[186] All English biblical quotations used in this work are from NRSV unless otherwise indicated.

other religions. At the end, the general conclusion will present the important findings of this study.

6. Presuppositions

This monograph presupposes that the Gospel as we have it today made good sense to its author for his particular purposes and to his community. Therefore, it tries to understand the Gospel in its present form, which is the final form. However, it neither rejects the possibility that it is the product of a longer compositional process nor accepts the view that the Gospel can only be interpreted in the light of attempts to reconstruct its redactional history.[187] The terms, "John", "evangelist" and "author" are used in this monograph to designate the person or persons responsible for the final form of the Gospel of John.

---

[187] Cf. R. A. Culpepper, "The Johannine *Hypodeigma*: A Reading of John 13", *The Fourth Gospel from a Literary Perspective*, ed. R. A. Culpepper and F. F. Segovia (Semeia 53; Atlanta 1991), 133.

Part One

A Study of Way Motif

Chapter I

Way Motif in Greek-Jewish Literature

As it has already been indicated in the general introduction, in this first part, the way/journey motif in Greek-Jewish literature is examined in view of grasping the general conceptual background for John's use of the way/journey motif in his Gospel. Besides this primary purpose, this exhaustive examination is undertaken to give the reader an objective picture of the concept of way in Greek-Jewish literature. In this attempt, only classical Greek literature, the Old Testament (Hebrew and Greek), the Dead Sea Scrolls, the works of Philo and Josephus and the New Testament are taken into account. This part will end with a concluding section, which will show how a study of the way/journey motif in the Old Testament can enlighten an understanding of the way/journey motif in the Gospel of John. The fruits of the study of the way/journey motif in Greek-Jewish literature will be made use of in the second part and will be further highlighted in the general conclusion of this monograph.

1. "Way" in Classical Greek Literature

1.1. Various Terminologies

The important way-lexemes in classical Greek literature are ὁδός, κέλευθος, οἶμος πόρος, πάτος and ἁμαξιτός. The terms κέλευθος and οἶμος are reserved for poets.[1] The literal meanings of κέλευθος are "path", "road", "journey", "voyage" and "walk" and it may metaphorically mean "way of life".[2] The term οἶμος literally means "way", "path", "road" and "stripe" and its metaphorical meaning is "the course or strain of song".[3] The term πόρος has both literal and metaphorical meanings. Its most common literal meanings are "pathway", "passage" and "opening", and metaphorically it can denote "a means of achieving, accomplishing or discovering something" or "journey",

---

[1] T. Fleischhauer, "Das Bild des Weges in der antiken griechischen Literatur: drei Streiflichter", *Symbolik von Weg und Reise*, ed. P. Michael (Schriften zur Symbolforschung 8; Bern 1992), 1.
[2] LSJ, 936.
[3] LSJ, 1206.

"voyage" or a personified cosmological principle.[4] The opposite of πόρος is the adjective ἄπορος. It means "without passage, having no way in, out, or through".[5] Besides other meanings, the term πάτος has the meanings of "trodden or beaten way, path, action of going and course".[6] The meaning of ἁμαξιτός is "carriage-road, high-road, highway".[7]

The term ὁδός is the oldest, the most frequently used and the most common word for "way" in classical Greek literature.[8] There is uncertainty with regard to the etymology of ὁδός. It is believed that ὁδός is connected with a Slavic word, *chodŭ/chód*, which means "course" or "progress".[9] *Chodŭ* itself is thought to be borrowed from Iranian.[10] There is also a proposal that the Indo-Iranian verbs like Sanskrit *ā-sad* (to tread on, to go on) or Avestan *apahad* (to go away) form the root for ὁδός.[11]

1.2 Meaning and Usage of ὁδός

The meaning and usage of ὁδός in classical Greek literature, dating from the time of Homer onwards, can be mainly classified into two categories: literal and metaphorical.[12]

1.2.1 Literal Meaning and Usage of ὁδός

Literally, ὁδός can denote a place for travelling or moving (from one place to another) and also the very act of travelling. As a place for travelling, it means "way", "road", "highway", "street".[13] It can be "a road for the chariot", ἱπ πηλασίη ὁδός, "a royal road", βασιλικὴ ὁδός or "a channel of a river",

---

[4] Cf. LSJ, 1450–1451.

[5] LSJ, 215. The state of being ἄπορος is known as ἀπορία. A problem that is difficult to solve can be called ἀπορία.

[6] LSJ, 1348.

[7] LSJ, 77.

[8] It is found as οὐδός once in Homer, *Odyssey*, 17.196. See O. Becker, *Das Bild des Weges und verwandte Vorstellungen im frühgriechischen Denken* (Berlin 1937), 15. In the following discussion, attention will be paid only to the meaning and usage of ὁδός. For further study on various other way-lexemes, including verbs of journey, see B. Snell, *Die Entdeckung des Geistes. Studien zur Entstehung des Europäischen Denkens bei den Griechen* (Göttingen 1993), especially chapter 13 on "Das Symbol des Weges"; Fleischhauer, "Das Bild des Weges", 1–17; Becker, *Das Bild des Weges*.

[9] R. Beekes, *Etymological Dictionary of Greek* (Leiden 2010) I, 1046–1047; P. Chantraine, *Dictionnaire Étymologique de la Langue Grecque. Histoire des Mots* (Paris 1984) II, 774–775. Becker, *Das Bild des Weges*, 15–16, has argued that ὁδός originates from ἕζομαι and ἕδος.

[10] Beekes, *Etymological Dictionary*, 1047.

[11] Beekes, *Etymological Dictionary*, 1047.

[12] Cf. LSJ, 1199.

[13] LSJ, 1199. Cf. Homer, *Odyssey*, 17.196; idem, *Iliad*, 12.168; 16.374.

ποταμοῦ ὁδός.[14] As an act of travelling, it means "course", "journey", "departure", "trip", "voyage".[15] In this sense, ὁδὸν ἐλθέμεναι means "to go on a journey",[16] and going τὰν νεάταν ὁδὸν implies making the "last journey" of life.[17] The expression τριήκοντα ἡμερέων ὁδός means "thirty days' journey".[18] When Heraclitus declares, ὁδὸς ἄνω κάτω μία καὶ ὡυτή, "the way up and down is one and the same",[19] it may refer to the two-fold journey of the soul as an ascent towards the heights, a knowledge of nature and gods, and as a descent, a knowledge of man, an introspective journey into the depths of the soul, both of which are one and the same.

1.2.2 Metaphorical Meaning and Usage of ὁδός

Since one must go some way in order to reach a goal, ὁδός becomes a metaphor and gets the meaning of "the means and the way of carrying out something".[20] Hence, as a metaphor, it denotes "the manner" of doing something or "the means" to achieve something.[21] Pindar can, therefore, speak of "many ways of success with the help of gods", πολλαὶ δ' ὁδοὶ σὺν θεοῖς εὐπραγίας.[22] Herodotus thinks of "three ways of telling the story" (τριφασίας ἄλλας λόγων ὁδοὺς φῆναι) of Cyrus.[23] In *Eumenides*, Athena would ask, "do they then intend to find the way of good speech?", ἆρα φρονοῦσιν γλώσσης ἀγαθῆς ὁδὸν εὑρίσκειν;[24] When Euripides states, τῆς δ' ἀληθείας ὁδὸς φαύλη τίς ἐστι· ψεύδεσιν δ' Ἄρης φίλος, he may be contrasting "the way of truth" (τῆς δ' ἀληθείας ὁδός) with the way of lies, whose friend is war.[25] However, he too thinks of "the way" for arriving at the truth. The expression ὁδὸς βίου was more often used to refer to "the manner of life" (form of life) than to "the path of life" (life, destiny).[26] Wrong human behaviour could be described as

---

[14] LSJ, 1199.

[15] LSJ, 1199. Cf. Homer, *Odyssey*, 2.273; 2.285; 8.150; Aeschylus, *Agamemnon*, 80. Since ὁδός stands for the missing abstract of ἰέναι (to go), the word carries in it an element of action. Cf. G. Ebel, "ὁδός", *NIDNTT*, III, 935.

[16] Homer, *Iliad*, 1.151.

[17] Sophocles, *Antigone*, 807.

[18] Herodotus, *The Histories*, 1.104.

[19] Heraclitus, *Fragments*, 60. The translation is mine.

[20] Cf. Ebel, "ὁδός", 935.

[21] LSJ, 1199.

[22] Pindar, *Olympian Odes*, 8.13.

[23] Herodotus, *The Histories*, 1.95.1.

[24] Aeschylus, *Eumenides*, 989.

[25] Euripides, *Fragments*, 289. This statement is from the existing constituent fragments of the play *Bellerophon*, most of which do not survive currently. It may be interesting to notice that Jesus contrasts truth (ἀλήθεια) with lie (ψεῦδος), whose father is the devil, the murderer (the friend of war) in John 8,44–45.

[26] See Plato, *Republic*, 10.600b; cf. Michaelis, "ὁδός", 43.

"following an unjust way".²⁷ Therefore, ὁδός also has the sense of "conduct" or "behaviour".

There is a lot of supporting evidence in classical Greek literature for the metaphor of two ways.²⁸ The earliest attestation is found in *Works and Days*, 286–292 of Hesiod (active between about 750–650 BCE). In this work, there is the allegory of two ways in the form of the difficult way of virtue (ἀερτή) and the easy way of vice (κακότης). According to Hesiod, wickedness can be obtained too easily and abundantly. She lives very nearby and the way (ὁδός) to her is smooth (λεῖος).²⁹ But the path (οἶμος) to virtue is lengthy (μακρός) and steep (ὄρθιος). It is rough (τρηχύς) and difficult (χαλεπός) at first, but when one reaches the summit (ἄκρον), it is easy (ῥήδιος).

There is also a metaphor of the two ways in "the fable of Hercules at the crossroads", which is recounted in Xenophon's *Memorabilia*.³⁰ "The fable of Hercules at the crossroads" is traced back to the Sophist Prodicus of Ceos (465–395 BCE). This fable is also known as "Prodicus fable" or "Judgement of Hercules" or "Choice of Hercules". According to this story, the young Hercules has a vision in which two women appear to him. One of them is of a voluptuous form and meretricious look and dress, and the other is of dignified beauty, adorned with purity, modesty and discretion. The first promises to lead him by the shortest way, without any toil, to the enjoyment of every pleasure, while the second shows him the long and difficult way. If the shortest and easiest way is the way of vice, the long and the difficult way is the way of virtue. The goal of virtue is most blessed happiness. The goal of vice is apparently happiness, but in reality, it is not so. Hence, she is nicknamed vice. Since both ways promise happiness, Heracles is in a dilemma to make a

---

[27] E.g., μετὰ γὰρ Ἀθηναίων ἄδικον ὁδὸν ἰόντων ἐχωρήσατε in Thucydides, *History of the Peloponnesian War*, 3.64.4.

[28] In Herodotus, *Histories*, 1.11.2, the phrase "two ways" is used metaphorically to make the choice between life and death. The context is that the wife of Candaules, the king of the Lydians, wanted to avenge herself upon Candaules for the shame that her husband prompted Gyges, his most pleasing spear man, to see her nakedness in secret (I.8–10). After the event, the wife of Candaules summoned Gyges and said to him: "Now, Gyges, you have two roads (τοί δυῶν ὁδῶν) before you; choose which you will follow. You must either kill Candaules and take me for your own and the throne of Lydia, or yourself be killed now without more ado; that will prevent you from obeying all Candaules' commands in the future and seeing what you should not see. One of you must die: either he, the contriver of this plot, or you, who have outraged all usage by looking on me unclad" (I.11.2). As translated by A. Godley, *Herodotus. An English Translation* (London 1975) I, 15. Gyges obeys her and kills Candaules and possesses her and the kingdom.

[29] Cf. Sir 21,10, "The way of sinners is paved with smooth stones, but at its end is the pit of Hades".

[30] Xenophon, *Memorabilia*, 2.1.21–34. Cf. E. W. Smith, *Dictionary of Greek and Roman Biography and Mythology* (Boston 1870) III, 542–543. Michaelis, "ὁδός", 46, believes that the metaphor of two ways is older than the fable of Prodicus.

choice between the two. The story and the metaphor of two ways remind one of the Greek letter Y, which Pythagoras is supposed to have used to give a picture of human life. The lower stroke represents unbroken childhood under the protection of parents and teachers. Then there are two branches to the left and right, which represent vice and virtue.[31]

In the course of time, ὁδός also became a technical term for the philosophical "way of enquiry or knowledge" and a "method" of thinking.[32] In Parmenides' poem *On Nature*, the notion of "way", represented by various terms, but mainly by ὁδός (9x), appears 15 times.[33] It shows that for Parmenides, knowledge is gained by a "route", a "journey", a conceptual course, that is, through a method.[34] For him, ὁδός represents the intellectual and philosophical path of investigation and knowledge. In this poem (1.1–30), Parmenides tells how he has been carried on a chariot, drawn by docile mares and driven by young girls, identified as the daughters of the Sun, on "the way of the goddess" (ὁδός δαίμονος). This "much spoken" (πολύφημος) way is capable to lead the man who knows through all things. It proceeds from "the abodes of the night" (δώματα Νυκτός) to "the light" (εἰς φάος), i.e., to the day. The poet claims that he was born on this way (1.5). There are also gates (πύλαι) between the ways of night and day, Ἔνθα πύλαι Νυκτός τε καὶ Ἤματός εἰσι κελεύθων (1,10). These gates, which are high in the air, are closed by mighty doors, and the avenging Justice holds the keys to open and shut them (1,10). The goddess is said to have unlocked the door for the traveller to enter the high road under the persuasion of the daughters of the Sun (1,20). The poet goes on to say that the goddess, probably the same Justice, then greets the traveller cordially, rejoicing with him that he has arrived on a road so little travelled by men, but "the divine law and justice" (θέμις τε δίκη τε) have brought him to travel on this way (1,25).[35] The image of the way lies at the centre of the poem as a trajectory leading from darkness to light, which is probably the symbol of the trajectory of human knowledge moving toward the truth.

After the preface (1.1–30), the author explains "the only (two) ways of inquiry into knowledge" (ὁδοὶ μοῦναι διζήσιός εἰσι νοῆσαι). The two ways which are called "the way of day" and "the way of night" in the preface seem to reappear in a different form in 2,1–5. The first way is "it is" and "it is impossible for it not to be" (ἡ μὲν ὅπως ἔστιν τε καὶ ὡς οὐκ ἔστι μὴ εἶναι). It is the way of persuasion (πειθοῦς κέλευθος), and it is accompanied by truth (ἀλήθεια). The second way is "it is not", and "it is necessary for it not to be"

---

[31] Michaelis, "ὁδός", 44, n. 7.
[32] Cf. Michaelis, "ὁδός", 43.
[33] Other way-lexemes that occur in this poem are κέλευθος (3x), πάτος (1x), ἀμαξιτός (1x), ἀταρπός (1x).
[34] N. L. Cordero, *By Being, It Is. The Thesis of Parmenides* (Las Vegas 2004), 23.
[35] Θέμις is the goddess of law and order.

(ἡ δ' ὡς οὐκ ἔστιν τε καὶ ὡς χρεών ἐστι μὴ εἶναι). This is an untrustworthy way, for one cannot know what is not and it amounts to nothingness. Thus, the only way of which we can speak is that "it is" (Μόνος δ' ἔτι μῦθος ὁδοῖο λείπεται ὡς ἔστιν, 8,1). Parmenides' metaphor of two ways may be based on a transfer of religious symbolism into a method (μέθοδος) of philosophical thinking. With Parmenides' poem, the image of the way, or more broadly, that of a "journey" as a method of access to the truth, makes its entry in definitive form into the domain of philosophy.[36]

The combination of ὁδός and μέθοδος is also used to refer to the philosophical way of enquiry and the system of thinking in the statement from Plato's *Republic*, ὡς αὐτοῦ γε ἑκάστου πέρι ὃ ἔστιν ἕκαστον ἄλλη τις ἐπιχειρεῖ μέθοδος ὁδῷ περὶ παντὸς λαμβάνειν.[37] The expression ὁδῷ or καθ' ὁδόν got the sense of "methodically".[38] In Plato's *Sophist*, during the dialogue between Theaetetus and the stranger, the stranger asks for a philosophical "method" (μέθοδος) of hunting the family of the sophists, who are troublesome and hard to catch.[39] The use of ὁδός can also be noticed in Plato's famous allegory of the cave.[40] People in the cave happen to see the shadows of the people who move along "the way" (ὁδός) behind the cave. Since the prisoners are not able to see "the way", "the way" belongs to the world of the real. Even though the metaphor of two ways is not stated here, there is at least a philosophical dualism between the world of appearances and the world of the real.

By the time of Lucian of Samosata (second centuary CE), the doctrine of philosophers like Pythagoras, Plato and Aristotle was called ὁδός ἐν φιλοσοφίᾳ. This is evident from the following passage from *Hermotimus*:

Well then, can you name me a man who has tried every path (ὁδός) in philosophy (ἐν φιλοσοφίᾳ), who knows what Pythagoras, Plato, Aristotle, Chrysippus, Epicurus, and the rest say, and, finally, has chosen one path out of them all, has proved it genuine, and has learnt by experience that it alone leads straight to happiness? If we found such a person, we should stop worrying. It would not be easy to discover such a person.[41]

---

[36] Cordero, *By Being, It Is*, 23.

[37] Plato, *Republic*, 7.533b.

[38] Notice Socrates' statement τὴν γὰρ διὰ τοῦ στοιχείου ὁδὸν ἔχων ἔγραφεν, ἣν δὴ λόγον ὡμολογήσαμεν in Plato, *Theaetetus*, 208b. Also see idem, *Phaedrus*, 263b; idem, *Republic*, 4.435a.

[39] Plato, *Sophist*, 218d.

[40] Plato, *Republic*, 7.514b.

[41] Lucian, *Hermotimus*, 46, as translated by K. Kilburn, *Lucian. With an English Translation* (LCL 430; Cambridge 1959) VI, 347. Though Lucian belonged to the second centuary CE, he wrote in Attic Greek and his works are regarded as part of classical Greek literature.

Thus, the image of way (ὁδός) turns into the "method" (μέθοδος = μετά + ὁδός), the trajectory of knowledge, in Greek philosophy.

1.3 Conclusion

There are various way-lexemes in classical Greek literature. These lexemes usually have literal and metaphorical meanings. Literally, they refer to "road" or "path" as a spatial reality. Some of them have the sense of "journey" or "voyage". Metaphorically, some of them have the meaning of "manner" or "means". Among the various way-lexemes, the most important and the most common one is ὁδός. An examination of the meaning and usage of ὁδός gives us adequate information about what the concept of way in classical Greek literature is. The term ὁδός has a variety of usages in the metaphorical sense. It may imply a "means of achieving something" or a "manner of doing something". The whole human conduct or behaviour can be referred to as ὁδός. Since human behaviour can be characterized either as good or evil, ὁδός has a moral sense. As a result, human morality is often described with the help of the metaphor of ways.[42] One can also notice that ὁδός gradually gets the meaning of a method of thinking, a trajectory of knowledge or a way of philosophical enquiry. Hence, the way of truth and the pursuit of truth are one and the same. We are not sure whether John is aware of the Greek philosophers' way of inquiry and truth when he presents Jesus as the way and truth in John 14,6. In Greek thought, there is a tendency to consider truth as a goal in itself and the Greek philosophers are concerned with the way of knowing the truth. In the course of this study, we will examine how John looks at truth and its relation to way and also to life. Let us now turn to the Jewish literature which provides the main literary background for John's language and thinking.

---

[42] There is no methodological justification for jumping to the conclusion that the metaphor of two ways in classical Greek literature influenced the use of the metaphor of two ways in Jewish and Christian writings. The metaphor of way is inherent in human thinking. It is a very suggestive and easily understandable metaphor, which offered itself independently in many different places and cultures in order to illustrate spiritual processes and religious and ethical developments. See Michaelis, "ὁδός", 46, 48.

2. "Way" in the Hebrew Bible

The concept of "way" in the Hebrew Bible is very profound and rich.[43] The lexical field connected to the idea of way is very vast.[44] Hence, only the most important way-lexemes that have considerable theological significance will be examined here.[45] In ancient times, Israelites were nomadic people. Their

---

[43] J. Muilenburg, *The Way of Israel. Biblical Faith and Ethics* (New York 1961), 33, says about the concept of way in the Old Testament, "No other image was more rich and manifold, none more diverse in nuance and connotation". Important literature on the way topic in the Old Testament are the following: Ø. Lund, *Way Metaphors and Way Topics in Isaiah 40–55* (WUNT II 28; Tübingen 2007); M. P. Zehnder, *Wegmetaphorik im Alten Testament. Eine semantische Untersuchung der alttestamentlichen und altorientalischen Weg-Lexeme mit besonderer Berücksichtigung ihrer metaphorischen Verwendung* (BZAW 268; Berlin 1999); J. K. Aitken, "דֶּרֶךְ", *Semantics of Ancient Hebrew*, ed. T. Muraoka (Abr-Nahrain Supplement Series 6; Leuven 1998), 11–37; D. J. A. Clines (ed.), "דֶּרֶךְ", *The Dictionary of Classical Hebrew* (Sheffield 1995), 464–473; F. Mathys, "Gott und Mensch auf dem Weg. Einige Hinweise zur hebräischen Bibel, ausgehend von Jes 55,9", *Symbolik von Weg und Reise*, ed. P. Michel (Symbolforschung 8; Bern 1992), 19–28; D. A. Dorsey, *The Roads and Highways of Ancient Israel* (Baltimore 1991); idem, "Another Peculiar Term in the Book of Chronicles: מסלה, 'Highway'?", *JQR* 75 (1985), 385–391; R. Ratner, "Derek: Morpho-Syntactical Considerations", *JAOS* 107 (1987), 471–473; N. Tidwell, "No Highway! The Outline of a Semantic Description of Mesilla", *VT* 45 (1995), 251–269; idem, "A Road and a Way. A Contribution to the Study of Word-Pairs", *Semitics* 7 (1980), 50–80; E. H. Merrill, "דֶּרֶךְ", *NIDOTTE*, I, 989–993; K. Koch, "דֶּרֶךְ", *TDOT*, III, 270–293; H. Wolf, "דָּרַךְ", *TWOT*, I, 196–197; G. Sauer, "דֶּרֶךְ", *TLOT*, I, 343–346; Gros, *Je suis la route*; J. Muilenburg, *The Way of Israel*; F. Nötscher, *Gotteswege und Menschenwege in der Bibel und in Qumran* (BBB 15; Bonn 1958); K. Kuschke, "Die Menschenwege und der Weg Gottes im Alten Testament", *ST* 5 (1951–1952), 106–119.

[44] Zehnder, *Wegmetaphorik*, 293–463, classifies the various way-lexemes broadly into an inner and an outer group. The inner group is the core group in which the central lexeme is דֶּרֶךְ. Other lexemes that belong to the inner group are ארח, מַהֲלָךְ, מְסִלָּה, מַסְלוּל, מַעְגָּל, מִשְׁעוֹל, נְתִיב/נְתִיבָה, שְׁבִיל and שׁוּק. Zehnder (pp. 430–463) includes 45 lexemes in the outer group like אֲשֶׁר, בָּאָה, הֲלִיכָה, הֵלֶךְ, מָבוֹא, מַעֲבָר, מֵרוֹץ, סֻלָּם, etc. He considers חוּץ as a special case without including it in any group because it is mostly used in the sense of "outside" or "outside of" (pp. 428–430). Finally, he examines briefly a special group, which he calls "Eschatologische Wunderstrasse" (pp. 463–472). In this group, he includes way passages like Isa 11,16; 19,23; 35,8; 40,3; 42,16; 57,14; 62,10; Jer 31,9; Mal 3,1.

[45] Our study of the way motif in the Hebrew Bible is in view of understanding John's conceptual background behind the usage of "way" in the Gospel. Since John uses the vocabulary for way only in the metaphorical sense, the way-lexemes which have only literal sense (e.g., מִשְׁעוֹל, שׁוּק, חוּץ) will not be considered here. Even though the step-lexemes like צַעַד, אָשֻׁר, פַּעַם and רֶגֶל are closely related to the way motif, they are not examined here because they do not add anything new or significant to the current discussion. The only way-lexeme that John uses is ὁδός. Here, only the most important Hebrew equivalents for ὁδός in the LXX which have considerable theological significance will be taken into account. Hence, only the following substantives will be examined: אֹרַח, דֶּרֶךְ, מַסְלוּל, מְסִלָּה, נְתִיב/נְתִיבָה.

primary means of journey on the way was walking/going on foot. Hence, the notion of "way" is inseparably intertwined with the activity of "walking/going". The Old Testament writers conceive life as a "journey/going" on "the way". The most prominent Hebrew term for way, דֶּרֶךְ, means not only "way" but also the very act of "journeying". Moreover, the Gospel of John also shows more interest in the use of verbs of journey than in the nouns for way. Therefore, it seems better to include in our study on the motif of way an examination of at least some of the important verbs of journey/movement.[46] Since the verbs of journey in the Hebrew Bible are numerous, only the theologically most important ones, which are relevant to this study, are selected here.[47]

2.1 Important Nouns and their Significance

2.1.1 דֶּרֶךְ

2.1.1.1 A Survey

The most frequently used and the most prominent word for "way" in the Hebrew Bible is דֶּרֶךְ.[48] דֶּרֶךְ is also the most commonly used term as a metaphor for life.[49] It is the way-lexeme with the broadest semantic usage too. It occurs

---

[46] F. Nötscher has included in his comprehensive study on "way" the analysis of six important verbs of journey like הָלַךְ, דָּרַךְ, עָלָה, נָחָה, נָהַל and נָהַג I under the title "Gott führt" (see Nötscher, *Gotteswege*, 32–42).

[47] To Nötscher's list, we add three more important verbs of journey, namely יָצָא, יָרַד and בּוֹא. The verb יָצָא is an important verb used for the exodus journey under God's leadership. Journey has usually two dimensions, an act of "going" and of "coming". Similarly, a way is not only for "going" but also for "coming". Hence, בּוֹא ("to come") and יָרַד ("to descend"), which is the antonym of עָלָה ("to ascend"), are also considered. Thus, we have to examine nine verbs: הָלַךְ, יָצָא, עָלָה, יָרַד, נָהַל, נָחָה, נָהַג I, דָּרַךְ and בּוֹא. These verbs are closely related to various way lexemes. Verbs like הָלַךְ (Gen 29,1; 42,37.38, also see the discussion below under הָלַךְ), יָצָא (Judg 19,27; 1 Sam 9,26; Jer 39,4; 52,7), עָלָה (Num 21,33; 2 Kgs 2,23), נָהַל (Gen 33,14), נָחָה (Exod 13,17; Gen 24,27), נָהַג I (Jer 23,12; cf. 1 Sam 30,2), דָּרַךְ (Pss 107,7; 119,35; Prov 4,11) and בּוֹא (2 Kgs 11,16.19; 19,33; Judg 9,37) tend to govern way-lexemes directly, in most cases the lexeme of דֶּרֶךְ. The verb יָרַד is found in close association with way-lexemes in 2 Kgs 11,19; Prov 7,27. For a brief examination of the relation of דֶּרֶךְ with other verbs of journey, see Aitken, "דֶּרֶךְ", 21–22; Dorsey, *The Roads and Highways*, 215–216. It should be kept in mind that an overlapping of various themes is likely to occur when we analyse various terminologies since they all circle around the same motif of "way".

[48] The root *drk* is employed as a verb and a noun in Phoenician and later in Egyptian Aramaic, Jewish Aramaic, Mandean and Syriac, also as a verb in Arabic and possibly in Ethiopic. However, it is impossible to get a convincing etymology for the root in Hebrew. See Koch, "דֶּרֶךְ", 276.

[49] E. H. Merrill, "הָלַךְ", *NIDOTTE*, I, 1032.

706 times, predominantly in the singular.⁵⁰ It is found in every book of the Old Testament except in Obadiah, Habakkuk, Zephaniah, Canticle of Canticles, Esther, Daniel and 1 Chronicles. About 58% of the occurrences of דֶּרֶךְ are found in prose and about 42% in poetry.⁵¹ In ca. 56.5% of the occurrences, דֶּרֶךְ has an adverbial function, and it is used as a direct object in ca. 22% of the cases, as a subject in ca. 11.6% and as a location in ca. 4% of the instances.⁵² In ca. 15% of all occurrences, דֶּרֶךְ is found in association with the verb הָלַךְ. דֶּרֶךְ is considered to be an outcome of the nominalization of the verb דָּרַךְ, which basically means "to tread" and occurs 63 times.⁵³ It is double gendered in Biblical Hebrew but is always used as masculine in the plural.⁵⁴ The greatest frequency of דֶּרֶךְ is found in Ezekiel (107x), Proverbs (75x), Psalms (66x),⁵⁵ Jeremiah (57x), Deuteronomy (48x), Isaiah (47x) and 1 Kings (46x). In the earlier strata of the books from Genesis through 2 Kings, דֶּרֶךְ is employed frequently in the literal sense of "road", "movement" and "journey".⁵⁶ In poetic literature, especially in Psalms and Proverbs, the word is used mostly in the figurative sense. As a whole, the term דֶּרֶךְ is used in the Hebrew Bible more frequently in its figurative sense than in its literal sense.

If one wants to translate דֶּרֶךְ by a single equivalent, there is no better option than to translate it as "way".⁵⁷ But דֶּרֶךְ can have various shades of mean-

---

⁵⁰ J. R. Kohlenberger III and J. A. Swanson, *The Hebrew English Concordance to the Old Testament* (Grand Rapids 1998), 419–424. According to G. Lisowsky, *Konkordanz zum hebräischen Alten Testament* (Stuttgart ³1993), 370–375, the frequency of דֶּרֶךְ is 690 times. Zehnder, *Wegmetaphorik*, 294, thinks that in ten instances (2 Sam 15,23; Isa 3,12; 35,8a; Jer 2,17; Ezek 42,1a; 42,4; Amos 8,14; Pss 50,23; 85,14; Lam 3,11) דֶּרֶךְ can be omitted. For Aitken, "דֶּרֶךְ", 12–13, the doubtful passages are Isa 3,12; 35,8; Jer 3,13; Hos 10,13; Amos 8,14; Prov 31,3 (also Sir 42,3; 49,9 in their Hebrew manuscripts). Sauer, "דֶּרֶךְ", 343, notices that דֶּרֶךְ appears 543 times in the singular.

⁵¹ Zehnder, *Wegmetaphorik*, 294.

⁵² Zehnder, *Wegmetaphorik*, 294.

⁵³ Cf. Kohlenberger and Swanson, *The Hebrew English Concordance*, 419. The other two derivatives from דָּרַךְ are מִדְרָךְ and דַּרְכְּמֹ(ו)נִים. While מִדְרָךְ means "footprint", "foot breadth" and occurs only in Deut 2,5, דַּרְכְּמֹ(ו)נִים means "drachma", "unit of measure" and is used only in Ezr 2,69 and Neh 7,69–71. Cf. *HALOT*, 232, 550.

⁵⁴ Ratner, "Derek: Morpho-Syntactical Considerations", 471–473, argues that דֶּרֶךְ is either masculine or feminine in independent clauses and some dependent clauses, but is always feminine in relative clauses. For various other proposals for gender problems, see Aitken, "דֶּרֶךְ", 18–21; Dorsey, *The Roads and Highways*, 220–222.

⁵⁵ דֶּרֶךְ occurs in the Psalms mostly in its metaphorical sense. In some Wisdom Psalms (Pss 1; 25; 37; 119), דֶּרֶךְ functions as an important theme. In these Psalms, the way lexemes are in content related to individual conduct or to the divine guidance of an individual's life. Cf. Koch, "דֶּרֶךְ", 284.

⁵⁶ Cf. Koch, "דֶּרֶךְ", 282–283.

⁵⁷ Koch, "דֶּרֶךְ", 277. Sauer, "דֶּרֶךְ", 344, thinks that the meaning of דֶּרֶךְ developed in many ways in both spatial-geographical as well as metaphorical-figurative senses from the primary meaning of "travelled and thus established way". He points out that from the

ings.⁵⁸ We may "broadly" classify the various meanings of דֶּרֶךְ into four groups: i. concrete-spatial meaning,⁵⁹ ii. meaning with focus on movement,⁶⁰ iii. meaning with focus on the course of human life and activity,⁶¹ iv. meaning with focus on God's activity and plan for human salvation.⁶² The following discussion will focus only on the metaphorical sense of דֶּרֶךְ, especially on its theological usage. This does not mean that human דֶּרֶךְ is played down, because it is the דֶּרֶךְ of God that determines how the human דֶּרֶךְ should be or should not be. For the Old Testament writers, the דֶּרֶךְ of God is always the ideal and the salvation towards which the human דֶּרֶךְ should orientate itself. It is in the light of the דֶּרֶךְ of God that the nobility or the misery of the human

---

concrete meaning of "way" imperceptibly evolved the meaning, "movement on the way" or "journey".

⁵⁸ Zehnder, *Wegmetaphorik*, 296, sees in דֶּרֶךְ about sixty various shades of meanings, which he classifies, according to their frequency, into the following four groups: i. usage relating to concrete-spatial aspect, ii. usage relating to the aspect of movement, iii. usage relating to moral aspect, iv. usage in the sense of "life as a way" (Lebensweg/Ergehen). But it is difficult to see a sharp distinction between the third and the fourth group in Zehnder's classification. *HALOT*, 231–232, gives the following list of meanings: i. way, road (Exod 4,24), ii. distance of journey (Gen 30,36), iii. journey, including the meaning of physical journey (Num 9,10), enterprise and business (2 Chr 13,22; Gen 24,21) and campaign (1 Sam 15,18), iv. manner, custom, behaviour (Gen 19,21; 31,35; Jer 10,2; Ps 50,23; Isa 55,7), v. divine ways: a. God's behaviour (Ezek 18,25; Hos 14,10) and action (Deut 32,4; Prov 8,22; Job 40,19), b. the conduct required by God (Gen 18,19; Jer 5,4; Deut 9,16), vi. condition, situation (Isa 40,27; Hag 1,5; Jer 10,23), vii. strength, power (Jer 3,13; Hos 10,13; Prov 31,3). The meanings suggested by *DCH*, 464–466, are the following: i. way, path, road, passage, ii. journey, iii. venture, mission, errand, iv. manner, v. course of life, conduct, morality, vi. way of Yahweh: a. commandments of Yahweh, b. activity of Yahweh, vii. hill, mountain pasture.

⁵⁹ E.g., "road" (Gen 38,16; Num 22,22; Prov 26,13; Jer 31,21), "way" associated with place names (Gen 16,7; Num 14,25; Deut 1,2; Josh 2,7; 1 Sam 6,9), "direction/toward" (Jer 4,11; Ezek 8,5; 21,2; 41,11; 42,1; 2 Chr 6,34.38), etc.

⁶⁰ E.g., "journey" (Gen 28,20; 42,25; 45,21; Num 9,10; Josh 9,11; 24,17; 1 Kgs 18,27), "on the way" (Gen 45,24; Exod 4,24; 18,8; 23,20; Num 21,4; Deut 23,4), with focus on movements like "flying" (Prov 30,19a), "moving" (Prov 30,19b.c), "going" (Nah 1,3), "mission/campaign" (1 Sam 15,18.20; 2 Sam 11,10), etc.

⁶¹ E.g., course of human life (Pss 91,11; 102,24[23]; Prov 3,23; Lam 3,9), human destiny (Jer 10,23; 23,12; Ps 35,6), way of life (Prov 22,6), manner (Gen 31,35; Isa 10,24.26; Jer 10,2; Amos 4,10; Qoh 11,5; 2 Chr 18,23), moral conduct/behaviour (Gen 6,12; Ps 50,23; Isa 3,12; 8,11; 55,7; 65,2; Hos 4,9; Ezek 3,18), death (Josh 23,14; 1 Kgs 2,2), etc. Apart from human life, דֶּרֶךְ can be used to refer to animals' way of life (Prov 6,6).

⁶² This includes, e.g., way in relation to God's leading (Exod 13,21; Deut 1,31.33; 8,2; Josh 24,17; Jer 2,17), God's statutes/commandments (Exod 18,20; Deut 8,6; Josh 22,5; 1 Kgs 2,3; 8,58), the conduct required by God (Gen 18,19; Jer 5,4; Deut 9,16), God's behaviour (Ezek 18,25; Hos 14,10[9]), God's action/work (Deut 32,4; Pss 138,5; 145,17; Prov 8,22; Job 40,19), God's plan (Exod 33,13; Isa 55,8–9), way in relation to future salvation (Isa 35,8; 40,3; 42,16; 43,19; 49,9.11; 57,14; 62,10; Jer 31,9; 32,39; Mal 3,1), etc.

דֶּרֶךְ is revealed. This is perhaps the best way to understand דֶּרֶךְ in the Old Testament.

2.1.1.2 Theological Usage

a. Way as God's Activity in Creation

Functioning as *nomen rectum*, דֶּרֶךְ refers to God's creative power in Job 26,14 (קְצוֹת דְּרָכָיו), 40,19 (רֵאשִׁית דַּרְכֵי־אֵל) and Prov 8,22 (רֵאשִׁית דַּרְכּוֹ). In Job 26,5–14, there is an account of God's creative work, which portrays God's dominion over the natural powers. Job is asked by Bildad to consider the facts of creation, if he wants to take the measure of God's power.[63] But even these acts of power are far from displaying the full sovereignty of God. These most spectacular exhibitions of his might are only קְצוֹת דְּרָכָיו, the "edges of his ways" (26,14). Here, דֶּרֶךְ is used to refer to God's power over the creation.[64] In Job 40,19, the beast Behemoth is called the "beginning/first of God's ways", רֵאשִׁית דַּרְכֵי־אֵל, i.e., the crown of the animal creation. In Prov 8,22, wisdom is characterized as the "beginning/first of his way", רֵאשִׁית דַּרְכּוֹ. Here דֶּרֶךְ signifies a collectivity of actions or deeds, referring to God's creative acts before the formation of the world.[65]

In Ps 145,17, Yahweh's "ways" stand in parallel with his "works" (cf. Deut 32,4). Ps 145, which celebrates the attributes of Yahweh, is described as a litany of divine names and appellatives.[66] V. 17 states that Yahweh is just "in all his ways" (בְּכָל־דְּרָכָיו) and kind "in all his deeds" (בְּכָל־מַעֲשָׂיו). The whole creation is dependent on Yahweh's providential care and deeds. In Nah 1,3, there is an association between דֶּרֶךְ and Yahweh's movement in the nature, "His way is in whirlwind and storm, and the clouds are the dust of his feet". The whirlwind, storm, and the clouds are not gods but only the willing and obedient servants of Yahweh, who reigns supremely over the nature.[67] As the creator of the universe and the controller of world history, God's deeds are above the human realm. He is infinitely greater than the created world (Isa

---

[63] There is a problem with the literary integrity in Job 24–27. It is suggested that the speaker of Job 26,14 is Bildad and not Job. See M. H. Pope, *Job. Introduction, Translation and Notes* (AB 15; New Haven 1974), xxiii–xxx.

[64] M. J. Dahood, "Some Northwest-Semitic Words in Job", *Bib* 38 (1957), 306–320, has shown that in this passage as well as in other places like Job 40,19; Jer 3,13; Hos 10,13; Amos 8,14; Pss 1,1; 110,7; 138,5; Prov 8,22; 31,3 the word דֶּרֶךְ has the meaning of "power" or "dominion", just as *drkt* in the Ugaritic mythological texts means "power" or "dominion". But this view is rejected by many scholars. See Sauer, "דֶּרֶךְ", 345. In the view of Zehnder, *Wegmetaphorik*, 385, the meaning of דֶּרֶךְ in the given instances can be satisfactorily explained without dependence on the Ugaritic *drkt*.

[65] Cf. M. V. Fox, *Proverbs 1–9* (AB 18A; New Haven 1974), 280–281.

[66] M. J. Dahood, *Psalms 101–150* (AB 17A; New Haven 1974) III, 335.

[67] In the context of Yahweh's judgement on his enemies (vv. 2–3), whirlwind, storm and clouds symbolize his judgement (cf. Ps 83,15; Isa 29,6).

40,12). No one has advised him either in the creation or in the administration of the natural world (Isa 40,12–14). No one has taught him "the path of justice", אֹרַח מִשְׁפָּט and "the way of intelligence", דֶּרֶךְ תְּבוּנוֹת (Isa 40,14; cf. Job 36,22–23). God's wisdom and creative power are so exclusively unique that no being can compete with him.

b. Way as God's Salvation in the Past

The first occurrence of דֶּרֶךְ appears in Gen 3,24. It is found in the context of humanity's separation from God and his presence (3,1–24). Adam and Eve are expelled from the garden of Eden on account of their sin of disobedience. The story beautifully narrates that "the way to the tree of life", דֶּרֶךְ עֵץ הַחַיִּים, is blocked and it remains unapproachable and inaccessible to them.[68] The wretchedness of the human condition (cf. 4,1–16) is again portrayed when Gen 6,12 states, "God looked upon the earth, and indeed it was corrupt; for 'all flesh' (כָּל־בָּשָׂר) had corrupted their 'way' (דַּרְכּוֹ) on the earth".[69] This situation of humanity necessitates the salvific plan of God; its purpose is to bring the estranged humanity back to "the way to the tree of life", i.e., to the presence of God. This requires a righteous community, who will be obedient to "the way of the Lord". The expression "way of the Lord" (דֶּרֶךְ יְהוָה) appears for the first time in the Old Testament in Gen 18,19. God chooses Abraham specially as his instrument for the fulfilment of his salvific plan and asks him to instruct his descendants to keep the "way of the Lord" (דֶּרֶךְ יְהוָה) by doing righteousness and justice like him. Thus, for human salvation, the Lord demands from the children of Abraham that they keep the way of the Lord by doing righteousness and justice.

Often דֶּרֶךְ is used in the book of Exodus in association with the redemption of Israel from Egypt (Exod 13,17.18.21; 18,8; 23,20; 33,3.13).[70] The Lord himself walks in front of them in a pillar of cloud by day "to lead them along the way" (לַנְחֹתָם הַדֶּרֶךְ), and in a pillar of fire by night to give them light, so that they might travel by day and by night (Exod 13,21; cf. 14,19).[71] He sends his angel in front of them to guard them "on the way" (בַּדָּרֶךְ) and to bring them to the place that he has prepared (Exod 23,20). Because of the rebellious nature of the Israelites, it is necessary for Moses to know the "ways" (דְּרָכִים)

---

[68] The Gospel of John presupposes the fundamental problem of humanity's separation from God as a consequence of the sin of Adam and Eve. See the comments on pp. 116–117, 398–400.

[69] This translation is according to NKJ.

[70] The term דֶּרֶךְ appears in the Book of Exodus only 13 times.

[71] Muilenburg, *The Way of Israel*, 50, says, "The hour of Exodus was the birth of a people, the people chosen and called to a destiny. Israel's consciousness of being a people was first awakened at the Exodus; the event was the *fons et origo* of her life" (cf. Josh 24; 1 Sam 12; Ps 105).

of the Lord, i.e., his intention, his decision about the fate of Israel.[72] Only if the Lord's "presence" (פָּנֶה) goes with him and Israel as they depart from Sinai, can Moses keep on finding favour in the Lord's sight[73] (33,13). The Lord promises him that his "presence" (פָּנֶה) will go with him and the people (33,14).

In the Deuteronomic and Deuteronomistic literature, דֶּרֶךְ is in the first instance bound with God's salvific deeds from the exodus to the conquest (Deut 1,31.33; 8,2). It is the Lord their God who brought them and their ancestors up from the land of Egypt, out of the house of slavery, and protected them "in all the way" (בְּכָל־הַדֶּרֶךְ) that they went and among all the peoples through whom they passed (Josh 24,17; cf. 5,4). The Lord redeemed the Israelites from the slavery in Egypt, so that they might walk in the "way" of the Lord (Deut 13,5). The salvation history of Israel can be called a דֶּרֶךְ on which the Lord has led his people (Jer 2,17; cf. 2,6).[74]

Exod 33,13; 34,6 function as the background for Ps 103,7, "He made known his ways to Moses, his acts to the children of Israel". Here דֶּרֶךְ is explicitly bound with Yahweh's saving acts for Israel. In Ps 77, the psalmist meditates over the exodus event and praises Yahweh for his salvific deeds for Israel.[75] In v. 14 (13), he describes Yahweh's "way" (דֶּרֶךְ) as "holy" (קֹדֶשׁ) and demonstrates that there is no other god like Yahweh, מִי־אֵל גָּדוֹל כֵּאלֹהִים, "what god is so great as our God?" In v. 20, the דֶּרֶךְ of Yahweh is said to be through the sea and his "path" (שְׁבִיל) through the mighty waters. The saving activity of Yahweh is stressed by the *inclusio* between, "you redeemed your people with your arm", גָּאַלְתָּ בִּזְרוֹעַ עַמֶּךָ (v. 16) and "you led your people like a flock", נָחִיתָ כַצֹּאן עַמֶּךָ (v. 21). The invisible Yahweh makes his presence visible in mighty deeds through the hands of Moses and Aaron and thus paves the "way" (דֶּרֶךְ) or "path" (שְׁבִיל) for the redemption of Israel. In Ps 67,2, Yahweh's "way" (דֶּרֶךְ) is synonymous with his "salvation" (יְשׁוּעָה). The psalmist prays, "Your way may be known on earth, your 'salvation' (יְשׁוּעָה) among all nations".[76] He wishes that all nations on earth should praise Yahweh for his saving work in and through Israel. Thus, דֶּרֶךְ refers to a divine history in which Israel comes from the land of Egypt and possesses the promised land.

---

[72] J. I. Durham, *Exodus* (WBC 3; Dallas 1987), 447.

[73] Durham, *Exodus*, 447.

[74] Koch, "דֶּרֶךְ", 288.

[75] The language of vv. 17(16)–19 is drawn from ancient Near Eastern mythology, which describes the conflict between the gods of order and creation, on the one hand, and the forces of chaos represented by water, on the other. Cf. M. J. Dahood, *Psalms 51–100* (AB 17; New Haven 1974) II, 231–233; R. Davidson, *The Vitality of Worship. A Commentary on the Book of Psalms* (Grand Rapids 1998), 250.

[76] This translation is according to NKJ. Some scholars understand דֶּרֶךְ in Ps 67,2 as power or dominion. E.g., Dahood, *Psalms* II, 123; M. E. Tate, *Psalms 51–100* (WBC 20; Dallas 1990), 154, 157. See the comments on p. 44, n. 64.

c. Way as Covenant Relationship

דֶּרֶךְ may refer to the whole course of life lived in conformity to covenant obligation.[77] The exodus is the prologue to the covenant at Sinai (Exod 19,3–6; cf. Deut 5,3). At Sinai, the people enter into a covenant relationship with the Lord, and they are called to make a decision, a choice between the God of Israel, the God of history (cf. Exod 19,4–6; 20,1–6; Deut 11,13–15.22–25; Josh 24,14–15) and the gods of the nations. It is a choice between one God and many gods, obedience and disobedience, curse and blessing, a future and no future (Deut 11,26–28; 28,1–45). The covenant with the Lord requires that Israel always walks in "his ways", בִּדְרָכָיו (Deut 26,17–19; 28,9). In Jeremiah as well, the covenant obligation is expressed through the image of way, "Obey my voice, and I will be your God, and you shall be my people; and walk only in the 'way' (דֶּרֶךְ) that I command (צוה) you, so that it may be well with you" (Jer 7,23).[78] If Israel walks in the way (דֶּרֶךְ) as laid down by the Lord at Horeb, it may go well with her and she will live long in the promised land (Deut 5,33; 8,6; 11,22–24; 13,6[5]; 19,8–9).

The Lord has given the Torah to Israel as his guidebook for their journey of life. It refers to a divine pointing out of "the way" in written form.[79] The דֶּרֶךְ of the Lord can stand in a synonymous relation with his law (תּוֹרָה), statues (חֻקָּה), commandments (מִצְוֹת), judgements (מִשְׁפָּטִים,), testimonies (עֵדֹת), precepts (פִּקּוּדִים), saying (אִמְרָה) and word (דָּבָר) (1 Kgs 2,3; 3,14; 11,33.38; 2 Sam 22,22; Pss 18,22–23[21–22];119; Isa 2,3; Mic 4,2; cf. Job 23,11–12). The commandments (מִצְוֹת) of the Lord are his ways (Deut 8,6; Ps 119,15; Jer 7,23). In the covenant, the Lord's will is communicated by his commandments/words (Exod 20,1–17; Deut 4,13). Hence, the execution of the Lord's will consists in keeping his commandments. The legal obligations of the דֶּרֶךְ of the Lord open up a future of salvation for Israel, but often Israel falls away from the way (דֶּרֶךְ) of the Lord by violating his commandments/covenant (Exod 32,8; Deut 9,12–16; Judg 2,17).

Blessing or curse depends on the following or not following the way of the Lord (Deut 11,26–28). The right ways are only those which go in accordance with his commandments. All those who violate his commandments stumble "on the ways" (Hos 14,10[9]). The wicked would say to God, "We do not desire to know your ways" (Job 21,14; cf. Isa 58,2). But the covenant fidelity

---

[77] Cf. Merrill, "דֶּרֶךְ", 989.

[78] The Old Testament frequently uses the imagery of journey (going/walking) as a metaphor for covenant obedience. About the significance of the expression "walking in the way/s of the Lord" and its relation to God's commandments, we will discuss under the terminology of הָלַךְ.

[79] L. C. Allen, *Psalms 101–150* (WBC 21; Dallas 2002), 184. S. E. Tesh and W. D. Zorn, *Psalms* (The College Press NIV Commentary; Joplin 1999) II, 373, view that Torah is a general term indicating "instruction", whose basic idea is "pointing the way".

is the hallmark of the blameless (Ps 119,1. cf. 119,30), who are a delight to the Lord (Prov 11,20).

d. God as the Moral Administrator of the Way

For the Israelites, what is good is what the Lord demands and what is evil is what the Lord forbids. In Israel, the Lord is the judge and the final arbiter (Isa 33,22; Gen 16,5; 1 Sam 24,15). He is the protector and the establisher of the right. His will is above the will of all human judges, leaders and rulers (Isa 3,13–15; 41,1– 42,4). It is he who determines what is right and wrong. Doing good consists in doing the will of the Lord, which is revealed through the word of the Lord. It is he who shows a man the way he should go. Without his leading, Israel does not know the way that she should go (Ps 16,11). The Lord is the teacher of Israel. He teaches and leads everyone the way that he should go (1 Kgs 8,36; 2 Chr 6,27; Pss 25,4.8–9.12; 27,11; 32,8; 86,11; 119,26.33; 139,24; 143,8; Prov 16,9; Isa 2,3; 48,17; Jer 42,3; Mic 4,2). All ways of man are in God's hand (Dan 5,23). In Jeremiah's plea, "I know, O Lord, that the way (דֶּרֶךְ) of human beings is not in their control, that mortals as they walk cannot direct their steps", דֶּרֶךְ may represent the whole human life and destiny (10,23; also see Job 23,10; 31,4; Ps 91,11; Prov 20,24; Lam 3,9), which stand under God's control. The psalmist will request, "Commit your way to the Lord; trust in him, and he will act" (Ps 37,5).

The Lord's way also includes directions for the moral conduct of his people. Instructions for the right moral conduct are found frequently (Prov 4,26; 5,8; 10,9; 14,2.8.12; 16,7.17.25; 19,3; 22,6; 23,19; Jer 4,18; 18,11; Ezek 3,18–19; 24,14; 33,11). The Lord sees and examines the ways of all and rewards or punishes everyone accordingly (Prov 5,21; 16,2; 21,2; Isa 57,17; Jer 6,27; 16,17; 17,10; 32,19; Ezek 7,3.8–9.27; 18,30; 24,14; 33,20). The way of the wicked may appear to prosper (Jer 12,1), but ultimately it will perish (Ps 1,6). "The way of the Lord is a stronghold for the upright but destruction for evildoers" (Prov 10,29). The Lord demands that the wicked should give up their way and turn to the Lord (Isa 55,7). The psalmist asks for the Lord's help on his way in a literal (Pss 91,11; 107,7) as well as in a figurative sense (Ps 139,24). Salvation is for those who go the right way (Ps 50,23). In order to avoid an evil end, one has to direct his mind in "the way" (דֶּרֶךְ) of the Lord (Prov 23,19; cf. 23,17).

e. The Way of Wisdom

Wisdom is necessary for proper conduct. The Lord is the only author of wisdom (Prov 2,6; 8,22). Hence, the success of human activity depends on one's relationship with the Lord (Prov 2,6–15). Wisdom wants that everyone should follow her way (Prov 8,32; 23,19.26). A synonym for the way of wisdom is the "way of understanding", דֶּרֶךְ בִּינָה (Prov 9,6). The place of those who fail to walk in the way of understanding is among the dead (Prov 21,16). Often adjectives like "blameless", תָּמִים (Prov 10,9; 13,6; 28,6) and "righteous", יָשָׁר (Prov 14,12; 21,29; 29,27) are used to qualify the way of wisdom. Hence, the "way of wisdom", דֶּרֶךְ חָכְמָה, is also synonymous with the "paths of righteousness", מַעְגְּלֵי־יֹשֶׁר (Prov 4,11; 8,20), and one who walks on her way finds peace (Prov 3,17). In order to direct the human mind to the ways and statutes of the Lord, the fear of the Lord should be present as the framework for practical conduct.[80] "The fear of the Lord is the beginning of wisdom" (Ps 111,10; Prov 1,7; 9,10; Sir 1,14), and it is the Lord who gives one wisdom to live uprightly and blamelessly (Prov 2,3-8).

f. Two Ways

Even though the concept of "two ways" (good and evil) is not systematically developed, the notion is present and it may sum up the moral conduct of Old Testament Judaism (Ps 1,6; Prov 2,20–22; 4,18–19; 15,9–10; 28,6; cf. Jer 21,8). The concept of "the way of the good/good way" (דֶּרֶךְ הַטּוֹבָה, 1 Sam 12,23; 1 Kgs 8,36) and "the way of the wicked" (דֶּרֶךְ רְשָׁעִים, Ps 146,9; Prov 4,19; 15,9; Jer 12,1; cf. Prov 4,14) does frequently appear. But, at the very outset, one must accept that the notion of moral conduct in the Old Testament is inseparably connected with covenant fidelity because "the fear of the Lord is hatred of evil" (Prov 8,13). Hence, in general, one may say that the good way consists in the faithfulness to the Torah/God's commandments (Pss 1,2; 119,29–33) and in the consequent practice of righteousness/justice (cf. Prov 8,20; 12,28). "The upright way" (1 Sam 12,23), "the blameless way" (Ps 101.2.6; Prov 10,29), etc., are synonyms of the good way. The good way leads to life or is "the way to/of life", דֶּרֶךְ חַיִּים (Prov 6,23; cf. path of life, חַיִּים אֹרַח in Ps 16,11; Prov 2,19; 5,6; 15,24).[81] On the contrary, "the way of the wicked" is the way of the sinners (Ps 1,1) and the way of the guilty (Prov 21,8). An important synonym for the wicked way is "evil way", דֶּרֶךְ רָע (1 Kgs 13,33; Prov 2,12; 28,10; Jer 18,11; 25,5; 26,3; 35,15; 36,3.7; Zech 1,4; cf. Ps 36,5[4]; Prov 16,29; Isa 65,2). It can be characterized as the way of darkness (Prov 2,13), the way of falsehood (Ps 119,29), the way of perversity (Prov 22,5) and the stubborn way (Judg 2,19). It leads to ruin (Pss 1,6; 146,9; cf. 49,14[13]) and to death (Prov 7,27; 12,28; 14,12; 16,25; cf. Prov 4,18–19). Between these two ways, everyone has the freedom to choose and also the responsibility for his decision. Anyone who wants to go on the good way

---

[80] Koch, "דֶּרֶךְ", 291.

[81] Jer 21,8 speaks of the choice between "the way of life" (דֶּרֶךְ הַחַיִּים) and "the way of death" (דֶּרֶךְ הַמָּוֶת) in the context of Nebuchadnezzar's conquest of Jerusalem. This is comparable with the choice between "life" and "death" in relationship with covenant fidelity in Deut 30,15–19 because this conquest is seen as an inevitable consequence of Judah's infidelity to the covenant/the Lord.

should commit himself to the Lord because there is no "goodness" (טוֹבָה) apart from the Lord (Ps 16,2). For Jeremiah, "the good way" (הַדֶּרֶךְ הַטּוֹב) is synonymous with "the ancient paths" (לִנְתִבוֹת עוֹלָם), those trodden by the righteous in the past (Jer 6,16).

g. Turning Aside from the Way

Even after the law was given to Israel, they "turned aside quickly from the way" (סָרוּ מַהֵר מִן־הַדֶּרֶךְ) that the Lord had commanded them, by making a golden calf and worshipping it (Exod 32,8; Deut 9,12.16).[82] The expression "turning aside from the way of the Lord" is used to refer to disobeying the commandments/covenant of the Lord (Deut 11,28; Mal 2,8–9; Job 23,11; cf. Ps 18,22[21]). In other words, worshipping other gods is called "turning aside from the way of the Lord" (Exod 32,8; Deut 9,12.16; 11,28; 13,1–6; 31,29; Judg 2,17–19; cf. 2 Sam 22,22–23; Isa 30,11) or "stumbling on the way" (Jer 18,15). Samuel taught the people the right way by asking them to turn away from idol worship and to worship the Lord with the whole heart (1 Sam 12,20–25).

The דֶּרֶךְ of the kings of Israel is decisive for the fate of the people. The fate of the Northern kingdom is determined by the sinful way of its first king, Jeroboam I, which is followed by his successors (1 Kgs 15,26.34). The fate of the Southern kingdom is not much different. Many of its kings turn away from the way of the Lord. There is a constant call by the Lord to repent and to renew the ways (Jer 7,3.5; 18,11; 25,5; 26,13; Ezek 33,11; Zech 1,4; Hag 1,5.7; cf. Lam 3,40) and to turn away from idol worship (Jer 35,15). Since Jehoshaphat's heart is courageous "in the ways of the Lord" (בְּדַרְכֵי יְהוָה), he eliminates idol worship by removing the high places and the sacred poles from Judah (2 Chr 17,3–6). When the Lord demands to go in his ways, people often refuse to go and rebel against the Lord's ways (Deut 31,29; 1 Sam 8,3; Jer 6,16; 18,15; cf. Job 24,13; 34,27). Complete destruction (2 Kgs 25) occurs because people refuse to obey the prophetic voice to turn from their evil ways (cf. 2 Kgs 17,13).

h. Way as God's Salvation in the Future

In the prophetic literature, דֶּרֶךְ is also mentioned with reference to God's future salvation (Isa 35,8; 40,3; 42,16; 43,19; 49,9.11; 57,14; 62,10; Jer 31,9; 32,39; Mal 3,1). Isa 35,8 speaks of a "highway" (מַסְלוּל) for God's holy and

---

[82] The verb סור is also an important verb of movement. It occurs 300 times. It means in qal form "to turn aside", "to retreat", "to abandon", "to leave off" and in hiphil "to remove" (see *HALOT*, 747–748). It is frequently used for "apostasy" from Yahweh and deviation from his ways.

2. "Way" in the Hebrew Bible

redeemed people, which will be called the "way of holiness" (דֶּרֶךְ הַקֹּדֶשׁ).[83] This verse is a part of the prophetic oracle of salvation (35,1–10), which is concerned with Yahweh's coming to save his people, "he will come and save you", יָבוֹא וְיֹשַׁעֲכֶם (35,4). Vv. 5–10 focus on the results of Yahweh's coming to his people, namely the restoration of sight to the blind, hearing to the deaf (v. 5), the capacity to walk to the lame and speech to the dumb (v. 6a), the turning of desert into green land (vv. 6b–7) and ultimately the restoration of the redeemed to Zion on the "way of holiness" (דֶּרֶךְ הַקֹּדֶשׁ) with "everlasting joy" and "gladness" (שִׂמְחַת עוֹלָם and שָׂשׂוֹן, vv. 8–10).

The "way of the Lord" in Isa 40,3 is presented in the context of Yahweh's coming to redeem his people (40,1–11). A central question, not only in the interpretation of Isa 40,3 but also in the interpretation of Isa 40–55 (Deutero-Isaiah) as a whole is the meaning of דֶּרֶךְ יְהוָה.[84] The expression דֶּרֶךְ יְהוָה in Isa 40,3 can be understood literally and figuratively. Literally, it may mean a way in the desert for the coming of the people from Babylon to Jerusalem. Figuratively, it may refer to the entry of God onto the historical and existential scene for the sake of all people.[85] The liberation from Babylon and the transformation of the people's situation are certainly in view, but the focal point of the image of the establishment of the way in the desert is the salvific coming of the Lord to humanity.[86] Therefore, at his coming the glory of his saving deeds will impress not only the people of Israel but also the whole humanity, כָּל־בָּשָׂר: "Then the glory of the Lord shall be revealed, and all people shall see it together, for the mouth of the Lord has spoken" (40,5).[87] It should be specially noted that "the preparation of the way" requires the removal of obstacles. "The mountains and hills" symbolize the hindrances and

---

[83] The connections between Isa 35 and Isa 40,1–11 are easily noticeable. U. F. Berges, *The Book of Isaiah. Its Composition and Final Form* (Hebrew Bible Monographs 46; Sheffield 2012), 235–236, underlines "the bridge character" of Isa 35. He believes that chapter 35 performs a "double duty" function. On the one hand, it describes the radiant future of Zion against the dark background of the judgement upon Edom and, on the other hand, it re-establishes the bridge from 1–33 to 40–66, broken by Isaiah 34. He regards chapters 36–39 as an insertion since there are no direct links between Isa 35 and Isa 36–39.

[84] U. F. Berges, *Jesaja 40–48* (HThKAT; Freiburg 2008), 103. B. H. Lim, *The 'Way of the Lord' in the Book of Isaiah* (Library of Hebrew Bible/Old Testament Studies 522; New York 2010), 116, considers the phrase "prepare the way" as a root metaphor within Isa 40–52. John cites Isa 40,3 in his own manner in 1,23, which has the only occurrence of "way" in the Gospel outside 14,4–6. The Isaianic phrase "prepare the way" plays a crucial role in John's presentation of Jesus as "the way" in 14,6. See the discussion on pp. 197–206.

[85] Lund, *Way Metaphors*, 94–95.

[86] Cf. Lund, *Way Metaphors*, 101.

[87] Muilenburg, *The Way of Israel*, 34, states, "In eschatological time, Israel is called to fulfil her mission in the world, to prepare the way of the Lord (Isa 40,3)".

the enemies that threaten Yahweh's plan (40,4).[88] The "levelling" and "breaking" of the mountains and hills function as an image of the elimination of the people's enemies (40,4; cf. 45,2).[89] The way of the Lord in Isa 40,3 is also a "way for the people" because 40,9–11 point out that the Lord will lead his people back to Zion along the way. The image of the shepherd in v. 11 may suggest that the Lord will lead his people on his salvific way as a shepherd leads his flock.

The "way" in Isa 42,16 is also uttered in the context of future salvation. In 42,1–9, God foretells how he and his מִשְׁפָּט will rule over the world through his chosen "Servant" (עֶבֶד).[90] This vision of salvation which God will accomplish through his Servant is so exciting that Deutero-Isaiah breaks into an ecstatic hymn of praise (vv. 10–12).[91] Vv. 13–17 function as an announcement or proclamation of salvation.[92] In vv. 13–17, the Lord shows himself as the God who acts and battles in stark contrast to the idol gods in which people trusted.[93] The Lord himself will lead his people, who are blind, on a way, which is unknown to them (v. 16). Various negative images in vv. 7.16 like darkness, prison, dungeons, crooked ways, rough places and blindness suggest the abject situation of the people, which will be reversed.[94] The blindness of the people refers to their lack of knowledge (vv. 7.16; cf. vv. 18–19; 35,5; 43,8; 56,10; 59,10) and calls for the need for leadership.[95] It involves a lack of ability to orientate oneself, to see the truth and to do what is right (cf. Exod

---

[88] Lund, *Way Metaphors*, 88. P. D. Akpunonu, *The Overture of the Book of Consolations (Isaiah 40:1–11)* (New York 2004), 106, comments, "The mountains, because of their size and stability can be symbols of pride, arrogance, and haughtiness. Yahweh will put to an end the arrogance of the haughty (Isa 13,11), all mountains and hills shall be laid low. Every obstacle, human or of nature, will be removed so that the king of glory may enter".

[89] Lund, *Way Metaphors*, 88.

[90] Isa 42,1–4 or 1–9 is the first of the so-called "Servant Songs". The others are 49,1–6; 50,4–9; 52,13–53,12. Isa 42,1–4 is cited by Matt 12,18–21.

[91] J. N. Oswalt, *Isaiah. Chapters 40–66* (NICOT; Grand Rapids 1998), 109.

[92] Cf. Lund, *Way Metaphors*, 126; C. Westermann, *Das Buch Jesaja. Kapitel 40–66* (Göttingen 1966), 87.

[93] Cf. Lund, *Way Metaphors*, 127.

[94] There are many passages in Isaiah 40–55, where the Lord promises comfort and a transformation of the difficult situation of the people (e.g., 40,11.29–31; 41,10.14; 43,1–2; 44,1–4; 50,10; 51,3; 52,7–10; 54,7–8). Isaiah 40–55 also includes many texts that speak of God forgiving the sins of the people and showing compassion for them (40,1–2; 43,25; 44,22; 55,6–7).

[95] People's inability/ability to "know" is a recurring theme in Isa 40–55. Its climax can be seen in 43,10, according to which, people in the future will know, believe and understand that the Lord is אֲנִי הוּא (ἐγώ εἰμι). In the view of W. A. M. Beuken, *Jesaja Deel IIA* (Nijkerk 1979), 148, blindness in Isa 42,7.18.19; 43,8 refers to the people's lack of ability to comprehend God's plan of salvation.

23,8; Deut 16,19; Job 9,24).[96] The "way" that is promised in v. 16 is a unique way, Lord's own way because no one has travelled on it so far and the Lord himself will guide them. The Lord will transform the situation of the people by turning their darkness into light.[97]

The promise of the Lord in Isa 43,19 that he will make a "way" in the desert is presented in a context (vv. 16–21) which states that the Lord has made a way (דֶּרֶךְ) in the sea and a path (נְתִיבָה) in the mighty waters (v. 16).[98] The language of vv. 16–17 has certainly roots in the exodus tradition. Nevertheless, the focus is not on the leading of the people but on the defeating of its enemies (the forces of chaos) by the Lord as a warrior.[99] The reference to "the new things", different from the past situation, suggests a new situation in the life of the people (vv. 18–19). The images of "way in the wilderness" and "rivers/water in the desert" (vv. 19–20) should be understood figuratively. The wilderness/desert is an image of the people's miserable situation, and the way in the desert provides an opportunity to escape from this situation (see Ps 107,4–5).[100] Water is also a conventional image of life/salvation (Pss 1,3; 23,2; Isa 35,7; 41,18; 44,3; Jer 17,8). The Lord is described as "the fountain of living water" (Jer 2,13; 17,13; cf. Ps 36,9; Isa 33,21), and a situation of separation from the Lord is like a barren desert (Pss 63,2[1]; 143,6). Hence, the combination of "way in the wilderness" and "rivers in the desert" indicates a transformed situation and a blessing in the life of the people. The honour from the wild animals and the praise from the people stress the joy of this transformed life (vv. 20–21).

The "way" in Isa 49,9.11 is regarded to be a part of an oracle of salvation (vv. 7–12).[101] The images of "prisoners" and "those in darkness" (v. 9), "hunger" and "thirst" (v. 10) may suggest the difficult situation after the fall of

---

[96] Lund, *Way Metaphors*, 135. Punishment with blindness is a part of God's judgement (Deut 28,28–29; Ps 107,1–16; Isa 59,8–10; Lam 3,1–20). On the contrary, the removal of blindness is related to his salvific actions (Ps 146,7–9; Isa 29,18; 32,3; 35,5).

[97] The word "darkness" (מַחְשָׁךְ) occurs 6 times in the Old Testament, only in the poetic compositions (Pss 74,20; 88,7.19; 143,3; Isa 29,15; Lam 3,6). It is used only in a figurative sense. It may refer to a sphere of evil where God's blessing is absent and to an outcome as a result of judgment and punishment. Cf. Lund, *Way Metaphors*, 139–140.

[98] It is worth mentioning that the pair of דֶּרֶךְ and נְתִיבָה is used in the Old Testament only in a figurative sense (see Job 24,13; Prov 1,15; 3,17; 7,25; 8,2; 12,28; Isa 42,16; 43,16; 59,8; Jer 6,16; 18,15; Lam 3,9; Hos 2,8).

[99] Lund, *Way Metaphors*, 186.

[100] Cf. Lund, *Way Metaphors*, 192. The situation after the fall of Jerusalem in 587 BCE is also described as a "desert" in Jer 31,1–2; Ezek 19,10–14; 20,32–38; Ps 126,4.

[101] Cf. Lund, *Way Metaphors*, 233. In vv. 9–11, other than דֶּרֶךְ there are various terminologies which belong to the semantic domain of "way" like מְסִלָּה, נָהַג I, נהל and בוֹא. Isa 49 also includes another "Servant Song" (vv. 1–6).

Jerusalem in 587 BCE.[102] The image of Yahweh as a shepherd and the people as his flock conventionally represents the relationship between Yahweh and his people (e.g., Gen 49,24; Ps 23,1–4; Ezek 34; Hos 4,16; Jer 31,10). The shepherd images in vv. 9–10 imply a bright future of salvation for Israel. The conversion of mountains into road and highway implies the elimination of hindrances and enemies that block the plan of the Lord.[103] The coming/return of people to Zion, to the presence of the Lord on his way and highway under his leadership, points out figuratively a renewed relationship with God (cf. Ps 84,5–8).[104]

The command to "prepare the way" in 57,14 is repeated verbatim from 40,3, but instead of a "highway", the verbal form סלל with no object is employed.[105] Here too, it is pointed out that the "preparation of the way" requires the removal of obstacles (cf. 40,4). The exhortation to "remove every obstruction (מִכְשׁוֹל) from my people's way" probably refers to the sins of the people mentioned in the immediate context. Vv. 3–13 refer to the people's indulgence in idolatrous practices. If v. 15 presupposes the sin of pride, v. 17 points out the sin of covetousness. In v. 15, the Lord asserts that he inhabits eternity and dwells in the high and holy place (cf. Isa 66,1–2). Hence, the final destination of "the way" for the humble and the contrite is not an earthly Jerusalem or temple but a peaceful relationship with the "holy" Lord who heals them (cf. 57,18–19).[106]

The concept of "way" (דֶּרֶךְ) in Isa 62,10 is no longer limited to the way back from the Babylonian diaspora, or even to the diaspora in general, but has been transformed into an eschatological concept.[107] In v. 10, a great eschatological procession into the holy city and the temple is envisaged. The command to "go through the gates" is an admonition to enter the city.[108] The eschatological procession and the entrance into the city require the prepara-

---

[102] The images of "hunger" and "thirst" are used to describe the conditions in the desert (2 Sam 17,39; Neh 9,15; Ps 107,5) or the situation as a result of judgement (e.g., Deut 24,48; Isa 5,13; 29,8; 65,13; Amos 8,11).

[103] Lund, *Way Metaphors*, 244.

[104] Cf. Lund, *Way Metaphors*, 242–246.

[105] Isa 57,14–21 and 62,10–12 are regarded as commentaries upon Isa 40–55. See Lim, *The Way of the Lord*, 114.

[106] B. Childs, *Isaiah* (OTL; Louisville 2001), 472, states, "The historical event of the end of exile serves for Third Isaiah as only an instance of God's mercy. However, true salvation is to enter into the holy presence of God. It is the path to his holy mountain offered only to those who take refuge in him" (cf. 57,13c).

[107] J. Blenkinsopp, *Isaiah 56–66. A New Translation with Introduction and Commentary* (AB 19B; New York 2003), 242. Isa 62,10–12 is often regarded as the conclusion of chapters 60–62. In these chapters, the goal of the way of the Lord is revealed in greater detail.

[108] The noun gate (שַׁעַר) occurs 12 times in Isaiah (14,31; 22,7; 24,12; 26,2; 28,6; 29,21; 38,10; 45,1; 54,12; 60,11.18; 62,10). In all these instances, שַׁעַר is a means of entrance and not exit.

tion of the way by removing all sorts of obstacles ("stones"). The salvation that the Lord promises is for all peoples of the earth (v. 11; see also 12,5–6; 14,1; 25,6–8; 30,31; 60,13, etc.).[109] The saying "See, your salvation comes; his reward is with him, and his recompense before him" (v. 11) suggests the personification of salvation. The salvation itself and the one who brings it about are inseparably bound together. Those who receive it will become "the holy and redeemed people of the Lord" and their city and temple will ever be "sought after" and never "forsaken" (v. 12).

Outside Isaiah, we may also notice the use of דֶּרֶךְ with eschatological overtones in Jer 31,9; 32,39; Mal 3,1. The use of דֶּרֶךְ in Jer 31,9; 32,39 in the context of "new covenant" (31,31–34) and "eternal covenant" (32,37–41) is possibly oriented to the future salvation.[110] In 31,9, God promises his people a smooth/straight "way" on which they will not stumble. One of the chief features of return theology is the removal of any obstacles that block the exiles' path to God.[111] Return is a spiritual journey back to God.[112] Certainly, ideas of literal return are present, but they fade into the background when the spiritual/ethical dimension comes to the fore.[113] Salvation in Jeremiah is not just a possibility for survival but the communion of the people with God.[114] This perspective is also likely to be present in the promise: "I will give them one heart and 'one way' (דֶּרֶךְ אֶחָד), that they may fear me for all time" (32,39). Mal 3,1 speaks in an eschatological context (2,17–3,6) of the imminent "coming of the Lord", for which "the way " is to be prepared (cf. Isa 40,3–5; Exod 23,20).[115] This preparation of the way involves salvation for those who seek the Lord and judgement for the wicked.

---

[109] The raising of "ensign" (v. 10) is intended to tell all nations to come to Zion to experience the salvation, which the Lord brings about.

[110] In Jer 31,9, there is similarity in ideas and phraseology to Second Isaiah (cf. Isa 35; 40,3–5.11; 41,18–20; 42,16; 43,1–7; 44,3–4; 48,20–21; 49,9–13). J. N. Moon, *Jeremiah's New Covenant. An Augustinian Reading* (JTISup 3; Winona Lake 2011), 260, states that the oracle of the new covenant is eschatological because "it describes the world as the way it ought to be and announces that it will be like that one day".

[111] W. J. Webb, *Returning Home. New Covenant and Second Exodus as the Context for 2 Corinthians 6,14–7,1* (JSNTSS 85; Sheffield 1993), 146–147.

[112] Webb, *Returning Home*, 148.

[113] Webb, *Returning Home*, 148.

[114] N. Kilpp, *Niederreißen und Aufbauen. Das Verhältnis von Heilsverheißung und Unheilsverkündigung bei Jeremia und im Jeremiabuch* (Biblisch-Theologische Studien 13; Neukirchen-Vluyn 1990), 180–181.

[115] Regarding the identity of the figures, "my messenger", "the Lord whom you seek" and "the messenger of the covenant in whom you delight", see the discussion in K. W. Weyde, *Prophecy and Teaching. Prophetic Authority, Form Problems and the Use of Traditions in the Book of Malachi* (BZAW 288; Berlin 2000), 284–291; A. Hill, *Malachi. A New Translation with Introduction and Commentary* (AB 25D; New Haven 1998), 286–289; E. H. Merrill, *Haggai, Zechariah, Malachi. An Exegetical Commentary* (Chicago

2.1.2 אֹרַח

After דֶּרֶךְ, אֹרַח is the most important term for "way" in the Old Testament. It occurs 56 times in biblical Hebrew and its Aramaic parallel אֹרַח twice in biblical Aramaic (Dan 4,34[37]; 5,23).[116] It appears most frequently in Proverbs (19x), Psalms (14x), Job (9x) and Isaiah (8x). Except the instance of Gen 18,11, אֹרַח occurs exclusively in poetic passages.[117] It is very often translated as "path" or "way". Other possible meanings are "ground", "dam", "behaviour", "condition" (of women), etc.[118] In sixteen cases, אֹרַח stands in parallel with דֶּרֶךְ, in four instances with מַעְגָּל and in four instances with נְתִיבָה.[119] It is used mostly in a figurative sense. When אֹרַח is used figuratively, the emphasis is more on the state or condition of the person under consideration than on his action.[120] "All the paths of the Lord" (כָּל־אָרְחוֹת יְהוָה) are steadfast love and faithfulness for those who keep his covenant (Ps 25,10).

As a metaphor, אֹרַח may stand for the whole life of a man. Hence, Job complains against God, "He has fenced up my way (אָרְחִי), so that I cannot pass; and he has set darkness in my paths (נְתִיבוֹת)" (19,8). אֹרַח is usually used for the expressions "path(s) of life" (אֹרַח חַיִּים, Prov 2,19; 5,6; 15,24; Ps 16,11) and "path to life" (אֹרַח לְחַיִּים, Prov 10,17; 12,28), which correspond with the "path of righteousness/the righteous/the upright (Ps 27,11; Prov 2,8.13.20; 4,18; 8,20; 15,19; 17,23; Isa 26,7; 40,14; cf. Prov 15,10). On the contrary, the "path of evil", אֹרַח רָע (Ps 119,101) is a "wrong path", אֹרַח שֶׁקֶר (Ps

---

1994), 370–376. Weyde, *Prophecy and Teaching*, 280–324, views that both theocracy and eschatology are central ideas in Mal 2,17–3,6.

[116] Kohlenberger and Swanson, *The Hebrew English Concordance*, 184, 1681.

[117] Because of its occurrence only in poetry with one exception, Dorsey, *The Roads and Highways*, 223, suggests that אֹרַח was no longer used in everyday speech during the Old Testament period.

[118] *HALOT*, 86–87.

[119] Cf. Dorsey, *The Roads and Highways*, 222. Even though אֹרַח and דֶּרֶךְ occur frequently in synonymous parallelism, they are not simply synonymous. Dorsey, *The Roads and Highways*, 222–223, considers אֹרַח as a poetic synonym for דֶּרֶךְ, with almost exactly the same range of meanings. However, some sort of distinction between the two can be noticed. אֹרַח occurs predominantly in the plural, whereas more than 75% of the occurrences of דֶּרֶךְ are in the singular. They can stand in construct relationship to each other. E.g., דֶּרֶךְ אָרְחֹתֶיךָ in Isa 3,12 means "course of your paths". Hence, a דֶּרֶךְ can be composed of many אֳרָחוֹת. While the construction אָרְחוֹת יְהוָה occurs only once (Ps 25,10), its singular form אֹרַח יְהוָה never appears. Meanwhile, the expressions דֶּרֶךְ יְהוָה, "way of the Lord" (Gen 18,19; Judg 2,22; Prov 10,29; Isa 40,3; Jer 5,4.5; Ezek 18,25.29; 33,17[2x].20) and יְהוָה דַּרְכֵי "ways of the Lord" (2 Sam 22,22; 2 Chr 17,6; Pss 18,21; 138,5; Hos 14,9[10]) are comparatively frequent. Moreover, if the Old Testament can speak of God's own דֶּרֶךְ, it can speak of God's אֹרַח only with reference to an אֹרַח which God has ordained for human beings (cf. Ps 44,19[18]). See Koch, "דֶּרֶךְ", 281.

[120] Koch, "דֶּרֶךְ", 281.

119,104.128). It endangers one's life (Prov 22,25) and leads to death (Prov 1,19). In short, the "path" which one chooses determines one's destiny.

2.1.3 נָתִיב and נְתִיבָה

The masculine noun נָתִיב appears 5 times, whereas its feminine counterpart נְתִיבָה 21 times.[121] נָתִיב is found only in Job and Psalms, and נְתִיבָה also appears only in poetic texts.[122] Both terms are usually translated as "path/pathway".[123] They stand in parallel with דֶּרֶךְ 12 times and with אֹרַח 6 times. They are mostly used in their metaphorical sense. They may represent the totality of human deeds or the whole human life (Job 19,8; 30,13; Ps 142,4[3]); Hos 2,8[6]) or the moral conduct (Job 18,10; 24,13; Prov 1,15; 3,17; 7,25; 8,20; 12,28; Isa 59,8; Jer 18,15). The way of wisdom is the way (אֹרַח) of righteousness and the path (נְתִיבָה) of justice (Prov 8,20). The psalmist describes his covenant relationship with God in terms of walking in the "path", נָתִיב (Ps 119,35) which is the "path" (נְתִיבָה) of light (Job 24,13), illuminated by the revelation of God's own word (Ps 119,105).[124] There is also a נָתִיב of God which he makes for his anger (Ps 78,50) and his נְתִיבָה for future deliverance (Isa 42,16). As the creator, he can make a נְתִיבָה through the mighty waters (Isa 43,16). In Jer 6,16, the good way, which the Lord prescribes, is called "ancient paths", נְתִבוֹת עוֹלָם.

2.1.4 מְסִלָּה and מַסְלוּל

The noun מְסִלָּה, which occurs 27 times, is usually translated as "highway". It means a prepared road leading across the country.[125] Other possible renderings are "public road", "raised way", "track", "pilgrimage" (Ps 84,5[6]).[126] It is cognate with the verb סָלַל, which can mean "to cast up/lift up a way/highway".[127] It is mostly used in the literal sense. There are מְסִלּוֹת for stars (Judg 5,20). In Prov 16,17, מְסִלָּה is used in association with moral con-

---

[121] Dorsey, *The Roads and Highways*, 225–226, considers נְתִיבָה and נָתִיב as actually one and the same, the singular being נָתִיב and the plural נְתִיבוֹת. In his view, נְתִיבָה is a ghost form, the creation of scribal error.

[122] Hence, Dorsey, *The Roads and Highways*, 227, suggests that נְתִיבָה and נָתִיב were no longer used in everyday speech even though their meaning was well known.

[123] *HALOT*, 732.

[124] E. H. Merrill, "נָתִיב", *NIDOTTE*, III, 202.

[125] Koch, "דֶּרֶךְ", 278.

[126] *BDB*, 700; *HALOT*, 606.

[127] *BDB*, 699. The root meaning of סלל ("to lift up") suggests that a מְסִלָּה should be a way that somehow reflects the concept of highness or heaping up. But Dorsey, *The Roads and Highways*, 229–233, has argued that the root meaning of סלל is "to clear away obstacles, flatten, level, make smooth". He stresses the idea of levelling and clearing away the obstacles in the preparation of a way and points out that מְסִלָּה "is, therefore, a public highway whose surface has been prepared by the clearance of obstacles and by grading and smoothing".

duct. מְסִלָּה stands with דֶּרֶךְ in synonymous (Isa 40,3; cf. 35,8) and also in antithetic parallelism (Isa 59,7–8). Deutero-Isaiah speaks of the great מְסִלָּה of Yahweh, which will be built between Babylon and Jerusalem (Isa 40,3; 49,11; cf. 11,16; 62,10). While Jeremiah laments that Israel has abandoned "God's highway" to follow false bypaths (18,15), Isaiah sees the time of future salvation, when all obstacles will be removed from the path of a repentant Israel, returning on the "highway" to Zion (Isa 57,14; 62,10).[128] In all three Old Testament passages where the preparation or construction of a highway is spoken of (Isa 40,3; 49,11; 62,10) the newly prepared way is called מְסִלָּה. The cognate word מַסְלוּל also means "highway". It occurs only once (Isa 35,8) and is designated as "way of holiness" (דֶּרֶךְ הַקֹּדֶשׁ) with reference to future salvation.

2.2 Important Verbs and their Significance

2.2.1 הָלַךְ

The verb which is semantically most associated with דֶּרֶךְ is הָלַךְ. It is the sixth most frequent verb in the Old Testament and also the second most frequent verb of movement.[129] It is the most frequently used verb to describe the act or process of living in the Old Testament.[130] It occurs totally about 1549 times in five conjugations, namely qal, niphal, piel, hiphil and hithpael.[131] The meanings of הָלַךְ in various conjugations are the following: "to go, walk, follow, go behind, behave, die" in qal, "to vanish" in niphal, "to go, walk, move about, vanish" in piel, "to bring, lead, escort" in hiphil and "to go to and fro, walk about, go up and down, part, disperse, behave" in hithpael.[132] As a verb of journey, it gives the image of way a dynamic character and a versatility of usage. The substantives which are derived from הָלַךְ are:[133] הֵלֶךְ (visitor/traveller), הָלִיךְ (step),[134] הֲלִיכָה (departure, way, caravan, procession)[135],

---

[128] R. D. Patterson, "סלל", *TWOT*, II, 627.

[129] The five verbs that occur more frequently than הָלַךְ are אָמַר (to say), הָיָה (to be), עָשָׂה (to do, to make), בּוֹא (to come) and נָתַן (to give). Cf. E. Jenni, "בוא", *TLOT*, I, 201.

[130] Merrill, "הָלַךְ", 1032.

[131] Kohlenberger and Swanson, *The Hebrew English Concordance*, 456–466. According to G. Sauer, "הָלַךְ", *TLOT*, I, 366, the verb הָלַךְ occurs 1547 times in the Hebrew Old Testament: 1412 times in the qal, 64 times in the hithpael, 45 times in the hiphil, 25 times in the piel and once in the niphal. It also occurs 7 times in Biblical Aramaic. The greatest frequency of הָלַךְ is found in 1 Sam (128x), 1 Kgs (120x), Gen (113x), Jer (111x) and Judg (110x).

[132] *HALOT*, 246–249.

[133] Cf. *HALOT*, 246–249; BDB, 237.

[134] The masculine noun הָלִיךְ occurs only once (Job 29,6).

[135] About the significance of the noun הֲלִיכָה, we have already discussed above. The term *Halakah*, which is derived from הָלַךְ, designates the entire early Jewish-rabbinical doctrine of proper conduct. Cf. Sauer, "הָלַךְ", 370.

2. "Way" in the Hebrew Bible

מַהֲלָךְ (walk, journey)[136] and תַּהֲלוּכָה (procession). But they do not have theological significance as the verbal form הָלַךְ. הָלַךְ has both secular and theological usages,[137] which will be dealt with below.

2.2.1.1 Secular Usage

In its secular use, הָלַךְ is employed literally and metaphorically. In its literal sense, it is used primarily to refer to the movement of persons, animals and inanimate things, e.g., the "walking" of Israelites (Exod 14,29), "creeping" of a snake (Gen 3,14), "prowling" of foxes (Lam 5,18), "flowing" of water (Gen 2,14), "sailing" of ships (Gen 7,18), "blasting" of trumpets (Exod 19,19), etc. Since human life is viewed as a journey or a way (cf. 1 Sam 12,2), הָלַךְ also necessarily entails metaphorical meanings.[138] E.g., it can be used to signify the growth, increase or progress of something (Gen 26,13; Judg 4,24; 1 Sam 2,26; 2 Sam 3,1; 5,10; 15,12; Jonah 1,11.13; Esth 9,4; Prov 4,18) and the end of human life too (Gen 15,2; 25,32; Job 7,9; 10,21; 14,20; 16,22; Ps 39,7[6].14[13]; Qoh 1,4; 3,20; 1 Chr 17,11). Death is also called "going the way of all the earth" (Josh 23,14; 1 Kgs 2,2).

2.2.1.2 Theological Usage

a. Walking of God

More significant and remarkable is the theological use of הָלַךְ. In theophanic accounts, the Lord is viewed as "walking in the garden" (Gen 3,8)[139] and "departing" when he has finished speaking to Abraham (Gen 18,33). These expressions are designed to point out the Lord's intimate relationship with humanity or with his people. The Lord is also portrayed anthropomorphically as "going on the wings of the wind" (Ps 104,3) or "walking on the dome of heaven" (Job 22,14).[140]

---

[136] The term מַהֲלָךְ appears 5 times in the Old Testament. It is used only in the literal sense.

[137] Cf. F. J. Helfmeyer, "הָלַךְ", *TDOT*, III, 390–403.

[138] The Akkadian cognate *alāku* has both literal ("go") and metaphorical ("live", "behave", "act") meanings. The going of a god with someone means divine protection. In the Ugaritic texts, *hlk* is most often used to refer to the "going" of gods. See Helfmeyer, "הָלַךְ", 388–389.

[139] In the case of Gen 3,8, the participle מִתְהַלֵּךְ can qualify either יְהוָה אֱלֹהִים or קוֹל. Since the verb הָלַךְ is frequently used to refer to the Lord's "moving/walking" with his people (Lev 26,12; Deut 23,15 [14]; 2 Sam 7,6–7), it is better to consider מִתְהַלֵּךְ in association with יְהוָה אֱלֹהִים than with קוֹל.

[140] It is believed that the concept of Yahweh's "going" or "walking" seems to have originated with J (Yahwist) in line with J's anthropomorphic representation of Yahweh and his action. See Helfmeyer, "הָלַךְ", 403.

b. Walking "with" (אֶת) and "before" (פְּנֵה) God

Righteous persons like Enoch and Noah are said to have "walked with God", וַיִּתְהַלֵּךְ אֶת־הָאֱלֹהִים (Gen 5,22.24; 6,9).[141] The expression "walking with God" reveals the intimate relationship between God and his devotees. The "walking" of Levi with Yahweh is mentioned in the context of the covenant between them (Mal 2,4–6). The "walking with God" in Mic 6,8 is not mentioned with reference to any particular individual. It has a universal appeal.[142] הָלַךְ in conjunction with לִפְנֵי וֶהְיֵה means the way of life which God requires[143] (Gen 17,1; 24,40; 48,15; 1 Sam 2,30; 1 Kgs 2,4; 3,6; 8,23.25; 9,4; 2 Kgs 20,3 = Isa 38,3; 2 Chr 6,16; 7,17; Pss 56,14[13]; 116,9). Yahweh turns his gracious countenance to the one who walks before him, and then this person need not fear the countenance and gaze of Yahweh in whatever he does.[144]

c. Leading of God in the Past

הָלַךְ is applied more frequently and more importantly to the Lord's coming to his people in order to save them. He "went to redeem" Israel as a people from Egypt and other nations (2 Sam 7,23; 1 Chr 17,21; cf. Ps 80,2[3]).[145] The Lord "went in front of them" (הֹלֵךְ לִפְנֵיהֶם) in a pillar of cloud by day to lead them along the way and in a pillar of fire by night to give them light, so that they might "travel" (הָלַךְ) by day and by night (Exod 13,21; Num 14,14; Deut 1,30.33).[146] During their wanderings in the desert, the Lord's "presence" (פָּנֶה) "goes" (הָלַךְ) with them, and they experience the leadership of the Lord (Ex 33,14; 34:9; cf. Lev 26,12; Deut 20,4; 23,14; 31,6.8; 2 Sam 7,6–7; 1 Chr 17,6). The ark of the covenant is a visible symbol of Yahweh's presence, "leading" the people on their way to the promised land (Josh 3,6–7; 6,9; Num 10,32–36; cf. 2 Sam 5,24; 6,3–4). The Lord is the subject of the hiphil forms of הָלַךְ (24x of 45), whereas Israel is the object of divine leadership and guidance (Lev 26,13; Deut 8,2.15; 29,4[5]; Josh 24,3; Isa 48,21; 63,13; Jer 2,6.17; Amos 2,10; Pss 106,9; 136,16).

---

[141] The hithpael form particularly expresses this relationship.

[142] Helfmeyer, "הָלַךְ", 395, considers Mic 6,8 to be a proverbial maxim, possibly having the preaching of the prophets as its locus.

[143] Helfmeyer, "הָלַךְ", 393.

[144] Helfmeyer, "הָלַךְ", 393.

[145] Sometimes, the Lord's "going" or "leading" is in order to punish Israel (Deut 28,36; Hos 5,14; Lam 3,2).

[146] Sometimes, it is the angel of the Lord/God who "goes" before the Israelites (Exod 14,19; 23,23; 32,34).

d. Walking in the Ways of God and Its Parallels

More frequently, הָלַךְ is used to refer to a life lived in obedience or disobedience to God's commandments/law/covenant. God tests Israel in the desert before he enters into covenant with them in order to know whether they will "walk" in his law (cf. Exod 16,4). Once they have become his people through the covenant, they are expected "to walk in his ways". The expression "walking in the ways of the Lord" serves to designate Israel's covenant obligation as the holy people of God (Jer 7,23). The covenant relationship between Israel and the Lord works to Israel's benefit only if Israel "walks in the ways of Lord" and obeys his voice (cf. Lev 26,1–46).[147] The locus of the expression "walking in the way/s of the Lord" is first seen in Deuteronomy (e.g., Deut 5,33; 8,6; 19,9; 26,17; 28,9; 30,16). It is the concern of Deuteronomy to show "the way of the Lord" that will effect and guarantee his blessing and the well-being for Israel.

The expression "walking in the ways of the Lord" is very frequently used as a synonym for "keeping the commandments of the Lord" (Deut 5,33; 8,6; 10,12–13; 11,22; 19,9; 26,17; 28,9; 30,16).[148] It also means "to walk in the law of the Lord" (Ps 119,1.3; Jer 5,4), "to fear the Lord" (Deut 8,6; Ps 128,1), "to love him" (Deut 10,12; 19,9; 30,16), "to obey his voice/law" (Deut 26,17; Isa 42,24) and "to serve him with one's whole heart and whole soul" (Deut 10,12). The meaning of the expression "walking in the ways of the Lord" in the Deuteronomistic History (Josh 22,1–6; Judg 2,22; 1 Kgs 2,3; 3,14; 11,33.38; 2 Kgs 21,22) corresponds to the meaning in Deuteronomy, i.e., the observance of his commandments.[149] As in Deuteronomy, the expression

---

[147] Helfmeyer, "הָלַךְ", 397.

[148] Also see Josh 22,5; 1 Kgs 2,3; 3,14; 8,58; 11,38; Ps 119,1–10; Zech 3,7; cf. Exod 18,20; Judg 2,22; Ps 119,27.32–33; Prov 19,16.

[149] When we speak of the correspondence between Deuteronomistic History and Deuteronomy here, we follow only the general assumption that the theology and the language of Deuteronomy might have influenced the books of Joshua, Judges, 1–2 Samuel and 1–2 Kings. Even though Martin Noth's hypothesis of the Deuteronomistic History continues to have a tremendous influence on the study of Deuteronomy and the Former Prophets, the notion of a "Deuteronomistic History" has itself come under attack more recently. For recent reviews of scholarship on the Deuteronomistic History, see T. Römer, *The So-Called Deuteronomistic History. A Sociological, Historical and Literary Introduction* (London 2005); R. F. Person Jr., *The Deuteronomic School. History, Social Setting, and Literature* (Studies in Biblical Literature 2; Atlanta 2002); A. de Pury et al. (ed.), *Israel Constructs Its History. Deuteronomistic Historiography in Recent Research* (JSOTSup 306; Sheffield 2000); G. N. Knoppers and J. G. McConville (ed.), *Reconsidering Israel and Judah. Recent Studies on the Deuteronomistic History* (Winona Lake 2000). For the latest discussion on the relationship between prophetical literature and Deuteronomistic history, see M. R. Jacobs and R. F. Person Jr. (ed.), *Israelite Prophecy and the Deuteronomistic History. Portrait, Reality and the Formation of a History* (Ancient Israel and Its Literature 14; Atlanta 2013). Helfmeyer, "הָלַךְ", 397, thinks that the origin of the expres-

"walking in the ways of the Lord" in the Deuteronomistic texts also refers to the worship of Yahweh alone, to the exclusion of foreign gods (cf. 2 Kgs 21,21–22).[150] In Ps 81,13, Israel is admonished to "walk in the ways" of the Lord in the light of the first commandment of the Decalogue: "There shall be no strange god among you; you shall not bow down to a foreign god. I am the Lord your God, who brought you up out of the land of Egypt" (Ps 81,9–10; cf. Exod 20,1–6; Deut 5,6–10). "Walking in the way" of the Lord's commandments is a prerequisite for the blessing that they may live and that it may be well with them in the promised land (Deut 5,33; Jer 7,23; Ps 128,1–6; cf. Ps 37,34).

In ancient times, each nation was walking in the name of its god, but Israel was walking in the name of the Lord God (Mic 4,5; Zech 10,12). It is not Israel alone, but the other nations, too, will learn and "walk in his (Lord's) paths", וְנֵלְכָה בְּאֹרְחֹתָיו (Mic 4,2). It is the Lord himself who teaches Israel and "leads them (you) in the way they (you) should go", מַדְרִיכְךָ בְּדֶרֶךְ תֵּלֵךְ (Isa 48,17). If the righteous "walk in the ways of the Lord" by keeping the covenant with him, the transgressors stumble "in the ways of the Lord" by breaking the covenant relationship with him (Hos 14,10[9]; cf. Zech 3,7; Jer 31,9). Sin, especially the sin of idol worship, is regarded as "not walking in the ways" of the Lord (1 Kgs 11,33; Isa 42,24). During the divided kingdom, the kings of Israel consistently "walked in the way" of Jeroboam and neglected the Lord (1 Kgs 16,26; 22,52–53). While David, Solomon in his early years, Jehoshaphat and Josiah "walked in the statutes of the Lord" (1 Kgs 3,3.6; 22,43; 2 Kgs 22,2; 2 Chr 17,3–4; 20,32; 34,2), kings like Manasseh and Amon "did not walk in the way of the Lord" (וְלֹא הָלַךְ בְּדֶרֶךְ יְהוָה, 2 Kgs 21,21–22; cf. Jeroboam in 1 Kgs 15,26; Baasha in 1 Kgs 15,34; the house of Ahab in 2 Kgs 8,27; 2 Chr 22,3; Jehoram in 2 Chr 21,12.13).

Parallels to the expression "walking in the way/s of the Lord" are abundant. There are many passages which speak of "walking in the good/upright/blameless way" or "walking in the paths of righteousness" (e.g., 1 Kgs 8,36; Isa 57,2; Jer 6,16; Ps 101,6; Prov 8,20). Even though in these passages the expression "walking in the way(s) of the Lord" is not explicitly mentioned, their context reveals that what is meant is conduct according to the will of God, which is revealed through his commandments.[151] The expression "walking in the law of the Lord" is equivalent to "acting according to/following the law of the Lord".[152] Other parallel expressions to "walking in

---

sion, "walking in the way(s) of the Lord" in the Deuteromistic History should be looked for in the prophetic circles (cf. 1 Kgs 11,33.38).

[150] Helfmeyer, "הָלַךְ", 397.

[151] Cf. Helfmeyer, "הָלַךְ", 398.

[152] Helfmeyer, "הָלַךְ", 398–399, suggests Deuteronomic origin for the expression "walking in" (הָלַךְ בְּ) the law/statutes in Jer 9,12(13); 26,4; 32,23; 44,10.23; Ezek 5,6.7; 11,12.20; 18,17; 20,13.19.21; 33,15; 36,27; 37,24. He thinks that the original locus of this

the way(s) of the Lord" are "walking in the fear of God" (Neh 5,9), "walking in the light of the Lord/Lord's countenance" (Isa 2,5; Ps 89,16[15]; cf. Job 29,3) and "walking in the truth of the Lord", which is associated with fearing God's name (Ps 86,11; cf. 26,3).

Expressions like "walking blamelessly" (הָלַךְ תָּמִים), "walking in integrity" (הָלַךְ בְּתֹם) or "walking in uprightness" (הָלַךְ בְּיֹשֶׁר) abound in Psalms and Proverbs (Pss 15,2; 26,1.11; 84,12[11]; 101,2; Prov 10,9; 14,2; 19,1; 20,7; 28,6). One should not think that they are just expressions of humanism. They are, rather, expressions of deep faith and trust in the Lord because those who walk blamelessly in uprightness/integrity are only those who fear the Lord (Prov 14,2). According to Old Testament theology, justice, righteousness or uprightness are not human virtues detached from faithfulness to God. A righteous (צַדִּיק) person is one who "walks in" (הָלַךְ בְּ) God' statutes (חֻקֹּת) and ordinances (מִשְׁפָּטִים) (Ezek 18,9). A person's walk is judged in terms of one's commitment to the covenant. Therefore, true righteousness is grounded in a walk that adheres to covenant principles.[153]

e. "Going after" (הָלַךְ אַחֲרֵי) Yahweh or other Gods

The expression "going after" (הָלַךְ אַחֲרֵי) is very fitting to the nomadic lifestyle of the Israelites. The Israelites are commanded to "go after" Yahweh (Deut 13,5[4]; 1 Kgs 14,8; 2 Kgs 23,3; 2 Chr 34,31; Jer 2,2; Hos 11,10; cf. to "go after a prophet" in 1 Kgs 19,20).[154] To "go after Yahweh" means fulfilment of God's law, especially the commandment to accept Yahweh exclusively.[155] Hence, apostasy is described as "going away" from Yahweh/the way of Yahweh (Deut 11,28; 1 Kgs 9,6; Hos 11,2; Jer 5,23) and "going after" other/false gods (Deut 4,3; 6,14; 8,19; 11,28; 13,3[2]; 28,14; Judg 2,12.19; 1 Kgs 11,5.10; 18,18; 21,26; 2 Kgs 13,2; 17,15) which involves cultic/idol worship.[156] Jeremiah criticizes Israel for her going after idols (Jer 2,5–8). The

---

expression was not the preaching of the prophets but the Deuteronomic and Deuteronomistic literature (cf. 1 Kgs 6,12; 8,58.61; 2 Kgs 10,31) and the circle of writers associated with this literature.

[153] E. H. Merrill, "הָלַךְ", 1033.

[154] Sauer, "הָלַךְ", 370, points out that during the desert wanderings and the conquest of the land, the notion of "going after" Yahweh was more prominent, but in the period of settlement, this idea was replaced by the knowledge that Yahweh dwells in the midst of his people.

[155] Helfmeyer, "הָלַךְ", 395.

[156] Also see Jer 2,5.8.23.25; 7,6.9; 8,2; 9,13[14]; 11,10; 13,10; 16,11; 25,6; 35,15; Ezek 20,16; cf. Exod 32,1.23; 1 Kgs 12,28–30). It is suggested that the frequent reference to and emphasis on the theme of "going after other gods" are due to the fact that this idea has its origin in the pagan cultic procession. Since Israel carefully avoided this expression, the theme of "going after Yahweh" is not as frequent as "going after other gods". See Sauer, "הָלַךְ", 369.

expression "to go backward/turn back" (אָחוֹר) is used to refer to the rejection of Yahweh (Jer 15,6). It is probably another expression for idol worship, which is also "a way" (דֶּרֶךְ) from which people refused to turn (Jer 15,7).

f. Leading on the Way of Future Salvation

The verb הָלַךְ is also found, especially in the prophetic literature, with reference to God's salvific "leading" in the future. Isa 35,8–9, in the context of God's coming to save, (35,4) speaks of a "way of holiness" (דֶּרֶךְ הַקֹּדֶשׁ) on which "the redeemed" (גְּאוּלִים) will "walk" (הָלַךְ). God's leadership role is much spoken of in the context of a new exodus or a new covenant (Isa 42,16; 45,2; 52,12; Jer 31,9). Isa 42,16 promises that God will "lead" (hiphil of הָלַךְ) the blind by a road they do not know, by paths they have not known. Similarly, Jer 31,9 foretells that God will make his people "walk" (hiphil of הָלַךְ) on a smooth/straight "way" (דֶּרֶךְ) on which they will not stumble. Ezek 37,24–25 speaks of a future shepherd-king, David who will rule eternally. During his rule, the people of Israel, who have "gone" (הָלַךְ) in dispersion, will be brought back and made into one nation (37,21). As a result of his rule, the people will "walk" (הָלַךְ) in the ordinances and the statutes of the Lord (37,24).

2.2.2 יָצָא

The verb יָצָא occurs about 1069 times in the Hebrew Bible.[157] Its most common meanings are "to go/come out/forth", "to proceed", "to set out" (qal, ca 750x) and "to bring out", "to lead out", "to bring forth" (hiphil, ca 280x).[158] It is used literally to speak of "the going out" from the presence of a person or a particular place (e.g., Gen 4,16; 11,31; 41,46). Its theological significance lies in its usage as a verb of deliverance. It is very frequently used to narrate the exodus events, especially using the causative function of the hiphil form (e.g., Exod 12,51; 13,3.9.14; 15,22; 16,3.6; 18,1). The God of Israel presents himself or is presented as "the Lord who brought Israel out of Egypt" (e.g., Exod 20,2; Lev 19,36; 22,33; Num 23,22; 24,8; Deut 4,37; 5,6; 6,21; 1 Kgs 8,16; 2 Chr 6,5; Pss 105,37.43; 136,11; Dan 9,15). In other words, he is the one who "caused Israel to go out/come out" of Egypt. He "brings" his believers "out" of their enemies or distress when they are in trouble (2 Sam 22,49; Ps 107,28). The verb is also used to indicate the source or origin of something (Gen 24,50; Lev 9,24; Job 8,10; Prov 10,18). From the Lord's mouth "comes/goes forth" his ever effective "word", דָּבָר (Isa 55,11; cf. Deut 8,3).

---

[157] Kohlenberger and Swanson, *The Hebrew English Concordance*, 720. According to E. Jenni, "יָצָא", *TLOT*, II, 562, the frequency of this verb is 1068 times.

[158] Cf. *HALOT*, 425–427; BDB, 422–425.

More importantly, the verb is used to refer to the future Saviour or future salvation (Isa 11,1; 42,1.7; 51,5; Mic 5,1[2]).

2.2.3 עָלָה and יָרַד

Since the roads in ancient Palestine had many ascents and descents, journey was often described either as "ascending" or "descending".[159] Two commonly used verbs for this upward and downward journey are עָלָה and יָרַד. The verb עָלָה occurs 892 times in the Old Testament.[160] Its most common meanings in the qal (612x) are "to go up", "come up", "ascend" and in hiphil (255x) "to lead up", "to bring up" (to cause to go up) and "to offer".[161] The verb is frequently used to describe the journey ("going up") from Egypt to Palestine or to the stations on the way there (Gen 13,1; 45,25; Exod 1,10; 12,38; 13,18; Num 32,11; Judg 11,13.16; 19,30; 1 Sam 15,2.6; 1 Kgs 9,16; Isa 11,16; Hos 2,17, etc.) and the entry from the desert into the land of Canaan (Exod 33,1; Num 13,17.21.30; Deut 1,21.26.41; Judg 1,1–4). It is also used to denote the return of the exiles as "going up" (Ezra 2,1.59; 7,6.28; 8,1; Neh 7,5.61; 12,1). The verb is often employed as a technical term for Yahweh's "leading out" the Israelites from Egypt and "bringing them up" to the land of Canaan. The fundamental faith of Israel as a nation in Yahweh is characterized by the affirmation, "it is Yahweh their God who has 'brought them up' out of the land of Egypt", which is expressed in various forms throughout the Old Testament (Lev 11,45; Deut 20,1; Josh 24,17; Judg 2,1; 6,8.13; 1 Sam 8,8; 10,18; 12,6; 2 Sam 7,6; 2 Kgs 17,7.36; Ps 81,11[10]; Jer 2,6; 11,7, etc.).[162] The verb עָלָה is also found to refer to the future restoration of Israel (Jer 30,17; Ezek 37,12).

The verb יָרַד appears 380 times.[163] Its most common meanings are "to come down", "to go down", "to descend" (qal) and "to bring down" (hiphil).[164] The journey from Canaan/Palestine to Egypt is described as "going down" or "descending" (Gen 12,10; 26,2; Deut 26,5). Since God is regarded as "the Most High", עֶלְיוֹן (e.g., Gen 14,19; Isa 14,14), a dweller in the highest world and human beings as dwellers on the earth, theophany is pictured as "God's descending or coming down" to the human realm. God hears the cry of the Israelites in Egypt and "comes down" to save them from the

---

[159] Since Jerusalem is situated on the hills, the journey towards it was known as "going up" or "ascending" (1 Kgs 12,27–28; Zech 14,16–19).
[160] Kohlenberger and Swanson, *The Hebrew English Concordance*, 1214.
[161] *HALOT*, 828–830; BDB, 748–750; G. L. Carr, "עָלָה", *TWOT*, II, 666.
[162] Even when the name of Moses is mentioned as the one who brought the people up from Egypt (Exod 17,3; 32,1.7.23; 33,1.12; Num 16,13; 20,5; 21,5), it is ultimately the Lord who is at work through him.
[163] Kohlenberger and Swanson, *The Hebrew English Concordance*, 735.
[164] *HALOT*, 434–435; BDB, 432–434.

Egyptian bondage (Exod 3,7–8). He "comes down" on Mt. Sinai in fire (Exod 19,18; Neh 9,13; cf. 2 Chr 7,1.3) and on the tent of meeting in a pillar of cloud (Exod 33,9; Num 12,5). In order to help Moses, God also comes down among the elders and distributes some of his spirit to them (Num 11,17). The discussion of God's descent is not merely an anthropomorphism but a stylistic means for expressing God's superiority over the world (cf. Gen 11,5.7).[165] There are many passages where עָלָה and יָרַד occur together to indicate the upward and downward journeys. E.g., Jacob sees in a vision a ladder set up on the earth, with its top reaching to heaven and the angels of God "ascending and descending" (עֹלִים וְיֹרְדִים) on it (Gen 28,12; also see Gen 24,16; Exod 19,24; Num 20,27; Deut 28,43; Judg 14,1, etc.).

2.2.4 נהל

The verb נהל appears 10 times, only in piel and hithpael forms. The primary meaning of נהל is "to lead", "to guide".[166] It denotes a shepherd's loving, concerned leading of his flock[167] (Gen 33,14; Isa 40,11; 51,18). It is like a shepherd that the Lord "led" (נהל) in steadfast love his people whom he redeemed from Egypt and brought to Canaan (Exod 15,13). The psalmist believes that the Lord, like a shepherd, leads him beside still waters (23,2) and asks the Lord "to lead" him evermore (31,4[3]). The model of the Lord's future salvation is portrayed using the language of a shepherd-sheep relationship, in which the leading role of the Lord is brought into light: "He will feed his flock like a shepherd; he will gather the lambs in his arms, and carry them in his bosom, and gently 'lead' (נהל) the mother sheep" (Isa 40,11; cf. 49,10).

2.2.5 נָחָה

The basic meaning of נָחָה is "to lead" and "to conduct".[168] It appears 39 times, mostly in the Psalms (18x). Various way-lexemes are found in association with נָחָה: 11 times with דֶּרֶךְ (Gen 24,27.48; Exod 13,17.21; Neh 9,12.19; Pss 5,9[8]; 27,11; 139,24[2x]; Isa 57,18), once with מַעְגָּל (Ps 23,3) and once with אֹרַח (Ps 27,11). It is used mainly to refer to the Lord's "leading" of his people in various circumstances (Gen 24,27.48; Exod 13,17.21; 15,13; Deut 32,12).[169] Abraham's servant confesses that it is the Lord who has "led" him

---

[165] G. Wehmeier, "יָרַד", *TLOT*, II, 891.
[166] BDB, 642; D. W. Baker, "נהל", *NIDOTTE*, III, 44. *HALOT*, 675, gives the following meanings: "to escort", "to transport", "to provide" in piel and "to move on further" in hithpael.
[167] L. J. Coppes, "נהל", *TWOT*, II, 559.
[168] *HALOT*, 685; BDB, 634.
[169] Also see Neh 9,12.19; Pss 5,9[8]; 23,3; 27,11; 31,4[3]; 43,3; 60,11[9]; 61,3[2]; 67,5[4]; 73,24; 77,21[20]; 78,14.53.72; 107,30; 108,11[10]; 139,10.24; 143,10; Isa 57,18; 58,11.

during his journey for searching a wife for Isaac (Gen 24,27.48). The verb is also used to refer to the Lord's "leading" of Israel in the exodus event protecting them from their enemies (Exod 13,21; 15,13; Neh 9,12.19; Pss 77,20; 78,14.53). The Lord's "guiding" in the future is promised in Isa 57,18 and 58,11. He is not only the guide of the people of Israel but also of all nations (Ps 67,5[4]).

2.2.6 נָהַג I[170]

Yet another verb similar to נהל and נָחָה is נָהַג I. It occurs 30 times. Its basic meaning is "to lead" and "to drive".[171] נָהַג I denotes an orderly conducting of animals (Gen 31,18; Exod 3,1; 1 Sam 23,5; 30,20; 2 Kgs 4,24; Job 24,3) or people (e.g., Gen 31,26; 1 Sam 30,22; 1 Chr 20,1; 2 Chr 25,11; Cant 8,2; Isa 20,4) to an intended destination either by forcible driving or leading.[172] The verb is used to refer to the Lord's "leading" of his people. He will be the guide of his people forever (Ps 48,15[14]). But a false prophet is one who leads astray the people from the way of the Lord by making them go after false gods (Deut 13,3[2].6[5]. The psalmist believes that it is the Lord who "leads" his faithful along the path of righteousness (Pss 5,9[8]; 23,3; 27,11; 143,10; cf. Prov 6,22; 11,3). The Lord is the one who "leads" (נָהַג) the Israelites like a shepherd (Pss 78,52; 80,2[1]) and will do the same in the future (Isa 49,10; 63,14). In the messianic kingdom, a child will be able to "lead" wild animals (Isa 11,6).

2.2.7 דָּרַךְ

The verb דָּרַךְ occurs 63 times. It means in qal "to tread", "to march", "to bend the bow", "to tread a wine/oil press" and in hiphil "to tread upon", "to cause to tread upon/walk", "to reach".[173] It is found mostly in poetical and prophetical books and is used in literal and figurative sense. Frequently, God is the subject of דָּרַךְ, especially when it is employed in a figurative sense. The verb דָּרַךְ in qal is used to describe God's movement on the heights of the earth (Amos 4,13; Mic 1,3), on the heights of the sea (Job 9,8; cf. Hab 3,15). The primary notion behind דָּרַךְ has to do with setting foot on a territory or objects, sometimes with the sense of trampling them.[174] The verb is used in Deuteronomy and Joshua with reference to taking possession of the promised land (Deut 1,36; 11,24; Josh 1,3; 14,9). דָּרַךְ is frequently applied in various idi-

---

[170] It is to be distinguished from נָהַג II, which means "to moan", "lament". See BDB, 624.
[171] HALOT, 675; BDB, 624.
[172] L. J. Coppes, "נָהַג", TWOT, II, 558.
[173] HALOT, 231; BDB, 201-202.
[174] H. Wolf, "דָּרַךְ", TWOT, I, 196.

oms.[175] The idiom "treading upon the high places of the earth" indicates control of the enemy (Deut 33,29; cf. Hab 3,15). When it is used of God, it refers to his sovereignty as creator of heaven and earth (Amos 4,13; cf. Job 9,8) or as judge (Mic 1,3). Another frequent idiom is to "tread" or "bend" the bow (Isa 5,28; 21,15; Jer 50,14; Pss 11,2; 37,14). The Lord himself bends his bow against his people because of their sin (Lam 2,4; cf. Lam 3,12; Zech 9,13). Yet other important idioms relating to agricultural life are "treading grapes", "treading the winepresses" (Amos 9,13; Judg 9,27; Isa 16,10; Jer 48,33) or "treading olives" (Mic 6,15; Job 24,11). The prophets speak of the Lord's "treading of the winepress" with reference to his judgment (Isa 63,2–3; Lam 1,15). The verb דָּרַךְ in hiphil is consistently used to refer to God as the one who leads his people, especially the righteous in straight paths (Pss 25,5.9; 107,7; 119,35; Prov 4,11). There is also mention of דֶּרֶךְ with reference to future "leading" in Isa 42,16; 48,17.

2.2.8 בּוֹא

The verb בּוֹא is the most frequently used verb of movement as well as the fourth mostly used verb in the Hebrew Bible. It occurs about 2557 times.[176] Its most common meanings are "to come to/in", "to enter", "to go" (qal) and "to bring", "to lead" (hiphil).[177] It is a significant term used to refer to Israel's coming to the promised land (e.g., Deut 9,5; 11,10; 23,21) and to God's "bringing" (hiphil of בּוֹא) them there (e.g., Deut 7,1; 8,7; Jer 2,7). The important theological significance of בּוֹא can be broadly summarized into the following three categories.[178]

2.2.8.1 Promise-Fulfilment

The verb בּוֹא is used in association with the fulfilment of God's promises. His promises "come" to pass/true (Josh 23,14). The proof of a true prophet is that his words will "come" to pass (Deut 18,22). By making his promises "come" true, the Lord establishes his dominion over the whole world (Josh 23,15; 2 Kgs 19,25; Isa 31,2). The Lord's superiority over the idol gods is established because of his capacity to make his predictions "come" to pass (Isa 41,22; 42,9). The verb בּוֹא is also used to promise the return of Israel to the land (Isa 35,10; 51,11; Ezek 11,16; 34,13; Mic 4,8; Zeph 3,20). The expression "Behold, days are coming" (הִנֵּה יָמִים בָּאִים) is frequently employed to refer to fu-

---

[175] See Wolf, "דֶּרֶךְ", 196.

[176] Kohlenberger and Swanson, *The Hebrew English Concordance*, 230. According to Jenni, "בּוֹא", 202 and E. A. Martens, "בּוֹא", *TWOT*, I, 93, the verb בּוֹא occurs 2570 times (1997x in qal, 549x in hiphil and 24x in hophal).

[177] *HALOT*, 112–114; BDB, 97–99.

[178] See Martens, "בּוֹא", 93–95. For further study of the theological significance of בּוֹא, see H. D. Preuss, "בּוֹא", *TDOT*, II, 20–49.

ture events (1 Sam 2,31; 2 Kgs 20,17; Isa 27,6; 39,6; Jer 7,32; 19,6; 23,5.7; 30,3; 31,27.38; Amos 8,11; 9,13), particularly to announce judgment (e.g., Jer 9,24[26]; 19,6; 48,12; 49,2), salvation (Jer 16,14), the establishment of the new covenant (Jer 31,31) and the appearance of a kingly Messiah (Jer 23,5).

2.2.8.2 Coming of God/a Saviour to His People

The Lord's visible presence is needed for the faith of Israelites at the formation of Israel as his nation. Hence, he "comes" in dense cloud, thunder and lightning while speaking to Moses (Exod 19,9; 20,20). He "comes" from Mount Sinai in order to fight for his people (Deut 33,2–5; Hab 3,3; cf. Isa 30,27). He promises to "come" and bless his people in every place which he chooses for the remembrance of his name (Exod 20,24). He will come to rule the world with justice (Pss 96,13; 98,9) and to judge the nations (cf. Isa 19,1; Jer 25,31) and the evil doers (Ps 50,3; Isa 66,15).

The salvation which the Lord promises is to come imminently (Isa 56,1). The purpose of the preparation of the "way" in the desert is for the "coming" of the Lord to his people (Isa 40,10; 62,10–11; Mal 3,1; cf. Isa 40,1–11) and to dwell with his people (Zech 2,14). The Lord himself will come to gather all nations and tongues so that they may see his glory (Isa 66,18; cf. 40,5). The coming of the Saviour to Zion is a notable theme (Isa 59,20; cf. 40,9; 62,11). Importantly, the verb בוא is used to refer to "the coming One"/"the One who comes" (Ps 118,26; Ezek 21,32; Dan 7,13; cf. Gen 49,10). It is used with reference to the "coming" Messiah who will bring salvation. This is explicitly stated in Zech 9,9: "Rejoice greatly, oh daughter Zion! Shout aloud, oh daughter Jerusalem! Lo, your king 'comes'(יָבוֹא) to you; triumphant and victorious is he, humble and riding on a donkey, on a colt, the foal of a donkey" (cf. Matt 21,5; John 12,15).

2.2.8.3 Coming of the People to God

The verb בוא is used not only to refer to God's coming to his people but also to point out the people's coming to God. A believer may come to the sanctuary in company with his community in order to pray and to bring sacrifices (Deut 12,5; 31,11; 2 Sam 7,18; Isa 30,29; Jer 7,2.10; Pss 5,8[7]; 42,3[2]; 43,4; cf. Gen 4,4). Before the temple was built, it was customary that people came to the Mount of Olives to worship the Lord (2 Sam 15,32). Priests have to fulfil special regulations in order to "come" before the holy place (Exod 28,29–35; 29,30, etc.). Foreigners from distant lands also can "come" to the holy place in order to pray (I Kgs 8,41). When the psalmist asks for God's help, his voice comes to God's ears (Ps 18,7[6]). In the future, the whole mankind will "come" to worship the Lord (Isa 66,23).

2.3 Conclusion

The analysis of important way/journey-lexemes is intended to give an independent and a complete picture of the way/journey motif in the Old Testament with regard to salvation history. The concept of way in the Old Testament is an overarching theme and has a variety of meanings. It is used as a major expression for history, ethics, monotheism, covenant fidelity, providence, piety, eschatology, etc.[179] It is an umbrella concept for the whole salvation history planned by God in the past and for the future.[180] The scope of the concept of way is not just restricted to a dead past. More importantly, it is oriented towards the future salvation that God plans. This is what the examination of various way lexemes and the verbs of journey discloses, and this is the major outcome of this survey, which can be confidently asserted.

The analysis of the various terminologies reveals that exodus, wandering in the desert, covenant and exile are only various stages of the journey on "the way of the Lord". This journey has a purpose, which consists in the future fulfilment of divine promises proclaimed by the prophets. The exile was indeed the decisive stage in the progressive internalization and spiritualization of the way which Israel carried out with the help of its prophets.[181] The way of the Lord will reach its culmination only when it reaches a situation in which there will be a unique intimacy between God and human beings (Jer 32,38–40). The ultimate destination of the way of the Lord is eternal joy in his presence (Ps 16,11).

The examination of important way-lexemes is helpful to understand better the relation of the way with the notions of truth and life in John 14,6.[182] Even though there are many way-lexemes in the Old Testament, the semantic range of the term דֶּרֶךְ is so broad and deep that it can explain everything what the concept of the way in the Old Testament is about. Other way-lexemes would support what דֶּרֶךְ intends to point out. דֶּרֶךְ in the Old Testament essentially has two dimensions: a human realm and a divine realm. Within the human realm, man's way and his deeds are one and the same. The way in which he should walk and what he should do are synonymous (Exod 18,20; Jer 7,3.5). In this respect, the whole life of a man can be described as his "way".[183]

---

[179] In some passages "way" may refer to God's creation as well.

[180] Zehnder, *Wegmetaphorik*, 517, remarks, "Im tiefsten wird der Weg der Geschichte dadurch zusammengehalten, dass sie in ihrer Gesamtheit als 'Werk JHWHs' verstanden wird. Gott ist das dominierende Subjekt der Geschichte; er ist in der Geschichte 'fortgesetzt' am Wirken; er waltet allmächtig in ihr. Geschichte ist sein 'Werk', sein 'Weg'".

[181] Gros, *Je suis la route*, 77.

[182] This aspect is highlighted on pp. 206–209, 255–260.

[183] Therefore, Gros, *Je suis la route*, 17, says, "Vivre, c'est être en route, sur la voie".

Unfortunately, "the way to the tree of life" is blocked due to the sin of Adam and Eve (Gen 3,24) and the human דֶּרֶךְ becomes corrupted (Gen 6,24). Hence, there is a necessity for the intervention of the divine realm to bring the estranged humanity back to "the way to the tree of life". This divine intervention in human history begins with the attempt to form a righteous community through Abraham (Gen 18,19). God's concern for the descendants of Abraham is well manifested through his mighty deeds at the exodus and his establishment of a covenant with them. Israelites are constantly asked by the prophets to walk in the way of the Lord by avoiding idol worship and by exclusive worship of the Lord. But they frequently turn away from the way of the Lord and indulge themselves in idolatry.[184] Turning away from the way of the Lord also implies walking on the way of wickedness because fear of the Lord and wisdom of the Lord are necessary to walk on the way of righteousness and justice. Consequently, there lies before the people a choice between two ways, either the righteous way in accordance with God's commandments or the wicked way.[185] In any case, God is the final court for the judgement of the right or wicked way.

Because of her infidelity to the way of the Lord (covenant) and her negligence to keep God's commandments and ways, Israel has to undergo punishment by being exiled from their homeland. But this punishment is re-creative and re-formative. Hence, the prophets proclaim a new covenant, an everlasting covenant, a new exodus, the restoration of the situation and "the preparation of the way of the Lord" in the desert. In the future, God will give his people "one heart and one way" and "lead" them like a shepherd (Jer 32,39; Isa 40,11; cf. Ezek 34,11–16). He will establish "the way of holiness" for his "redeemed" "to walk" (Isa 35,8–9). The motif of the preparation of the way in the desert is an overarching theme of Deutero-Isaiah, which deserves our special attention in our forthcoming discussions.

The study of various verbs of journey also reveals the dynamic character of the relationship between God and his people. The way in the Old Testament is not an abstract and a static reality. The examination of the most important verb הָלַךְ and other verbs reveals the intimate relationship between God and his people. The various activities of journey like "coming down", "leading", "bringing out", "bringing up", "walking", "going up", etc., manifest what happens on the way and thus point out the dynamic character of the way. The God of Israel is a God who "walks" with his people like a friend,

---

[184] Turning from the way of the Lord is a synonym for idol worship.

[185] It should be specially kept in mind that in the Old Testament the Lord's way is the standard according to which the human way should be measured. Set apart from the Lord's way, human ways are evil. Hence, Kuschke, "Die Menschenwege", 114, rightly states, "Es gibt für Israel nur einen Weg, das ist der von Jahwe im Bund gewiesene Weg. Alle Wege, die von diesem im Bunde gewiesenen Weg abweichen, sind selbst erdachte Wege, Menschenwege. Auf ihnen liegt der Fluch" (Lev 26,14–46; Deut 28,15–68; Jer 4,18).

one who "comes down" to save his people in their plight (Exod 3,8), one who "leads" them on the way and promises "to come" again to save them eternally. Most of the nouns and the verbs we have examined have a future dimension. They are somehow oriented towards the future salvation that God is planning.

The theme of way in the Old Testament begins with a reference to "the way to the tree of life", which is blocked due to the sin of Adam and Eve (Gen 3,24). It is worthwhile to pay attention to the last occurrence of the way-lexeme (דֶּרֶךְ) in the prophetical books of the Old Testament.[186] It is found when the prophet Malachi restates the Isaianic exhortation in Isa 40,3 "to prepare the way" for the immediate coming of the Lord: "See, I am sending my messenger to prepare the way before me, and the Lord whom you seek will suddenly come to his temple. The messenger of the covenant in whom you delight – indeed, he is coming, says the Lord of hosts" (Mal 3,1). It is with this theme of preparing/straightening the way of the Lord that the ministry of Jesus in the New Testament opens (Matt 3,3; Mark 1,3; Luke 3,4; John 1,23). Thus, the motif of way crucially and decisively connects the Old Testament with the New Testament in which Jesus himself is the way (John 14,6).[187]

3. "Way" in the Septuagint

The concept and the theology of way in the LXX are basically and essentially the same as in the Hebrew Bible. Hence, it is unnecessary to repeat what we have already discussed in the previous section. Nevertheless, it is essential to know the most important Greek equivalents of Hebrew terms for way and journey. Hence, the purpose of this section is to introduce the important Greek way-lexemes and their usages with special attention to the Deutero-Canonical books and to discuss some relevant Greek verbs, which correspond to the Hebrew verbs of journey mentioned previously. Familiarity with the LXX vocabularies for the way and journey motif is necessary to understand better the Johannine vocabularies for the way and journey motif in the Gospel.

---

[186] Prophet Malachi is considered to be the last of all prophets in the history of the Old Testament.

[187] The overall contribution and outcome of an examination of the way motif in the Old Testament will be discussed at the end of this part and also in the course of this study, especially in the general conclusion.

3.1 Important Way-Lexemes

3.1.1 Ὁδός

3.1.1.1 In General

The term ὁδός which is found in the LXX 891 times both in literal and figurative senses represents 18 Hebrew equivalents.[188] The most significant Hebrew term for way, namely דֶּרֶךְ is predominantly translated as ὁδός in the LXX. The term ὁδός corresponds in more than 600 instances to דֶּרֶךְ, which occurs 706 times. Other important Hebrew equivalents to ὁδός are אֹרַח (35x), חוּץ (15x) and מְסִלָּה (12x). There are also many instances in which דֶּרֶךְ is not translated in the LXX (e.g., Gen 19,31; 31,35; Exod 33,13; 1 Kgs 18,27; Job 38,19; 40,19; Prov 8,22; Amos 8,14).

In its literal sense, ὁδός is used to refer to "way", "path" or street" for the sake of travel (e.g., Gen 16,7; Deut 3,1; Num 20,17; 21,4; Ezek 11,6; Sir 49,6) or to "journey" (e.g., Gen 30,36; 42,25; Exod 3,18; Num 9,13; Judg 17,8; Tob 5,17; 1 Macc 5,24). The figurative use of ὁδός is found frequently throughout the LXX. The whole human life is viewed as a ὁδός (Job 23,10; 31,4; Prov 4,10; 20,24; Sir 33,13; Isa 40,27; Jer 10,23; Dan 5,23). Ὁδός can refer to God's creation (Job 26,14; Ps 144,17; Prov 8,22), God's salvific deeds at the exodus by leading Israel to the promised land[189] (Exod 13,17.18.21; 18,8; 23,20; 33,3; Deut 1,31.33; 8,2, etc.) and to the covenant relationship (Deut 5,33; 26,17; 28,9; Jer 7,23). The ὁδοί of the Lord are synonymous with his ἐντολαί (e.g., Deut 8,6; 11,22; 19,9; Josh 22,5; Ps 118,15; Bar 4,13; cf. with ῥήματα in Sir 2,15).[190] God is the moral administrator of the ὁδός (1 Kgs 8,36; Pss 24,4; 26,11; Isa 2,3, etc.) and the author of the way of wisdom (Prov 2,6–8; 8,22). Idol worship is called turning aside "from the way", ἐκ τῆς ὁδοῦ of the Lord (Exod 32,8; Deut 9,12, etc.). More importantly, ὁδός is oriented to God's future salvific plan for Israel and the entire world (Isa 35,8; 40,3; 42,16; 43,19; 49,9.11; 57,14; 62,10; Jer 38,9; 39,39; Mal

---

[188] The term ὁδός is most frequently found in Prov (100x), Pss (81x), Ezek (73x), Isa (67x) and Jer (61x). See E. Hatch and H. Redpath, *A Concordance to the Septuagint and the Other Greek Versions of the Old Testament* (Oxford 1897) II, 962; J. Lust et al., *A Greek-English Lexicon of the Septuagint* (Stuttgart 2003), 842; Michaelis, "ὁδός", 48.

[189] The important derivative of ὁδός which is closely associated with Israel's journey from Egypt into the promised land in the LXX is ἔξοδος (Exod 19,1; Num 33,38; 1 Kgs 6,1). The noun ἔξοδος occurs 70 times and is equivalent to 7 Hebrew terms. Cf. Lust, *Lexicon of the Septuagint*, 477; Hatch and Redpath, *A Concordance to the Septuagint*, 497.

[190] They also stand in parallel relationship with ὁδὸς ἀγαθή (1 Sam 12,23; 1 Kgs 8,36; Jer 6,16), ὁδὸς εὐθεῖα (1 Sam 12,23; Isa 33,15), ὁδὸς δικαιοσύνης (Job 24,13; Prov 8,20; 21,16), ὁδοὶ σοφίας (always plural, Prov 3,17; 4,11; 8,34; Sir 6,26; 14,21), ὁδὸς ἀληθείας (Ps 118,30; Wis 5,6; Tob 1,3), ὁδοὶ ζωῆς (Ps 15,11; Prov 5,6; 6,23; 10,17; 15,24), etc.

3,1).[191] In short, God will give his people in the future "another way and another heart", ὁδὸν ἑτέραν καὶ καρδίαν ἑτέραν (Jer 39,39[32,39]).

3.1.1.2 In the Deutero-Canonical Books

The concept of way in the Deutero-Canonical books corresponds well with that in other books of the LXX and they have not developed any new way-lexeme.[192] The term ὁδός occurs in the Deutero-Canonical books about 101 times, both in its literal and metaphorical senses.[193] Literally, ὁδός is used as "road" (Tob 1,15; 5,2.4–5; Jdt 5,14; Sir 49,6; 1 Macc 5,4.46; 6,33) or as "journey" (Tob 5,6; 10,14[13]; 11,15; Jdt 2,21; 1 Macc 5,24; 7,45; 8,19). The metaphorical sense of ὁδός is predominantly noticed in Tobit, Judith, Wisdom, Sirach and Baruch. It is used with regard to fidelity to God and to human moral conduct.

God's ὁδοί are synonymous with his "deeds", ἔργα (Tob 3,2). Ὁδός can stand for covenant fidelity (Jdt 5,18). Fidelity to the covenant is sometimes judged in terms of following the ways of the ancestors (Sir 48,22; cf. 47,23). In some cases, true worship of God involves abandoning "the ways" of the ancestors, namely idol worship (Jdt 5,8). Accepting other gods (idol worship) is called wandering from the way (Wis 12,24). Morality and fear of God go together. Hence, revering the Lord also implies not "walking" (πορεύομαι) "in the ways of wrongdoing", ταῖς ὁδοῖς τῆς ἀδικίας (Tob 4,5). Walking "in the ways of God's commandments" (ὁδοῖς ἐντολῶν θεοῦ) is identical with following "the path of discipline" (τρίβος παιδείας), which is rooted "in righteousness", ἐν δικαιοσύνῃ (Bar 4,13). It is God who "makes straight" (εὐθύνω) one's way "in truth", ἐν ἀληθείᾳ (Sir 37,15; Tob 4,19), directs and protects it (Jdt 12,8; 13,16).

In Wis 5,6–7, "the way of the Lord" (ὁδὸς κυρίου) stands in parallel with "the way of truth" (ὁδὸς ἀληθείας). God is the author of "the way of wisdom" (ὁδὸς τῆς σοφίας) and "the way of knowledge" (ὁδὸς ἐπιστήμης, Bar 3,23.27). God's wisdom can "guide" (ὁδηγέω) holy people "on a way" (ἐν ὁδῷ) which is marvellous (Wis 10,17). The fear and love of the Lord consist in keeping his "ways", i.e., his law (Sir 2,15–16), which is synonymous with the ways of wisdom (Sir 6,26; 14,21–22). According to Bar 3,13, one who "walks" (πορεύομαι) "in the way of God" (τῇ ὁδῷ τοῦ θεοῦ) lives in eternal peace. God rewards everyone "according to his ways", κατὰ τὰς ὁδοὺς αὐτοῦ (Sir 11,26). Human ways (behaviour) are known to God and he observes

---

[191] See the comments on these texts under "Way as God's Salvation in the Future" on pp. 50–55.

[192] Nötscher, *Gotteswege*, 69.

[193] The frequency is as follows: Tob (28x), Sir (26x), Jdt (12x), Bar (10x), Wis (9x), Ep Jer (1x), Dan (1x), 1 Macc (12x) and 2 Macc (2x). This counting is based on Hatch and Redpath, *A Concordance to the Septuagint*, II, 963–966.

them (Sir 17,15.19; 23,19). But God's ways are beyond the reach of the human mind (Sir 16,20).

3.1.2 Other Way-Lexemes

The noun τρίβος, which means "path", occurs 70 times in the LXX.[194] It is equivalent to seven Hebrew way-lexemes like דֶּרֶךְ, אֹרַח, מְסִלָּה, מַעְגָּל, נְתִיבָה, נָתִיב, שְׁבִיל.[195] It is used both in a literal (e.g., Gen 49,17; Judg 5,20; 1 Sam 6,12) and a figurative sense (e.g., referring to the course of action, conduct, covenant fidelity, Tob 4,19; Prov 1,15; 2,15; Jer 6,16; 18,15). More significant and notable is the use of τρίβος with reference to the future salvific plan of God (Isa 40,3; 42,16; 49,9.11; 58,12).

The substantive πλατεῖα, which occurs about 52 times, is an equivalent to חוץ. Its meaning is "street" and it is used only literally (e.g., Gen 19,2; Judg 19,15; Ps 17,42). The noun ἴχνος is used as an equivalent to דֶּרֶךְ and צַעַד. It occurs 34 times and has the meanings of "foot", "route" and "trace". It is used literally and figuratively denoting human conduct (e.g., Ps 17,36; Prov 5,5; Sir 21,6; 37,17). The LXX equivalent of מַעְגָּל (path) is τροχιά (6x). It is used mostly figuratively with reference to human conduct (e.g., Prov 2,15; 4,11.26.27). The noun ἀτραπός (path, 5x), which is an equivalent of הֲלִיכָה and נְתִיבָה, is used figuratively referring to human conduct (Judg 5,6; Job 19,8; Sir 5,9).

3.2 Some Important Verbs of Journey

An examination of the important verbs of journey in the LXX becomes especially relevant because John uses more frequently the verbs of journey than the nouns for "way". Since the verbs of journey in the LXX are numerous, some kind of reservation is to be made with regard to the selection of these verbs. The Hebrew verbs of journey discussed previously can be broadly classified into verbs for "to and fro movement" and verbs for "leading" or "guiding". Hence, some important verbs for "to and fro movement" and for "leading" or "guiding" are examined. Since the way motif in the Gospel of John is closely associated with the journey motif, Johannine preference is taken into consideration by paying attention to those verbs of journey to which John attaches some theological significance in the Gospel.

---

[194] Lust, *Lexicon of the Septuagint*, 1190.
[195] Hatch and Redpath, *A Concordance to the Septuagint*, II, 1372.

3.2.1 Verbs for "to and fro Movement"

3.2.1.1 Πορεύομαι and Ἔρχομαι

The verb πορεύομαι, which occurs 1263 times in the LXX, is equivalent to 13 Hebrew verbs of movement.[196] It translates the Hebrew verb הָלַךְ about 947 times.[197] The verb πορεύομαι takes on the rich significance of הָלַךְ and acquires a broader sense in the LXX than in secular Greek.[198] The most important meanings of πορεύομαι in the LXX are "to leave a place and head for another", "to go", "to walk", "to walk after", "to seek", "to march", "to grow", "to function", "to pass away" (to die), "to conduct oneself", "to follow a certain moral lifestyle", etc.[199] Πορεύομαι attains a more metaphorical sense in the LXX than in secular Greek, where the transferred sense is very seldom.[200] Since human life is viewed as a journey in the Old Testament, human conduct is called "walking" (e.g., 1 Kgs 3,14; 2 Kgs 13,6; 2 Chr 7,17). Death is also regarded as a journey or passing away.[201] Hence, David may say, ἐγώ εἰμι πορεύομαι ἐν ὁδῷ πάσης τῆς γῆς (1 Kgs 2,2; cf. Hos 6,4).

When πορεύομαι is used in association with "way" or "ways", it is often characterized and qualified. E.g., ἐν ταῖς ὁδοῖς Δαυιδ (2 Chr 11,17), ἐν ὁδοῖς τοῦ πατρός (2 Chr 17,3), ἐν ὁδοῖς σκότους (Prov 2,13), ὁδοὺς διε- στραμμένας (Judg 5,6), ἐν ὁδῷ ἀμώμῳ (Ps 100,6), ὁδῷ ἀληθινῇ (Isa 65,2). The most important Old Testament view that man should "go" on the "ways" of God is foreign to the Greek world.[202] Parallel to בְּ הָלַךְ, the expression πορεύεσθαι ἐν is frequently found with reference to various qualifications, e.g., "walking in (your/the ways of) truth" (Ps 85,11; Prov 28,6; Tob 1,3;), "walking in (my) innocence" (Pss 25,1; 83,12), "walking in the house of the Lord/God" (Pss 54,15; 121,1), etc. The Israelites are constantly asked to "go after" the Lord (1 Sam 12,14; 2 Kgs 23,3; Sir 46,10; Hos 11,10) or "to walk in the ways" of the Lord, πορεύεσθαι ἐν ταῖς ὁδοῖς αὐτοῦ, i.e., to keep his commandments (Deut 8,6; 10,12; 11,22, etc.). The Hebrew expression אַחֲרֵי הָלַךְ, which is very frequently used for apostasy, is usually translated as πορεύεσθαι ὀπίσω in the LXX (e.g., Deut 4,3; 6,14; Judg 2,12; 1 Kgs 11,10).

---

[196] It also translates the Hebrew step-lexeme צָעַד. Cf. Hatch and Redpath, *A Concordance to the Septuagint*, II, 1189.

[197] Other important Greek equivalents of הָלַךְ are ἀπέρχομαι (136x), βαδίζω (47x), ἔρχομαι (26x) and περιπατέω (24x). Besides these, there are about 48 other verbs to render הָלַךְ. See Lust, *Lexicon of the Septuagint*, 990; Helfmeyer, "הָלַךְ", 389.

[198] F. Hauck and S. Schulz, "πορεύομαι", *TDNT*, VI, 570.

[199] T. Muraoka, *A Greek-English Lexicon of the Septuagint* (Louvain 2009), 577–578; Lust, *Lexicon of the Septuagint*, 990.

[200] Hauck and Schulz, "πορεύομαι", 570.

[201] It should be kept in mind that it is in terms of journey that John frequently presents Jesus' death.

[202] Hauck and Schulz, "πορεύομαι", 570.

Very importantly, πορεύομαι is also related to God's promise of future salvation (Isa 35,8; 45,2; 52,12; Ezek 37,24).

The verb ἔρχομαι occurs 1054 times in the LXX and is equivalent to 35 Hebrew terms, mostly to בוא.[203] Its significant meanings in the LXX are "to come", "to go", "to come to pass", "to happen and become a reality".[204] The important theological uses of ἔρχομαι are with reference to God's coming to individuals (Gen 31,24; Num 22,9.20; 1 Sam 3,10), the coming of the day(s) of the Lord (Joel 2,31; Zech 14,1; Mal 3,19.22; Isa 13,9; Jer 7,32), people's coming to the house of God (2 Chr 30,1; Jer 7,10; 33,2; Ezra 3,8), God's coming in relation to his salvific plan for the future (Isa 40,10; Zech 2,10[14]; Mal 3,1) and the coming of the Messiah (Zech 9,9; cf. Dan 7,13).[205] Ps 117,26 speaks of "the coming One" (ὁ ἐρχόμενος) who is regarded as a promised messianic or eschatological figure by all evangelists (Mark 11,9; Matt 21,9; 23,39; Luke 13,35; 19,38; John 12,13). As a result of God's salvific plan for the future, all nations will come to see the glory of God (Isa 66,18). The compound verbs of ἔρχομαι, which are often used to refer to believer's "coming into/to" God's presence, are εἰσέρχομαι (2 Sam 12,20; 2 Kgs 19,1; Pss 70[71],16; 72[73],17; 117[118],20; Isa 30,29; Jer 43[36],5)[206] and προσέρχομαι (Exod 16,9; 22,8[7]; Lev 21,17.21; Num 18,4; Jer 7,16; Ezek 44,16; Sir 2,1). The verb εἰσέρχομαι is also used to speak of God's coming to human beings (Gen 20,3; 31,24; Num 22,9; 1 Sam 3,10; 5,10.12; 2 Chr 8,11; Ps 23[24],7.9; Ezek 43,4; 44,2). The verb ἐξέρχομαι, however, is used to refer to the coming forth of the Messiah in Isa 11,1; Mic 5,2 (cf. Matt 2,6). The promise of a righteous kingdom in Isa 32 is related to the coming (ἐπέρχομαι) of the Spirit (32,15).

3.2.1.2 Ἀναβαίνω and Καταβαίνω

The verb ἀναβαίνω that occurs 685 times in the LXX is an equivalent to 21 Hebrew terms.[207] Israel's cry in Egypt is said to have gone up to God (Exod 2,23), and their journey from Egypt to the promised land is an ascension (Exod 13,18). There are instances which speak of God's ascension (Gen 35,13; 1 Sam 2,10; Ps 46,6).[208] There are also frequent references to Moses' ascension to the mountain of the Lord (Exod 19,3.20; 24,13) or to the Lord

---

[203] Hatch and Redpath, *A Concordance to the Septuagint*, I, 548; J. Schneider, "ἔρχομαι", *TDNT*, II, 667.

[204] Lust, *Lexicon of the Septuagint*, 531; Muraoka, *Lexicon of the Septuagint*, 292–293.

[205] The verb ἥκω is found in Isaiah (35,4; 59,20) to refer to God's coming as Saviour.

[206] The verb εἰσέρχομαι is also used to refer to the coming of prayers into God's presence (Pss 87,3[88,2]; 78[79],11; 118[119],170; cf. Isa 26,2).

[207] Lust, *Lexicon of the Septuagint*, 147; Hatch and Redpath, *A Concordance to the Septuagint*, I, 70.

[208] 1 Sam 2,10 speaks of God's ascension into the heavens.

(Exod 19,24; 24,1.12; 32,30) and people's ascension to the Lord (Judg 21,5.8; 1 Sam 10,3; Jer 38,6), to the mountain of the Lord (Ps 23,3; Mic 4,2; Isa 2,3) or to the house of the Lord (1 Sam 1,7; 2 Kgs 19,14; 2 Chr 29,20; 34,30; Isa 37,1).

The verb καταβαίνω occurs 349 times in the LXX and is equivalent to 21 Hebrew terms.[209] There are many passages which say that the Lord comes down to his people. He comes down to see the city and the tower built by the people (Gen 11,5.7) and the people's way of life (Gen 18,21). He comes down to save the Israelites from the hand of the Egyptians and to lead them into the promised land (Exod 3,8). During their journey, the Lord enters into a covenant relationship with them by coming down on Mt. Sinai (Exod 19,11.18.20) and in the pillar of cloud (Exod 34,5; Num 11,25; 12,5; Deut 31,15). Isa 63,14 says that the Spirit of the Lord comes down and guides his people. Gen 28,12 where the terms ἀναβαίνω and καταβαίνω come together presents the image of angels ascending and descending, which is reflected in John 1,51.

3.2.2 Verbs for "Leading"

3.2.2.1 Ἄγω

An important verb in the LXX which is used with reference to the motif of God's "leading" is ἄγω. It occurs 274 times and is equivalent to 26 Hebrew verbs.[210] It includes verbs like הָלַךְ, עָלָה, נהל, נָחָה, נָהַג, יָצָא, יָרַד and בוא, which we have previously discussed. The important meanings of ἄγω are "to cause to move with someone", "to lead" and "to bring".[211] It is used to refer to God's "leading" of Israel from Egypt through the wilderness to the promised land (Lev 26,13; Num 14,13; Deut 8,2.15; 29,5; 32,12; Josh 24,8; Ps 77[78],52; Isa 63,12.13; cf. Exod 15,22). He can also "guide" individually (Tob 11,17). It is God's "light" (φῶς) and "truth" (ἀλήθεια) which "guide" (ὁδηγέω) and "bring" (ἄγω) the psalmist to God's holy mountain (Ps 42[43],3). The verb ἄγω is found in Isaiah in association with God's future salvific plan with focus on God's leading (Isa 9,6; 11,6; 42,16; 43,5–6; 48,21; 49,10; 63,14; cf. Jer 38[31],8–9). In Isa 63,14, there is a reference to God's "guiding" and "leading" with his spirit, κατέβη πνεῦμα παρὰ κυρίου καὶ ὡδήγησεν αὐτούς, οὕτως ἤγαγες τὸν λαόν σου ποιῆσαι σεαυτῷ ὄνομα δόξης ("The spirit descended from the Lord and guided them, thus you led your

---

[209] Lust, *Lexicon of the Septuagint*, 647; Hatch and Redpath, *A Concordance to the Septuagint*, II, 727.

[210] Lust, *Lexicon of the Septuagint*, 95; Hatch and Redpath, *A Concordance to the Septuagint*, I, 9.

[211] Muraoka, *Lexicon of the Septuagint*, 8; Lust, *Lexicon of the Septuagint*, 95.

people in order to make for yourself a name of glory").[212] The Servant of the Lord is said to be "led" (ἤχθη, passive of ἄγω) to death (Isa 53,7.8).

3.2.2.2 Ἐξάγω

The verb ἐξάγω occurs 221 times in the LXX and is equivalent to 16 Hebrew terms.[213] It is frequently used to refer to the deliverance of Israel from Egypt. It is the Lord himself who brings out his people from Egypt and leads them into the promised land (Exod 3,8; 6,6–8; Lev 19,36; Num 15,41; Deut 1,27; Ezek 20,6). Moses, Aaron and the angel are only Lord's instruments (Exod 3,11–12; 6,26–27; Num 20,16). The Lord will also lead Israel from exile into their own land (Ezek 20,38; 34,13). Furthermore, it is the Lord who leads the sinner into the light (Mic 7,9).

3.2.2.3 Ὁδηγέω

The verb ὁδηγέω is used as an equivalent to דָּרַךְ (hiphil), הָלַךְ (qal and hiphil), יָצָא (hiphil), יָרָה, (hiphil), נָהַג and נָחָה (qal and hiphil).[214] It occurs 44 times and has the meanings of "to guide" and "to lead".[215] It is also used along with way-lexemes like ὁδός, τρίβος or other equivalents (Pss 22,3; 26,11; 85,11; 106,7; 118,35; 138,24). In most cases, God is the subject of ὁδηγεῖν. More importantly, it is at the exodus event that Israel experiences God's guidance and leading (Exod 13,17; 15,13; Num 24,8; Pss 76,20; 77,53; 105,9; Isa 63,14). The psalmist frequently confesses his trust in "the leading and guidance" of the Lord or asks for his "guidance" (e.g., 22,3; 24,5; 26,11; 30,3; 60,2; 72,24; 118,35). It is wisdom that "guides" (ὁδηγέω) the righteous man "on the straight paths" (ἐν τρίβοις εὐθείαις) and shows the kingdom of God (Wis 10,10). Other important verbs for "leading" in the LXX are ἡγέομαι (166x), εἰσάγω (158x), ἀνάγω (114x), ἀπάγω (52x), etc.

3.3 Conclusion

An important observation is that the Greek equivalents of Hebrew way-lexemes and other verbs of journey receive a special metaphorical sense in the LXX, which is absent or rare in secular Greek. Obviously, ὁδός, the most important way-lexeme in the LXX, receives a salvific significance and becomes an important salvific term of the LXX. The use of ὁδός in the LXX is

---

[212] The LXX translation is mine.

[213] Lust, *Lexicon of the Septuagint*, 463; Hatch and Redpath, *A Concordance to the Septuagint*, I, 483.

[214] The verb ὁδηγέω is used in 25 instances as an equivalent to נָחָה. It occurs 27 times in the Psalms. Cf. Hatch and Redpath, *A Concordance to the Septuagint*, II, 962; Michaelis, "ὁδός", 97.

[215] Lust, *Lexicon of the Septuagint*, 841–842.

very strongly stamped by God's salvific deeds and promises. It has two dimensions with regard to God's salvific plan. On the one hand, it is related to God's leading and guiding of his people on the way from the Egyptian bondage to the promised land. On the other hand, it is oriented towards God's promise of future salvation. It is in the book of Isaiah, specifically in Deutero-Isaiah, that ὁδός strongly emphasizes God's salvific plan for the future. The use of ὁδός in the Deutero-Canonical books is more focused on covenant fidelity and right moral conduct under the guidance of God's wisdom. Moral conduct is judged in terms of one's fidelity to God's commandments. The verbs of journey, especially πορεύομαι, ἄγω and ἔρχομαι, have salvific dimensions which are oriented to the future. The verb ὑπάγω, which John uses synonymously with πορεύομαι in his Gospel, occurs only 6 times and does not receive any theological significance in the LXX. The verbs ἀναβαίνω and καταβαίνω demonstrate the distance between the human and the divine realms. Human beings have to go up to reach God and God has to come down in order to suit himself to the level of human beings. The causative function of the Hebrew verbs of journey is often rendered in the LXX by the use of separate verbs for "leading" like ἄγω, ἐξάγω and ὁδηγέω. The God of Israel not only "goes" with his people but also "makes them go". The significance of many of the verbs presented above will become clear when we discuss the journey motif in John.

4. "Way" in the Dead Sea Scrolls

The important way-lexemes with theological implications in the DSS are דֶּרֶךְ (276x), נְתִיבָה (10x), מְסִלָּה (7x), שְׁבִיל (4x) and מַעְגָּל (2x).[216] As in the Hebrew Bible, in the DSS the most important way-lexeme with a variety of theological implications is דֶּרֶךְ. It is mostly found in 1QS (40x), 1QH[a] (25x) and CD

---

[216] The calculation of the frequency of the occurrence of these terms as well as the numbering system for the inner divisions within each document followed here are based on M. G. Abegg Jr., *The Dead Sea Scrolls Concordance Volume I. The Non-Biblical Texts from Qumran* Parts 1–II (Leiden 2003). The original texts used here are according to F. G. Martínez and E. J. C. Tigchelaar, *The Dead Sea Scrolls. Study Edition. Transcriptions* (Leiden 1997–1998) I–II. It should be kept in mind that in many instances the texts are either incomplete or corrupt. Here only the important uses of way-lexemes, especially of דֶּרֶךְ, will be mentioned. For further reading on the theme of way in the DSS, see H-D. Neef, "דרך", *Theologisches Wörterbuch zu den Qumrantexten*, ed. H-J. Fabry and U. Dahmen (Stuttgart 2011) I, 716–725; E. Repo, *Der Weg als Selbstbezeichnung des Urchristentums. Eine traditionsgeschichtliche und semasiologische Untersuchung* (Helsinki 1964); Nötscher, *Gotteswege*, 72–96.

(22x).²¹⁷ It is used in the literal sense of "road" (e.g., CD XI,1; 1QM III,10; 1Q17,4; 4Q158 1–2,10) or journey (e.g., 4Q180 5–6,3; 11Q19 [11QT] LII,14). More frequently, however, דֶּרֶךְ is used in its figurative sense with reference to God's way or human way.²¹⁸ The human way has to comply with God's way, which implies God's plan for human salvation.²¹⁹

In the *Damascus Document*, the author sets out to demonstrate from the history of Israel and the Qumran Community that fidelity to the covenant is always rewarded and apostasy punished. He gives a description of the origin and the goal of the community in CD I,1–II,1. The sinful or helpless condition of the people is compared to "blind people" groping for a "way" (CD I,9; 4Q268 1,16). God established for them a "Teacher of Righteousness" (צדק מורה) to "guide" (hiphil of דרך) them "in the way" (בדרך) of his heart (CD I,11).²²⁰ Those who were unfaithful to the covenant are called "the congregation of traitors", who strayed from "the way" and made Israel wander in the desert without a "way" and diverge "from the ways of righteousness", צדק מנתיבות (CD I,13–16; cf. II,6; III,17). The way of the traitors is the way of the wicked, the way of licentiousness and wicked wealth (CD VIII,4–5.9; cf. XIX,17.21). But the remnant, those who are faithful to the covenant, are admonished "to walk (הָלַךְ) in the ways of God", that is, in the commandments and testimonies of God (CD II,16). CD III,13–16 testify that when God made the covenant with Israel, he revealed "the ways of his truth" (ודרכי אמתו) so that they might "live" (חיה) by them. Everyone who keeps the covenant is asked to make his brother holy so that his steps become steady "in the way of God", בדרך אל (CD XX,18). The expression "the way of the people" has a negative connotation implying infidelity to the covenant (CD VIII,16; XIX,29; XX,24; 11Q13 II,24).

In *The Community Rule*, the members are advised to refine their knowledge in the truth of God's decrees and order their powers according to his ways of perfection (1QS I,13). He who is stubborn in his heart regards darkness as way to light (1QS III,3). The "ways of God" (דרכי אל) are identified with his commandments (1QS III,10). דֶּרֶךְ is often used to set forth the dualistic beliefs. "All the children of righteousness are ruled by the Prince of Light and walk in the ways of light, but all the children of injustice are ruled

---

²¹⁷ For the names and abbreviations of various manuscripts of DSS used in this study, see B. J. Collins (ed.), *The SBL Handbook of Style. For Biblical Studies and Related Disciplines* (Atlanta ²2014), 126–128, 269–330.

²¹⁸ Very frequently דֶּרֶךְ is employed to refer to human behaviour or moral conduct (e.g., 1QS IX,2.5; 4Q184 1,9.14.16.17; 4Q200 2,5; 4Q223–224 2,ii.6; 4Q256 IX,4; XVIII,4).

²¹⁹ The expression "the way of your heart" (דרך לבכה) is frequently used to refer to God's way (plan) of salvation for human beings (1QHª XII,17–18.21.24; XIV,6–7.20.21; 4Q429 4,i.10; 4Q434 1,i.11).

²²⁰ Unless necessary, the Hebrew terms are presented here without vowel pointings as it is found in the original texts.

by the Angel of Darkness and walk in the ways of darkness" (1QS III,20–21).[221] The ways of the sons of light are contrasted with the ways of the sons of darkness by means of a list of their virtues and vices (1QS III,26–IV,11). The difference in the history of all people lies in the division between these two "ways" in which they walk (1QS IV,15). He who enters the covenant has to be separated from all the men of injustice who walk "in the ways of wickedness", בדרך הרשעה (1QS V,11).

The very text of Isa 40,3 is used in *The Community Rule* to explain why the Qumran community is in the desert:

And when these become members of the Community in Israel according to all these rules, they shall separate from the habitation of unjust men and shall go into the wilderness to prepare there the way of Him; as it is written, *Prepare in the wilderness the way of* **** [Yahweh], *make straight in the desert a path for our God* (Isa 40,3). This (path) is the study of the Law which He commanded by the hand of Moses, that they may do according to all that has been revealed from age to age, and as the Prophets have revealed by His Holy Spirit (1QS VIII,12–16).[222]

The life of the covenant community is named "the way" and their main purpose is called "preparation of the way into the desert". This is clearly stated in 1QS IX,17–20:

He shall conceal the teaching of the Law from men of injustice, but shall impart true knowledge and righteous judgement to those who have chosen the Way. He shall guide them all in knowledge according to the spirit of each and according to the rule of the age, and shall thus instruct them in the mysteries of marvellous truth, so that in the midst of the men of the Community they may walk perfectly together in all that has been revealed to them. This is 'the time for the preparation of the way into the wilderness' (פנות הדרך למדבר עת).[223]

References to the need "to prepare the way in the desert" can also be found in 4Q258 VIII,4; 4Q259 III,4–5. The members of the covenant community are advised to "walk" (הָלַךְ) "in the perfect way" (בתמימ דרך) as commanded by God (1QS VIII,18.21). In God's hand are the perfection of one's "way" (דרך) and the uprightness of one's heart (1QS XI,2). Hence, it is said, "For mankind has no way, and man is unable to establish his steps since justification is with God and perfection of way is out of His hand" (1QS XI,10–11).[224] That "the truth of God" (אמת אל) has a guiding role in human life is testified in 1QS XI,4–5: "What always is, is support for my right hand, the path of my steps

---

[221] As translated by G. Vermes, *The Complete Dead Sea Scrolls in English* (London 2004), 101.
[222] Vermes, *The Complete Dead Sea Scrolls*, 109.
[223] Vermes, *The Complete Dead Sea Scrolls*, 111.
[224] Vermes, *The Complete Dead Sea Scrolls*, 116.

goes over firm rock, it does not waver before anything. For the truth of God is the rock of my steps, and his might the support of my right hand".[225]

In the *Thanksgiving Hymns*, rejecting the covenant is identified with walking along the ways which are not good (1QH[a] VII,22). In 1QH[a] XII,4, there is a reference to the "eternal way" (דרך עולם) which belongs to the realm of God. Since God is eternal, his "ways" also are eternal (1QH[a] XV,31–32). The way of God's heart is contrasted with idol worship and other sins (1QH[a] XII,18–19). The way of man is not secure except by the spirit which God creates for him (1QH[a] XII,31). It is striking to notice that the notions of "way" (נְתִיבָה, שְׁבִיל), "truth" (אֱמֶת) and "life" (חַיִּים) occur together in one sentence (1QH[a] XV,13b–15):

> You establish my heart [with] your [tea]chings and with your truth, to straighten my steps on the paths of justice, to walk in your presence on the frontier of [lif]e along tracks of glory {and life} and peace without e[nd] which will ne]ver stop.[226]

It should be noted that while the notion of "truth" has a guiding role, the notion of "life" appears here as the destination or the goal of one's journey of life. That the goal or the destination of the way is life is very explicitly asserted in the wisdom text of 4Q185 II,1–2: "search for yourself a 'way towards life' (דרך לחיים), a 'highway' (מסלה) [towards ...] a remnant for your sons after you".[227]

1Q19 1,3 (1Q Noah) states probably with reference to Gen 6,12 that "all humanity" (כול בשר) has lost their way on the earth. In the view of 4Q88 VIII,4 and 11Q5 XXII,10, man is examined according to his path and is rewarded according to his deeds. The Documents like 4Q420 and 4Q421, which are entitled *Ways of Righteousness*, uphold the moral virtues to walk in the ways of God. Document 4Q473 is called *Two Ways*. It speaks of "two ways", good and evil that bring blessing and destruction respectively. Expressions like "way/ways of life", דרך/דרכי חיים (4Q270 2,ii.20; 4Q299 79,3), "ways of truth", דרכי אמת (CD III,15; 4Q416 2,iii.14; 4Q418 9+9a–c.15) frequently appear. In the Aramaic manuscripts, expressions like "eternal path" (4Q212 1,iv.22) and "paths in truth" (4Q246 1,ii.5) are found.

As a conclusion, the following points can be pointed out. The way topic in the DSS can be broadly grouped into two categories, which are closely interrelated: the way of God and the human way.[228] God's way is the way of truth and the way of life. It is the perfect and eternal way. To go on God's way means to live according to his Torah. Man needs God for the perfection of his way. Hence, separated from God's way, the human way is imperfect and evil.

---

[225] As translated by F. G. Martínez and E. J. C. Tigchelaar, *The Dead Sea Scrolls. Study Edition. Translations* (Leiden 1999) I, 97.
[226] Martínez and Tigchelaar, *The Dead Sea Scrolls. Translations*, 179.
[227] Vermes, *The Complete Dead Sea Scrolls*, 419–420.
[228] Cf. Neef, "דרך", 725.

The basic reason for the formation of the Qumran community is the awareness that "the way of the people" is corrupt and evil. Hence, every member is asked to turn away from "the way of the people" (cf. Isa 8,11) and to live in accordance with God's way.

The theology of two ways in the DSS is rooted in the covenant theology of the Old Testament.[229] Blessing and curse depend on one's fidelity or infidelity to the covenant. Those who follow God's way will attain "eternal life", נצח חיי (CD III,20; cf. III,15–20).[230] The goal of "the way" is always life. In the journey towards life, truth has a guiding role. Since human beings are spiritually blind, there is the need for a guide on the way. The role of "the Teacher of Righteousness" is to guide the community in the way of God's heart.

Special attention should be given to the fact that the Qumran community gave a very prominent place to the book of Isaiah in the formation of their community.[231] Isa 40,3 is the basic source of inspiration for the very foundation of the Qumran community. The citations in *The Consolations* begin with Isa 40,1–4, a passage which figures prominently as an expression of the community's latter-day vocation in the wilderness.[232] The community had the aim "to prepare the way in the desert", that is, to prepare for the imminent coming of the eschatological salvation through ardent study and strict following of the Torah.[233] The thinking and belief of the Qumran community were focused upon this goal.[234] If the Qumran community is called "the way", the destination of this "way" is the coming of the Lord.

---

[229] Cf. Neef, "דרך", 721.

[230] Repo, *Der Weg als Selbstbezeichnung*, 178, states, "Jedenfalls war der 'Weg' der Essener auf ein ewiges Leben ausgerichtet". Nötscher, *Gotteswege*, 90, points out that the way terminology in the Qumran texts as a whole have nothing to do with gnostic thinking.

[231] C. D. Elledge, *The Bible and the Dead Sea Scrolls* (SBL Archaeology and Biblical Studies 14; Atlanta 2005), 89, asserts, "Without question, the most impressive biblical manuscript from Qumran is the *Great Isaiah Scroll* (1QIsaª)". The most abundantly attested book among the prophets in the biblical documents of DSS is the book of Isaiah. There are about 21–24 copies of Isaiah in the DSS. The numerous copies of this book reflect its predominant role as a prophetical writing. Besides the *Great Isaiah Scroll*, there are also an anthology from the book of Isaiah, called *The Consolations* (4QTanḥumim = 4Q176) and translatable fragments of four commentaries on Isaiah, discovered in Cave 4 (4Q161–4). The anthology is called *The Consolations* according to a title given in the manuscript itself that identifies the content of this work as "Consolations from the book of Isaiah". It includes a number of quotations that highlight the theme of consolation so important to Isa 40–55. It begins with the opening verses, Isa 40,1–5. *The Consolations* contain a series of quotations that offer comfort for the Community in the latter days. Cf. Elledge, *The Bible and the Dead Sea Scrolls*, 87–88, 91.

[232] Elledge, *The Bible and the Dead Sea Scrolls*, 91.

[233] Repo, *Der Weg als Selbstbezeichnung*, 177.

[234] Cf. Repo, *Der Weg als Selbstbezeichnung*, 177.

5. "Way" in the Works of Philo and Josephus

5.1 Philo of Alexandria

The term ὁδός occurs 211 times in the writings of Philo.[235] Even though Philo uses ὁδός frequently, he does not follow the usual pattern of Old Testament usages. He uses ὁδός in the literal sense of "road", "path" in the sea and on the land[236] or in the planetary system.[237] The metaphorical sense of "procedure" or "method" is also found.[238] There are instances where he regards human life as ὁδός.[239] Very frequently, ὁδός is used to refer to the moral conduct, either wicked or good.[240] It can also be synonymous with God's commandments.[241]

The notion of two ways frequently appears in Philo even though he uses the expression δύο ὁδοί only once.[242] They are the ways which lead to wickedness (κακία) or to virtue (ἀρετή).[243] If the way of virtue has for its end "life" (ζωή) and immortality (ἀθανασία), the end of the way of vice is the loss of "life" and "immortality", that is to say, "death" (θάνατος).[244] There are frequent references to the way to virtue (ἀρετή).[245] It is said that only a few walk along the way of virtue.[246] Sometimes Philo contrasts the way to piety or the way of virtue with "a way which is no way at all" (ἀνοδία).[247] There are exhortations to follow the way of/to piety (εὐσέβεια).[248] Inspired by Greek poets and thinkers, Philo demonstrates that the way to virtue is long and steep.[249] In the beginning, it is difficult, but gradually it becomes easy. For Philo, the way to virtue is philosophy.[250]

---

[235] P. Borgen et al., *The Philo Index. A Complete Greek Word Index to the Writings of Philo of Alexandria* (Grand Rapids 2000), 237.

[236] *Mos.*, 1.177; *Contempl.*, 86; *Spec.*, 4.154; *Opif.*, 114; *Spec.*, 1.335; 4.111. For the full names of the woks of Philo and Josephus used in this study, see Collins, *The SBL Handbook of Style*, 129–130.

[237] *Opif.*, 101; *Her.*, 149; *Aet.*, 109.

[238] E.g., *Post.*, 7; *Deus*, 180.

[239] *Leg.*, 3.253; *Deus*, 61; *Mos.*, 1.195.

[240] *Ios.*, 212; *Spec.*, 1.192.243; *Det.*, 19.24; *Plant.*, 97–98; *Agr.*, 104; *Mos.*, 2.189.

[241] *Spec.*, 1.300.

[242] *Somn.*, 1.237.

[243] *Spec.*, 4.108; *Leg.*, 2.98; *Abr.*, 204; *Mos.*, 2.138; cf. *Abr.*, 269.

[244] *Plant.*, 37.

[245] *Congr.*, 10; *Fug.*, 21; *Somn.*, 1.179.246; *Spec.*, 1.215.

[246] *Agr.*, 104.

[247] *Spec.*, 3.29; *Mos., 2.138*; cf. *Somn.*, 2.161.

[248] *Det.*, 21; *Spec.*, 1.132; 3.29; *Agr.*, 177; *Legat.*, 216.

[249] *Ebr.*, 150; *Post.*, 154; cf. Hesiodus, *Opera et Dies*, 286–292.

[250] *Leg.*, 1.57.

Philo gives an allegorical interpretation of the passage about דֶּרֶךְ הַמֶּלֶךְ/ὁδὸς βασιλικός in Num 20,17–21.[251] According to him, the way to God may be called "the King's way", ἡ ὁδὸς βασιλέως. The King's way is the way of philosophy and of "the word of God" (θεοῦ ῥῆμα).[252] It is the way of wisdom and its goal is knowledge and understanding of God. In *Quod Deus sit Immutabilis*, 142–144, he interprets the King's way in association with the expression κατέφθειρεν πᾶσα σὰρξ τὴν ὁδὸν αὐτοῦ ἐπὶ τῆς γῆς of Gen 6,12 thus:

> All flesh corrupted the perfect way of the everlasting and incorruptible being, which conducts to God. And know that this way is wisdom. For the mind being guided by wisdom, while the road is straight and level and easy, proceeds along it to the end; and the end of this road is the knowledge and understanding of God. But every companion of the flesh hates and repudiates, and endeavours to corrupt this way; for there is no one thing so much at variance with another, as knowledge is at variance with the pleasure of the flesh. Accordingly, the earthly Edom is always fighting with those who wish to proceed by this road, which is the royal road for those who partake of the faculty of seeing who are called Israel; for the interpretation of the name Edom, is 'earthly', and he labours with all earnestness, and by every means in his power, and by threats, to hinder them from this road, and to make it pathless and impracticable forever.[253]

Abraham is said to have used the King's way, "the way of the only King" (ἡ ὁδός τοῦ μόνου βασιλέως) who governs all things, turning aside and deviating neither to the left hand nor to the right.[254] It is also "the way of virtue" (ἡ ὁδός ἀρετῆς).[255] To go along the King's way is to go along "the middle way" (ὁδῷ τῇ μέσῃ), which God has widened to be a most suitable abode for the souls that love virtue.[256] It is called "the middle way" because it lies between excess and deficiency.[257]

Philo's notion of way betrays the influence of the exodus motif, especially God's leading in the desert when he refers to Moses' words, "Thou shalt remember all the road by which the Lord God led thee in the wilderness (μνησθήσῃ πᾶσαν τὴν ὁδὸν ἣν ἤγαγέ σε κύριος ὁ θεὸς ἐν ἐρήμῳ).[258] God's

---

[251] *Deus.*, 142–183; cf. *Post.*, 101–102. For a detailed study on the theme of King's way and its mystical significance, see J. Pascher, *Hē Basilikē Hodos. Der Königsweg zu Wiedergeburt und Vergottung bei Philon von Alexandreia* (Paderborn 1931).

[252] *Post.*, 102. It should be kept in mind here that for Philo the way of philosophy is the way of wisdom and his philosophy is religious philosophy.

[253] As translated by C. D. Yonge, *The Works of Philo. Complete and Unabridged* (Peabody 1993), 170.

[254] *Gig.*, 64.

[255] *Deus.*, 180.

[256] *Migr.*, 146.

[257] *Spec.*, 4.168.

[258] *Congr.*, 170; Yonge, *The Works of Philo,* 425. Philo here immediately relates "the way that God led" to keeping God's "commandments" (ἐντολαί). This is a significant Old Testament usage of the way motif. Hence, the sweeping comment of Michaelis, "ὁδός", 63, n. 61 that "the many passages where the reference is to the ways of God which men should

guidance in the context of the exodus is a part of Philo's way motif.[259] No one by himself knows the way to God. Hence, God himself is the guide to his seekers on the way that leads to him.[260] Since God is the king, the ruler and the controller of the world, he is more frequently regarded as the guide on the way.[261] In *De Posteritate Caini*, 31, there is a view that God is the guide who makes the way that leads to heaven. He is called ἡγεμὼν τῆς ἀνόδου.[262] He is the "fellow traveller/guide" (συνοδοιπόρος) on the way to virtue.[263] The notion of a way that goes up to heaven is also present in *De Confusione Linguarum*, 4. The divine λόγος comes as an angel and a guide and removes the obstacles on the royal way of virtue.[264] According to *De Vita Mosis*, 2.265, "the divine spirit" (τὸ πνεῦμα θεῖον) leads one to the truth (also see *Gig.*, 55). The goal of the way is also "holiness of life" (ὁσιότης).[265]

To conclude, in Philo's concept of way we find the mixed influence of Greek philosophy and the Old Testament.[266] He does not just follow and emphasize the usual pattern of the Old Testament usage of the way motif. He goes deeper and brings out the inner meaning of the way concept. He spiritualizes the concept of way and gives it a mystical colour. This he often does through an allegorical interpretation of Old Testament passages. He is a philosopher in the sense that he loves the way of wisdom. But he is not an abstract thinker. He is interested in the way of wisdom that leads to a virtuous and holy life. For Philo, all philosophy must be subordinate to Jewish tradition, and the primary source of his philosophy is not Greek philosophers but Moses.[267]

---

follow had not the slightest influence on Philo" is not correct. It is true that his emphasis is different, but the Old Testament usage stands in the background.

[259] *Mos.*, 1.86.164.166.290.

[260] *Migr.*, 170-171: "On which account Moses prays that he may have God himself as his guide to the road which leads to him" (see Yonge, *The Works of Philo*, 362). In *Conf.*, 95, Moses is called "the governor of the way", ἡγεμὼν τῆς ὁδοῦ. Philo regards in *Migr.*, 174 the divine λόγος as ἡγεμὼν τῆς ὁδοῦ.

[261] *Leg.*, 2.85; 3.40; *Migr.*, 143.171; *Det.* 29.114-118; *Decal.*, 81; *QE.*, 1.10; 2.40. Philo also points out God's promise of his presence with his people on the way (*Somn.*, 1.3.179).

[262] *Det.*, 114. The term ἄνοδος is a double-meaning word. It can mean "way up" and "having no way". See LSJ, 145.

[263] *Somn.*, 1.179; *Det.*, 29. Cf. Gen 28,15.

[264] *Deus.*, 181-182. There are passages where the guiding role of λόγος is emphasized. E.g., *Somn.*, 1.71; *Migr.*, 173-174. See B. L. Mack, *Logos und Sophia. Untersuchungen zur Weisheitstheologie im hellenistischen Judentum* (SUNT 10; Göttingen 1973), 135-138.

[265] *Abr.*, 172. In *Praem.*, 1.167, Philo speaks of a beaten road, whose end is nothing other than pleasing God as sons please their father.

[266] M. Scott, *Sophia and the Johannine Jesus* (JSNTSS 71; Sheffield 1992), 58, points out that Philo's writings exhibit a unique blend of Jewish monotheism with middle-Platonic and Stoic philosophy.

[267] Cf. Scott, *Sophia and the Johannine Jesus*, 92.

5.2 Josephus Flavius

The term ὁδός appears 185 times in the writings of Josephus.[268] However, Josephus employs ὁδός mostly in its literal sense. Very frequently, it is used in the sense of "road" or "path".[269] There are references to the way of Israel through the Red Sea.[270] The sense of "journey" or "military march" is also common.[271] The sense of "manner of life" is, however, less frequently attested.[272] The metaphorical sense of ὁδός with theological implication is very rare in Josephus. Hence, the use of the way motif characteristic of the Old Testament has no significant role in the writings of Josephus.

6. "Way" in the New Testament

Since the only way-lexeme in John is ὁδός, in this discussion our focus is exclusively on the term ὁδός. The term ὁδός occurs 101 times in the New Testament. Its distribution in the New Testament is as follows: Matt (22x), Mark (16x), Luke (20x), John (4x), Acts (20x), Rom (3x), 1 Cor (2x), 1 Thess (1x), Heb (3x), Jas (3x), 2 Pet (4x), Jude (1x) and Rev (2x). The most frequent usage is found in Matt, Luke, Acts and Mark. As in classical Greek literature and the Old Testament, ὁδός has both literal and figurative senses in the New Testament. In the Synoptic Gospels, ὁδός is used most frequently in its literal sense and rarely in its figurative sense. There are altogether 58 occurrences of ὁδός in the Synoptic Gospels. Among them, in 43 instances ὁδός is employed in a literal sense and only in 15 instances in the figurative sense.[273] Hence, most of the literal usage of ὁδός in the New Testament is found in the Synoptic Gospels. Literally, ὁδός may mean "road", "street" (e.g., Matt 2,12; Mark 4,4; Luke 18,35; Acts 8,26) or journey (Matt 10,10; Mark 6,8; Luke 11,6; Acts 1,12). Figurative usage is seen in all writings of the New Testament where ὁδός occurs. Here only the figurative usage outside the Gospel of John will be discussed. Johannine usage of the journey/way motif will be later examined.

---

[268] This calculation is based on K. H. Rengstorf and B. Justus, *A Complete Concordance to Flavius Josephus* (Leiden 1979) III, 166–168.

[269] E.g., *A.J.*, 8.235; 8.330; 9.84; *B.J.*, 2.212; *Vita*, 108.118.241.253.

[270] *A.J.*, 2.338; 3.86. It is called θεία ὁδός in *A.J.*, 2.339.

[271] *A.J.*, 2.133; 2.175; 8.227; 12.198; 17.84; *B.J.*, 2.551.

[272] *A.J.*, 6.34; 7.31; 13.290; *B.J.*, 5.402.

[273] The figurative use is found 6 times each in Matthew (3,3; 7,13.14; 11,10; 21,32; 22,16) and Luke (1,76.79; 3,4.5; 7,27; 20,21) and 3 times in Mark (1,2.3; 12,14).

6.1 Synoptic Gospels

The use of Isa 40,3 by all three Synoptists is identical with the LXX wording except for the alteration of τὰς τρίβους τοῦ θεοῦ ἡμῶν into τὰς τρίβους αὐτοῦ. It implies that they identify "the paths of our God" with the paths of Jesus. The citation in Mark 1,2–3, which seems to be a conflation of Mal 3,1, Exod 23,20 and Isa 40,3, presents John the Baptist and Jesus as the eschatological fulfilment of biblical hope.[274] By placing these quotations at the very beginning of the Gospel, Mark sets the entire Gospel in the framework of the fulfilment of Old Testament prophecy. Matthew and Luke, too, place Isa 40,3 before the beginning of Jesus' public ministry and indicate that the promise of future salvation found in the second half of Isaiah is fulfilled with the coming of Jesus. Luke alone extends the Isaianic citation up to Isa 40,5 (Luke 3,4–6). In the Synoptic Gospels, John the Baptist is identified with Elijah who is to come in accordance with Mal 3,1.23 (cf. Mark 9,11–13; Matt 11,10.14; Luke 1,17.76; 7,27) and to prepare the people for the coming of Jesus by proclaiming a baptism of repentance and by teaching them about the one who would come after him (Mark 1,4–8; Matt 3,2.4–12; Luke 3,7–18).[275]

In Matt 7,13–14 (cf. Luke 13,23–24), the imagery of two ways is contrasted with regard to their character (broad and narrow), popularity (followed by many and few; cf. Matt 22,14) and destination (destruction and life; cf. Deut 11,26–29; Jer 21,18).[276] It is possible to view that 'gate' and 'way' here function synonymously.[277] If those who do evil and come to destruction are many, those who do good and attain "eternal life" (cf. Matt 18,8–9; 19,16–17) are a minority. As Matt 7,24–27 suggests, the whole sermon on the mount can be regarded as "the way to eternal life", and to live by the words of Matt 5–7 is not an easy task but a challenge.[278] It is very difficult to be a disciple of Jesus, but it alone leads to life.[279] It should be specially noted that the words in Matt

---

[274] J. Marcus, *Mark 1–8. A New Translation with Introduction and Commentary* (AB 27A; New Haven 2000), 143. Here Mark 1,2 refers to Exod 23,20 and Mal 3,1. Mark 1,3 refers to Isa 40,3. Matthew also uses a conflation of Mal 3,1 and Exod 23,20 in 11,10. But he adds ἔμπροσθέν σου to the form seen in Mark.

[275] R. A. Guelich, *Mark 1–8* (WBC 34A; Dallas 1989), 11, writes, "'Prepare the way of the Lord' reflects Isaiah's call to make ready for a triumphal march to be led by God himself".

[276] The teaching on two ways is well developed in *Didache* 1–6. *Did* 1.1 says, "There are two ways, one to life and one to death, but the difference between the two ways is great". See K. Niederwimmer and H. W. Attridge, *The Didache. A Commentary* (Hermeneia; Minneapolis 1998), 58.

[277] W. D. Davies and D. C. Allison, *A Critical and Exegetical Commentary on the Gospel According to Saint Matthew* (ICC; London 2004) I, 698.

[278] Cf. Davies and Allison, *Matthew*, I, 699.

[279] Michaelis, "ὁδός", 74.

7,13–14 are attributed to Jesus. The relation of "way" with "life" is also worth noticing. Life is regarded as the goal of the way.

In Matt 21,32, John the Baptist is regarded to have come "in the way of righteousness" (ἐν ὁδῷ δικαιοσύνης). "The way of righteousness" is an expression used frequently in the Old Testament (e.g., Prov 8,20; 12,28; 21,16; Tob 1,3; cf. Ps 23,3; Prov 2,20). It means the righteous way of life in accordance with God's commandments. The baptism of Jesus by John is "to fulfil all righteousness", that is, God's will (3,15). In Matt 21,32, "the way of righteousness" would refer primarily to John's preaching of righteousness even though it includes his righteous life as well. John preached and lived righteousness, but he was rejected. Those who reject John will also reject Jesus.

Another expression parallel to "the way of righteousness" is "the way of God upon/in truth" (ἐπ' ἀληθείας τὴν ὁδὸν τοῦ θεοῦ/τὴν ὁδὸν τοῦ θεοῦ ἐν ἀληθείᾳ) found in all the Synoptic Gospels (Mark 12,14; Matt 22,16; Luke 20,21). It can mean "the way", i.e., the behaviour demanded by God (cf. Gen 18,19).[280] Jesus is the teacher of God's righteousness or God's will. "The way of peace" (ἡ ὁδὸς εἰρήνης) in Luke 1,79 is the way that leads to peace, especially peace between God and his people (cf. Rom 3,17; Pss 29,11; 85,9; 119,165; Jer 14,13). It is one of the many blessings which the Messiah is to bring (Luke 2,14; 10,5; 24,36).[281] In the Synoptic Gospels, the whole public life of Jesus can be broadly viewed as a journey along the way from Galilee to Jerusalem (Mark 10,32; Matt 20,17; Luke 9,51.53; 19,28). The climax of this journey is called "the departure" (ἔξοδος) in Jerusalem (Luke 9,31; cf. 13,33; 22,22) and his entry into glory (Luke 24,26; cf. 24,32). Discipleship is following Jesus "on the way" (ἐν τῇ ὁδῷ) that he goes (Mark 10,52; cf. Matt 20,34; Luke 18,43), wherever he may go (Matt 8,19; Luke 9,57).[282]

6.2 Acts

In Acts 2,25–28, Luke cites Ps 15,8–11 from the LXX and in 2,28 he speaks of "ways to life" (ὁδοὶ ζωῆς), which in the context would refer to the risen

---

[280] Davies and Allison, *Matthew*, III, 213.

[281] A. Plummer, *A Critical and Exegetical Commentary on the Gospel According to S. Luke* (ICC; London ³1909), 44.

[282] J. A. Fitzmyer, *The Gospel According to Luke. Introduction, Translation and Notes* (AB 28; New Haven 1974) I, 241, explains the Lukan notion of discipleship in relation to the way motif as follows: "Underlying this notion is the Lucan view of God's revelation of salvation in Jesus as the revelation of a way. For salvation is not made manifest in merely isolated saving events in Jesus' ministry – in cures, exorcisms, or resuscitations – or even in Jesus' suffering or death on the cross understood in an isolated way. All of these elements must be seen as parts of a pattern described as a way (*hodos*), on which Jesus has entered (*eisodos*), moves along (*poreuesthai*), and heads for its outcome (*exodos*, the transit to the Father). Christian discipleship, then, suits this pattern by being a close following of Jesus *en route*".

life that Christ now enjoys. Luke thinks here of the way out of death back to life. It is striking to notice that in Acts there are six instances (9,2; 19,9.23; 22,4; 24,14.22) where ὁδός is used with the definite article in the absolute sense to refer to the Christian movement.[283] This designation will include not only the Christian message but also a particular way of life in accordance with the Christian message.[284] In these texts, ὁδός functions as a symbol that defines the identity of the Christians over against the identity of the non-believing Jews.[285] There is no certainty with regard to the origin of the designation, "the Way". But Isa 40,3 can be regarded as the primary source of inspiration for this designation because it is a fact that the early Christian community regarded the Christ event as the fulfilment of this prophetic voice (Mark 1,2–3; Matt 3,3; Luke 3,4–5; John 1,23).[286] In Acts, one can also find expressions like "way of salvation", ὁδὸς σωτηρίας (16,17), "the way of the Lord", ἡ ὁδὸς τοῦ κυρίου (18,25) and "the way of God", ἡ ὁδὸς [τοῦ θεοῦ] (18,26). The Christian claim that theirs is the true way to salvation might have led to the absolute use of "the Way".[287] If the early Christian community knew or had contact with Qumran/the Essenes, then there is more reason to believe that the absolute use of "Way" by the Qumran community (e.g., 1QS IX,17–18.21; X,21; CD 1,13; 2,6) might have influenced the early Christians in designating their movement as "the Way".[288]

---

[283] It is only with the beginning of the story of Saul that the designation "Way" is used (9,2). In 24,14, "the Way" is regarded as a "sect" (αἵρεσις) by the enemies of Christians.

[284] Cf. G. Ebel, "ὁδός", *NIDNTT*, III, 942.

[285] D. W. Pao, *Acts and the Isaianic New Exodus* (WUNT II 130; Tübingen 2000), 64–65.

[286] Pao, *Acts*, 66–68; S. V. McCasland, "The Way", *JBL* 77 (1958), 226, 228; J. Pathrapankal, "Christianity as a Way according to the Acts of the Apostles", *Les Actes des Apôtres. Traditions, Rédaction, Théologie*, ed. J. Kremer (Leuven 1979), 536.

[287] I. H. Marshall, *The Acts of the Apostles. An Introduction and Commentary* (Leicester 1980), 168–169. J. MacArthur, *John 12–21* (MacArthur NT Commentary; Chicago 2008), 103, views that since the early Christians taught that Jesus Christ is the only way to salvation, Christianity came to be known as "the Way". P. Mallen, *The Reading and Transformation of Isaiah in Luke-Acts* (Library of New Testament Studies 367; London 2008), 72, emphasizes the Christological basis of way (Luke 1,76; 3,15–17) and points out that the Christian movement is called "the Way" because it is none other than the way of Jesus.

[288] McCasland, "The Way", 228–230, believes that there was a real contact in ideas and persons between Qumran and early Christianity and that John the Baptist was an important means of that contact. There is also a view that some Essenes were possibly included among the priests mentioned in Acts 6,7. See J. A. Fitzmyer, "Jewish Christianity in Acts in Light of the Qumran Scrolls", *Studies in Luke-Acts*, ed. L. E. Keck and J. L. Martyn (Nashville 1966), 239. After pointing out the various differences between the early Christian community and Qumran community, Fitzmyer, "Jewish Christianity", 253, would state regarding the relationship between the two thus, "The most that one can say is that the early Jewish Christian church was not without some influence from the Essenes". In his commentary on Luke, Fitzmyer also views that, given the existence of such a Palestinian

In Acts 13,10, the activity of a false prophet (cf. 13,6), which is the same as that of the devil (διάβολος), is described as "making crooked" the straight ways of the Lord. This is to be contrasted with a true prophet whose chief role is to make straight the ways of the Lord (Luke 3,4; cf. Isa 40,3). In Acts 14,16, Paul says that in the past all nations or gentiles were allowed "to go in their own ways" (πορεύεσθαι ταῖς ὁδοῖς αὐτῶν), which means the practice of idol worship, but now they should turn to the living God (14,15; cf. 1 Thess 1,9). The "way of salvation" (ὁδὸς σωτηρίας) in Acts 16,17 means the way to salvation or the way to achieve salvation. Parallel to the journey of Jesus in Luke, in Acts there is the journey of the word of God as the agent of salvation.[289]

6.3 Letters

The "inscrutable ways" of God in Paul's exclamation in Rom 11,33 may mean God's deeds for the accomplishment of his plans (Ps 10,5 [9,26]). Paul's expression "my ways in Christ [Jesus]" in 1 Cor 4,17 may mean his Christian directives, i.e., instructions and teachings.[290] It is his way of life in conformity with Christ. The "more excellent way" in 1 Cor 12,31 may refer to the life governed by love, which is valued above all other gifts (13,1–8).

One of the dominant thoughts of the Letter to the Hebrews is that "the way to the holy place" (τὴν τῶν ἁγίων ὁδόν) or "the direct access to God", which was impossible during the age of the old covenant (Heb 9,8)[291], has been made possible in Jesus through his sacrificial death (10,19–25). The author of Hebrews is concerned with the act of God himself in Jesus, which opens up "the new and living way" to the heavenly sanctuary (10,20).[292] A counterpart to John 14,6 can be noticed in Heb 10,19–20, "Therefore, my friends, since we have confidence to enter the sanctuary by the blood of Jesus, by 'the new and living way' (ὁδὸν πρόσφατον καὶ ζῶσαν) that he opened for us through the curtain (that is, through his flesh)...".[293] Here the reader is reminded to see an implicit allusion to the rending of the temple curtain from top to bot-

---

designation for a community, it is not impossible that early Christians would have borrowed this designation ("Way") for their way of life, too. See Fitzmyer, *Luke*, I, 243.

[289] See Pao, *Acts*, 147–176.

[290] J. A. Fitzmyer, *First Corinthians. A New Translation with Introduction and Commentary* (AYB 32; New Haven 2008), 224.

[291] The idea behind Heb 9,8 is that "the earthly sanctuary with all its ceremonies had to be rendered invalid if the way to the heavenly sanctuary were to be opened". See N. A. Dahl, "'A New and Living Way' – the Approach to God according to Hebrews 10,19–25", *Interpretation* 5 (1951), 405.

[292] B. Lindars, *The Theology of the Letter to the Hebrews* (Cambridge 1991), 46.

[293] Dahl, "New and Living Way", 405, writes, "The flesh of Jesus is the point where the heavenly and the earthly worlds meet, but meet in a way which leaves the heavenly world hidden".

tom at the moment of Jesus' death (Mark 15,38; Matt 27,51; Luke 23,45). What is symbolically expressed by the Letter is realistically narrated by the Synoptic Gospels. Through the death of Jesus, the blockage between God and man is removed and the direct access to God's presence is established.

The basis for the "confidence" (παρρησία) to enter the presence of God is "the blood of Jesus", i.e., his death on the cross (10,19).[294] The way that Jesus opens up is "a new way" because it did not exist before and "a living way" because it is established by the ever-living Christ and leads to salvation, to the presence of God. It is a way which leads "through the curtain" into the Holy of Holies. The way by which Jesus the High Priest has entered into the presence of God is open for all people who follow him.

The "way" in Jas 1,8; 5,20 refers to human conduct and behaviour. The term ὁδός also appears 4 times in its metaphorical sense in 2 Pet 2 in the context of an exposition on false prophets and their punishment. In this chapter, there are three synonymous expressions like "way of truth" (2,2), "straight way" (2,15) and "way of righteousness" (2,21). These expressions refer to "the Christian way of life, Christianity considered not as a body of doctrine but as a way of life, a religious message which takes effect in an ethical lifestyle".[295] "The way of truth" (ἡ ὁδὸς τῆς ἀληθείας) is the way which is based on and corresponds to the truth of the gospel" (cf. 2 Pet 1,12).[296] The "straight way" of the Lord is contrasted with "the way of Balaam", which leads to destruction (2 Pet 2,15–16; cf. Num 22,21–35; 25,1–9; 31,14–16; Josh 13,22). "The way of Cain" in Jude 11 is similar to "the way of Balaam". Cain is the first murderer and the prototype of hatred and envy. "Going the way of Cain" would mean following his footsteps by imitating his sin.

6.4 Revelation

In the Book of Revelation ὁδός occurs twice (Rev 15,3; 16,12). In 15,3, the angels praise God for his "just and true ways", which may refer to his salvific deeds (cf. Deut 32,4; Ps 145[144],17). In 16,12, ὁδός is used in conjunction with ἑτοιμάζω to refer to the preparation of "the way of the kings" (ἡ ὁδὸς τῶν βασιλέων) from the east. The sixth angel pours the bowel of God's wrath on the river Euphrates, and its water is dried up so that the way is prepared for the kings. This may suggest a military invasion from the east, specifically from the area of the Euphrates River.[297]

---

[294] Dahl, "New and Living Way", 403, views that the Greek word παρρησία must be assumed to mean both the God-given permission and the personal confidence and frankness arising from it.

[295] R. J. Bauckham, *2 Peter, Jude* (WBC 50; Dallas 2002), 242.

[296] Bauckham, *2 Peter*, 242.

[297] The Euphrates was traditionally the boundary between the Roman and the Parthian Empires. Parthia was the ever dreaded enemy of the Romans (cf. Rev 9,13–19). Hence, the

6.5 Conclusion

It is to be specially noted that all the evangelists cite Isa 40,3 and assert that the eschatological salvation promised by Isaiah is fulfilled by the coming of Jesus. The expression "prepare the way of the Lord" in the Synoptic Gospels have more ethical overtones. There is an emphasis on repentance and renewal of hearts, whose agent is John the Baptist. A notable difference between the Synoptic Gospels and the Gospel of John is that John does not use the verb "prepare" (ἑτοιμάζω) but rather "make straight" (εὐθύνω), while citing Isa 40,3 in 1,23. About the significance of this change, we will discuss in the second part. Strictly speaking, there is no parallel to John 14,6 in the Synoptic Gospels. But the notions of "way to life" and "way of truth" can be found in them. It is possible to assume that Isa 40,3 might have inspired the early Christians in designating their movement as "the Way". A comparatively better parallel of John 14,6a can be found in Heb 10,19–20. It is striking that the notions of "way" (ὁδός) and "living" (ζάω) occur together in Heb 10,20.[298] In both John and Hebrews, it is the death of Jesus that makes possible the access to God. The notion that Jesus goes ahead and the believers have to follow him also appears in both of them.

7. Journey Motif in the Gospel of John

John uses ὁδός, the key LXX term for way, only 4 times (1,23; 14,4–6). Even though the Synoptic Gospels frequently employ the term ὁδός, it is not used exclusively to refer to God's salvific plan in Jesus.[299] But in the Gospel of John, ὁδός is exclusively a salvific term in all its four occurrences.[300] One should not so narrowly think that the theme of way in the Gospel is restricted to those four texts where the term "way" (ὁδός) is mentioned. On the contrary, the way motif is inseparably connected to the journey motif, which is employed pervasively from the beginning until the end of the Gospel.

"kings of the East" can be a reference to the Parthian rulers. There is also a view that the Nero *redivivus* myth lies underneath the interpretation of a military invasion against Rome. See D. E. Aune, *Revelation 6–16* (WBC 52B; Dallas 1998), 891–894.

[298] The occurrences of terms like εἴσοδος (v. 19), οἶκος τοῦ θεοῦ (v. 21), ἀληθινός (v. 22), καρδία (v. 22) in the immediate context of Heb 10,20 become specially notable if the immediate context of John 14,6 is called to mind.

[299] See pp. 89–90 for a survey of ὁδός in the Synoptic Gospels.

[300] It should be noticed that, unlike the Synoptic Gospels, John never uses the term ὁδός in a literal sense. Even though in 14,5 Thomas may misunderstand and think of a way in the geographical sense, in the mind of the evangelist the way that Jesus goes has only a salvific sense.

Way and journey are inseparable concepts. The way metaphor belongs to the semantic domain of journey. Way is for going and coming. Apart from the purpose of a journey, way has no meaning and significance. Jesus' being the way is inseparable from his going the way.[301] It is in the context of Jesus' journey from the Father to this world, from this world to the Father and finally with the Father to the believers that John's presentation of Jesus as the way to the Father is to be understood (cf. John 13–14). Hence, an examination of the way motif in the Gospel should take into account the journeys that Jesus makes in the Gospel. The following discussion is intended to show how John depicts Jesus' journey in the Gospel in general, then his cosmic journey in John 13–14, which provides the backdrop for his claim to be the way to the Father in 14,6, and finally the journey of the believers towards Jesus.[302]

7.1 Jesus' Journeys in General

The journey of Jesus is one continuous journey. But it has two levels, otherworldly and this-worldly. For practical reasons, they can be called the cosmic and the geographical journeys. They do not exclude each other. Even Jesus' geographical journey is part of his cosmic journey and its mission. John's presentation of Jesus as the way belongs to the network of Jesus' cosmic journey. Hence, more attention will be given to his cosmic journey.

7.1.1 Cosmic Journey

The story of Jesus in John has the cosmos as its setting and eternity as its time frame (1,1–14).[303] It is indeed "a story of a human on the plane of history, but it is at the same time the story of one who comes from beyond the world and from the beginning of all existence".[304] The prologue portrays the cosmic journey of the Logos from the other world, the world above, to this world, the world below, ultimately becoming flesh as Jesus of Nazareth (1,14).[305] It is a

---

[301] In the Old Testament, one's way and journey (going/coming) are inseparable. E.g., the psalmist says, "In the path (ὁδός) where I walk (πορεύομαι) they have hidden a trap for me" (Ps 142,3; LXX 141,4).

[302] This will be a sketchy presentation of the journey motif in the Gospel of John. Other themes and issues involved in the texts will not be the concern of this discussion.

[303] For a good discussion on the theme of the cosmological tale in the Gospel of John, see A. Reinhartz, *The Word in the World. The Cosmological Tale in the Fourth Gospel* (SBLMS 45; Atlanta 1992).

[304] R. Kysar, *John's Story of Jesus* (Philadelphia 1984), 18.

[305] B. Lindars, *The Gospel of John* (NCBC; Grand Rapids 1972), 76, observes in his comment on the prologue, "John has felt it desirable to place Jesus in the cosmic setting of his relationship to the Father, which is everywhere presupposed but not treated systematically". In the view of R. E. Brown, *The Gospel According to John. Introduction, Translation, and Notes* (AB 29; New Haven 1966) I, 18, "The Prologue is not concerned with the earthly origins of Jesus but with the heavenly existence of the Word in the beginning".

journey that starts from the Father and ends apparently in this world with a return to the Father, but still continues by coming to the believers and making home with them (cf. 14,23). It is a mission undertaken upon the wish of the Father. At the completion of Jesus' mission, he goes from this world to the other world with the promise of coming again. This cosmic journey of Jesus provides an overall framework for his geographical journeys in the Gospel. Three stages can be discerned in the cosmic journey of Jesus: the journey from the Father into this world, the departure from this world to the Father and the return to the believers.

7.1.1.1 Journey from the Father into this World

The significance of Jesus and the nature of his mission are displayed in sayings concerning his coming and being sent.[306] Jesus' journey from his Father into this world is described by means of verbs of "coming" (ἔρχομαι, ἐξέρχομαι, καταβαίνω and ἥκω) and verbs of "sending" (ἀποστέλλω and πέμπω).

a. In Terms of Coming

The theological importance of Jesus' coming into the world is more emphasized in the Gospel of John than in the Synoptic Gospels. The self-attestation of Jesus about his coming is more in number in John than in the Synoptic Gospels. The verb ἔρχομαι occurs in the Gospel of John 157 times. About 28 times, it is used to refer to Jesus' coming into this world.[307] In the prologue, he is identified with the true light that was coming into the world (1,9). He came to his own, but his own did not receive him (1,11).[308] Jesus is frequently identified as ὁ ἐρχόμενος, "the One who comes". This expression occurs 7 times with reference to Jesus (1,15.27; 3,31[2x]; 6,14; 11,27; 12,13). It is an appellative that indicates an ambassadorial mission from God to the people and refers to God's promise that a Saviour would come.[309] It is a messianic designation and when Jesus is called ὁ ἐρχόμενος, his messiahship is in-

---

[306] Cf. J. Schneider, "ἔρχομαι", *TDNT*, II, 671.

[307] In addition to the reference to Jesus' coming into this world, ἔρχομαι is twice used to refer to Jesus' departure to the Father (17,11.13) and 7 times with reference to Jesus' return to the believers (14,3.18.23.28; 21,22–23). About 14 times, it is used in relation to the coming/not coming of the "hour" (ὥρα) and once in relation to the coming of "night" (9,4). There are four references each to the coming of the Holy Spirit (15,26; 16,7–8.13) and to the coming (appearance) of the risen Jesus (20,19.24.26; 21,13).

[308] This can refer to the rejection by Israel or more broadly by the very humanity, which came into being through him (1,3.10).

[309] E. Arens, *The HΛΘΟΝ-Sayings in the Synoptic Tradition. A Historico-Critical Investigation* (Freiburg 1976), 297.

voked.³¹⁰ Hence, it corresponds to Jesus' real appearance on earth.³¹¹ John the Baptist identifies Jesus as "the One who comes" (ὁ ἐρχόμενος) after him, but admits that Jesus is greater than him in rank (1,15.27.30; cf. 1,29). Isa 40,3, which John the Baptist uses to interpret his role in John 1,23, would call to mind the coming of Yahweh in the coming of Jesus (cf. Isa 40,10).³¹²

Nicodemus identifies Jesus as a teacher who has come from God, on account of Jesus' signs (3,2; cf. 16,28). But his statement ἀπὸ θεοῦ ἐλήλυθας has a different nuance, strictly meaning, "from the part of God" since he explains it by ὁ θεὸς μετ' αὐτοῦ.³¹³ Since "from God" is a traditional way of speaking of God's emissaries, Nicodemus' statement cannot be regarded as a perfect confession of faith.³¹⁴ John the Baptist is from the earth, but Jesus comes from heaven/above (3,31). Jesus' heavenly origin is, therefore, a proof of his superiority over John. The Samaritan woman believes that the Messiah is coming and when he comes, he will proclaim all things (4,25).³¹⁵ Jesus immediately presents himself to her as the coming Messiah, using an ἐγώ εἰμι-saying (4,26). In 5,43, Jesus demonstrates his authority from the Father before the Jews by saying that he has come not in his own name but in the name of the Father. After the miraculous feeding, the crowd regards him as the prophet who is to come into the world (6,14). The people's belief serves to continue the exodus imagery of the miracle because it recalls the promise of a prophet like Moses of Deut 18,15.³¹⁶

The crowd speculates that when Christ comes, no one will know where he is from (7,27; cf. 7,31), and Jesus makes clear to them that he has come not on his own (7,28; 8,42). In fact, Jesus' origin is hidden to the crowd since he comes from God. When the crowd thinks that Christ cannot come from Galilee but from Bethlehem (7,41–42), their speculation can be an instance of Johannine irony or the evangelist's concern with Jesus' heavenly origin. When Jesus says that he has come into this world for judgment (9,39), it may mean that his coming necessarily involves judgement. But 9,39 is not a con-

---

[310] Arens, *The ΗΛΘΟΝ-Sayings*, 288, 295.

[311] Arens, *The ΗΛΘΟΝ-Sayings*, 300, states, "If ὁ ἐρχόμενος is a *terminus technicus* for the Messiah, used in the New Testament to point to the actualization of God's promise of a Saviour and final revealer of his designs for men, then it is highly probable that behind the ἦλθον-form of speech the expression ὁ ἐρχόμενος is present. In other words, ἦλθον would be a self-revelatory affirmation of the presence of the Messiah; the ἦλθον-sayings would be concrete statements of messiahship in the mouth of the ὁ ἐρχόμενος".

[312] A. C. Brunson, *Psalm 118 in the Gospel of John. An Intertextual Study on the New Exodus Pattern in the Theology of John* (WUNT II 158; Tübingen 2003), 241.

[313] Arens, *The ΗΛΘΟΝ-Sayings*, 310, n. 30.

[314] Cf. G. O'Day, *The Gospel of John. Introduction, Commentary and Reflections* (NIB IX; Nashville 1995), 549.

[315] Since the Samaritans regarded their Messiah as a teacher, they believed that he would proclaim all things. Cf. O'Day, *John*, 568.

[316] O'Day, *John*, 594.

tradition to 3,17 and 12,47 because in 9,39 it is not said that Jesus himself will judge, but that judgment will take place because of him.[317] The ultimate purpose of his coming is not to judge but to save (cf. 3,17–19; 12,47). He has come as the good shepherd so that all who follow him may have life in abundance (10,10; cf. 3,16; 5,24; 6,40.51; 11,25; 20,31). When Martha proclaims that Jesus is the Christ, the Son of God, the One who comes into the world, the evangelist anticipates the very purpose of the Gospel (cf. 20,31) through her words (11,27). The designation "the One who comes into the world" recalls the theme of eschatological expectation that has dominated Jesus' conversation with Martha.[318]

At Jesus' entry into Jerusalem, the people shout, "Hosanna! Blessed is the One who comes in the name of the Lord, the King of Israel!" (12,13; Ps 118,26). Even though this verse in its original context is applied to every pilgrim who enters the temple, it is interpreted messianically in the Gospels (Matt 21,9; Mark 11,9; Luke 19,38; John 12,13; cf. Matt 11,3; Luke 17,19–20) and in the Midrash to the Ps 118.[319] In 12,15, the citation "Do not be afraid, daughter of Zion. Look, your king is coming, sitting on a donkey's colt" can be seen as a conflation of Zeph 3,16 or Isa 40,9 and Zech 9,9. In Zeph 3,16, the words "Do not fear, O Zion" are immediately associated with the promise, "The Lord, your God, is in your midst" (Zeph 3,17), and in Isa 40,9, the words "Do not be afraid" are found in association with "here is your God". In Zech 9,9, the cited words are found in connection with the salvation which the righteous kings brings, צַדִּיק וְנוֹשָׁע הוּא (δίκαιος καὶ σῴζων αὐτός). If so, in John 12,15 it is likely that the evangelist is aware of the context of these quotations and that he sees in Jesus the coming of Yahweh who is at the same time the Saviour as well. In the person of Jesus, it is Yahweh, the true king of Israel who has returned to Jerusalem.[320] Thus, the new exodus promises related to eschatological salvation are fulfilled in Jesus.[321] It is as light that he has come into the world so that those who believe in him will not remain in darkness (12,46; cf. 1,4.5.9; 3,19; 8,12; 9,5.39). Since Jesus is the light (8,12), this promise is a natural and an abiding outcome of a positive response to Jesus. In Jesus' reply to Pilate in 18,37, there is an emphasis on the purpose of Jesus' coming into the world, namely to bear witness to the

---

[317] Arens, *The ΗΛΘΟΝ-Sayings*, 312.

[318] O'Day, *John*, 689.

[319] Brown, *John*, I, 457, thinks that for John "he who comes in the Lord's name" has special significance since according to 17,11–12 the Father has given Jesus the divine name, Ἐγώ εἰμι.

[320] Brunson, *Psalm 118*, 258.

[321] In the view of Brunson, *Psalm 118*, 264, Jesus' entry into Jerusalem not only symbolizes and represents but actually is the new exodus coming of Yahweh to end the exile and to defeat Israel's enemies.

truth (cf. 8,46; 14,6).³²² It is by making God known in his very person through his words and deeds that Jesus bears witness to the truth.

The verb ἐξέρχομαι is used 30 times in the Gospel. In six occurrences, it is employed to refer to Jesus' origin from God (8,42; 13,3; 16,27.30) or the Father (16,28; 17,8). While the verb ἔρχομαι expresses an independent personal initiative, ἐξέρχομαι denotes a direct relation and dependence on the source of origin.³²³ The frequent appeal to Jesus' origin is a means of correcting false and inadequate Christology.³²⁴ One's relationship with Jesus is the measure of one's relationship with God because of Jesus' divine origin (8,42).³²⁵ Within the farewell discourse, the term ἐξέρχομαι is used 5 times with reference to Jesus' origin. In two instances, there is an emphasis on his divine destination as well (13,3; 16,28). Jesus' mission in the world is completed only with his return to God the Father, the source of his origin. In 13,3, there may be an indication that it is God's Son who humiliates himself in foot-washing, which symbolizes his death. In three passages, Jesus' divine origin is the content of the disciples' belief (16,27.30; 17,8). Even though the disciples confess Jesus' divine origin in 16,30, their confession is incomplete because they do not acknowledge the necessity of Jesus' death and departure to the Father.³²⁶

The verb καταβαίνω occurs 17 times in the Gospel. Twice it is used to refer to the descending of the Holy Spirit (1,32.33), which is the sign for John the Baptist to identify "the One who comes" (1,30–34). Καταβαίνω is found twice along with ἀναβαίνω to mention the ascending and descending of the angels (1,51) and of the Son of Man (3,13).³²⁷ John 1,51 is a part of Jesus' dialogue with Nathanael (1,47–51). Perceiving Jesus' supernatural knowledge, Nathanael comes to believe in Jesus and identifies him correctly as "the Son of God" and "the king of Israel" (1,47–49). Jesus' words in 1,50 are, therefore, not a rebuke but a promise. Nathanael is now only at the initial stage of belief in Jesus. In the future, he will see greater things which will deepen his belief (1,50). The double ἀμήν-saying is used to draw attention to an important point that follows. Jesus reveals and identifies himself in 1,51 as

---

[322] "For this I was born" and "for this I came into the world" are synonyms.

[323] Arens, *The HΛΘON-Sayings*, 310.

[324] G. C. Nicholson, *Death as Departure. The Johannine Descent-Ascent Schema* (SBLDS 63; Chico 1983), 55.

[325] Brown, *John*, 1, 357, thinks that the focus of ἐξέρχομαι in 8,42 is on the mission of the Son, i.e., incarnation. For him, "I came from God and now I am here" is all one idea. However, the value of the mission depends on his divine origin.

[326] O'Day, *John*, 782.

[327] Even though the use of καταβαίνω in John 1,51 is about the ascent and descent of the angels, the descent of the Son of Man is implied in the context. Moreover, the image of the ladder, which the text presupposes, parallels well with John's presentation of Jesus as the gate in 10,9 and as the way in 14,6. Hence, it is relevant to pay some attention to 1,51.

the Son of Man who bridges the distance between heaven and earth. This verse may remind the reader of two images of the descent of the Son of Man[328] in Dan 7,13 and the ladder in Jacob's dream in Gen 28,12. The title "Son of Man" can be seen as a conflation of concepts of humanity and divinity, reflecting the human and divine aspects in the person and mission of Jesus.[329] The Johannine Son of Man replaces the ladder of Genesis and becomes the meeting point between heaven and earth. He is the mediator between heaven and the earth and the gate of heaven.[330] Hence, the Son of Man imagery in 1,51 corresponds well with the image of Jesus as the gate in 10,9 and the way to the Father in 14,6.

The Son of Man saying in 3,13 parallels with that in 1,51. In both instances, there is a reference to heavenly ascent and descent. As the Son of Man, Jesus moves between heaven and earth and brings the two together.[331] No one else has ascended into heaven and only Jesus has the access to heaven (cf. 8,35). Thus, there is a good correspondence between the exclusivism in 3,13 and that in 14,6b. The verb καταβαίνω is also used 7 times in the discourse on the bread of life (6,33.38.41.42.50.51.58). Except in 6,38, according to which the purpose of his coming is to do the will of the Father, in all other instances καταβαίνω is associated with the bread of life. Jesus presents himself as the bread that comes down from heaven. But the Jews, like the Samaritan woman, misunderstand Jesus' words and are unable to grasp their real sense. Unlike the manna, he is the bread that can satisfy the spiritual hunger of the people by giving them eternal life. The motif of Jesus' heavenly descent comes to an end in chapter 6. The verb ἥκω, which occurs 4 times in the Gospel, is used in 8,42 in relation to Jesus' origin. It is found in pagan literature to refer to the coming of a deity who makes a solemn appearance (cf. 1 John 5,20).[332]

b. In Terms of Sending

The verbs for sending belong to the journey motif since the language of sending in itself implies a movement of one who is sent from one place/realm to another. The Gospel of John uses two verbs for sending, ἀποστέλλω and πέμπω. The verb ἀποστέλλω occurs 28 times, while the verb πέμπω occurs 32

---

[328] For a study on the theme of the Son of Man in John, see the literature given in A. J. Köstenberger, *The Missions of Jesus and the Disciples According to the Fourth Gospel* (Grand Rapids 1998), 50, n. 26.

[329] Köstenberger, *The Missions of Jesus,* 127.

[330] The image of "heaven opened" may remind the reader of the image of the gate in 10,7.9.

[331] O'Day, *John,* 551.

[332] Brown, *John,* 1, 357.

times. They are synonymously used by the evangelist.³³³ His choice for these verbs can be better explained as a preference for a verb in a certain grammatical form or by stylistic variation.³³⁴ Both verbs point out the initiative of the sender and suggest obedience by the one sent.³³⁵ They mostly refer to the origin of Jesus' mission.³³⁶ To indicate that the Father has sent Jesus into this world, the verb ἀποστέλλω is used 17 times³³⁷ and the verb πέμπω 24 times.³³⁸

The purpose of God's sending his Son into the world is that the world might be saved through him (3,17) because it is out of love for the world that God gives his Son (3,16). Because of his union with the Father, Jesus can say that his food is to do the will of the Father who sent him (4,34; 6,38). The proof that God has sent Jesus is to be seen in his works (5,36; cf. 11,42), which include not only his miracles but also his whole ministry (cf. 17,4). The right way to honour the Father is to honour the Son whom he has sent (5,23).³³⁹ Jesus is not alone in his mission (8,16.29), the Father who sent him is with him as his witness (5,37; 8,18). One who believes in Jesus believes in the Father who sent him (12,44) and this belief is initiated by the Father himself (6,44). As Jesus is sent by the Father, so also will he be returning to the one who sent him (7,33; 16,5). The expression ὁ πέμψας με occurs 9 times. 8 times it stands for God who reveals himself through Jesus (5,37; 6,44; 7,28; 8,16.18.26.29; 12,49) and once for John the Baptist (1,33). It refers to Jesus' relationship with the Father and has its origin in the awareness that Jesus' coming into the world is completely due to the Father's initiative.³⁴⁰

7.1.1.2 Departure from this World to the Father

The verbs of journey used to describe Jesus' departure from this world to his Father are ἀναβαίνω, ὑπάγω, ἀφίημι, μεταβαίνω, πορεύομαι, ἀπέρχομαι and ἔρχομαι. The verb ἀναβαίνω, which occurs 16 times in John, is used 4 times with reference to Jesus' ascension (3,13; 6,62; 20,17[2x]).³⁴¹ The ascent that

---

[333] For the debate on evangelist's use of these verbs, see Köstenberger, *The Missions of Jesus*, 97–106.

[334] Köstenberger, *The Missions of Jesus*, 106.

[335] Arens, *The ΗΛΘΟΝ-Sayings*, 309.

[336] Arens, *The ΗΛΘΟΝ-Sayings*, 311.

[337] Those texts are: 3,17.34; 5,36.38; 6,29.57; 7,29; 8,42; 10,36; 11,42; 17,3.8.18.21.23.25; 20,21.

[338] Those texts are: 4,34; 5,23.24.30.37; 6,38.39.44; 7,16.18.28.33; 8,16.18.26.29; 9,4; 12,44.45.49; 13,20; 14,24; 15,21; 16,5. Thrice there are references to the "sending" (πέμπω) of the Holy Spirit (14,26; 15,26; 16,7).

[339] In the ancient Mediterranean world, to dishonour the one sent is equal to dishonour the sender. Cf. O'Day, *John*, 584.

[340] Arens, *The ΗΛΘΟΝ-Sayings*, 321. For a distinction between the functions of ἀποστέλλω/πέμπω and ἔρχομαι, see Arens, *The ΗΛΘΟΝ- Sayings*, 321–322.

[341] For comments on 3,13, in comparison with 1,51, see pp. 99–100.

6,62 mentions is Jesus' return through his death, resurrection and ascension to his Father and thus to his pre-existent glory (cf. 17,5). The ascension in 20,17 should be regarded as the glorification of Jesus in the Father's presence, and therefore, it should be distinguished from the ascension which is understood as a levitation symbolizing the end of the appearances of the risen Jesus (Acts 1,1–11).[342] John is not concerned with the ascension as an end of Jesus' appearances, but rather with the completion of "the hour" in which Jesus goes from this world to the Father (13,1).[343] Jesus' words to Mary Magdalene may suggest that Jesus' glorification is not yet completed and that the disciples should be prepared for receiving the Holy Spirit.[344] The bestowal of the Holy Spirit to the disciples is the culmination of Jesus' glorification (cf. 7,39). Moreover, Jesus' ascension to the Father is part of his preparing a place in the Father's house, a possibility of communion with the Father for the disciples (14,2) and thus preparing a way to the Father.

The verb ὑπάγω, which appears 32 times in John, is used 17 times in relation to Jesus' departure to the Father.[345] During his public ministry, Jesus tells the Jews repeatedly that he will be present in this world only for a little while. He will be going back to the one who sent him, and where he goes, they cannot come (7,33–34; 8,21–22). Jesus also informs his own disciples that he will soon be going away from them (13,33; 14,4.28; 16,5.10). But even his own disciples cannot follow him at the moment when Jesus goes (13,33.36). Therefore, Jesus' departure is unique and has a special purpose. It is intended to prepare a place and thus a way to the Father through his death and resurrection (14,2–6). But the astonishing fact is that neither the Jews (7,35–36; 8,22) nor his own disciples (16,17) are able to understand what his departure to the Father means. In fact, only Jesus knows where he is going (8,14).

Even though the verb ἀφίημι occurs 15 times in John, it is used only twice to refer to Jesus' departure (14,18; 16,28). In 14,18, Jesus makes clear that his departure will not make the disciples orphaned because he will be coming back to them.[346] In 16,28, Jesus points out that his origin and destination is the Father. Jesus' journey is incomplete just with his descent. It should be completed with his departure to the Father and return to the believers. The verb μεταβαίνω, which occurs 3 times in this Gospel, is used only once to refer to Jesus' departure to the Father (13,1). 13,1 introduces the book of

---

[342] R. E. Brown, *The Gospel According to John. Introduction, Translation, and Notes* (AB 29A; New Haven 1970) II, 1012. Also, see the comment on 20,17 on pp. 284–286.

[343] Brown, *John*, II, 1012.

[344] Brown, *John*, II, 1016, comments, "By speaking of his ascension in 20,17, Jesus is not drawing attention primarily to his own glorification – that process has been going on throughout 'the hour' – but to what his glorification will mean to men, namely, the giving of the Spirit that makes them God's children".

[345] Those texts are: 7,33; 8,14(2x).21(2x).22; 13,3.33.36(2x); 14,4.5.28; 16,5(2x).10.17.

[346] The theme of Jesus' return to the believers we will discuss below.

glory. It is the arrival of Jesus' hour that marks the end of his public ministry and prepares the disciples through the farewell meal and speech for his departure to the Father.[347]

The verb πορεύομαι, which is synonymous with ὑπάγω, occurs 16 times in John. It is used 9 times in relation to Jesus' departure (7,35[2x]; 10,4; 14,2.3.12.28; 16,7.28). In 7,35, the issue is that the Jews do not understand what Jesus' imminent departure means (cf. 7,33). They think of Jesus' departure in a geographical sense, believing that Jesus will be going to the dispersion (διασπορά) to teach the Greeks. The questions of the Jews are significant like the unconscious prophecy of Caiaphas (11,49–52), which foresees the gathering of the dispersed children of God into one family as a result of Jesus' departure. In 10,4, which is a part of the shepherd discourse (10,1–18), Jesus is not speaking about his departure. But the imagery of the shepherd who "goes ahead" and of the sheep who "follow him" (ἔμπροσθεν αὐτῶν πορεύεται, καὶ τὰ πρόβατα αὐτῷ ἀκολουθεῖ) has great significance in relation to Jesus' journey in the Gospel. In fact, the journey of Jesus ahead of his disciples in the Gospel is like the journey of the shepherd ahead of his sheep in 10,4 (cf. 14,2–3.28; 16,28). Just as the shepherd goes ahead and the sheep follow him, Jesus is going ahead through his death and resurrection to prepare the way to the Father, so that the disciples can come to the Father along this way (cf. 14,2–6). The advantage of Jesus' departure is that the Holy Spirit, the advocate, will come (16,7)[348] and the disciples will be able to do still greater works (14,12). Even though the verb ἔρχομαι is used mostly to refer to Jesus' coming into the world, in Jesus' prayer to the Father it is used twice to denote Jesus' coming/going to the Father (17,11.13).

7.1.1.3 Return to the Believers

Even though the motif of Jesus' coming into this world and going to the Father is prominent in the Gospel, there are also references to Jesus' return to the believers (14,3.18.23.28; 21,22–23). It means that Jesus' journey does not come to an end with his departure to the Father.[349] It is worth noticing that

---

[347] See also the comments on 13,1 on p. 139.

[348] In 16,7, there is also the occurrence of the verb ἀπέρχομαι. It is used only twice to refer to Jesus' departure, even though it appears 21 times in this Gospel.

[349] One notable limitation in the model of the "Botenweg" suggested by J. A. Bühner, *Der Gesandte und Sein Weg im 4. Evangelium. Die kultur- und religionsgeschichtlichen Grundlagen der johanneischen Sendungschristologie sowie ihre traditionsgeschichtliche Entwicklung* (WUNT II 2; Tübingen 1977), 118–267, is that the mission and the journey of the messenger come to an end with his return to the sender. In the Gospel of John, the journey and the mission of Jesus do not terminate with his departure to the Father. He will not leave his believers orphaned (14,18) and is going to dwell inwardly with the believers (14,23). Unlike Mark and Luke, but like Matthew, John does not narrate the disappearance

Jesus' promises concerning his return are given only to his disciples. During his public ministry, he never speaks explicitly of his return after his departure even though his return through resurrection is implied in some instances (e.g., 3,14; 8,28; 12,23.32). It is in the farewell speech (14,3.18.23.28)[350] and in the epilogue (21,22–23) that explicit references to his return appear. It can be said that 14,3 is a Johannine adaptation of the traditional expectation about Parousia. At the same time, both traditional and realized eschatology are juxtaposed in John 14. In 14,18, there is an indication of the post-resurrectional appearances. However, the promise that he will not leave his disciples orphaned may also imply additionally a permanent presence of the risen Christ with his disciples (cf. Matt 28,20). This promise is further supported and complimented by an explicit reference to the indwelling by the Father and the Son in the believers who love Jesus and keep his word (14,23). The motif of departure and return in 14,28 seems to parallel with that mentioned in 14,3. The rebuke of Jesus in 21,22–23, especially the expression "until I come" (ἕως ἔρχομαι), may presuppose an early Christian expectation that Parousia would happen before the first generation of Christians had disappeared (cf. 1 Thess 4,15; 1 Cor 15,51).[351] Jesus reveals that the future of the beloved disciple should not be a concern for Peter, he should rather follow the Lord and feed his sheep (21,15–17).[352]

Some of the expectations regarding Jesus' return to the believers, promised in chapter 14 (cf. v. 18), are fulfilled in Jesus' resurrection appearances (20,19.24.26). It should be specially noticed that Jesus' promises of his return in chapter 14 are described using the verb ἔρχομαι, and it is by using this verb that the evangelist presents Jesus' first resurrection appearances (20,19.24.26; cf. 21,13). The use of ἔρχομαι for the appearance of the risen Lord is unique to the Gospel of John, and it may be intended to reaffirm the reality of the resurrection as well as the continuity between the earthly Jesus and the risen Christ.[353]

It is also noteworthy that besides the references to the coming of Christ, there are also explicit references to the coming of the Holy Spirit. The promise that the Paraclete will be given is first mentioned in 14,16–17. In 14,26, it is pointed out that he will be "sent" (πέμπω) by the Father in Jesus' name in

---

of the risen Jesus. The Gospel of John assumes that Jesus is spiritually ever present and active in his believers (cf. Matt 28,20).

[350] For a discussion on these verses, see pp. 161–163, 173–176.

[351] C. K. Barrett, *The Gospel According to St. John. An Introduction with Commentary and Notes on the Greek Text* (London ²1978), 586; Brown, *John*, II, 1109; Schnackenburg, *John*, III, 369.

[352] John 21,22–23 may also deal with the problem that the Parousia which was still expected during the beloved disciple's life had not happened. See Schnackenburg, *John*, III, 370–371.

[353] Arens, *The HΛΘON-Sayings*, 307.

order to teach the disciples everything and to remind them of whatever Jesus has spoken (14,26). It is in terms of "coming" (ἔρχομαι) that the Holy Spirit is promised in 15,26; 16,7.8.13. In 15,26, it is also mentioned that he will be "sent" (πέμπω) by Christ (cf. 16,7) and "proceed" (ἐκπορεύομαι) from the Father.[354] Jesus' going is necessary for the coming of the Spirit (16,7; cf. 7,39). It is to be noted that the work of the Spirit is described in 16,13 in terms of a guide on the way during a journey. He will "guide" (ὁδηγέω) the disciples to all truth because he is the Spirit of truth (16,13). The promises that Jesus makes about the coming of the Holy Spirit during his farewell speech are fulfilled in 20,22.

7.1.2 Jesus' Geographical Journey

Besides the cosmic journey of Jesus, John also narrates a number of geographical journeys of Jesus.[355] Broadly speaking, there are two main poles between which Jesus travels, namely Judea/Jerusalem and Galilee. John presents the beginning of Jesus' public ministry in the context of John the Baptist's witness to Jesus in Bethany beyond Jordan in the region of Judea (1,19–34). The first geographical journey of Jesus in the Gospel is from the region of Judea to Galilee. There are three journeys to Galilee and three corresponding journeys from Galilee to Jerusalem. Therefore, we can notice three "Galilee/Jerusalem cycles" (1,43–3,21; 4,1–5,47; 6,1–10,39). Each of these cycles includes a journey from Judea/Jerusalem to Galilee and then a return journey to Jerusalem. After his third journey to Jerusalem, Jesus does not return to Galilee anymore. Instead, he goes to Bethany beyond Jordan (10,40), to Bethany (11,15), to Ephraim (11,54) and then back to Bethany (12,1). The final journey of Jesus takes place between Bethany and Jerusalem (12,12–19,42). This is the fourth and last journey of Jesus to Jerusalem. It comes to an end with Jesus' death and burial since the earthly body of Jesus disappears

---

[354] The difference of agency in sending the Holy Spirit in 14,26 and 15,26 may reflect various stages in the development of Johannine thought. Since the Father and the Son are one (10,30), on the theological level this difference is not significant. Cf. Brown, *John*, II, 689.

[355] Scholars have already recognized the significance of the journey motif in discerning the structure and plot of the Gospel. See M. Rissi, "Der Aufbau des Vierten Evangeliums", *NTS* 29 (1983), 48–54; J. F. Staley, "The Structure of John's Prologue: Its Implications for the Gospel's Narrative Structure", *CBQ* 48 (1986), 241–264; F. F. Segovia, "The Journey(s) of the Word of God: A Reading of the Plot of the Fourth Gospel", *The Fourth Gospel from a Literary Perspective*, ed. R. A. Culpepper and F. F. Segovia (Semeia 53; Atlanta 1991), 23–54; idem, "John", *A Postcolonial Commentary on the New Testament Writings*, ed. F. F. Segovia and R. S. Sugirtharajah (London 2009), 156–193; J. Beutler, "Jesus on the Way to Galilee. The Movement of the Word in John 1–4", *Melita Theologica* 62 (2012), 7–22. For a detailed analysis of Jesus' geographical journeys, see Segovia, "The Journey(s) of the Word of God", 37–49; idem, "John", 175–182.

from the scene with his burial in 19,42. All journeys of Jesus to Jerusalem are directly associated with the celebration of a Jewish feast (2,13; 5,1; 7,10; 12,12).[356] Other cities and places to which Jesus goes during his public life are Cana (2,1–2; 4,46), Capernaum (2,12; 6,17), the Judean countryside (2,22), Sychar in Samaria (4,5), the other side of the sea of Galilee (6,1), the garden near Kidron valley (18,1) and finally Golgotha (19,17).

Jesus' journey through Samaria is very significant. It is worthwhile to notice that in 4,6 John uses the term ὁδοιπορία, which means "walking" or "journey". This term appears only twice in the entire New Testament (cf. 2 Cor 11,26) and is used only in a literal sense. It is out of tiredness from his journey that Jesus comes to sit by Jacob's well. This occasion paves the way for him to introduce himself to the Samaritans. His presence among the Samaritans, who are marginalized in the society, highlights the universal dimension of his way, i.e., that he is the Saviour of the world (4,42). In other words, Jesus' "journey" (ὁδοιπορία) through Samaria gives the Samaritans the opportunity to accept him as "the way" (ὁδός). The miracle of Jesus' walking over the sea (lake) of Galilee along with his ἐγώ εἰμι-saying and admonition not to fear (6,16–21) has theophanic overtones and may remind the reader of the God of the Old Testament who makes his way through the sea, "Your way was through the sea, your path, through the mighty waters; yet your footprints were unseen" (Ps 77,19[20]).[357]

The final journey of Jesus to Jerusalem is worth noticing (12,12–19). Through his triumphal entry into the city, Jesus fulfils the Old Testament messianic expectations and presents himself as the Saviour who is to come (Zech 9,9). His admonition at the end of the first part of the farewell speech, "Arise, let us go from here" (Ἐγείρεσθε, ἄγωμεν ἐντεῦθεν, 14,31), suggests his determination to go ahead and to lead the way. He takes the initiative to go out into the garden (18,1) in order to be arrested and tried by his enemies (18,12–19,16). He carries the cross by himself without anyone's help and goes out to Golgotha to open the way to the Father (19,17; 20,17). Only John says that Jesus carries the cross by himself and goes out to Golgotha to be crucified and to die. But the portrayal of Jesus' passion is quite different in the Synoptics. According to them, the enemies lead Jesus away to crucify him and he is helped by Simon of Cyrene to carry the cross (Mk 15,20; Matt 27,31–32; Luke 23,26). Thus, Johannine Jesus *goes* the way and *is* the way to the Father so that the believers may follow him (cf. 21,22).

---

[356] The first and the fourth/last journey is associated with the feast of Passover. The second journey is related to an unidentified feast and the third journey is on the occasion of the feast of Tabernacles and extends through the feast of Dedication (10,22).

[357] See pp. 306–308 for more discussion on John 6,20.

7.2 Jesus' Cosmic Journey in John 13–14

Jesus' geographical journeys between Jerusalem (Judea) and Galilee (1,43–7,10) and between Jerusalem and its neighbouring places (10,40–12,12) come to an end in 12,12. After his entry into Jerusalem, he does not leave the city. From chapter 13 onwards, the evangelist is intensively focusing on the cosmic journey of Jesus, which is already introduced in the prologue (1,9.11.14) and frequently referred to in the first part of the Gospel. The unifying and decisive theme in the farewell discourse is Jesus' cosmic journey, i.e., Jesus is going from this world to the Father (13,1 ἐκ τοῦ κόσμου τούτου πρὸς τὸν πατέρα), from where he came, and the negative and positive consequences of Jesus' journey for the disciples. In his speech, Jesus teaches the disciples the destination of his journey and provides for them the way to the Father, which is he himself (14,6). It is in the context of Jesus' cosmic journey motif that his claim as the way to the Father in 14,6 is placed and is to be understood. As it is seen in the whole Gospel, the motif of Jesus' cosmic journey in chapters 13–14 is illustrated by the evangelist through various verbs of "going", "coming" and other related verbs of journey like "sending", "following" and "leaving".[358] The following table will show the distribution of the various verbs of journey used in John 13–14, arranged in the order of their first appearance.

Verbs of journey/movement within John 13–14	Frequency	Place of occurrence
μεταβαίνω[359]	1	13,1
ἔρχομαι	9	13,1.6.33; 14,3.6.18.23.28.30
ἐξέρχομαι	3	13,3.30.31
ὑπάγω	7	13,3.33.36(2x); 14,4.5.28
πέμπω[360]	5	13,16.20(2x); 14,24.26
εἰσέρχομαι	1	13,27
ἀκολουθέω[361]	3	13,36(2x).37

---

[358] In this cosmic journey of Jesus, the devil (Satan, the ruler of the world), Judas, the disciples who will follow him later, the Holy Spirit and the Father have their own roles to play. Hence, the verbs of journey related to these characters are also taken into account. All the verbs given in the table belong to the semantic domain of journey or movement. See J. P. Louw and E. A. Nida, *Greek-English Lexicon of the New Testament Based on Semantic Domains* (New York ²1989) I, 180–211.

[359] Μεταβαίνω can mean "to effect a change of location in space, with the implication that the two locations are significantly different – to move from one place to another, to change one's location". See Louw and Nida, *Greek-English Lexicon* I, 181.

[360] Louw and Nida, *Greek-English Lexicon*, I, 190, defines πέμπω as "to cause someone to depart for a particular purpose", "to send".

πορεύομαι	4	14,2.3.12.28
ἀφίημι	2	14,18.27
ἄγω	1	14,31

The above table shows that there are 10 verbs used in these two chapters to refer mostly to Jesus' cosmic journey.[362] The following sketch of passages based on the verbs of journey will reveal clearly how vehemently the motif of Jesus' cosmic journey controls these two chapters from the beginning till the end.

13,1 - Jesus knows that the hour <u>came</u> for him to <u>go</u> from this world to the Father.
<u>ἦλθεν</u> αὐτοῦ ἡ ὥρα ἵνα <u>μεταβῇ</u> ἐκ τοῦ κόσμου τούτου πρὸς τὸν πατέρα.

13,2 - The devil had already <u>moved (put into)</u> the heart of Judas to betray Jesus.[363]
τοῦ διαβόλου ἤδη <u>βεβληκότος</u> εἰς τὴν καρδίαν ἵνα παραδοῖ αὐτὸν Ἰούδας Σίμωνος Ἰσκαριώτου ...

13,3 - Jesus knows that he <u>came</u> from the Father and <u>is going</u> to the Father.
ἀπὸ θεοῦ <u>ἐξῆλθεν</u> καὶ πρὸς τὸν θεὸν <u>ὑπάγει</u>.

13,6 - Jesus <u>came</u> to Simon Peter[364].
<u>ἔρχεται</u> οὖν πρὸς Σίμωνα Πέτρον.

13,16 - The <u>messenger (apostle)</u> is not greater than the one who <u>sent</u> him.
... οὐδὲ <u>ἀπόστολος</u> μείζων τοῦ <u>πέμψαντος</u> αὐτόν.

---

[361] According to Louw and Nida, *Greek-English Lexicon*, I, 201, ἀκολουθέω can mean "to follow or accompany someone who takes the lead in determining direction and route of movement, to accompany as a follower, to follow, to go along with".

[362] These 10 verbs occur altogether 36 times. In some instances, they refer to the journey of the disciples/believers (13,20.33.36.37; 14,6), Satan (13,27), Judas (13,30–31), the Holy Spirit (14,26) and the ruler of the world (14,30).

[363] This verse is included here to show the role of the devil in the cosmic journey of Jesus and the corresponding relationship between the devil and the ruler of the world at the end of the first part of the farewell speech (14,30). Although the verb βάλλω is not a verb of journey, according to Louw and Nida, *Greek-English Lexicon*, I, 207, it is a verb of linear movement, which "involves actions in which an agent causes something to move through space by means of an initial force". E.g., John 5,7; 8,7; 8,59; 12,6; 13,5; 15,6; 18,11. In the case of 13,2, the verb βάλλω refers to the movement within the heart of Judas, initiated by the devil. Judas yields himself to the initial force of the devil and later allows Satan "to enter into" him (13,27 εἰσέρχομαι). His yielding to the movement in his heart caused by the devil facilitates the "coming" of the ruler of the world (14,30).

[364] That Jesus came to Peter (ἔρχεται οὖν πρὸς Σίμωνα Πέτρον) during the footwashing scene is also included here. Even though the verb ἔρχομαι in 13,6 is not directly associated with Jesus' cosmic journey, it has special significance in the resurrection appearances. It is used to refer to the risen Jesus' coming to the disciples (20,19.24.26; 21,13) and also to his final coming (21,22.23).

13,20 - "Whoever receives one whom I <u>send</u> receives me; and whoever receives me receives him who <u>sent</u> me".
ὁ λαμβάνων ἄν τινα πέμψω ἐμὲ λαμβάνει, ὁ δὲ ἐμὲ λαμβάνων λαμβάνει τὸν πέμψαντά με.

13,27 - Satan <u>entered</u> (went/moved) into Judas.
εἰσῆλθεν εἰς ἐκεῖνον ὁ Σατανᾶς.

13,30 - Judas <u>went out</u> into the night.
ἐκεῖνος ἐξῆλθεν εὐθύς. ἦν δὲ νύξ.

13,31–32 - When Judas had <u>gone out</u>, Jesus said, "Now the son of man has been glorified ..."[365]
Ὅτε οὖν ἐξῆλθεν, λέγει Ἰησοῦς, Νῦν ἐδοξάσθη ὁ υἱὸς τοῦ ἀνθρώπου ...

13,33 - Where Jesus <u>is going</u> the disciples cannot <u>come</u>.
ὅπου ἐγὼ ὑπάγω ὑμεῖς οὐ δύνασθε ἐλθεῖν.

13,36a - Peter asks Jesus where he <u>is going</u>.
λέγει αὐτῷ Σίμων Πέτρος, Κύριε, ποῦ ὑπάγεις;

13,36bc - Where Jesus <u>is going</u> Peter cannot <u>follow</u> him now, but he will <u>follow</u> later.
ὅπου ὑπάγω οὐ δύνασαί μοι νῦν ἀκολουθῆσαι, ἀκολουθήσεις δὲ ὕστερον.

13,37 - Peter asks Jesus why he cannot <u>follow</u> him now.
λέγει αὐτῷ ὁ Πέτρος, Κύριε, διὰ τί οὐ δύναμαί σοι ἀκολουθῆσαι ἄρτι;

14,2 - Jesus <u>is going</u> to prepare a place for the disciples.
πορεύομαι ἑτοιμάσαι τόπον ὑμῖν.

14,3 - After <u>going</u> and preparing a place, Jesus will <u>come</u> again.
ἐὰν πορευθῶ καὶ ἑτοιμάσω τόπον ὑμῖν, πάλιν ἔρχομαι.

14,4 - Jesus assumes that the disciples know the <u>way</u> to where he <u>is going</u>.
ὅπου [ἐγὼ] ὑπάγω οἴδατε τὴν ὁδόν.

14,5 - Thomas states that they know neither where he <u>is going</u> nor the <u>way</u>.
Λέγει αὐτῷ Θωμᾶς, Κύριε, οὐκ οἴδαμεν ποῦ ὑπάγεις· πῶς δυνάμεθα τὴν ὁδὸν εἰδέναι;

14,6 - Jesus claims, "I am the <u>way</u> and the truth and the life. No one <u>comes</u> to the Father except through me".
λέγει αὐτῷ [ὁ] Ἰησοῦς, Ἐγώ εἰμι ἡ ὁδὸς καὶ ἡ ἀλήθεια καὶ ἡ ζωή· οὐδεὶς ἔρχεται πρὸς τὸν πατέρα εἰ μὴ δι' ἐμοῦ.

14,12 - Since Jesus <u>is going</u> to the Father, the believer will do greater works.
μείζονα τούτων ποιήσει, ὅτι ἐγὼ πρὸς τὸν πατέρα πορεύομαι.

---

[365] Even though the verb δοξάζω is not a verb of movement, it has a special significance in the cosmic journey of Jesus. It also refers to the glorification of Jesus through his death, resurrection and ascension, which is actually the crucial part of his cosmic journey.

14,18 - Jesus will not <u>leave</u> the disciples orphaned and he <u>is coming</u> to them.
Οὐκ <u>ἀφήσω</u> ὑμᾶς ὀρφανούς, <u>ἔρχομαι</u> πρὸς ὑμᾶς.
14,23 - Jesus and the Father will <u>come</u> and make dwelling among those who love Jesus.
πρὸς αὐτὸν <u>ἐλευσόμεθα</u> καὶ μονὴν παρ' αὐτῷ ποιησόμεθα.
14,24 - The word of Jesus is of the Father who <u>sent</u> him.
ὁ λόγος ὃν ἀκούετε οὐκ ἔστιν ἐμὸς ἀλλὰ τοῦ <u>πέμψαντός</u> με πατρός.
14,26 - The Father will <u>send</u> the Holy Spirit in Jesus' name.
τὸ πνεῦμα τὸ ἅγιον, ὃ <u>πέμψει</u> ὁ πατὴρ ἐν τῷ ὀνόματί μου ...
14,27 - "Peace I <u>leave</u> with you".[366]
Εἰρήνην <u>ἀφίημι</u> ὑμῖν.
14,28 - Jesus <u>is going away</u> and <u>coming</u> to the disciples. The disciples should rejoice because he <u>is going</u> to the Father.
Ὑπάγω καὶ ἔρχομαι πρὸς ὑμᾶς. εἰ ἠγαπᾶτέ με ἐχάρητε ἂν ὅτι πορεύομαι πρὸς τὸν πατέρα.
14,30 - The ruler of the world <u>is coming</u>.
ἔρχεται γὰρ ὁ τοῦ κόσμου ἄρχων.
14,31 - "Get up, let's <u>go</u> from here".
Ἐγείρεσθε, <u>ἄγωμεν</u> ἐντεῦθεν.

The most frequently used verbs of journey within John 13–14 are ἔρχομαι (9x) and ὑπάγω (7x), which also has its synonym, πορεύομαι (4x). The motif of Jesus' journey ("going") begun in 13,1.3 is continued through the verb ὑπάγω in vv. 33.36; 14,4.5.28 and through the verb πορεύομαι in 14,2.3.12.28. Verbs of journey occur at the beginning (13,1 μεταβαίνω[367]) and the end (14,31 ἄγω) of this sub-section. We can even notice an *inclusio* between 13,1 and 14,31, formed by the presence of the nouns πατήρ and κόσμος, the verb ἀγαπάω, the verbs of journey μεταβαίνω (13,1) and ἄγω (14,31) and the verbs of knowing οἶδα (13,1) and γινώσκω (14,31). There is also a correspondence between "the coming" of the hour in 13,1 and "the coming" of the ruler of the world in 14,30 and between the "devil" in 13,2 and "the ruler of the world" in 14,30. In 13,1, the evangelist indicates that Jesus is going from this world to the Father. In 14,28, there is also a reference that Jesus is going to the Father, and the sub-section ends with Jesus' admonition "let's go" (14,31). Jesus' "coming from" and "going to" God in the beginning (13,3) is matched by his "going" and a new "coming" at the end of the sub-section (14,28; cf. 14,3), forming an *inclusio*. V. 28 repeats the theme

---

[366] Even though the verb ἀφίημι in 14,27 has the sense of "imparting", it is the "leaving" Jesus who imparts the disciples the peace. Peace is, therefore, closely associated with Jesus' cosmic journey. It is not the peace of "this world" but of "the other world" that Jesus "leaves" with the disciples. After the resurrection, the first words of Jesus to the disciples are "peace with you", εἰρήνη ὑμῖν (20,19).

[367] Μεταβαίνω is used also in 5,24 and 1 John 3,14 for passing from death to life.

of departure and return, and along with v. 3, it forms an *inclusio*. The verb ἐξέρχομαι in 13,31a and the verb ἄγω in 14,31 in its literal sense will form an *inclusio*, too.

The following diagram will make it clear how 13,1–3 and 14,28.30–31 function as the frames of these chapters, emphasizing the motifs of cosmic journey and cosmic conflict of Jesus with the devil (Satan, ruler of the world).

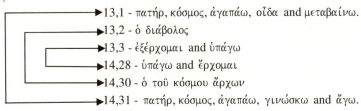

7.3 Believers' Journey to Jesus

Just as in the Old Testament people come to God, so also in the Gospel of John people from all walks of life come to Jesus.[368] He is accessible and approachable to all. There are many passages in the Fourth Gospel where the people's journey or approach to Jesus is literally or figuratively described.[369] The people may not be able to understand whatever Jesus teaches, but many come to him with an open heart. Even though Nicodemus may be a man of cowardice and misunderstanding, he is open to confess with his imperfect knowledge that Jesus has come from God (3,2; cf. 7,50). Towards the end of the Gospel, he comes with courage to show his faith in Jesus openly when he joins Joseph of Arimathea, who also comes and openly confesses his faith in Jesus by giving a royal burial to him (19,38–42). Their act, thus, fulfils the prophecy of Jesus, "And I, when I am lifted up from the earth, will draw all people to myself" (12,32).

The disciples of John the Baptist are envious of the success of Jesus' ministry and complain that "all are coming/going to him" (πάντες ἔρχονται πρὸς αὐτόν, 3,26). The Baptist's reply, however, points out the fact that all those who come to Jesus are given to him by the Father (6,37.39.65; 10,29; 17,9.24). A Johannine irony, therefore, may be noticed in the complaint of the disciples of the Baptist since Johannine thought demands that all should come to Jesus in order to reach the Father (14,6b). The Samaritans who are margin-

---

[368] There is a correspondence between people's journey to God in the Old Testament (see p. 69) and believers' journey to Jesus.

[369] The most commonly used verb to describe the people's journey to Jesus is ἔρχομαι (3,2.26; 4,30.40; 6,5; 7,50; 8,2; 10,41; 11,29.32; 12,9.22). Other verbs are περιπατέω (6,66; 8,12; cf. 11,9–10; 12,35), ἐξέρχομαι (12,13; cf. 10,9), ἀπέρχομαι (6,66–68; 12,19), εἰσέρχομαι (10,9), ἥκω (6,37) and μεταβαίνω (5,24).

alized in the society are open to come to Jesus and to recognize him as the Saviour of the world (4,30.40). The royal official's coming to Jesus to ask for Jesus' healing touch for his dying son is an act of faith in Jesus (4,47; cf. 4,50).

In Galilee, a large crowd comes to Jesus on account of his signs, acknowledges him as the prophet who is to come into the world and even wants to make him their king (6,2–5a.14–15). Since Jesus is the gate to life, those who seek life should "go through" (εἰσέρχομαι) him (10,9). There are many in Judea who come to Jesus to see him or to listen to him or to believe in him (10,41–42; 12,9.13).[370] There are also women disciples who come to Jesus or are found near Jesus like Martha and Mary (11,20–32), the Mother of Jesus (19,25b–27) and Mary Magdalene (20,1–18). The theme that Jesus is the universal Saviour is ironically depicted in the comment of the Pharisees in 12,19, "Look, the world has *gone after* him!" (ἴδε ὁ κόσμος ὀπίσω αὐτοῦ ἀπῆλθεν). There are gentiles like the Greeks who come from far to see him (12,20–22).[371] But there are also unbelievers who come to him to humiliate him and make his death sure (19,3.32.33).

In a number of passages, "coming to Jesus" is synonymous with "believing in him" (5,40; 6,35.37.44.45.65; 7,37; 14,6). Hence, faith in Jesus is seen as a journey. The gift of faith in Jesus is the work and the gift of the Father (6,37.44.45.65). It is in accordance with the will of the Father that people come to Jesus (6,37). It is his initiative to make people come to Jesus (6,44). He teaches all, but those who hear and learn from him come to Jesus (6,45). Therefore, it can be said that no one can come to Jesus except through the Father (6,65), just as no one can come to the Father except through Jesus (14,6). The result of coming to Jesus is eternal satisfaction and eternal life (5,40; 6,35; 7,37; cf. 10,9). A believer in Jesus can "pass" (μεταβαίνω) from death to life and experience eternal life as a present reality (5,24).

The verb ἀκολουθέω, which occurs 19 times in the Gospel, is used 16 times with reference to following Jesus.[372] Following Jesus can be meant literally (1,37–40; 6,2; 18,15) and figuratively (8,12; 10,27; 12,26; 13,36–37, etc.).[373] Jesus is said to follow no one else. Since Jesus is the way, his believers are called to follow him. It is by calling the disciples to follow him that Jesus begins his public ministry (1,37–43). Since Jesus is the light, if anyone follows him, he will not "walk" (περιπατέω) in darkness, but will have the light

---

[370] Within the pericope of the adulteress, there is a reference to the coming of all people to Jesus (πᾶς ὁ λαὸς ἤρχετο πρὸς αὐτόν) to listen to his teaching (8,2).

[371] See the comments on the Greeks' visit (12,20–22) on pp. 385–386.

[372] Those texts are: 1,37.38.40.43; 6,2; 8,12; 10,4.27; 12,26; 13,36(2x).37; 18,15; 21,19.20.22.

[373] In some instances, literal and figurative meanings may go hand in hand, e.g., 1,40; 13,36–37.

of life (8,12; cf. 11,9–10; 12,35–36).³⁷⁴ The imagery of the sheep hearing the voice of the shepherd and following him, in fact, refers to Jesus who goes the way ahead and to his disciples who follow his way (10,4.27). But not all disciples follow him (6,60–71). In 6,66, it is pointed out that many of his disciples "depart" (ἀπέρχομαι) from him and are no longer ready to "walk with him" (μετ' αὐτοῦ περιπατέω). Jesus asks his own inner circle of disciples whether they too wish to "go away" (ὑπάγω) from him. Peter's reply is worth noticing, "Lord, to whom can we *go*? You have the words of eternal life" (6,68). There is an element of exclusivism in 6,68 as there is in 14,6. The question "Lord, to whom can we *go*?" means "Besides Jesus, there is no one else to go to!" (cf. Acts 4,12; Isa 40,25; 43,11; 46,9). This is because the disciples have come to believe and know that he is the Holy One of God (6,69). Since Jesus himself is the way, they need not go to anyone else (14,6). Many Jews are leaving their Jewish leadership and believing in Jesus because of the miracle of raising Lazarus from the dead (12,11).

Jesus predicts that when his hour comes even his closest disciples will be scattered and will "go away" (ἀφίημι) from him (16,32). A true following of Jesus is impossible before Jesus' glorification (13,36–37) because the Spirit is given only after Jesus' glorification, and the work of the Holy Spirit is necessary to remind the disciples of whatever Jesus has said (cf. 2,22; 7,39; 12,16; 14,26). This fact is very dramatically presented within the passion narrative, especially when Peter, who literally "follows" (ἀκολουθέω, 18,15) Jesus during his trials, denies to be a follower (μαθητής) of Jesus (18,15–18.25–27). But after Jesus' glorification, Peter is enabled to follow Jesus even until death (21,19.22). The follower of Jesus will be honoured by the Father and is promised the gift of being where Jesus is (12,26).

The journey and mission of Jesus continue through his disciples. Hence, they are sent just as Jesus is sent. This is mentioned in the post-resurrectional perspective of the evangelist in 4,38; 15,16; 17,18, but becomes a present reality when the risen Jesus sends them as apostles to carry out his mission in 20,21 (cf. 13,20).³⁷⁵ The mission of the disciples is also a journey. They are appointed to "go" (ὑπάγω) and bear lasting fruits (15,16; cf. Luke 10,3).

---

³⁷⁴ The urgency of walking in the light of Jesus is highlighted in 11,9–10; 12,35. It is an admonition to believe in him and to follow his way. The figurative sense of περιπατέω in John is not used primarily to refer to human conduct but to belief in Jesus and to discipleship.

³⁷⁵ Cf. T. Okure, *The Johannine Approach to Mission. A Contextual Study of John 4,1–42* (WUNT II 31; Tübingen 1988), 158–159. For a different view, see Köstenberger, *The Missions of Jesus*, 180–184.

7.4 Conclusion

The Gospel presupposes that life is a journey. Hence, John presents the life of Jesus in terms of a journey. The story of Jesus in John is a story of his journey into this world from his Father who sent him. It is a journey with a mission to save the world. Unlike the Synoptic Gospels, John attaches a preeminent role to the figurative sense of the verbs of journey. He uses the spatial language of journey to highlight Jesus' heavenly and divine origin and destination. Jesus' cosmic journey firmly establishes the divine provenance of his message. The exclusive assurance of his origin from the Father and his destination to the Father, demonstrated in the Gospel from its beginning till the end, verifies and certifies that he alone is the way to the Father (14,6). The exclusive claim of 14,6b is not an isolated case in the Gospel. It is differently expressed even in the journey language of 3,13 and 6,68 (cf. 3,26). It should be noticed that just as no one can come to the Father without the Son, so can no one come to the Son without the Father.

The most commonly used verb for Jesus' journey into this world is ἔρχομαι. In various accounts, the evangelist portrays the expectation of the people about the coming eschatological figure and tries to show that Jesus' identity transcends their various speculations. The ἦλθον-sayings of Jesus may express that in Jesus the coming of the expected Saviour is realized.[376] In the coming of Jesus, it is the coming of Yahweh himself that the evangelist sees. It is not in terms of his being raised up from the dead but in terms of his going to the Father that John describes the victory of Jesus (14,12.28; 16,5.10.28).[377] Like the good shepherd, Jesus goes ahead and makes the way for his believers in order that they may come and receive the life of the Father (10,1–16), who is the original source of life (5,26).

In John 13–17, Jesus prepares his disciples for his final journey and presents himself as the way for them to come to the Father. Jesus' claim to be the way in 14,6 is closely interrelated to the network of Jesus's cosmic journey portrayed in the Gospel, particularly in John 13–14. Jesus will go ahead to prepare the way to the Father and the disciples can follow him later (13,36). Here, the Old Testament imagery of Yahweh or his messenger going ahead and leading the people of Israel to the promised land (e.g., Exod 13,17–22; 23,20) and also the promise of future guidance (Isa 40,11) can be brought in comparison with Jesus' journey. Thus, all the promises of a new exodus related to eschatological salvation are fulfilled in Jesus (cf. Isa 35,8; 40,1–11; 45,2; 52,12; Ezek 37,24).[378]

By identifying Jesus as the Son of God and witnessing to him, John the Baptist makes straight the way for the journey of Jesus (1,19–34). Jesus is

---

[376] Arens, *The ΗΛΘΟΝ-Sayings*, 286.
[377] Cf. Brown, *John*, II, 1018.
[378] See the concluding remarks on the theme of new exodus in John on pp. 400–402.

also the ladder between heaven and earth (1,51) and the universal way on which all can go (cf. 12,19). The way that Jesus goes is prepared by himself through his journey. As a result of his journey, the way to the Father is made available to all. He can, therefore, authoritatively claim that he himself is the way to the Father (14,6).

Through his geographical journeys, thereby confronting various persons in various episodes, Jesus presents himself as the way for them. Even though his geographical journeys are often confronted with opposition and rejection, they serve to build up a community of believers. Other than his disciples, Nicodemus, the Samaritans, the royal official, the blind man and the household of Lazarus belong to the community of believers. In his dialogue with Nicodemus, Jesus makes clear that he is the only one who has access to heaven, and therefore, everyone needs to come to him in order to have access to heaven and eternal life (3,13–14).

Jesus' decision to go from Jerusalem, the heart of the Jewish faith, to Galilee is notable (1,43). It is a decision to go from the centre to the region and people on the margin. It is in Samaria that Jesus is recognized as the Saviour of the world. The first three geographical journeys of Jesus are mentioned by the evangelist in terms of "ascending" to Jerusalem (2,13; 5,1; 7,10). But the fourth and the last geographical journey to Jerusalem is not called "ascending" because it is not just an ascending to Jerusalem but an ascending to his Father (cf. 20,17).

The journey of Jesus does not end with his departure. It continues through the disciples and their mission. There is no dichotomy between discipleship (following) and mission (being sent) in the Gospel. Mission is preceded by discipleship, and discipleship entails mission. The disciples of Jesus are asked to follow Jesus because he himself is the way. After Jesus' physical departure, the believers are not abandoned. They also have the abiding presence of the Spirit, the Son and the Father (14,16–17.23). A journey needs a way, a guide and a goal. In the future, the belief in Jesus will be their way and the Spirit of truth will be their guide on the way (16,13) to the goal of the Father's life.

8. Contribution to the Study of Way/Journey in John

A comprehensive, independent and objective understanding of the way/journey motif in Greek-Jewish literature, especially in the Old Testament, is a requirement to grasp the Johannine usage. The outcome of this examination will be made use of in the course of this monograph. Nevertheless, two important points are worth mentioning here.

8.1 Prophetic Fulfilment of Future Salvation in Jesus as the Way

When John speaks of Jesus' journeys and presents him as the way in 14,6, he must have in mind the whole Old Testament picture of the way/journey motif in relation to God's salvific deeds in the past and his salvific plan for the future. It is very important to pay attention to the situation where the notion of way occurs for the first time in the Bible. The concept of way in the Bible begins when the author of Genesis narrates how "the way to the tree of life" is blocked and separated from the humankind (3,24). It is also worthwhile to take into consideration the last prophetic voice of the Old Testament on the notion of way in Mal 3,1, which restates the Isaianic exhortation "to prepare the way" for the immediate coming of the Lord (Isa 40,3). If the former occurrence is found in a negative situation of human alienation from God (Gen 3,24), the latter is found in a positive context of the promise of salvation for the estranged humanity through the coming of the Lord himself (Mal 3,1). The very emergence of the Qumran community in the desert "to prepare the way of the Lord" under the inspiration of Isa 40,3 reveals how seriously "the preparation of the way" for the coming of the Lord was taken into consideration by the people of the intertestamental period.[379] The fact that along with all other evangelists John cites Isa 40,3 before the public ministry of Jesus shows that like all other evangelists he sees in Jesus the fulfilment of the salvific coming of the Lord as foreseen by the prophets of the Old Testament.

In the examination of the way motif in the Old Testament, it has been affirmed that way is a salvific term. It is frequently used to refer to God's salvific deeds in the past and to his commandments. In the prophetic literature, it is employed to emphasize God's promise of future salvation. The study of the way motif in Jewish literature becomes remarkably relevant and fully meaningful when the salvific significance of the way motif is placed in the context of the Gospel of John. This becomes especially clear when we notice that only the Gospel of John in the New Testament calls Jesus "the way" (14,6). For John, Jesus alone is the way. Therefore, he uses the term "way" only to say that Isa 40,3 is fulfilled in the coming of Jesus in John 1,23 and to present Jesus as the way in 14,4–6. He does not use the term "way" in any other manner and occasion in the Gospel.

It is likely that John presupposes humanity's estrangement from God as a result of the sin of Adam and Eve, which blocks "the way to the tree of life" (Gen 3,24). It is John's view that sin causes separation from God (John 9,31; cf. 3,19–20).[380] Jesus' mission is to take away the blockage of sin and liberate the people from the slavery of sin (John 8,34.36). Hence, John portrays Jesus

---

[379] John's perspective on "the preparation of the way" will be discussed later. See pp. 182, 197–206.

[380] That sin separates man from God is an established view in the Bible (e.g., Josh 7,11–12; Ps 66,18; Isa 59,2; Ezek 14,5.7; 39,23; Rom 11,22; Eph 2,12; 4,18).

as the lamb of God who takes away "the sin of the world" (1,29; cf. 1 John 3,5). The singular noun "the sin" in "the sin of the world" (ἡ ἁμαρτία τοῦ κόσμου) may imply the very separation and alienation of humanity from God.[381] Jesus is the reconciler between God and humanity. The expression "the way to the tree of life" in Gen 3,24 may denote the way to the source of life.[382] Since John regards the Father as the ultimate source of life (5,26) and Jesus as the way to the Father (14,6), it can be argued that Jesus opens "the way to the tree of life", which was blocked due to the sin of Adam and Eve (cf. Gen 3,24). [383] It should be noted that the Isaianic preparation of the way of the Lord also involves the removal of the obstacles of sin and evil (Isa 57,3–18; cf. 40,3–4; 62,10) and in Mal 3,1–3 too, the Lord's coming is intended to purify and to cleanse.

It is also possible to assume that the Johannine Jesus is "the way of holiness" which Isaiah foresees for the redeemed to walk (Isa 35,8–9) because he is the "holy one of God" (John 6,69), "the one sanctified by the Father" (John 10,36; cf. 17,19) and the way for the believers to walk (14,6). It is a way on which even the blind can walk (Isa 42,16; John 9). Some important results of the coming of Yahweh in the Old Testament are the restoration of the capacity of walking to the lame and of sight to the blind and above all the leading of the redeemed to Zion. The first two promises are literally fulfilled by the Johannine Jesus (5,1–9; 9,1–41). The third promise will be fulfilled at a spiritual level by the Johannine Jesus by taking all the believers to the Father's house (14,2–3). It is also a way on which no one has so far travelled (Isa

---

[381] M. Hasitschka, *Befreiung von Sünde nach dem Johannesevangelium. Eine bibeltheologische Untersuchung* (Innsbrucker theologische Studien 27; Innsbruck 1989), 125, explains the meaning of "sin" in John 1,29 thus, "Es handelt sich um eine Grundverfehlung, in der die Menschheit sich befindet, eine verfehlte Grundeinstellung gegenüber Gott, in der die einzelnen konkreten Sündentaten wurzeln und die in ihnen zur Erscheinung kommt". The theme of humanity's alienation from God presupposed in the Gospel of John and Jesus' role as the way is again discussed in the general conclusion.

[382] H. N. Wallace, "Tree of Knowledge and Tree of Life", *ABD*, VI, 658, points out that "the concepts of a supernatural tree as a source of life and of eating and drinking some substance to gain divine powers seem to have coalesced in the tree of life in Gen 2,4b–3,24". The notion of "eating" and "drinking" in order "to live forever" or "to have eternal life" is clearly demonstrated in John 6, precisely in 6,52–58.

[383] S. Brock, "The Two Ways and the Palestinian Targum", *A Tribute to Geza Vermes. Essays on Jewish and Christian Literature and History*, ed. P. R. Davies and R. T. White (JSOTSS 100; Sheffield 1990), 145, writes, "Whereas Jewish texts such as Enoch 25 and the Palestinian Targumim have an eschatological interest in Gen 3,24, for early Christianity there were soteriological overtones as well. This was largely the result of typological considerations; the way to the Tree of Life, cut off by the sword of the cherubim as a consequence of the wrong choice (or, in Christian terms, disobedience or sin) of the First Adam, was seen as being opened up again by the Second Adam (and more specifically, by the lance which opened up the side of the Second Adam on the cross, John 19,34), thus enabling Adam/humanity to have full access to the Tree of Life, identified as Christ".

42,16). Frequently, the Johannine Jesus informs the public and his inner circle of disciples that where he goes no one can go with him (8,21; 13,33). On the way that Jesus walks, no one has travelled so far. Therefore, John's presentation of Jesus as the way in 14,6 can be understood as a fulfilment of the eschatological salvation promised in the prophetical literature, particularly in Deutero-Isaiah. It is in the light of this finding that the possible background behind the formulation in 14,6 and its context in the second part is discussed.[384] Moreover, a study of the way motif in the Jewish literature, especially in the Old Testament, also will contribute to a better explanation of the relation of the way with truth and life in John 14,6, which is done in the second part.[385]

8.2 The Literary Background of Johannine Journey Language

The various verbs of journey we analysed in the Old Testament and the Gospel of John reveal the truth that there is a closer affinity between the salvific dimension of journey language in the Old Testament and Jesus' salvific journey in the Gospel of John. When John narrates Jesus's salvific journey, he is likely to see in it the fulfilment of the Old Testament promises of God's salvific coming. We may even assume that the basic literary background for John's journey language is the Old Testament.[386] It is during the exile that the conception of the future coming of God developed because it was only with the actual experience of the destruction of Jerusalem and the exile that a more concrete coming of God in the near future was prophetically announced and expected (Ezek 43,2; Hab 3,3; Zech 14,5).[387] Since exile, God's coming is hoped for in a more concrete fashion to bring salvation.[388] This line of

---

[384] See the discussion on pp. 197–225.

[385] See the discussion on pp. 255–260.

[386] The model of a gnostic redeemer for John's language of journey is rejected today. E.g., C. H. Talbert, *The Development of Christology During the First Hundred Years. And Other Essays on Early Christian Christology* (NovTSup 140; Leiden 2011), 83–112, rejects the past view of a myth of a gnostic redeemer and suggests the possibility of a myth of an ascending-descending redeemer from Hellenistic Judaism for John's ascent-descent language. Bühner, *Der Gesandte und Sein Weg,* believes that the Jewish rabbinic and esoteric speculation on the relation between the Old Testament prophet and the angel messenger is the *religionsgeschichtliche* background for Johannine "sending Christology". J. P. Miranda, *Der Vater mich gesandt hat. Religionsgeschichtliche Untersuchungen zu den johanneischen Sendungsformeln. Zugleich ein Beitrag zur johanneischen Christologie und Ekklesiologie* (Frankfurt/M 1972), 372–386, suggests the Old Testament prophetic model for the sending formula in John. Also see idem, *Die Sendung Jesu im vierten Evangelium. Religions- und theologiegeschichtliche Untersuchungen zu den Sendungsformeln* (SBS 87; Stuttgart 1977), to know more about the conceptual background of the sending Christology of John's Gospel.

[387] Arens, *The HΛΘON-Sayings*, 276.

[388] Arens, *The HΛΘON-Sayings*, 286.

thought, which is kept alive in the Pseudepigraphic writings and within the Qumran community, may have influenced the Johannine journey language.[389]

Hence, it is possible that the expectation of God's future coming is given an actualizing expression in Jesus' ἦλθον-sayings in the Gospel of John.[390] It should be noted that prophets never use the formula "I came/have come". Instead, they are conscious of their having been sent by Yahweh (e.g., Jer 23,28; 26,12). Along with the idea of the future coming of God, in the Old Testament there is also a notion of the coming of an eschatological salvific figure (Deut 18,15.18; Zech 9,9; cf. Gen 49,10–12). The New Testament identifies "the One who comes"/"the coming One" (ὁ ἐρχόμενος) of Ps 117,26 in the LXX as Jesus Christ (Matt 21,9; 23,39; Mark 11,9; Luke 13,35; 19,38; John 12,13). The expression ὁ ἐρχόμενος is applied to Jesus 7 times in the Gospel of John (1,15.27; 3,31[2x]; 6,14; 11,27; 12,13; cf. Matt 11,3; Luke 7,19–20). The participial phrase with the definite article suggests that ὁ ἐρχόμενος is intended as a title.[391] The combination of ἔρχομαι and ὄνομα is unique to Ps 117,26 in the LXX (ὁ ἐρχόμενος ἐν ὀνόματι κυρίου). It is worth noticing that only the Gospel of John specifically claims that Jesus has come in Father's name, ἐγὼ ἐλήλυθα ἐν τῷ ὀνόματι τοῦ πατρός μου (5,43; cf. 12,13). "Coming" is the action of the "coming One". John attaches more significance to Jesus' self-attestation about his coming than the Synoptic Gospels. In John, Jesus identifies himself very explicitly as "the coming Messiah" (4,25-26).

The future coming of God in the Old Testament is intended to judge (Pss 96,13; 98,9; 1 Chr 16,33) and to save (Isa 62,11; Zech 2,14; cf. Isa 40,10). John associates these two functions with the purpose of Jesus' coming. Even though the ultimate purpose of his coming is not to judge, he has the power to judge (John 5,22.27.30; cf. 8,15–16; 12,47). Likewise, he has come with the power to save (3,17; 10,9; 12,47). When John speaks of Jesus' cosmic journey, he may be aware of the God of Israel who "comes down" to save his people (Exod 3,8), "goes ahead" of them "to lead them along the way" (Exod 13,21; Deut 1,30–33; 8,2) and "brings" them from the land of slavery to the promised land (Josh 24,17). This is what Jesus does in the Gospel of John at the spiritual level. Jesus "comes down" from above/the Father into this world to save it from the slavery of sin and "goes ahead" and prepares the way to "lead" all to the Father. It is by going the way of death-resurrection that Jesus prepares the way to the Father, "leads" the believers to the Father's house and thus becomes the way to the Father. Indeed, Jesus leads the new exodus as a

---

[389] Cf. Arens, *The ΗΛΘΟΝ-Sayings*, 286.

[390] E. Arens points out that behind the ἦλθον-sayings in the New Testament there lies certainly the Old Testament expectation of a final and unsurpassable personage who would come to inaugurate the Messianic era. See Arens, *The ΗΛΘΟΝ-Sayings*, 279–280.

[391] Cf. Brunson, *Psalm 118*, 260.

warrior (cf. John 12,31; 14,30; 18,3–6; Isa 40,10; 42,13; 43,16–17) and as a shepherd (cf. John 10,11–16; 13,36; Isa 40,11).[392]

During the examination of the journey motif in the Old Testament, it was pointed out that the verbs of journey can be broadly grouped into the verbs for "to and fro movement" and the verbs for "leading" or "guiding".[393] An analysis of the journey motif in the Gospel of John also shows that more frequently John uses the verbs of journey than the noun ὁδός. Jesus' cosmic journey is presented in terms of "to and fro" movement. Very often John uses the verbs of "to and fro movement" to refer to Jesus' coming into this world, his departure to the Father through his death-resurrection and his return to the believers. Even though John uses the verbs for "leading" or "guiding" only occasionally, the images of Jesus' "leading" or "guiding" are clearly detectable in the Gospel. In fact, the images of light, gate, shepherd and sheep and the verbs for believers' journey to Jesus (discipleship) demonstrate Jesus' guidance and leadership.

He is the light so that the believers can "follow" (ἀκολουθέω) him (8,12). As the gate, he offers the believers the direction to salvation (10,7.9). As the shepherd, he "leads out" (ἐξάγω) his followers (10,3) and "goes ahead of them" (ἔμπροσθεν αὐτῶν πορεύεται), so that they may "follow" (ἀκολουθέω) him like the sheep (10,4.27). In 14,31, Jesus takes the initiative to "arise" (ἐγείρω) and to "go forward" (ἄγω). This literally happens when Jesus "goes out" and "enters" the garden with his disciples, who supposedly follow him (18,1). Jesus' leadership becomes much clearer when he "goes out" (ἐξέρχομαι) and asks his enemies, "Whom are you looking for?" (18,4) and when he protects his disciples from harm (18,8–9), just as a shepherd safeguards his sheep. After Jesus' physical departure, the Spirit of truth will "guide" (ὁδηγέω) his disciples into all the truth (16,13). In short, it is possible to assume that John sees in Jesus the image of a God who comes down from above to save his people and to lead them along the way to the promised land of the Father's house. Hence, we may suppose that the salvific journey language in the Old Testament is the literary background for the salvific journey language in the Gospel of John.

---

[392] The theme of "leading the new exodus" by Jesus will be explained in the general conclusion. See pp. 400–402.

[393] See pp. 75–79.

Part Two

A Study of John 14,6 in Its Context

Chapter II

John 14,6 in Its Literary Context

1. Preliminary Observations

1.1 Genre of the Farewell Discourse

The purpose of this discussion is not to suggest something new regarding the genre of John 13–17 but to offer a brief overview of the current understanding and to show how far it is relevant for the present study.[1] John 13–17 is usually called the farewell discourse(s) of Jesus. This is based on the general assumption that this part of the Gospel is modelled on the literary genre of farewell speeches or testaments found in biblical or non-biblical literature. Jacob's farewell speech to his sons in Gen 49 and Moses' speech to the assembled Israelites in Deuteronomy 34 are notable examples of biblical farewell speeches.[2] *Testaments of the Twelve Patriarchs* is an important model of farewell speech in the extra-biblical literature.

Martin Winter has tried to isolate a genre that he calls "Vermächtnisrede" (legacy speech), which he distinguishes sharply from farewell speeches and the testament form.[3] In his study, Winter investigates the formal elements of the legacy speech like language, style, structure (with fictional and historical

---

[1] For a detailed study of the genre of the farewell discourse in dialogue with current approaches, see R. Sheridan, "John's Gospel and Modern Genre Theory: The Farewell Discourse (John 13–17) as a Test Case", *ITQ* 75 (2010), 287–299; G. L. Parsenios, *Departure and Consolation. The Johannine Farewell Discourses in Light of Greco-Roman Literature* (NovTSup 117; Leiden 2005); P. A. Holloway, "Left Behind: Jesus' Consolation of His Disciples in John 13,31–17,26", *ZNW* 96 (2005), 1–34; M. Winter, *Das Vermächtnis Jesu und die Abschiedsworte der Väter. Gattungsgeschichtliche Untersuchung der Vermächtnisrede im Blick auf Joh 13–17* (Forschungen zur Religion und Literatur des Alten und Neuen Testaments 161; Göttingen 1994). These works include references to other important studies of the past on the genre of John 13–17. Also see Beutler, *Do not Be Afraid*, 18–21; Dettwiler, *Die Gegenwart des Erhöhten*, 14–33; F. F. Segovia, *The Farewell of the Word. The Johannine Call to Abide* (Minneapolis 1991), 5–20, for an overview of the past studies on the genre of John 13–17.

[2] A. Lacomara, "Deuteronomy and the Farewell Discourse (John 13,31–16,33)", *CBQ* 36 (1974), 65–84, thinks that the deuteronomic discourses of Moses form the model for the Johannine farewell discourse.

[3] Winter, *Das Vermächtnis Jesu*, 36–44.

levels), intention, argumentation and motivation of texts.[4] He tries to reconstruct a history of the genre (Gattungsgeschichte) of the legacy speeches in the Old Testament as well as in the Old Testament Apocryphals/Pseudepigraphs and to show how they influenced John 13–17. He considers John 13,1–30 as the opening scene, 13,31–14,31 as the first legacy speech composed by the evangelist and 15–17 as further additions by the members of the Johannine school.[5] Winter's approach to John 13–17 is based on strict redaction-critical presuppositions, which are vehemently contested. His reconstruction of the Johannine school in association with the expulsion from the synagogue as a result of the application of *Birkath ha-Minim* is questionable today.

There are also considerable differences between the Johannine farewell discourse and Jewish testamentary/farewell literature as a whole.[6] In the traditional form of deathbed speeches attributed to great figures of the Old Testament, consolation does not have an important role to play as it is found in John 13–17 (cf. Gen 49; Deut 31; 1 Sam 12; 1 Chr 28).[7] In the Gospel, Jesus is not presented as sick or on his deathbed like the Jewish patriarchs (cf. Gen 48,2; T. Reu. 1,2–4; T. Sim. 1,2; T. Jos. 1,1). His death is not a natural one but his free choice (John 10,18). Unlike the Jewish heroes, his departure through death is not a permanent one. There is an emphasis in the Gospel on Jesus' return and abiding presence (14,2–3.18.23; cf. 21,22). In the Jewish testamentary literature, the appointed successor will expire and, in turn, appoint another member of the family as the successor. But the Paraclete as the successor of Jesus abides forever, without having a further successor (14,16). The theme of Jesus' departure is not limited to John 13–17 alone. Even during his public ministry, he announces that he will be soon going away (7,33–36; 8,21–22). The whole Gospel is, in fact, on the verge of being turned into a farewell discourse.[8] Jesus' departure is not his joining with the fathers like a patriarch but an ascent to his Father. Moreover, materials like the allegory of the vine (15,1–8) and the parable of the woman in labour (16,21) are absent in Jewish farewell literature.[9]

---

[4] Winter, *Das Vermächtnis Jesu*, 43.

[5] Winter considers 15,1–17; 15,18–16,4a; 16,4b–33 as three distinct additional legacy speeches and 17,1–26 as the farewell prayer. See Winter, *Das Vermächtnis Jesu*, 257–290.

[6] Cf. Sheridan, "John's Gospel and Modern Genre Theory", 290.

[7] But consolatory speeches of a dying person can be found in the classical Greco-Roman literature, e.g., at the end of Plato's *Apology* and *Phaedo* and in Tacitus' account of the death of Seneca (*Annals* 15.62). See G. A. Kennedy, *New Testament Interpretation through Rhetorical Criticism* (Chapel Hill 1984), 77.

[8] E. Bammel, "The Farewell Discourse of the Evangelist John and its Jewish Heritage", *TynB* 44 (1993), 106.

[9] Bammel, "The Farewell Discourse", 116, thinks that from a literary point of view the farewell discourse is the product of a transitional phase.

Scholars have noticed various examples of farewell scenes or speeches in Greco-Roman literature as well.[10] George L. Parsenios believes that John bends and twists the testament form by blending various literary forms of consolation, dramatic exit and symposium found in ancient Greek-Roman literature.[11] He notices that the farewell discourse in John includes themes and techniques of classical consolation literature to soften the disciples' grief.[12] In the farewell discourse, the consolatory work is done by the Paraclete who will make Jesus and his words present to the disciples. Parsenios also believes that John presents the farewell discourse of Jesus in the literary form of a symposium.[13] He notices parallels between Judas' departure followed by an intimate conversation of Jesus and the departure of an offensive figure during meals, followed by a more friendly conversation, in ancient classical literature. There the speakers may even neglect food and entertainment common to a symposium and focus more on speech, thus making the symposium a feast of words, not a feast of food. Moreover, he also sees Jesus' hesitation to depart in 14,31 as a delayed dramatic exit to death found in ancient Greek tragedy and comedy, where the dramatic figures delay their announced exits.[14]

According to the current understanding, the farewell discourse in John reveals a polyphony of genres and a play on genres.[15] John Ashton believes that along with the testament genre, the commission form lies behind the farewell discourse in John.[16] In his opinion, the generic combination of the commission form and the testament form is the basis for the two roles of the Paraclete as a guarantor of the abiding presence of Jesus and as Jesus' successor.[17] Ruth Sheridan posits the theoretical conditions for John's deliberate 'skewing' of generic conventions, using the Jesus-Paraclete relationship of John 13–17 as a test case. She appreciates "John's employment of the farewell

---

[10] Some of the latest examples are Parsenios, *Departure and Consolation*; Holloway, "Left Behind", 1–34; M. Lang, "Johanneische Abschiedsreden und Senecas Konsolationsliteratur. Wie konnte ein Römer Joh 13,31–17,26 lesen?", *Kontexte des Johannesevangeliums. Das vierte Evangelium in religions- und traditionsgeschichtlicher Perspektive*, ed. J. Frey and U. Schnelle (WUNT 175; Tübingen 2004), 365–412.

[11] Parsenios, *Departure and Consolation*, 35–36. H. W. Attridge, "Genre Bending in the Fourth Gospel", *JBL* 121 (2002), 18, believes that John has substantially bent the literary genre of testament in the farewell discourse by insisting on Jesus' abiding presence.

[12] See Parsenios, *Departure and Consolation*, 77–109. Holloway, "Left Behind", 1–34, also tries to illuminate Jesus' consolation of his disciples in John 13,31–16,33 in comparison with Greco-Roman sources and Lang, "Johanneische Abschiedsreden", 365–412 in comparison with Seneca's consolation literature.

[13] See Parsenios, *Departure and Consolation*, 111–149.

[14] See Parsenios, *Departure and Consolation*, 49–76.

[15] Cf. Sheridan, "John's Gospel and Modern Genre Theory", 292.

[16] J. Ashton, *Understanding the Fourth Gospel* (Oxford [2]2007), 420.

[17] Ashton, *Understanding*, 444.

discourse genre for his own unique purposes by understanding how genre itself 'works' and how the theorization of genre affects the interpretation of John 13–17 as a 'farewell discourse'".[18] She notices that the second generation Christians lived not only at a time when cultural influences freely mixed, but also at a time of great transition from their adherence to Judaism and paganism to a united community held together by the guidance of the Paraclete.[19] The shift from living in the presence of the fleshly Jesus to living in a new, post-resurrection era characterized by the presence of the risen Christ in the Spirit-Paraclete reflects itself in the 'tension' between the form and content of the Johannine farewell discourse.[20] As a result, a bit of 'genre-bending' is to be expected.[21]

Jerome H. Neyrey has tried to give a cultural interpretation of John 14–17. According to his perspective, the Johannine farewell discourse should be understood not as a form of farewell address but as a model of worship.[22] Neyrey sees prayer as a form of worship in John 14–17 and examines these chapters in terms of two directions of worship: speaking to God (prayers) and listening to God (prophecy, homily and oracles of salvation/judgement).[23] While the repeated instructions for petitionary prayer in John 14–16 (14,13–14.16; 15,7.16; 16,23–24.26) and Jesus' multi-purposed prayer in chapter 17 constitute the aspect of speaking to God, the aspect of listening to God is present in Jesus' prophecy, homily, words of salvation, judgement, etc.[24]

From this brief examination of the current discussion on the genre of John 13–17, the following observations and conclusions can be made. Among various influences, the tendency of scholars is to regard the biblical testament as the single most important literary influence on the Johannine farewell discourse. But they are aware that this discourse cannot be solely interpreted as an ancient testament or a farewell speech. Hence, they often suggest a variety of influences or models for understanding the genre of the Johannine farewell discourse.

---

[18] Sheridan, "John's Gospel and Modern Genre Theory", 292.

[19] Sheridan, "John's Gospel and Modern Genre Theory", 297.

[20] Sheridan, "John's Gospel and Modern Genre Theory", 297.

[21] Sheridan, "John's Gospel and Modern Genre Theory", 298, views, "John certainly extends the possibilities of the farewell discourse genre with his version of the 'protagonist-successor' motif, and this simply illustrates that the relationship between text and genre is not that of direct correspondence requiring a logical 'fit,' but of creative elaboration. Texts are 'uses' of or performances of genres, but they do not 'belong' to them. And as much as texts are shaped by genres, texts work upon genres. The 'farewell discourse' genre of antiquity was thus 'modified' when John created his 'performance' of it".

[22] J. H. Neyrey, *The Gospel of John in Cultural and Rhetorical Perspective* (Grand Rapids 2009), 377–411, originally published in idem, "Worship in the Fourth Gospel: A Cultural Interpretation of John 14–17", *BTB* 36 (2006), 107–117.

[23] Neyrey, *The Gospel of John*, 383.

[24] Neyrey, *The Gospel of John*, 387–405.

Indeed, John's farewell discourse is unique in its formulation. It surpasses all literary genres of ancient literature, whether Jewish or Greco-Roman. It may bear a close resemblance to the literary forms of testament, drama, consolation and symposium, but it exceeds all these literary forms. This is due to the surpassing character of the figure who speaks in these chapters. Therefore, Raymond Brown rightly states, "The one who speaks here speaks as no man has spoken".[25] Jesus is, for the evangelist, more than a holy man of God like Jacob or Moses. He is the Word made flesh (1,14) and the One sent by God/the Father (3,34; 5,37). Being uniquely one with the Father, Jesus is beyond any comparison (10,30). John 13,31–17,26 are the utterances not of a dying person or a victim of tragedy but of a victorious person who has full command and authority over everything (cf. 13,1a.3; 16,33). It may be regarded as the Christian genre of "the Speeches of the Risen Lord".[26] In his formulation, the evangelist may be variously influenced by the Old Testament literature. His concern is to show that in Jesus the eschatological salvation promised in the Old Testament is fulfilled. Hence, unlike any Jewish patriarchs or ancient heroes, only Jesus can say, "I am the way and the truth and the life. No one comes to the Father except through me".

Even though scholars have rarely paid attention to the element of worship in the farewell discourse, there is some truth in Neyrey's cultural interpretation. The focus on prayer is very intensive in this section of the Gospel. The motif of prayer is present in every chapter within John 14–17. The cultic setting behind the Gospel has some significance in understanding the exclusive claim in John 14,6. This will be made clear when we try to understand the exclusivism of 14,6 in its historical context.[27]

1.2 Unity of the Farewell Discourse

The purpose of this discussion is not to suggest a new solution to the problem of the unity of the Johannine farewell discourse but to take a stance on this problem.[28] Much scholarly attention has been paid to the *aporias* of the Johannine farewell discourse. Scholars have noticed some difficulties in reading 13,31–17,26 as one single speech of Jesus due to the presence of some *apori-*

---

[25] Brown, *John*, II, 582.
[26] Bammel, "The Farewell Discourse", 115–116. According to L. S. Kellum, *The Unity of the Farewell Discourse. The Literary Integrity of John 13,31–16,33* (JSNTSS 256; London 2004), 126–132, the Johannine farewell discourse can be characterized as an eschatological discourse, somewhat along the lines of the Olivet Discourse in the Synoptic Gospels.
[27] See pp. 363–378.
[28] The problem of the unity of the farewell discourse has no direct or crucial role within the concern of the present study.

as.[29] There are two notable *aporias* in the farewell discourse, which are found in 14,31 and 16,5. In 14,31, Jesus says, "Rise, let us be on our way", but it is only in 18,1 that Jesus with his disciples goes out across the Kidron valley into the garden. In John 15–17, Jesus further continues his speech and prayer until 17,26. In 16,5, Jesus asks his disciples, "But now I am going to him who sent me; yet none of you asks me, 'Where are you going?'" This question seems to be in conflict with Peter's question in 13,36 and Thomas' similar query in 14,5. The natural flow between 14,31 and 18,1 poses a challenge to the unity of the farewell discourse of Jesus. Besides these, there are many duplications, repetitions and a variety of theological outlooks in the farewell discourse.

Various solutions and approaches have been suggested to solve the *aporias* and the inconsistencies in the farewell discourse.[30] It is likely that in the farewell discourse the evangelist brought together various traditions which had originally existed independently of this unit, and hence, one can find in these chapters a combination of many once distinct units of tradition whose prior history is beyond recovery.[31] In the farewell discourse, there are many paradoxes, inconsistencies and incongruities which may have a prehistory, but John's fundamental character largely conceals that prehistory from us.[32] The meaning of the present text of the farewell discourse is not in any way

---

[29] It was since the publication of a series of articles by Eduard Schwartz that scholars paid serious attention to the *aporias* in the Gospel of John. See E. Schwartz, "Aporien im 4. Evangelium I–IV", *Nachrichten von der Königlichen Gesellschaft zu Göttingen* (Berlin 1907–1908), 342–72; 115–48; 149–88; 497–560.

[30] For a detailed study of various approaches with regard to the problem of the unity of the farewell discourse, see R. Bultmann, *The Gospel of John. A Commentary* (Philadelphia 1971), 459–61; Brown, *John*, II, 581–597; Schnackenburg, *John,* III, 90–91; Barrett, *John*, 454–55; Segovia, *Farewell*, 20–58, 283–330; Kellum, *Unity of Farewell Discourse*; Dettwiler, *Die Gegenwart*; J. Zumstein, *Kreative Erinnerung. Relecture und Auslegung im Johannesevangelium* (Zurich 1999), 115–124; K. Scholtissek, *In ihm Sein und Bleiben. Die Sprache der Immanenz in den johanneischen Schriften* (HBS 21; Freiburg 1999), 131–139, 278; idem, "Abschied und neue Gegenwart. Exegetische und theologische Reflexionen zur johanneischen Abschiedsrede Joh 13,31–17,26", *EThL* 75 (1999), 332–358; Y. Simoens, *La Gloire d'Aimer. Structures stylistiques et interprétatives dans le discours de la Cène (Jn 13–17)* (Rome 1981); Kennedy, *New Testament Interpretation,* 73–85; D. F. Tolmie, *Jesus' Farewell to the Disciples. John 13,1–17,26 in Narratological Perspective* (BIS 12; Leiden 1995); Parsenios, *Departure and Consolation*, 49–76; J. C. Stube, *A Graeco-Roman Rhetorical Reading of the Farewell Discourse* (Library of New Testament Studies 309; London 2006)

[31] O'Day, *John*, 737. In the view of D. Rensberger, "Sectarianism and Theological Interpretation in John", *What Is John? Literary and Social Readings of the Fourth Gospel*, ed. F. F. Segovia (Atlanta 1998) II, 150, we should be "skeptical about our ability to sort out stages in the literary redaction and communal and theological history behind the Gospel of John based on contradictory statements in the text".

[32] Cf. Rensberger, "Sectarianism", 150.

directly dependent on understanding its process of growth and composition.[33] The text in its final form undoubtedly appeared to its original readers, not only to be a unified and coherent literary whole but also a proper and meaningful form of communication by the author(s) and an artistic and strategic whole.[34] We should not look for today's standards of historical accuracy and perfection in such an ancient literature. This study prefers a synchronic approach to the farewell discourse, which is at the same time sensitive and open to its diachronic dimensions.[35]

1.3 The Structure and Organization of John 13–14[36]

From a narrative and theological point of view, the first verse of John 13 can be considered as the introduction to the second part of the Gospel, often called "the book of glory" (John 13–20). The key ideas in this introduction are the festival of Passover, Jesus' foreknowledge, the arrival of his hour, the departure from this world to the Father and Jesus' love for his own to the end, which direct the reader to the culmination of the Gospel, i.e., the passion, death, resurrection and ascension of Jesus narrated in the final chapters of the second part of the Gospel (18–20). Along with v. 1, vv. 2–3 provide a brief setting for the farewell discourse. The temporal particle ὅτε in 13,12 and 13,31 and the temporal participle εἰπών in 13,21 give us clear signals to divide 13,4–30 into three units, 4–11; 12–20; 21–30.[37] In 13,4–20, John pre-

---

[33] Segovia, *Farewell*, 49.

[34] Segovia, *Farewell*, 48. At this juncture, it is worth paying attention to the comments of Brown, *John*, II, 582, "it has been wisely said that the Last Discourse is best understood when it is the subject of prayerful meditation and that scientific analysis does not really do justice to this work of genius. Just as a great painting loses its beauty when the individual parts are studied under a microscope, so the necessary discussion of the composition and division of the Last Discourse may tend to mar the overall realization that one is dealing with a masterpiece".

[35] M. de Jonge, *Jesus: Stranger from Heaven and Son of God* (Missoula 1977), viii, states, "the first task of an exegete should be to interpret the documents as they lie before him; even if in some cases the present text cannot be explained without some knowledge of its history, one can never be content with simply describing that history and restrict oneself to the 'original' meaning and function of the constituent parts".

[36] When we speak here of the organization of John 13–14, we do not refer to the compositional and redactional history of the text but rather to the inner cohesion and relations within the text in its final state. We consider 13,1–30 as the larger setting for the farewell speech and prayer of Jesus, 13,31–14,31 as the first part of the farewell speech, chapters 15–16 as the second part of the farewell speech and chapter 17 as the farewell prayer of Jesus. We use the term "farewell discourse" to refer to the whole section of John 13–17 and the term "farewell speech" to refer to Jesus' speech in 13,31–16,33.

[37] It is also possible to consider 13,2–11 as a unit with the help of an *inclusio*. In v. 2, the evangelist focuses on the character of Judas, the son of Simon Iscariot, with a reference to his betrayal (ἵνα παραδοῖ αὐτόν) and in v. 11 he concludes the scene of foot-washing

sents the scene of foot-washing, which prefigures the way that Jesus has to go (vv. 4–5) and the meaning of foot-washing (vv. 6–20), with its two explanations (vv. 6–11; vv. 12–20).[38]

Vv. 21–30 form the next unit in which Jesus plainly foretells the betrayal by Judas. In v. 30, Judas Iscariot leaves Jesus' presence and goes out into the darkness. The departure of Judas plays a crucial and decisive role in the literary design of the book of glory. It marks the starting point for the continuous and lengthy speech and prayer of Jesus (13,31–17,26). The temporal clause ὅτε οὖν ἐξῆλθεν in 13,31 functions as a boundary marker of a new section. The particle οὖν is frequently used in John to begin new units with significant change or development.[39]

The narrative part of the farewell discourse begins in 13,2 with a reference to Judas, the betrayer and to the devil (διάβολος), and it ends in 13,30 with another reference to Judas and to the night (νύξ), the symbol of evil. In this Gospel night (11,10; cf. 9,4) and darkness (1,5; 3,19; 8,12; 12,35) are used as symbols of evil. The devil has prompted Judas to betray Jesus (13,2) and when he receives the piece of bread, Satan (Σατανᾶς) enters him (13,27; cf. Luke 22,3), and he goes out into night/darkness (13,30). The betrayal by Judas is seen by the evangelist as a deed of darkness, a work of the devil and he is called διάβολος (6,70). Thus, clearly through the references to Judas and the evil one (v. 2 διάβολος and v. 30 νύξ), 13,2 and 13,30 form an *inclusio*, concluding the narrative section and making it coherent to a certain extent.[40]

---

with another reference to Judas and to his betrayal (τὸν παραδιδόντα). Thus, vv. 2 and 11 form an *inclusio*. However, we consider vv. 2–3 along with v. 1 as a part of the setting in order to pay special attention to the motif of cosmic journey and cosmic conflict.

[38] In 13,12, the transitional marker οὖν along with the temporal particle ὅτε introduces the unit of vv. 12–20. J. Zumstein, *Das Johannesevangelium* (Kritisch-exegetischer Kommentar über das Neue Testament 2; Göttingen 2016), 487–493, regards 13,6–11 and 13,12–17 as the two interpretations of the foot-washing.

[39] See R. Buth, "*Oun, De, Kai* and Asyndeton in John's Gospel", *Linguistics and New Testament Interpretation*, ed. D. A. Black et al. (Nashville 1992), 157.

[40] John 13,30 is the end of the narrative part in the farewell discourse. The evangelist has mentioned about nineteen physical actions with movements within the narrative of 13,2–30. They are ἐγείρω, τίθημι, λαμβάνω, διαζώννυμι (v. 4), βάλλω, νίπτω, ἐκμάσσω (v. 5), ἔρχομαι (v. 6), λαμβάνω, ἀναπίπτω (v. 12), βλέπω εἰς ἀλλήλους (v. 22), ἀνάκειμαι (v. 23), νεύω (v. 24), ἀναπίπτω (v. 25), βάπτω, [λαμβάνω], δίδωμι (v. 26), λαμβάνω and ἐξέρχομαι (v. 27). But there are no physical actions in the following section of 13,31–17,26. The last action described by the evangelist is found in 13,30: "So, after receiving the piece of bread, he immediately *went out*" (ἐξῆλθεν), and the next action is in 18,1, "When he had said this, Jesus *went out* (ἐξῆλθεν) with his disciples across the Kidron valley to where there was a garden...". Obviously, the evangelist places the farewell speech and prayer of Jesus, which are focused on the motif of *departure*, between two *departures*, exactly speaking, between two actions of physical movement: ἐξῆλθεν in 13,30 and ἐξῆλθεν in 18,1. The *inclusio* between 13,30 and 18,1 will enable us to consider 13,31 reasonably as the beginning of the farewell speech of Jesus.

1. Preliminary Observations

Along with the majority view in contemporary scholarship,[41] we may consider 13,31 as the starting point of the farewell speech and 13,31–14,31 as the first part of Jesus' farewell speech.[42] The departure of Judas gives Jesus the occasion to announce his hour of glorification (v. 31) and departure (v. 33). Judas' departure (v. 30) is a pre-requisite for the departure of Jesus (cf. 18,1). Jesus is now in dialogue with his "own" (ἴδιοι), his own sheep who will hear his voice (10,27). Even though the theme of Jesus' departure in John 13,31–38 is closely related to the themes in John 14, we can notice some demarcations between 13,38 and 14,1. In John 13,36–38, there is a dialogue between Peter and Jesus. But this dialogue does not continue in 14,1, where Jesus' speech is addressed to all the disciples. The plural forms like ὑμῶν, πιστεύετε are some indications. In 13,38, Jesus is speaking about the fate of one disciple, namely Peter. In 14,1, Jesus is addressing all the disciples to console

---

[41] E.g., Tack, *John 14,6 in Light of Jewish–Christian Dialogue*, 21–23; F. Back, *Gott als Vater der Jünger im Johannesevangelium* (WUNT II 336; Tübingen 2012), 25; Kirchschläger, *Nur Ich bin die Wahrheit*, 200; Zumstein, *Saint Jean 13–21*, 46–47; U. Schnelle, *Das Evangelium nach Johannes* (ThHKNT 4; Leipzig ³2003), 246; A. J. Köstenberger, *John* (BECNT; Grand Rapids 2004), 420; H.-U. Weidemann, *Der Tod Jesu im Johannesevangelium. Der erste Abschiedsrede als Schlüsseltext für den Passions- und Osterbericht* (BZNW 122; Berlin 2004), 79–80; Kellum, *The Unity of the Farewell Discourse*, 149; C. S. Keener, *The Gospel of John. A Commentary* (Peabody 2003) II, 895, 899; J. Frey, *Die johanneische Eschatologie* (WUNT 117; Tübingen 2000) III, 119; K. Wengst, *Das Johannesevangelium* (ThKNT 4,2; Stuttgart 2001) II, 106; C. Dietzfelbinger, *Der Abschied des Kommenden. Eine Auslegung der johanneischen Abschiedsrede* (Tübingen 1997), 12; Dettwiler, *Die Gegenwart*, 19; L. Schenke, *Johannes. Kommentar* (Düsseldorf 1998), 277; C. Hoegen-Rohls, *Der nachösterliche Johannes: Die Abschiedsreden als hermeneutischer Schlüssel zum vierten Evangelium* (WUNT II 84; Tübingen 1996), 91–92; Tolmie, *Jesus' Farewell*, 105; Segovia, *Farewell*, 62; J. Becker, *Das Evangelium nach Johannes. Kapitel 11–21* (ÖTK 4.2; Gütersloh ³1991), 523; G. R. Beasley-Murray, *John* (WBC 36; Dallas ²1999), 240; Schnackenburg, *John*, III, 48; Brown, *John*, II, 586, etc. F. Schleritt, *Der vorjohnneische Passionsbericht. Eine historisch-kritische und theologische Untersuchung zu Joh 2,13–22; 11,47–14,31 und 18,1–20,29* (Berlin 2007), 282–328, considers 13,31–38 as "die kleine Abschiedsrede Jesu" and 14,1–31 as "die große Abschiedsrede Jesu". Barrett, *John*, 449, sees in 13,31–38 the distinctive Johannine theme of departure and glory, which is developed throughout the farewell speech of Jesus.

[42] There are also scholars who consider 13,31–38 as still belonging to the narrative section of foot-washing and separated from John 14 and regard 14,1 as the beginning of the farewell speech of Jesus. E.g., J.-N. Aletti, "Jn 13 – Les problèmes de composition et leur importance", *Bib* 87 (2006), 263–272; M. L. Coloe, "Sources in the Shadows: John 13 and the Johannine Community", *New Currents through John. Global Perspective*, ed. F. Lozada Jr. and T. Thatcher (Resources for Biblical Study 54; Atlanta 2006), 73–74; H. Thyen, *Das Johannesevangelium* (HNT 6; Tübingen 2005), 603; F. J. Moloney, *The Gospel of John* (Sacra Pagina 4; Collegeville 1998), 385; Simoens, *Selon Jean. 3*, 571–600; O'Day, *John*, 731; Culpepper, "The Johannine *Hypodeigma*", 133. Beutler, *Do not Be Afraid*, 106, regards 13,31–33.36–38 as a transition and an introduction to John 14.

them and to encourage them. Thus, John 13,31–38 can be taken as the first unit of 13,31–14,31.

In many and varied ways 13,31–38 can be regarded as belonging more to John 14. It introduces the important themes of Jesus' farewell speech, namely his glorification (13,31–32; 16,14; 17,1.5) and departure (13,33.36; 14,2–5.12.28). If the negative consequences of this glorification and departure are the focus during the dialogue with Peter in 13,36–38 (cf. 15,18–21; 16,1–2.32), the positive outcome of Jesus' glorification and departure in the form of various promises are the concern of the evangelist in John 14.[43] One of the most important positive consequences of Jesus' glorification is the giving of the Holy Spirit (7,39). Since Jesus announces his imminent glorification in 13,31, he can also announce the coming of the Holy Spirit in 14,16–17.26. Just as the narrator reminded the reader in 7,39 to look forward and to relate the glorification of Jesus with the giving of the Holy Spirit (cf. 20,19–23), in 13,31 he asks him to look forward and to relate Jesus' announcement of his glorification with his announcement of the promise of the Holy Spirit in the following speech (14,16–17.26; cf. 15,26; 16,7–15). The departure of Judas is a must for the glorification of Jesus. Hence, the timing mentioned in the temporal clause ὅτε οὖν ἐξῆλθεν in 13,31 prompts the reader not just to turn back, as some scholars think,[44] but more to look forward to its outcome promised in John 14. This is clearly expressed through the adverb νῦν (13,31), which draws the attention towards the future glory and its effects, as narrated in John 14.

It is very clear that the new commandment given in 13,34–35 is closely associated with the message of the foot-washing episode (13,2–20). The ὑπόδειγμα set by Jesus is his own example, "as I *loved* you", καθὼς ἠγάπησα ὑμᾶς (13,34). The other occurrence of the verb ἀγαπάω in this chapter is only in the introduction (13,1), where the narrator states that "he *loved* (ἠγάπησεν) them *to the end* (εἰς τέλος)". The example set by Jesus draws the reader's

---

[43] Throughout the second part of the farewell speech (15,1–16,33) as well, the negative and positive consequences of Jesus' glorification and departure go hand in hand. E.g., in 16,32, there is the mentioning of the negative impact of Jesus' departure upon the disciples that they will be scattered, each to his own home. There is also the positive impact of Jesus' departure, namely the promise of the Holy Spirit (15,26; 16,7–15).

[44] E.g., Moloney, *John,* 385; O'Day, *John,* 731. The limitation of the arguments of Moloney, Culpepper (see Culpepper, "The Johannine *Hypodeigma*", 146) and Coloe (see Coloe, "Sources in the Shadows", 74) is that they restrict the meaning of the verb δοξάζω, which occurs in 13,31–32 four or five times (see the dilemma of the Committee with regards to the retention of εἰ ὁ θεὸς ἐδοξάσθη ἐν αὐτῷ in v. 32), to the death of Jesus or to the glory on the cross alone and neglect its aspect of resurrection and ascension and its relation to the giving of the Holy Spirit in accordance with John 7,39, which is the concern of the evangelist in John 14. The glorification/hour of Jesus is not complete on the cross even from a narrative point of view. It is the risen and *glorified* Jesus who gives his disciples the Holy Spirit (20,19–23).

attention not only to the foot-washing scene but also through the following chapters to the *end* scene on the cross, where, before his life of love comes to an end, he utters τετέλεσται (19,30).[45] Jesus' life of love extends from the past through the present till the end. The promises given in chapter 14 are also manifestations of his love for his disciples. Thus, the model set in the new commandment in 13,34 demands the reader not only to turn backward but also to look forward.

The use of the literary device of dialogue in the form of questioning and answering introduced through Peter (13,36) is continued in John 14 through Thomas (v. 5), Philip (v. 8) and Judas, not Iscariot (v. 22). Moreover, the expression ὅπου ἐγὼ ὑπάγω found in 13,33.36 is repeated in 14,4 (cf. 16,5), and it alerts the reader to look forward in order to know the way and the destination of Jesus' journey as stated in 14,6. On account of these reasons, we may claim that the farewell speech of Jesus begins in 13,31, and 13,31–38 as a unit is not closed within chapter 13.

The material of 13,31–38 seems to be composite in nature, and scholars have raised doubts with regard to its internal unity.[46] The various themes of glorification, departure, love commandment and Peter's denial may appear to be juxtaposed. Since the love commandment (vv. 34–35) disturbs the natural flow of thought between the mention of Jesus' going (v. 33) and Peter's question as to where Jesus is going (v. 36), it is often considered to be an interpolation.[47] However, it is possible to find the logic that relates these themes inseparably. The arrival of the hour of Jesus' glorification (vv. 31–32) implies his immediate departure and absence (v. 33). If v. 33 announces Jesus' immediate departure, vv. 34–35 point out what this means for the disciples. The love commandment (vv. 34–35) dictates what the disciples are to do in Jesus' absence. They are to love one another as Jesus has loved them, so that they may continue his life of love by their example among the non-believers, even in his physical absence (v. 35).

The word order given for emphasis in v. 33 and v. 34 is perhaps an indication that v. 34 is not the work of a later redaction. Both v. 33 (τεκνία, ἔτι μικρὸν μεθ' ὑμῶν εἰμι) and v. 34 (ἐντολὴν καινὴν δίδωμι ὑμῖν) begin with an accusative object followed by the verb. The connection of the love commandment in vv. 34–35 with its preceding and following passages is not easily negligible. The implications of the injunction associated with καθὼς ἐγὼ

---

[45] The commandment to love one another is also found in 15,12–14.

[46] See Brown, *John*, II, 609.

[47] E.g., Weidemann, *Der Tod Jesu*, 95; Dietzfelbinger, *Der Abschied*, 26; Schnackenburg, *John*, III, 53; Becker, *Johannes*, 536; F. F. Segovia, "The Structure, Tendenz and Sitz im Leben of John 13,31–14,31" *JBL* 104 (1985), 491. But later Segovia recanted his position and tried to read 13,34–35 as an integral part of 13,31–38. See Segovia, *Farewell*, 76–77. Beutler, *Do not Be Afraid*, 14, thinks that it belongs to the post-Johannine redaction.

ἐποίησα ὑμῖν (13,15) and καθὼς ἠγάπησα ὑμᾶς (13,34) are one and the same.[48] For John, love entails not just a feeling but action.[49] The ἐντολή of 14,15 is not different from that of 13,34. Those who love Jesus (14,15) have to keep his ἐντολή of loving one another (13,34). Thus, the love commandment may fit well in the current place without an appeal to editorial work.[50]

John 14 distinguishes itself from chapter 15 not only due to the well-known *aporia* in 14,31, "Rise, let us be on our way", but also due to many other features. There is a shift from the theme of departure and return to the theme of mutual relationship between Jesus and his disciples, which is demonstrated through the parable of vine and branches at the beginning of John 15. Unlike John 14, in chapter 15 there are no forms of dialogues between Jesus and his disciples. They reappear only in chapter 16. Jesus who speaks in chapter 15 appears more to be the one already glorified with the Father than the one who is yet to undergo the "hour" of his glorification. Thus, the first part of the farewell speech (13,31–14,31) remains distinct from the remaining part of the farewell speech (chapters 15–16) as a coherent unit.

Scholars have often observed certain tensions and many repetitions within John 14. This is mainly due to the evangelist's references to various ways of "coming" of Jesus in vv. 3.18.23 and also to the Paraclete sayings in vv. 16.26, especially due to their present context. Hence, source and redaction critics have suggested various proposals with regard to the compositional history of John 14.[51] The present study, however, assumes the literary unity of this chapter, taking into account only its final form without appealing to its redactional history, along with the new literary critics who prefer to read it synchronically.[52]

It is very difficult to determine in John 14 where one unit ends and another begins. The train of thoughts in this chapter is circular, turning around certain concepts and ideas by means of objections and associations.[53] There is no

---

[48] Both verbs are in active aorist indicative form. Moloney, *John*, 385–386, views that if the foot-washing is marked by Jesus' example (ὑπόδειγμα), the sharing of the bread is marked by Jesus' new commandment (ἐντολή).

[49] Regarding the relationship of 13,34 with 13,15, Dettwiler, *Die Gegenwart*, 76, writes, "Die als Tat verstandene Liebe wird durch die Fusswaschung im weiteren inhaltlich qualifiziert".

[50] Kellum, *The Unity of the Farewell Discourse*, 154, points out that the abrupt break in 13,34 could be the intent of the author rather than the evidence of a redactor. For various arguments to consider vv. 34–35 as an integral part of the present text, see Tack, *John 14,6 in Light of Jewish-Christian Dialogue*, 34–38; Frey, *Eschatologie*, III, 128–130; J. Augenstein, *Das Liebesgebot im Johannesevangelium und in den Johannesbriefen* (BWANT 134; Stuttgart 1993), 38; Back, *Gott als Vater der Jünger*, 30.

[51] For a survey of some important proposals, see Beutler, *Do not Be Afraid*, 14–16.

[52] See the discussion on pp. 128–129 for reasons for a synchronic approach.

[53] Schnackenburg, *John*, III, 58. We may notice in this chapter, as BROWN, *John*, II, 623, observes, the Johannine technique of overlapping, where the conclusion of one unit is

consensus among scholars with regard to the structuring of this chapter.[54] We may consider both the content and the formal division markers in our approach to the structure of this chapter.[55] Accordingly, we can give three major divisions for this chapter: vv. 1–14; vv. 15–24; vv. 25–31.[56]

---

the beginning of the next. O'Day, *John*, 739, comments on the nature of John 14 thus, "this unit does not develop according to a strict linear logic. Rather, its logic is more circular, developing its perspective through repetition of key themes and words".

[54] For a survey of various proposals for the division of John 14, see Back, *Gott als Vater der Jünger*, 27; Beutler, *Do not Be Afraid*, 16–17, 106; Frey, *Eschatologie*, III, 119–121; Segovia, *Farewell*, 64–68; idem, "The Structure, *Tendenz* and *Sitz im Leben*", 476–478; Brown, *John*, II, 623, 642–643.

[55] Dettwiler, *Die Gegenwart*, 112–118 (also see Weidemann, *Der Tod Jesu*, 79–81), suggests five criteria (Merkmale) for structuring the chapter, namely dialogical elements, catch words and bridge verses, *inclusiones*, semantic relations and finally John 14,2f. as the criteria for the division of the chapter. In order to structure the chapter, we will consider these criteria except the dialogical elements. In 13,36–38, there is a perfect dialogue between Peter and Jesus. But we cannot notice this perfect dialogical character in 14,8–21. Here the questions of the disciples function as literary devices and just help the discourse to move along. An observation of the four questions of the disciples will make this point clear. In all instances, the question of the disciple is prompted by the previous statement of Jesus, which, in fact, introduces the particular motif in question. In 13,36, Peter's question depends on Jesus' statement in v. 33. In 14,4, it is Jesus who introduces the theme of way. Thomas' question just picks up it. In v. 7, Jesus introduces the theme of knowing the Father, which Philip's question picks up in v. 8. The same can be applied to Judas' question in v. 22, which harks back to Jesus' statement in v. 21. In short, the questions are not employed to introduce the theme but to advance it. Moreover, only the question of Peter has a personal character (13,36–38). Thomas, Philipp and Judas ask questions not in a personal manner but as representatives of all disciples, and their questions function as literary means to develop Jesus' speech. Cf. D. B. Woll, *Johannine Christianity in Conflict. Authority, Rank and Succession in the First Farewell Discourse* (SBLDS 60; Chico 1981), 14. Dettwiler, *Die Gegenwart*, 113, points out, "Es ist allerdings deutlich, dass diese Dialogelemente nicht als ein hinreichendes Gliederungsprinizip betrachtet werden können".

[56] This is one of the various ways of dividing this chapter. E.g., this perspective is held by T. Popp, "Die konsolatorische Kraft der Wiederholung: Liebe, Trauer und Trost in den johanneischen Abschiedsreden", *Repetitions and Variations in the Fourth Gospel. Style, Text, Interpretation*, ed. G. Van Belle et al. (Leuven 2009), 542; Schnelle, *Johannes*, 250; Beutler, *Do not Be Afraid*, 16–17, 106; Tolmie, *Jesus' Farewell*, 28–29; Moloney, *John*, 392; Brown, *John*, II, 623; Bultmann, *John*, 595–631 (with a minor variation, 13,36–14,4.5–14.15–24.25–31). There are scholars who do divide the chapter at v. 15 but differ regarding the division of the introductory or concluding unit. E.g., 14,1.2–14.15–26.27.28–31 (Back, *Gott als Vater der Jünger*, 27–28); 14,1–14.15–26.27–31 (Tack, *John 14,6 in Light of Jewish–Christian Dialogue*, 25; J. A. Du Rand, "The Johannine 'Group' and 'Grid': Reading John 13,31–14,31 from Narratological and Sociological Perspectives", *Miracles and Imagery in Luke and John*. Festschrift U. Busse, ed. J. Verheyden et al. [Leuven 2008], 126); 14,1–14.15–31 (Köstenberger, *John*, 420; Kellum, *The Unity of the Farewell Discourse*, 159–161); 14,1–14.15–27.28–31 (Weidemann, *Der Tod Jesu*, 143–

The motifs that unite 14,1–14 as a single unit are the command to believe and Jesus' journey to the Father.[57] The internal unity and the coherence of this pericope can be established by two *inclusiones* found in this unit. The command to believe (πιστεύετε) forms an *inclusio* between 14,1 and v. 11, and the theme of Jesus' "going" (πορεύομαι) to the Father forms an *inclusio* between 14,2 and 14,12. The vv. 12–14 deal with the fruits of believing in Jesus. Those who believe in Jesus can ask in his name and do even greater works, which will manifest Jesus' oneness with the Father. Thus, the contents of vv. 12–14 remain in harmony with the preceding verses.

In 14,15, there is a shift of theme.[58] New themes of loving Jesus, keeping his commandments and the coming of the Paraclete are introduced from 14,15 onwards. There are also linguistic reasons for separating vv. 1–14 from vv. 15–24. While the verb πιστεύω occurs 6 times in vv. 1–14, it is not found in vv. 15–24. The verb ἀγαπάω occurs 8 times in vv. 15–24, but it is absent in vv. 1–14. In the same way, excepting the conclusion (vv. 25–31), we may notice that while the verbs like λαλέω, οἶδα, ὁράω, πορεύομαι and ὑπάγω occur only in vv. 1–14, verbs like δίδωμι, λαμβάνω, εἰμὶ μετά, ἐρωτάω, γίνομαι, θεωρέω and τηρέω are found only in vv. 15–24. We can also find an *inclusio* between v. 15 and vv. 23–24. In these verses, the theme of loving Jesus and keeping his commandments/words is presented.

---

212); 14,1–3.4–14.15–26.27–31 (Dettwiler, *Die Gegenwart*, 124–125); 14,1–3.4–14.15–27.28–31 (Segovia, *Farewell*, 58–59). Other than those who follow the structure adopted in this study, there are also scholars who consider John 14,25–31 as the conclusion of the chapter but differ with regard to the division of the main body of the chapter. E.g., 14,1–3.4–11.12–20.21–24.25–31 (Schleritt, *Der vorjohanneische Passionsbericht*, 303); 14,1–11.12–24.25–31 (O'Day, *John*, 739); 14,1–4.5–7.8–14.15–20.21–24.25–31 (J. H. Bernard, *A Critical and Exegetical Commentary on the Gospel According to St. John* [Edinburgh 1929] II, 530–557); 14,1–7.8–14.15–17.18–24.25–31 (L. Morris, *The Gospel According to John* [NICNT 4; Grand Rapids 1995], 565–587) and 14,1–3.4–11.12–17.18–24.25–31 (Schnackenburg, *John*, III, 48–88). Holloway, "Left Behind", 22, considers 14,1–31 as Jesus' first consolatory speech for his disciples, which is divided into three parts, based on the consolatory speech of Greek literature: the consolation that comes from faith (14,1–14), the consolation that comes from love (14,15–24) and consolation from various sources (14,25–31).

[57] The verb referring to Jesus' "coming back" (ἔρχομαι) occurs only once (v. 3) in this unit. Vv. 1–3 can be regarded as the announcement of the theme of the chapter, namely Jesus' "going" to the Father and his "coming back" to the believers. In 13,31–38, even though the theme of Jesus' "going" is already announced, there is not any reference to Jesus' "coming back". While vv. 4–14 focus on the motif of Jesus' "going" to the Father, vv. 15–24 concentrate on the "coming" of the Trinitarian God, presented through three alternative models of indwelling (vv. 15–17.18–21.22–24).

[58] U. Schnelle, "Die Abschiedsreden im Johannesevangelium", *ZNW* 80 (1989), 67, also notices, "V. 15 eröffnet einen neuen Abschnitt, denn die Thematik des Folgenden wird wesentlich durch ἀγαπᾶν (Joh 14,15.21.23.24.28.31) und τηρεῖν (Joh 14,15.21.23.24) bestimmt".

V. 25 introduces a caesura through the formal division marker ταῦτα λελάληκα ὑμῖν παρ' ὑμῖν μένων, separating vv. 15–24 from the following unit of vv. 25–31.[59] Many recapitulatory formulas like "I have said these things to you" in v. 25, "all that I have said to you" in v. 26, "you heard me say to you" in v. 28, "and now I have told you this before it occurs" in v. 29 and "I will no longer talk much with you" in v. 30 confirm the recapitulatory nature of this unit. They look back on the previous speech of Jesus. Hence, we may consider vv. 25–31 as a conclusion to what Jesus has explained in 13,31–14,24.[60] This conclusion includes themes like the promise of the Paraclete (v. 26; cf. vv. 16–17), which is closely associated with Jesus' glorification (13,31–32; cf. 7,39), words of consolation (v. 27c; cf. v. 1a), Jesus' "going" (v. 28; cf. 13,33.36; 14,2–5.12) and "coming" (v. 28; cf. vv. 3.16–23), his relationship with the Father (vv. 28.31; cf. vv. 7–11), the motif of love (vv. 28.31; cf. 13,34–35; 14,15.21–24) and the motif of belief (v. 29; cf. vv. 1b.10–12). Along with this recapitulation, we may also notice the new motifs of peace (v. 27) and joy (v. 28), which together with the promise of the Holy Spirit are characterized as the "eschatological gifts" of Jesus.[61] In parallel to the character of the devil in 13,2, there is the character of the ruler of the world in 14,30, with whom Jesus enters into conflict. 13,1–3 and 14,28.30–31 function as the frames of chapters 13–14, emphasizing the motifs of cosmic journey and cosmic conflict of Jesus with the devil (Satan, ruler of the world).[62] Considering this organization and movement, we can give the following outline for John 13–14:

13,1–30 The Backdrop of the Farewell Discourse
    13,1–3 The Setting: The Cosmic Journey and the Cosmic Conflict
    13,4–5 "The Way to Go" Prefigured
    13,6–20 Meaning of "the Way to Go" Explained
        13,6–11 The First Explanation
        13,12–20 The Second Explanation
    13,21–30 Judas' Journey into Darkness
13,31–14,31 The Farewell Speech of Jesus
    13,31–38 Announcement of Jesus' Glorification
    14,1–14 The Command to Believe and Jesus' Journey to the Father

---

[59] The refrain "These things I have spoken to you" is used in 16,4a and 16,33 to mark the end of a subdivision, and in 15,11; 16,1.25 it is found a few verses before the end of the units.

[60] Schenke, *Johannes*, 293, opines about 14,25–31 thus, "Fast jeder Satz hat abschließenden Charakter".

[61] See Beutler, *Do not Be Afraid*, 79.

[62] See the diagram on p. 111 that portrays how the motifs of Jesus' cosmic journey and cosmic conflict control John 13–14.

14,15–24 The Command to Love and Trinitarian God's Journey to
the Believers
14,25–31 Recapitulation/Conclusion

2. Analysis of the Near and Immediate Context (13,1–14,31)

At the end of chapter 12, Jesus' revelation to the world and to the Jews comes to an end.[63] In chapter 13, he is turning to his own who, except Judas Iscariot, the betrayer, believe in him (cf. 1,12–13). We analyse John 13–14 to understand better the near and immediate context of Jesus' claim as the way to the Father in 14,6. The farewell speech of Jesus cannot be read separately from the entire setting provided in chapter 13. John 13,1–30 forms an inseparable backdrop of the farewell discourse. Since 14,6 is placed within Jesus' farewell speech in 13,31–14,31, an analysis of this whole passage becomes inevitable for a comprehensive view of the context of 14,6. A short examination of the journey motif in John 13–14 has already shown us that the motifs of Jesus' journey and conflict with the devil control these chapters and provide the fitting context to understand Jesus' claim to be the way in 14,6.[64] In this analysis, we follow basically the general outline given above. Since our purpose is to study the context in relation to John 14,6, we may make use of this outline accordingly. Therefore, chapter 13 and 14,15–31 are regarded as the preceding and following near contexts respectively and 14,1–14 as the immediate context. More attention will be paid to the exegesis of the immediate context. Our aim in the following discussion is only to see how 14,6 is placed in its literary context and how it is related to its immediate and near context. A close examination of various issues related to 14,6, like the unity and integrity of 14,6, the interrelation among the nominative predicatives in 14,6a, the significance of the Father metaphor in 14,6b in relation to Jesus and the believers, possible background for the formulation of 14,6, etc., will be carried out only after an analysis of the literary context of 14,6.

---

[63] For an overview of the function of the farewell discourse and its relation to the Gospel as a whole, see Tack, *John 14,6 in Light of Jewish–Christian Dialogue*, 17–19.

[64] See pp. 107–111.

2.1 The Preceding Near Context (John 13)

2.1.1 The Backdrop of the Farewell Discourse (13,1–30)

2.1.1.1 The Setting: The Cosmic Journey and the Cosmic Conflict (vv. 1–3)[65]

In 13,1, the author prepares the reader for the hour of Jesus' cosmic journey from "this world" to the Father through his death-resurrection-ascension, which is the subject matter of the entire book of glory. Two systems of time form the temporal setting for the events and for Jesus' speech and prayer narrated in chapters 13–17, namely the time of the Jews represented by the feast of Passover (cf. 2,13.23; 6,4; 11,55; 12,1; 18,28.39; 19,14) and the hour of Jesus set by the Father (cf. 2,4; 4,21.23; 7,30; 8,20; 12,23.27; 17,1). Jesus' last supper with his disciples in Jerusalem before his arrest in the garden (18,1–12) provides the spatial setting.

It is after the arrival of the Greeks that the evangelist says for the first time that the hour of Jesus is arrived: "The hour has come for the Son of Man to be glorified" (12,23; cf. 17,1). The glorification refers to Jesus' passion, death and resurrection. This hour is also the hour of overthrowing the ruler of the world. Hence, Jesus says in the same context, "Now is the judgment of this world; now the ruler of this world will be driven out" (12,31). John does not describe the acts of exorcism by Jesus as the Synoptics do. For John, the only act of exorcism is Jesus' death and resurrection in his hour, which is the hour of the preparation of the way to the Father (14,1–6).

13,1 can be seen as an introduction to the whole book of glory.[66] Jesus is acting out of his union with the Father and with full knowledge of his origin and destination. Jesus' fore-knowledge about what would happen to him is a frequent theme in the Gospel (13,3; 18,4; 19,28). It implies that no one could take his life from him until he would lay it down of his own accord (10,18). The death of Jesus is the hour of his Passover to the Father and the culmination of his self-giving love for his own. These two ideas of his love for his

---

[65] Jesus' journey is "cosmic" because it is a journey from "this world" to the world of the Father (13,1). It is inseparably related to "cosmic conflict" because it necessarily involves a fight with "the ruler of the world" (cf. 12,31; 14,30). Judas is the agent of the devil because he obeys the devil's voice (13,2), just as Adam and Eve obey the voice of the serpent (Gen 3,1–13). Judas is deceived by the devil, like Adam and Eve. That Judas is deceived is dramatically portrayed in Matt 27,3–10 (cf. Acts 1,15–19).

[66] V. 1 is a long complex sentence with one independent (main) clause and four dependent (subordinate) clauses. The main clause which is placed at the end of the sentence states, εἰς τέλος ἠγάπησεν αὐτούς. The expression εἰς τέλος can be understood temporarily or quantitatively, "to the end" or "fully". In relation to 15,13 and 19,30, a temporal sense is preferable here. See G. Delling, "τέλος", *TDNT*, VIII, 55. The entire second part of the Gospel can be hence entitled, "He loved them to the end". Schnackenburg, *John*, III, 16, considers 13,1 as the heading of the whole of the second main part of the Gospel. Cf. Brown, *John*, II, 563.

disciples and of his journey from "this world" to the Father intertwine to form the leitmotif of the book of glory.[67]

The story that John tells deals with a battle between Jesus and Satan, acted out in the sphere of human history.[68] 13,2–30 portrays Jesus' cosmic conflict with the devil and prefigures his passion. Vv. 2–3 can be seen as an introduction to the entire scene of vv. 4–30.[69] V. 2 and v. 30 frame the whole narrative emphasizing the role of Judas and the devil in his hour (cf. 13,27).[70] 13,2 makes clear that the human heart is the sphere of the devil's activity. According to Jub. 12,20, evil spirits have dominion over the thoughts of human hearts. Judas allows the devil to control his thoughts and decisions. By presenting in the introductory verses Jesus and the Father in contrast with the devil and Judas, the evangelist indicates the conflict between good and evil (cf. 12,31; 14,30), between the love of Jesus and the betrayal of Judas. Jesus undertakes the action of foot-washing symbolic of his death only after the dark forces have been set in motion that will lead to his crucifixion.[71] The events of the last supper are enacted against the backdrop of a cosmic conflict between the powers of good and evil which will be manifested in Judas' betrayal of Jesus.[72]

Jesus knows that the Father has handed over all things to him (13,3a; cf. 3,35; 6,39; 10,29). Hence, he has complete mastery over his death and life. Coming from God and going to God is a common theme in John (13,3b; cf. 7,28.33; 8,14; 16,28.30).[73] Jesus comes from the Father (8,42; 13,3; 16,28; 17,8). The Father is with him during his ministry (8,16; 8,29; 14,10) and he returns to the Father (13,3; 14,28; 16,10.28). It is the awareness of his prove-

---

[67] Cf. Brown, *John*, II, 563.

[68] J. L. Kovacs, "'Now shall the ruler of this world be driven out': Jesus' Death as Cosmic Battle in John 12,20–36", *JBL* 114 (1995), 233.

[69] The verses 2–4 form a very long compound-complex sentence. It should be noted that vv. 2–3 constitute an amalgamation of seven subordinate clauses and there are no main (independent) clauses in them. The main clauses are given only in verse 4. Therefore, the vv. 2–3 are inseparably bound with v. 4 and they should be read in relation to the following passage. Here, vv. 1–3 are presented separately from vv. 4–5 for the practical purpose of emphasizing the motif of Jesus' cosmic journey and conflict with the devil.

[70] Brown, *John*, II, 563, thinks that the betrayal of Judas is mentioned precisely in v. 2 so that the reader may connect the foot-washing and the death of Jesus.

[71] Brown, *John*, II, 563.

[72] O'Day, *John*, 722. H.-J. Klauck, *Judas ein Jünger des Herrn* (Quaestiones Disputatae 111; Freiburg 1987), 81, writes, "Das Teuflische an Judas besteht darin, daß er den Plan gefaßt hat, Jesu Vernichtung zu betreiben, und so das Bestreben der Kräfte des Bösen zu seinem eigenen macht".

[73] "To come from God and go to God" is the formula used in Gnosticism to describe the self-consciousness of the perfect gnostic. But the humble attitude on the part of Jesus stands in contrast to the status of a perfect gnostic. See E. Haenchen, *John. A Commentary on the Gospel of John* (Philadelphia 1984), II, 106.

2. Analysis of the Near and Immediate Context (13,1–14,31)

nance and destination of his journey that make him claim to be the way to the Father. He is the only one who has ever seen the Father (6,46; cf. 8,38). It is notable that throughout the Gospel the words πατήρ and θεός are interchangeably used (e.g., 6,46; 13,1–3; 17,1–3). If Jesus is portrayed as the one who comes out (ἐξῆλθεν) from the Father, Judas is depicted as the one who goes out (ἐξῆλθεν) of the way of Jesus into darkness (13,30). Jesus finally goes out (ἐξῆλθεν) to confront him and the dark forces (18,1).

2.1.1.2 "The Way to Go" Prefigured (vv. 4–5)

The way Jesus has to go is demonstrated beforehand symbolically through washing the feet of his disciples. During the supper, Jesus gets up and lays aside (τίθησιν) his garments. The verb τίθημι is used in the Gospel for the laying down of life (10,11.15.17.18; 13,37.38; 15,13) and for the burial of Jesus (19,41–42; 20,2.13.15). Thus, the verb τίθημι serves to relate the foot-washing to the humiliating death of Jesus and thus to his love until the end. Jesus, who comes from God, humiliates himself and takes the role of the Suffering Servant of Isaiah (Isa 52,13–53,12) that John has just mentioned (John 12,38).[74]

2.1.1.3 Meaning of "the Way to Go" Explained (vv. 6–20)

a. The First Explanation (vv. 6–11)

The Gospel itself gives two interpretations for the meaning of foot-washing, namely in 13,6–11 and in 13,12–20.[75] Peter's embarrassment (v. 6) paves the way for Jesus' first explanation regarding the meaning of foot-washing. Peter will be able to understand the significance of foot-washing only after "the hour" is over. After Jesus' death and resurrection, the disciples will recognize the full significance of Jesus' words and actions (cf. 2,22; 12,16). Foot-washing is the means for the disciples to have μέρος with Jesus.[76] It means

---

[74] Cf. Keener, *John*, II, 902.

[75] Due to the existence of these two interpretations and the lack of inner harmony among them, scholars have questioned the unity of 13,1–20 and have suggested various theories of composition. See the discussions in G. Richter, *Die Fußwaschung im Johannesevangelium. Geschichte und Deutung* (Regensburg 1967), 3–284; Brown, *John*, II, 559–562; C. Niemand, *Die Fußwaschungserzählung des Johannesevangeliums. Untersuchungen zu ihrer Entstehung und Überlieferung im Urchristentum* (StAns 114; Rome 1993); B. Mathew, *The Johannine Footwashing as the Sign of Perfect Love: An Exegetical Study of John 13,1-20* (WUNT II 464; Tübingen 2018), 167-181.

[76] Μέρος is the word used in LXX to translate the Hebrew word חלק, the word that describes the God-given heritage of Israel (cf. Num 18,20; Deut 12,12; 14,27). Brown, *John*, II, 565, views that when the hopes of Israel turned to an afterlife, the μέρος of God's people was portrayed in heavenly terms. The Book of Revelation speaks of eternal reward in terms

that foot-washing is a symbol of Jesus' salvific death. It is an action-parable, a sign pointing to Jesus' death.[77] The salvific factor is not the physical washing itself but what it symbolizes, that is his humiliating death on the cross (v. 10a).[78] His death provides for the disciples the possibility to have eternal life with him.

On the one hand, this unit is a story of Jesus' act of love, service and humility pre-figuring his sacrificial death on the cross. On the other hand, it is the story of an unclean disciple, who is under conflict. By presenting the character of Judas Iscariot at the beginning and the end of the scene of foot-washing (13,2.11) and contrasting his uncleanliness (13,11) with Peter's cleanliness (13,10), this unit emphasizes that inner cleanliness is a necessary quality to follow Jesus' way to the Father. It is clear from the context (vv. 5.12) that Jesus washes the feet of all his disciples, including those of Judas, his betrayer. When Jesus, the master, washes the feet of Judas, there is not any sign of repentance in him. But when Jesus comes to Peter to wash his feet, he is conscious of his unworthiness and nothingness. Thus, showing the hard-heartedness of Judas and the simplicity of Peter, the author makes a contrast between them. The foot-washing scene is also a story of a master who loves unconditionally the disciple who acts inimical to his master. Even though Jesus washes the feet of Judas, this disciple is not moved by the loving and humble act of Jesus. His heart is filled with evil intent to betray Jesus and hence remains unclean (13,10b–11).

b. The Second Explanation (vv. 12–20)

The second interpretation of the foot-washing points out that Jesus, their Lord and teacher, has set an example before them and the disciples are to imitate it (cf. 1 Tim 5,10).[79] However, this interpretation does not rule out the association of foot-washing with the death of Jesus. "As I have done..." refers not just to the event of foot-washing but also to Jesus' sacrificial and humiliating death on the cross, which the foot-washing symbolizes. The spirit of the example of foot-washing, which is to be imbibed by the disciples, is the spirit of

---

of μέρος (Rev 20,6; 21,8; 22,19). The farewell discourse envisages the union of the disciples with Jesus in the Father's house (14,2–3; 17,24).

[77] F. J. Matera, "On Behalf of Others, Cleansing and Return: Johannine Images for Jesus' Death", *LS* 13 (1988), 171.

[78] Brown, *John*, II, 566. Some scholars notice a secondary baptismal symbolism for the foot-washing. The use of the verb λούω in v. 10 is seen to be the main evidence for this interpretation. The cognates of λούω are standard New Testament vocabulary for baptism (Acts 22,16; Titus 3,5; 1 Cor 6,11; Eph 5,26; Heb 10,22 and the variant in Rev 1,5). Brown points out that the idea of inheritance (κληρονομία, not μέρος) is mentioned in the New Testament in a baptismal context (1 Pet 1,3–4; Titus 3,7). See Brown, *John*, II, 566.

[79] The change in the order of the titles (ὁ κύριος καὶ ὁ διδάσκαλος) in v. 14 may emphasize the true identity of Jesus.

humility and love. There is no greater love than to lay down one's life for his fellow-beings (15,13). Jesus' death on the cross is an act of supreme humility and love. The disciples are to follow his example of love and humility even at the cost of their own lives.

Like the first interpretation, the second one also ends with a reference to Judas who has not been touched by what Jesus has done (13,10b–11; 13,18–20). Jesus allows the betrayal of Judas and considers it necessary because the Scripture has to be fulfilled (13,18). The Scripture to be fulfilled here refers to Ps 41,9, "Even my bosom friend in whom I trusted, who ate of my bread, has lifted the heel against me". Judas' lifting his heel against Jesus contrasts with Jesus' washing of Judas' feet.[80] Jesus foretells this event beforehand (cf. 14,29; 16,4), so that after his death and resurrection the disciples may realize that he is the Lord, the one who can say ἐγώ εἰμι (cf. 8,58).[81] Jesus foresees that his death, resurrection and ascension will lead the disciples to complete belief in him. The disciples, too, will undergo the same sort of sufferings which Jesus is to experience. They are not greater than their master. They are the agents of Jesus, just as Jesus is the Father's agent.

2.1.1.4 Judas' Journey into Darkness (vv. 21–30)

In the previous sections of the Gospel, there are many references to the betrayal of Judas (6,70–71; 12,4; 13,2.10b–11.18–19). But in 13,21 Jesus explicitly announces and prophecies Judas' betrayal. Jesus is troubled in spirit when he declares this, as at the death of Lazarus (11,33) and at the coming of the hour (12,27).[82] In 13,23, there is the first appearance of the beloved disciple, whose role is mentioned only in the second part of the Gospel (cf. 19,26; 20,2; 21,7.20).[83] He is characterized by his intimacy with Jesus and his friendship with Peter. He is reclining on Jesus' "bosom" (κόλπος), just as in 1,18 Jesus is described as being (ὤν) in the Father's "bosom" (κόλπος). In other words, the beloved disciple enjoys a special intimacy with Jesus just as Jesus with his Father (cf. 17,23).

By offering Judas a piece of bread after dipping, on the one hand, Jesus points out his betrayer, and on the other hand, this gesture shows Jesus' love and affection for Judas. Jesus' act can be seen as a gesture of feeding, which

---

[80] Keener, *John*, II, 912–913, points out that betrayal by a friend was considered by people in ancient Mediterranean society far more heinous than any insult by an enemy.

[81] Brown, *John*, II, 571, thinks that 13,19 is very close to the claims of God expressed in Ezek 24,24 and Isa 43,10. There is also an echo of the declaration, אֶהְיֶה אֲשֶׁר אֶהְיֶה in Exod 3,14. See A. E. Nida, *Lexical Semantics of the Greek New Testament* (Atlanta 1992), 20.

[82] John 12,27 (cf. Matt 26,38; Mark 14,34) seems to cite Ps 42,5 and 13,21 seems to be influenced by the next verse of this psalm (42,6).

[83] According to Brown, *John*, II, 571, the reason for the absence of the beloved disciple in the first part of the Gospel is that the evangelist wished to introduce him as an antithesis to Judas, showing the good and bad extremes in the spectrum of discipleship.

in itself implies care and nourishment.[84] It is a crucial and decisive moment for Judas, a time to choose either for Jesus or for Satan. The fact that he receives the bread without changing his wicked plan to betray Jesus is clear from the evangelist's statement that Satan enters into him (13,27; cf. Luke 22,3). V. 27 reveals that Judas wholeheartedly decides for the devil (cf. 13,2).

There is a definite development with regard to the influence of the devil upon Judas in v. 27. While he is only induced by the devil to betray Jesus in v. 2, he is portrayed as fully mastered by Satan and completely in his power in v. 27.[85] This is very evident when we compare his first appearance with his last appearance in the Gospel. In 6,71, he is said to be with the disciples as one among the twelve (εἷς ἐκ τῶν δώδεκα), but in 18,5 he is depicted to be with the enemies of Jesus (εἱστήκει δὲ καὶ Ἰούδας ὁ παραδιδοὺς αὐτὸν μετ' αὐτῶν). There is a Johannine irony in the portrayal of the character of Judas in chapter 13.[86] Even though his feet are washed by Jesus, he remains still unclean. He receives the bread of life from Jesus, but he still remains dead. He abandons "the way of truth and life" (cf. 14,6) and joins "the way of the devil", which is "the way of falsehood and death" (cf. 8,44). Judas does not receive Jesus (cf. 13,20). So Satan enters him. Judas is possessed by Satan and he joins the satanic programme, which is opposed to the divine programme. When Jesus recognizes the irrevocability of Judas' malice, he allows Judas to betray him saying, "Do quickly what you are going to do" (13,27). Here we can notice Jesus' control and mastery over his destiny because no one can take his life from him unless he consents (10,18).

John indicates that "and it was night" (ἦν δὲ νύξ) when Judas went out. In this Gospel, night (11,10; cf. 9,4) and darkness (1,5; 3,19; 8,12; 12,35) are symbols of evil. The betrayal by Judas is seen by the evangelist as a deed of darkness (cf. 3,16–21; Luke 22,53), a work of the devil, and therefore, Judas is called διάβολος (6,70). That he has chosen for Satan, for the darkness/night rather than for Jesus the light, becomes much more evident when he appears next time with the police from the authorities to arrest Jesus (18,2–5; cf. 3,16–21).

2.1.2 Announcement of Jesus' Glorification (vv. 31–38)

The decisive moment of the farewell scene is "the going out" of Judas so that Jesus can "go" (cf. 14,31; 18,1). Judas' determination to betray Jesus actually

---

[84] This interpretation is possible considering the broad metaphorical network in the Gospel as a whole and the immediate context within which the gesture is introduced, especially the scriptural citation in v. 18. See the discussion in D. F. Tolmie, "Jesus, Judas and a Morsel: Interpreting a Gesture in John 13,21–30", *Miracles and Imagery in Luke and John*. Festschrift U. Busse, ed. J. Verheyden et al. (Leuven 2008), 118–120.

[85] Tolmie, "Jesus, Judas and a Morsel", 111–112.

[86] Cf. Tolmie, "Jesus, Judas and a Morsel", 123.

inaugurates the process of Jesus' journey from this world to the Father because Judas goes out to bring the police and soldiers who will arrest Jesus and finally put him to death. In 13,31a, the evangelist prepares the reader for the transition. Until v. 31, Jesus has not explicitly mentioned his journey to the Father. Jesus' announcement of his journey is explained in terms of his relationship with the Father (vv. 31–32) and in terms of his relationship with his disciples (vv. 33–38). His journey implies for him his glorification with the Father and for his disciples the need to love one another.

2.1.2.1 Glorification (vv. 31–32)

Jesus' farewell speech begins with a proclamation of the glorification of the Son of Man. The coming of the Greeks heralded the beginning of the glorification (12,20–23) because they foreshadowed all people who would be drawn to Jesus once he had been lifted up to the Father (12,32).[87] Jesus' glorification is an act of legitimation (cf. 8,54) and vindication of his claims to be from above (cf. 3,31). The Father and the Son are glorified in one another. Their reciprocal glorification must be understood in the light of their reciprocal indwelling and oneness described in 14,10–11. In the process of glorification, there is a blurring of borders between the Father and the Son. Hence, the confusing repetition of αὐτός in 13,31–32 can be considered as a literary description of the Father and Son becoming one and less distinguishable in the process of glorification.[88]

In the events of Jesus' death and resurrection, God's majesty and glory are visibly manifested through powerful deeds. The change from a past tense in v. 31 (ἐδοξάσθη) to a future tense in v. 32 (δοξάσει) is noticeable. It is suggested that the aorist ἐδοξάσθη is complexive referring to the whole passion, death, resurrection and ascension that take place in "the hour", and the future δοξάσει refers to the glory that will follow when the Son returns to the Father's presence (cf. 17,5).[89] The use of the aorist ἐδοξάσθη along with the adverb νῦν is a strong reason to relate this glorification to the "hour".[90] The idea of the glorification of the Son of Man in v. 31 is comparable to the suf-

---

[87] Brown, *John*, II, 610. Brown thinks that John's interpretation of Jesus' glorification related to his suffering and death is foreshadowed in Isa 52,13. See Brown, *John*, II, 146, 478, 610.

[88] N. Chibici-Revneanu, "Variations on Glorification: John 13,31f. and Johannine δόξα Language", *Repetitions and Variations in the Fourth Gospel. Style, Text, Interpretation*, ed. G. Van Belle et al. (Leuven 2009), 513, 515.

[89] Brown, *John*, II, 477, 610.

[90] Cf. Chibici-Revneanu, "Variations on Glorification", 519; Schnackenburg, *John*, III, 49. In 12,28, the aorist ἐδόξασα may be a reference to all the past glorifications of the divine name through the signs that Jesus did during his ministry (2,11; 11,4), and the future πάλιν δοξάσω may be a reference to all the glorification of the hour through his death, resurrection and ascension. See Brown, *John*, I, 476.

fering of the Son of Man (cf. Mark 8,31) and in v. 32 to the future glory and Parousia of the Son of Man in judgment (cf. Mark 13,26; John 17,24) found in the Synoptic tradition.[91]

2.1.2.2 Departure (v. 33)

It is only here in John's Gospel that the disciples are explicitly called by Jesus "little children" (τεκνία).[92] The address "little children" (τεκνία) after the departure of Judas is very significant, especially in relation to 1,12. It is only those who believe in Jesus become the children of God (τέκνα θεοῦ). Jesus' words of departure do not differ from his earlier words to the Jews (7,33–36; 8,21). But he does not tell his disciples that they will not find him (cf. 7,34) and will die in their sin (cf. 8,21). Jesus' words to the Jews were spoken in the context of conflict (7,32) and condemnation (8,26). But Jesus' words to the disciples are intended to initiate a new relationship with him and with one another. The expression ἔτι μικρόν may indicate the urgency of God's salvation.[93] Jesus' death-resurrection-ascension is expressed by the evangelist in terms of "going" (ὑπάγω). The disciples cannot accompany him in his death and in the glory of his resurrection and ascension. The access of the disciples to the Father requires the prior journey of Jesus to the Father, which is intended to prepare the way for them to the Father.

2.1.2.3 Commandment of Love (vv. 34–35)

The principle behind Jesus' commandment is his experience of the Father's love, "As the Father has loved me, so I have loved you" (15,9; cf. 15,12.17; 1 John 2,7–9; 3,23; 4,21; 5,2–3; 2 John 5). In the Old Testament, the Israelite is commanded to love his neighbour as himself (Lev 19,18). But the expression "as I have loved you" in 13,34 indicates that Jesus is the standard of Christian love. He loves them to the point of laying down his life (13,1; 15,13; Rev 1,5). Therefore, it is Jesus' mode of maximum love that makes the love commandment new. 13,35 affirms that the identity of the followers of Jesus is mutual love among them. The non-Christians will recognize then the distinc-

---

[91] In the Synoptic tradition, there are three types of Son of Man sayings: i. those that refer to the earthly activity of the Son of Man (e.g., eating, dwelling, saving the lost); ii. those that refer to the suffering of the Son of Man; iii. those that refer to the future glory and Parousia of the Son of Man in judgment. See Brown, *John*, II, 84, 611.

[92] "Little children" is a common form of address used for the members of the community in 1 John (2,1.12.28; 3,7.18; 4,44; 5,21).

[93] It suggests little about chronological duration because it is used both in 7,33 when Jesus has at least six months more to live and in the present context when Jesus has only a few hours to live (cf. 12,35; 14,19; 16,16). Brown thinks that it is an Old Testament expression used by the prophets to express optimistically the shortness of time before God's salvation would come (Isa 10,25; Jer 51,33). See Brown, *John*, II, 607.

2. Analysis of the Near and Immediate Context (13,1–14,31)

tiveness of the Christian love and come to know Jesus (17,23). Thus, Jesus' presence will be felt even in his physical absence as long as there is Christian love in the world. Christian love is the medium for the world to encounter Jesus.

2.1.2.4 Prediction of Peter's Denial (vv. 36–38)

V. 36 continues the theme of Jesus' journey mentioned in v. 33. Peter wants to go with Jesus, but Jesus promises that Peter will follow him only later. Jesus' promise to Peter will be fulfilled in 21,15–19 when he predicts his future death and says to him finally, "Follow me" (21,19). Peter is offered the role of the shepherd, who will lay down his life for his sheep and thus become a true follower of the good shepherd (10,14–15). But Peter is very overconfident and wants to follow Jesus at once at the expense of laying down his life for him like a model shepherd (10,11). Such an element of overconfidence can also be seen on the part of all the disciples in 16,29–32. Peter does not recognize that the death to which Jesus goes involves a struggle with the ruler of this world, and only when Jesus has overcome him, others can follow.[94] This is how the way is prepared by him. In Jesus' response to Peter, "Will you lay down your life for me?", we can notice an element of irony and an awareness of human fragility. Like the Synoptic tradition, John records Jesus' prediction of Peter's denial (cf. Mark 14,29–31; Matt 26,33–35; Luke 22,31–34) and also its fulfilment (John 18,17–18.25–27; cf. Mark 14,66–72; Matt 26,69–75; Luke 22,54–62).[95]

2.2 The Immediate Context: Exegesis of John 14,1–14

2.2.1. Textual Criticism

According to GNT^5, there are seven units of variant readings within the pericope 14,1–14.[96] They are found in vv. 2.4.7 (twice), 11 and 14 (twice). Some manuscripts omit the conjunction ὅτι in 14,2. The presence of ὅτι in this verse has been a problem for the scribes in the past and is still so for contemporary interpreters. The conjunction ὅτι may be rendered recitative ("that") or causal ("because"). Besides this, 14,2b can be read as a question or a statement.[97] Because of these difficulties, an omission of ὅτι may appear to

---

[94] Brown, *John*, II, 616.

[95] It is notable that before recording Jesus' prediction of Peter's denial, Mark (14,27) and Matthew (26,31) cite Zech 13,7 stating, "I will strike the shepherd, and the sheep will be scattered" (cf. John 16,32).

[96] The minor variants under each unit are not taken into account here if they seem to be insignificant.

[97] According to N-A[28] and GNT^5, this verse is a question. We can find only a conjecture with regard to punctuation in order to read it as a statement.

be an easy solution.⁹⁸ But there is excellent, if not absolutely conclusive, manuscript evidence for the retention of ὅτι.⁹⁹ Moreover, the reading with ὅτι should be seen as the *lectio difficilior* and it should be retained. The verse in 14,2b can be read as a statement or a question rendering ὅτι a causal or an explicative meaning or εἰ δὲ μη, εἶπον ἂν ὑμῖν can be read parenthetically linking ὅτι to the preceding verse in 14,2a.¹⁰⁰ Accordingly, this verse can be translated in the following ways:

i. If it were not so, I would have told you because I am going to prepare a place for you.

ii. If it were not so, would I have told you so because I am going to prepare a place for you?

iii. In my father's house there are many dwelling places (if it were not so, I would have told you) because I am going to prepare a place for you.

iv. If it were not so, I would have told you that I am going to prepare a place for you.

v. If it were not so, would I have told you that I am going to prepare a place for you?

To take ὅτι causally (i, ii, iii) does not make any significant sense and has its own logical problems. The fact that there are many dwelling places in the Father's house and the fact that Jesus is going to prepare a place for the disciples are two different things. In other words, the existence of the Father's house with many dwelling places and the preparation of a (dwelling) place in it are different things. That Jesus is going to prepare a place for the disciples cannot be the cause for the fact that there are many dwelling places in the Father's house. It should be the other way round. Jesus' preparation of a place for the disciples presupposes the existence of the Father's house with many dwelling places. The sense of this metaphorical language can be understood in this way: there is eternal life with the Father; Jesus' death and resurrection is the preparation through which Jesus is securing eternal life for his disciples.

---

⁹⁸ B. M. Metzger, *A Textual Commentary on the Greek New Testament* (Stuttgart ²1994), 206, explains the omission of ὅτι as a simplification introduced by copyists who took it as ὅτι *recitativum* which is often omitted as superfluous. Brown, *John*, II, 620, omits ὅτι from the text.

⁹⁹ N-A²⁸, Merk and *GNT*⁵ and the majority of the scholars and commentators retain ὅτι.

¹⁰⁰ Bultmann, *John*, 601, suggests along with Noack that a μή has been omitted before εἶπον through haplography and reads this verse as a question. Schnackenburg, *John*, III, 59, also reads this verse as a question. But he conjectures that the ὅτι was originally followed by a ὑπάγω which was omitted at quite an early stage because the word which followed it has the same meaning. But there is no manuscript evidence for these two conjectures. Barrett, *John*, 457, reads it parenthetically. In this case, ὅτι should be rendered a causal meaning.

If we read this verse as a statement rendering ὅτι an explicative meaning (iv), then it would contradict the following verse (v. 3) because immediately Jesus is saying clearly that he is going to prepare a place. Therefore, the last option (v), i.e., reading this verse as a question and rendering ὅτι an explicative meaning, needs to be taken into consideration.[101] One objection to this reading is that Jesus has not explicitly said before that he is going to prepare a place for the disciples. But this is not a fatal objection because many sayings of Jesus have not been recorded by the evangelist (cf. 21,25). He has the style of repeating or quoting Jesus' sayings for the development of the narrative and argument. It is not his concern to cite Jesus' former sayings always accurately (e.g., 6,65; 8,24; 10,25; 12,34b; 14,28; 18,9), and it is sometimes difficult to trace the place of their first occurrence (e.g., 6,36; 8,54b; 9,41; 10,36b; 11,40). A reference to Jesus' former sayings can function as a summary reformulation or explication of earlier statements in the narrative.[102] It does not always concern specific words but can be related to a motive or a chain of thought. The evangelist's report here is meant to be so condensed that he has chosen not to record the fact that Jesus is going to prepare a place for his disciples other than by the rhetorical question itself.[103] It is also possible that the evangelist intends a reference to a traditional saying, which is not included in the narrative but known to his readers.[104]

We can also find an implicit reference for 14,2b in 12,26 and 13,33.36. But one needs to make here a major inference in order to find the notion of a place being prepared. Moreover, Jesus' question, linked to a contrary to fact condition in 14,2b, is placed between two factual statements in 14,2a and 14,3 and its significance is to be understood rhetorically. Finally, it should be kept in mind that the different translations of 14,2b do not considerably affect the meaning and theology of the passage.

---

[101] This position is held by many interpreters like Bernard, *John,* II, 534; W. Bauer, *Das Johannesevangelium* (HzNT 6; Tübingen ³1933), 177–178; G. Fischer, *Die himmlischen Wohnungen. Untersuchungen zu Joh 14,2f* (Bern 1975), 35–56; J. McCaffrey, *The House with Many Rooms. The Temple Theme of Jn. 14,2–3* (Rome 1988), 38–40; Segovia, *Farewell*, 83. n. 46; Dettwiler, *Die Gegenwart,* 143–145; Y. Simoens, *Selon Jean 1. Une Traduction* (CIET 17; Brussels 1997), 73; Dietzfelbinger, *Der Abschied,* 28; Wengst, *Johannesevangelium,* II, 117; Schnelle, *Johannes,* 250; Kellum, *The Unity of the Farewell Discourse,* 160; Thyen, *Johannesevangelium,* 615–616. Moreover, some of the modern English versions like NRSV, NLT and NAB and the German versions like EÜ and MNT support this translation.

[102] Segovia, *Farewell,* 83, n. 46. Also see Fischer, *Wohnungen,* 53–56, for his conclusions.

[103] D. A. Carson, *The Gospel According to John* (Grand Rapids 1991), 490.

[104] A. T. Lincoln, *The Gospel According to Saint John* (London 2005), 389. Segovia, *Farewell,* 83, asserts that "there is nothing intrinsically defective about a character's referring to a previous declaration not recorded in the narrative itself".

In 14,4, some witnesses add καὶ τὴν ὁδὸν οἴδατε so as to read ὅπου ἐγὼ ὑπάγω οἴδατε καὶ τὴν ὁδὸν οἴδατε. This is to be seen as an amelioration by the copyists to solve the syntactical harshness of the shorter reading ὅπου ἐγὼ ὑπάγω οἴδατε τὴν ὁδόν.[105] It is also possible to assume that copyists expanded this verse because Thomas distinguished in v. 5 between "knowing where you are going" and "knowing the way". According to the transcriptional probabilities of internal evidence, the principles of *lectio brevior* and *lectio difficilior* should be applied here to prefer the shorter reading most probably as the original one.

In 14,7a, we find mainly two variants ἐγνώκειτέ με instead of ἐγνώκατέ με and ἐγνώκειτε ἄν or ἄν ἤδειτε instead of γνώσεσθε and also other various derivatives. As a result, v. 7a can be read as a condition of fact or as a contrary to fact condition. If it is read as a contrary to fact condition, "if you had known me, you would have known my Father also", then it is a reproach by Jesus. This variant reading is notably influenced by 8,19 and 14,8-9. But in 8,19 Jesus is addressing the public who are often sceptic of his teachings and behave as his opponents, and in 14,9 Jesus is answering an imprudent question of Philip. Hence, a reproach was necessiated in 8,19 and 14,9, but it is not inevitable in 14,7a. In addition to that, this reproach will not agree with the positive statement of v. 7b. Moreover, if the text that offers a condition of fact is taken as the original one, it can be seen as a positive explanation of "no one comes to the Father except through me" of the preceding v. 6b. Hence, we can neglect this variant and read 14,7a as a promise, "if you know me, you will know my Father also".

The variant reading in 14,11b (πιστεύετέ μοι) should be seen as an attempt to harmonize with the expression πιστεύετέ μοι of the preceding v. 11a. Some manuscripts omit the complete v. 14. It can be a mistake in transcription when the eye of the scribe passed from ἐάν in 14,14 to ἐάν in v. 15. Another reason for the omission of this verse is its similarity with v. 13a. It is also possible to assume that the scribe omitted this verse purposely to avoid the contradiction with 16,23. Some witnesses omit v. 14 along with ἵνα δοξασθῇ ὁ πατὴρ ἐν τῷ υἱῷ of v. 13b. This can be regarded as an example for omission by *homoioteleuton* when the eye of the copyist passed from ποιήσω in v. 13a to ποιήσω in v. 14. Among the manuscripts that preserve v. 14, there are also some textual witnesses which omit με after αἰτήσητέ. This can also be considered as an attempt to avoid a contradiction with 16,23. A few manuscripts try to avoid this contradiction by replacing με with τὸν πατέρα. There is, however, adequate textual evidence for the retention of με in the

---

[105] Metzger, *A Textual Commentary*, 207. Bultmann, *John*, 603, n. 2, remarks that it is a clarificatory correction, which spoils the rhythm.

2. Analysis of the Near and Immediate Context (13,1–14,31)

text.[106] As a result of this textual critical analysis, we can establish the text as it is given in N-A[28] and GNT[5].

2.2.2 Structure

In 14,1–14, we can notice some kind of concatenation of ideas, i.e., the art of linking together the concepts in the form of a series or chain. In every verse there are words taken up from the previous one. In some verses, not only the idea of the previous verse is literally repeated, but also a new idea is introduced, which will be taken up again in the next verse.[107] V. 1 as a command to believe stands, to some extent, independently. However, "in me" (εἰς ἐμέ) in v. 1 is taken up in "in my" (ἐν... μου) of v. 2.[108] Again, πορεύομαι ἑτοιμάσαι τόπον ὑμῖν of v. 2 is repeated in πορευθῶ καὶ ἑτοιμάσω τόπον ὑμῖν of v. 3, and ὅπου... ἐγώ of v. 3 is taken up in ὅπου [ἐγώ] of v. 4 and so on. Below, the text is presented showing how the key concepts or motifs of a verse are repeated in the next verse, sometimes leading to new concepts or motifs. The repeated terms, which are either taken from the previous verse or taken up in the next verse, are underlined.

¹ Μὴ ταρασσέσθω ὑμῶν ἡ καρδία· πιστεύετε εἰς τὸν θεὸν καὶ εἰς ἐμὲ πισ τεύετε.
² ἐν τῇ οἰκίᾳ τοῦ πατρός μου μοναὶ πολλαί εἰσιν· εἰ δὲ μή, εἶπον ἂν ὑμῖν ὅτι πορεύομαι ἑτοιμάσαι τόπον ὑμῖν;
³ καὶ ἐὰν πορευθῶ καὶ ἑτοιμάσω τόπον ὑμῖν, πάλιν ἔρχομαι καὶ παραλήμψομαι ὑμᾶς πρὸς ἐμαυτόν, ἵνα ὅπου εἰμὶ ἐγὼ καὶ ὑμεῖς ἦτε.
⁴ καὶ ὅπου [ἐγὼ] ὑπάγω οἴδατε τὴν ὁδόν.
⁵ Λέγει αὐτῷ Θωμᾶς, Κύριε, οὐκ οἴδαμεν ποῦ ὑπάγεις· πῶς δυνάμεθα τὴν ὁδὸν εἰδέναι;
⁶ λέγει αὐτῷ [ὁ] Ἰησοῦς, Ἐγώ εἰμι ἡ ὁδὸς καὶ ἡ ἀλήθεια καὶ ἡ ζωή· οὐδεὶς ἔρχεται πρὸς τὸν πατέρα εἰ μὴ δι' ἐμοῦ.
⁷ εἰ ἐγνώκατέ με, καὶ τὸν πατέρα μου γνώσεσθε· καὶ ἀπ' ἄρτι γινώσκετε αὐτὸν καὶ ἑωράκατε αὐτόν.
⁸ λέγει αὐτῷ Φίλιππος, Κύριε, δεῖξον ἡμῖν τὸν πατέρα, καὶ ἀρκεῖ ἡμῖν.
⁹ λέγει αὐτῷ ὁ Ἰησοῦς, Τοσούτῳ χρόνῳ μεθ' ὑμῶν εἰμι καὶ οὐκ ἔγνωκάς με, Φίλιππε; ὁ ἑωρακὼς ἐμὲ ἑώρακεν τὸν πατέρα· πῶς σὺ λέγεις, Δεῖξον ἡμῖν τὸν πατέρα;

---

[106] Metzger, A Textual Commentary, 208, opines that με is appropriate because of its correlation with ἐγώ later in the verse.

[107] This style is not present in 13,31–38 and 14,15–31. No words are taken from the previous verse in 14,1 and 14,15.

[108] The basis for the command to believe in Jesus (v. 1) is Jesus' free access to his Father's house (v. 2). Only Jesus can call the Father's house "my" Father's house since he belongs to the Father's house permanently (cf. 8,35).

¹⁰ οὐ πιστεύεις ὅτι ἐγὼ ἐν τῷ πατρὶ καὶ ὁ πατὴρ ἐν ἐμοί ἐστιν; τὰ ῥήματα ἃ ἐγὼ λέγω ὑμῖν ἀπ' ἐμαυτοῦ οὐ λαλῶ, ὁ δὲ πατὴρ ἐν ἐμοὶ μένων ποιεῖ τὰ ἔργα αὐτοῦ.
¹¹ πιστεύετέ μοι ὅτι ἐγὼ ἐν τῷ πατρὶ καὶ ὁ πατὴρ ἐν ἐμοί· εἰ δὲ μή, διὰ τὰ ἔργα αὐτὰ πιστεύετε.
¹² ἀμὴν ἀμὴν λέγω ὑμῖν, ὁ πιστεύων εἰς ἐμὲ τὰ ἔργα ἃ ἐγὼ ποιῶ κἀκεῖνος ποιήσει καὶ μείζονα τούτων ποιήσει, ὅτι ἐγὼ πρὸς τὸν πατέρα πορεύομαι·
¹³ καὶ ὅ τι ἂν αἰτήσητε ἐν τῷ ὀνόματί μου τοῦτο ποιήσω, ἵνα δοξασθῇ ὁ πατὴρ ἐν τῷ υἱῷ·
¹⁴ ἐάν τι αἰτήσητέ με ἐν τῷ ὀνόματί μου ἐγὼ ποιήσω.

Thus, the thought-flow of this unit is not linear but more circular, developing its perspective through the repetition of important motifs and words. Hence, it is difficult to impose a neat and perfect structure on this unit. We may, however, look for key concepts and motifs within this unit and find the logic and the thought-flow within the text. The most frequently used term in this unit is πατήρ (13x). The Father is the destination of Jesus' journey, and his oneness with the Father becomes the ground for his claim to be the exclusive way to the Father. The motifs of the command to believe in Jesus and his journey to the Father control this pericope. The language of journey is prominent in this unit. There are seven occurrences of verbs of journey like πορεύομαι (3x), ὑπάγω (2x) and ἔρχομαι (2x) and three occurrences of the noun ὁδός, which belongs to the semantic domain of journey. Another important motif is the command to believe, using the verb πιστεύω (6x). The unit begins with a command to believe (v. 1) and introduces the theme of Jesus' "going" and "coming back" together for the first time (vv. 2–3).[109] The important motif within vv. 4–6 is the way (ὁδός). There is certainly continuity of thought between v. 6b and v. 7 and the following verses. The division is made here between v. 6b and v. 7 for the practical purpose of highlighting the motif of way in vv. 4–6. The unifying theme within vv. 7–11 is Jesus' oneness with the Father in which the disciples are asked to believe. The fruits of believing in Jesus are explained in vv. 12–14. Consequently, we can give the following outline for this pericope:

Command to Believe (v. 1)
Jesus' Going and Coming Again (vv. 2–3)
Jesus as the Way to the Father (vv. 4–6)
Jesus' Oneness with the Father (vv. 7–11)
Fruits of Belief in Jesus' Oneness with the Father (vv. 12–14)

---

[109] While the motif of Jesus' "going" is again taken up in vv. 4–14, the motif of Jesus' "coming" is not mentioned in vv. 4–14 but discussed in the following unit of vv. 15–24 with different models.

2.2.3 Syntactical Analysis

The plural verbs in 14,1–4 show that Jesus is addressing the group of disciples. Μή with the present imperative is a prohibitive imperative, which is generally used to forbid the continuance of an action in progress or under way. The usage of the singular noun ἡ καρδία with the plural possessive pronoun (ὑμῶν) in a distributive sense is due to Semitic style.[110] The two occurrences of πιστεύετε in 14,1 can function as indicative as well as imperative with regard to belief in God and in Jesus. An imperative sense is more appealing to the context. Belief in God is indeed a true consolation for a troubled man (2 Chr 20,20; Pss 27,13–14; 141,8; Sir 2,5–6). The occasion of the last supper has created an atmosphere of uncertainty and sorrow among the disciples. The immediate context suggests a progressive or an ongoing situation of being disturbed on the part of the disciples on account of Jesus' unusual way of washing the disciples' feet, his indication of an unclean disciple, his prediction of the betrayal and denial by Judas and Peter respectively and the announcement of his imminent departure.[111] For the disciples who have left everything for their master, it is something shattering when they hear that Jesus is about to leave them.[112] The imminent suffering and death of Jesus are likely to disturb them. Hence, they need to be strengthened with belief in God and in Jesus.

In 14,11, Jesus also urges his disciples to believe (πιστεύετε) in him (cf. 12,36).[113] An indicative sense is not possible there. The introductory imperative (μὴ ταρασσέσθω) is also a clue to read the other two verbs as imperatives in v. 1. If an indicative sense of πιστεύετε were intended by the evangelist in 14,1, why should he use the imperative in 14,11? Moreover, immediately after a prohibition (μὴ ταρασσέσθω) imperatives make a more natural flow of thought than the indicatives because "don'ts" naturally presuppose "do's" or "do's" follow "don'ts".[114] Therefore, Jesus' command to believe in God and

---

[110] See J. H. Moulton and N. Turner, *A Grammar of New Testament Greek Syntax* (London ²1963), III, 23. John uses καρδία in this way in the singular 5 times (including one quotation from LXX) but never in the plural (cf.12,40; 14,21; 16,6.22). He employs the Semitic preference for a distributive singular probably in the Septuagintal idiom (Deut 5,29; 6,5–6; 7,17; 8,2.5.14.17; 9,4–5; 10,12; 11,13.18; 13,13). See Keener, *John*, II, 930.

[111] Jesus himself is mentally disturbed when he speaks of the imminent betrayal (note the same verb ἐταράχθη in 13,21; cf. 12,27), and it may have a consequent effect upon the disciples.

[112] Morris, *John*, 566.

[113] Compare with Mark 11,22 where Jesus during his final days urges his disciples "to have faith in God" (ἔχετε πίστιν θεοῦ).

[114] E.g., Jesus says to the leader of the synagogue (Mark 5,36 cf. Luke 8,50), "Do not fear, only believe" (μὴ φοβοῦ, μόνον πίστευε).

in him in the context of disciples' anxiety and wavering faith[115] makes more sense and seems to be more logical.

The condition in v. 2 with an indicative aorist (εἶπον) in the apodosis with ἄν is a second class condition, particularly a past contrary to fact (unreal) condition.[116] Εἰ δὲ μή is an abbreviation of the protasis where the verb is to be supplied, "if there were not many dwelling places in the house of my Father". The fact of 14,2a that "there are many dwelling places in my Father's house" indicates that the protasis of 14,2b is an unreal (counterfactual) condition. The infinitive ἑτοιμάσαι with πορεύομαι forms an infinitive of purpose.

In 14,3, the conjunction ἐάν with the aorist subjunctives (πορευθῶ and ἑτοιμάσω) forms a third-class condition of futurity.[117] As a marker of the prospect of an action in a point of time, coordinated with another point of time, ἐάν has the meaning of ὅταν.[118] Even though ἐάν can be rendered a hypothetical meaning from a grammatical point of view, it could be given a temporal sense because Jesus' departure is without any doubt after the announcement of his departure in John 7,33–36; 13,33.36–38.[119] The present tense of the verbs of going and coming, namely πορεύομαι (14,2.12), ἔρχομαι (14,3) and ὑπάγω (14,4) denote futuristic present used with a future reference, and the future of παραλήμψομαι (14,3) indicates a further consequence.[120] The certainty of this future return in the mind of Jesus causes him to express it with the present, and it reflects theologically a divine resolve, which cannot fail to occur without impinging the character of God.[121]

In 14,5, εἰδέναι is the complementary infinitive of δυνάμεθα. The particle εἰ together with the indicative ἐγνώκατε in the protasis in 14,7 indicates a

---

[115] In the Synoptic Gospels, the disciples are often accused of their lack of belief.

[116] Moulton and Turner, *A Grammar of New Testament Greek*, III, 91; M. Zerwick and M. Grosvenor, *A Grammatical Analysis of the Greek New Testament* (Rome ⁵2010), 330; D. B. Wallace, *Greek Grammar Beyond the Basics. An Exegetical Syntax of the New Testament* (Grand Rapids 1996), 695.

[117] Wallace, *Greek Grammar Beyond the Basics*, 696. According to Moulton and Turner, *A Grammar of New Testament Greek*, III, 114, ἐάν with aorist subjunctive "represents a definite event as occurring only once in the future and conceived as taking place before the time of the action of the main verb. It is expectation but not fulfilment as yet".

[118] BDAG 268. B. M. Newman and E. A. Nida, *A Handbook on the Gospel of John* (New York 1980), 456, suggest to translate this conjunction here in the temporal sense of "after", "when" or in the causal sense of "since". Fischer, *Wohnungen* 89, n. 89, points out that in John καὶ ἐάν is used to lead the thought further.

[119] See Beutler, *Do not Be Afraid*, 37; W. Bauer, *Das Johannesevangelium* (HNT 6; Tübingen ³1933), 178.

[120] Cf. BDF, 168 (§323.1); R. A. Young, *Intermediate New Testament Greek. A Linguistic and Exegetical Approach* (Nashville 1994), 111. The use of the present tense of the verb ἔρχομαι with a future sense is common in this Gospel. E.g., 1,15.30; 4,21.23.25; 14,18.28; 16,2.13.25; note the use of ἔρχομαι in Rev 1,4.7.8; 22,20.

[121] Young, *Intermediate New Testament Greek*, 111.

first-class condition, which here functions as a tool of persuasion. The idea seems to be an encouragement to respond in which the evangelist attempts to get his audience to come to the conclusion of the apodosis.[122] The future of γνώσεσθε (14,7) is predictive. The preposition ἀπό with the adverb ἄρτι (14,7) marks a point of time. In 14,8, δεῖξον is an imperative of entreaty and ἀρκεῖ is an impersonal use of ἀρκέω. In 14,9, the temporal dative of τοσούτῳ χρόνῳ expresses an expanse of time, and εἰμι with this temporal indicator is a durative present, where an action that began in the past continues into the present.[123] It refers to the quantity of time. Jesus tells Philip that he has been with him for a long time. The perfect of ἔγνωκας is intensive and it indicates the present state of affairs resulting from the past action.[124] Λέγει in 14,8.9 is a historical present used as an ordinary narrative tense form.[125] In 14,10, the interrogative indicative with the negation οὐ πιστεύεις expects an affirmative answer. The condition in 14,11b is a first class condition to persuade. In 14,13, ὅ τι ἂν with the subjunctive can be translated as "whatever".[126] In 14,14, ἐάν with the subjunctive αἰτήσητε in the protasis is a future condition.

2.2.4 Translation

The text is divided and translated according to the structure and the syntactical analysis given above.

Command to Believe (v. 1)
¹"Stop letting your hearts be distressed; keep on believing in God, and keep on believing in me".[127]

Jesus' Going and Coming Again (vv. 2–3)
²"In my Father's house there are many dwelling places. But if it were not so, would I have told you that I am going to prepare a place for you? ³And after I go and prepare a place for you, I will come again and take you to myself, so that where I am, there you may be also".

Jesus as the Way to the Father (vv. 4–6)
⁴ "And where I am going you know the way". ⁵Thomas said to him, "Lord, we do not know where you are going. How are we able to know the way?"

---

[122] Wallace, *Greek Grammar Beyond the Basics*, 692.

[123] Cf. Young, *Intermediate New Testament Greek*, 111.

[124] M. Zerwick, *Biblical Greek. Illustrated by Examples* (SPIB 114; Rome 1963), §285.

[125] Cf. BDF, 167 (§321).

[126] Zerwick, *A Grammatical Analysis*, 330.

[127] Μή with the present imperative ταρασσέσθω and the present imperative πιστεύετε may allow us this translation. Beasley-Murray, *John*, 241, translates v. 1 as, "Do not let your hearts continually be in turmoil; keep on believing in God, and keep on believing in me".

⁶Jesus said to him, "I am the way and the truth and the life. No one comes to the Father except through me".

Jesus' Oneness with the Father (vv. 7–11)

⁷"If you know me, you will also know my Father. And from now onward you know him and have seen him". ⁸Philip said to him, "Lord, show us the Father. And that is enough for us". ⁹Jesus said to him, "I have been with you so much time, and have you not known me, Philip? The one who has seen me has seen the Father. How do you say, 'Show us the Father'? ¹⁰Do you not believe that I am in the Father and the Father is in me? The words which I speak to you I do not speak to you from myself, but the Father who abides in me does his works. ¹¹Believe me that I am in the Father and the Father is in me. Otherwise, believe on account of the works themselves".

Fruits of Belief in Jesus' Oneness with the Father (vv. 12–14)

¹²"Truly, truly, I say to you, the one who believes in me will also do the works which I do, and he will do greater than these because I am going to the Father. ¹³I will do whatever you ask in my name, so that the Father may be glorified in the Son. ¹⁴If you ask me anything in my name, I will do it".

2.2.5 Interpretation: The Command to Believe and Jesus' Journey to the Father

2.2.5.1 Command to Believe (v. 1)

John 14 presents the disciples in an atmosphere of sorrow, uncertainty and despair. In order to depict the mental state of the disciples, the evangelist uses the verb ταράσσω along with the noun καρδία.[128] John uses the verb ταράσσω 6 times, but outside of his Gospel, it is not common (Acts with 3x has the next most frequent use).[129] The verb is used literally to refer to the "troubling" of the waters of Bethesda in 5,7 and figuratively to depict the mental agony of Jesus in 11,33; 12,27; 13,21 and to strengthen the courage of the disciples in 14,1.27 (cf. Tob 12,16). Jesus' predictions of the betrayal of Judas, his imminent departure, and of the denial of Peter lead his disciples into deep sorrow. The only remedy to their troubled hearts is belief in God and in Jesus. Hence, Jesus requests the disciples to believe in God and in him. These two imperatives also indicate the Christological core of Jesus' minis-

---

[128] In the New Testament, καρδία is more importantly used as the seat of feelings, emotions, desires, passions, understanding and will. In this context, the emotional aspect is highlighted. See BDAG, 509; J. Behm, "καρδία", *TDNT*, III, 611–612.

[129] The verb ταράσσω can mean literally "to shake together" or "to stir up" and figuratively "to disturb" or "to throw into confusion". See BDAG, 990–991. According to C. Spicq, "ταράσσω", *TLNT*, III, 374, the verb ταράσσω usually expresses simple uneasiness mixed with fear with respect to persons.

try, the unity of Jesus with the Father (10,30) and provide the theological basis for the exhortation.[130]

Johannine predilection for πιστεύω with the preposition εἰς is worth noting. This usage is found 36x in the Fourth Gospel, 3x in 1 John and 8x elsewhere in the New Testament.[131] The verb πιστεύω with the preposition εἰς here has the meaning of "to believe in", "to entrust oneself to an entity in complete confidence", "to trust" (cf. Is 7,9; 28,16) and implies a total commitment to the one who is trusted.[132] It is used in John exclusively for belief in a person: in the Father (2x), in Jesus (31x) and in the name of Jesus (4x).[133] Believing in Jesus is identical with believing in God (12,44; 14,1) just as knowing (14,7) and seeing (12,45; 14,9) Jesus is identical with knowing and seeing God. John refers in 14,1 to one's faith in Jesus and God at the same time, with the implication that trust in God is shaken if belief in Jesus is not maintained.[134] Belief in Jesus is not something additional to belief in God because belief in the Father in any meaningful sense is impossible apart from belief in Jesus.[135] It will be much more difficult for the disciples to continue to believe in Jesus as the Messiah and the Son of God when he is dragged off to the courts, condemned by the rulers, nailed to a cross and mocked by the onlookers.[136]

---

[130] O'Day, *John*, 740.

[131] We do not find any real parallel for this usage in the secular Greek or in the LXX.

[132] BDAG, 817. Cf. O. Michel, "πίστις", *NIDNTT*, I, 594. It is to be noted that John never uses the noun πίστις. Instead, he prefers the verb πιστεύω. Among its 241 occurrences in the New Testament, a great number of them (98x) occur in John's Gospel. The evangelist's preference for πιστεύω suggests that he is not thinking of faith as an internal disposition but as an active commitment. However, this is not an emotional commitment. It entails a willingness to respond to God's demands as they are presented by and in Jesus (cf. 1 John 3,23). In other words, it is an acceptance of Jesus and of all that he claims to be and a dedication of one's life to him. See Brown, *John*, I, 512–513.

[133] According to BDAG, 817, "God and Christ are the objects of this kind of faith that relies on their power and nearness to help, in addition to being convinced that their revelation or disclosures are true".

[134] Schnackenburg, *John*, III, 59. E. A. Abbott, *Johannine Vocabulary. A Comparison of the Words of the Fourth Gospel with Those of the Three* (London 1905), 72, remarks that belief in the Father is inseparable from belief in the Son.

[135] Morris, *John*, 566. According to Carson, *The Farewell Discourse*, 18, the first-centuary Jews did not urge others to believe in them as they believed in God.

[136] Beasley-Murray, *John*, 249. Morris, *John* 567, views that it is one thing for the disciples to have faith in the God who acted in days of old, and it is another to have faith in the Jesus who stands before them, especially when he is even being betrayed, denied and abandoned by his followers and crucified by his enemies.

2.2.5.2 Jesus' Going and Coming Again (vv. 2–3)

a. The Father's House

Jesus consoles his disciples before his death with the promise that he is going to prepare a place for them in his Father's house.[137] The noun οἰκία has generally the literal sense of a structure used as a dwelling or a house (11,31; 12,3) and the figurative sense of household or family (4,53; 8,35; cf. Gen 24,38; 28,21; 46,31; Josh 2,13; Judg 6,15; 9,18; 1 Sam 22, 15).[138] Here it can have the meaning of household, family of God.[139] Behind the imagery of the Father's house, there is a Jewish tradition which identifies the heaven with God's dwelling place (Pss 2,4; 113,5–6; 123,1; Isa 66,1; cf. Luke 16,9).[140] Philo calls the heaven "paternal house".[141] The Father's "house" with its many dwellings reminds us of the heavenly Jerusalem, the city of God in Heb 11,16; 12,22 (cf. 6,20) and Rev 21,9–22,5.

The reference of ὁ οἶκος τοῦ πατρός μου in John 2,16 is to the Jerusalem temple. For John, Jesus is the new temple (2,19.21; cf. Rev 21,22). Just as the

---

[137] A somewhat similar promise could be noticed in Luke 22,29–30, given in the context of the Last Supper, "And I confer on you, just as my Father has conferred on me, a kingdom, so that you may eat and drink at my table in my kingdom, and you will sit on thrones judging the twelve tribes of Israel". The Hebrew verb ישׁע (cf. Arab. *wasi'a*) originally means "to be roomy, broad", especially in contrast to oppression in the spatial sense of "narrowness", "choking" or "constricting". Since oppression is viewed as a kind of spatial hemming in or imprisonment, so rescue from it is a moving out into the open. Hence, the hiphil form of ישׁע means "to make it spacious" for one who is constricted. This takes place through the saving intervention of a third party in favour of the oppressed and in opposition to his oppressor (see G. Fohrer, "σῴζω" *TDNT*, VII, 973). Johannine language of dwelling places and the preparation of a place in 14,2–3 reflect this aspect of the meaning of the verb ישׁע.

[138] BDAG, 695. Cf. LSJ, 1203.

[139] Back, *Gott als Vater der Jünger*, 49. Back thinks that the Johannine use of the metaphor οἰκία in 14,2 is inspired by the idea of family relationship. Jesus' journey to the Father is intended to create a family relationship between the disciples and God. A parallel to παραλαμβάνω in 14,3 can be found in 19,27. Jesus directly creates a family relationship between his mother and the beloved disciple before his death on the cross. When the beloved disciple receives the mother of Jesus into his own home (εἰς τὰ ἴδια), he carries out what Jesus has demanded. See also J. G. van der Watt, *Family of the King: Dynamics of Metaphor in the Gospel According to John* (BIS 47; Leiden 2000), 347. Jesus' journey to the Father gives the believers a new status as the children of God in the Father's house (cf. 8,35; 20,17).

[140] According to Beutler, *Do not Be Afraid*, 26–47, behind John 14,1–9 there is an early Christian tradition, which interprets the passion of Jesus in the light of Ps 42/43. For a criticism of his views, see pp. 194–195.

[141] Philo, *Somn.*, I.256. But Philo uses the imagery of the father's house in relation to the soul's long and profitless wandering in this foreign world, and it is not same as the Johannine thought. See Fischer, *Wohnungen*, 192.

earthly temple was an asylum for fugitives, so also the Father's house has places of rest for the afflicted disciples.[142] To be in the Father's house can mean to be in Jesus and the Father (17,21; Rev 21,22). The reference to the Father's house can be read in the context of the mutual indwelling of God and Jesus, a form of "residence" that has been stressed in the other parts of the Gospel (e.g., 1,1; 1,18; 14,23).[143] Hence, οἰκία indicates an inner spiritual space, where Jesus himself already abides as the Son in a close union with the Father and which is to be shared by all believers in union with Jesus later.[144]

b. Dwelling Place

The noun μονή occurs only twice in the New Testament, and both occurrences are found in John's Gospel. It has the meaning of "staying" and "a place in which one stays", namely "dwelling place", "room" or "abode".[145] It seems better to understand μονή here as a permanent dwelling place or abode in relationship to the cognate verb μένειν, which plays a significant role in John and is also used with reference to staying or remaining with Jesus (1,39; 2,12; 4,40; 11,54).[146] In the Old Testament, God's dwelling among his people is narrated in the context of the cult (Ex 25,8; 29,45; Lev 26,11) and is seen as a promise for the last time (Ezek 37,26f.; Zech 2,14; cf. Rev 21,3.22f.). In the New Testament, parallel imageries to μονή are found in the forms of the "eternal tents" (αἰώνιαι σκηναί) in Luke 16,9 and of the places "to sit at the right hand and the left of Jesus in his glory", prepared by the Father in Mark 10,37–40. The closest apocryphal parallels to μονή can be found in apocalyptic texts like 1 Enoch. 1 En. 39,4 speaks of "the dwelling places of the holy and the resting places of the just", which are situated in the extremities of the heavens (also see 41,2; 71,16).[147]

---

[142] O. Michel, "οἰκία", *TDNT*, V, 132.

[143] A variant reading found in patristic writings for "in my Father's house" is "with my Father". See M.-E. Boismard, "Critique textuelle et citations patristiques", *RB* 57 (1950), 388–391. Even though this variant reading is negligible, it may support the idea of indwelling in the chapter.

[144] McCaffrey, *The House*, 246.

[145] BDAG, 658.

[146] In the LXX (1 Macc 7,38 πεσέτωσαν ἐν ῥομφαίᾳ μνήσθητι τῶν δυσφημιῶν αὐτῶν καὶ μὴ δῷς αὐτοῖς μονήν), it is confirmed that μονή is used to refer to a permanent abiding or dwelling place. In the Vulgata, *mansiones* also refer to the dwelling places. The noun *mansio* comes from the verb *manere* which means "to dwell". Originally, the term did not have the connotation of a palatial house. F. Hauck, "μονή", *TDNT*, IV, 580, opines, "The word seems to be deliberately chosen to express the fact that our earthly state is transitory and provisional compared with eternal and blessed being with God". For a study of the religious-historical background of the concept μονή, see Fischer, *Wohnungen*, 115.

[147] There are good and bad dwellings mentioned in the Slavonic Book of Enoch for the situation at the end of time (see 2 En. 61,2; cf. 1 En. 39,4; 2 Esd 7,80; T. Ab. 20,14; Jos. Asen. 8,11). In the *Mandean Liturgy* (139,9ff), the gnostic redeemer takes souls to their

In the Gospel of John, location is a symbol of relationship (1,18; 8,35–36). The verb μένειν is used to describe the mutuality and reciprocity of the relationship of Jesus with his Father (14,10; 15,10). To "remain" (μένειν) with Jesus (15,4–10) is a great virtue and requirement for Christian discipleship. His return to the Father will enable his disciples to join in the relationship that Jesus shares with his Father. Jesus' departure is intended to provide the disciples with a permanent possibility of an abiding communion with his Father. Johannine μονή refers to the permanence, indestructibility and continuation of union with God, which begins here on earth through the immanence of God in the believers.[148] Hence, the "many dwelling places in my Father's house" can be parabolically interpreted as the possibilities for permanent union with the Father in and through Jesus. All those who abide in him now will be able to abide in him in the future.

c. Going to Prepare a Place

In the New Testament, πορεύομαι is used to refer to one's death (Luke 22,22; Acts 1,25). John also uses this verb to refer to Jesus' death figuratively as "going away" (14,2–3; 16,7) and as "going to the Father" (14,12.28; 16,28; cf. Acts 1,10–11). It is used along with the preposition πρός to indicate a journey with a specific point of departure or destination.[149] In 14,2, the infinitive ἑτοιμάσαι suggests the purpose of going. The term ἑτοιμάζω, which occurs 40 times in the New Testament, is found in John only twice (14,2–3). It has the meaning of "to cause to be ready, put/keep in readiness, prepare".[150] It is used in the New Testament to refer to the preparation of something or someone. The language of "preparing" and "way" in John 14,2–6 may remind the reader of Isa 40,3, which the evangelist cites in 1,23 with alteration.[151] It is by going the way of cross, death and resurrection that Jesus prepares a place for the believers and admits them into heavenly life (cf. Heb 11,16).

---

heavenly dwellings. The original home of the souls is often called "the house of life" or "the house of fulfilment". But it is difficult to establish a direct relationship between John 14,2 and gnostic literature. The dwelling places in John have only symbolic meanings in accordance with the views current at the time and do not necessarily have to coincide with the return of souls to their heavenly house, found in the apocryphal apocalyptic and gnostic literature. See Schnackenburg, *John*, III, 60–61. In 8,35 too, the evangelist uses the figurative language of "house" (οἰκία) and "to dwell" (μένειν) to refer to the Son's eternal dwelling (μένει εἰς τὸν αἰῶνα) in the house (ἐν τῇ οἰκίᾳ) and thus to his permanent relationship with the Father.

[148] Cf. F. Hauck, "μονή", *TDNT*, IV, 580.
[149] Cf. BDAG, 853.
[150] BDAG, 400–401.
[151] The influence of Isa 40,3 upon 14,2–6 and the reasons for the evangelist's alteration of the Isaianic quotation in 1,23 will be discussed later. See pp. 197–206.

The word τόπος refers to a place of habitation like a room.[152] In the New Testament, it has both literal (e.g., Matt 14,35; John 11,48; 2 Cor 2,14) and metaphorical senses (e.g., Luke 16,28; Acts 1,25). It has the metaphorical sense of "a favourable circumstance for doing something, a possibility, opening, occasion, opportunity or a chance" (e.g., Eph 4,27; Rom 12,19; Heb 12,17).[153] The term τόπος occurs 16 times in John. It is used in John mostly to refer to some kind of physical space (5,13; 6,10.23; 10,40; 11,6.30; 18,2; 19,13.17.20.41; 20,7.25), twice to the Jerusalem temple (4,20; 11,48; cf. Matt 24,15; Acts 6,13; 21,28) and twice to the heavenly or spiritual space (14,2.3). In Rev 12,8, τόπος is used for a place in heaven.

The purpose of Jesus' journey is to open up the possibility of dwelling in the Father's house or to make the Father's house accessible to all.[154] Jesus' death and resurrection offer his disciples the opportunity to be united with the Father. The goal of Jesus is also the goal of the believers, and his departure will make it possible for them to reach that goal.[155] The Father's house which is now inaccessible to the disciples (13,36) will become accessible to them after the preparation by Jesus. Jesus restores the right relationship with God and makes man at home with the Father.[156] If John the Baptist comes to "make straight" (εὐθύνω) the way of the Lord (John 1,23; cf. Isa 40,3), Jesus is the one who "prepares" (ἑτοιμάζω) the way to the Father by removing the obstacles on the way through his passion, death and resurrection.[157]

d. Coming Again

It is difficult to understand the meaning of v. 3, "And after I go and prepare a place for you, I will come again and take you to myself, so that where I am, there you may be also". The expression πάλιν ἔρχομαι can have various layers of meanings in John.[158] Firstly, it can refer to the Parousia of the end

---

[152] BDAG, 1011.

[153] See BDAG, 1012; LSJ, 1806.

[154] According to James McCaffrey, the new temple of the risen body of Jesus becomes the spiritual space where all believers can occupy eternal dwelling places in the Father's house. See McCaffrey, *The House*, 248.

[155] Schnackenburg, *John*, III, 59.

[156] Haenchen, *John*, II, 124. St. Augustine in his commentary on the Gospel of John (Tractate 68,2) says, "He is in a certain sense preparing the dwellings by preparing for them the dwellers". See P. Schaff (ed.), *A Select Bibliography of the Nicene and Post-Nicene Fathers of the Christian Church. St. Augustine: Homilies on the Gospel of John, Homilies on the First Epistle of John, Soliloquies* (Edinburgh 1887), VII, 323.

[157] The significance of the expression "prepare a place" will be further examined while discussing the background of the way in John 14,6. See pp. 197–206.

[158] For an examination of various interpretations by different authors, see Frey, *Eschatologie*, III, 148–153. According F. J. Moloney, *Glory Not Dishonor. Reading John 13–14* (Minneapolis 1998), 34 and McCaffrey, *The House*, 34–35, there is no need to resolve the

times (1 Thess 4,16–17; cf. John 21,22–23).[159] Secondly, it may allude to the coming of Jesus through his resurrection (cf. 14,18–19). The accounts of the resurrection appearances in John are introduced by the words ἔρχεται and ἦλθεν (20,19.26; 21,13). Thirdly, it can suggest the coming of Jesus at the hour of death of the believer (especially through martyrdom) to take him into heaven as it is indicated in Acts 7,55–60.[160] Fourthly, there is a view that it is a reference to Christ's coming in the person of the Holy Spirit (14,16–17; 26).[161] Finally, it may point out his coming together with the Father to make his dwelling (μονή) with those who love him (14,23).[162]

The language of Jesus' coming again and taking believers to be with him is that of early Christian imminent expectation. Hence, 14,3 appears to be a Johannine adaptation of the tradition reflected in 1 Thess 4,16–17 and Mk 13,24–27 (cf. Matt 24,30–31) about the expectation of the Parousia (cf. John 21,22–23).[163] It is more likely that traditional future eschatology and a more

---

tension regarding the "when" of Jesus' return mentioned in 14,3 and it is better to leave it open. According to Brown, *John*, II, 603, various predictions about Christ's coming and references to various indwellings in the farewell discourse are left side by side without an attempt at reconciling them. He thinks that these sayings are composed or rephrased at various stages in the history of Johannine eschatological thought and early sayings are reinterpreted in a way consonant with later thought.

[159] However, in the view of Thyen, *Johannesevangelium*, 620, "Wenn Jesus hier dem intimen Kreis seiner um ihn versammelten Jünger verheißt daß er wiederkommen und sie zu sich nehmen werde, damit sie da, wo er ist, ihre ewige Bleibe finden, so darf man diese Verheißung trotz ihrer fraglos apokalyptischen Metaphorik keinesfalls unmittelbar oder gar ausschließlich auf seine endzeitliche Parusie und das Gericht über Lebende und Tote beziehen".

[160] See K. Kundsin, "Die Wiederkunft Jesu in den Abschiedsreden des Johannesevangeliums", *ZNW* 33 (1934), 210–215. It is through death that Peter is asked to follow Jesus who is returning to the Father (13,36–37; 21,15–19). The idea that through death the Christians are taken to the Father's house is also reflected in 2 Cor 5,1. However, John 14,2–3 do not seem to speak of the individual destiny of the disciples but of the community in a collective sense. The plural expressions like μοναὶ πολλαί, τόπον ὑμῖν, παραλήμψομαι ὑμᾶς and ὑμεῖς ἦτε support this view. Cf. Frey, *Eschatologie*, III, 150.

[161] The return of Jesus does not refer to the coming of the Paraclete because the evangelist keeps up a distinction between Jesus/the Father and the Paraclete in vv. 16–17. What Jesus promises is that he will ask the Father to send "another Paraclete" to the disciples. See Schnelle, "Die Abschiedsreden", 69–70, n. 27; Frey, *Eschatologie*, III, 150. Moloney, *John*, 398, views that the reader is not yet informed about the gift of the Paraclete in v. 3.

[162] The structure of vv. 2–3, which is shaped by the traditional formula about the Parousia, may not allow this interpretation. The use of ἔρχομαι along with παραλήμψομαι indicates this fact. See Frey, *Eschatologie*, III, 152.

[163] See Zumstein, *Johannesevangelium*, 520–524; Frey, *Eschatologie*, III, 147. Holloway, "Left Behind", 23. Schnackenburg, *John*, III, 62, thinks that evangelist wanted to consider the universal early Christian expectation of the Parousia, but consciously reinterpreted it to apply to the presence of Christ and his spiritual coming after the resurrection (14,18–23). For Schnackenburg, παραλαμβάνειν is not a distinctive term for the Parousia,

realized version have been juxtaposed in John 14 as it is found elsewhere in the Gospel.[164] The idea of realized eschatology goes along with Jesus' promise of the Paraclete (14,15–17; 16,7) and the indwelling of the Trinitarian God (πρὸς αὐτὸν ἐλευσόμεθα καὶ μονὴν παρ' αὐτῷ ποιησόμεθα) here on earth (14,23). Thus, the ideas of a heavenly dwelling with Jesus and of earthly divine indwelling go side by side in John 14. The Johannine expression "where I am there you may be also" may refer to the union of the disciples with Jesus (12,26; 17,24). Jesus' journey is intended to prepare for them the universal and permanent possibility of an everlasting communion with the Father.[165]

2.2.5.3 Jesus as the Way to the Father (vv. 4–6)

In 14,4, when Jesus tells the disciples that they "know" the way he is going, there is a reference to his previous statements of his imminent death (e.g., 12,23–25.32–33) and to the preceding foot-washing event, where the way to go is prefigured (13,4–5) and its meaning is explained (13,6–20). Thomas has not understood from foot-washing the way Jesus will be going. He is presented in the Gospel as a loyal and courageous disciple but endowed with a lack

---

but the evangelist employs it since he has previously used the image of a house and the verb can also mean "to receive into a house" in accordance with John 1,11. According to Schnackenburg, "to be where Jesus is" is a Johannine expression for the union of the disciples with Jesus (cf. 12,26; 17,24), and the reality of "I will take you to myself" begins after Easter in the existence of the believers, in so far as that existence is an experience of communion with Jesus in the present, but it is completed only after death or the Parousia. If Jesus' "coming again" primarily refers to his coming after Easter, then "taking to himself" may imply the restoration of the personal communion which will be completed in heaven. See Schnackenburg, *John*, III, 63, 410, n. 49.

[164] We can notice throughout the Gospel that John maintains the notions of futuristic (5,28; 6,39–40.44.54; 12,48) and realized eschatology (4,23; 5,25; 11,24–26) side by side. There is eschatological judgment occurring in the immediate encounter of humans with Jesus (e.g., 3,19; 9,39) and also a judgment in the future – on "the last day" (12,48). "Eternal life" is not only an immediate experience of the believer (3,36; 5,24; 8,51) but also a future hope (12,25). On the one hand, there is the possibility that the dead will "now" hear the voice of the Son of God and live (5,24–25). On the other hand, there is the resurrection of the dead on the last day (5,28–29; 6,39–40.44.54). It seems that the evangelist purposefully intended the juxtaposition of the future and present eschatology in a kind of paradoxical manner. J. Beutler, *Das Johannesevangelium. Kommentar* (Freiburg 2013), 403, thinks that the evangelist has consciously placed both future and present eschatology in John 14 to complement each other. Scholtissek, *In ihm Sein und Bleiben*, 267, remarks, "Die Metaphorik von der 'Aufnahme in das Haus' wird in 14,2–3 futurisch-eschatologisch und in 14,23 präsentisch-eschatologisch entfaltet". In the view of X. Léon-Dufour, *Lecture de l'Évangile selon Jean. Les adieux du Seigneur: Chapitres 13–17* (Paris 1993), III, 94, "Il convient, ... de lire le texte comme intégrant à la fois l'existence postpascale et le futur ultime de la communauté".

[165] Moloney, *John*, 394.

of understanding and doubts (cf. 11,16; 20,24). In 11,16, he says, "Let us also go, that we may die with him". But he cannot understand the death of Jesus as a salvific journey to the Father for the disciples. He only regards it as a termination of existence. Just as the Jews of 7,3; 8,22, Thomas cannot understand where Jesus is going. His question echoes that of Peter in 13,36 and reflects a failure to grasp the implications of 14,2–3, where Jesus has just spelled out his destination. However, the plural form "we do not know" indicates that he is a representative of his fellow disciples. His question shows that he interprets Jesus' words in a literal way. It is naturally difficult to think of a way without any idea of the destination. He seems to want to know precisely where Jesus is going and where the Father's house is located. Above all, his question functions as a literary means to provide Jesus with an opportunity to articulate precisely the goal of his journey and the way to it. Even though there is apparently no attempt to answer Thomas' first difficulty regarding the destination of Jesus' journey ("Lord, we do not know where you are going"), Jesus' statement in 14,6b implies that the Father is the destination of his journey.

The revelatory formula ἐγώ εἰμι with three predicates occurs only here in John. The repeated use of the verbs of "going" (πορεύομαι vv. 2.3; ὑπάγω vv. 4.5)[166] and "coming" (ἔρχομαι vv. 3.6), the other two occurrences of ὁδός in the immediate context (vv. 4.5) and the statement in v. 6b "no one comes (goes) to the Father except through me" point out the fact that the way is the primary focus in this unit (14,4–6). Jesus' saying in v. 6 has two parts, a positive statement (v. 6a) and a negative one (v. 6b). The negative part clarifies the focus of the positive one. The issue is how one comes to the Father. Jesus is the only way to the Father (cf. John 10,9; Acts 4,12; 1 Tim 2,5; Heb 9,15).[167] In other words, the Father is the goal to which the way leads.[168]

Jesus identifies himself with a concrete reality and with two abstract realities in 14,6a. The "way" is an unusual metaphor to apply to a person. Moreover, there is a difficulty in explaining the interrelation among the three nouns, namely "the way and the truth and the life".[169] Among these three concepts, the emphasis is placed entirely on ἡ ὁδός because (καὶ) ἡ ἀλήθεια καὶ ἡ ζωή in spite of their coordination are not literally involved in the context (13,1–14,14). Jesus is the way for the believers to attain the many dwelling-

---

[166] Fischer thinks that there is a difference between ὑπάγω and πορεύομαι. According to him, ὑπάγω indicates a separation, and πορεύομαι points out a movement in the sense of "going there". See Fischer, *Wohnungen*, 75–84.

[167] The idea that the believers in Christ have direct access to God through Christ is present throughout the New Testament. E.g., Rom 5,2; Eph 2,18; Heb 4,16.

[168] The possible literary background for the claim in John 14,6 is discussed at length in chapter IV and the important motifs in 14,6 are studied in detail in chapters V, VI.

[169] We will discuss in detail the interrelation between way, truth and life after an examination of John's usage of truth and life in the Gospel. See pp. 255–260.

places in the Father's house.[170] His mission has as its purpose to bear witness to the truth (18,37) and to bring life (10,10). He so mediates God's truth and God's life that he is the very way to God.[171]

After the Christological statement in v. 6a, a soteriological one follows in v. 6b.[172] Jesus alone reveals the Father (1,18; 3,13; 10,30–38; 12,45; 14,9; cf. Col 1,15.19; 2,9; Heb 1,3). Anyone who rejects Jesus cannot legitimately claim to know the Father (5,23; 8,42–45; 15,23; 1 John 2,23; 2 John 9; cf. Matt 11,27). The Christological claim of vv. 6b–7 is first introduced in the concluding affirmation of the prologue (1,18) and sounds throughout Jesus' discourses (e.g., 5,19–29; 7,28–29; 8,24–29.54–58; 10,30.34–38; 12,44–45).[173] As the Son who exists and acts in the closest association with the Father, he must make the full and exclusive claim to be the only way to the Father.[174] The preposition διά in 14,6b probably marks the agentship (cf. 1,3.10.17; 1 John 4,9). It also reminds the reader of Jesus' identification of himself with the "gate" in 10,7.9. In Jesus' reply to Thomas, there is a change of topic. The topic is no longer the way of Jesus but the way of the disciples to the Father. The change of access from "the Father's house" in 14,2–3 to "the Father himself" in 14,6 should be seen as a climax and a precision of the promise of 14,2–3.[175]

2.2.5.4 Jesus' Oneness with the Father (vv. 7–11)

In 14,7–11, the significance of the Christological-soteriological statement of v. 6 is explained in terms of Jesus' relationship with the Father, especially his oneness with the Father.[176] These verses give the reasons for Jesus' absolute claim in the previous verse, "No one comes to the Father except through me" (14,6b). They reveal the fact that the way and the goal meet in Jesus. V. 7 emphasizes the realized eschatology of John. It is a positive explanation of v. 6b, and it aims to emphasize what is said in v. 6b. John speaks of Jesus' mediation of knowledge of the Father (cf. 8,19; 10,15.38) and of his mediation of the vision of the Father (cf. 1,18; 5,37–8; 6,46; 8,38). The term γινώσκω is

---

[170] Carson *John*, 491.

[171] Carson, *John*, 491. Cf. De la Potterie, "Je suis la Voie", 938. See also pp. 232, 252 for a discussion on Jesus' identification with truth and life respectively.

[172] Back, *Gott als Vater der Jünger*, 60, writes, "Auf die christologisch akzentuierte Äußerung des Thomas gibt Jesus in Joh 14,6 eine soteriologisch ausgerichtete Antwort". Cf. Zumstein, *Saint Jean 13–21*, 65.

[173] Thyen, *Johannesevangelium*, 624–625, thinks that 14,6 is to be understood in relation to 6,44, "No one can come to me unless drawn by the Father who sent me" and also to 5,23; 15,23.

[174] Schnackenburg, *John*, II, 88.

[175] Back, *Gott als Vater der Jünger*, 60, n. 109.

[176] Dettwiler, *Gegenwart*, 160, considers vv. 7–11 as "ein konzentriertes Kompendium joh Theologie".

used in the Old Testament sense of intimate personal relationship (cf. Gen 4,1; Jer 1,5), not of cognitive or external knowledge.[177] John employs γινώσκω in a theological sense, parallel to "believe" or "love God" or "see God", thereby giving this gnostic term an Old Testament and Christian meaning.[178] Because of his oneness with the Father (10,30), the knowledge of Jesus is knowledge of the Father (cf. Luke 10,22).

The contracted pair of words ἀπ' ἄρτι in 14,7 could be read as one word, namely as ἀπαρτί with the meaning "certainly", since there were usually no spaces between words in the early uncial manuscripts.[179] It is, however, difficult to think that this is what Jesus here means because the disciples are full of ignorance, misunderstanding and doubts. It is better to understand this expression in the light of the schema of Johannine eschatology, which is begun in the present and oriented towards the future. In agreement with v. 9, v. 7b should be taken as a statement of realized eschatology (cf. 4,23; 5,25; 11,24–26). The revelation of the Father in and through the person of Jesus already took place during his ministry. But it will be much more brilliantly revealed at the hour of his death and resurrection.

Philip's question in v. 8 suggests that the disciples still do not understand the revelation in Jesus sufficiently. Philip seems to think of a direct access to the Father. In John's Gospel, δείκνυμι has the meaning of "to reveal", "to disclose" and it is used for the revelation of the Father (cf. 5,20; 10,32).[180] Philip's demand is a rhetorical device that enables Jesus to affirm his oneness with the Father and his unique role as the revelation of the Father.[181] His request reveals ironically his dissatisfaction despite his experience of the miracles of Jesus (cf. 6,7).[182] It reminds us of Moses' request, "Show me your glory, I pray" (Exod 33,18). In Judaism, to look upon the face of God would be deadly for any mortal being (Exod 33,20). John has reminded his readers early that "no one has ever seen God" (1,18).

Jesus' statement "the one who has seen me has seen the Father" (14,9) is a highly Christological statement. For John, to see Jesus is to see God (1,14–

---

[177] In the Old Testament, people are frequently exhorted to "know God" (e.g., Pss 46,10; 100,3). The verb "know" in the sense of "acknowledge" was part of Near Eastern covenantal language (Hos 13,4; Jer 24,7; 31,34). See Brown, *John*, II, 631. After Jesus' hour of glorification, Thomas, representing the disciples, will acknowledge him as "my Lord and my God" (20,28).

[178] W. Schmithals, "γινώσκω", *EDNT*, I, 250.

[179] BDAG, 97. Beasley-Murray, *John*, 241–243, favours this reading.

[180] H. Schlier, "δείκνυμι", *TDNT*, II, 27.

[181] Moloney, *John*, 393.

[182] The verb ἀρκέω occurs only twice in John (6,7; 14,8). In both occasions, it is uttered by Philipp. He shows his dissatisfaction with Jesus' suggestion to buy the bread for the people (6,5–7). The irony is that he cannot recognize the true identity of Jesus even after the experience of the miracle in 6,1–13.

18; 5,24; 12,44–45; cf. 2 Cor 4,4; Col 1,15; Heb 1,3).[183] Jesus is the place where the Father is to be seen and known. The reference is here not merely to sensual or intellectual perception but to a further seeing, i.e., the decision which is taken in the encounter with Jesus and is a turning to faith.[184] It is a spiritual comprehension (cf. 6,46; 12,45). For John, seeing and believing are closely interrelated. Johannine seeing implies a submission in faith to the revelation of God in Jesus Christ.[185] To see is to believe and to see oneself confronted by the message of revelation.[186] Jesus is the perfect revelation of the invisible Father. Therefore, no one who rejects Jesus can claim to know the Father (cf. 1 John 5,9–12). The way to see the Father is to see Jesus. The vision of Jesus is the vision of the Father as well. Hence, for John there is no possibility of a direct vision of the Father unmediated by Jesus (1,18; 5,37; 6,46). Jesus is the only one who has seen the Father, and in Jesus the believer is able to see the Father (6,46).

Jesus' correction of Philip warns the disciples not to look for any visionary experience of God or any form of direct union with God while being on earth, but to be satisfied with their belief in Jesus and his word.[187] The failure to see the Father in Jesus is the failure to know Jesus. The truth is that the disciples have not yet known Jesus himself sufficiently well. They have not understood that in Jesus God has made himself known. Their knowledge of him is not perfect. Jesus is to be seen with the eyes of faith. Only through faith one can see the presence of the Father in Jesus. However, the disciples have not completely failed to know Jesus like the Jews in 8,19. It is only after Jesus' death and resurrection and the coming of the Holy Spirit (14,17.26; 15,26; 16,13–15) that the disciples will finally understand the revelation in Jesus (20,28). But the perfect vision of the Father is a matter of futuristic eschatology.

Jesus has already spoken about his unity with the Father and the mutual indwelling between them during his confrontations with the Jewish leaders (e.g., 5,18; 10,30.38). This thought is continued in 14,10–11, which show specifically that Jesus' words and works reveal his union with the Father. The sequence of thought in 14,10b–c has always been a puzzle for scholars. The motivation for the immediate shift from words to works is to be understood in the light of the Isaianic influence.[188] It is likely that the words of Jesus are

---

[183] According to M.-J. Lagrange, *Évangile selon Saint Jean* (Paris 1936), 376, to see the Father in the Son is to believe that the Son has the divine nature.

[184] W. Michaelis, "ὁράω", *TDNT*, V, 362. Brown, *John*, I, 502, views that ὁράω refers to the sight accompanied by real understanding (cf. 1,50.51; 3,11.32; 11,40; 14,7.9; 16,16; 19,35.37; 20,29). When the reader confronts Jesus in the Gospel, he is seeing the Father.

[185] W. Michaelis, "ὁράω", *TDNT*, V, 363.

[186] W. Michaelis, "ὁράω", *TDNT*, V, 361.

[187] Schnackenburg, *John*, III, 69.

[188] See p. 222.

part of the Father's works, which are wrought through Jesus. His works include both his miracles and his words. The whole ministry of Jesus, including his words and deeds, is called "the work" (τὸ ἔργον) given him by his Father to do (17,4). His work is always related to the will of the Father (4,34) and is consummated with his death on the cross (cf. 19,30). The plural form πιστεύετε in 14,11 indicates that Jesus addresses the disciples collectively. V. 1 and v. 11 form an *inclusio*. "Believe in me" implies a personal commitment, and "believe me" refers to the acceptance of the message.[189]

Jesus' oneness with the Father means that when Jesus speaks, it is the Father's words that one hears (3,34; 7,16–17; 8,26–28.38.47; 12,49–50; 14,24) and when Jesus acts, it is the Father's works that one sees (5,17–20.36; 9,3–4; 10,32.37–38; 17,4). Thus, it is in his words and works that his oneness with the Father is to be seen.[190] The faith which is generated by his works is not the highest type of faith. But it is better to believe on behalf of them than not to believe at all. Even though both words and works are equally revelatory from Jesus' point of view, for the public, the works have more confirmatory value than the words.[191] Jesus' words are sufficient for people to recognize him as the bringer of salvation, but his works are additional help to those who have only weak faith.[192]

2.2.5.5 Fruits of Belief in Jesus (vv. 12–14)

In 14,12–14, the focus moves beyond the question of Jesus' departure, destination and his unity with the Father to the disciples' future mission as a result of Jesus' glorification. These verses explain the reasons for the exhortation to believe, found in v. 11. V. 12 serves as a transition from the topic of belief (vv. 10–11) to the topic of getting favours from the Father in Jesus' name (vv.

---

[189] Brown, *John*, II, 513.

[190] Köstenberger, *John*, 431, claims that the unity here clearly implies ontological unity (unity of being); but the emphasis is on functional unity, that is, the way in which the Father is revealed in Jesus' words and works (cf. 10,38). Brown, *John*, II, 632, opines that the motif of Jesus' oneness with the Father refers to his mission to human beings and has only secondary metaphysical implications about life within the Godhead. Schnackenburg, *John*, III, 69, thinks that this reciprocal formula of immanence is a linguistic way of describing the complete unity between Jesus and the Father. Scholtissek, *In ihm Sein und Bleiben*, 256, comments, "Das tertium comparationis der reziproken Relation ist nicht die Identität der Subjekte, sondern ihre durch ἐν angezeigte wechselseitige Immanenz. Die Immanenz hebt die Unterschiedenheit beider Subjekte, beider Personen, nicht auf, sondern begründet und charakterisiert ihre Unterschiedenheit in aller denkbar intensiven Bezogenheit: Gerade als der im Vater Immanente spricht der Sohn die Worte des Vaters (v. 10de); gerade weil der Vater in ihm 'bleibt' (v. 10f), wirkt der Vater 'seine Werke' durch den Sohn".

[191] Brown, *John*, II, 622.

[192] Schnackenburg, *John*, III, 70.

2. Analysis of the Near and Immediate Context (13,1–14,31)   169

13–14).[193] The participial phrase ὁ πιστεύων embraces all believers and is not restricted to the group of the disciples. Jesus demonstrates to them the benefits of belief in him on account of his oneness with the Father. Throughout vv. 12–14 the future tense is used. Hence, the period in view is the post-resurrectional period, the post-Easter era of the Church.

There are two promises for those who believe.[194] Firstly, the believers will do the kind of works that Jesus did and even greater ones. Secondly, they will be able to make requests in Jesus' name and their requests will be answered. The idea that the disciples are capable of performing miraculous deeds is found in many New Testament writings (e.g., Mark 16,17–18; Matt 21,21). They have the power to heal (Acts 3,6; 9,34), to take life (Acts 5,1–11) and to give life (Acts 9,40). However, the reference to "greater works" does not mean that the believers will perform more astonishing miracles than those of Jesus. The contrast here is not ultimately between Jesus' works and his disciples' works but between the works of Jesus in his limited circumstances of earthly ministry and the works that the risen Jesus will be doing through his disciples in the post-Easter situation.[195] It is the same Jesus who will be continuing his ministry by doing "greater works" through his disciples after his death and resurrection.[196] The repeated use of ποιήσω ("I will do") in vv. 13–14 makes clear that it is Jesus who will be at work in the mission of his disciples after his exaltation. The works of the disciples are the works of the risen Jesus through the Holy Spirit. The ministry of the disciples will be based on

---

[193] According to S. H. Levinsohn, *Discourse Features of New Testament Greek* (Dallas ²2001), 266, when ὅτι does not follow ἀμὴν ἀμὴν λέγω ὑμῖν/σοι, a new point is developed. Lincoln, *John*, 392, remarks that the ἀμὴν ἀμὴν formula signals a saying from the tradition (cf. Mark 11,22–23; Matt 21,21).

[194] Schnackenburg, *John*, III, 70–71, thinks that the promise of the Paraclete should also be included among these promises because it is also linked to them in content. He also notices the tradition of Mark 11,23–24 and Matt 21,21–22 in John 14,12–14.

[195] Carson, *John*, 497; Beasley-Murray, *John*, 255. The disciples' works will be greater because of the geographical scope of the Gentile mission and the work of the Spirit. They will not have the geographical and temporal limitations of the historical Jesus. Jesus' deeds were restricted to a particular place and a specific time. But when he goes to the Father, his help will be available to all the believers in all parts of the world and at all times. Moreover, the greater works can also refer to the greater number of converts from all over the world and the far-reaching spiritual effects of the apostolic ministry. See Bernard, *John*, II, 543; Morris, *John*, 574; Newman and Nida, *John*, 462. G. D. Fee, "John 14,8–17", *Interpretation* 43 (1989), 173–174, remarks that John is referring to the ongoing activity of the disciples under the guidance of the Paraclete since he will not write "Acts of the Apostles".

[196] Dettwiler, *Gegenwart*, 160, writes, "Die Verheißung der Gebetserhörung in vv. 13.14 macht klar dass letztlich nicht die Jünger sondern der erhöhte Jesus Subjekt dieses nachösterlichen Offenbarungswirkens ist". For B. F. Westcott, *The Gospel According to St. John. Introduction and Notes on the Authorized Version* (Cambridge 1881), 204, the "greater works" are also the works of Christ being performed by those who believe in him.

Jesus' completed salvific work (12,24; 15,13; 19,30), and it belongs to a more advanced stage in God's economy of salvation (cf. Matt 11,11).[197]

Even though, for John, the emphasis may be on the eschatological nature of the "greater works" (cf. 5,20), their miraculous character cannot be disregarded.[198] The immediate context of v. 12 suggests two reasons why the believers' works will be greater. Firstly, the greatness of the works depends on their performance "in Jesus' name" after his departure (vv. 13–14). Secondly, Jesus' return to the Father through his death and resurrection will facilitate the coming of the Holy Spirit (14,16–17.26; 15,26; 16,13; 20,22; cf. 7,39; Acts 1,5) to indwell believers (14,17; cf. Rom 8,9–11) and to empower them for ministry (20,23; cf. Acts 1,8; 1 Cor 12,4–11). The lives of the disciples will be the continuation of Jesus' life in this world.

The sayings in 14,13–14 have many parallels in vocabulary and pattern in other parts of the New Testament (Mark 11,24; Matt 7,7–8; 18,19; 21,22; Luke 11,9–10; 1 John 3,21–22; 5,14–15).[199] In v. 13, it is not said that to whom the prayer is addressed. But in v. 14 the prayer is addressed to the Son, and in 15,16; 16,23 τὸν πατέρα is the object of prayer.[200] According to Johannine perspective, this difference is not very significant. The prayer addressed to the Father is also a prayer addressed to the Son because of the intimate union between the Father and the Son (10,30). Since Jesus is the way to the Father (14,6), the prayers to the Father are to be addressed through Jesus. The expression ἐν τῷ ὀνόματί μου occurs 7 times in John and is found only in the farewell discourse (14,13.14.26; 15,16; 16,23.24.26). It is usually understood

---

[197] Köstenberger, *John*, 433. Carson, *The Farewell Discourse*, 42, observes that the disciples' works are greater because they participate in the newer and greater phase of redemptive history after the completion of Jesus' earthly work. C. Dietzfelbinger, "Die größeren Werke (Joh 14,12f)", *NTS* 35 (1989), 27, views that the promise of "greater works" invites John's community to look not only backward but also to the present, in which Christ continues to be active through his presence by the Paraclete and his proclaimed word.

[198] Brown, *John*, II, 633, stresses the eschatological nature of "the greater works".

[199] Brown, *John*, II, 635, maintains that some differences between John and the Synoptics may be attributable to various attempts to translate original Aramaic sayings into Greek. C. H. Dodd, *Historical Tradition in the Fourth Gospel* (Cambridge 1963), 349–52, views that John and the Synoptics preserve independent echoes of older sayings. Lincoln, *John*, 392, notices that unlike in the Synoptic Gospels, the Johannine Jesus gives no instruction on prayer to his disciples during his public ministry. All teachings on prayer are clustered in the farewell discourse indicating that prayer will be important for the disciples in the period after his departure.

[200] According to Bernard, *John*, II, 543–544, the difference between δώσει ("he will give") of 16,23 and ποιήσω ("I will do") of 14,13 is the difference between the Jewish and the Christian doctrine of prayer.

2. Analysis of the Near and Immediate Context (13,1–14,31) 171

as "in union with Jesus".²⁰¹ In accordance with this general meaning of ἐν τῷ ὀνόματί μου in the larger context of the Gospel, it may imply that the disciples, by uniting themselves with Jesus, will do the same works that Jesus performs.²⁰² Their request "in Jesus' name" will be granted because of Jesus' loving intimacy with his Father. The requests of the disciples, however, should be of such a nature that when they are granted, the Father is glorified in the Son (14,13; cf. 17,4). The goal of Jesus' mission on earth is the glorification of the Father (7,18; 11,4; 12,28; 13,31–32; 17,1). The presence and mission of Jesus will be continued and the Father will be glorified even after Jesus' departure when the disciples pray "in his name".

2.3 The Following Near Context (vv. 15–31)

2.3.1 The Command to Love and Trinitarian God's Journey to the Believers (vv. 15–24)

The motif of love binds vv. 15–24 together. The verb ἀγαπάω occurs 8 times in these verses. If Jesus is an object of belief in vv. 1–14, he is an object of love in vv. 15–24. In these verses, the fruits of love are described in terms of the coming and indwelling of the Trinitarian God in the believers. The conditions for the indwelling of the Trinity are loving Jesus and keeping his commandments. Loving God and keeping his commandments are the conditions for God's promises in the Old Testament covenant theology.²⁰³ Jesus' promises in vv. 15–24 thus remind the reader of God's promises in Jer 31 and Ezek 36–37 in the forms of bestowing new hearts, the gift of the Spirit and the dwelling of God in his people. The conditional sentence in v. 15 has the semantic force of a mitigated command.²⁰⁴ It functions as the main exhortation in this unit, just as the command to believe in v. 1 of the previous unit. The motifs of the coming of the three persons of Trinity and of loving Jesus and keeping his commandments/word in vv. 21.24 provide the signals to divide vv. 16–24 into three subunits, vv. 16–17; vv. 18–21; vv. 22–24.

---

[201] Brown, *John*, II, 622. Morris, *John*, 646, explains prayer "in Jesus' name" thus, "It means that prayer is to be in accordance with all that the name stands for. It is prayer proceeding from faith in Christ, prayer that gives expression to a unity with all that Christ stands for, prayer which seeks to set forward Christ Himself".

[202] Since the "greater works" can have a miraculous element within it and the expression ἐν τῷ ὀνόματί μου in vv. 13–14 is closely related to the "greater works" in v. 12, ἐν τῷ ὀνόματί μου may have in this particular context (vv. 13–14) the sense of invoking the name of Jesus (cf. ἐν τῷ ὀνόματί μου in Mark 16,17). This aspect of ἐν τῷ ὀνόματί μου will be highlighted when we examine the exclusivism of 14,6 in its historical context. See p. 372.

[203] Beutler argues that the covenant theology of Deuteronomy forms the underlying layer for vv. 15–24. See Beutler, *Do not Be Afraid*, 52–78. Cf. Beutler, *Das Johannesevangelium*, 410.

[204] Kellum, *The Unity of Farewell Discourse*, 161.

2.3.1.1 The Command to Love (v. 15)

Parallel to the command to believe in Jesus in v. 1, there is a command to love him in v. 15. While the love of God is a frequent motif in both Testaments, the motif of the Christian's love of Jesus occurs only occasionally in the New Testament (cf. John 8,42; 16,27; 21,15–17; Matt 10,37; 1 Cor 16,22; Eph 6,24; 1 Pet 1,8).[205] The verb τηρέω is often used in John for keeping the words (8,51; 14,23.24; 15,20) and the commandments of Jesus (14,15.21; 15,10).[206] In contrast with the singular "new commandment" of 13,34, Jesus speaks of the plural "my commandments" in 14,15.21. The same alteration of plural and singular is also found in 15,10.12. The commandments of Jesus are not simply moral precepts, rather they involve a whole way of life in loving union with him.[207] A close parallel of 14,15 can be found in 1 John 5,3, "For the love of God is this, that we obey his commandments". The demand to keep Jesus' commandments in John is matched in 1 John by an insistence on observing God's commandments, which leads to God's indwelling within the believer (1 John 3,24; cf. 4,12–16).[208] The fruits of love are expressed in terms of the coming of the Father, the Son and the Spirit to the believers and their indwelling in them.

2.3.1.2 The Coming of the Paraclete/the Spirit of Truth (vv. 16–17)

John 14,16–17 constitutes the first of five Paraclete passages (14,16–17.26; 15,26–27; 16,7–11.12–14) in the farewell speech of Jesus.[209] We should not identify the coming of the Paraclete with that of Jesus.[210] The Paraclete is promised to those who love Jesus. There is a reciprocal relation between the gift of the Paraclete and the love of Jesus because the Paraclete will enable the believers to love Jesus and to keep his commandments, by reminding

---

[205] But the motif of belief in Jesus is a frequent one. Brown, *John*, II, 643, comments that the view that the Christian must love Jesus even as he loves the Father may be a facet of a gradual theological development in the realization of who Jesus is. He also notices that Jesus' demand to be loved is perfectly in harmony with the covenant atmosphere of the farewell discourse and the last supper (cf. Deut 6,5).

[206] In 14,15, there are three equally well attested variant readings: i. future indicative τηρήσετε, ii. aorist subjunctive τηρήσητε, iii. aorist imperative τηρήσατε. In agreement with ἐρωτήσω in the next verse, the future indicative is preferable here.

[207] Brown, *John*, II, 638.

[208] Brown, *John*, II, 643.

[209] Brown, *John*, II, 644, thinks that the introduction of the theme of the Paraclete in 14,16–17 need not be seen as too abrupt since the gift of the Paraclete is associated with the theme of making petitions in prayer (14,13–14; cf. Luke 11,9–13).

[210] M. Hasitschka, "Die Parakletworte im Johannesevangelium: Versuch einer Auslegung in synchroner Textbetrachtung", *SNTU* 18 (1993), 110, speaks of "einer geheimnisvollen Deckung" in the coming of the Paraclete and Jesus.

everything which Jesus has said.[211] There is a variation in John with regard to the attribution of the sending of the Holy Spirit. In some texts (14,16; 14,26) it is the Father who sends the Spirit, and in some other passages (15,26; 16,7) the sending is done by Jesus.[212] This kind of variation can be found also in Luke–Acts (Luke 24,49; Acts 2,33). The reference in John 14,16 to "another Paraclete" may imply that Jesus has been a Paraclete (cf. 1 John 2,1). When Jesus departs, another Paraclete comes (16,7).

He is called "the Spirit of truth" because he will guide the disciples into all the truth (16,13). There is an opposition between the Paraclete and the world. The world cannot accept the Spirit of truth because it has no the spiritual insight to recognize him (cf. 1 Cor 2,14). He is a Paraclete precisely because he will continue the earthly work of Jesus by indwelling in the believers.[213] He will dwell within all believers who love Jesus and keep his commandments (vv. 15–17). The Paraclete is the ongoing presence of the revelation of God to the believers.

2.3.1.3 Coming of the Son (vv. 18–21)

The image of "orphans" (ὀρφανοί) in v. 18 fits well in the context of the farewell discourse, where Jesus addresses his disciples as "little children" (13,33).[214] We may take the expression ἔτι μικρόν in v. 19 literally to refer to the post-resurrectional appearances of Jesus. This may well explain the idea that the world will not see Jesus (cf. Acts 10,40–41). Moreover, the statement ἐγὼ ζῶ shows the characteristic terminology of the resurrection (cf. Luke 24,5.23; Mark 16,11; Acts 1,3; Rev 1,18). However, the statement in v. 18, "I will not leave you orphaned; I am coming to you", may imply not only a brief period of post-resurrectional appearances but also a continued and permanent presence (cf. Matt 28,20).[215] The metaphor of orphan points out the relationship of the disciples to God as the Father.

---

[211] Cf. Hasitschka, "Die Parakletworte", 101.

[212] Brown, *John*, II, 638, thinks that the attribution of the action to the Father may be more original.

[213] Brown, *John*, II, 644, comments that the Old Testament theme of "God with us" (the Immanuel of Isa 7,14) is realized in the Paraclete who remains with the disciples forever (14,16). There is confusion regarding the tenses of the verbs in the last clause of v. 17. Some important early manuscripts favour ἐστίν instead of ἔσται and understand all three verbs as present. Various versions prefer μενεῖ (future) to μένει (present) along with ἔσται. Probably, we have to consider the present tenses here to be proleptic. See BDF, 168 (§323).

[214] The disciples of the rabbis were said to be orphaned at their death as well as the disciples of Socrates at his death (Plato, *Phaedo* 116a). See Str-B., II, 562.

[215] Brown, *John*, II, 645–646. Brown comments, "If originally these verses referred to Jesus' coming back in a series of post-resurrectional appearances, they were soon reinterpreted in Johannine circles to refer to a more abiding and non-corporeal presence of Jesus

The statement "because I live, you also will live" (v. 19) implies that Jesus' life is the basis and source of the Christian life (cf. Rom 5,10; 1 Cor 15,22). This is a life which is mutually shared by the Father and the Son (v. 20; cf. 5,26; 6,57), and the disciples are given a participation in this life (v. 19) through indwelling (v. 20).[216] The pre-requisite for this indwelling is keeping Jesus' commandments and thus loving him (v. 21). Vv. 1–20 have been addressed to the disciples in the second person. But there is a change to the third person in vv. 21.23–24a. V. 21a repeats v. 15 in inverse manner. Those who keep the commandments are those who love Jesus. Those who love Jesus will be loved by the Father (cf. 16,27) and Jesus will directly reveal himself to them.[217]

2.3.1.4 The Coming of the Father with the Son (vv. 22–24)

The question raised by Judas (not Iscariot)[218] is similar to the problem posed by Jesus' brothers in 7,4 that he should show his miracles to the world. In the

---

after the resurrection. (And seemingly this happened before they were associated with the promise of the Paraclete and still further reinterpreted to refer to Jesus' presence in his Spirit.) This reinterpretation grew out of the profound insight that the real gift of the post-resurrectional period was a union with Jesus that was not permanently dependent on bodily presence... John has also realized that the appearances are not an end in themselves; they initiate and point to a deeper type of presence". See Brown, *John*, II, 646. According to Holloway, "Left Behind", 24, it is better to think of the resurrection initiating Jesus' spiritual presence in the community, which continues until the Parousia.

[216] The expression ἐν ἐκείνῃ τῇ ἡμέρᾳ occurs 3 times in John (14,20; 16,23.26). Brown, *John*, II, 640, thinks that even though in the Old Testament "that day" is a traditional formula to describe the time of God's final intervention (cf. Mark 13,32), in the final form of Johannine thought the expression appears to be applied to the period of Christian existence made possible by "the hour" of Jesus. According to Beutler, *Das Johannesevangelium*, 408, ἐν ἐκείνῃ τῇ ἡμέρᾳ does not refer to the end of the times but to the post-Easter period.

[217] Often the Old Testament sapiential background is suggested for the Johannine thought and vocabulary in v. 21 (cf. Wis 1,2; 6,12.18).

[218] The departure of Judas Iscariot in 13,30 might have prompted the scribe to indicate that this Judas was not Judas Iscariot. It is suggested that the original may simply have had "Judas" and the parenthesis, as well as the versional variants, may be scribal attempts to clarify. The New Testament indicates that besides Judas Iscariot, there are at least two other important men named Judas who had contact with Jesus. The first one is Judas, the relative or brother of Jesus (Mark 6,3; Matt 13,55). He is the brother of James of Jerusalem and is traditionally identified as the author of the Epistle of Jude. The second one is Judas of James (the son of James). His name is found in the two Lucan lists of the Twelve (Luke 6,16; Acts 1,13) but not in the Marcan or Matthean lists. The later hagiography identifies him with the Thaddaeus or Lebbaeus whose name appears in the Marcan and Matthean lists of the Twelve (Mark 3,18; Matt 10,3), but is missing from the Lucan lists. It is assumed, therefore, that Judas of James in Luke is the same as Thaddaeus or Lebbaeus in

previous verses Jesus has mentioned that after a little while the world will not see him any longer, but the disciples will see him and he will reveal himself to them by indwelling in them (vv. 19–21). This is what Judas does not understand. Jesus' answer in v. 23 shows that loving him and keeping his word are the necessary conditions for the indwelling of the Father and the Son in the believers. The theme of keeping Jesus' word(s) in 14,23.24 (cf. 8,51; 15,20; 1 John 2,5) can be seen as synonymous with the theme of keeping Jesus' commandments in 14,15.21.[219] The one who has known and seen Jesus has also known and seen the Father (14,7–9). Hence, the presence of Jesus after his resurrection will also mean the Father's presence. The post-resurrectional divine indwelling mentioned in 14,23 is an act of the Father's love for Jesus' disciples, just as Jesus' incarnation and death was an act of divine love for the world (3,16).[220]

In v. 2, the term μονή was employed for the dwelling place in the Father's house, to which Jesus would take his disciples. It is to be noted that John uses the verb μένω for the presence of Jesus with his disciples during his speech (v. 25) as well as for the dwelling of the Holy Spirit with his disciples (v. 17) and its cognate noun μονή to describe the dwelling places in the Father's house (v. 2) as well as the dwelling of the Father and the Son with the disciples (v. 23). However, the dwelling of the Father and the Son with those who love him and keep his word in v. 23 does not replace the "coming again" of Jesus and "taking of the believers to himself" in v. 3, but rather precedes them.[221] For John, the Old Testament promise of God's dwelling in the midst of his people is fulfilled in the divine indwelling, which is the outcome of the realization of the hour and will enable the believers to worship God in Spirit and truth (4,21–24; cf. Ezek 37,27; Zech 2,14; Exod 25,8; 1 Kgs 8,27–66). The revelation through divine indwelling is not given to the world because it neither loves Jesus nor keeps his words (14,24; cf. 12,48–49).

2.3.2 Recapitulation/Conclusion (vv. 25–31)

These verses have a recapitulatory nature as well as a concluding character. They may conclude not only the farewell speech of Jesus in 13,31–14,31 but also chapters 13–14.[222] The formulas in v. 25 and v. 29 and the motifs of

---

Mark and Matthew. It is usually believed that the Judas mentioned by John in 14,22 is Judas of James and that he was one of the Twelve. See Brown, *John*, II, 641.

[219] In the Old Testament, the ten commandments are referred to as הַדְּבָרִים, "the words" of God (Exod 20,1; Deut 5,5.22). We can also notice that the terms "commandments", "word", and "words" are interchangeably used in the Greek of Ps 119,4.25.28.

[220] Brown, *John*, II, 648.

[221] Scholtissek, *In ihm Sein und Bleiben*, 269. Brown, *John*, II, 648, assumes that in the indwelling some of the expectations of the last period are fulfilled.

[222] We can look at 14,28 from two different perspectives. If we look at it from the perspective of the initial setting of the farewell discourse and of the framing verses of 13,1–3,

cosmic conflict and cosmic journey in vv. 30–31 may help us to divide vv. 25–31 into vv. 25–29 and vv. 30–31. While vv. 25–29 have an analeptic (flashback) nature, vv. 30–31 have a proleptic sense. Vv. 25–29 recapitulate the important motifs of the farewell speech of Jesus, namely the promise of the Holy Spirit (v. 26; cf. vv. 16–17), call to fearlessness (v. 27; cf. v.1), journey (vv. 28.31; cf. 13,33; 14,2–6.12.18.23), love (v. 28; cf. vv. 15.21.23–24) and belief (v. 29; cf. vv. 1.10–12). The new motifs of peace (v. 27) and joy (v. 28) also appear in this unit. The gifts of peace and joy along with the promise of the Holy Spirit can be called the eschatological or Easter gifts of Jesus, whose fulfilment is found in 20,19–23.[223] 14,30–31 are oriented towards the future and open to the passion of Jesus. As we mentioned already, the section (chapters 13–14) begins (13,1–2) and ends (14,30–31) with the motif of Jesus' cosmic journey (13,1; 14,31) and cosmic conflict (13,2; 14,30).[224]

2.3.2.1 The Eschatological Gifts of Jesus (vv. 25–29)

a. The Gift of the Holy Spirit (vv. 25–26)

The formula ταῦτα λελάληκα ὑμῖν ("I have said these things to you") occurs like a refrain in the farewell speech of Jesus (15,11; 16,1.4a.6.25.33; cf. 14,29). In v. 25, it paves the way for the second passage on the Paraclete.[225] There is a contrast between the mode of Jesus' presence at the moment (v. 25) and the spiritual presence of the Holy Spirit in the future (cf. v. 17). In v. 26, the Paraclete is known as the Holy Spirit, ὁ δὲ παράκλητος, τὸ πνεῦμα τὸ ἅγιον. This is the only passage in the Gospel which makes this identification explicit. The adversative particle δέ in v. 26 shows that this verse is closely related to the previous verse. As a teacher, the Holy Spirit will continue the teaching activity of Jesus. The Holy Spirit will reveal to the disciples the full meaning of what Jesus has taught (cf. 16,13; 1 John 2,27). They cannot grasp the full meaning of what they see in Jesus and what they hear from him (cf.

---

this verse is to be seen as a part of the framing verses (vv. 28–31) of chapter 14. If 13,3 indicates that Jesus has "come from" (ἐξέρχομαι) God and "goes" (ὑπάγω) to God, 14,28 reveals that Jesus not only "goes" (ὑπάγω, πορεύομαι) to the Father but also "comes (back)" (ἔρχομαι) to the disciples, forming an *inclusio* with 13,3. If we look at this verse from the perspective of the farewell speech of Jesus (13,31–14,31), it well concludes through recapitulation the motif of Jesus' "going" (13,33.36; 14,3.4–5.12) and "coming again" (14,3) to the disciples, especially forming an *inclusio* along with 14,3.

[223] Beutler sees in vv. 26–29 the prophetic tradition of the eschatological gifts of salvation. See Beutler, *Do not Be Afraid*, 82–93; idem, *Das Johannesevangelium*, 411.

[224] See the discussion on pp. 110–111 regarding the function of 13,1–3 and 14,28.30–31 as frames of chapters 13–14.

[225] Beutler, *Do not Be Afraid*, 89–90, notices behind the promise of the Holy Spirit the tradition from Isa 11,1–10; 32,15–20; 44,3; 61,1–11 (cf. Luke 4,18–19); Ezek 36,26–28; 37,1–14; Joel 3.

14,9–10) while he is physically living with them. It is only the post-resurrectional gift of Jesus, namely the Holy Spirit (20,22–23) who will enable them to grasp the full meaning of what they see in Jesus and hear from him, by constant reminding (2,22; 12,26; 14,26), guiding them into all truth (16,13) and declaring the things to come (16,13).

In the first Paraclete passage (14,16) it is said that the Father will give another Paraclete at the request of Jesus. But the second Paraclete passage (14,26) says that the Father will send the Paraclete in Jesus' name. Both verses imply the union of the Father with Jesus in sending the Holy Spirit (cf. 14,20.23–24).[226] The phrase ἐν τῷ ὀνόματί μου may also indicate that the Paraclete's mission is the continuation of Jesus' mission. He will continue the teachings of Jesus by taking what is Christ's and declaring it to the disciples (cf. 16,14).[227] With the physical absence of Jesus, his revealing mission does not terminate. The Paraclete will continue the revealing mission of Jesus.[228]

b. The Gift of Peace (v. 27)

The departing Jesus gives peace (εἰρήνη) to his disciples. The Hebrew word שָׁלוֹם was used traditionally to greet each other. The peace that Jesus offers is not worldly peace in the sense of absence of wars and conflicts but inner peace which is the gift of God (cf. Ps 29,11; Isa 57,19; Wis 3,1–3; Rom 1,7; 1 Cor 1,3; Col 3,15). It is the fruit of salvation (cf. Luke 2,14). In the Old Testament prophecies, the messianic king sent by God is called a prince of peace (Isa 9,6; cf. 52,7; Eph 2,14), and he will command peace to the nations (Zech 9,10). Peace is one of the covenantal promises to the disciples who are asked to enter into a covenantal relationship with Jesus by believing in him, loving him and keeping his commandments (cf. Ezek 34,25; 37,26a; Hag 2,9).[229] Jesus' promise of peace will remove the fear of the disciples who are troubled in their hearts. The final clauses of v. 27 repeat the consolation given by Jesus in 14,1. The advice "do not to fear" (μηδὲ δειλιάτω) is appropriate because Jesus' journey and the preparation of the way involve a combat with the ruler

---

[226] See Brown, *John*, II, 652–653.

[227] There is no contrast between ταῦτα in v. 25 and πάντα in v. 26, rather a sense of completion. What restricts Jesus to teach his disciples *everything* (πάντα) is not the limitations of time, as Brown, *John*, II, 652, points out, but rather the inability of the disciples to understand *everything* (16,12).

[228] Beutler, *Das Johannesevangelium*, 411, writes, "Er wird der Lehrmeister der Jünger sein, aber nicht selbständig oder als Bringer neuer Offenbarungen, sondern nur dadurch, dass er die Jünger an die Worte Jesu erinnert".

[229] Other notable covenantal promises in John 14 are divine indwelling (vv. 12–21.23.28; cf. Exod 25,8; Ezek 37,26b–27) and the knowledge of the divine (vv. 7.17.20–21.26; cf. Exod 29,45–46; Lev 26,11–12). See S. Brown, *Gift upon Gift. Covenant through Word in the Gospel of John* (Eugene 2010), 185; R. Chenattu, *Johannine Discipleship as Covenant Relationship* (Peabody 2006), 101–111; Beutler, *Do not Be Afraid*, 91.

of the world (14,30–31).²³⁰ This promise of peace is fulfilled when the risen Jesus repeatedly uses the greeting formula εἰρήνη ὑμῖν to greet his disciples, who have gathered within a locked house "due to fear of the Jews" (διὰ τὸν φόβον τῶν Ἰουδαίων), and imparts them his peace (20,19.21.26).

c. The Gift of Joy (vv. 28–29)

The purpose of Jesus' "going" is for a new "coming", for a permanent dwelling with the disciples. Therefore, if they really understood it, they would rejoice. The love of the disciples is, however, possessive and imperfect because they fail to recognize the significance of Jesus' journey and its advantages (cf. 16,7). Hence, they are not able to rejoice at his departure. The statement "the Father is greater than I" has created much Christological and trinitarian debate.²³¹ The key to explain this statement should be found in its context. The context says that the disciples should rejoice (χαίρω) that Jesus is going to the Father because the Father is greater than Jesus. As the messenger, he is lesser than the one who sent him (13,16). His departure implies that the Father will glorify him in his own presence with the glory which he had in his presence before the world existed (17,5; cf. 17,24). This should make the disciples rejoice because when Jesus is glorified, he will glorify his disciples as well by granting them eternal life (17,2).²³² We can also notice the motif of joy when the risen Jesus appears to the disciples in 20,20, "Then the disciples 'rejoiced' when they saw the Lord" (ἐχάρησαν οὖν οἱ μαθηταὶ ἰδόντες τὸν κύριον). Here in v. 29 Jesus is foreseeing his death, resurrection, ascension, and giving of the Spirit. When the disciples receive the Holy Spirit, he will remind them all that Jesus has spoken to them (v. 26) and enable them to see the fulfilment of Jesus' words and thus truly to believe in him.

2.3.2.2 Cosmic Conflict and Cosmic Journey (vv. 30–31)

John uses the expression ὁ τοῦ κόσμου ἄρχων for Satan or the devil (cf. 12,31; 16,11; 1 Cor 2,6–8; 2 Cor 4,4; Eph 2,2; 6,12), who acts against Jesus through his agents, namely Judas, the betrayer and the Jewish authorities who plan to kill Jesus.²³³ The statement "the ruler of this world is coming" is

---

[230] Brown, *John*, II, 654. We may here call to mind the admonition given by Moses in his last days, "Do not fear or be dismayed" (Deut 31,8).

[231] The view of Loisy is worth mentioning here, "From the very fact that Christ compares himself to the Father, it is taken for granted that he is of divine nature". As quoted in Brown, *John*, II, 654.

[232] Cf. Brown, *John*, II, 655.

[233] The identification of devil/Satan with the ruler of this world is clear from the context within the Gospel. The Gospel does not give any indication that these three titles refer to three distinct realities. In fact, the devil, Satan and the ruler of the world form a unity because these characters are always presented in opposition to Jesus. No reconciliation is

2. Analysis of the Near and Immediate Context (13,1–14,31)

meaningful here in the context of Jesus' imminent arrest in the garden by the soldiers and the police from the chief priests and the Pharisees (18,2–3), facilitated by the betrayal of Judas, who is called "devil" (6,70; cf. 13,2.27; Mark 14,42).[234] Judas and the Jewish and the Roman rulers who are involved in the death of Jesus are the agents of the devil, who rules and controls them as "the ruler of the world". In the light of 13,2, the rulership of the devil should be understood as the rulership over human hearts (cf. Jub 12,20). Hence, in the coming of Judas who is ruled by the devil the evangelist sees the coming of the ruler of the world. However, this ruler of the world has no power over Jesus because Jesus is doing what the Father has commanded him and acting in accordance with the Father's will (14,31; cf. 4,34; 8,55). He lays down his life of his own accord, and no one can take it away (10,18). Hence, Jesus can say to Pilate, who is also under the influence of evil, "You would have no power over me unless it had been given you from above" (19,11). Thus, since the Father is controlling the situation, "the ruler of the world" has no power over Jesus.[235] From Jesus' obedience to the Father, the world will come to

---

possible between them and Jesus. The devil is a murderer (8,44) and "the ruler of this world" also seeks to murder Jesus. In the Gospel, Judas Iscariot is called a devil (6,70) and is controlled by the devil (13,2) and possessed by Satan (13,27). When Judas goes out of the supper room, it is night (13,30). In the Gospel, darkness refers to the evil realm (3,19–20). It is to this evil realm that Judas goes out. In 8,44, Jesus accuses the Jews thus, "You are from your father the devil, and you choose to do your father's desires" because the Jews attempt to arrest Jesus (7,30.32.44–45; 10,39; 11,57) and want to murder him (5,18; 7,1.19.25; 8,37.40) and thus ally themselves with the devil, the murderer who is their father (8,44). When John says that the ruler of the world is "coming" (ἔρχεται γὰρ ὁ τοῦ κόσμου ἄρχων), he has in mind the "coming" of Judas, who "comes" (ἔρχεται) with a band of armed soldiers and police in order to arrest and "murder" Jesus (14,30; 18,1–12). Their falling down on the ground at Jesus' words, Ἐγώ εἰμι is a sign that the ruler of the world has no power over Jesus (18,5–6). Similarly, the Book of Revelation identifies the ancient serpent, the dragon with the devil, Satan and the deceiver of the whole world, who is thrown out from heaven (12,9; 20,2). Above all, it should be kept in mind that the evangelist is not concerned to give a systematic presentation about the devil/Satan/the ruler of the world as modern readers would often desire. He expects the pre-understanding of the readers that these three names refer to the one and the same evil reality.

[234] Beutler, *Do not Be Afraid*, 95, points out that when the evangelist refers to the "coming of the ruler of the world" instead of the coming of the betrayer (cf. Mark 14,42), he is, on the one hand, following a consistent tendency to bring the role of Judas into relation with the activity of the devil and, on the other hand, following the early Christian *theologoumenon* that sees the devil or Satan as the decisive inspirer of evil (cf. 13,2.27; Luke 22,3.31; Acts 5,3).

[235] Unlike the Synoptic Gospels, John does not mention any acts of exorcisms during the public ministry of Jesus. As the hour of Jesus' death and resurrection approaches, Jesus declares, "Now is the judgment of this world; now the ruler of this world will be driven out" (12,31). Jesus' death on the cross and his resurrection are for John the only acts of exorcism (cf. Koester, *Symbolism*, 230). Hence, Jesus' death in John can be called a "cosmic battle" against Satan. See Kovacs, "The Ruler of this World", 227–247; A. van

know that he loves the Father.[236] It is in doing what the Father has commanded that Jesus' love for the Father consists (cf. 14,15.21a).[237] The coming of the ruler is, therefore, an occasion for Jesus to show the world his love and obedience to the Father. The term "world" in v. 31 refers positively to the creation of God (cf. 3,16; 4,42) and does not have the negative implications as in vv. 17.19.22.

The first part of the farewell speech ends with the command, "Rise, let us be on our way". This can also be seen as an invitation to the disciples to follow him on the way of suffering. The farewell speech of Jesus serves indeed to prepare the disciples for the death of Jesus and the persecution they themselves will experience in this world. For John, the devil or Satan is not a mere figure of speech or a mythological conception but an effective power, who is active on the stage of human history.[238] Jesus' prayer in 17,15, "I am not asking you to take them out of the world, but I ask you to protect them from the evil one", indicates that the conflict with the evil one will continue even after Jesus' departure. Jesus will continue the conflict with the evil one by sending the Paraclete.

2.4 Conclusion

John 14,6, especially Jesus' self-identification with the way, intrinsically belongs to the network of Jesus' journey depicted in John 13–14. An examination of the near and the immediate context of 14,6 within these chapters certainly broadens our horizons in interpreting this verse. The theme of Jesus as the way to the Father is explicitly stated only in 14,6. But John 13–14 as a whole answers the questions of how (journey motif, conflict with the ruler of the world) and why (oneness with the Father) Jesus becomes the exclusive way to the Father.

Oudtshoorn, "Where Have All the Demons Gone?: The Role and Place of the Devil in the Gospel of John", *Neot* 51 (2017), 65–82.

[236] The only text in the New Testament that states that Jesus loves the Father is John 14,31.

[237] It is notable that John does not present the agony of Jesus in Gethsemane as seen in the Synoptic tradition. But some parallel elements to that event can be found in John 14,30–31 (cf. 12,27–29). The notion of the coming of the ruler of the world is similar to Luke 22,53, where the moment of his arrest is characterized as the hour and the power of the darkness. The command, "Rise, let us be on our way" in v. 31 is the same as the command in Mark 14,42, as Judas approaches the garden, "Get up, let us be going. See, my betrayer is at hand". Jesus' words in v. 31, "I do as the Father has commanded me", parallel with Luke 22,42, "Father, if you are willing, remove this cup from me; yet, not my will but yours be done". See Brown, *John*, II, 652.

[238] Kovacs, "The Ruler of this World", 234. Beutler, *Das Johannesevangelium*, 413, comments, "Für Johannes ist der eigentliche Gegner nicht ein Mensch, sondern der Böse in Person, der in der Kraft der Liebe zu Gott besiegt werden kann".

2. Analysis of the Near and Immediate Context (13,1–14,31) 181

Jesus' claim to be the exclusive way to the Father is placed in the context of his imminent journey to the Father, which is the demonstration of the truth of his claims to be from God. It is certainly the motif of Jesus' cosmic journey which controls these chapters from the beginning till the end. 14,6 itself contains the terms of the semantic domain of journey, namely ἡ ὁδός and ἔρχομαι. Jesus, who comes from the Father into this world and goes from this world to the Father and again comes to the disciples in order to dwell with and within them, can alone claim to be the way to the Father.

The language of journey implies a distance between the traveller and his destination. The evangelist frequently uses the terminology of "going" and "coming" to point out the distance between God and man, the estrangement between God and mankind. Jesus removes this distance through his passion, death, resurrection and ascension. In Jesus this distance is removed because in him the way and the destination, the Son and the Father converge. Jesus' journey will traverse the distance which separates the sphere of the disciples from the transcendent heavenly sphere of God. When Jesus says that he is going to prepare a place in his Father's house, he offers a definite security, which all mankind seeks, not in this world, but in the world thereafter.[239]

Since the journey of Jesus is a cosmic journey, it involves inevitably a cosmic conflict, the battle with "the ruler of this world", also called Satan and the devil, who blocks the way to God (cf. 12,31; 13,2.27; 14,30; 16,11; 17,15).[240] Jesus came into this world to remove the obstacles and to open the way to the Father and thus to provide access to God for all people. In fact, the real antagonist of Jesus is not chief priests and Pharisees, Judas Iscariot or Pilate but the devil. John 13–14 portrays in the background the story of Jesus' battle with this ultimate enemy. These chapters are framed by a conflict over power between Jesus and the devil. It is in the context of his reference to Jesus' conflict with the devil (13,2.27;14,30; cf. 16,11; 1 John 5,19) and to Jesus' "preparation of a place in the Father's house" that John presents Jesus as the way to the Father. Since Jesus and his kingdom are not of "this world"

---

[239] H. Koester, "John 14,1–20: A Meditation", *ExpTim* 73 (1961), 88.

[240] According to 1 John 3,8, "Everyone who commits sin is a child of the devil; for the devil has been sinning from the beginning. The Son of God was revealed for this purpose, to destroy the works of the devil" (cf. John 6,70; 8,44; 13,2; Heb 2,14). The sin "from the beginning" may refer to the sin inspired by the devil in the whole complex of Gen 1–4. This section starts with "in the beginning" (Gen 1,1). God created all things good, but the diabolic serpent persuaded Adam and Eve to sin, which led to further sin among their sons, Cain and Abel (Gen 4,1–16). Thus, the devil has been active from the beginning of human history in the emergence of sin. There is a remorseless antithesis in nature and operation between the devil and the Son of God. The battle between the two is an everlasting one and the believers in Christ must relinquish the devil and his works. Cf. Brown, *The Epistles of John*, 406; R. Schnackenburg, *The Johannine Epistles. A Commentary* (New York 1992), 174. In the Book of Revelation as well the destruction of the devil is foreseen (Rev 20) before the believers are given access to the tree of life (Rev 22,14; cf. 4 Ezra 8,52–53).

(8,23; 17,14.16; 18,36), the world hates him (7,7; 15,18; cf. 15,19).[241] He himself is the truth (14,6) and he came into this world to bear witness to the truth (18,37). But the devil is the father of lies; there is no truth in him, and he does not stand in the way of truth (8,44). Jesus himself is the life (11,25; 14,6), and he has come to give life abundantly (10,10). But the devil is a murderer from the beginning (8,44). That is why there is always a conflict between Jesus and the devil, who is "the ruler of this world".

It is already mentioned that the preparation of the way, which is an overarching theme in Deutero-Isaiah, necessarily entails the removal of obstacles (Isa 40,4; 57,14; 62,10).[242] In the Gospel of John too, Jesus' "preparation of a place in the Father's house" necessitates the removal of obstacles. Jesus does this through his death and resurrection, which is the hour of glorification (12,27–28; 13,31–32) and also the hour of "the overthrow of the ruler of this world" (12,31; 16,11; cf. Col 2,15; Heb 2,14; Rev 12,1–18).[243] When "the ruler of this world" is overthrown, the glorified Christ can draw all people to himself, (12,32) and the devil will lose authority and rulership over the human hearts (cf. 6,70; 13,2.27). Hence, the hour of Jesus is the hour of preparation of the way to the Father by overthrowing the ruler of the world.

The devil achieves his purposes through human beings, who work as his agents. John 13–14 portrays Judas as an agent of the devil. On the one hand, the Father puts all things in the hands of Jesus, who is his agent (13,3), and on the other hand, the devil puts the idea of betrayal into the heart of Judas, who is his agent (13,2). The last action narrated in the farewell discourse is an act of satanic possession (13,27.30) of Judas, which is to be contrasted with the cosmic exorcism of Satan by Jesus, "Now is the judgment of this world; now the ruler of this world will be driven out" (12,31; cf. 16,11). The true disciple, thus, stands in stark contrast to Judas. If Judas is indwelt by Satan, the true disciple is indwelt by the Father, the Son and the Spirit (14,15–24).

Through the foot-washing, Jesus is showing his disciples the way he will be going to the Father (cf. 14,4). He grants the disciples the share with him, and his death becomes the means for the disciples to come to the Father (13,7–8). Judas does not believe in and love Jesus, at least as other disciples do. Jesus is, however, showing him his love unto death by washing his feet and giving him the bread. He is unclean because he decides to betray Jesus. Judas, who refuses to believe in Jesus and to love him, goes out of the way of Jesus into darkness, the world of the devil. He has to "go out" of Jesus' inner circle so that Jesus can speak to his own (13,31). When Judas departs in

---

[241] Since Jesus' disciples also do not belong to the world, the world hates them as well (15,19).

[242] See pp. 51–55. In As. Mos. 10,1–4, the elimination of Satan is paralleled with the levelling of high mountains and hills, which is an allusion to Isa 40,4.

[243] Also see the discussion on pp. 197–206 regarding Jesus' preparation of the way.

13,30, the remaining disciples form a group that is receptive to Jesus' word and are to become the children of God (13,33; cf. 1,11). The difference between Judas and Peter is shown in the pre-meditation and pre-planning of Judas' actions (13,2.10–11.18).[244] The disciples, who are frightened at the news of Jesus' physical departure, are asked to take courage and to believe in him because his journey is intended to prepare a place for them in the Father's house (14,1–3).

Jesus knows everything that is going to happen, but the disciples do not know at all. The questions of the disciples indicate their lack of knowledge and insight into Jesus' teachings. Hence, they are in need of the help of the Paraclete who will remind them and teach them all things. If they believe in Jesus, they can continue his work by asking everything in his name. Jesus is the only way to the Father because of his exclusive relationship with the Father, i.e., his oneness with the Father. The disciples should believe in the oneness of Jesus with the Father. The greater works done by Jesus' disciples will prove that Jesus is one with the Father and thus the true way to the Father.

There is a difference between Jesus and the disciples in their relationship to the Father or to the Father's house.[245] This distinction is found firstly in their position in the Father's house and secondly in their sequence of journeys. Firstly, with regard to the position, Jesus is the Son of the Father. He belongs to the Father's house originally. He has an original and a permanent place there, which the disciples do not have (cf. 8,35).[246] Secondly, with regard to the sequence of journeys, Jesus goes first (13,33.36; 14,3). He goes first to the Father's house because he is from there. The disciples cannot go with him now but only afterwards (13,33.36). The journey of the disciples depends on Jesus' prior journey and his "preparation of a place" for them. His place is original and theirs is secondary, derived from and dependent upon him. Jesus goes first because he is first (1,1). The disciples have only a mediated position in relation to the Father. Hence, no one can come to the Father except through Jesus (14,6b).

The authority over access to the Father in the Son is expressed explicitly in the vocabulary of investiture in 13,3 (also in 3,35; implicitly in 16,15; 17,10) and in the ἐγώ εἰμι-saying of 14,6.[247] Even after Jesus' physical departure, his claim to be the exclusive way to the Father remains valid. The identity of

---

[244] It is understandable from 18,12–18.25–27 that Peter's failure is due to the pressure of circumstances and the fear of persecution.

[245] Cf. Woll, *Johannine Christianity*, 38.

[246] The imagery in 8,35 points out the privileged status of the son in the house (οἰκία), where he abides for ever (μένει εἰς τὸν αἰῶνα). Jesus is the privileged Son of the Father, but the disciples are not. The saying also serves to prove that Jesus is the pre-existent Son of God.

[247] Woll, *Johannine Christianity*, 49.

Jesus as the way to the Father serves as a backup for the disciples' confidence in the future and as an authoritative basis for their obedience to the new commandment (13,34) and the Paraclete (14,16–17.26).[248] The basis for Jesus' claim to be the exclusive way is the reciprocal formula, "I am in the Father and the Father is in me" in 14,10.11.[249] In other words, the unity of Jesus and the Father or their mutual indwelling is the basis for Jesus' claim of exclusive authority over access to the Father.

A triadic pattern is discernible in 14,6 and in its near context (John 13–14). It is to be noted that 14,6 is the only ἐγώ εἰμι-saying in the Gospel with three predicate nominatives, namely the way, the truth and the life. It is three times that the name of Judas Iscariot, who is the betrayer of Jesus and the agent of the evil one, is mentioned referring to his presence and function (13,2.26.29).[250] Peter is warned that he will deny Jesus "three times" (τρίς, 13,38). There are three distinct names for the evil one, namely devil (13,2), Satan (13,27) and ruler of the world (14,30). The three persons of the Holy Trinity, namely the Father (vv. 2.6–13.16.20–21.23–24,26.28.31; cf. 13,1.3), the Son (v. 13) and the Spirit (vv. 16–17.26) play their roles in John 14. Three names are given for the third person of the Trinity, namely παράκλητος (14,16.26), τὸ πνεῦμα τῆς ἀληθείας (14,17) and τὸ πνεῦμα τὸ ἅγιον (14,26).

Jesus' claim in 14,6 is placed between two commands, the command to believe (14,1) and the command to love (14,15). In fact, these commands dominate the surrounding context of 14,6. Hence, the two important conditions on the way of discipleship are belief and love. Belief is only a beginning. It should lead one to love in order to experience the indwelling of the Trinitarian God. While the motif of "going" dominates 14,1–14, the motif of "coming" dominates 14,15–24. The consequence of Jesus' "going" to the Father is the "coming" of the Trinitarian God to the believers. In fact, his journey provides the possibility for the Father, the Son and the Spirit to come to the disciples (vv.15–24). Hence, the purpose of Jesus' journey is not only to bring the believers to the Father's house, but also to bring along with him the Father and the Spirit to the disciples. Therefore, the way of Jesus is not a one-way but a two-way – a way that enables both the believers and the triune God (the Father, the Son and the Spirit) to make an up and down journey (cf. 1,51).

---

[248] Du Rand, "The Johannine Group", 131.

[249] Woll, *Johannine Christianity*, 47, thinks that the introductory words "don't you believe..." (v. 10) and "believe me that..." (v. 11) and the use of the formula in the context of an argument (v. 9) may suggest that the formula had a confessional status in the Johannine community.

[250] In 14,22, the reference is not to the betrayer but to another disciple who is also known as Judas. The name of Judas Iscariot is mentioned here only to distinguish the other Judas from the betrayer. Moreover, Judas Iscariot is not in the scene. He has already gone out of the supper room (13,30).

Chapter III

The Unity and Integrity of John 14,6

Generally speaking, in Johannine scholarship there is no doubt regarding the unity and integrity of John 14,6. However, very few authors like J. H. Charlesworth and M. Theobald have cast suspicion regarding the unity of John 14,6. J. H. Charlesworth is embarrassed by the exclusivism found in v. 6 and believes that it is caused by a social setting different from that of Jesus, i.e., the expulsion of the Johannine Christians from the synagogue.[1] He thinks that v. 6 is composed of two strata (v. 6a and v. 6b) and that v. 6b can be accurately assigned to a later stratum of tradition. In his view, v. 6b is a later addition to the developing traditions. The approach of Theobald is very different from that of Charlesworth. He is not disturbed by the exclusivism of v. 6b but finds it difficult to understand the role of ἡ ἀλήθεια καὶ ἡ ζωή in v. 6a since they are like intruders in the context. Hence, he thinks that the original saying in v. 6 was short in form, i.e., Ἐγώ εἰμι ἡ ὁδός· οὐδεὶς ἔρχεται πρὸς τὸν πατέρα εἰ μὴ δι' ἐμοῦ.[2] According to him, the evangelist has expanded the original saying with the addition of καὶ ἡ ἀλήθεια καὶ ἡ ζωή because for the evangelist the original saying seemed to represent only inadequately his own Christological perspective. But we do have neither external nor internal evidence to support Theobald's claim. Moreover, the association of way with truth and life in the biblical and other Jewish literature, the mediating role of truth and the theological correspondence between life and the Father in the Gospel are evidences to reject Theobald's proposal.[3] We shall now examine

---

[1] See Charlesworth, "The Gospel of John: Exclusivism", 479–513. Charlesworth's view that the exclusivism of John 14,6 is caused by the social setting of expulsion from the synagogue will be critically evaluated later. See pp. 352–353.

[2] See Theobald, *Herrenworte*, 311–312.

[3] Since Theobald's problem is regarding the role of ἡ ἀλήθεια καὶ ἡ ζωή in 14,6, we will be able to give an answer to his difficulty when we discuss the background of the formulation, "the way and the truth and the life" and the relation of ἡ ἀλήθεια καὶ ἡ ζωή with ἡ ὁδός after an examination of the usage of ἀλήθεια and ζωή in the Gospel. See pp. 206–209, 255–260. However, the role of ἡ ἀλήθεια καὶ ἡ ζωή is mentioned below briefly while discussing the relation between v. 6a and v. 6b on pp. 187–188.

whether the text shows any signs of redactional activity, taking into account its vocabulary, grammar, structure, context and the theology of the Gospel.[4]

1. Vocabulary in v. 6b

There is not a single word in v. 6b that is peculiar and distinct from the rest of the Gospel. The frequency of the occurrences of the words of v. 6b in John, except the definite articles, are given in the following table.

Vocabulary in 14,6b	
Words	Frequency in the Gospel of John
οὐδείς	53
ἔρχομαι	157
πρός	102
πατήρ	136
εἰ	49
μή	117
διά	59
ἐμοῦ	26

The expression οὐδεὶς ἔρχεται πρός in v. 6b is not much different from οὐδεὶς δύναται ἐλθεῖν πρός in 6,44 and 6,65. Among 136 occurrences, the noun πατήρ refers to God 119 times. The phrase πρὸς τὸν πατέρα is found 10 times in the Gospel. Among these, only once it occurs without a verb of movement (5,45) but 9 times with following verbs of movement: μεταβαίνω (13,1), ἔρχομαι (14,6), thrice with πορεύομαι (14,12.28; 16,28), twice with ὑπάγω (16,10.17) and twice with ἀναβαίνω (20,17). It should be noted that πρὸς τὸν πατέρα with a verb of movement occurs 3 times in chapter 14 (vv. 6.12.28) and most of its occurrences (7x) are found in chapters 13–16. The similar expression πρὸς τὸν θεόν is found 3 times (1,1.2; 13,3), once with the verb ὑπάγω (13,3). Even though the expression εἰ μὴ δι' ἐμοῦ is used only in 14,6, the construction εἰ μὴ is very common in the Gospel (12x). There is a clear exclusive sense in Jesus' sayings in 3,13, καὶ οὐδεὶς ἀναβέβηκεν εἰς τὸν οὐρανὸν εἰ μὴ ὁ ἐκ τοῦ οὐρανοῦ καταβάς, ὁ υἱὸς τοῦ ἀνθρώπου and in 6,46, οὐχ ὅτι τὸν πατέρα ἑώρακέν τις εἰ μὴ ὁ ὢν παρὰ τοῦ θεοῦ, οὗτος ἑώρακεν τὸν πατέρα. The preposition διά occurs 14 times with the genitive, implying "through". The prepositional phrase δι' ἐμοῦ is also found in anoth-

---

[4] The following discussion is mainly an answer to Charlesworth's difficulty. For a critical evaluation of Charlesworth's views, also see Tack, *John 14,6 in Light of Jewish-Christian Dialogue*, 154–156.

er ἐγώ εἰμι-saying, i.e., in 10,9 in which exclusivism might be seen. Exclusivism can be noticed in the phrase δι' ἐμοῦ and in the image of gate with the definite article because the sheepfold about which Jesus speaks here has only one gate (cf. 10,1–16). The corresponding phrase δι' αὐτοῦ also appears 4 times referring to Jesus (1,3.7.10; 3,17). Thus, from the observation of the vocabulary we find that v. 6b employs only the usual words that the evangelist frequently uses and that their usage is totally in agreement with his style. Therefore, v. 6b is not intrusive from the viewpoint of its vocabulary.

2. Relation between v. 6a and v. 6b

It is evident that v. 6 has two parts, v. 6a and v. 6b. If the first part is a self-identification of Jesus in positive terms, the second part negatively explains v. 6a. Moreover, it is possible to observe an *inclusio* and a *chiasmus* within v. 6:[5]

A Ἐγώ εἰμι
   B ἡ ὁδὸς καὶ ἡ ἀλήθεια καὶ ἡ ζωή
   B¹ οὐδεὶς ἔρχεται πρὸς τὸν πατέρα
A¹ εἰ μὴ δι' ἐμοῦ.

Jesus' saying begins with the first person personal pronoun ἐγώ and ends with the same pronoun in its genitive case ἐμοῦ, forming an *inclusio*.[6] The appearance of the personal pronoun ἐγώ at the beginning and at the end of the verse attracts special attention because it emphasizes that Jesus himself is the way (v. 6a), and it is only through him that one can reach the destination, the Father (v. 6b). *Chiasmus* is discernible if we pay attention to the correspondence between the personal pronouns in A and A¹ and the correspondence between ὁδός and ἔρχεται and between ζωή and πατήρ in B and B¹. Both ὁδός and ἔρχεται belong to the semantic domain of journey. The purpose of ὁδός is to enable the traveller to "come" and to "go". Jesus as the "way" (ὁδός) enables the believer to "come" (ἔρχομαι) to the Father. It is also possible to notice a theological correspondence between πατήρ and ζωή. Accord-

---

[5] Scholars are often aware of the *inclusio* and *chiasmus* in this verse. E.g., see De la Potterie, "Je suis la voie", 916; Theobald, *Herrenworte*, 307.

[6] It is a commonplace that if an author begins and ends a sentence with the same word, we call it an *inclusio* or inclusion. E.g., according to B. M. Dupriez, *A Dictionary of Literary Devices. Gradus A–Z* (Toronto 1991), 229, an inclusion is "a device consisting of beginning and ending a poem, story or play with the same word". But Charlesworth, "The Gospel of John: Exclusivism", 493, insists that an *inclusio* in 14,6 would be evident only if the author had written, "Through me is the way, the truth, and the life; no one comes to the Father except through me". This is a very rigid and also a wrong approach to the understanding of inclusion.

ing to John, only the Father has life in himself independently (5,26). In Johannine soteriology, both πατήρ (e.g., 14,6b–8; 17,3) and ζωή (e.g., 3,16; 17,3; 20,31) function as the final goal for the believer. In Johannine schema, the believer's journey to the Father (14,6) and the journey to the life (e.g., 5,24) are inseparable.[7]

The relation between v. 6a and v. 6b can be further supported by noticing some sort of correspondence between "way" (v. 6a) and "through me" (v. 6b). If Jesus is the "way" (v. 6a), it is "through me" (v. 6b), i.e., through the way of Jesus that the believer has to come to the Father. The correspondence between "the way" (ἡ ὁδός) and "through me" (δι' ἐμοῦ) in 14,6 is similar to the correspondence between "the gate" (ἡ θύρα) and "through me" (δι' ἐμοῦ) in 10,9. Since Jesus is the gate, the sheep has to go "through him" in order to be saved (10,9) and to have abundant life (10,10).

Apparently, it is difficult to see any correspondence between ἀλήθεια and any element in v. 6b. However, a correspondence at a theological level is discernible if we pay attention to the special role of ἀλήθεια in the journey of the believer towards salvation. This requires an explanation and a correct understanding. In the Gospel, truth is never regarded as an ultimate goal, but has only a mediating or guiding role. It is a means or an agent of salvation (e.g., 8,32; 17,17.19). Therefore, the position of ἀλήθεια in the middle after ὁδός is meaningful. The theological role of ἀλήθεια is comparable with the role of the preposition πρός in v. 6b. The preposition πρός with accusative is a marker of movement or orientation towards someone/something.[8] As a means of salvation, truth also gives an orientation in the journey of the believer and leads him "towards" (πρός) salvation (the life/the Father).[9] As truth, Jesus guides or leads the believer to the goal, i.e., to the life of and with the Father. Thus, the inseparable relation between the two constitutive parts of v. 6 in the form of *inclusio*, *chiasmus* and correspondence in various ways demonstrate the unity of this verse and argue against the redactional approaches given by Charlesworth and Theobald. Theobald's way of examining only the literal role/relationship of the words is not sufficient to understand John 14,6. The theological perspective of the evangelist as well should be taken into account.

---

[7] I. de la Potterie considers the Father, not the life as the goal of the way. His view that nothing in v. 6a corresponds with what is said in v. 6b is not correct (see de la Potterie, *La vérité dans Saint Jean*, I, 252). The correspondence between life and the Father is further explained on pp. 258–260.

[8] BDAG, 874–875.

[9] John 14,6b is interpreted as an invitation to experience the fatherhood of God through the begetting of the Holy Spirit (see pp. 280–292). The Holy Spirit who is called the Spirit of truth in the Gospel (14,17; 15,26; 16,13; cf. 1 John 5,6) plays a mediating role in the work of salvation. Thus, there is correspondence between the mediating role of truth in John 14,6a and the function of the Spirit of truth.

3. Relation between v. 6 and v. 7

The relation between v. 6 and v. 7 is grammatically reflected in the *chiasmus* of non-conditional sentences in vv. 6a.7b (A, A¹) and conditional phrase/sentence in vv. 6b.7a (B, B¹).

A   λέγει αὐτῷ [ὁ] Ἰησοῦς, Ἐγώ εἰμι ἡ ὁδὸς καὶ ἡ ἀλήθεια καὶ ἡ ζωή.
B   οὐδεὶς ἔρχεται πρὸς τὸν πατέρα εἰ μὴ δι' ἐμοῦ.
B¹   εἰ ἐγνώκατέ με, καὶ τὸν πατέρα μου γνώσεσθε.
A¹   καὶ ἀπ' ἄρτι γινώσκετε αὐτὸν καὶ ἑωράκατε αὐτόν.

The relationship between v. 6 and v. 7 is established by the fact that v. 7 begins (εἰ ἐγνώκατέ με) where v. 6 ends (εἰ μὴ δι' ἐμου). This is achieved through the use of a conditional phrase in v. 6b and a conditional sentence in v. 7a. The conditional element εἰ... ἐμοῦ of v. 6b is literally repeated in εἰ... με of v. 7. They reveal that Jesus is the mediator between the disciples and the Father, as shown below:

v. 6b: The disciples come to the Father through Jesus.
    <u>Disciples</u>   (coming through)   <u>Jesus</u>   (coming to)   <u>Father</u>
———————————————————————▶

v. 7a: The disciples know the Father through Jesus.
    <u>Disciples</u>   (knowing through)   <u>Jesus</u>   (knowing)   <u>Father</u>
———————————————————————▶

While the concern of v. 6b is "coming to the Father through me (Jesus)", the focus in v. 7 is "knowing the Father through me (Jesus)". This intimate relationship between v. 6b and v. 7a reveals that v. 7a is an explanation of v. 6b. What is said negatively in v. 6b, is stated positively in v. 7a. Indeed, v. 7a explains v. 6b with the help of the motif of knowing (γινώσκω), which functions in parallel to ἔρχομαι πρός. At a deeper level, there is a relation between these two verbs. Both involve a reference to the realm of belief. If ἔρχομαι πρός is synonymous with the active element in believing, γινώσκω is partially synonymous with the receptive element in believing.[10]

It was already mentioned that throughout the unit of 14,1–14 there is some kind of concatenation of ideas or movement of ideas through the repetition of key words taken from the previous verse.[11] The *only* key word that is taken from v. 6 and repeated in v. 7 is πατήρ. In fact, vv. 7–11 as a whole are an explanation of v. 6, centred on the chief motif of the Father, which continues

---

[10] Brown, *John*, I, 513.
[11] See pp. 151–152.

to occur in every verse until v. 13. In the tapestry of Johannine thought found within 14,1–14, the motif of πατήρ functions as the key thread that weaves v. 6 together with v. 7. If v. 6b is omitted, the flow of thought which is maintained in its immediate context is lost, and the connecting thread between v. 6 and v. 7 is broken. Therefore, we can ascertain that v. 6b is an inseparable part of v. 6 and not a later addition.

4. Thrust of John 14,4–7

If we examine the thrust of the whole pericope (vv. 1–14), it becomes evident that v. 6b is an integral part of it. In v. 1, there is a command to believe in God and in Jesus. The following verses (vv. 2–14) give the motivation to believe. This motivation to believe is presented in the context of Jesus' journey. Every journey presupposes a way to go and a destination to reach. In vv. 2–3, the journey motif is introduced, and the destination is set as the Father's house. But the disciples have not understood Jesus' language. In vv. 4–7, the thrust of the dialogue is on two things, the way and the destination.[12] The content of vv. 4–7 can be grouped into these two categories of motifs, as given in the following table:

Verses	Way	Destination
v. 4	οἴδατε τὴν ὁδόν.	καὶ ὅπου [ἐγὼ] ὑπάγω
v. 5	πῶς δυνάμεθα τὴν ὁδὸν εἰδέναι;	Λέγει αὐτῷ Θωμᾶς, Κύριε, οὐκ οἴδαμεν ποῦ ὑπάγεις·
v. 6	λέγει αὐτῷ [ὁ] Ἰησοῦς, Ἐγώ εἰμι ἡ ὁδὸς καὶ ἡ ἀλήθεια καὶ ἡ ζωή·	οὐδεὶς ἔρχεται πρὸς τὸν πατέρα εἰ μὴ δι' ἐμοῦ.[13]
v. 7	εἰ ἐγνώκατέ με,[14]	καὶ τὸν πατέρα μου γνώσεσθε· καὶ ἀπ' ἄρτι γινώσκετε αὐτὸν καὶ ἑωράκατε αὐτόν.

If we examine the dialogue in vv. 4–7 through the lens of the motifs of way and destination, we can notice the following chiastic pattern of these motifs:

---

[12] V. 7 has a transitional nature. In it, the way and the destination gradually merge together. But it is from v. 8 that we understand that the disciples' attention is fully focused on the Father, the destination.

[13] The conditional phrase might be better placed under the motif of way. It is placed here under the motif of destination to give a complete sense to v. 6b.

[14] The conditional clause εἰ ἐγνώκατέ με is placed under the motif of way because it can be understood as "if you know me who is the way" (cf. v. 6). There is a correspondence between με in v. 7 and ἐγώ, ἐμοῦ in v. 6 which are identified with Jesus the way.

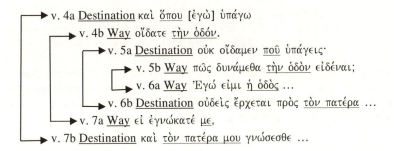

As far as Jesus is concerned, his destination is his Father (v. 4a) and his way is death-resurrection-ascension (v. 4b). But, as Thomas' question in v. 5 indicates, the disciples understand neither his destination (v. 5a) nor his way (v. 5b). In v. 6, Jesus declares that he himself is the way for them (v. 6a) and that the Father is their destination (v. 6b). In v. 7a, the motifs of Jesus as the way or the means (εἰ ἐγνώκατέ με) and the Father as the destination (καὶ τὸν πατέρα μου γνώσεσθε) are repeated through a conditional construction. The motif of Jesus' oneness with the Father is then clearly articulated in vv. 7b–11. After v. 7 there are no more questions regarding the way from the part of the disciples. They want to know more about the Father, their destination, as Philip's question in v. 8 points out. Thus, the thrust of the passage (vv. 4–7) is not about "knowing" but about the way and the destination.[15]

If the thrust of vv. 4–7 is centred on the motifs of way and destination, it is easy to recognize the role and function of v. 6b. Even though in v. 5 there is only one question, Thomas is, in fact, concerned with two things: the destination of Jesus' journey (v. 5a) and the way of Jesus' journey (v. 5b). V. 6a is Jesus' answer to Thomas' concern about the way and v. 6b is the answer to his concern about the destination. If Jesus is the way (v. 6a), the Father is the destination (v. 6b). To make sure that v. 6b is an answer to Thomas' concern about Jesus' destination, it is enough to observe that the destination is always expressed in vv. 4–6 in association with verbs of movement and a destination marker, as shown below.[16]

---

[15] Even though the verb οἶδα (vv. 4.5) and γινώσκω (v. 7) occur 3 times each, the thrust of the passage (vv. 4–7) is not about knowing in itself as Charlesworth, "The Gospel of John: Exclusivism", 498, thinks, but about *where* Jesus and the disciples go and *how* they go, namely the destination and the way. While v. 4 is concerned with the destination and way of Jesus, vv. 5–7 deal with the destination and the way of the disciples.

[16] In v. 7, the language of journey is not used because in v. 6b the destination, the Father, is announced in relation to a verb of movement (ἔρχομαι πρός) and it is not necessary to use it again. Nevertheless, as we have already seen, ἔρχομαι πρός is not only a verb of movement but also a synonym for πιστεύω εἰς. In v. 7, the evangelist employs the verb γινώσκω which is also, to a certain extent, interchangeable with πιστεύω εἰς.

ὑπάγω + ὅπου in v. 4a: ὅπου [ἐγὼ] ὑπάγω
ὑπάγω + ποῦ in v. 5a: οὐκ οἴδαμεν ποῦ ὑπάγεις
ἔρχομαι + πρός in v. 6b: οὐδεὶς ἔρχεται πρὸς τὸν πατέρα

Thus, v. 6b answers the issue about the destination of Jesus' journey that is begun in v. 4 and also about the destination of the disciples, which are one and the same, i.e., the Father.[17] Therefore, Charlesworth's claim that v. 6b is not the answer to the question in v. 5 is baseless.[18]

5. John 14,6 as an ἐγώ εἰμι-Saying

It is very important to notice that John 14,6 is an ἐγώ εἰμι-saying with images. Many of the ἐγώ εἰμι-sayings with images have a common two-fold structure, a Christological saying immediately followed by a soteriological statement (6,35.51; 8,12; 10,9; 11,25; 14,6; 15,5).[19] While the first sentence deals with Jesus, the second sentence concerns the believer. The first sentence describes who Jesus is in relation to the believer. The second sentence is concerned with the salvation of the believer. It tells what the believer has to do in order to be saved. This two-fold structure of the ἐγώ εἰμι-sayings with images is well supported by the Christological and soteriological claim in the purpose statement of the Gospel (20,31). Obviously, the ἐγώ εἰμι-saying in 14,6 has a two-fold structure. While v. 6a is a Christological saying, v. 6b is a soteriological statement. V. 6a says who Jesus is for the believer, and v. 6b states what the believer has to do in order to reach the Father. V. 6b states that the believer has to "come to" Jesus first in order to reach the Father. In this Gospel, the Father and the life are regarded as the soteriological goal of the believer because the Father is the ultimate source of life (5,26). Thus, from the view point of the two-fold structure of 14,6, supported by many other ἐγώ εἰμι-sayings with images in the Gospel itself, it can be well established beyond doubt that v. 6b is not redactional.

6. Conclusion

Whatever may be the historical or social setting one tries "to construct" for the composition of the Gospel of John, it is impossible to regard v. 6b as a

---

[17] The phrase πρὸς τὸν πατέρα is frequently used in the Gospel as the destination in association with the verbs of movement (13,1; 14,6.12.28; 16,10.17.28; 201,17).

[18] See Charlesworth, "The Gospel of John: Exclusivism", 504.

[19] See the views about the structure of ἐγώ εἰμι-saying with images on p. 315.

6. Conclusion

later addition to v. 6a from the viewpoint of grammar, vocabulary, structure, context and theology of the text. It is not possible to show that structurally v. 6b is untied from the context. Philologically, there is no reason to assume that v. 6b stems from different scribal hands or that it was an interpolation. Charlesworth's redactional approach to the exclusivism of 14,6 is, in fact, a child of his own whims and fancies. We will discuss later at length how the exclusivism of 14,6 is to be approached and handled.[20]

---

[20] See pp. 352–395.

Chapter IV

Possible Background of John 14,6 and Its Context

1. Introductory Views

The following discussion is a proposal for an alternative approach to the literary background of John 14,6 and its context.[1] Before discussing it, it is worthwhile to consider a notable view emphasized by Johannes Beutler with regard to the tradition behind 14,1–9.[2] Beutler claims that behind 14,1–9 there is an early Christian tradition, which interprets the passion of Jesus in the light of Pss 42–43 (LXX Pss 41–42). In many respects, Beutler's views are not convincing. The apparent aporias mentioned by Beutler in 14,1–9 can be resolved without any recourse to Pss 42–43.[3] The possibility of using this psalm to interpret the passion of Jesus in conjunction with the Synoptic tradition (Mark 14,34; Matt 26,38) is detectable only in John 12,27 and to some extent in 13,21. In 11,33, there is not any indication about the passion of Jesus. It is in the context of the sorrow as a result of the death of Lazarus that Jesus is said to be troubled in spirit (11,33). Even if we assume that John used Pss 42–43 to present the distress of Jesus in 12,27 and 13,21, the focus of the evangelist in 14,1 is not on the distress of Jesus but of the disciples. The Synoptic tradition does not use this psalm to present the distress of the disciples.

---

[1] This proposal does not necessarily rule out other possible influences, which are not discussed here. Even though the main purpose of this discussion is to examine the possible influences behind John 14,6, the surrounding context is also taken into account. This is only to support the argument in favour of the possible influences behind John 14,6, which are discussed here and thus to show that John 14,6 does not stand in isolation, rather it is related to a possible network of influences behind the text.

[2] See Beutler, *Habt keine Angst*, 25–50; idem, *Do not Be Afraid*, 26–47. The views of J. Beutler are closely followed by Léon-Dufour, *Lecture de l'Évangile selon Jean*, 89–102 and A. I. Wilson, "Send your Truth: Psalms 42 and 43 as the Background to Jesus' Self-description as 'Truth' in John 14,6", *Neot* 41 (2007), 220–234.

[3] Some important aporias are addressed in this study during the examination of 14,1–14. Beutler, *Do not Be Afraid*, 24, disregards a psychological explanation of 14,1 and asks, "Where else does the Fourth Evangelist show himself to be concerned with psychology?" But there are passages in the Gospel like, e.g., 11,33.35–36; 20,11.13 where the evangelist is concerned with human emotions, and they may require psychological explanations. What theological explanation can be given for the weeping of Jesus and Mary Magdalene at the tombs of Lazarus and Jesus respectively?

It is unlikely that John interprets and uses the same word ταράσσω of this psalm (LXX Ps 41,7), on the one hand, to present the distress of Jesus in 12,27; 13,21 and, on the other hand, to denote the distress of the disciples in 14,1. It should be noted that the term ταράσσω is not something peculiar to Pss 41–42. The motif of "troubling (ταράσσω) of one's heart (καρδία)" can be seen in many other psalms (LXX Pss 6,3; 37,11; 54,5; 75,6; 108,22; 142,4). Moreover, the term ταράσσω is found in Pss 41–42 in association with ψυχή and not with καρδία as in the Gospel (John 14,1). Furthermore, John does not use in 14,1 the verb ἐλπίζω from the proposed psalm (LXX Ps 42,5). Instead, he uses the verb πιστεύω. Since the evangelist has used the term πιστεύω in 5,46–47 (4x) immediately after using the term ἐλπίζω in 5,45, it is clear that he makes some sort of distinction between ἐλπίζω and πιστεύω. Since he is already familiar with the term ἐλπίζω, he would have used it in 14,1 if LXX Pss 41–42 provided the tradition for him.

The most decisive motifs within 14,1–14 are way and Jesus' relationship with the Father. Hence, various translations, commentators and interpreters entitle this pericope as "Jesus as the way to the Father". But the crucial and decisive term "way" never occurs in this psalm. Beutler's attempt to notice in the verb ὁδηγέω (LXX Ps 42,3) the notion of way is not strong enough to reach the Johannine thought. Even though a few other Johannine terms like "truth", "life", "house", "see" occur here and there in this psalm, they look like jigsaw pieces and do not exactly correspond to Johannine thought. Their occurrence can be regarded as coincidental since these terms frequently appear in many other psalms. Moreover, the sequence of thought followed in Pss 42–43 does not correspond with the Johannine thought flow. Beutler has not clearly and adequately shown the background behind the formulation in John 14,6, which is the core of our present discussion.[4]

Even though the focus of this discussion is to study the possible literary background of John 14,6, it is not wise to examine 14,6 in isolation. Therefore, we need to carefully observe its immediate context (14,1–4) and, to a certain extent, the near context (chapters 13–14) and the possible influences upon them as well. It is clear that 14,6 contains two independent sentences, "I am the way and the truth and the life"[5] and "No one comes to the Father except through me". Even though both sentences are exclusive claims, the exclusivity of the second sentence is much stronger. Why does Jesus make the claim, "No one comes to the Father except through me" here? Nobody asked him, "Are there other ways to come to the Father?" It means that the second sentence is a natural consequence of the first. The force of the second claim

---

[4] For a criticism of Beutler's views, see also E. D. Freed, "Ps 42/43 in John's Gospel", *NTS* 29 (1983), 62–73; Tack, *John 14,6 in Light of Jewish-Christian Dialogue*, 108–109.

[5] The consistent use of the definite article in the predicative statement in 14,6a expresses Jesus' exclusivity.

(v. 6b) depends on the significance and background of the first claim (v. 6a).[6] It seems that there is some relationship between the background of the first claim and the second one. Hence, we need to observe first the possible background of the first claim, which will give us the clues to understand the background of the second claim.

The first claim is an "I am"-saying with three predicate nouns – "way" (ὁδός), "truth" (ἀλήθεια) and "life" (ζωή). It is very clear from the context that among these three nouns the focus is on the first one, "way", despite the fact that "truth" and "life" are more significant terms in the Gospel. It should be noted that neither ἀλήθεια nor ζωή nor their cognates occur in the immediate context (14,1–14) or in the previous near context (13,1–14,5).[7] Thomas' question, "How can we know the way?" does not necessarily require a statement about "truth" and "life". Jesus' answer, "I am the way", is quite sufficient. "Way" is a significant term in the context because it is closely related to the theme of Jesus' imminent departure/journey, which is a dominant topic not only in the immediate context but also in the large context of the farewell discourse (13–17).[8] This is an indication that the term "way" has a unique role in the context and should be examined apart from "truth" and "life". The natural temptation of scholars and commentators is to seek a place in the Bible where "way", "truth" and "life" occur together and to establish all possible ways of connections. Such an approach disregards the unique role which "way" plays and the unique significance which "way" deserves in the context. It should be noted that the term "way" occurs in 14,4–5 twice before its occurrence along with "truth" and "life" in 14,6 and that the way motif is strongly predominant in the form of various verbs of journey in the immediate and near context (13,1–14,30). Therefore, it is reasonable, justifiable and even recommendable to examine the background of "way" independently of "truth" and "life".[9]

In the entire Bible, there is not an equal parallel to the formulation, "I am the way and the truth and the life" or to the paratactic construction "the way and the truth and the life". It is not yet known that an exact parallel to the claim, "I am the way and the truth and the life", exists in any of the world

---

[6] Similarly, the exclusivity of 14,6b is inseparably bound with the claims in 14,7–14, about which we shall discuss later.

[7] The last occurrence of ἀλήθεια is in 8,46, ἀληθής in 10,41, ἀληθινός in 8,16 and ἀληθῶς in 8,31. The last occurrence of ζωή is in 12,50, ζάω in 11,26 and ζῳοποιέω in 6,63. It is only in the following near context that ἀλήθεια in the construct form "the Spirit of truth", τὸ πνεῦμα τῆς ἀληθείας (14,17), and the verb ζάω (14,19) are found.

[8] In order to understand the significance of the way motif in the larger context, it is enough to observe the verbs of journey that occur very frequently in chapters 13–17. We have already examined various verbs of journey in chapters 13–14 on pp. 107–111.

[9] Beutler, *Do not Be Afraid*, 40, admits the possibilities of looking for the parallels of the "way" motif separately or together with the concepts of "truth" and "life".

literature. Thus, it is really a unique formulation of the Gospel of John. In order to know better the possible literary background behind John 14,6, the best way is not to seek immediately parallels outside the Gospel of John, but to carefully observe the intra-textual connections that the evangelist himself provides in the Gospel. It is through the observation of intra-textuality that we can better find out the intertextuality of John 14,6. Therefore, we need a two-fold examination in order to understand the background of 14,6a. At the first level, we need to examine the background of "way" independently of "truth" and "life", and then at the second level, we may observe the possible background of the paratactic construction "the way and the truth and the life". Once we know the background of 14,6a, we will be able to determine the background of 14,6b.

2. Background of "Way" (14,4–6) and its Context (14,2–3)

To understand the background of "way" in 14,6 and its context, the best approach is to recognize the fact that "the Gospel of John is a self-interpreting narrative".[10] It is, therefore, always better to interpret John with John himself. It is noteworthy that John uses only once the term "way" (ὁδός) outside 14,4–6.[11] This usage is found in the expression "the way of the Lord" in 1,23, and this verse is the key that the evangelist himself gives the reader to understand his usage in 14,6a.[12] It is important to notice that the first and only appearance of ὁδός outside 14,4–6 is found in a citation from Isa 40,3, which is quoted by all other evangelists as well (Mark 1,3; Matt 3,3; Luke 3,4).[13] This verse deserves careful observation.

---

[10] Cf. Zumstein, "Intratextuality and Intertextuality", 122.

[11] Lindars, *John*, 471–472, comments on 14,4, "Apart from an allusion to Isa 40,3 in 1,23, 'way' occurs only in this and the next two verses in the Fourth Gospel, and never in the Johannine epistles. This is surprising, considering the wide range of meanings of this word in general and the importance of the idea of 'going' in John's presentation of the Passion. But the fact that the word here comes as a non-Johannine intruder suggests that we should look for a specific saying in the underlying tradition to account for it". Even though Lindars suggests the possibility of a Synoptic tradition, he is aware of the peculiarity of the Johannine usage of ὁδός. In the Synoptic Gospels, there is no exact parallel to John 14,6a, and the Synoptic tradition cannot explain the reasons for the statement in 14,6b. About the possible role of the Synoptic tradition, we will discuss below.

[12] The situation in the Synoptic Gospels is quite different. The term ὁδός is an ordinary term there. It occurs very frequently both in its literary and figurative senses. But in John, ὁδός is never used in literal sense and it has a unique importance.

[13] The LXX rendering of Isa 40,3 quoted by all evangelists slightly differs from MT. In the LXX, "in the desert" qualifies "the voice", whereas in the MT "in the desert" is attached to "prepare the way of the Lord". Since the ministry of John the Baptist is presented

John 1,23 is a part of the first interrogation by priests and Levites from Jerusalem regarding the identity of John the Baptist (1,19–23). The questions raised by them indicate various popular eschatological expectations of that time.[14] It is striking to notice how John has employed this verse in relation to John the Baptist. In John's Gospel, it is John the Baptist himself who utters, "I (am) the voice of the one crying in the wilderness", whereas in the Synoptic Gospels it is the evangelists who apply the Isaiah quotation to John the Baptist.

Most probably the source of quotation in John 1,23 is the LXX rendering of Isa 40,3, "The voice of one crying in the wilderness, prepare the way of the Lord, make straight the paths of our God" (φωνὴ βοῶντος ἐν τῇ ἐρήμῳ ἑτοιμάσατε τὴν ὁδὸν κυρίου εὐθείας ποιεῖτε τὰς τρίβους τοῦ θεοῦ ἡμῶν).[15] But John has made significant changes to Isa 40,3 in his quotation in 1,23 by condensing the two parallel lines of the original into one and by replacing the initial command "prepare" (ἑτοιμάσατε) with the command of the second line, "make straight" (εὐθύνατε), which varies slightly from "make straight" (εὐθείας ποιεῖτε) of the LXX.[16] Hence, it is important to ask why John has replaced ἑτοιμάσατε with εὐθύνατε.

The attempt to find out the background of the way motif in 14,4–6 and the attempt to answer the question why John has replaced ἑτοιμάσατε with

---

in the geographical setting of a desert, the alteration in the LXX is suitable for the purpose of the evangelists.

[14] The questions directed to John the Baptist refer to the fact that the majority of the Jews at that time were expecting the coming of a Messiah, whatever might be their views of the Messiah. The Qumran community seems to have expected three eschatological figures: a prophet, a priestly Messiah and a royal Messiah. Cf. Brown, *John*, I, 46.

[15] Cf. C. H. Williams, "The Testimony of Isaiah and Johannine Christology", *'As Those Who Are Taught'. The Interpretation of Isaiah from the LXX to the SBL*, ed. C. M. McGinnis and P. K. Tull (Leiden 2006), 109; idem, "Isaiah in John's Gospel", *Isaiah in the New Testament*, ed. S. Moyise and M. J. J. Menken (London 2005), 103. For various reasons to prefer the LXX version to the possible translation of the Hebrew text by the evangelist, see M. J. J. Menken, *Old Testament Quotations in the Fourth Gospel. Studies in Textual Form* (Kampen 1996), 22–25; B. G. Schuchard, *Scripture Within Scripture. The Interrelationship of Form and Function in the Explicit Old Testament Citations in the Gospel of John* (SBLDS 133; Atlanta 1992), 3–6.

[16] Εὐθύνατε is an obvious equivalent of εὐθείας ποιεῖτε. The alteration of εὐθείας ποιεῖτε into εὐθύνατε by the evangelist can be explained by the possibility that John's source text had εὐθύνατε instead of εὐθείας ποιεῖτε. Since Aquila's translation in ms. 86 has in Isa 40,3c εὐθύνατε for ישרו, Menken, *Old Testament Quotations*, 24–25, suggests the possibility that John quoted from a pre-Aquila recension. According to Schuchard, *Scripture Within Scripture*, 11–12, John has intentionally inserted εὐθύνατε in order to present the identity and message of John the Baptist from a sapiential standpoint (cf. e.g., Prov 4,25–26; 9,15; 13,13; Sir 2,6).

2. Background of "Way" (14,4–6) and its Context (14,2–3)

εὐθύνατε are closely related.[17] It is possible that John has intentionally avoided ἑτοιμάσατε and used εὐθύνατε in 1,23 because according to him, it is only Jesus who can prepare "the way of the Lord", and not John the Baptist. For John, Jesus himself is "the way" and the activity of preparing the way is reserved to Jesus alone and not to John the Baptist or to anyone else.[18] It is a style of the evangelist to retain only those words or clauses in scriptural citations which are of direct relevance to their new surrounding context.[19] The role of the Baptist is "to make straight" the way of the Lord by pointing to

---

[17] R. A. Culpepper, *Anatomy of the Fourth Gospel. A Study in Literary Design* (Philadelphia 1983), 201, remarks, "Various parts of the gospel are interrelated by the recurrence of core symbols. The themes to which they are related are repeated and interrelated with challenging and enriching variations which cause various passages and contexts to resonate simultaneously, thereby allowing the sensitive reader to grasp the whole with increasing appreciation".

[18] It should be noted that the appellative "Baptist" is used only in the Synoptic Gospels, but never in the Gospel of John. In this monograph, it is used for easy identification. Menken, *Old Testament Quotations*, 26–35, tries to understand John's redaction in 1,23 in the light of the evangelist's overall presentation of the relationship of John the Baptist with Jesus. Even though John the Baptist is historically prior to Jesus (1,15.27.30; 3,28), from the perspective of meta-historicity he is inferior to Jesus because Jesus existed prior to John as the Logos and is superior to him (1,1–2; 1,15.30; 3,31–36). The eternal "being" (εἰμί) of the Logos is contrasted with the historical "becoming" (γίνομαι) of John the Baptist (1,1.6). Hence, John the Baptist identifies himself with the voice mentioned in Isa 40,3 and denies any messianic claims (1,19–28). Menken also points out that when the verb ἑτοιμάζω is used with an explicit or implicit indirect object, it has a peculiar connotation, which prevents the evangelist to use it in relation to John the Baptist. It can be explained with the following example. The subject A prepares something for B (indirect object). Only when the preparation is done by A, B can come there where A already is, to participate in what has been prepared. In this case, A precedes B in time at a certain place and fulfils his task of preparing before B arrives. According to Menken, the reason for the alteration of ἑτοιμάσατε into εὐθύνατε is that the evangelist wanted to avoid the idea that the task of John the Baptist had been accomplished when Jesus appeared on the scene. The Baptist was not so much Jesus' precursor, as a witness to Jesus contemporaneous with him. Menken's views are acceptable, but his attention is exclusively on John 1,23 and its context. Therefore, his focus is on the relationship between John the Baptist and Jesus. He does not pay sufficient attention to John's exclusive use of ἑτοιμάζω in 14,2–3, which is closely related to the way motif in 14,4–6. This is understandable because the concern of Menken's work is the study of the Old Testament quotations in John's Gospel. In fact, John's omission of ἑτοιμάζω in 1,23 should be understood and interpreted also in the light of John's exclusive use of it in 14,2–3. Menken has failed to notice it. In the view of *Tack, John 14,6 in Light of Jewish-Christian Dialogue,* 140, "The Logos has already entered the world (cf. 1:11). Therefore, the way no longer needs to be prepared". But John 1,11 is a programmatic statement about what is going to happen to Jesus. Hence, it is not logically correct to say that the Logos has already entered the world. If the Logos had already entered the world, then one has to show when his own had rejected him (1,11) before the Logos became flesh (1,14).

[19] Williams, "Isaiah in John's Gospel", 103.

Jesus who remains unknown (1,26.31.33) and in whom the coming of the Lord for salvation is finally realized.[20] Unlike the Synoptic Gospels, John interprets Isa 40,3 christologically with exclusive focus on Jesus in the description of the Baptist's testimony and activity (cf. 1,6–8.15.26–27.29–36) and gives it a new definition.[21]

It should be noted that, unlike the Synoptic Gospels, John adds ἐγώ to the quotation from Isa 40,3. While John the Baptist identifies himself with "the voice" (ἐγὼ φωνή) of the one crying out in the wilderness (John 1,23; Isa 40,3), Jesus identifies himself in John 14,6 with "the way" (ἐγώ εἰμι ἡ ὁδός) promised in Isa 40,3 for the salvation of humanity. Both 1,23 and 14,6 are answers to the questions of interrogators. In both cases, the speaker reveals his identity using the images, "voice" and "way" found in Isa 40,3. The utterance by John the Baptist and Jesus begins with ἐγώ. Unlike Jesus, the Baptist does not utter ἐγώ εἰμι. Even though ἐγώ εἰμι in 14,6a is predicated, it will remind the reader of the ἐγώ εἰμι formula frequently found in Deutero-Isaiah. By identifying the role of John the Baptist with a voice, the evangelist seems to lay more emphasis on the witnessing role (μαρτυρία) of John the Baptist (cf. 1,6–8.19).[22] In John, it is the coming of Jesus that is made straight through the Baptist's testimony. This he does by recognizing the unknown Messiah who is also the Son and the Lamb of God and by making him known to the people of Israel (1,26–34). While the Baptist is the "voice" that speaks (witnesses) on behalf of Jesus (1,15.29–36), Jesus is the "way" to the Father on behalf of the believers.

That the evangelist does not use ἑτοιμάζω in 1,23 should draw the reader's attention to examine where and how the evangelist employs ἑτοιμάζω elsewhere in the Gospel. He uses the verb ἑτοιμάζω only in 14,2–3 (2x), in the very immediate context of 14,6. We may assume that if John has intentionally omitted ἑτοιμάζω along with ὁδός in 1,23, he has intentionally used ἑτοιμάζω in 14,2–3, which stands in close relationship with ὁδός in 14,4–6. There exists an inseparable relation between the "preparation" in 14,2–3 and "the way of

---

[20] Williams, "Isaiah in John's Gospel", 104.

[21] Williams, "Isaiah in John's Gospel", 103–104. M. Stowasser, *Johannes der Täufer im Vierten Evangelium. Eine Untersuchung zu seiner Bedeutung für die johanneische Gemeinde* (ÖBS 12; Klosterneuburg 1992), 131, remarks, "Da die Bußpredigt des Täufers nicht entfaltet wird, erfolgt eine Neudefinition von Jes 40,3 durch seinen joh. Kontext. ...Die vv. 22f. bezwecken demnach weder eine Korrektur des joh. Täuferbildes noch eine Reverenz an die synoptische Konzeption, sondern versuchen die Neudefinition eines traditionellen Elementes der urchristlichen Überlieferung von Johannes d. T".

[22] Mark also regards John the Baptist as a witness to Jesus, though not as rigidly as does the Gospel of John. See C. S. Keener, "Historical Tradition in the Fourth Gospel's Depiction of the Baptist", *Jesus Research. The Gospel of John in Historical Inquiry*, ed. J. H. Charlesworth and J. G. R. Pruszinski (Jewish and Christian Texts in Contexts and Related Studies 26; London 2019), 155, n. 1.

2. Background of "Way" (14,4–6) and its Context (14,2–3)

Jesus/the Lord" in 14,4. The immediate shift from the motif of "preparing" (14,2–3) to the motif of "way" (14,4–6), especially to "Jesus'/the Lord's way" (14,4), may remind the reader of the Isaianic phrase "prepare the way of the Lord" (Isa 40,3), which is well-known during the intertestamental period. In the Gospel, Jesus is frequently called "the Lord" (4,1 *l.v.*; 6,23; 11,2; 13,13.14; 20,2.13.18.20.25.28; 21,7.12). Hence, "the way" that Jesus "goes" in 14,4 can be regarded as "the way of the Lord". For John, it is same as "the way of the Lord" promised in Isa 40,3 and proclaimed by John the Baptist in 1,23 because the evangelist has not mentioned any other way in the Gospel. Thus, the themes of "preparation" in 14,2–3 and "the way of the Lord" in 14,4 are brought together to present Jesus as the one who prepares the way of the Lord. Since what Jesus prepares is a soteriological and eschatological way through his death-resurrection, Jesus can claim, "I am the way" in 14,6. Since Jesus' "preparation" belongs to his hour, the evangelist speaks of it only after Jesus' hour has come (13,1; cf. 12,23). Thus, John sees the fulfilment of the Isaianic exhortation (Isa 40,3) "prepare the way of the Lord" (ἑτοιμάσατε τὴν ὁδὸν κυρίου) only in Jesus.

Isa 40,3 may, at a first glance, just refer to the preparation of the way in the desert for the return of the Israelites from Babylonian captivity to their homeland. But its use by the Qumran community (cf. 1QS VIII,14; IX,20) and the New Testament writers make clear that Isa 40,3 was an object of intense eschatological speculation during the period of second temple Judaism and carried a reference to the eschatological salvation.[23] John's citation in 1,23 indicates that, for John, the eschatological salvation promised in Isa

---

[23] J. Blenkinsopp, *Isaiah 40–55. A New Translation with Introduction and Commentary* (AB 19A; New Haven 1974), 182, comments on the eschatological dimension of way in Isa 40,3 thus, "Viewed within the context of the book of Isaiah as a whole, the figure of the way or the journey indicates a broader development from historical particularities to an eschatological and, eventually, apocalyptic perspective". C. F. D. Moule, "Fulfilment-Words in the New Testament: Use and Abuse", *NTS* 14 (1968), 294, points out that the citation from Isa 40,3 in the Qumran scrolls (cf. 1QS VIII,13–16) is used as an injunction or authorization, whereas in the Gospels it is regarded as a prediction. From the geographical context and the ideology, it is possible to assume that John the Baptist had some kind of relationship or contact with the Qumran community. For an examination of the possible relationship between the Qumran community and John the Baptist, see J. H. Charlesworth, "John the Baptizer and the Dead Sea Scrolls", *The Bible and the Dead Sea Scrolls. The Scrolls and Christian Origins* (Waco 2006), III, 1–35; J. A. Fitzmyer, *The Dead Sea Scrolls and Christian Origins* (Grand Rapids 2000), 18–21. However, at present there is no scholarly unanimity regarding this topic. For a different view, see S. E. Porter, "Was John the Baptist a Member of the Qumran Community? Once More", *Christian Origins and Hellenistic Judaism. Social and Literary Contexts for the New Testament*, ed. S. E. Porter and A. W. Pitts (TENT 10; Leiden 2013), II, 283–313.

40,3–5 is fulfilled in Jesus.[24] It is likely, then, that John understands and (re)interprets the Isaianic expression "prepare the way of the Lord" eschatologically in 14,2–3 in the light of Jesus' death, resurrection and the traditional belief about Parousia (1 Thess 4,13–17; cf. Mark 13,24–27; Heb 9,28). It is by "going" and "preparing a place" in the Father's house and "coming again" to take his disciples to himself (14,2–3) that Jesus prepares and becomes the way (14,6).[25] The sudden change from the theme of preparing (14,2–3) to the way motif (14,4–6), especially to Jesus'/the Lord's way (14,4), is worth noticing. It helps one to think of the Isaianic text.[26] For John, the new exodus promised in Isa 40,3 takes place with Jesus' death on the cross when God delivers his people from the power of Satan.[27] However, the way of the Lord does not end with Jesus' death and resurrection, but continues until the believers are with him where he is or in the place prepared by him.

The term τόπος is usually translated as "place".[28] In John 14,2–3, τόπος does not have a literal meaning but maintains an eschatological sense. It should be noted that the text does not say that after preparing a place Jesus will take his disciples to the prepared place, rather it says, "And after I go and prepare a place for you, I will come again and take you to myself, so that where I am, there you may be also" (14,3). Since Jesus is where the Father is and he has a permanent place in the Father's house (8,35), what is envisaged here is communion with the Father through Jesus. Hence, τόπος gradually gets the sense of "a possibility" for communion with the Father as a result of Jesus' death-resurrection.[29] The term τόπος also has both in the biblical and non-biblical literature the sense of "a favorable circumstance for doing some-

---

[24] In Isaiah, "the way" signifies "the coming" of God to save his people and his saving presence (40,3; 42,16; 43,19; 49,10–11).

[25] It is a view of Deutero-Isaiah that the Lord himself will make or prepare the way. It is clearly said in Isa 43,19: "I am about to do a new thing; now it springs forth, do you not perceive it? I will make a way in the wilderness and rivers in the desert". See T. R. Briley, *Isaiah* (The College Press NIV Commentary; Joplin 2004), II, 117.

[26] It is the repetition of the key terms "prepare" (ἑτοιμάζω 2x) and "way" (ὁδός 3x) which makes the allusion to Isa 40,3 discernible in the immediate context of 14,6.

[27] C. J. Davis, *The Name and the Way of the Lord* (JSNTSS 129; Sheffield 1996), 180.

[28] The term τόπος is found along with ἑτοιμάζω in 1 Chr 15,1.3.12; 2 Chr 3,1 with reference to the preparation of a place for the ark of God and in Rev 12,6.14 with an eschatological significance.

[29] Brown, *John*, II, 627, explains the preparation of a place/the dwelling places thus, "Jesus is on his way to be reunited with the Father in glory (13,1) and *to make it possible* for others to be united to the Father – this is how he prepares the dwelling places". According to Barrett, *John*, 457, "John is thinking here of the whole process of the passion and glorification of Jesus as *the means* by which believers are admitted to the heavenly life". The emphasis in italics in both instances is mine. C. Dietzfelbinger, *Das Evangelium nach Johannes. Kapitel 13–21* (Züricher Bibelkommentare NT 4.2; Zurich 2001), 30, argues that τόπος in 14,2–3 means not only "place" but also "Gelegenheit, Möglichkeit für jemanden".

2. Background of "Way" (14,4–6) and its Context (14,2–3)

thing, possibility, opportunity, chance" (e.g., Sir 4,5; 19,17; Wis 12,10; 1 Macc 9,45; Acts 25,16; Eph 4,27; Rom 12,19; 15,23; Heb 12,17; Jos., *A.J.*, 16.258; 1 Clem. 7,5).[30] This sense is close to the figurative sense of "way".[31] Hence, Jesus' "preparation of a place" in its context can be understood as "preparation of the way" to the Father.

What Jesus does through his death for the believers is "preparing the possibility or the way" to come to the Father. This becomes clearer when John 14,2–6 is read in the light of a parallel text from Heb 10,19–20, "Therefore, my friends, since we have confidence to enter the sanctuary by the blood of Jesus, by the new and living way that he opened for us through the curtain (that is, through his flesh)...". Here too, what Jesus' death provides the believers is an opportunity for entrance (εἴσοδος) into God's sanctuary (cf. προσαγωγή in Rom 5,2; Eph 2,18; 3,12; Heb 7,25; 1 Pet 3,18).[32] In both Hebrews and John, it is the death of Jesus that makes possible the access to God. In both texts Jesus *goes ahead* as "the high priest" and "the good shepherd", and the believers have to follow him. When Jesus claims that he is the way to the Father in 14,6, he is claiming that he can give the believers an opportunity to come to the Father. Thus, we can assume that Jesus' "preparing a place" in the Father's house is not much different from his preparation of the way to the Father/Father's house.

Nobody else can "go" and "prepare" a place in the Father's house because only Jesus belongs to the Father's house eternally (8,35). The preparation of the way requires the removal of obstacles (Isa 40,4; 57,14; 62,10). According to John, Jesus' ultimate enemy is the devil and the greatest obstacle between God and human being is sin caused by the rulership of the devil over human hearts (John 8,44–46; 13,2; cf. 1 John 3,8). Jesus' death and resurrection is the hour of preparation of the way to the Father in which the rulership of the devil will be overthrown (John 12,31; 16,11; cf. Col 2,15; Heb 2,14; 1 John 3,8; Rev 12,1–18). Since Jesus alone can prepare the way by taking away the sin of the world (John 1,29) and by overthrowing the rulership of the devil (12,31; 16,11), the evangelist does not ascribe this salvific activity to John the Baptist in 1,23. For John, the notion of the way to the Father and its preparation by Jesus is much more important than the concept of the preparation of the way for Jesus by John the Baptist, as found in the Synoptic Gospels. At the same time, this is yet another case to argue for "the competition hypothesis" concerning the relationship between the disciples of John the Baptist and

---

[30] BDAG, 1012.

[31] NAB translates τόπος in 1 Macc 9,45 as "way", "The battle is before us, and behind us are the waters of the Jordan on one side, marsh and thickets on the other, and there is no *way* (τόπος) of escape".

[32] Ebel, "ὁδός", 941 and M. Völkel, "ὁδός", *EDNT*, II, 493, point out that "way" (ὁδός) in Heb 10,19–20 (cf. 6,20) has almost the sense of "access" (εἴσοδος).

the disciples of Jesus.[33] If this hypothesis is true, we may assume that the evangelist may be trying to ascertain the superiority of Jesus' preparation of the way over the preparation of the way by the Baptist, as popularly known in other Gospel traditions, and thus to present Jesus as the real preparer of the way.[34]

Throughout the Gospel, John has alerted the readers that Jesus' "going" (πορεύομαι/ὑπάγω) is something unique and that no one can "go" along with him (ὑπάγω 8,21; 13,33.36)[35] and no one knows what his "going" really means (cf. πορεύομαι 7,34–35; ὑπάγω 8,14.22; 14,5). He must go first because he is the good shepherd who alone can "go ahead" of the sheep (10,4) and lay down his life for them (10,11). Jesus' "going" and "preparing a place" are not two activities but only one. They are inseparable and refer to his death-resurrection and its outcome for the believers.[36]

The preparation of the way of the Lord in Isa 40,3 has the result that "the glory of the Lord shall appear and all flesh shall see the salvation of God" (ὀφθήσεται ἡ δόξα κυρίου καὶ ὄψεται πᾶσα σὰρξ τὸ σωτήριον τοῦ θεοῦ). Just as "the appearance of the glory of the Lord" as a result of "the preparation of the way of the Lord" is mentioned in Isa 40,3–5, so also the theme of glory/glorification occurs in the context of both occasions when John uses the Isaianic terms, "make straight", "prepare" and "way".[37] In the context of 1,23, John has already said that the glory of the Lord appeared, "We saw his glory,

---

[33] According to the "competition hypothesis", there existed a friendly competition or a rivalry between the followers of John the Baptist and the followers of Jesus. It is clear from the very beginning of the Gospel itself that the Fourth Evangelist tries to assert the superiority of Jesus over John the Baptist and to put the Baptist in his place (1,6–9.15.19–34; 3,25–30; 4,1; 5,36; 10,41). W. Wink, *John the Baptist in the Gospel Tradition* (Cambridge 1968), 98, thinks that the Fourth Evangelist has set out a systematic correction of Baptist Christology and those Synoptic traditions which were open to misuse by the Baptist sect as a means of combating a false estimation of John. J. Ernst, *Johannes der Täufer: Interpretation, Geschichte, Wirkungsgeschichte* (BZNW 53; Berlin 1989), 212, says, "Der Evangelist wendet sich vom Anfang bis zum Ende gegen eine Überwertung des Täufers". For a discussion over the "competition hypothesis" and over the theme of polemic and apologetic attitude against the Baptist sect, see J. Marcus, *John the Baptist in History and Theology* (Columbia 2018), 11–26; C. S. Keener, *The Gospel of John. A Commentary* (Peabody 2003), I, 388–393; Wink, *John the Baptist*, 98–106; Ernst, *Johannes der Täufer*, 212–215.

[34] There is a difference between John the Baptist and Jesus in their preparation of the way. While the preparation of the way by John the Baptist is, as we find in the Synoptic Gospels, intended for the coming of Jesus, the preparation of the way by Johannine Jesus is meant for the coming of believers to God (John 14,6) and for the coming of God to the believers (John 14,15–24).

[35] The predictions of the betrayal and denial respectively by Judas Iscariot and Peter highlight the incapability of the disciples to go along the way of Jesus.

[36] Πορεύομαι is used in the sense of Jesus' death in Luke 22,22 (cf. Luke 22,33; 1 Kgs 2,2; 2 Sam 12,23; Job 10,21; 16,22; Qoh 12,5).

[37] Cf. Ball, *I Am*, 234.

the glory as of the Father's only Son" (1,14).[38] The theme of glorification also occurs in the very near and immediate context (13,31–32; 14,13) when John speaks of the Isaianic theme of preparation and way in 14,2-6. In 13,31–32, Jesus says, "Now is the Son of Man glorified, and God is glorified in him. (If God is glorified in him,) God will also glorify him in himself, and he will glorify him at once".[39] As a result of Jesus' "going" to the Father (14,12), the petition of the disciples in Jesus' name will eventually lead to the glorification of the Father in the Son (14,13).

"The way of the Lord" in Isa 40,3 is also a "way for the people" because 40,9–11 points out that the Lord will lead his people back to Zion along the way. Moreover, what has begun as "the way of the Lord" in Deutero-Isaiah (Isa 40,3) becomes later "the way for the people" (Isa 57,14; 62,10).[40] Thus, in the context of the new exodus in Isaiah, the way of the Lord has a two-fold meaning. On the one hand, it is the way that the Lord has to go beforehand for the redemption of his people, and on the other hand, it is the way by which people must pass in their return from exile.[41] In the Gospel too, this transition is notable. What has begun as the way of the Lord in John 1,23 (cf. 14,4) becomes a way for the people in 14,6. On the one hand, it is the way that Jesus has to go beforehand to make possible the believers' access to the Father's house (14,4), and on the other hand, it is the way which the believers must go to reach the Father (14,6).

Finally, there is also an external evidence from the Qumran community for the possibility of the influence of Isa 40,3 in John's characterization of Jesus as the way in 14,6.[42] As it has already been discussed, the Qumran community called itself "the Way" (1QS IX,17–18.21; CD 1,3).[43] The basic reason for this is most probably their interpretation of Isa 40,3 (1QS VIII,12–16).[44] It is

---

[38] The translation given here is according to NAB.

[39] Glorification is a key theme in Deutero-Isaiah, where the term δοξάζω occurs 8 times (42,10; 43,4.23; 44,23; 49,3.5; 52,13; 55,5). The mutual glorification between the Father and the Son in John 13,31-32 is comparable with the mutual glorification between God and his Servant in Isa 49,3–5 (cf. 52,13).

[40] Ball, *I Am*, 236, says, "The way of the Lord in Isaiah is also the way that the people will pass on their journey from exile to Jerusalem".

[41] Ball, *I Am*, 236.

[42] This view is still supported by the current "apparent consensus" in Johannine scholarship that the Gospel of John was in some way influenced by Qumran or Essene thought. However, this influence need not be necessarily a direct one. For a detailed study on this topic and literature, see M. L. Coloe and T. Thatcher, *John, Qumran, and the Dead Sea Scrolls. Sixty Years of Discovery and Debate* (Atlanta 2011). Cf. Theobald, *Herrenworte*, 320; Ball, *I Am*, 237.

[43] See the discussion under "Way in the Dead Sea Scrolls" on pp. 80–84.

[44] Scholars have suggested the possibility of the influence of Isa 40,3 upon the characterization of the Christian movement as "the Way" in Acts. See pp. 90–91; Blenkinsopp, *Opening the Sealed Book*, 178–185. In his study, Pao, *Acts*, 67–68, has pointed out that the

likely that John's interpretation of Isa 40,3 has influenced him in applying the salvific Old Testament image of the way to Jesus.[45] Unlike the Qumran writings and the Acts of the Apostles, the focus of John is not on the identity of the community but on the identity of Jesus (cf. 20,31). It is crucial for John to present Jesus as the way since Jesus is the only possibility of access to the Father.

3. Background of "the Way and the Truth and the Life"

After having detected the influence of Isaiah upon the way motif in John, it is possible to look at the background behind the paratactic formulation "the way and the truth and the life". Since there is no exact parallel to John 14,6a in the entire Bible and non-biblical literature, we need to assume that 14,6a is a unique Johannine formulation. To understand the background of this formulation, we have to observe the association of way with truth and life throughout the Bible and other Jewish literature.[46]

In the Old Testament, the association of way with truth and life is very common. In Ps 85,11 (LXX), the psalmist prays, "Guide, O Lord, on your way and I will walk in your truth" (ὁδήγησόν με κύριε τῇ ὁδῷ σου καὶ πορεύσομαι ἐν τῇ ἀληθείᾳ σου). Here, "Lord's guidance on the way" stands in parallel relationship with "walking in his truth". It is the Lord's guidance on the way that enables the psalmist to walk in the truth. According to Sir 37,15, it is God who "makes straight" (εὐθύνω) "the way in truth" (ἐν ἀληθείᾳ τὴν ὁδόν). Tobit is presented as the man who "walked in the ways of truth" (ὁδοῖς ἀληθείας ἐπορευόμην, Tob 1,3). "Keeping the commandments" of the Lord is synonymous with "walking in the truth" before him (Tob 3,5). In Wis 5,6–7, "the way of the Lord" (ὁδὸς κυρίου) stands in parallel with "the way of truth", ὁδὸς ἀληθείας (cf. Ps 119,30). The idea that truth guides human beings or God guides human beings in his truth is prevalent in the Old Testament. E.g., it is God's "light" (φῶς) and "truth" (ἀλήθεια) which "guide" (ὁδηγέω) and "bring" (ἄγω) the psalmist to God's holy mountain (LXX Ps 42,3). The psalmist asks God "to guide" (ὁδηγέω) him in his (God's) truth (LXX Ps 24,5). It implies that "walking in truth" is not a goal in itself but only a means to the goal.

---

recurrence of Isa 40,3–5 throughout the Lukan writings confirms the dependence of the way-terminology on Isa 40,3.

[45] Cf. Brown, *John*, II, 629–630.

[46] The association of way with truth and life in Jewish literature is already indicated while analysing the way motif in the first part of this monograph. Below various scattered texts are brought together to highlight the association of way with truth and life.

3. Background of "the Way and the Truth and the Life"

The idea that way leads to life is present in the Old Testament. The very first occurrence of the way in the Bible is found in association with life. The way that Gen 3,24 speaks of is "the way of/to the tree of life" (ἡ ὁδὸς τοῦ ξύλου τῆς ζωῆς). The psalmist asks the Lord to show him the "path of life" (ὁδὸς ζωῆς), which is to be experienced in the presence of the Lord (Ps 16[15],11). In Proverbs, the expressions "way/ways of life" (2,19; 5,6; 6,23; 15,24) and "way to life" (10,16–17; 12,28) occur frequently. The expression "the way of life" in Proverbs can be interpreted as an objective genitive, meaning "the way that leads to life".[47] The "way of life" that the Lord sets before the people of Israel is actually the way to life, which consists in doing the will of the Lord (Jer 21,8; cf. Deut 30,15–20). The view that the following of the way of Lord will lead to a long life is expressed in Deut 5,33.[48] Generally, in the Old Testament the Lord's way may stand for his words and commandments. That the Lord's commandments lead to a long life is a dominant view of the Old Testament (e.g., Deut 5,33; 6,2; 11,8–9; 30,16; 32,46–47; 1 Kgs 3,14; Neh 9,29; Ezek 33,15; Bar 4,1; Prov 4,4.10; 7,2; cf. Matt 19,17; John 6,63.68). It should be noted that life in the Old Testament is very frequently equated with blessing, success, happiness, peace, health or longevity. The notion of eternal life, which is central to the New Testament teaching, comes to the fore only at the very end of the Old Testament period (see Dan 12,2; 2 Macc 7,9; Wis 2,22–23).

In the Dead Sea Scrolls too, the association of way with truth and life can be noticed (see CD III,13–16).[49] That "the truth of God" (אמת אל) has a guiding role in human life is testified in 1QS XI,4–5. It is striking to find that the notions of "way" (שְׁבִיל, נְתִיבָה), "truth" (אֱמֶת) and "life" (חַיִּים) occur together in one sentence in 1QH[a] XV,13b–15. In this verse, while the notion of "truth" has a guiding role, the notion of "life" appears as the destination of one's life journey. Expressions like "way/ways of life", דרך/דרכי חיים (4Q270 2ii20; 4Q299 79,3), "ways of truth", דרכי אמת (CD III,15; 4Q416 2,iii.14; 4Q418 9+9a–c.15) also frequently appear. In the wisdom text of 4Q185 1–2ii,1–2, the expression "way towards life" (דרך לחיים) is used.[50] For Philo, the end of the way of virtue is "life" (ζωή) and immortality (ἀθανασία).[51] God is frequently regarded as the guide on the way.[52]

---

[47] Koch, "דֶּרֶךְ", 287.

[48] Deut 5,33 says, "You must follow exactly *the path* that the Lord your God has commanded you, so that you may *live*, and that it may go well with you, and that you may *live long* in the land that you are to possess". The words in italics are for emphasis.

[49] See the section "Way in the Dead Sea Scrolls" where the texts are cited. See pp. 80–84.

[50] Repo, *Der Weg als Selbstbezeichnung*, 178, states, "Jedenfalls war der Weg der Essener auf ein ewiges Leben ausgerichtet".

[51] *Plant.*, 37.

[52] *Leg.*, 2.85; 3.40; *Migr.*, 143.170–171; *Det.*, 29.114–118; *Decal.*, 81; *QE.*, 1.10; 2.40.

The association of way with truth and life is prevalent in the New Testament as well. All the Synoptic Gospels report that Jesus teaches the way of God in accordance with truth (Matt 22,16; Mark 12,14; Luke 20,21). In these three instances, the prepositional phrase ἐν ἀληθείᾳ/ἐπ' ἀληθείας modifies the verb διδάσκω. It may indicate how Jesus teaches the way of God. In saying that Jesus teaches in accordance with truth/truthfully the way of God, there is an underlying view that what Jesus teaches about God's way is truth.[53] In 2 Pet 2,2, the Christian way is characterized as "the way of truth" (ἡ ὁδὸς τῆς ἀληθείας), which is dishonoured by the false prophets and teachers (cf. 2 Pet 2,15). The association of the way motif with truth is also found in the Johannine letters (2 John 1,4; 3 John 1,3–4) in the expression "walking in truth" (περιπατέω ἐν ἀληθείᾳ).

The idea that "the way leads to life" (ἡ ὁδὸς ἡ ἀπάγουσα εἰς τὴν ζωήν) is explicitly noticeable in the teaching of Jesus in Matt 7,14: "For the gate is narrow and the road is hard that leads to life". Acts 2,28 clearly speaks of "ways to life" (αἱ ὁδοὶ ζωῆς), which in the context is a reference to the life of Christ risen from the dead. According to Heb 10,20, the access to the presence of God, which the believers have attained through the death of Jesus, is called "the living way" (ἡ ὁδὸς ζῶσα). It is certain that in the New Testament "life" (ζωή) is regarded as the goal or the end result of God's salvific plan through Christ for humanity.[54]

The above given examination shows that the association of way with truth and life is a matter of fact in biblical and other Jewish literature. The notion of way is incomplete in itself.[55] Similarly, Jesus' identification with the way alone is not sufficient. Hence, truth and life are immediately added to give additional information about him and thus a complete sense to the notion of way. In 14,6a, John has only made use of the common association of way with truth and life in the Jewish and biblical tradition.[56] Hence, it is unnecessary and pointless to look for an individual text and to suggest it as the primary literary background for the paratactic construction of "the way and the truth and the life". In the Bible, truth is not an ultimate goal, as it is found in Greek philosophy. In the Old Testament, truth often corresponds with fidelity

---

[53] Cf. B. M. Newman and P. C. Stine, *A Handbook on the Gospel of Matthew* (New York 1988), 683.

[54] E.g., Matt 18,8–9; 19,16–17; 19,29; 25,46; Mark 9,43–45; 10,17.30; Luke 10,25; 18,18.30; Acts 2,28; 11,18; 13,46.48; Rom 2,7; 5,18.21; 6,22–23; Gal 6,8; 1 Tim 1,16; 6,12; Titus 1,2; 3,7; 1 John 5,13.16; Jude 1,21; Rev 2,10; 7,17; 21,6.

[55] According to biblical understanding, the notion of way becomes complete when there is some sort of information about the means (guidance/guide) and the destination for the journey.

[56] Cf. P. F. Bartholomä, *The Johannine Discourses and the Teaching of Jesus in the Synoptics. A Contribution to the Discussion Concerning the Authenticity of Jesus's Words in the Fourth Gospel* (TANZ 57; Tübingen 2012), 271–272.

4. Background of John 14,6b

In the entire Bible, there is no exact parallel to the formulation, "No one comes to the Father except through me" (14,6b).[58] Therefore, this statement should be regarded as a unique Johannine formulation, which presents an exclusive claim. It should be specially noted that unlike the Synoptic Gospels (Mark 1,3; Matt 3,3; Luke 3,4), John 1,23 shows no interest in quoting the phrase τὰς τρίβους τοῦ θεοῦ ἡμῶν of Isa 40,3. From this, it is possible to assume that in John's mind there is an exclusive concentration on "the way of the Lord". It is this exclusive concentration that prompts him to consider Jesus as the only way and to state, "No one comes to the Father except through me". It is important to know the possible background behind this formulation. If we can suggest Isa 40,3 within the overarching theme of the way in Isa 40–55 as the background behind the way metaphor in 14,6a, the context of the same text is likely to be the background behind the statement in 14,6b. Isa 40–55 is well known for the exclusive claims of Yahweh. There-

---

[57] Michael Theobald has failed to recognize in proper perspective the association of way with truth and life in the biblical and other Jewish literature. Therefore, he is unable to understand the role of "the truth and the life" in John 14,6 and is compelled to think that "I am the way" is the original saying and "truth and life" are addition by the evangelist to the existing tradition. See Theobald, *Herrenworte*, 311–312. For a detailed discussion on the role of truth and life in John 14,6 and on the interrelation between way, truth and life, see pp. 255–260.

[58] The nearest possible Synoptic parallel is found in Matt 11,27, "No one knows the Son except the Father, and no one knows the Father except the Son and anyone to whom the Son chooses to reveal him" (cf. Luke 10,22). Despite the differences in formulation, this parallel shows that John 14,6b is not, as some think, purely an invention or imagination of John. It is an indication that in the core sayings of Jesus that spread in the early Church, there were sayings that served as a catalyst for the discourses in John. Cf. R. A. Culpepper, *The Gospel of Luke. Introduction, Commentary and Reflections* (NIB 9; Nashville 1995), 224. But the Synoptic parallel does not carry the same exclusive force as John's formulation in 14,6b. It should be noted that in the Synoptic text Jesus' role is rendered in the third person. But, in John, Jesus' role is rendered in the first person, "through me" (δι' ἐμοῦ). The verse also begins with an emphatic "I am...", ἐγώ εἰμι. Therefore, the possible background behind Jesus' exclusive claim to salvation in John 14,6b in the form of first person speech is still to be found out.

fore, it is likely that John is aware of the near and broader context of Is 40,3 and the exclusive monotheistic claims found in them.[59]

The most important source of monotheism in the Old Testament outside the Torah is Deutero-Isaiah.[60] God's exclusive claim to divinity as creator and redeemer/Saviour is demonstrated in Isa 40–55 with the help of the notions of God's incomparability, the hollowness of idols, God's sole existence and the formula "no other gods besides me". In this section of Isaiah, Yahweh is portrayed as the unique, incomparable and the sole living God. He cannot be compared to the false gods, which are merely products of human hands. No god is able to equate to Yahweh, who is the only creator and the Saviour.

Immediately after the prologue (Isa 40,1–11), from which John cites 40,3, Isa 40,12–31 describes the unequalness and incomparability of Yahweh. In this section, one can find the exclusive claims of Yahweh in the form of first person speech like, "To whom then will you compare me, or who is my equal?, says the Holy One" (Isa 40,25). Isa 40,12–31 has a rhetorical frame of five sets of questions and answers which play a crucial role in demonstrating Yahweh's uniqueness and incomparability. These five sets of questions and answers can be shown as follows:[61]

Questions	Answers
40,12–14	40,15–17
40,18	40,19–20
40,21	40,22–24
40,25	40,26
40,27–28a	40,28b–31

As a whole, John 13–14 also uses the rhetoric of questions and answers. Within the narrative section (13,1–30), there are questions by Jesus, Peter and the Beloved Disciple, but answers only by Jesus. With the departure of Judas Iscariot, the narrative section of the farewell discourse ends in 13,30 and Jesus begins a long speech. The speech in 13,31–14,30 also follows a pattern of questions/request and answers, where Peter, Thomas, Philip and Judas (not Iscariot) are involved in interaction with Jesus. The pattern of questions/requests by the five disciples and Jesus' answers to them in John 13–14

---

[59] Regarding the exclusivity of 14,6b, A. T. Lincoln states, "Its exclusivity is rooted in the claims of Jewish monotheism". See Lincoln, *John*, 391.

[60] R. Bauckham, *Jesus and the God of Israel. God Crucified and other Studies on the New Testament's Christology of Divine Identity* (Grand Rapids 2008), 9.

[61] See E. W. Conrad, *Reading Isaiah* (OBT; Minneapolis 1991), 65.

is comparable in a certain way to the five sets of questions and answers in Isa 40,12–31.[62]

Questions/Requests	Answers
By the Beloved Disciple: 13,25	By Jesus: 13,26
By Peter: 13,6.8a.9.36a.37	By Jesus: 13,7.8b.10.36b; 13,38–14,4
By Thomas: 14,5	By Jesus: 14,6–7
By Philip: 14,8	By Jesus: 14,9–21
By Judas: 14,22	By Jesus: 14,23–31

The rhetorical questions in Isa 40,18, "To whom then will you liken God, or what likeness compare with him?" and in Isa 40,25, "To whom then will you compare me, or who is my equal?" highlight the incomparability of Yahweh and his exclusive status of divinity.[63] The series of rhetorical questions in Isa 40,12–31 are repeatedly posed in a manner that requires the answer, "No one . . . absolutely no one".[64] The prophet is exhorting the captives to remain steadfast in their loyalty to Yahweh in the context of their idolatrous environment. Thus, Isa 40,12–31 argues against Israel's pessimism and wavering faith.[65] Similarly, Jesus's claim in John 14,6b is uttered in the context of the disciples' despair and wavering faith. Jesus is admonishing his disciples to believe in him, their only way to the Father, in the context of their internal and external tribulations. In Isaiah, it is after the words of consolation and encouragement that God's uniqueness/incomparability is discussed. Similarly, in John 14, it is after words of consolation and encouragement that the exclusive claim of 14,6b is made with an emphasis on Jesus' uniqueness and incomparability as the Saviour.

---

[62] What is comparable in general is the pattern of questions/requests and answers and not the inherent structures and contents. In particular, the exclusive claims of John 14,6b and Isa 40,12–31 are also comparable.

[63] The incomparability texts in Isa 40,12–31 are, in fact, expressions of the "monotheizing" dynamic that is constantly driving a line of absolute distinction between Yahweh and other gods. The effect of "there is none like Yahweh" is precisely to put Yahweh in a class of his own, exactly as the monotheistic texts do in denying that there is any other besides Yahweh. Hence, the effect of incomparability texts is the same as that of monotheistic texts. Moreover, the distinction between incomparability texts and monotheistic texts is not significant since both notions of incomparability and monotheism appear in the same texts. E.g., Isa 46,9 says, "Remember the former things of old; for I am God, and there is no other; I am God, and there is no one like me". Also see 2 Sam 7,22. Cf. Bauckham, *Jesus and the God of Israel*, 89–90.

[64] E.g., C. Stuhlmueller, *Creative Redemption in Deutero-Isaiah* (AnBib 43; Rome 1970), 146, points out that the past perfect tense in v. 12 in the Hebrew text would lead to the answer, "Yahweh alone and no one else" has measured the earth's water and determined the size of the heavens. Also see D. O. Wenthe, "The Rich Monotheism of Isaiah as Christological Resource", *CTQ* 71 (2007), 57.

[65] Cf. Stuhlmueller, *Creative Redemption,* 146.

Closely related to the theme of incomparability is the use of the formula of high exclusivism, "There is no god/Saviour, besides me", which appears frequently in Deutero-Isaiah (Isa 43,11; 44,6; 45,5–6.18.21–22; 46,9; cf. 45,14 in third person) or the formula, "I am, and there is not another", ἐγώ εἰμι καὶ οὐκ ἔστιν ἑτέρα (Isa 47,8.10). It is noteworthy that in these texts the formula is expressed in the first person, and it is Yahweh himself who is the speaker. It is the major concern of Deutero-Isaiah to present Yahweh as the sole creator and sole redeemer/Saviour of the universe.[66] Likewise, John asserts very clearly the unique and exclusive role of Jesus in creation and salvation. The prologue describes the role of the pre-existent Christ as the mediator of creation (1,1–5; cf. 1 Cor 8,6; Col 1,15–16; Heb 1,2–3.10–12; Rev 3,14). Jesus is also called "the Saviour of the world" (4,42) and his mission is to "save the world" (3,17; 5,34; 10,9; 12,47). Just as Deutero-Isaiah proclaims that there is no god capable of saving Israel from the captivity in Babylon like Yahweh, John affirms that no one can take the disciples to the Father like/except Jesus. Thus, the exclusive claim of Jesus in 14,6b is similar to the exclusive claim of Isa 43,11, "I, I am the Lord, and besides me there is no Saviour" (LXX: ἐγὼ ὁ θεός καὶ οὐκ ἔστιν πάρεξ ἐμοῦ σῴζων).[67] For John, Jesus is like the Saviour of Isa 43,11, who is none other than Yahweh and who is frequently identified as "I Am" (ἐγώ εἰμι) in Deutero-Isaiah, and there is no salvation apart from him.[68] In the Gospel, Jesus is many times identified as "I Am", ἐγώ εἰμι (8,24.28.58; 13,19; 18,5–8; cf. 4,26; 6,20) like Yahweh in Deutero-Isaiah. The influence of Deutero-Isaiah upon the ἐγώ εἰμι-sayings in John is a further support to see the influence of the same source upon the exclusive claim in John 14,6, which is also attached to an ἐγώ εἰμι-saying.[69] In short, it is likely that the monotheistic exclusive claims of Yahweh due to his incomparability/uniqueness in Isa 40,12–31 and in other texts of Deutero-Isaiah have greatly influenced John's formulation of Jesus' exclusive claim in 14,6b.

---

[66] The most frequent occurrence of the verb בָּרָא in the Hebrew Bible is found in Deutero-Isaiah (16x), where Yahweh is portrayed as the creator of not only Israel but of the whole universe (e.g., 40,28; 42,5; 43,1.5, etc.). The most frequent use of the verb גָּאַל in the Hebrew Bible, with reference to Yahweh as the redeemer of Israel, is attested in Deutero-Isaiah. The very substantive "redeemer" (גֹּאֵל) occurs 10 times, while the noun "Saviour" (מוֹשִׁיעַ) is found 6 times in Deutero-Isaiah alone. In the LXX of Deutero-Isaiah, the frequency of the occurrence of terms related to salvation and redemption (based on Hatch and Redpath, *A Concordance to the Septuagint*) is as follows: σῴζω (13x), σωτηρία (8x), σωτήριον (4x), σωτήρ (3x), ῥύομαι (12x), λυτρόω (8x), λύτρον (1x).

[67] Cf. Lincoln, *John*, 391; Stube, *A Graeco-Roman Rhetorical Reading*, 108.

[68] Lincoln, *John*, 391.

[69] The influence of Deutero-Isaiah upon the ἐγώ εἰμι-sayings in John and the meaning of John 14,6 in the context of ἐγώ εἰμι-sayings are discussed on pp. 298–302, 304–314, 340–351.

5. Parallels Between the Contexts of Isa 40,3 and John 14,6

It is possible to find parallels between the contexts of Isa 40,3 and John 14,6 in the form of thematic connections and verbal links. A comparison can be made between the immediate contexts of both texts, namely Isa 40,1–11 and John 14,1–14 and between their near contexts. Isa 40–55 is traditionally called "the Book of Consolation". It is with the thoughts of consolation that this part of Isaiah begins and ends (40,1; 55,12–13). The overall message of Deutero-Isaiah is clearly one of encouragement to renew trust in Yahweh.[70] These chapters address the exiled community that is enfeebled and dispirited and their primary focus is comfort and reassurance (e.g., 49,13; 51,3.12–13; 52,9) followed by exhortation and challenge.[71] The people are constantly supported with the words, "Do not fear" (40,9; 41,10.13–14; 43,1–2.5; 44,2.8; 54,4). Isa 40,1 begins with the words, "Comfort, comfort my people, says God" (LXX). As a whole, John 14 can also be called a "Text of Consolation". It consists of comfort, consolation, exhortation and promises. It is addressed to the distressed disciples. It begins with words of consolation and encouragement, "Do not let your heart be troubled, believe in God and believe in me" (14,1), which are partly repeated at the ending section of the chapter, "Let not your heart be troubled, neither let it be afraid" (14,27), and the whole chapter is full of eschatological promises.[72]

In particular, Isa 40,1–11 introduces the themes of consolation, return from exile (vv. 1–2)[73], universal revelation of God's glory and salvation (vv. 3–5), power of the word of God (vv. 6–8) and the coming of Yahweh to Jerusalem (vv. 9–11). If seen from an eschatological perspective, one can notice the presence of these themes in John 14. The chapter begins with and repeats the words of consolation (14,1.27). Jesus' return from this world of exile (cf. 8,23; 13,1) is to go beforehand (cf. 13,36), to prepare a place and to take his disciples from this world of exile to the Father's house (14,2–3). In the LXX of Isa 40,5, the term "glory" (δόξα) is used synonymously with "salvation"

---

[70] P. S. Johnston, "Faith in Isaiah", *Interpreting Isaiah. Issues and Approaches*, ed. D. G. Firth and H. G. M. Williamson (Downers Grove 2009), 117.

[71] Johnston, "Faith in Isaiah", 119.

[72] Both Isa 40 (LXX) and John 14 begin with imperatives. In Isa 40,1, there are two imperatives, while there are three imperatives in John 14,1. If we limit the search within Isa 40,1–11 and John 14,1–14, it can be noticed that there are 12 imperatives in Isa 40,1–12 and 7 imperatives in John 14,1–14. Similarly, within the same pericopes there are many promises (cf. Isa 40,10–11; John 14,2–3.12–14). In John 14,15–31, there are promises of the coming of the Holy Spirit, the Father and the Son to dwell in the believers and of the gifts of peace and joy.

[73] The theme of return from exile is implied when these verses speak of the end of the exile.

(σωτήριον).⁷⁴ In John 14,13, (cf. 13,31–32) Jesus makes clear that his return will result in the "glorification" (δοξάζω) of the Father/God in the Son. The term "way" (ὁδός) is a salvific term in Isaiah, and it points to the return of the people from exile and also to the coming of Yahweh to his people.⁷⁵ As in Isaiah, there is a reference to the theme of salvation when John speaks of "way" (ὁδός) in 14,4–6. In 14,6, Jesus declares himself as "the way" for people's coming to God. There is an indirect reference to the universal salvation in 14,6b. Positively expressed, 14,6b means that everyone comes to the Father/God through Jesus (cf. 4,42).

Isa 40,8 speaks of the endurance of "the word of God", "But the word of our God will abide (μένω) forever" (τὸ δὲ ῥῆμα τοῦ θεοῦ ἡμῶν μένει εἰς τὸν αἰῶνα). In John 14,10.23–24, there are three references to the term "word" (ῥῆμα). Jesus' words are not his own but God's own words (14,10.24). Even after Jesus' departure, Jesus' words will endure forever when his disciples keep them (14,23) and when his words "abide" (μένω) in the disciples (15,7; cf. 17,8). The coming of Yahweh to Jerusalem, the city of his dwelling, is to dwell with his people (Isa 40,9–10). The expression "my Father's house" (ἡ οἰκία τοῦ πατρός μου) in John 14,2 may remind the reader of the Jerusalem temple, which is already called "my Father's house" (ὁ οἶκος τοῦ πατρός μου) in 2,16. The "way" that Jesus prepares implies a two-fold coming. Through the way of Jesus, on the one hand, people can come to God (14,6) and on the other hand, God can come to his people and make his "dwelling" (μονή) with them (14,23).⁷⁶ It should be noted that the second half of John 14 speaks of God's coming to the people in the persons of the Holy Spirit (vv. 16–17.26), the Son and the Father (vv. 18.23.28). God's dwelling with his people begins on earth. Isa 40,11 states that the Lord who is coming will lead his people like a shepherd. Jesus' role as the shepherd is demonstrated in John 10,11–16. In chapter 14 the role of Jesus as the shepherd is present when he speaks of his going to the Father ahead of his disciples to prepare a place for them in the Father's house in order that they may follow him (14,2–3; cf. 10,1–16.27; 13,36–37). Besides these thematic parallels, there are also

---

[74] L. H. Brockington, "The Greek Translator of Isaiah and his Interest in Δόξα", *VT* 1 (1951), 30–31, points out that "glory" is often associated with "salvation" in Isaiah (12,2; 40,5; 44,23; 45,21–25; 60,1–7). Also see, J. Frey, "The Use of Δόξα in Paul and John as Shaped by the Septuagint", *The Reception of Septuagint Words in Jewish-Hellenistic and Christian Literature*, ed. E. Bons et al. (WUNT II 367; Tübingen 2014), 92.

[75] Cf. Pao, *Acts*, 53.

[76] The Father's house in 14,2 can be understood as an eschatological temple (cf. the heavenly Jerusalem in Heb 12,22; the new Jerusalem in Rev 3,12; 21,2). In 2,18–22, Jesus calls his own body the temple. McCaffrey, *The House*, 256, views, "Jesus enters through his passion-resurrection into the heavenly temple of the Father's House by the sacrificial transformation of his body into the New Temple of his risen body in which believers have permanent and abiding at-one-ment with God".

5. Parallels Between the Contexts of Isa 40,3 and John 14,6

verbal links between John 14 and Isaiah 40. Below is given a survey of important verbal links between John 14 and Isa 40 (LXX).

John 14
μὴ ταρασσέσθω, μηδὲ δειλιάτω (vv. 1.27)
καρδία (vv. 1.27)
θεός (v. 1)

πολλή (v. 2), πολύς (v. 30)
μονή 2x (vv. 2.23), μένω 3x (vv. 10.17.25)
λέγω 13x (vv. 2.5–6.8, etc.)
πορεύομαι (vv. 2–3.12.28), ὑπάγω (vv. 4.28)
ἑτοιμάζω 2x (vv. 2–3)
ἔρχομαι 6x (vv. 3.6.18.23.28.30)
ὁδός 3x (vv. 4–6)
κύριος 3x (vv. 5.8.22)

οὐδείς (v. 6), οὐδέν (v. 30)
γινώσκω 8x (vv. 7.9.17.20.31)

ὁράω 3x (vv. 7.9)
δείκνυμι 2x (vv. 8–9)
ἀρκέω (v. 8)
ῥῆμα (v. 10)
ἔργον 3x (vv. 10–12)
ποιέω 8x (vv. 10.12–14.23.31)
λαλέω 3x (vv. 10.25.30)
ὄνομα 3x (vv. 13–14.26)
δοξάζω (v. 13; cf. 13,31–32)
δίδωμι 4x (vv. 16.27)
παράκλητος 2x (vv. 16.26)[77]

εἰς τὸν αἰῶνα[78] (v. 16)
κόσμος 4x (vv. 17.19.27.31)

ἔχω 2x (vv. 21.30)
ὁ τοῦ κόσμου ἄρχων (v. 30)

Isaiah 40
μὴ φοβεῖσθε (v. 9)
καρδία (v. 2)
θεός 10x (vv. 1.3.5.8–9.27–28.31)

πολλή (v. 26)
μένω (v. 8)
λέγω 6x (vv. 1.6.9.25.27)
ἀναβαίνω (v. 9)
ἑτοιμάζω (v. 3)
ἔρχομαι (v. 10)
ὁδός 3x (vv. 3.14.27)
κύριος 6x (vv. 2–3.5.10.13.18)

οὐδέν 4x (vv. 17.23.26)
γινώσκω 4x (vv. 13.21.28)

ὁράω 3x (vv. 5.26)
δείκνυμι 2x (v. 14)
ἱκανός 2x (v. 16)
ῥῆμα (v. 8)
ἔργον (v. 10)
ποιέω 3x (vv. 3.19.23)
λαλέω 3x (vv. 2.5.27)
ὄνομα (v. 26)
δόξα (v. 5)
δίδωμι 2x (vv. 23.29)
παρακαλέω 4x (vv. 1–2.11)

εἰς τὸν αἰῶνα (v. 8)
κόσμος (v. 26), γῆ 6x (vv. 12.21.24.28)
ἔχω (v. 11)
ἄρχων (v. 23), ἄρχειν τὴν γῆν (v. 23)

---

[77] It is worth noticing that in the Hebrew text of Isa 40,7.13 the expression רוּחַ יְהוָה occurs twice. This expression is found only in these passages in Deutero-Isaiah.

[78] There is a correspondence when "the Spirit of truth" in John 14,16–17 and "the word of God" in Isa 40,8 are said to "abide" (μένω) "for ever" (εἰς τὸν αἰῶνα).

The above discussion has shown various thematic connections and verbal links between the immediate and near contexts of John 14,6 and Isa 40,3. It is not intended to argue for a direct dependence of John 14 upon Isaiah 40, but only to support the previous argument that the literary background behind Jesus' identification as the way in 14,6a and his exclusive claim in 14,6b is provided respectively by Isa 40,3 and its context.

6. Influence of Isaiah Quotations in John 12,38–41 upon John 14,7–14

It has already been shown how Isa 40,3, cited in John 1,23, and its Deutero-Isaianic context influenced Jesus' self-identification as the way and his exclusive claim in John 14,6. Moreover, the thematic connections and verbal links between the contexts of Isa 40,3 and John 14,6 are pointed out in order to strengthen this view. There is still further literary evidence from the Gospel to show the influence of Isaiah upon John 14,6 and its immediate context. The Isaianic quotations in 12,38–41 also shape the thinking and language of the evangelist in the near and immediate context of 14,6, specifically in 14,7–14. We will first examine 12,38–41 briefly and then observe its influence upon the context of 14,6.

6.1 A Brief Examination of John 12,38–41

John 12,37–50 is regarded as an epilogue to Jesus' public ministry. It can be divided into an evaluation by the evangelist (12,37–43) and a summary discourse by Jesus (12,44–50). In the evaluation, John states the problem of unbelief (v. 37) and gives two reasons for the unbelief of the people (vv. 38–41; vv. 42–43). Firstly, in vv. 38–41 he explains the unbelief of the people as the fulfilment of two prophecies from Isaiah (Isa 53,1 in John 12,38; Isa 6,10 in John 12,40).[79] Secondly, in vv. 42–43 he explains the unbelief as a result of the love of human glory.[80]

---

[79] The first quotation is exactly from the LXX. But the second quotation varies considerably from the MT, the LXX and other versions. It reflects John's theological interests and seems to be his own creation. Cf. D. J. Brendsel, *'Isaiah Saw His Glory'. The Use of Isaiah 52–53 in John 12* (BZNW 208; Berlin 2014), 109.

[80] The following discussion will be only on the quotations from Isaiah and the evangelist's comment on them.

The evangelist's appeal to Isa 53,1 in 12,38 is to explain that people were not believing in Jesus (v. 37) so that Jesus as the servant might experience rejection (v. 38).[81] According to the majority view, "the message" and "the arm of the Lord" refer to Jesus' public ministry, which consists of his "words" and "works".[82] In the context, "the message"[83] stands for Jesus' words and "the arm of the Lord"[84] may stand for his works. While the speaker in Isa 53,1 is Isaiah representing his believing remnant community, in the Gospel (12,38) it is Jesus.[85] Jesus has during his ministry passed on to the Jews what he has heard from the Father and revealed God's saving power through his signs. Despite these, Jesus faces unbelief like Isaiah's Servant of God. John views the unbelief encountered by Jesus as the direct prophetic fulfilment of the negative experiences of the Servant described in Isa 53.[86] The evangelist removes any reference to "hearing" and "ears" while citing Isa 6,10 in 12,40 and focuses on "seeing" (ὁράω) and "understanding" (νοέω). According to the majority view, God is the agent of blinding and hardening in John's quotation 12,40.[87] Consequently, the pre-existent Christ is the speaker and the healer in the Isa 6,10 quotation.[88]

When John says, "Isaiah said these because he saw his glory and spoke about him", he must be thinking of both Isaiah quotations and their contexts.[89] The antecedent of "these" (ταῦτα) is most likely the two-fold quota-

---

[81] Brendsel, *Isaiah Saw His Glory*, 119.

[82] Cf. Brendsel, *Isaiah Saw His Glory*, 112; R. Kühschelm, *Verstockung, Gericht und Heil. Exegetische und bibeltheologische Untersuchung zum sogenannten "Dualismus" und "Determinismus" in Joh 12,35–50* (BBB 76; Frankfurt am Main 1990), 33. Even though Brendsel accepts the majority view, he gives his own nuances. See Brendsel, *Isaiah Saw His Glory*, 112–113. It should be kept in mind that even though Jesus' ministry can be divided into "words" and "works", one need not be very rigid with regard to this categorization. Sometimes, even Jesus' whole ministry can be called "the work" which the Father gave him to do (John 17,4).

[83] In the original context of Isa 53,1, שְׁמוּעָה means "that which is heard and passed on to others". Cf. Brendsel, *Isaiah Saw His Glory*, 104.

[84] "The arm of the Lord" is in the exodus traditions often linked with God's signs and wonders (Exod 6,6; Deut 4,34; 5,15; 7,19; 2 Kgs 17,36; Jer 32,21; Ps 136,12) and may refer to his saving power. In Deuero-Isaiah, the arm of the Lord is also linked with exodus motifs (40,10–11; 51,9; cf. 63,12). Cf. Brendsel, *Isaiah Saw His Glory*, 105–106.

[85] Brendsel, *Isaiah Saw His Glory*, 103, 110.

[86] Brendsel, *Isaiah Saw His Glory*, 116.

[87] E.g., Kühschelm, *Verstockung*, 188–192; Brendsel, *Isaiah Saw His Glory*, 90; Williams, "Isaiah in John's Gospel", 110; Menken, *Old Testament Quotations*, 109–115; R. Schnackenburg, *The Gospel According to St. John* (London 1980), II, 415–416.

[88] Kühschelm, *Verstockung*, 194–195; Brendsel, *Isaiah Saw His Glory*, 90–91.

[89] Brendsel, *Isaiah Saw His Glory*, 130. The reference to Isaiah's vision of "his glory" is in accordance with the Gospel's view that no one has ever seen God (1,18; 5,37; 6,46). This perspective is also maintained by Targum Isaiah 6:1, "I saw the glory of the Lord". John has already spoken of two great Old Testament figures in relation to the life of Jesus,

tion in 12,38–40. "His" in "Isaiah saw his glory" (12,41) refers to the "I" in "I would heal them" (12,40), and therefore, "his glory" refers to Christ's glory. The glory seen by Isaiah is the future glory of Christ, a glory attained by way of rejection, death and exaltation (Isa 52,13–14).[90] John's reference to Isaiah's vision of glory is related to the "glory" of Isaiah's temple vision (Isa 6,1.3).[91] Since John understands the glory of Isa 52–53 as linked with and a development of the glory in Isa 6, the glory mentioned in John 12,41 includes not only the glory of the suffering and exalted Servant (LXX Isa 52,13–14), but also the glory filling the temple at the time of Isaiah's calling (LXX Isa 6,1; cf. MT 6,3).[92] John's assertion, "Isaiah saw his glory", implies that John capitalizes on the repetition of the phrase "exalted and lifted up" in Isa 6,1 and 52,13.[93] The unique expression "exalted and lifted up" (נשא + ו + רום) is found in the Hebrew Bible only in Isa 6,1; 52,13 and 57,15. In Isa 6,1 and 57,15, it is used to describe Yahweh and in Isa 52,13 to describe Yahweh's Servant.[94] The verbal repetition in Isa 6,1 and Isa 52,13 reveals a close relationship between Yahweh and his Servant.

---

namely Moses and Abraham. In 5,46, Jesus argues, "If you believed Moses, you would believe me, for he wrote about me". This may refer to an individual passage like Deut 18,18 (cf. John 6,14; 7,40.52; 9,17). But Jesus' role as a prophet is not sufficient to portray John's full picture of Jesus. It is more likely that it is a reference to all writings of Moses, as 5,47 suggests. There is ambiguity regarding the meaning of Abraham's joy in seeing the day of Jesus in 8,56, "Your ancestor Abraham rejoiced that he would see my day; he saw it and was glad". There are two main possible ways of interpretations. Firstly, Abraham's joy can be a reference to his laughter in Gen 17,17 (cf. 18,9–15; 21,6), which is interpreted as a laughter of joy in some Jewish traditions. The future hopes promised to Abraham were linked to Isaac. A Christian Midrash on Abraham might have influenced the evangelist to think that the day of Isaac aroused in Abraham the joyful hope of the day of the Messiah. Secondly, in the post-biblical Jewish traditions there is a view that Abraham saw the future or at least some aspects of it in his vision in Gen 15,12–21 (see Schnackenburg, *John*, II, 221-223; Keener, *John*, I, 766–768). However, some also argue that it is in his heavenly life that Abraham saw Jesus' day (e.g., Lindars, *John*, 334–335). But, in the case of John 12,41, there is better clarity from the context that John's reference is to Isaiah's temple vision. Moreover, it is evident that it is in linking the contexts of the two quotations in 12,38–40 that the vision of Christ's glory in the temple vision becomes possible.

[90] Brendsel, *Isaiah Saw His Glory*, 125–130; Kühschelm, *Verstockung*, 201.

[91] Brendsel, *Isaiah Saw His Glory*, 130.

[92] Brendsel states, "We may say that John believes the glory seen by Isaiah (12,41b) is especially the glory of the rejected and crucified Servant who is 'high and lifted up' (Isa 52,13), but the full significance of this belief can only be realized when the relationship between this glory of the Servant and the glory of the Lord seen during Isaiah's temple vision (Isa 6,1.3) is recognized". See Brendsel, *Isaiah Saw His Glory*, 131.

[93] Brendsel, *Isaiah Saw His Glory*, 131.

[94] Modern Old Testament scholars think that Isa 52,13 and Isa 57,15 must be dependent on 6,1. See Bauckham, *Jesus and the God of Israel*, 36.

The early Christians seem to have capitalized on this connection, concluding that in the light of the connections with Isaiah 6,1 and 57,15, the meaning of Isa 52,13 is that the Servant is exalted to the heavenly throne of God, not to be beheld as merely a human being distinguished from God, but as actually belonging to the identity of the unique God (cf. Phil 2,6–11; Rev 5,13–14).[95] Through the identification of Jesus as Isaiah's Servant of the Lord and by applying the Jewish exegetical principle of *gezerah shawah*[96] to Isa 6,1 and 52,13, John has found biblical warrant for his assertions, repeated throughout the Gospel, that the Son is transparent to the Father (12,45; 14,7–11) and that the glorification of the Father and the glorification of the Son are a unified act (12,27–28; 13,31–32; 14,13; 17,1–5).[97] The question of how Isaiah could see not only the glory of God but of Jesus can be explained from this scriptural combination.[98]

Jesus' glory foreseen by Isaiah contains his rejection and death *and* is the very glory of Yahweh himself.[99] In other words, Isaiah saw Christ's glory in the glory of God. Therefore, to reject the glory of Jesus is to reject the glory of God out of love for human glory (12,43), and to believe in him is to believe in the One who sent him (12,44–45). Thus, the focus of John in 12,41 is on Jesus' oneness with the one God of Israel, based on the book of Isaiah, which is the bedrock of Jewish monotheism. The Christology and monotheism that John pinpoints here can be called respectively the Christology of divine identity and Christological monotheism.[100]

---

[95] See Brendsel, *Isaiah Saw His Glory*, 132; Bauckham, *Jesus and the God of Israel*, 35–37; Williams "The Testimony of Isaiah", 117–118.

[96] According to the principle of *gezerah shawah*, the passages in which the same words occur should be interpreted with reference to each other. Cf. Bauckham, *Jesus and the God of Israel*, 36.

[97] Brendsel, *Isaiah Saw His Glory*, 132. According to Bauckham, *Jesus and the God of Israel*, 36, the most early Christian exegesis of the Old Testament was done with reference to the Hebrew text, even when the Greek text was also employed. Williams "The Testimony of Isaiah", 118, points out that even if one were to adopt the minority view that it cannot be proved that John knew Hebrew or Aramaic, the combination of the two passages could have been done some time prior to its adoption in John's Gospel. Even though the connection between the texts in the LXX is not as impressive as in the Hebrew text, the correspondences between the texts can still be identified.

[98] Frey, "The Use of Δόξα", 102. J. Beutler, *Judaism and the Jews in the Gospel of John* (Subsidia Biblica 30; Rome 2006), 79, states, "On seeing the glory of God, the prophet sees already the glory of Jesus, and so can speak of him prophetically".

[99] Brendsel, *Isaiah Saw His Glory*, 133.

[100] The notions of Christology of divine identity and Christological monotheism are highlighted in recent New Testament scholarship by Richard Bauckham. Christology of divine identity and Christological monotheism refer to the inclusion of Jesus in the identity of the one God. See Bauckham, *Jesus and the God of Israel*, 30–31. A. T. Lincoln, *Truth on Trial. The Lawsuit Motif in the Fourth Gospel* (Peabody 2000), 421, points out, "Since

6.2 Influence of John 12,38–41 upon John 14,7–14 and its Context

John 12,38–41 is regarded as "the tip of the iceberg" of Isaianic influence in John 12.[101] D. J. Brendsel affirms, "There is reason to believe that the 'iceberg' of Isaiah's influence stretches both backward and forward from the 'tip' in John 12,38–41".[102] The presence of this "iceberg of Isaianic influence" (12,38–41) can be detected in John's presentation of Jesus and his identity in chapters 13–14, especially in the immediate context of John 14,6. By citing Isa 53,1 in 12,38, John introduces the theme of the Isaianic suffering Servant of God into his Gospel. In chapter 13, it is as the Servant of God that John presents Jesus. Among the evangelists, it is only John who speaks of the washing of the disciples' feet by Jesus. By washing the feet of his disciples, Jesus literally fulfils his role as the Servant of God (13,4–20).[103] The scene of foot-washing is proleptic of his humiliating death as God's Servant. John continues the theme of rejection of the Servant (cf. Isa 53,6) in a way when Jesus predicts the betrayal by Judas Iscariot (13,21–30) and the denial by Peter (13,36–38).

The problem that John deals with in 12,37–41 is the unbelief of the people. Even though Jesus' disciples are open to the revelation in him, there is still some sort of unbelief and lack of understanding in them. It is only after Jesus' death-resurrection that the disciples will be able to believe in the true identity of Jesus as the ἐγώ εἰμι (13,19).[104] This indicates that the current belief of the disciples is not a perfect one. As there is an appeal to believe in Jesus in the context of citing the Isaianic texts (12,44–50), in the immediate context of 14,6 one can also notice an urgent appeal to believe. It seems that John's reflections on the theme of unbelief, based on Isa 53,1, continue in chapter 14. The verb "believe" (πιστεύω) occurs 6 times in the immediate context of 14,6, i.e., within 14,1–14.[105] It is with the exhortation to believe that chapter 14 begins (14,1)[106] and there is a reference to belief in the concluding section of the chapter (14,29).

---

for John there remains only one true God, Jesus, in his relationship as Son to the Father, must be intrinsic to this one God's identity".

[101] Brendsel, *Isaiah Saw His Glory*, 213–214.

[102] Brendsel, *Isaiah Saw His Glory*, 214.

[103] Brendsel, *Isaiah Saw His Glory*, 114, n. 73.

[104] In the absolute ἐγώ εἰμι in 13,19, there is a clear echo of the absolute ἐγώ εἰμι which appears most frequently only in Deutero-Isaiah in the Old Testament.

[105] It appears in 14,1(2x).10.11(2x).12.

[106] There is a correspondence between 12,42 and 14,1, created by the motifs of belief and fear. In 12,42, the notion of belief is linked with that of fear. Even though the authorities believed in Jesus, because of fear of the Pharisees, they could not confess it. In 14,1, the disciples are asked not to be troubled in heart but to believe (cf. 14,27).

6. Influence of Isaiah Quotations in John 12,38–41 upon John 14,7–14 221

Jesus' exclusive claim in 14,6b, "No one comes to the Father except through me", cannot be separated from his claims in 14,7–14. The exclusivity of Jesus' claim in 14,6b is based on his oneness with the Father, which, rooted in Jewish monotheism, is further explained in vv. 7–14. It is to be noted that while quoting Isa 6,10 in 12,40 John has eliminated any reference to "hearing" and "ears" and concentrated on "seeing" (ὁράω) and "understanding" (νοέω). A synonym of νοέω is the verb γινώσκω.[107] In John 14,7, the important Johannine motifs of "knowing" (γινώσκω) and "seeing" (ὁράω) appear together. If the unbelieving Jews are unable to see and understand (12,40), the believing disciples are invited to know and see the Father in and through Jesus (14,7). In 14,7–9, the theme of Jesus' oneness with the Father is centred around the motif of simultaneous "seeing" of Jesus and the Father. The notion of simultaneous vision of the Father and Jesus in the Gospel is mentioned only in 12,45 and 14,9. In the first case, the simultaneous vision of the Father and Jesus is spoken in the epilogue to Jesus' public ministry, which is evaluated on the basis of Isaianic texts. The claims of a simultaneous vision of the Father and Jesus in 12,45 and 14,9 should draw the readers' attention to Isaiah's vision mentioned in 12,41, "Isaiah said these because he saw his glory and spoke about him".[108]

In the interpretation of 12,41 given above, it is clearly shown that Isaiah's vision of the glory of "the exalted and lifted up" Servant in Isa 52,13 cannot be separated from his vision of the glory of "the exalted and lifted up" Yahweh sitting on the throne in Isa 6,1. This implies that John conceives a simultaneous vision of the glory of Yahweh sitting on the throne and the glory of his exalted and lifted up Servant. John's view of the unity between Yahweh and his Servant (based on Isaiah's vision) seems to function as a model for his understanding of the unity between the Father and Jesus. Hence, when the Johannine Jesus states, "The one who has seen me has seen the Father" (14,9), John is probably thinking about the simultaneous vision of Isaiah (implicitly mentioned in 12,41), who saw Christ's glory in God's glory as well as God's glory in Christ's glory.[109] For John, "Jesus not only is associat-

---

[107] See W. Schenk, "νοέω", *EDNT*, II, 469.

[108] The verb used in 14,7–9 and 12,41 to refer to the vision is ὁράω. The first use of ὁράω after 12,41 is found in 14,7. The verb used in 12,45 is θεωρέω, which is a synonym of ὁράω. "Seeing" in John 14,7–9 may refer to a spiritual perception. However, the point of comparison between Isaiah and John is not the vision alone, but also the unity of Yahweh and his Servant, of the Father and the Son.

[109] M. J. J. Menken, "Observations on the Significance of the Old Testament in the Fourth Gospel", *Neotest* 33 (1999), 137; R. E. Watts, "Isaiah in the New Testament", *Interpreting Isaiah. Issues and Approaches*, ed. D. G. Firth and H. G. M. Williamson (Downers Grove 2009), 223. L. W. Hurtado, *Lord Jesus Christ. Devotion to Jesus in Earliest Christianity* (Grand Rapids 2003), 380, states, "The Johannine treatment of Jesus amounts to him being the one in whom God's glory is manifested, the unique human em-

ed with the glory of God, he *is* the glory of God *manifest*".[110] Therefore, the vision of Jesus is the same as the vision of the Father, just as Isaiah's vision of the glory of Christ in 12,41 cannot be separated from the vision of Yahweh's glory.[111] Thus, the oneness motif demonstrated in 14,7–11 is an assertion of the Christology of divine identity and Christological monotheism pinpointed in 12,41.

In 12,38, John cites the Isaianic text, "Lord, who has *believed our message*, and to whom has *the arm of the Lord* been revealed?" (Isa 53,1). We have already suggested the majority view that "message" and "arm of the Lord" refer in the context to Jesus' words and works. The combination of "words" (τὰ ῥήματα) and "works" (τὰ ἔργα) of Jesus in relation to an appeal to "believe" (πιστεύω) is found only in 14,10, "Do you not *believe* that I am in the Father and the Father is in me? The *words* that I say to you I do not speak on my own; but the Father who dwells in me does *his works*".[112] The sequence of thought in 14,10b–c has created difficulties for the scholars.[113] We expect something like this, "The words that I say to you I do not speak on my own; but the Father who dwells in me speaks his words". Even though scholars have adequately explained 14,10, especially the relation between Jesus' words and works, none of them has satisfactorily given the reason for the anomalous shift from words to works in this verse. This difficulty can be easily solved if we make a recourse to Isa 53,11 cited in John 12,38, where the evangelist is concerned with the issue of belief whose object is the words and works of Jesus. We may assume that the evangelist's reflections upon Isa 53,1 cited in 12,38, continue here. In the context of 12,38, the issue is that the Jews did not believe in Jesus in spite of his words and works. In 14,10–11, Jesus appeals to his disciples to believe in his words and works, which are the manifestations of his oneness with the Father. This oneness is already fore-

---

bodiment of God's glory on earth. This is why the Johannine Jesus can say, in reply to Philip's request to be shown the Father, 'Whoever has seen me has seen the Father' (14,9)".

[110] Hurtado, *Lord Jesus Christ*, 380.

[111] It is worthwhile to notice the assertion of Yahweh in Isa 42,8, "I am the Lord, that is my name; my glory I give to no other" (also cf. Isa 48,11). John 17,1–5.24 make clear that Jesus was always included in the identity and glory of the one God, even before the foundation of the world.

[112] In both cases (12,38; 14,10), there are references to the issue of belief (cf. 14,10–12), to the message/words and the arm of the Lord/Father's works. Just as Isa 53,1/John 12,38 is a question, John 14,10a is also a question. Jesus' words (2,22; 4,41; 5,24.47; 8,30) and signs/works (2,23; 4,48; 10,38) are often either object or cause of belief. The direct object of "believe" in 14,10a is the Father's presence in Jesus, which is manifested through his "words" and "works" (14,10b–c).

[113] Brown, *John*, II, 622, himself admits that the relation of "the words" in v. 10b to "the works" in v. 10c is not clear. Also see Beutler, *Do not be Afraid*, 45; Morris, *John*, 572.

seen by Isaiah as the evangelist already indicated in 12,41, and as a result of his oneness with the Father, the disciples can do still greater works and pray in "Jesus' name" (14,12–14).

7. Conclusion

The above given discussion is a proposal for an alternative approach to the understanding of the literary background of John 14,6 and its context. The important findings of this examination are as follows. The Gospel of John is self-interpretative. Intratextuality is a better way to understand John's intertextuality. The Isaianic citations which John has used in 1,23 and 12,38–41 have some kind of influence upon John 14,6 and its context.[114] It seems that the evangelist's reflections on these Isaianic texts continue in the context of 14,6 as well. John's peculiar way of using ὁδός and the verb ἑτοιμάζω in the immediate context can make us think that there is an eschatological and Christological interpretation of Isa 40,3 in the background. It is by preparing a place in the Father's house through his death-resurrection that Jesus prepares the way for the people to come to the Father. This salvific act can be done only by Jesus and not by anyone else. Therefore, after 1,23 John speaks of ὁδός only in 14,4–6 when he thinks of the true preparation (ἑτοιμάζω) in 14,2–3. There is also correspondence between "the way of the Lord" in 1,23 and "the way of Jesus" in 14,4 since Jesus is called "the Lord" in the Gospel. Thus, for the evangelist's presentation of Jesus as the way, the basic text of inspiration seems to be Isa 40,3. The underlying influence for the paratactic construction "the way and the truth and the life" is more likely the common association of way with truth and life found in the Bible and other Jewish literature.

---

[114] The quotation found in John 6,45 is exclusively from Isa 54,13. Cf. Williams, "Isaiah in John's Gospel", 106; A. Obermann, *Die christologische Erfüllung der Schrift im Johannesevangelium. Eine Untersuchung zur johanneischen Hermeneutik anhand der Schriftzitate* (WUNT II 83; Tübingen 1996), 151–167; Menken, *Old Testament Quotations*, 77; Schuchard, *Scripture Within Scripture*, 57. There is some kind of relationship in language and thought between the Deutero-Isaianic quotation in John 6,45 and John's reference to the future activity of the Holy Spirit in 14,26. What establishes the relationship is the motif of "teaching" in both texts (διδακτός in 6,45 and διδάσκω in 14,26). Schnackenburg, *John*, II, 52, explains 6,45 thus, "The word of Jesus, helped by the inner action of the Father in a person, is for the reader of the gospel not a word from the past, but one which endures into the present, which indeed is made plain only by the Paraclete (14,26; 16,13–14)". Moreover, Jesus' promise of the Spirit in 14,16–17.26 can be seen in connection with the pouring out of the Spirit promised in Isa 44,3.

For understanding the background of exclusivism in 14,6b, we need to take into account the uniqueness and the incomparability of Yahweh in Isa 40 and the exclusive monotheistic claims in Isa 40–55 like Isa 43,11. Immediately after the exclusive claim in 14,6b, John speaks of Jesus' oneness with the Father (14,7–11), which is an expression of his divine identity. For John, Jesus belongs to the divine identity of the one God of Israel. Thus, the exclusivism in John 14,6b is rooted in Jewish monotheism and it should be understood in the light of Jewish monotheism, which John presents in Christological terms. The notion of the simultaneous vision of the Father and Jesus in 14,7–9 may draw the readers' attention to Isaiah's vision of the glory of Jesus and Yahweh mentioned in 12,41. There is also some sort of correspondence between 12,38 and 14,10. In short, there appears to be some kind of influence of the Isaianic quotations in 1,23 and 12,38–41 upon the language and thinking of the evangelist in John 14,6 and in its immediate and near context. The main advantage of this approach is that it can satisfactorily explain at a literary level the background of the exclusivism expressed in 14,6, which former approaches could not. This approach will be further supported when we discuss the historical setting for the emergence of exclusivism in John 14,6.

The above discussion underscores the influence of Isaiah upon the Gospel of John, which has already become a prominent topic in Johannine studies.[115] The name "Isaiah" ('Ησαΐας) occurs 4 times in the Gospel (1,23; 12,38.39.41). "Isaiah" is the only book from the Old Testament, used with its title by the evangelist. It is worthwhile to pay attention to the words of G. Reim, "Kein Buch des AT hat die Theologie des Johannes stärker geprägt als

---

[115] Some important studies in this area are the following: Brendsel, *Isaiah Saw His Glory*; C. H. Williams, "Seeing the Glory: The Reception of Isaiah's Call-Vision in John 12,41", *Judaism, Jewish Identities and the Gospel Tradition. Essays in Honour of Maurice Casey*, ed. J. G. Crossley (London 2010), 186–206; idem, "The Testimony of Isaiah", 107–124; idem, "Isaiah in John's Gospel", 101–116; J. Hamilton, "The Influence of Isaiah on the Gospel of John", *Perichoresis* 5 (2007), 139–162; J. Painter, "Monotheism and Dualism. Reconsidering Predestination in John 12,40", *Transcending Boundaries. Contemporary Readings of the New Testament*, ed. R. M. Chennattu and M. L. Coloe (Biblioteca Di Scienze Religiose 187; Rome 2005), 119–139; Lincoln, *Truth on Trial*; M. J. J. Menken, "The Quotation from Isa 40,3 in John 1,23, *Bib* 66 (1985), 190–205; F. W. Young, "A Study of the Relation of Isaiah to the Fourth Gospel", *ZNW* 46 (1955), 215–233; D. R. Griffiths, "Deutero-Isaiah and the Fourth Gospel", *ET* 65 (1954), 355–360. The following works also include studies with regard to the influence of Isaiah upon John's Gospel: J. J. F. Coutts, *The Divine Name in the Gospel of John. Significance and Impetus* (WUNT II 447; Tübingen 2017); Menken, "Observations", 125–143; idem, *Old Testament Quotations*; Obermann, *Die christologische Erfüllung der Schrift im Johannesevangelium*; Schuchard, *Scripture Within Scripture*; A. T. Hanson, *The Prophetic Gospel. A Study of John and the Old Testament* (Edinburgh 1991); G. Reim, *Studien zum alttestamentlichen Hintergrund des Johannesevangeliums* (Cambridge 1974); E. D. Freed, *Old Testament Quotations in the Gospel of John* (NovTSup 11; Leiden 1965).

Dtjes und keiner der Verfasser neutestamentlicher Schriften ist von Dtjes so stark beeinflußt wie Johannes".[116]

---

[116] Reim, *Hintergrund des Johannesevangeliums,* 183. Young, "A Study of the Relation of Isaiah", 222, asserts that John "consciously utilized Isaiah as a source of language and ideology in his own effort to interpret the meaning of Jesus Christ in the Gospel which he produced". Bauckham, *Jesus and the God of Israel,* 34, points out the influence of Deutero-Isaiah in the New Testament thus, "What has not been recognized sufficiently is that, behind many of the New Testament texts, lies an integrated early Christian reading of these chapters (Isa 40–55) as a connected whole". In the view of Hurtado, *Lord Jesus Christ,* 378, Isa 40–55 is "a body of material that was richly mined in earliest Christian circles as a resource for Christological reflection".

Chapter V

Important Motifs of John 14,6 in the Gospel Context

There is no *hapax legomenon* in John 14,6. All words are found in the rest of the Gospel. The important motifs and concepts in this verse are "I am" (ἐγώ εἰμι), way (ὁδός), journey (ἔρχομαι), truth (ἀλήθεια), life (ζωή) and Father (πατήρ).[1] Besides the usage and significance of truth (ἀλήθεια), life (ζωή) and Father (πατήρ) in the Gospel, the interrelation between way, truth and life will also be discussed below.

1. Truth (ἀλήθεια) in the Gospel of John

Etymologically, ἀλήθεια means non-concealment.[2] An event is true (ἀληθής) when it is unveiled, and a person is true if he conceals nothing and does not try to deceive.[3] Ἀλήθεια can be translated variously, firstly as the quality of being in accord with what is true, truthfulness, dependability, uprightness in thought and deed (cf. Gen 24,27; Judg 9,15; Rom 15,8; 1 Cor 5,8), secondly as the content of what is true, truth in opposition to ψεῦδος (cf. Zech 8,16; Eph 4,25; Rom 9,1; 1 Tim 2,7; Mark 5,33; Eph 4,21) and thirdly as an actual event or state, reality (cf. Mark 12,14; Acts 10,4; Rom 2,2; 2 John 1).[4]

Often Greek-Hellenistic and Semitic backgrounds are suggested for understanding the meaning of John's concept of truth.[5] In Greek philosophy,

---

[1] The way/journey motif in John has already been discussed at length on pp. 94–115. See also pp. 163–165, 194–209 and also 255–260. The significance of ἐγώ εἰμι-sayings and their relation to John 14,6 will be discussed later. See pp. 293–351.

[2] G. Quell et al., "ἀλήθεια", *TDNT*, I, 238.

[3] C. Spicq and J. D. Ernest, "ἀλήθεια", *TLNT*, I, 66.

[4] BDAG, 42.

[5] For a study of the socio-historical-religious background of the notion of truth, see Kirchschläger, *Nur Ich bin die Wahrheit*, 23–94; Quell, "ἀλήθεια", *TDNT*, I, 232–251; A. C. Thiselton, "Truth", *NIDNTT*, III, 874–883; Schnackenburg, *John*, II, 225–237; Brown, *John*, I, 499–501. While scholars like Quell, "ἀλήθεια", 241–251 and C. H. Dodd, *The Interpretation of the Fourth Gospel* (Cambridge 1968), 170–178, emphasize the Greek influence on the Johannine notion of truth, scholars like I. de la Potterie, L. J. Kuyper and R. E. Brown think that ἀλήθεια reflects the Old Testament and Jewish background. See I. de la Potterie, "La verità in San Giovanni", *RivBib* 11 (1963), 3–24; idem, "Je suis la voie", 907–942; idem, *La vérité dans Saint Jean*, I; L. J. Kuyper, "Grace and Truth: An

ἀλήθεια is understood in the sense of "true or genuine reality" in opposition to "reflection" or "appearance".[6] Since the only thing which is truly ἀληθής is that which always is, the divine ἀλήθεια was used to refer to the eternal and divine reality.[7] The term ἀλήθεια in the LXX is a representation of אֱמֶת of the Old Testament, which means "firmness", "faithfulness", "reliability" or "stability".[8] Hence, אֱמֶת is that on which others can rely. It is often argued that truth in the Old Testament is not merely theoretical or abstract, but is rooted in the faithfulness of God.[9] God reveals his truth to the Israelites not only in his words but also in his deeds, and this truth is proved in practice in the experience of his people.[10] In the Deutero-Canonical books, ἀλήθεια is used mostly but not always to mean truth in contrast to falsehood (cf. Tob 7,10; Wis 3,9).[11] Truth is used in a variety of ways in the Qumran writings. It is used as a quality of moral behavior, an attribute of God, from the point of view of revelation to refer to "the revealed Torah" and from a dualistic perspective in opposition to lie, deceit and wickedness.[12] The expression "spirit of truth" is also found in the Qumran writings (cf. 1QS IV,20–21).

Truth is one of the most important and also one of the most studied concepts of the Gospel of John.[13] There are altogether 55 occurrences of the

---

Old Testament Description of God and Its Use in the Johannine Gospel", *Interpretation* 18 (1964), 3–19; Brown, *John*, I, 500.

[6] Quell, "ἀλήθεια", 239.

[7] Quell, "ἀλήθεια", 239–240.

[8] BDB, 54. It should be kept in mind that the LXX translates אֱמֶת not only as ἀλήθεια but also as πίστις.

[9] Thiselton, "Truth", 877. Brown, *John*, I, 499, views that while the Greek concept of truth is intellectual, there is a moral element in the Hebrew notion of truth.

[10] Thiselton, "Truth", 881.

[11] Cf. Thiselton, "Truth", 882. In the view of I. de la Potterie, the immediate background for the Johannine notion of ἀλήθεια is to be sought in the apocalyptic and wisdom literature. In these writings, truth is understood as the revealed teaching or wisdom, i.e., the revelation of the mystery of God, the divine plan revealed to the human beings (e.g., Prov 23,23; Sir 4,28; Wis 3,9; 6,22; cf. 1 En. 21,5; 1 QH 7,26–27; 1 QS 4,6). See I. de la Potterie, "The Truth in Saint John", *The Interpretation of John*, ed. J. Ashton (Edinburgh 1997), 68–69.

[12] Schnackenburg, *John*, II, 233–234; Thiselton, "Truth", 882.

[13] Studies on the Johannine notion of truth are plenty. For recent studies on the topic, see Tack, *John 14,6 in Light of Jewish-Christian Dialogue*, 160–219; P. G. Kirchschläger, "'Ich bin der Weg, die Wahrheit und das Leben' (Joh 14,6). Der Wahrheitsanspruch des johanneischen Christus und Wahrheit in anderen Religionen", *BLit* 85 (2012), 123–147; idem, *Nur Ich bin die Wahrheit*; idem, "Spannung und Interaktion: Das Begriffsfeld 'Wahrheit'", *Repetitions and Variations in the Fourth Gospel. Style, Text, Interpretation*, ed. G. Van Belle et al. (Leuven 2009), 213–234; J. van der Watt, "The Good and the Truth in John's Gospel", *Studien zu Matthäus und Johannes/Études sur Matthieu et Jean. Festschrift J. Zumstein*, ed. A. Dettwiler and U. Poplutz (Zurich 2009), 317–333; B. Kowalski, "Was ist Wahrheit? (Joh 18,38a): Zur literarischen und theologischen Funktion

ἀληθ-word group in John. The ἀληθ-word group consists of ἀλήθεια (25x), ἀληθής (14x), ἀληθινός (9x) and ἀληθῶς (7x).[14] Since from this group only the noun ἀλήθεια occurs in John 14,6, our focus will be mainly on the usage of ἀλήθεια. The 25 occurrences of ἀλήθεια in John are found in 1,14.17; 3,21; 4,23.24; 5,33; 8,32(2x).40.44(2x).45.46; 14,6.17; 15,26; 16,7.13(2x); 17,17(2x).19; 18,37(2x).38.[15] The Johannine usage of ἀλήθεια is discussed below.

---

der Pilatusfrage in der Johannespassion", *Im Geist und in der Wahrheit: Studien zum Johan-nesevangelium und zur Offenbarung des Johannes sowie andere Beiträge*. Festschrift für Martin Hasitschka SJ zum 65. Geburtstag, ed. K. Huber and B. Repschinski (Münster 2008), 201–227; J. A. Glancy, "Torture: Flesh, Truth, and the Fourth Gospel", *BInterp* 13 (2005), 107–136; Köstenberger, "What is Truth?", 33–62; H. Hübner, "Wahrheit und Wort: Heideggers 'Vom Wesen der Wahrheit' und Wahrheit im Johannes-Evangelium", *Testimony and Interpretation: Early Christology in Its Judeo-Hellenistic Milieu: Studies in Honour of Petr Pokorný*, ed. J. Mrázek and J. Roskovec (London 2004), 201–222; H. C. Kee, "Knowing the Truth: Epistemology and Community in the Fourth Gospel", *Neotestamentica et Philonica: studies in honor of Peder Borgen,* ed. D. E. Aune et al. (Leiden 2003), 254–280; R. Gebauer, "'Aletheia' im Johannesevangelium", *Theologische Wahrheit und die Postmoderne*, ed. H. H. Klement (Wuppertal 2000), 233–254; T. Söding, "Die Wahrheit des Evangeliums: Anmerkungen zur johanneischen Hermeneutik", *EThL* 77 (2001), 318–355; idem, "Die Macht der Wahrheit und das Reich der Freiheit: Zur johanneischen Deutung des Pilatus-Prozesses (Joh 18,28–19,16)", *ZTK* 93 (1996), 48–49; D. R. Lindsay, "What is Truth? *Alētheia* in the Gospel of John", *ResQ* 35 (1993), 129–145; D. J. Hawkin, "The Johannine Concept of Truth and its Implications for a Technological Society", *EvQ* 59 (1987), 3–13. Other comparatively older but important studies are R. J. Campbell, *The Concept of Truth in Johannine Writings, Related to Modern Critical Tensions* (Diss. Strasbourg 1970); Y. Ibuki, *Die Wahrheit im Johannesevangelium* (BBB 39; Bonn 1972); J. O. Zimmermann, *Die johanneische ἀλήθεια* (Dissertation, Freiburg 1977); de la Potterie, *La vérité dans Saint Jean*, I; idem, *La vérité dans Saint Jean. Le croyant et la vérité* (AnBib 74; Rome 1977), II; idem, "The Truth in Saint John", 67–82; Dodd, *Interpretation*, 170–178; Schnackenburg, *John*, II, 225–237; Brown, *John*, I, 499–501; S. Aalen, "'Truth,' A Key Word in St. John's Gospel", *SE* 2, ed. F. L. Cross (Berlin 1964), 3–24; J. Blank, "Der Johanneische Wahrheitsbegriff", *BZ* 7 (1963), 163–173; F. Büchsel, *Der Begriff der Wahrheit in dem Evangelium und den Briefen des Johannes* (Gütersloh 1911). Besides these proper Johannine studies, the following dictionary articles on ἀλήθεια also include the analysis of the Johannine notion of truth: Quell, "ἀλήθεια", 241–251; H. Hübner, "ἀλήθεια", *EDNT*, I, 57–60; Thiselton, "Truth", 889–894; Spicq and Ernest, "ἀλήθεια", 66–86.

[14] In the Synoptics, the frequency of their occurrence is comparatively very less: ἀλήθεια (7x), ἀληθής (2x), ἀληθινός (1x) and ἀληθῶς (8x). We may also add the frequently used ἀμὴν ἀμὴν sayings in John's Gospel to the semantic field of "truth".

[15] We will now examine very briefly these occurrences of ἀλήθεια to disclose its meaning in its particular context without entering into a detailed study of the passages.

1.1 Grace and Truth in Jesus Christ (1,14.17)

In the prologue (1,14.17), the evangelist says that the Word who became flesh is "full of grace and truth" (πλήρης χάριτος καὶ ἀληθείας) and that "grace and truth" (ἡ χάρις καὶ ἡ ἀλήθεια) came (ἐγένετο) through Jesus Christ. It is commonly suggested that the use of ἡ χάρις καὶ ἡ ἀλήθεια here reflects in a unique way the famous Old Testament pairing of חֶסֶד וֶאֱמֶת (e.g., Exod 34,6; Pss 25,10; 61,8; 86,15; Prov 20,28), which can be translated as "steadfast love"/"kindness" and "fidelity"/"faithfulness".[16] The fidelity to the covenant promised by God to the Israelites is fulfilled in the event of sending his Son, which is given the status of the definitive revelation of salvation.[17] The divine life is revealed through Jesus Christ who is the actual person of the incarnate Word. Thus, ἡ ἀλήθεια is essentially the revelation of salvation fulfilled in Jesus.

1.2 Doing the Truth (3,21)

In 3,21, the believer is characterized as "the one who does the truth" (ὁ ποιῶν τὴν ἀλήθειαν).[18] He acts in accordance with the truth and thus comes to the light. His deeds have been done through the grace of God in Christ, and he would acknowledge God's grace before the world.[19] He will live in faithful obedience to God and will respond faithfully to the revelation of light that God has given concerning himself.[20] Since Jesus is the embodiment of truth, doing the truth equates to actions performed in a faithful and obedient relationship with Jesus.[21] In conjunction with 3,20 and 1 John 1,6, we may notice in 3,21 not only an allusion to the way of Christian revelation but also a reference to the contrast between truth and falsehood.[22]

---

[16] Cf. Brown, *John*, I, 14. Kirchschläger, *Nur Ich bin die Wahrheit*, 253, writes, "Wahrheit wird in Joh 1,14 im Sinne der Offenbarung und – mit dem AT-Rückverweis und der damit verbundenen Betonung der 'Treue' – in der Menschwerdung im relationalen Sinn verstanden".

[17] Schnackenburg, *John*, II, 228. In the words of Kirchschläger, *Nur Ich bin die Wahrheit*, 120, "'Ἀλήθεια, die in der jüdischen Tradition in dem von JHWH durch Moses gegebenen Gesetz steckt, wird in Joh 1,14–18 christologisiert".

[18] The expression "doing the truth" is often viewed as a Semitic usage, also noticeable in the Qumran literature. Cf. Schnackenburg, *John*, II, 227. Brown, *John*, I, 135, reports that in the Old Testament "to do truth" (*'aśāh 'emet*) means "to keep faith".

[19] Beasley-Murray, *John*, 51.
[20] Newman and Nida, *John*, 93.
[21] Van der Watt, "The Good and the Truth", 331.
[22] Cf. Thiselton, "Truth", 891.

1.3 Worship in Spirit and Truth (4,23.24)

In 4,23–24, Jesus urges that the Father/God should be worshipped "in spirit and truth" (ἐν πνεύματι καὶ ἀληθείᾳ). The preposition ἐν may indicate the means or manner of worship.[23] The contrast between worship in Jerusalem or on Gerizim and worship in spirit and truth should be regarded as part of the familiar Johannine dualism between "earthly" and "heavenly", "from below" and "from above", "flesh" and "Spirit".[24] The worship of the Father/God in Spirit will replace the worship in the temple, attached to a particular place. Here there is a reference to the theme of replacement of the temple through Jesus mentioned in 2,13–22. The anarthrous use of the nouns, "spirit and truth" can be viewed as a hendiadys equivalent to the "Spirit of truth" (14,17; 15,26; 16,13; 1 John 4,6).[25] If it is Jesus himself who is to take the place of the Temple (2,21), it is the Spirit given by Jesus who will animate the worship that replaces worship at the Temple.[26] God can be worshipped as Father only by those who are born of the Spirit and possess the Spirit (3,5; cf. 1,12; Rom 8,15–16).[27] In Jesus, who is the truth incarnate and the place where God is truly and fully present, the believer can worship the Father in Spirit and truth.[28]

1.4 Witness to the Truth (5,33)

The reference to ἀλήθεια in 5,33 is placed in the context of the unit 5,31–40, which is dominated by the motif of witness (μαρτυρία) and witnessing (μαρ̂τυρέω). The Jewish legal system was based on the examination of witnesses, where one's own testimony was not valid and the testimony of two or more witnesses was a requirement (Deut 17,6; 19,15; Num 35,30). Hence, Jesus lists here four witnesses, namely the Father (v. 32), John the Baptist (v. 33), his own works (v. 36) and the Scriptures (v. 39). In v. 31, Jesus accepts the human principle that the witness on behalf of oneself is not a true evidence even though his own witness is valid (8,13–18). Since Jesus does not consider the testimony of human beings as important (v. 34), the witness mentioned in v. 32 is not John the Baptist. The other One (ἄλλος) who bears witness on behalf of Jesus in v. 32 is the Father as explicitly mentioned in v. 37, and the other three witnesses are dependent on the Father. The testimony of John the

---

[23] For the use of the preposition ἐν in this sense, see BDAG, 328–330.

[24] Brown, *John*, I, 180.

[25] Dodd, *Interpretation*, 223; Brown, *John*, I, 180. See the discussion under 1.8 in this section for the various nuances of the meaning of "Spirit of truth".

[26] Brown, *John*, I, 180.

[27] Cf. Brown, *John*, I, 180. According to Dodd, *Interpretation*, 175, ἐν ἀληθείᾳ means "on the plane of reality", i.e., τὰ ὄντα as distinct from εἴδωλα or φαντασίαι.

[28] Cf. B. Thettayil, *In Spirit and Truth. An Exegetical Study of John 4,19–26 and a Theological Investigation of the Replacement Theme in the Fourth Gospel* (Leuven 2007), 165.

Baptist is true because he was a man sent by God (1,6) and came as a witness to testify to the light (1,7). He was faithful to the mission given by God to bear witness to Jesus (1,15.19–36; cf. 18,37). He testified to the truth concerning Jesus that Jesus existed before him (1,30), that he baptizes with the Holy Spirit (1,33) and that he is the Son of God (1,34) and the Lamb of God (1,36). The truth that he witnessed is God's eschatological revelation manifested through Jesus.

1.5 Knowing and Saying the Truth (8,32.40.45.46; 16,7)

The most occurrences of ἀλήθεια are found in chapter 8 (7x). They occur during Jesus' confrontation with the Jews, beginning in 8,31 and ending in 8,59. By opposing Jesus, the Jews are setting themselves in opposition to the truth and in slavery to the devil. In the statement "You will know the truth, and the truth will make you free" (8,32), the reference is to the recognition of the revelation of God in Jesus (cf. 8,28) and to the freedom from sin (cf. 8,34) brought about by this revelation. Truth functions here as a means of liberating the person from the slavery of sin. "Knowing the truth" can mean inwardly accepting the saving truth brought by Jesus (8,40.45–46; 14,6), internalizing it (cf. 1 John 1,8; 2,4) and doing it (John 3,21; 1 John 1,6).[29] Truth has salvific power. "Knowing the truth" will lead one to true freedom. The freedom mentioned here is not freedom in any worldly sense but the divine freedom, the freedom of the children of God (1,12; 8,34–35; cf. 1 John 3,1–2). "Saying" (λαλέω) or "speaking" (λέγω) the truth in 8,40.45–46 implies not only the correctness and reliability of what is said but also the revelatory aspect of Jesus' preaching. Truth in 16,7 can probably refer to the truth in opposition to falsehood. The statement "Nevertheless, I tell you the truth; it is to your advantage that I go away" (16,7) removes any suspicion that Jesus' words may have been tailored to provide some illusory comfort.[30]

1.6 Truth and Life (8,44)

John 8,44 is a part of the polemical dialogue between Jesus and the Jews, recorded in 8,31–59. In 8,44, Jesus characterizes the Jews as having their origin from the devil. There is a radical opposition between truth represented by Jesus and falsehood represented by the devil, who is a liar and the father of lies. The sons of the devil cannot believe in Jesus because Jesus tells the truth, and their heart is dominated by lie (cf. 1 John 1,8; 2,4). The devil not simply "tells lies" but utters the Lie, the final denial of divine reality because he has no standing-ground in the world of eternal reality, and there is, there-

---

[29] Schnackenburg, *John*, II, 205.
[30] Thiselton, "Truth", 890.

fore, nothing in him which corresponds with the eternal reality.[31] Lie may also refer to the denial of God's revelation in Jesus and thus to unbelief.[32] Just as the sons of darkness hate the light (3,20), so also the sons of the devil hate the truth, who is Jesus himself. The accusers of Jesus are not truly Abraham's descendants. If they were so, they would not have hated Jesus.

1.7 Jesus as the Truth (14,6)

The use of ἀλήθεια with the definite article as the nominative predicate of the ἐγώ εἰμι-saying in 14,6 implies that Jesus is the enfleshment of truth.[33] "Wahrheit wird durch Jesus für den Menschen erkennbar, verortbar und erreichbar".[34] He embodies in himself the divine truth which means life for the believers and thus becomes the way for all who seek salvation.[35] Jesus not only reveals the truth in his words and deeds but also embodies it in his own person. "God is true" (ὁ θεὸς ἀληθής ἐστιν 3,33) and the truth of God is present in the person of Jesus. The identification of Jesus with the truth truly means his oneness with the Father, that he is in the Father and the Father is in him (14,7–11). As the incarnation of truth, Jesus is the revelation of the Father.

1.8 The Spirit of Truth (14,17; 15,26; 16,13)

The Paraclete is called "the Spirit of truth" (τὸ πνεῦμα τῆς ἀληθείας) in 14,17; 15,26; 16,13 (cf. 1 John 4,6). The genitive in the phrase τὸ πνεῦμα τῆς ἀληθείας can be viewed variously.[36] Firstly, it can be seen as a descriptive/attributive genitive, where the genitive denotes quality. Accordingly, the Holy Spirit is characterized by truth and truth is his essential quality. He is a true Spirit. This becomes clearer in relation to 1 John 4,6, where the Spirit of truth (τὸ πνεῦμα τῆς ἀληθείας) is placed in opposition to the Spirit of error (τὸ πνεῦμα τῆς πλάνης).[37] Secondly, we may regard this genitive as an appos-

---

[31] Dodd, *Interpretation*, 177.

[32] Kirchschläger, *Nur Ich bin die Wahrheit*, 182–183, thinks, "Wenn die 'Juden' den Glauben an Jesus nicht finden, stehen sie nicht mehr in der Tradition des gültigen Bundes der göttlichen Verheißung, sondern in der Nachfolge dessen, der Gott entgegengesetzt ist".

[33] Brown views, "In calling himself the truth, Jesus is not giving an ontological definition in terms of transcendentals but is describing himself in terms of his mission to men". He insists that "I am the truth" should be interpreted in light of 18,37, and it tells us what Jesus is in relation to men. See Brown, *John*, II, 630.

[34] Kirchschläger, *Nur Ich bin die Wahrheit*, 228.

[35] Schnackenburg, *John*, II, 228.

[36] For various functions of the genitive case, see BDF, 89–100 (§§162–186); Young, *New Testament Greek*, 23–41; Wallace, *Greek Grammar*, 72–136.

[37] We can assume from the context (1 John 4,1–6) that the reference to τὸ πνεῦμα in two instances indicates an allusion to superhuman spirit. Cf. R. E. Brown, *The Epistles of John. Translated, with Introduction, Notes and Commentary* (New Haven 1982), 501.

itive genitive, where the genitive is translated with the paraphrase "which is", "that is" or "who is". This view can be upheld in consideration of 4,23–24 and 1 John 5,6, where it is written, "the Spirit is the truth" (τὸ πνεῦμά ἐστιν ἡ ἀλήθεια). Thirdly, it can be considered as an objective genitive. Accordingly, τὸ πνεῦμα τῆς ἀληθείας can be translated as "the Spirit for the truth", "the Spirit who communicates/reveals the truth". In the case of τὸ πνεῦμα τῆς ἀληθείας in John, these various nuances of the genitive do not necessarily exclude each other but complement one another.

The Spirit of truth will be sent to the believers to be with them (παρ' ὑμῖν μένει) and to be within them (ἐν ὑμῖν ἔσται, 14,17).[38] He will bear witness to Jesus (15,26; cf. 1 John 5,6) through the disciples (15,27; cf. Matt 10,20; Acts 5,32) and guide them into the full truth of what Jesus has said (16,13).[39] The Paraclete's guidance into all truth involves not just a deeper intellectual understanding of what Jesus has said, but also a way of life in conformity with Jesus' teaching.[40] The function of the Spirit of truth is revelatory because the Spirit's truth is the truth about Jesus, the revelation brought by Jesus.[41] John does not regard truth as the ultimate goal or destination when he states that the Spirit of truth will lead the disciples into all truth (16,13). It only means that the Spirit will lead the disciples to the full understanding of the revelation made by Jesus (14,26).

1.9 Sanctification in the Truth (17,17.19)

In 17,17.19, the evangelist deals with the theme of the holiness of the disciples, where the Father is asked to sanctify or consecrate them "in the truth" (ἐν τῇ ἀληθείᾳ).[42] Just as the Father sanctified the Son and sent him into the world, so also Jesus wants to sanctify his disciples and send them into the

---

[38] In 2 John 2, the truth is said to abide in (τὴν μένουσαν ἐν ἡμῖν) and to be with (μεθ' ἡμῶν ἔσται) the believers.

[39] The witness of the Spirit to Jesus will be an inner one in the hearts of the disciples, so that they may be able to bear witness to Jesus before the world. The interior activity of the Spirit in the conscience of the believers can be called "witness" here (15,26). Cf. de la Potterie, "The Truth in Saint John", 75.

[40] Brown, *John*, II, 715.

[41] Van der Watt, "The Good and the Truth", 329.

[42] In v. 17, ἀλήθεια is used with the article and in v. 19 without an article. But we need not interpret ἐν ἀληθείᾳ in v. 19 in the sense of ἀληθῶς as Bultmann, *John*, 511, does, but rather in the sense of ἐν τῇ ἀληθείᾳ in v. 17. It should be noted that the evangelist has used ἀληθῶς in the near context (v. 8). In the case of ἀλήθεια a transition from the use of an arthrous substantive to an anarthrous substantive can be found in 8,44 (also in 3 John 3). The anarthrous prepositional phrase ἐν ἀληθείᾳ is common in the letters of John (1 John 3,18; 2 John 3.4; 3 John 1.3). The prepositional phrase ἐν ἀληθείᾳ in v. 19 can be seen in parallel to ἐν τῇ ἀληθείᾳ in v. 17. Cf. Schnackenburg, *John*, III, 188.

world (10,36; 17,18). The preposition ἐν can be translated as "by" or "for".[43] Since the evangelist immediately says, "Your word is truth" (ὁ λόγος ὁ σὸς ἀλήθειά ἐστιν), an instrumental sense of ἐν should be preferred. Thus, truth becomes an agency of sanctification. The disciples are to be sanctified in the truth, which is God's word (v. 17). In Jewish prayers, it is said that God sanctifies his people through his commandments.[44] It is noticeable that John uses "word" and "commandment" interchangeably (14,15.21.23.24). For John, Jesus is both the word (1,14) and the truth (14,6). Hence, sanctification in the truth implies an aspect of belonging to Jesus and thus to God (17,10).[45] The disciples are characterized as those who receive God's word through Jesus (17,14) and keep it (17,6). The disciples are, therefore, clean (καθαροί) through Jesus' word (15,3). Jesus also prays for the sanctification of the future believers who will believe in him through the word of his present disciples (17,20). The purpose of Jesus' consecration through his death for others (ὑπὲρ αὐτῶν; v. 19; cf. 10,11.17–18; 11,51; 15,13) is the sanctification of his disciples (cf. Heb 9,12–14; 10,10). The disciples become holy through the acceptance of the revelation of God in Jesus.

1.10 Truth on Trial (18,37.38)

In the episode of Jesus' trial before Pilate, the term ἀλήθεια occurs 3 times (18,37–38), which are the last occurrences in the Gospel. Jesus states before Pilate that he came into the world to testify to the truth, and everyone who belongs to the truth listens to his voice. In 5,33, it was said that John the Baptist testified to the truth. In 18,37, Jesus uses the same language to describe his mission in this world. The revelation of the Father is Jesus' testimony to the truth. Jesus' words and deeds are not his own. They reveal the Father because he does what the Father does (5,19) and speaks what he hears from the Father (8,26). But only those who belong to the truth can listen to Jesus' voice (18,37). He is the good shepherd (10,11.14), but only his sheep hear his voice (10,3.27). Those who belong to the truth are the sheep given to Jesus by the Father.[46] Those who do not belong to Jesus' sheep do not believe in him (10,26) and those who do not hear his words do not belong to God (8,47).

When Pilate asks Jesus, "So you are a king?", Jesus does not refuse categorically to be a king. But he is concerned to explain his role in terms of

---

[43] Brown, *John*, II, 761, assumes here both "by" and "for".

[44] Str-B., II, 566.

[45] Brown, *John*, II, 762. Barrett, *John*, 510, views that the saving truth revealed in the teaching and activity of Jesus separates and designates the disciples for their mission. Brown, *John*, II, 766, also sees in v. 17 the possibility of identifying the truth with the Holy Spirit (the Spirit of truth) and thus the sanctification by the Spirit (cf. 2 Thess 2,13).

[46] 1 John 3,18–19 states that those who belong to the truth will show their love in action rather than in speech.

bearing testimony to the truth. He is not a political king having an earthly kingdom and people as his subjects. His subjects are those who belong to the truth and listen to his voice. It is only those who belong to the truth can understand in what sense Jesus is a king having a kingdom. Jesus has been handed over to Pilate mainly because he has testified to the truth and the world has hated his testimony to the truth (7,7).

On the one hand, Jesus' statements bring comfort to Pilate because Jesus' kingship poses no threat to him and to the political interests of Rome. On the other hand, they make Pilate disturbed because with his statement "Everyone who belongs to the truth listens to my voice" (18,37) Jesus implicitly challenges Pilate to recognize the truth and to belong to the truth. By raising the issue of truth, Jesus subtly reminds Pilate of his highest obligation to find out the truth.[47] In reality, the one who is tried is not Jesus but Pilate. The issue here is whether or not Pilate will belong to the truth and listen to Jesus' voice. Pilate's question, "What is truth?" (Τί ἐστιν ἀλήθεια;) put to Jesus who is the truth himself (14,6), reveals that he fails to recognize and to belong to the truth. John does not record any answer to Pilate's question, but this silence speaks louder than words.[48]

1.11 Conclusion

The term ἀλήθεια is used in various ways and contexts in the Gospel of John. It is an overarching concept that covers everything that belongs to God and how it impacts on the believer.[49] The Johannine use of ἀλήθεια seems to combine both the Semitic and Greek-Hellenistic meanings of truth[50] and even

---

[47] Cf. M. Volf, *Exclusion and Embrace. A Theological Exploration of Identity, Otherness, and Reconciliation* (Nashville 1996), 266.

[48] Morris, *John*, 682, thinks that "the whole of the following narrative of the death and resurrection of Jesus is John's answer in action. On the cross and at the empty tomb we may learn what God's truth is". Cf. John 19,35. According to Köstenberger, "What is Truth?", 45, "Pilate's question, 'What is truth?' remains open-ended, and still rings through the ages, calling for an answer from every reader of the Gospel". J. A. Glancy does a "carnal reading" (expression as used by the author) of the Johannine passion narrative. She considers the Johannine passion account as an account of torture as defined in Roman law: "By torture we mean the infliction of anguish and agony on the body to elicit the truth" (cf. *The Digest of Justinian* 48.10.15.41). For her, "Jesus' tortured body is a truth telling corpus. The crucifixion squeezes out the bloody truth. The flesh of the Johannine Jesus is flush with truth (John 1,14)". See Glancy, "Torture: Flesh, Truth, and the Fourth Gospel", 108.

[49] Cf. R. Schnackenburg, *The Gospel According to St. John* (New York 1968), I, 407; van der Watt, "The Good and the Truth", 332.

[50] Cf. van der Watt, "The Good and the Truth", 325; Beasley-Murray, *John*, 14; Thiselton, "Truth", 874–875. Quell, "ἀλήθεια", 238, states that the New Testament use of ἀλήθεια is partly determined by the Semitic use of אֱמֶת and partly by the Greek and Hellenistic use of ἀλήθεια.

transcends them. The concept is taken from the language of the time and flexibly used to sustain and illuminate John's theology of the saving revelation in Jesus Christ.[51] An important discovery of this word analysis is that truth is never regarded by the evangelist as an ultimate goal. It is only a manner of doing something or a means or an agent of salvation (e.g., 4,23–24; 8,32; 17,17.19).

For John, truth is primarily a theological and perhaps even more accurately a Christological concept, which is inextricably related to God and to Jesus' relationship with God.[52] We can notice a strong Christological orientation of truth in John's Gospel in line with the evangelist's purpose of proving that Jesus is the Christ and the Son of God (20,30–31), and therefore, truth is to be understood as an affirmation of these two central claims of the Gospel.[53]

John uses the term ἀλήθεια to interpret the event of revelation in Jesus Christ.[54] Truth has become an event in the life of Jesus. Jesus is full of grace and truth (1,17). He not only reveals the truth in his words and actions but also embodies it in his own person (14,6). God's reality becomes manifest in him.[55] For John, truth is intensely personal because Jesus represents the truth in his very own person and calls people to respond to him in faith.[56] The episode of Jesus' trial before Pilate points out the profound relation between Jesus and the truth. The more one comes to know Jesus, the more one knows the truth. Hence, the rejection of truth is not a rejection of a set of abstract propositions but of Jesus.[57] It is to be specially noted that truth in John is related to the function of the Holy Spirit in a distinct manner. He is the Spirit of truth and after the physical departure of Jesus the Spirit will guide the believers into all truth about Christ. In short, truth in John has to be understood in his own terms.

---

[51] Schnackenburg says, "It was a suitable concept for John as an extension of the biblical understanding of revelation and a contrast with that of Judaism, and also for winning a hearing from his Hellenistic readers". See Schnackenburg, *John*, II, 237.

[52] Köstenberger, "What is Truth?", 34–35. Tack, *John 14,6 in Light of Jewish-Christian Dialogue*, 219, understands Johannine truth "as the loving unity of being between the Father and the Son, brought to life in an exemplary way by the incarnated Logos, in which also the faith community participates, not least through the mediation of the Spirit of truth after Jesus's departure". For Barrett, *John*, 538, "Truth is, as it were, truth in motion, entering the world, addressing the world, liberating (8,32) those who are capable of hearing it".

[53] Köstenberger, "What is Truth?", 58.

[54] Schnackenburg, *John*, II, 236.

[55] Schnackenburg, *John*, II, 228.

[56] Köstenberger, "What is Truth?", 59.

[57] Cf. Köstenberger, "What is Truth?", 59.

2. Life (ζωή) in the Gospel of John

The Gospel of John is the Gospel of life. Life (ζωή) is one of the most importantly theologically loaded words in this Gospel.[58] It is the unifying theme par excellence in John's Gospel.[59] It is the framing theme of the Gospel appearing in the beginning (1,4) and at the end of the Gospel (20,30–31), form-

---

[58] Ζωή is very less frequently attested in the Synoptic Gospels, altogether 16 times (4x in Mark; 7x in Matthew; 5x in Luke).

[59] For a detailed study of this Johannine theme from various angles, consult M. Stare, "Der Lebensbegriff als ethische Norm im Johannesevangelium", *Ethische Normen des frühen Christentums: Gut – Leben – Leib – Tugend,* ed. F. W. Horn et al. (WUNT 313; Tübingen 2013), 257–279; idem, "Ethics of Life in the Gospel of John", *Rethinking the Ethics of John. "Implicit Ethics" in the Johannine Writings,* ed. J. van der Watt and R. Zimmermann (WUNT 291; Tübingen 2012), 213–228; M. Hasitschka and M. Stare, "'...damit sie Leben haben und es in Fülle haben' (Joh 10,10): Der zentrale Heilsbegriff im Johannesevangelium und seine aktuelle Bedeutung", *Gutes Leben - für alle? Theologisch-kritische Perspektiven auf einen aktuellen Sehnsuchtsbegriff,* ed. A. Findl-Ludescher et al. (Kommunikative Theologie - inter-disziplinär 16; Vienna 2012), 259–271; C. Hoegen-Rohls, "Ewigkeit und Leben. Der biblische Vorstellungskreis III: Johannes", *Das Leben: Historisch-systematische Studien zur Geschichte eines Begriffs: Band 1,* ed. P. Bahr and S. Schaede (Religion und Aufklärung 17; Tübingen 2009), 129–152; J. van der Watt, "Repetition and Functionality in Johannine Research: A General Historical Survey", *Repetitions and Variations in the Fourth Gospel. Style, Text, Interpretation,* ed. G. van Belle et al. (Leuven 2009), 87–94; idem, *Family of the King,* 201–245; idem, "The Use of Ἀιώνιος in the Concept Ζωή Ἀιώνιος in John's Gospel", *NovT* 31 (1989), 217–228; J. Becker, "Die Hoffnung auf ewiges Leben im Johannesevangelium", *ZNW* 91 (2000) 192–211; P.-M. Jerumanis, *Réaliser la communion avec Dieu: Croire, vivre et demeurer dans l'évangile selon S. Jean* (Etudes bibiliques 32; Paris 1996); M. M. Thompson, "Eternal Life in the Gospel of John", *ExAud* 5 (1989), 35–55; J. Heer, *Leben hat Sinn. Christliche Existenz nach dem Johannesevangelium* (Stuttgart 1974); H. Lasic, *Recherches sur la notion de la vie chez S. Jean et les influences sur lui* (Dissertation, Freiburg 1970); Schnackenburg, *John,* II, 352–361; Brown, *John,* I, 505–508; R. W. Thomas, "The Meaning of the Terms 'Life' and 'Death' in the Fourth Gospel and in Paul", *SJT* 21 (1968), 199–212; U. E. Simon, "Eternal Life in the Fourth Gospel", *Studies in the Fourth Gospel,* ed. F. L. Cross (London 1957), 97–109; F. Mussner, *Zoe. Die Anschauung vom "Leben" im vierten Evangelium unter Berücksichtigung der Johannesbriefe. Ein Beitrag zur biblischen Theologie* (MThS 1.5; Munich 1952); E. Smilde, *Leven in de Johanneische Geschriften* (Kampen 1943); A. J. Appasamy, *The Johannine Doctrine of Life. A Study of Christian and Indian Thought* (London 1934); H. Pribnow, *Die johanneische Anschauung vom Leben* (Greifswald 1934); J.-B. Frey, "Le Concept de Vie dans l'Évangile de St. Jean", *Bib* 1 (1920), 37–58, 211–239; V. Schrenck, *Die johanneische Anschauung vom 'Leben' mit Berücksichtigung ihrer Vorgeschichte* (Leipzig 1898). Besides these general studies, there are many literature based on the theme of life in chapters 6 and 11 of John. E.g., R. A. Culpepper (ed.), *Critical Readings of John 6* (Leiden 1997); M. Stare, *Durch ihn leben. Die Lebensthematik in Joh 6* (NTA.NF 49; Münster 2004); J. Wagner, *Auferstehung und Leben. Joh 11,1–12,19 als Spiegel johanneischer Redaktions- und Theologiegeschichte* (Regensburg 1988).

ing an *inclusio* for the whole Gospel. In the New Testament, the noun ζωή can refer either to physical life (Luke 16,25; Rom 8,38; Phil 1,20) or to transcendent/eternal life (Mark 10,30; Matt 7,14; Luke 18,18; Rom 2,7; Gal 6,8; Jude 21; cf. Dan 12,2; 2 Macc 7,14). But John uses ζωή only to refer to transcendent/eternal life. To refer to physical life he uses exclusively the term ψυχή 10 times (10,11.15.17.24; 12,25(2x).27; 13,37.38; 15,13) and does not employ βίος at all, which can be found in the Synoptic Gospels (Mark 12,44; Luke 8,14.43; 15,12.30; 21,4). However, the natural life is used as a symbol to refer to the most precious divine gift lying beyond man's reach.[60] Eternal life is a way of existence which can be known through the analogy with earthly life, but differs from it on account of its divine nature.[61]

The background for the Johannine notion of ζωὴ αἰώνιος can be traced in the later writings of the Old Testament. In Dan 12,2, it is stated, "Many of those who sleep in the dust of the earth shall awake, some to *everlasting life* (לְחַיֵּי עוֹלָם), and some to shame and *everlasting contempt* (לְדִרְאוֹן עוֹלָם)".[62] The belief in a life after death is attested in the later period of Old Testament thought in terms of the resurrection of the dead (2 Macc 7,14; 12,43–44) and the immortality of the soul (Wis 3,1–4; 5,15).[63] The noun ζωή occurs in John's Gospel 36 times (1,4 [2x]; 3,15.16.36 [2x]; 4,14.36; 5,24 [2x].26 [2x].29.39.40; 6,27.33.35.40.47.48.51.53.54.63.68; 8,12; 10,10.28; 11,25; 12,25.50; 14,6; 17,2.3; 20,31). The other cognate words related to the theme of life in John are ζῶ (17x) and ζῳοποιέω (3x).[64] It should be noted that the

---

[60] Brown describes the motivation behind the theological notion of life thus, "Since man thinks analogically of God, it was appropriate to speak of God's 'life' on the analogy of man's life; and God's greatest act of friendship to man was described in terms of man's receiving a share in God's life". See Brown, *John*, I, 506.

[61] Cf. M. Vellanickal, *The Divine Sonship of Christians in the Johannine Writings* (AnBib 72; Rome 1977), 210–211.

[62] The Hebrew expression חַיֵּי עוֹלָם is translated in the LXX as ζωὴ αἰώνιος. Even though עוֹלָם is not an adjective rather a noun, it should be noted that in classical Hebrew nouns are often employed to qualify a preceding noun. Cf. Ashton, *Understanding*, 401, n. 34.

[63] Ashton, *Understanding*, 404, argues that John has two sources for his notion of ζωὴ αἰώνιος, namely the Jewish eschatology, from which he derives his concept of a life that surpasses human life, and the Synoptic tradition, which allows him to replace the preaching of the kingdom with a term more suggestive of the benefits that follow upon the acceptance of the gospel. For the Greek/Hellenistic-Jewish background and the New Testament usage of the term ζωή, see R. Bultmann et al., "ζωή", *TDNT*, II, 832–875; H. G. Link, "Life", *NIDNTT*, II, 476–484; Ashton, *Understanding*, 399–405; Dodd, *Interpretation*, 144–150; E. Percy, *Untersuchung über den Ursprung der johanneischen Theologie. Zugleich ein Beitrag zur Entstehung des Gnostizismus* (Lund 1939), 307–343; L. Schottroff, "ζῶ/ζωή", *EDNT*, II, 105–109.

[64] The verb ζῳοποιέω does not occur at all in the Synoptic Gospels. The verb ζῶ appears altogether 18 times in the Synoptic Gospels (3x in Mark; 6x in Matthew; 9x in Luke). Since we are confronting only the noun ζωή in John 14,6, our focus will be mainly on its usage.

most of the occurrences of ζωή are found in the first part of the Gospel (1–12), i.e., 32 times. Within the farewell discourse, it occurs only 3 times. It never appears in the passion-resurrection narratives (18–20), except in the concluding statement (20,30–31). The Johannine usage of ζωή is discussed below.

2.1 Light and Life (1,4; 8,12)

The initial section of John's prologue (1,1–5) as a whole deals with the participation of the λόγος in creation. The Word was not only with God but was God himself (cf. Rev 19,13). In v. 3, the Word is presented both positively (v. 3a) and negatively (v. 3b) as the mediator of creation. All things came into being through the Word.[65] The relative clause ὃ γέγονεν can be joined either to the preceding clause (καὶ χωρὶς αὐτοῦ ἐγένετο οὐδὲ ἕν) or to the following clause (ἐν αὐτῷ ζωὴ ἦν). We prefer to read it in conjunction with the following clause, implying "what came into being through him was life".[66] The ζωή here can refer both to physical and eternal life. But John emphasizes the latter because throughout the Gospel he is concerned with the saving activity of the Word, which provides light of life to all people who follow him (cf. 8,12).[67] Jesus has life in himself (5,26) and his resurrection will bring this life to the believers (14,19). The statement ἡ ζωὴ ἦν τὸ φῶς τῶν ἀνθρώπων has ethical undertones because light makes people able to see and act correctly.[68] The light of revelation in Jesus will eradicate darkness and lead people to the final goal of eternal life.

Another passage where life is used in association with light is 8,12, one of the ἐγώ εἰμι-sayings of the Gospel. It is set within the context of Jesus' conflict with the Jews in Jerusalem at the time of the feast of Tabernacles (7,14–8,59). It begins the unit vv. 12–20, where the pattern of conversation evident in 7,1–52 continues.[69] In the context of the feast of Tabernacles which is a

---

[65] The "word of the Lord" has a creative role in the Old Testament (Gen 1; Ps 33,6; Wis 9,1) even as has the Word of the Prologue. Heb 1,2 speaks of the creation through the Son, referring to his powerful word. In 1 John 1,1, Jesus is considered as the Word of life. Brown, *John*, I, 26, views that the Father may be said to create through the Word since the Word is related to the Father (cf. 5,26).

[66] The texts of N-A[28] and *GNT*[5] maintain this reading, which preserves the rhythmical balance of the clauses in the unit (vv. 1–5) and its style of the "staircase parallelism". Moreover, creation and life are inseparable themes. Cf. Beasley-Murray, *John*, 2; Brown, *John*, I, 6–7.

[67] In Prov 8,35, Wisdom says, "For whoever finds me, finds life and obtains favour from the Lord".

[68] Cf. van der Watt, *Family of the King*, 236–237.

[69] The pericope of the adulteress (7,53–8,11) is not considered by the scholars as original to the Gospel of John on account of its absence in the earliest Greek manuscripts and due to the evidence for its non-Johannine origin (see Metzger, *Textual Commentary*, 187–

feast of lights, Jesus declares that he himself is the light of the world.[70] There are two consequences if anyone follows Jesus. Negatively, he will not walk in the darkness, and positively, he will have the light of life. John gives a new meaning to the symbol of light identifying it with the revelation of God in Jesus (cf. 1,1–18).[71] The light of revelation in Jesus will lead one to life. Through the dualistic categories of light and darkness, Jesus is giving his audience the choice either to accept or to refuse the revelation of the Father in him. In 8,12, life is found in association with the journey motif (ἀκολουθέω, περιπατέω) and is regarded as the ultimate goal of the human journey. Since Jesus is regarded as the way and the life (11,25; 14,6), an imagery of following the way who is Jesus and reaching the goal of life is envisaged here.

2.2 Belief and Life (3,15–16.36)

In chapter 3, the term ζωή appears 4 times (vv. 15–16.36), among them 3 times with its epithet αἰώνιος. In these four instances, it is closely associated with the motif of belief (πιστεύω). V. 15 is a part of Jesus' conversation with Nicodemus (3,1–21),[72] where Jesus explains to him how the rebirth through the Holy Spirit becomes an actuality. Jesus refers here to his salvific death on the cross, resurrection and ascension for the salvation of humanity. In order to impart the Holy Spirit, the Son of Man must be lifted up, just as Moses lifted up the serpent in the desert (Num 21,8–9). The crucified and glorified Jesus is the giver of the Holy Spirit (John 7,39; 20,22) and eternal life (17,2; 1 John 5,11). The bestowal of the Holy Spirit will inaugurate an era of eternal life for

---

188). However, in its current canonical location, it makes sense when it is viewed as a narrative of conflict in the context of Jesus' conflict with the Jewish authorities in Jerusalem.

[70] For a study of the background of the theme of light, see H. Conzelmann, "φῶς", *TDNT*, IX, 309–358; H. -C. Hahn and C. Brown, "Light", *NIDNTT*, II, 484–496. For a study of John 8,12 in the light of the feast of Tabernacles, see T. Marottikaparambil, *John 8,12–20: Jesus the Light of the World. A Study of the Johannine Christological Reinterpretation of the Feast of Sukkot* (Dissertation, Pontificia Universitas Urbaniana; Rome 2011).

[71] O'Day, *John*, 632.

[72] Of course, it is not easy to discern who is speaking in vv. 16–21, whether Jesus or the evangelist. There is not any indication of the change of speaker, and the theme of vv. 16–21 is closely related to the previous verses. The connective γάρ indicates the continuity of the speaker. Moreover, there is homogeneity of style. The use of the third person pronoun is not a sufficient reason to distinguish between Jesus and the evangelist as the speaker because in many instances Jesus speaks of himself in the third person (e.g., 1,51; 3,13–15; 8,28; 12,23; 13,31). Here we need to be aware that the words of the Johannine Jesus and the evangelist often overlap. We have access to the words of Jesus only through the understanding and rethinking of the evangelist. The threads of tradition and homiletic development are too interwoven to make sometimes the distinction between the words of Jesus and those of the evangelist. See O'Day, *John*, 548; Brown, *John*, I, 136–137, 149.

those who believe in Jesus.[73] This eternal life is the life of the children of God (1,12) and the life born of the Holy Spirit and born from above (3,5–8).

In v. 16, the role of the Father comes into the scene. The purpose of the Father in giving his Son in incarnation and death is the eternal life of those who believe in the Son, and the motivating force behind it is the love of the Father for the world (cf. 1 John 4,9).[74] The condition of humanity is presented in dualistic terms, either "to have eternal life" or "to perish". Humanity can escape from its destruction and attain eternal life only by believing in the Son of God. The term ζωή occurs twice in the concluding verse of chapter 3 in association with the motif of belief. This verse is part of the concluding discourse of the chapter (vv. 31–36).[75] It states the consequences of believing and not believing in Jesus. By believing in Jesus, one attains salvation at once (cf. 5,24) and for all eternity. For John, access to eternal life is a present reality (ὁ πιστεύων εἰς τὸν υἱὸν ἔχει ζωὴν αἰώνιον) and not something reserved for the future (cf. Mark 10,17.30; Matt 25,46; Luke 10,25). Unbelief in the Son is disobedience to the Son and leads to the deprival of eternal life. Unbelief is an act of will, the decision to refuse Jesus' claims. The expression "not to see life" is equivalent to "not to see the kingdom of God" (3,3). Thus, the kingdom of God and eternal life are the same reality for John. To persist in unbelief is to bring God's judgment upon oneself.

2.3 The Living Water and the Life (4,14)

The term ζωή is also found in Jesus' dialogue with the Samaritan woman (4,7–26), which is centred around the topics of living water and true worship. In this scene, we find the struggle of a soul to rise from the things of this world to the belief in Jesus.[76] From natural water, Jesus shifts the theme of

---

[73] The ἵνα clause in vv. 15–16 explicitly indicates that the goal of belief is eternal life.

[74] Here the reader is reminded of the sacrifice of Abraham, who was willing to offer "his only son" (אֶת־בִּנְךָ אֶת־יְחִידְךָ; cf. John 3,16 τὸν υἱὸν τὸν μονογενῆ), Isaac to the Lord as a sacrifice (Gen 22,2.12), which would become a means of blessings for all the nations of the earth (Gen 22,18; Sir 44,21).

[75] Here also, it is difficult to recognize the speaker of this discourse. It resembles closely the style of speech attributed to Jesus in the Gospel and has close parallels with Jesus' words to Nicodemus. Hence, it can be regarded as a displaced discourse of Jesus. It is placed at its current position by the evangelist as a recapitulation of the chapter (in chapter 4 there is a clear change of setting in describing Jesus' encounter with the woman of Samaria and the royal official) and to summarize both the Nicodemus and the John the Baptist scenes. We may assume that what was once an isolated discourse of Jesus has been attached to the scenes of chapter 3 as an interpretation of those scenes. See Brown, *John*, I, 159–160. It is worthwhile here to consider the comment of Schnackenburg, "We have here the Johannine kerygma, which to the mind of the evangelist is none other than the revelatory testimony of Jesus". See Schnackenburg, *John*, I, 381.

[76] Brown, *John*, I, 178.

the dialogue to the living water which is the heavenly water of eternal life. V. 14 makes clear that the living water itself is not the eternal life but leads to it.[77] The imagery of the living water which leads one to eternal life, supported by its Old Testament background, can within the scope of Johannine theology refer to the revelation (the teaching/wisdom) which Jesus brings to the people and to the Holy Spirit which Jesus imparts to the believers.[78] Thus, John presents Jesus as the divine wisdom (cf. 1,1–18)[79] and as the giver of the Holy Spirit (cf. 7,37–39; 20,22).[80] The revelation and the activity of the Holy Spirit are closely interrelated because it is through Jesus' words that the believers attain Spirit and life (5,24; 6,63.68; 8,51), and it is the Spirit of truth who will continue the revelation of Jesus by teaching everything and guiding them into all the truth (14,26; 16,13).

2.4 Reaping for Eternal Life (4,36)

After Jesus' dialogue with the Samaritan woman (4,7–26), there is a change of scene through the appearance of the disciples (4,27–38). V. 36 is placed within the context of Jesus' dialogue with the disciples (4,27–38), where the discussion about food leads to the imagery of harvest (vv. 35–38). The harvest imagery consists of two proverbs and their explanations, the first one about the time of harvesting (vv. 35–36)[81] and the second about the distinction between sower and reaper (vv. 37–38). Normally, there is a time gap between sowing and reaping and a distinction between sower and reaper. But in the case of Jesus there is something unusual. He is reaping on the very day of sowing, and he himself is the sower and the reaper. Jesus' dialogue with the Samaritan woman leads her to believe in Jesus, and through her the whole village comes to believe in Jesus (vv. 28–30.39.42). To believe in Jesus is to attain eternal life (3,15–16.36). The believers whom Jesus wins in Samaria are the fruits for eternal life. Jesus' presence and his doing the will of the Father make the harvest of eschatological fulfilment a present reality.

---

[77] Brown, *John*, I, 178, writes, "water is to natural life as living water is to eternal life".

[78] Cf. Schnackenburg, *John*, I, 429–432; Brown, *John*, I, 178–180.

[79] In the Old Testament, water is a symbol of divine wisdom that gives life (Prov 13,14; 18,4; Isa 55,1–3; Sir 24,21; cf. John 6,35).

[80] In the immediate context, there are allusions to the Holy Spirit. The expression "gift (of God)" (ἡ δωρεά τοῦ θεοῦ) is used to refer to the Holy Spirit in the New Testament (Acts 2,38; 8,20; 10,45; 11,17; Heb 6,4). In vv. 23–24, there is an explicit reference to the Spirit.

[81] This proverb might mean, "Labour hard in sowing now, and in four months we shall reap". See Keener, *John*, I, 625.

2.5 Jesus' Authority over Life (5,24.26.29)

Chapter 5 introduces the conflict between Jesus and the Jewish authorities. It consists of Jesus' healing of a paralytic on the day of the Sabbath and the Jews' reactions to it (vv. 1–18) and a discourse by Jesus (vv. 19–47), which draws out the theological implications of vv. 1–18. We may divide the discourse into two parts: i. the authority of the Son based on his relationship with the Father (vv. 19–30) and ii. the witnesses to Jesus and the Jews' refusal to believe in Jesus (vv. 31–47). In vv. 19–30, Jesus explains that the Father has given him the authority to give life and to judge because he is the Son. The Father is present in the Son. Hence, if anyone does not honour the Son, he does not honour the Father (v. 23). The words of the Son are the words of the Father. He who listens to the Son believes in the Father. The Son has the power to give eternal life to anyone who listens to him (cf. 3,15–16.36). His word is life-giving (cf. 6,63.68) and the believer who gains eternal life does not come under judgment. He is transferred from the realm of death to the realm of divine life (cf. 8,51; 11,26). Johannine dualism of death and life is used here metaphorically to refer to spiritual death and life.[82] The focus of v. 24 is on the effect of belief in the present life of the believer and thus on realized eschatology. It should be noted that in v. 24 life is found in association with a verb of journey (μεταβαίνω) and presented as the ultimate destination of the human journey.

The voice of the Son has the power to raise the dead to life (v. 25) because he has life in himself like his Father (v. 26). Only God has uncreated and unbegotten life in himself. Hence, he is called "the living God" in the Old Testament (e.g., Deut 5,26; Josh 3,10; 1 Sam 17,26; 2 Kgs 19,4; Ps 42,2; Isa 37,4; Jer 10,10; Hos 1,10) and also in the New Testament (e.g., Matt 16,16; 26,63; Acts 14,15; Rom 9,26; 2 Cor 3,3; 1 Thess 1,9; Heb 3,12). In Rev 1,18, Jesus is called "the living one" (ὁ ζῶν). The Father has given the Son the authority to have life in himself. Hence, by claiming "to have life in himself", Jesus makes a claim to deity (v. 26). However, the life of the Son is dependent on that of the Father. The Son has a share in the life of the Father so that the Son can give life to whomever he wishes (v. 21), and he also has the power to judge (v. 27).

If v. 25 is focused on realized eschatology, the language of vv. 28–29 is that of future eschatology, referring to the resurrection of the dead at the end and final judgment. Those who are spiritually dead in v. 25 are said to be physically dead ("in the graves") in vv. 28–29. Thus, in vv. 19–30 we have a combination of Johannine and traditional eschatological statements to show that Jesus has "God's full eschatological power".[83] V. 29 reminds that the

---

[82] Van der Watt, *Family of the King*, 211, states that death is a metaphorical description of a state of alienation from God.

[83] Cf. O'Day, *John*, 585.

believer's decisions in the present also have future consequences because when the believer hears the voice of Jesus, his life is transformed from death to life in the present (vv. 24–25) as well as in the future (v. 29).[84] Acceptance or refusal of the Son now will be decisive for the entry from death to life in the future.

2.6 Witnesses to Jesus and Life (5,39–40)

As we mentioned earlier,[85] the unit vv. 31–40 is dominated by the motif of witness (μαρτυρία) and witnessing (μαρτυρέω). To support his claims in vv. 19–30, Jesus lists four witnesses, namely the Father (v. 32), John the Baptist (v. 33), his own works (v. 36) and the Scriptures (v. 39). The expression "(you) search the Scriptures" (ἐραυνᾶτε τὰς γραφάς) is a typical and technical way to refer to scriptural study in rabbinic Judaism and the Qumran community.[86] The Jews believe that they will attain eternal life from the study of the Scriptures (cf. Sir 17,11; 45,5; Bar 4,1). But they refuse to accept that it is about Jesus, who is the only way to eternal life (14,6), that these Scriptures speak. For John, the individual sayings of the Scripture are fulfilled in the person of Jesus (12,38; 13,18; 15,25; 17,12; 19,24.36). The whole Scripture is directed towards him (cf. 12,41), and it is about him that Moses has written (v. 46).[87] The phrase "come to Jesus" is a Johannine expression used to refer to "believe in Jesus", and its result is eternal life (5,40; 6,35; 7,37; cf. 1,47; 3,2; 4,30.40.47). The irony is that the Jews refuse the very thing for which they search. As God's Word (1,1–18), Jesus represents the whole Scripture, and hence, the rejection of him is the repudiation of the very heart of the Scripture. It should be noted that in 5,40 life is found in relation to the journey motif (ἔρχομαι) and regarded as the goal.

---

[84] Cf. O'Day, *John*, 585.

[85] See the discussion under "Witness to the Truth" on pp. 230–231.

[86] The Hebrew term דָּרַשׁ was used technically to refer to scriptural study. See Str-B., II, 467; O. Betz, *Offenbarung und Schriftforschung in der Qumransekte* (WUNT 6; Tübingen 1960), 15–36; G. Jeremias, *Der Lehrer der Gerechtigkeit. Studien zur Umwelt des Neuen Testaments* (Göttingen 1963), 271–275.

[87] Jesus' words here reflect the life situation of the early Christians in confrontation with Judaism. V. 24 is a statement of the Christian community's understanding of Scripture as opposed to the use of Scripture in Judaism. See Schnackenburg, *John*, II, 125. Brown, *John*, I, 228, observes that the whole chapter of John 5 fits in well with the purpose of the Gospel to persuade the Jewish Christians to leave the Synagogues and to profess openly their faith in Jesus.

2.7 The Bread of Life (6,27.33.35.40.47.48.51.53.54)[88]

The highest number of occurrences of ζωή in the Gospel is found in chapter 6 (11x). Jesus' signs of the multiplication of loaves (vv. 1–15) and his walking over the water (vv. 16–21) and the crowd's search after Jesus (vv. 22–24) provide the narrative background for Jesus' long discourse on the theme of life, centred on the bread of life (vv. 25–72). The interventions of various groups of people and Jesus' interactions with them provide the clues to structure the discourse. Thus, this longest chapter of the Gospel can be divided as follows:[89]

6,1–15 Jesus' Multiplication of Loaves
6,16–21 Jesus' Walking over the Water
6,22–24 Crowd's Search after Jesus
6,25–71 Jesus' Dialogue
        6,25–40 Jesus' Dialogue with the Crowd
        6,41–59 Jesus' Dialogue with the Jews
        6,60–66 Jesus' Dialogue with the Disciples
        6,67–71 Jesus' Dialogue with the Twelve.

In Jesus' dialogue with the crowd (vv. 25–40), we can notice four questions/interventions from the part of the crowd and Jesus' corresponding answers to them (vv. 25–27; vv. 28–29; vv. 30–33; vv. 34–40). The crowds are seeking for Jesus, not because they understood the deeper meaning of Jesus' signs, but because they seek for sensual satisfaction (vv. 25–26). Jesus' multiplication of loaves, however, is a sign of his power to provide life through imperishable food. This food creates life for eternity. It is a food which the Son of Man will give when he has ascended to where he was before (vv. 62). It is similar to "the living water", which is capable of providing eternal life (4,14).

---

[88] The discussions here and on pp. 315–317 on the theme of bread of life may complement each other.

[89] Cf. Stare, *Durch ihn Leben*, 19. For various approaches to the structure of John 6, see M. Labahn, *Offenbarung in Zeichen und Wort. Untersuchungen zur Vorgeschichte von Joh 6,1–25a und seiner Rezeption in der Brotrede* (WUNT II 117; Tübingen 2000); J. Beutler, *Studien zu den johanneischen Schriften* (SBAB 25; Stuttgart 1998), 247–262; idem, "The Structure of John 6", *Critical Readings of John 6*, ed. R. A. Culpepper (Leiden 1997), 115–127; P. N. Anderson, *The Christology of the Fourth Gospel. Its Unity and Disunity in the Light of John 6* (WUNT II 78; Tübingen 1996); H. Weder, *Einblicke ins Evangelium. Exegetische Beiträge zur neutestamentlichen Hermeneutik* (Göttingen 1992), 363–400; J. D. Crossan, "It is Written: A Structuralist Analysis of John 6", *Narrative Discourse in Structural Exegesis. John and I Thessalonians*, ed. D. Patte (Semeia 26; Chico 1983), 2–20.

In 6,33, Jesus is presented as "the bread of God" in contrast with the manna of the Old Testament (Exod 16; Num 11,9). The description of Jesus as "the bread of God" together with two predicates, "comes down from heaven" and "gives life to the world", reminds the reader of 3,13.31, where he is said to have descended from heaven and of 5,21, where he is said to be capable of giving life to whomever he wishes. The manna of Moses gave physical nourishment to the people of Israel, but "the bread of God" gives eternal life to the whole world (cf. 3,14–16). Since this bread comes down from heaven, the realm of divine life, it has the power to give divine life to the world. In v. 35, Jesus reveals that he himself is the very bread that the crowd asks for (cf. v. 34). "I am the bread of life" is the first occurrence of the ἐγώ εἰμι-statement with a predicate nominative in John's Gospel. The expression ὁ ἄρτος ὁ ζῶν may refer to the plenitude and the power of life in the heavenly bread.[90] "To come to Jesus" and "to believe in him" are synonymous (cf. 7,37). "The bread of life" can here refer to Jesus' teaching and revelation in the light of the Jewish wisdom traditions, where wisdom is represented by food and drink (Prov 9,5; Sir 15,3; 24,19–21; cf. John 6,45), and also to the Eucharistic symbolism, which is explicitly enumerated in vv. 51–58.[91] In v. 40, there is a combination of realized and future eschatological beliefs. Everyone who believes in the Son has eternal life at present, and he will be raised up on the last day. The scope of the mission of Jesus is universal because it is to give life to all who believe in him.

In vv. 41–59, Jesus' speech is addressed to the complaining and disputing Jews, who know only his human origin (vv. 41–42) and are concerned about the manner of giving his flesh to eat (v. 52). But Jesus points out his divine origin, asserting that he is sent by the Father (v. 44) and is from God (v. 46). He reaffirms that the one who believes in him has eternal life (v. 47; cf. 3,16.36; 5,24; 6,40) and that he himself is the bread of life (v. 48; cf. v. 35). It is not like the manna that could not give imperishable life (v. 49). The death of the ancestors is contrasted here with the life of the living bread. Just as everyone requires bread for life, the person who wants to sustain eternal life needs Jesus.[92] Jesus' passion and his sacrificial-salvific death on the cross are reflected in the clause, "The bread that I will give for the life of the world is my flesh" (v. 51). The vv. 51–58 have Eucharistic tones and remind the reader of the Last Supper in which Jesus gives himself as the bread to be eaten (cf. Mark 14,22; Matt 26,26; Luke 22,19; 1 Cor 11,24).[93] It is likely that John

---

[90] Schnackenburg, *John*, II, 54.

[91] Cf. Brown, *John*, I, 272–275.

[92] Cf. van der Watt, *Family of the King*, 223.

[93] With the term "Eucharist", we refer to the communal meals of the first Christians. John does not use the noun εὐχαριστία in his Gospel. However, it should be noted that the non-occurrence of εὐχαριστία is not only in John but also in the Synoptic Gospels. John uses the verb εὐχαριστέω 3 times (6,11.23; 11,41; Mark 2x; Matthew 2x; Luke 4x) and the

2. Life (ζωή) in the Gospel of John   247

presupposes the Eucharistic institution and desires only to explain its meaning.[94] The Johannine Eucharistic section (6,51–58) refers to the relation between the Eucharist and the death of Jesus.[95] In his crucifixion, Jesus gives

---

noun δεῖπνον 4 times (12,2; 13,2.4; 21,20), which Paul uses while referring to "Lord's Supper" in Corinth (1 Cor 11,17–34). It is extremely difficult to think that neither the writer nor the readers of the Gospel of John had some idea about the communal meals of the first Christians (Luke 24,35; Acts 2,42; 1 Cor 11,17–34). John presents three scenes of meals (6,1–13; 13,1–30; 21,1–14), which remind us of the communal meals of the first Christians. In all of them "eating" has only a literal meaning. Remarkable is also the use of the verb τρώγω in 13,18, which occurs 4 times in the Eucharistic section of chapter 6 (vv. 54.56.57.58). In 13,18, the verb τρώγω is used literally. Therefore, eating Jesus' flesh and drinking his blood cannot be merely "a metaphor" for believing in Jesus and accepting his revelation. O'Day, *John*, 607, considers vv. 53–58 as "the institution text" in John but presented in Johannine, not Synoptic categories. The vocabularies that carry Eucharistic overtones in 6,51–58 are ἐσθίω, σάρξ, πίνω and αἷμα (cf. Matt 26,26–28). It is true that John uses σάρξ rather than the Synoptic σῶμα. There is no Hebrew or Aramaic word for σῶμα, as we understand this term. It is, therefore, believed that what Jesus actually said at the Last Supper was the Aramaic equivalent of "this is my flesh". If this is true, then, John in this respect is the closest of the Gospels to the original Eucharistic language of Jesus. Moreover, Ignatius of Antioch, one of the earliest ecclesiastical writers (Rom 7,3; Phil 4,1; Smyr 7,1), and Justin (Apol 1,66) use σάρξ to refer to the Eucharist. Cf. Brown, *John*, I, 284–285. Barrett, *John*, 298, thinks that John might have substituted σάρξ for σῶμα partly because it corresponded with the use of his own church and partly because it fitted his theology of incarnation.

[94] It is a phenomenon in the Gospel that the evangelist sometimes presupposes that the readers have some basic information about Christian traditions. In chapter 1, the baptism of Jesus is not narrated, but it is presupposed. In John 6,67.70.71; 20,24, John speaks of "the twelve" disciples. Who are they? When are they chosen? The evangelist neither narrates the election of the twelve disciples nor gives their names as it is found in Mark 3,13–19; Matt 10,1–4; Luke 6,12–16. In 18,24.28, John scantily mentions that Jesus was taken to and from Caiaphas. But he does not narrate the trial before Caiaphas, which has an important role in the Synoptic Gospels (cf. Mark 14,53–65 without mentioning the name of Caiaphas but the parallel accounts in Matt 26,57–68; Luke 22,66–71 with his name). In short, we must believe that John makes many presuppositions. Therefore, he does not narrate the institution of the Eucharist as we find it in the Synoptic tradition. His purpose is to lead to the deeper meaning and importance of the Eucharist. Brown, *John*, I, 292–293, states, "While the Synoptic Gospels record the institution of the Eucharist, it is John who explains what the Eucharist does for the Christian".

[95] For a non-Eucharistic interpretation of John 6,51c–58, see M. J. J. Menken, "John 6,51c–58: Eucharist or Christology?", *Critical Readings of John 6*, ed. R. A. Culpepper (Leiden 1997), 183–204. It is not the concern of this study to argue for the Eucharistic interpretation and to expose the flaws of Menken's article. However, some general observations can be made here. Menken himself clearly admits that the evangelist uses Eucharistic language. Then, it is difficult to think that the evangelist uses Eucharistic language without any intention of referring to Eucharistic participation because the evangelist uses Eucharistic language (6,51–58) in a context where he speaks about Jesus' "giving thanks" (εὐχαριστέω in 6,11.23) and feeding of the five thousand (6,1–14). Otherwise, the evange-

his "flesh" (σάρξ) for the life of the world. The Eucharist, thus, provides a vivid picture of what it means to receive Christ by faith.[96] It will maintain and strengthen the divine life in the believers. Even though ὁ ἄρτος ὁ ζῶν is synonymous with ὁ ἄρτος τῆς ζωῆς, ὁ ἄρτος ὁ ζῶν is more suitable for the Eucharist.[97] That Jesus' flesh and blood give life to those who consume them is stated negatively and positively in vv. 53–54. The life that the Eucharist provides will not pass away with one's physical death, but will lead one to the final resurrection on the last day (v. 54).[98]

2.8 Jesus' Words and Life (6,63.68)

In vv. 60–66, Jesus' speech is addressed to the larger group of his disciples, who find his teaching difficult to accept. Jesus wants that his discourse on the bread of life should be understood in the light of his ascension and the bestowal of the Spirit. The reference to "flesh" in v. 63 is not to the Eucharistic flesh, but to the natural principle in man which cannot give eternal life (cf.

---

list should have given a warning to the readers as he does often, indicating that this Eucharistic language he used does not refer to the Eucharistic participation but only to Jesus' death (cf. 2,21–22; 7,39; 12,32–33). Menken looks at the text, as the title of his article suggests, through "either or" categories, either Eucharist or Christology. But it is not reasonable to examine the text through "either or" categories. It is hard to think that for the evangelist, belief in Jesus and Eucharistic participation are mutually exclusive. If "flesh" and "blood" refer only to Jesus' death, then is it possible to separate this view from the Christian understanding of the Eucharist as a commemoration of Jesus' death? The very basis of the Eucharist is the death of Christ. Therefore, Apostle Paul says, "For as often as you eat this bread and drink the cup, you proclaim the Lord's death until he comes" (1 Cor 11,26). Moreover, those who interpret John 6,51–58 christologically suggest that "to eat" and "to drink" indicate metaphorically belief in Jesus. Then, it is to be noted that there is no attempt at all from the part of Jesus to correct his disciples who left him during his discourse on the bread of life (6,66–69). If they went wrong in taking a metaphor in a literal sense, why didn't he call them back and rectify their misunderstanding? Those disciples who had accepted everything up to this point would not have abandoned him, had he said that he was speaking only "metaphorically". The views of Menken are followed by Stare, *Durch ihn leben*, 196–217. Schnackenburg, *John*, II, 61, comments, "The Eucharist bears witness to the Cross of Jesus as the enduring and unsurpassable source of salvation (cf. 19,34; 1 John 5,6–8) and to the historical redeemer who came in the flesh (1,14; 6,51c; 1 John 4,2–3)". In the view of Colacrai, "Gesu. Cristo Salvatore e Signore", 161, the words "flesh" and "blood" in 6,51–58 suggest a close relationship between the incarnation (cf. 1,14) and the Eucharist. For more arguments in favour of Eucharistic allusions in the Gospel of John and for more literature on this topic, see E. Kobel, *Dining with John. Communal Meals and Identity Formation in the Fourth Gospel and Its Historical and Cultural Context* (BIS 109; Leiden 2011) 173–188, 205–214.

[96] Barrett, *John*, 297.
[97] Brown, *John*, I, 291.
[98] V. 54 is also a blend of two types of eschatology.

1,13; 3,6a; Matt 16,17).[99] The Spirit which is the gift of the risen-ascended Jesus (v. 62; cf. 7,39; 20,22) is the divine life-giving principle (cf. 3,6b–8). The one who accepts the words of Jesus receives his life-giving Spirit.[100] The words of Jesus are not something that is spoken (sounds) and then disappears, but the creative effect of what is being said (cf. 15,3.25).[101] The flesh as the flesh is useless, but the Spirit and the flesh should be held together.[102] The flesh has salvific power only because it is inseparably bound to the life-giving, Spirit-filled words of Jesus.[103]

In vv. 67–71, Jesus is finally turning to his twelve apostles and asking them whether they wish to go away like other disciples. Peter as the spokes-man of the Twelve (cf. 13,6–10.36–37) answers that Jesus has words of eter-nal life and accepts Jesus as the Holy One of God. In v. 68, there is an echo of v. 63b: "The words that I have spoken to you are spirit and life". The effect of Jesus' words is life and this life is present and effective in the disciples.[104] For the Twelve (except Judas Iscariot), Jesus is the only way to eternal life. Peter's question "Lord, to whom can we go?" implies that there is no one upon whom they can rely for eternal life. Hence, nobody who has come to know Jesus' life-giving word would ever abandon him. In Peter's question "Lord, to whom can we *go* (ἀπέρχομαι)? You have the words of *eternal life*", we can again notice the association of life with the journey motif, where life is viewed as the final destination of the human journey.

2.9 Gate/Shepherd and Life (10,10.28)

The shepherd discourse (10,1–18) continues the words of Jesus begun at 9,41 and is placed in the narrative as Jesus' reflection on what has just taken place with the blind man and the Pharisees/Jews (9,1–41).[105] The two occurrences of the introductory expression Ἀμὴν ἀμὴν λέγω ὑμῖν (10,1.7) help us to divide the discourse into two parts: vv. 1–6 and vv. 7–18. Vv. 1–6 consists of a figure of speech (vv. 1–5) and the evangelist's comment (v. 6). Vv. 7–18 consists of a series of four ἐγώ εἰμι-sayings. Vv. 7–10 are centred around Jesus' self-identification as the gate for the sheep (vv. 7.9) and vv. 11–18

---

[99] Brown, *John*, I, 300. According to Moloney, *John*, 231, σάρξ in v. 63 refers to the su-perficiality of the limited human expectations, which disciples have about Jesus.

[100] Brown, *John*, I, 300.

[101] Van der Watt, *Family of the King*, 225. Words have a performative power (cf. 15,25; 18,9.32).

[102] O'Day, *John*, 610.

[103] O'Day remarks that Jesus is not demanding his disciples to eat flesh and drink blood, but to eat the Spirit-filled flesh and blood of the Son of Man (cf. 6,27). See O'Day, *John*, 610. Newman and Nida, *John*, 214, annotates 6,63b as follows, "By means of the words which I have spoken to you, I have caused God's life-giving Spirit to come to you".

[104] Cf. van der Watt, *Family of the King*, 226.

[105] Cf. O'Day, *John*, 666. The shepherd discourse is examined on pp. 319–336.

around his self-identification as the good shepherd (vv. 11.14). V. 10 states that while the thief comes to take life away, Jesus comes to give life to the sheep in abundance.[106] Thus, v. 10 reasserts the very purpose of Jesus' mission, which is to give life to the world (cf. e.g., 3,16; 20,31). It is a life of the eschatological kind, the attainment of that sphere where the Godhead dwells and hence fullness and superabundance.[107]

Vv. 26b–29 also deal with shepherd-sheep imagery, but are set within the context of Jesus' confrontation with the Jews at the feast of Dedication in Jerusalem (vv. 22–39). To believe in Jesus is to belong to his sheep and to hear his voice (vv. 26–27). The relation between belief and eternal life is repeated here (cf. 3,15.16.36; 6,40.47). Those who believe in Jesus have eternal life and shall never perish (cf. 3,16). No one can snatch them away from Jesus because the life that Jesus gives them is the gift of the Father (cf. 5,26) and they are secure in the Father's hand (cf. v. 29).

2.10 Resurrection and Life (11,25)

The Lazarus episode (11,1–44) can be broadly divided into the following units: the setting (vv. 1–6), the decision to go to Judea (vv. 7–16), the encounter with Martha (vv. 17–27), the encounter with Mary (vv. 28–37) and the raising of Lazarus from the dead (vv. 38–44). Jesus' statement "I am the resurrection and the life;[108] those who believe in me, even though they die, will live" (v. 25) is placed within Jesus' dialogue with Martha. In this ἐγώ εἰμι-saying, Jesus identifies himself as the fulfilment of eschatological expectations, affirming his sovereignty over the present and future lives of believers.[109] The meaning of v. 25a is explained in vv. 25b–26. Physical death has no power over believers, and their future is determined and secured here and now by their faith in Jesus. The life that Jesus offers is the life from above, begotten through the Spirit and conquers physical death.[110] He who believes in Jesus will never die spiritually but live eternally. Jesus is, therefore, the giver of this indestructible life (cf. 5,21) here and now and not only on the last day. The giving of natural life to Lazarus is an external sign of his power to give eternal life.

---

[106] Since the devil is called a murderer (8,44), it is possible to consider the opposition between the thief and Jesus as an opposition between the devil and Jesus.

[107] Schnackenburg, *John*, II, 293.

[108] Some manuscripts omit καὶ ἡ ζωή. But taking into account the age, weight, and diversification of witnesses that include these words, it is preferable to retain them in the text. See Metzger, *Textual Commentary*, 199.

[109] O'Day, *John*, 688.

[110] Brown, *John*, I, 434.

2.11 Earthly Life (ψυχή) and Eternal Life (12,25)

John 12,25 is located in 12,20–36, which deals with the visit of the Greeks and Jesus' declaration of his death. The arrival of the Greeks marks for Jesus the coming of the hour of his glorification (vv. 20–23). The announcement of the arrival of his hour is followed by his teachings about the meaning of his death (vv. 24–26). In v. 24, the significance of Jesus' death is explained in terms of an agricultural parable of the grain of wheat. In this parable, the quality of a grain's dying and being fruitful is contrasted with its non-dying and remaining unfruitful. The parable reveals the salvific power of Jesus' death on the cross. The purpose of Jesus' death is to bear abundant fruits by bringing life to all people on earth, irrespective of race, creed, ethnicity and nationality (cf. v. 32). From the example of Jesus' death, the disciple has to appreciate the value of sacrifice in this world and follow the path of Jesus (cf. Mark 8,34–35; Matt 10,39; Luke 9,24). In v. 25, there is a contrast between earthly life (ψυχή) and eternal life (ζωή αἰώνιος). Anyone who gives undue importance to earthly life will lose eternal life. When the disciple loses his earthly life on account of hatred and persecution in this world (cf. 15,18–21; 16,1–3), he will be gaining eternal life of the communion with God.

2.12 Commandment and Eternal Life (12,50)

John 12,37–50 can be regarded as a conclusion to Jesus' public ministry. This unit can be divided into two parts: an evaluation of his ministry (vv. 37–43) and a summary of his teachings (vv. 44–50). V. 50 is placed in the concluding teaching of Jesus towards the end of the chapter. Since Jesus is sent by the Father, belief in Jesus is ultimately belief in his Father (v. 44). He has come as light (cf. 1,4–5; 8,12; 9,5; 12,35–36) into the world to save it (cf. 3,16–17). Since Jesus' words are spoken under the command of the Father, they serve as judge on the last day. The statement that "Father's commandment is eternal life" can be regarded as elliptical for "obedience to the Father's command produces eternal life".[111] Since the Father's commandment is eternal life, the words of Jesus, which are spoken under the Father's command, are a source of eternal life for those who accept them (12,50; cf. 5,39–40; 6,68).

---

[111] Cf. Keener, *John*, II, 889. Kühschelm, *Verstockung*, 261, states, "'Seine ἐντολή ist ewiges Leben' heißt also, daß im Christusereignis Gottes liebendes und rettend-erlösendes Handeln für uns (paulinisch: 'Gottes Gerechtigkeit') zum Ausdruck kommt, das durch gläubige Akzeptanz an sein ureigenstes Ziel gebracht werden kann".

2.13 Jesus as the Life (14,6)[112]

The use of ζωή with the definite article as nominative predicate of the ἐγώ εἰμι-saying in 14,6 implies that Jesus is the embodiment of life. As the Word, he possessed life before the creation (1,4). The life of God is present in the person of Jesus. As the incarnation of life, Jesus is the revealer of the life of the Father. In him life is audible and visible because in his words and deeds life is present. The identification of Jesus with the life implies his oneness with the Father because the Father is the source of life (5,26; cf. 14,7–11). Jesus as the way leads one to the life of the Father. The view that Jesus is the life should be understood in terms of his mission to the world. The very purpose of his mission is to give life to the world (3,16; 5,21; 10,10.28). Jesus' gift of natural life to Lazarus is an external sign of his claim to be the life (11,25–26).

2.14 Knowledge of God/Jesus and Eternal Life (17,2.3)

The final prayer of Jesus in chapter 17 can be broadly divided into three units: prayer for his glorification (vv. 1–5), prayer for his disciples (vv. 6–19) and prayer for the future believers (vv. 20–26). Jesus opens his prayer with a reference to the arrival of his hour of glorification (v. 1). It is the only time that Jesus explicitly speaks of the arrival of his hour within the farewell discourse (John 13–17). The motif of glorification frames the motif of eternal life in vv. 2–3, forming an *inclusio* between v. 1 and vv. 4–5. The glorification of Jesus at his hour is simultaneously the glorification of the Father. In Jesus' death-resurrection-ascension the mutual glorification of the Father and the Son will occur. V. 2 indicates that the Father is the source of eternal life. He has given the Son "the authority over all flesh" (ἐξουσίαν πάσης σαρκός) to give eternal life.[113] The act of glory that will manifest the unity of the Father and the Son will be the bestowal of eternal life to the believers.[114]

V. 3 should be considered as yet another instance where the voice of Jesus overlaps with that of the evangelist.[115] For John, γινώσκω is sometimes interchangeable with πιστεύω.[116] Hence, in knowing God and Jesus Christ the emphasis is not on the intellectual dimension, but on the believing aspect that

---

[112] Since we have already discussed the context and structure of the text in which 14,6 occurs, we do not repeat them here. See pp. 129–184.

[113] The expression πάσης σαρκός here is regarded as a Hebraism (כָּל־בָּשָׂר) for "all people" (e.g., Gen 6,12; Num 18,15; Deut 5,26; Isa 40,5–6; Jer 12,12; Ezek 21,4; cf. Rom 3,20).

[114] Brown, *John*, II, 751.

[115] See the discussion on p. 240, n. 72.

[116] This is evident in the immediate context. V. 8 places the verb γινώσκω in parallelism with the verb πιστεύω, implying the correspondence between the knowledge that Jesus came from the Father and the belief that Jesus was sent by the Father (cf. 14,7.10).

in Jesus God is revealed. This knowledge refers to an intimate relationship with the Father and the Son through faith in Jesus. Knowledge of God cannot be separated from knowledge of Jesus Christ because the knowledge of the true God comes through the revealing words and deeds of Jesus (1,18; 3,32–34; 14,7–11). The "one true God" is the God who is known through his Son, Jesus Christ, and if anyone does not confess the Son, he also does not confess the "one true God".[117] By giving eternal life to the believers, Jesus is completing the work that the Father has given him to do and thus glorifying the Father (17,4).

2.15 Purpose of the Gospel and Life (20,31)

The last occurrence of ζωή is found in 20,31, where the evangelist explicitly states the purpose of the Gospel.[118] The intention of the evangelist is not to write a biographical account of Jesus (v. 30), but a document of testimony with an appeal for faith (cf. 19,35). He records that his purpose is two-fold, Christological and soteriological: to believe that Jesus is the Christ and the Son of God[119] and, through believing, to have life in his name. That those who believe in Jesus have eternal life is many times explicitly stated in the Gospel (3,15–16.36; 6,40.47). "Life in his name" denotes the eschatological life lived in this life and in the world to come in union with Christ. For John, there is no Christology apart from soteriology. Jesus who is Christ and the Son of God is the bringer of life for humanity.

---

[117] Brown, *John*, II, 752.

[118] Along with the scholarly consensus, we may regard vv. 30–31 as the original conclusion to the Gospel and chapter 21 as the epilogue to the Gospel. However, there are also some scholars who consider vv. 30–31 as the conclusion only to chapter 20. E.g., E. C. Hoskyns, *The Fourth Gospel* (London 1947), 549–550; H. Thyen, "Aus der Literatur zum Johannesevangelium", *ThR* 42 (1977), 213–261; S. S. Smalley, "The Sign in John 21", *NTS* 20 (1974), 275–288; P. S. Minear, "The Original Functions of John 21", *JBL* 102 (1983), 85–98; O'Day, *John*, 851–852. In his commentary, Thyen considers 20,30–21,25 as the epilogue of the Gospel. See Thyen, *Johannesevangelium*, 771.

[119] The manuscript evidence is divided on whether the verb πιστεύω is to be read as an aorist subjunctive (πιστεύσητε) or a present subjunctive (πιστεύητε). The aorist subjunctive πιστεύσητε can be translated as "that you may come to believe" and this reading may suggest that the Gospel is a missionary document, written for the purpose of bringing people to faith in Jesus. The present subjunctive πιστεύητε can be translated as "that you may (continue to) believe" and this reading would suggest that the Gospel is written to support and sustain the faith of those who already believe in Jesus. We prefer to consider the present subjunctive πιστεύητε as the original reading. For arguments in favour of this reading, see Thyen, *Johannesevangelium*, 775–776; Keener, *John*, II, 1215–1216; G. D. Fee, "On the Text and Meaning of John 20,30–31", *The Four Gospels*. Festschrift F. Neirynck, ed. F. van Segbroeck et al. (Leuven 1992), III, 2193–2206; H. Riesenfeld, "Zu den johanneischen *Hina*-Sätzen", *ST* 19 (1965), 213–220; Schnackenburg, *John*, III, 338.

2.16 Conclusion

John's doctrine of salvation is centred on the notion of life.[120] The above given brief analysis of the term ζωή reveals that ζωή is spread throughout the Gospel in many different contexts. Its main concentration is noticed in chapters 5–6. Among the 36 occurrences of ζωή, 17 of them are found along with the epithet αἰώνιος. John uses interchangeably ζωή and ζωή αἰώνιος, and we cannot find any semantic difference between the two.[121] The absence of the epithet αἰώνιος with ζωή can be explained chiefly on the basis of style except in the references to God.[122] Ζωή is found in association with other major Johannine theological concepts like belief, knowledge, witness, word, resurrection, truth, commandment and metaphors like light, water, harvesting, bread, gate, shepherd and way.

It is to be noted that ζωή in John is specially related to the function of the Father. It is the divine life which the Son possesses from the Father, who is the source of all life (5,26; 6,57). It is the gift of the Father through Jesus to those who belong to the Father. It is a life which death cannot destroy (11,26). The very purpose of the mission of Jesus in the world is to give life to everyone (3,16; 10,10). That Christ gives life to the world is the central thought of the Fourth Gospel (cf. 20,31). Belief in Jesus is the only means to attain life (3,15–16.36; 6,40.47; 20,31). This life is sustained and nourished through the bread of life, the Eucharist (6,56). Since Jesus is the fullest embodiment of the wisdom of God and the giver of the Holy Spirit, he is also the gateway to God's life (cf. 4,14; 14,6).

Life is an eschatological notion in the Fourth Gospel, which the evangelist places firmly in the present. He who believes in the Son has eternal life and has already passed from death to life here and now. Life is presented in dualistic categories, especially in contrast with perishing (3,16; 6,27; 10,28), death (5,24), the wrath of God (3,36) and judgment (5,24.29). Moreover, the life that Jesus promises is a cosmic principle because it is the life of the world to come. It has a universal dimension because it is the light of humanity (1,3.4.9), the illumination of their otherwise dark and doom-ridden way on

---

[120] Mussner, *Zoe. Die Anschauung vom 'Leben'*, 186 evaluates, "Ζωή αἰώνιος ist für Johannes der umfassende Heilsbegriff, der alles enthält, was der gottgesandte Retter der Welt den Menschen bringt".

[121] Brown, *John*, I, 508; Newman and Nida, *John*, 105. H. Pribnow, *Die johanneische Anschauung vom 'Leben'* (Greifswald 1934), 27, asserts, "Leben und ewiges Leben ist für Johannes überhaupt ein und dieselbe Grösse".

[122] There are three cases in which the evangelist does not employ ζωή with αἰώνιος: where ζωή is used with the Father and the Son; where ζωή is used in close conjunction with other nouns and where the immediate context makes a repetition of αἰώνιος unnecessary. The use of αἰώνιος in references to God (the Father and the Son) is avoided because God is not a transitory being and the specific semantic dimension of αἰώνιος is already present in God and need not be mentioned. See van der Watt, "The Use of 'Αἰώνιος'", 218–219, 227.

earth with meaning (cf. 8,12).¹²³ It is the answer to man's search for the meaning of his existence and his true salvation.¹²⁴ The ultimate goal of man's existence is eternal life, and it is realized in the knowledge of God and Jesus Christ (17,3). In some instances (5,24.40; 6,68; 8,12), life is found in association with the journey motif. This will support the view that the final result of following the way of Jesus is eternal life and he is certainly the way to life (14,6).

3. Relation of Way with Truth and Life in John 14,6

After the examination of the background of the paratactic construction in 14,6a and the analysis of the notions of "truth" and "life" in the Gospel, we are in a position to find the relation between way, truth and life.¹²⁵ In the statement ἐγώ εἰμι ἡ ὁδὸς καὶ ἡ ἀλήθεια καὶ ἡ ζωή, it is evident from the context that the focus is on ὁδός. The term ὁδός is already introduced in 14,4 by Jesus and taken up by Thomas in 14,5 and finally applied by Jesus to his own person in 14,6a. In 14,6b also, the motif of way is present because one has to "come" (ἔρχομαι) to the Father through Jesus who is the way. But the presence of ἀλήθεια and ζωή in 14,6a may confuse the readers because they appear like intruders and their role is to be examined.¹²⁶

Usually, scholars attach an epexegetical role to the first καί in 14,6 and interpret "truth" and "life" as explanation of "way".¹²⁷ It means that Jesus is

---

¹²³ Schnackenburg, *John*, II, 355.

¹²⁴ Schnackenburg, *John*, II, 355.

¹²⁵ The following discussion is my proposal for understanding the interrelation between way, truth and life in John 14,6. For the latest summary of the various discussions on the interrelation between way, truth and life by various authors in the past, see Tack, *John 14,6 in Light of Jewish-Christian Dialogue*, 272–286.

¹²⁶ The seemingly intruding nature of ἀλήθεια and ζωή has prompted Theobald, *Herrenworte*, 311–312, to think that the evangelist has expanded the original saying ἐγώ εἰμι ἡ ὁδός with the addition of καὶ ἡ ἀλήθεια καὶ ἡ ζωή in order to represent adequately his Christological perspective. The following discussion will expose the role and function of of ἀλήθεια and ζωή as an original part of 14,6 without resorting to any redactional approach.

¹²⁷ E.g., Tack, *John 14,6 in Light of Jewish-Christian Dialogue*, 280, 285–286; Zumstein, *Johannesevangelium*, 528–529; idem, *Saint Jean*, 66; Thyen, *Johannesevangelium*, 621; Keener, *John*, II, 943; Beasley-Murray, *John*, 252; Moloney, *John*, 398; Léon-Dufour, *Lecture de l'Évangile selon* Jean, 99; Schnackenburg, *John*, III, 64–65; Barrett, *John*, 458; Brown, *John*, II, 620–621; 628–631. The contemporary scholarship holds this view, which is, to a great extent, based on the work of I. de la Potterie. See de la Potterie, *La vérité dans Saint Jean*, I, 253; idem, "Je suis la Voie", 917. Potterie has based his view on the possibility of an epexegetical use of καί shown in BDF, 228 (§442.9). It is true that Blass and Debrunner have mentioned the epexegetical use of καί, but they have not sug-

256   Chapter V: Important Motifs of John 14,6 in the Gospel Context

the way because (that is) he is the truth and the life. This interpretation is not wrong in itself, but it has certain limitations. It cannot precisely explain why John uses the word order "the way and the truth and the life". Why does he not write, "I am the way and the life and the truth"? An epexegetical reading does not take into account the interrelation between truth and life. There are examples of three coordinate nouns in John where there is no suggestion that the second and third nouns explain the first (2,14; 16,8).[128] Moreover, there is no evidence in the biblical and Jewish literature that "truth" and "life" explain "way", as scholars often attempt to do so in John 14,6. Hence, an alternative reading can be suggested here.

In order to explain the importance of the word order in 14,6a and the significance of the occurrence of truth and life along with way, an observation of the association of way with truth and life in the Bible and other Jewish literature is very helpful.[129] Therefore, the question of the interrelation between way, truth and life in 14,6 is closely associated with the issue of the background of this paratactic construction. It is already mentioned that in the biblical and other Jewish literature the association of truth and life with the metaphor of way gives an additional information about it.[130] There are two basic assumptions associated with the metaphor of way in the biblical and Jewish literature. Firstly, every way presupposes a destination or goal. There is no way or journey without a destination. This is a practical wisdom in daily life too. No one can think of a way without a destination. This is actually the problem of Thomas, "Lord, we do not know where you are going, and how can we know the way?" (14,5). Secondly, every way presupposes that the one who journeys has some information/guidance to reach the destination or a means/mode to reach the destination (e.g., Isa 42,16; Wis 18,3; Luke 1,79; As. Mos. 11,10). This is actually the work of a guide. The guide leads the traveller to the destination. These commonplace biblical assumptions associated with way are at work when Jesus says, "I am the way and the truth and the life".[131] If Jesus' reply is reduced to "I am the way", the questions may

---

gested that any of the καί in John 14,6 should be read epexegetically. Hence, the epexegetical reading of καί in 14,6 is to be regarded as one of the possible ways of reading 14,6 and need not be seen as an absolute norm for interpreting it.

[128] In 2,14, "sheep and doves" do not explain further "cattle", and in 16,8, "righteousness and judgment" do not further explicate "sin". Cf. Köstenberger, *John*, 429.

[129] Bernard, *John*, II, 537–538, also believes that the juxtaposition of ἀλήθεια and ζωή with ἡ ὁδός is due to a reminiscence of Old Testament phraseology and that the close association in Old Testament phraseology between ὁδός and ἀλήθεια and between ὁδός and ζωή may account for the introduction of ἡ ἀλήθεια καὶ ἡ ζωή at this point.

[130] See pp. 206–209. The role and function of truth and life in John 14,6 are scantly mentioned on pp. 187–188.

[131] J. Blenkinsopp, *Opening the Sealed Book. Interpretations of the Book of Isaiah in Late Antiquity* (Grand Rapids 2006), 179, comments on the notion of the way in the Bible

3. Relation of Way with Truth and Life in John 14,6

still arise: "Is Jesus just the way alone?", "Where does the way lead to?", "Is there any guidance on the way or how does one reach the goal?" In fact, the role of "truth" and "life" in 14,6a is to answer these questions. If "truth" fulfils the role of a guide, "life" fulfils the role of a destination. Therefore, the notions of truth and life are immediately added to the notion of way in 14,6 even though "truth" and "life" are not the subject matter in the preceding and immediate context. Truth and life, which appear like intruders in the context, are added to give a complete sense to the metaphor of way.[132] Since truth and life are, for John, theologically more significant concepts than "way", an ascensive sense of the first καί ("even") can be discerned here.[133] As a result, Jesus' statement can be translated as "I am the way, even the truth and the life". It means that Jesus is much more than the way. Truth and life are added to indicate that Jesus is not only the way but also (even) the truth and the life.[134] In fact, the reader does not need an "explanation" about the way at this juncture. Instead, the reader may be curious to know whether Jesus is just the way alone and not the destination to which the way leads. The concern of the evangelist at this point is not to "explain" what the way is or why Jesus the way is, but to add that Jesus is more importantly also the truth and the life, whose association with the way has a strong background in the Bible and other Jewish literature. Jesus' statements and question in the following verses like, "If you know me, you will know my Father also" (v.7), "The one who has seen me has seen the Father" (v. 9) and "Do you not believe that I am in the Father and the Father is in me?" (v. 10. cf. v. 11) are attempts of the

---

thus, "In the biblical context, the word is almost always qualified. It is the way of something, the way of somebody, the way to somewhere".

[132] Bernard, *John*, II, 537, also observes, "καὶ ἡ ἀλήθεια καὶ ἡ ζωή, being not directly involved in the context, but [are] added to complete the great declaration".

[133] See BDF, 228 (§442.12); Young, *Intermediate New Testament Greek*, 188–189; W. J. Perschbacher, *New Testament Greek Syntax. An Illustrated Manual* (Chicago 1995), 79. A. T. Robertson, *A Grammar of the Greek New Testament in the Light of Historical Research* (London ³1919), 1180–1183, notices three main uses of καί in the New Testament: connective ("and"), ascensive ("even") and adjunctive ("also"). According to Robertson, the ascensive use of καί is wholly dependent on the context. Some examples for ascensive use are Matt 5,46; 10,30; Mark 1,27; John 14,12; 1 Cor 2,10.

[134] Theobald's view that ἐγώ εἰμι ἡ ὁδός in itself is incomplete and does not adequately and satisfactorily express the evangelist's Christological perspective is a support to interpret the first καί as ascensive. Cf. Theobald, *Herrenworte*, 311–312. Although unintentionally, the comment of Schnelle, *Johannes*, 252, corresponds with the ascensive sense of the first καί in 14,6, "Johannes verwendet diese Metapher, um die Frage nach dem Sinn und Ziel menschlichen Lebens zu stellen und gleichzeitig Jesus als den alleinigen Zugang zum Heil zu qualifizieren. *Jesus ist aber nicht nur der Weg zu Gott*, er ist die Verkörperung göttlicher Wahrheit und göttlichen Lebens". The same view is differently expressed by Lagrange, *Saint Jean*, 375, "Déjà les termes de vérité et de vie, étant absolus, suggéraient que *Jésus n'était pas seulement la voie qui conduit à Dieu, mais Dieu lui-même*". The emphasis in italics in both quotations is mine.

evangelist to show clearly that Jesus is not just the way alone but much more than that.[135]

Like other biblical literature, for John, truth is not the final goal or destination of human life. Truth is the revelation of the Father or the revelation of salvation in Jesus. Jesus is the truth because revelation has taken place in him through his words and deeds. Hence, belief in Jesus implies belief in the truth. As an agent of salvation, truth has only a mediating role like a guide or a means in the Gospel (e.g., 4,23–24; 8,32; 17,17.19). Therefore, the position of ἀλήθεια in 14,6 in the middle after ὁδός is meaningful. As truth, Jesus guides or leads the believer to the goal, i.e., to the life of and with the Father.[136] Jesus is the life because the life of the Father is in him and he can give it to anyone who believes in him. When Jesus claims to be the truth and the life, the reader is to see Jesus as the fulfilment of all that has been asserted by these terms throughout the Gospel.[137]

The view that, as the way and the truth, Jesus leads the believer to life does not contradict the perspective that Jesus is the way to the Father.[138] For John, the Father is the author of life. Life is the basic feature of the Father because the Father is the ultimate source of life (5,26).[139] Thus, the Father is charac-

---

[135] Following R. E. Brown, Theobald understands the first καί in John 14,6 as epexegetical (explanatory). See Theobald, *Herrenworte*, 322. It is already explained that an epexegetical reading of the first καί is not sufficient to understand the relation of way with truth and life in 14,6. Moreover, Theobald's epexegetical reading will make his proposal more problematic and will lead even to self-contradicting positions about which Theobald himself is not aware. On the one hand, Theobald holds an epexegetical understanding of the first καί, but on the other hand, he thinks that "the truth and the life" are added to "I am the way" because "the way alone" does not sufficiently present the Christological perspective of the evangelist. Here Theobald is turning away from the epexegetical to the ascensive sense of the first καί and thus contradicting himself.

[136] There are also authors who consider life in 14,6 as the goal of the way. E.g., Cebulj, *Ich bin es*, 226, comments on 14,6 thus, "Als Ziel dieses Weges wird auch die Gabe der ζωή verheißen, die schon im Jetzt die Fülle des eschatologischen Heils verheißt". Beutler, *Das Johannesevangelium*, 402, considers the mediating/guiding role of "truth" and the role of "life" as final destination when he states, "In johanneischer Sicht ist Jesus der Weg, insofern er die 'Wahrheit', die von Gott herkommende Offenbarung kundtut, die zum Leben führt". O'Day, *John*, 742, comments, "In v. 6a Jesus reveals himself to be simultaneously the access to and the embodiment of life with God".

[137] Ball, *I Am*, 205.

[138] The correspondence between v. 6a and v. 6b, specifically between "life" (v. 6a) and "the Father" (v. 6b), is already mentioned. See p. 187–188. In the view of Becker, *Johannes*, 551-552, "'Wahrheit' und 'Leben' gelten als das Heilsziel, wie es im Nachsatz mit dem Vater benannt ist".

[139] Thompson, "The Living Father", 20, writes, "In John it is not a particular characteristic or attribute of God that shapes understanding of him as Father, but rather the fundamental reality that a father's relationship to his children consists first in terms simply of giving them life. What it means to be a father is to be the origin or source of the life of

terized as ὁ ζῶν πατήρ in 6,57.[140] He has life in the absolute sense, without depending on anyone. The Son has life because of the Father (6,57). Moreover, there is a close link between κἀγὼ ζῶ διὰ τὸν πατέρα in 6,57 and ὅτι ἐγὼ ζῶ καὶ ὑμεῖς ζήσετε in 14,19. It indicates a chain of the relationship between the life of the Father and the life of the disciples in and through Jesus (cf. 1 John 4,9). We cannot separate the affirmation that God is "the Father" from the affirmation that God is the source of life and from the conviction that the life of the Father has been given to, and comes to human beings through the Son.[141] If Jesus is the life, it is because of the Father, and the life that he gives is the life of the Father. Therefore, the view that Jesus is the way to the Father is not separable from the view that he is the way to the life because he is the way to the life of the Father and eternal life consists in knowing the Father through the Son (17,3; cf. 14,7).

It has already been said that the verbal expression ἔρχομαι πρός is also a synonym for πιστεύω εἰς in John's Gospel (5,40; 6,35.37.44.45.65; 7,37; 14,6). The end result of "coming to" or "believing in" Jesus is "eternal life" (e.g., 3,15–16.36; 6,40.47; 20,31; cf. 1 John 5,13). One who comes to the Father through Jesus is coming to life. Hence, it can be said that "coming to the Father" is synonymous with "coming to life". The similarity between the images of way and gate will further corroborate the correspondence between the life and the Father. Just as Jesus as the gate leads the believer to the life (10,9–10), as the way he leads the believer to the life of the Father. That Jesus as the shepherd "leads" (ὁδηγέω) the saved ones "to the springs of the water of life" (ἐπὶ ζωῆς πηγὰς ὑδάτων) is clearly mentioned in Rev 7,17.

Hence, the position of ζωή at the end in John 14,6a is not pointless and accidental. It should be seen as well planned by the evangelist because according to him ζωή is the ultimate goal and destination of the journey of the believer. This is very explicitly stated by him in the purpose statement of the Gospel in 20,31, "But these are written so that you may believe that Jesus is the Messiah, the Son of God, and that through believing you may have *life* (ζωή) in his name".[142] Moreover, the evangelist often places the noun ζωή in

---

one's children. For John, this pertains to the fact that the Father has given life to the Son and through the Son mediated life to others, who become 'children of God'".

[140] The expression ὁ ζῶν πατήρ in 6,57 implies that the Father is the ultimate giver of life, the creator. Cf. Newman and Nida, *John*, 209. God is described in the Old Testament as "the living God" (אֱלֹהִים חַיִּים; ὁ ζῶν θεός). E.g., Deut 5,26; 1 Sam 17,26; Jer 10,10; Hos 2,1; 2 Kgs 19,4 Josh 3,10. Thompson, "The Living Father", 21, explains, "The basic view of God as the one who lives eternally and so is the only source of life for the world fits integrally with John's view of God as the life-giving Father, crystallized in the phrase 'the living Father'".

[141] Cf. Thompson, "The Living Father", 23.

[142] This translation is based on the supposition that πιστεύητε is the original reading. See the discussion on p. 253, n. 119.

the ἵνα clauses with the subjunctive to show that life is always the ultimate goal and destination of the believer (3,15–16; 5,40; 6,40; 10,10; 17,2; 20,31). Thus, in Jesus' claim "I am the way, and the truth, and the life", there lies underneath an imagery of a way that leads in truth to the life, as often found in the Bible and other Jewish literature. Therefore, we may annotate that Jesus is the way that leads the believer in the truth to the life of the Father. That is how Jesus becomes the way to the Father.[143] Nevertheless, as Bultmann suggests, the way and the goal are not to be separated because "he is the way in such a manner as to be at the same time the goal".[144] The paradox that the way and the goal meet in Jesus is stated explicitly in the immediately following verses (14,7–11). Moreover, the view that Jesus as the way leads the believer to life can be further supported by the close relation between the journey motif and life in the Gospel. The journey of the believer is always a journey to life (5,24.40; 6,68; 8,12; cf. 10,9–10).

4. The Father in the Gospel of John

The invocation of a deity under the name of "father" is one of the basic phenomena of ancient civilizations, cultures and religions. However, it is the New Testament that gives more emphasis in characterizing God as the Father than any other ancient writings.[145] This study on "Jesus as the Way to the

---

[143] Gollwitzer, "Außer Christus", 172, says, "Das Verbum 'kommen' scheint nur die Bedeutung Christi als des Weges zum Leben, das mit dem Vater identisch ist, auszusprechen". However, the focus here is not that the Father is identical with life, but that in Johannine soteriology having access to the Father is identical with having access to the life.

[144] Bultmann, *John*, 605–606. Dietzfelbinger, *Johannes*, 45, states, "Weg und Ziel sind also miteinander verschränkt. Damit wird die Thomasfrage gründlich umgebogen". St. Augustine in his exposition on John 14,6 (Tractate 69,2) says, "After knowing the way by which he went, they had still to learn whither he was going, but just because it was to the truth and to the life he was going?" See Schaff, *A Select Bibliography. St. Augustine: Homilies on the Gospel of John*, 325. St. Thomas Aquinas comments on John 14,6 thus, "Because this way is not separated from its destination but united to it, he adds, and the truth, and the life. So Christ is at once both the way and the destination. He is the way by reason of his human nature, and the destination because of his divinity. Therefore, as human, he says, I am the way; as God, he adds, and the truth, and the life. These last two appropriately indicate the destination of the way". See T. Aquinas, *Commentary on the Gospel of John. Chapters 13–21*, tr. F. Larcher and J. A. Weisheipl (Washington 2010), 55. It seems that when St. Augustine and St. Thomas Aquinas regard truth along with life as the destination, they do it so from the viewpoint of philosophy and not from the view point of the evangelist. In the Gospel, truth is never considered as the destination.

[145] For the use of "father" in ancient religious writings, especially in Greek-Jewish literature and the New Testament, see G. Schrenk and G. Quell, "πατήρ", *TDNT*, V, 945–1014.

Father in the Gospel of John" will be incomplete without a discussion on the motif of Father in the Gospel. The most important designation of God in the Gospel of John is πατήρ.[146] The noun πατήρ occurs 136 times in the Gospel. Among these occurrences, 119 times it refers to God.[147] Most of the references to God as the Father are found in the words of Jesus, especially in Jesus' dialogue with the Jews in chapters 5–6, 8, 10 and in his dialogue with his disciples in the farewell discourse, mainly in chapters 14–17. There are no references to God as the Father in chapters 7, 9, 19 and 21. The following table illustrates the distribution of the term πατήρ referring to God in John's Gospel. The number within the bracket indicates the total number of the term within a specified chapter, including the references to characters other than God.

Chapters of John's Gospel	Number of Occurrences of πατήρ
1	2 (2)
2	1 (1)
3	1 (1)
4	3 (6)
5	14 (14)
6	11 (15)
7	0 (1)
8	11 (20)
10	13 (13)
11	1 (1)
12	5 (5)

[146] Some attempts have been made for a study of the concept of the Father/God in John's Gospel from various perspectives. See E. Zingg, *Das Reden von Gott als "Vater" im Johannesevangelium* (HBS 48; Freiburg 2006); M. Stibbe, "Telling the Father's Story: The Gospel of John as Narrative Theology", *Challenging Perspectives on the Gospel of John*, ed. J. Lierman (WUNT II 219; Tübingen 2006), 170–193; D. R. Sadananda, *The Johannine Exegesis of God. An Exploration into the Johannine Understanding of God* (BZNW 121; Berlin 2004); M. M. Thompson, *The God of the Gospel of John* (Grand Rapids 2001); idem, *The Promise of the Father. Jesus and God in the New Testament* (Louisville 2000), 133–154; idem, "'God's Voice You Have Never Heard, God's Form You Have Never Seen': The Characterization of God in the Gospel of John", *Characterization in Biblical Literature*, ed. A. Berlin and E. S. Malbon (Semeia 63; Atlanta 1993), 177–204; idem, "Thinking about God: Wisdom and Theology in John 6", *Critical Readings of John 6*, ed. R. A. Culpepper (Leiden 1997), 221–246; A. Reinhartz (ed.), *God the Father in the Gospel of John* (Semeia 85; Atlanta 1999); D. F. Tolmie, "The Characterization of God in the Fourth Gospel", *JSNT* 69 (1998), 57–75; P. W. Meyer, "'Father:' The Presentation of God in the Fourth Gospel", *Exploring the Gospel of John*, ed. R. A. Culpepper and C. C. Black (Louisville 1996), 255–273.

[147] In the following instances where the term πατήρ occurs, there is no reference to God: 4,12.20.53; 6,31.42.49.58; 7,22; 8,19.38–39.41.44(3x).53.56.

13	2 (2)
14	23 (23)
15	10 (10)
16	11 (11)
17	6 (6)
18	1 (1)
20	4 (4)

The Father motif is not presented in the Gospel indifferently. It is either in terms of Jesus' relationship with the Father or in terms of believers' relationship with the Father that the notion of the Father is envisaged in the Gospel.[148] Jesus' statement "No one comes to the Father except through me" (14,6b) is an example of these two sides of the Father's relationship. On the one hand, it speaks of Jesus' relationship with the Father, and on the other hand, it manifests the possibility of believers' relationship with the Father attainable through Jesus. These two aspects will be discussed below.

4.1 Jesus' Relationship with the Father/God

In the Gospel of John, God is identified most characteristically in relation to Jesus and in that relationship the term "Father" figures prominently.[149] In the words of Jesus, God is referred to as πατήρ 111 times. The expression ὁ πατήρ μου occurs 32 times. Only once Jesus calls God πατήρ ὑμῶν, imparting a new status to his disciples (20,17). But there is no single occurrence of "our Father". Jesus' relationship with the Father is exclusive.[150] The statement "No one comes to the Father except through me" testifies it. We shall now examine briefly how the evangelist has presented Jesus' exclusive and unique relationship with the Father in the Gospel.[151]

---

[148] The only other relationship that the Father has is with the Holy Spirit (15,26; cf. 14,26).

[149] Thompson, *The God of the Gospel of John*, 50.

[150] Meyer, "Father", 260, views that the expression "my Father" makes it clear that God is Jesus' Father as no one else's.

[151] We will examine very briefly the occurrences of πατήρ pertaining to Jesus' exclusive relationship with the Father without entering into a detailed study of the passages. More attention is given to those instances, where Jesus' exclusive relationship with the Father is highlighted. Since we are confronting the term πατήρ in 14,6, at first, we will give priority to the use of πατήρ in the Gospel. Then at the end, we will also consider the use of θεός for examining Jesus' exclusive relationship with God.

4.1.1 Jesus' Exclusive Relationship with the Father

4.1.1.1 Jesus as the Only Son of the Father (1,14)

The first appearance of πατήρ occurs in the prologue (1,14), where Jesus' exclusive relationship with the Father as his only Son is explicitly expressed. The unique relationship of Jesus with the Father is depicted in the words, ἐθεασάμεθα τὴν δόξαν αὐτοῦ, δόξαν ὡς μονογενοῦς παρὰ πατρός (v. 14). Jesus is described here as the μονογενής from the Father. The adjective μονογενής can mean here "being the only one of its kind", "unique".[152] Hence, the expression implies that Jesus is the only and the unique Son of the Father (cf. 1,18; 3,16.18). The relationship between the Logos and God, described in 1,1–2, is articulated as an exclusive relationship in v. 14 in terms of "Son" (implied by μονογενής) and "Father". V. 14 refers to a revelation of glory that proceeds alone from the μονογενής from the Father, i.e., God's only Son.[153] The evangelist will have in mind the glory of the Christ, which is manifested in the signs he performed (e.g., 2,11), in his being lifted up on the cross (19,35) and in the Easter resurrection (20,24–29).[154]

4.1.1.2 Jesus as the Exegete of the Father (1,18)

Jesus' superiority mentioned in 1,17, his identity as God and his exclusive relationship with the Father are more powerfully emphasized in 1,18: θεὸν οὐδεὶς ἑώρακεν πώποτε· μονογενὴς θεὸς ὁ ὢν εἰς τὸν κόλπον τοῦ πατρὸς ἐκεῖνος ἐξηγήσατο.[155] Perhaps, the evangelist cannot better express Jesus' divine identity and his relationship with the Father in any other terms than these.[156] 1,1 and 1,18 form a beautiful *inclusio*. In v. 1 the Word is said to be God and with God, and in v. 18 the Son is said to be God and with God, being in the bosom of the Father. The expression θεὸν οὐδεὶς ἑώρακεν πώποτε

---

[152] According to BDAG, 658, "only", "unique" are adequate renderings for μονογενής. For further study on μονογενής, see G. Pendrick, "Μονογενής", *NTS* 41 (1995), 587–600; M. Theobald, *Die Fleischwerdung des Logos. Studien zum Verhältnis des Johannesprologs zum Corpus des Evangeliums und zu 1 Joh* (NTA.NF 20; Münster 1988), 250–254; J. V. Dahms, "The Johannine Use of *Monogenes* Reconsidered", *NTS* 29 (1983), 222–232; T. C. de Kruijf, "The Glory of the Only Son (John 1,14)", *Studies in John*, ed. M. C. Rientsma et al. (NovTSup 24; Leiden 1970), 111–123.

[153] Beasley-Murray, *John*, 14.

[154] Cf. Beasley-Murray, *John*, 14.

[155] There are no stronger reasons to consider the variants in 1,18 as better readings. P[66] and P[75] support μονογενὴς θεός to be the more original reading. Moreover, since μονογενὴς υἱός appears to be more fitting to "in the bosom of the Father", μονογενὴς θεός should be regarded as the *lectio difficilior*. Schnackenburg, *John*, I, 279, comments, "Whether one reads θεός or υἱός after (ὁ) μονογενής makes no essential difference".

[156] Therefore, Schnackenburg, *John*, I, 278, says, "The absolute claim of the Christian revelation could not be put more definitely".

reminds us of the Old Testament view that no one shall see God and stay alive (e.g., cf. Exod 33,20–23; Deut 4,12; Sir 43,31). The expression refers not only to God's invisibility but also to his incomprehensibility, inaccessibility and hiddenness (cf. 14,6b).[157] The present participle ὤν may indicate the eternal presence of the Son in the bosom of the Father.[158] The Son's intimacy with the Father is beyond the categories of time. Not only in his pre-existence and glorified existence, but also in his earthly existence, the Son is said to be intimate/one with the Father (10,30; 14,7–11). The phrase εἰς τὸν κόλπον τοῦ πατρός points out the Son's exclusive and privileged intimacy of a deeply affectionate interpersonal relationship.[159] Since Jesus as the Son has direct and intimate experience of the Father, he alone can reveal the Father with complete authority and authenticity. This verse affirms once more the full divine dignity of Jesus as the Son of God on earth and also his unique capacity as the revealer and the interpreter.[160] Since Jesus expounds and interprets the Father, we may call him "the exegete of the Father".

4.1.1.3 Jesus' Authority from the Father over Everything (3,35; 13,3a; 17,2)

In the concluding unit of the third chapter (3,31–36), there is a statement of Jesus' exclusive relationship with the Father in v. 35.[161] In this pericope, Jesus' authority and greatness are pointed out in dualistic terms. Since he comes from above, he is greater than all those who belong to the earth (v. 31). The statement "The Father loves the Son and has placed *all things* in his hands" reveals Jesus' exclusive relationship with the Father (cf. 13,3; Matt 11,27; Luke 10,22).[162] In the course of the Gospel, we come to know that the things that the Father has given Jesus are judgment (5,22.27), power to have life in himself (5,26), works (5,36; 17,4), disciples/believers (6,37.39; 10,29; 17,6–7.12.22.24; 18,9), power to give life (17,2), the words (12,49; 17,8), the divine name (17,11–12), glory (17,22) and the cup of suffering (18,11). Thus, Jesus has complete authority to act in the Father's name and his revelation is authoritative.

---

[157] Cf. Sadananda, *The Johannine Exegesis of God*, 209.

[158] The Greeks and Philo call God τὸ ὄν ("that which is"), but the Johannine expression ὁ ὤν ("he that is") reveals that God is a person, not a thing or an abstract idea. Cf. E. A. Abbott, *Johannine Grammar* (London 1906), 55.

[159] Cf. Sadananda, *The Johannine Exegesis of God*, 214.

[160] Schnackenburg, *John*, I, 280. The verb ἐξηγέομαι can mean "to set forth in great detail", "expound", "report", "describe" (see BDAG, 349), "to tell at length", "to interpret" (see LSJ, 593).

[161] It is not easy to identify the speaker of 3,31–36. It can be regarded as the words of John the Baptist or Jesus or the evangelist. The situation is almost like that in 3,16–21. See the comments on p. 240, n. 72. Also see Brown, *John*, I, 159–160.

[162] Schnackenburg, *John*, I, 388, thinks that the Semitic phrase "to give something into the hands of another" implies in general the conferring of power and authority.

Parallel to 3,35, in 13,3a and 17,2 there are statements about Jesus' authority given to him by the Father over all things and people.[163] In 13,3a, the evangelist states that Jesus knows that the Father has given all things into his hands. This statement indicates a counterbalance to the previous observation about the devil in 13,2.[164] It represents his unassailable sovereignty over everything including his adversary, the devil and his agents.[165] Therefore, Jesus says that the ruler of the world has no power over him (14,30). The authority that Jesus has over all things and all people is an outcome of his exclusive relationship with the Father.

4.1.1.4 God as Jesus' Own Father and Jesus' Equality with God (John 5)

Jesus' divine identity and his exclusive relationship with the Father are presented in chapter 5 in the context of Jesus' healing of a paralytic on the Sabbath and its aftermath (vv. 1–18), which leads to a discourse (vv. 19–47).[166] The point of conflict between Jesus and the Jews is that it is on the Sabbath that Jesus does this miracle (vv. 9.16) and that the healed man carries his mat at Jesus' command (vv. 9–11). Thus, the healing story becomes a conflict story. The Jews' complaint about the Sabbath violation causes Jesus to speak about his exclusive relationship with the Father. Jesus defends his deed on theological grounds, claiming, "My Father is still working, and I also am working" (v. 17).[167] If the Father is working on the Sabbath, then Jesus as his Son also should work. From the Jews' point of view, Jesus is a blasphemer since he calls God his own Father and thus equates himself with God (v. 18).

Jesus' claim in v. 17 should be placed against the background of the relation of God to the Sabbath in Jewish theology (later rabbinic thought).[168] The

---

[163] In the discussion below, under "Jesus' Prayer to the Father", we will mention the significance of 17,2.

[164] Schnackenburg, *John*, III, 17.

[165] Schnackenburg, *John*, III, 17.

[166] We have already presented the structure of chapter 5. See pp. 243–244. The chapter has the pattern of an event followed by a discourse, which draws out the theological implications of that event. See O'Day, *John*, 576–577. Brown, *John*, I, 216, evaluates the sayings of Jesus in this discourse as follows, "Moreover, embedded in the discourse are sayings that have every reason to be considered genuine traditional sayings of Jesus. Therefore, it is not at all impossible that parts of this discourse have solid foundations in the controversies with the Pharisees that were part of Jesus' ministry, even if the evangelist has given to the final product an organization and theological depth that reflects a later and more mature insight".

[167] In the view of Dodd, *Interpretation*, 326, the words in v. 17 "seem to imply collateral action with God in a field where God's competence is exclusive".

[168] The Jewish theologians believed that God did not really stop to work on the Sabbath for the protection of life on earth. The divine activity is seen to be visible in two ways: some people are born and some die on the Sabbath. This is a sign that God is active on the Sabbath because only God can give life (2 Kgs 5,7; 2 Macc 7,22–23) and judge the dead

saying Ὁ πατήρ μου ἕως ἄρτι ἐργάζεται implies that the Father is active even on the Sabbath by giving life and doing judgment. Jesus' words κἀγὼ ἐργάζομαι point out that what he does on the Sabbath is an instance of the life-giving work of God, which is exempt from Sabbath rules. As the only Son of the Father, Jesus has the power to give life and to do judgment. The work of giving life necessarily involves the work of judgment (cf. 3,16–21) and the Son has the authority to judge (v. 27).

In the following unit of 5,19–30, Jesus illustrates his relationship with the Father and his authority as the Son pointing out God's perpetual activity. These verses also make clear that Jesus' claim in vv. 17–18 should not be understood as a claim to be a second God, being a rival to the one God because he acts in complete unity with the Father and in total obedience to his will (v. 30).[169] As a result of this unity, every act of the Son is an act of the Father. The model for the work of the Son is the work of the Father. Vv. 19–20 can be considered as a parable of the apprentice relationship between a father and his son found in the Near Eastern culture of Jesus' time. According to this parable, a father shows his apprenticed son all the process that belongs to his craft (cf. v. 20) and the son does only what he sees his father doing (cf. v. 19).[170] Jesus' relationship with God is that of a son to his own father. The Father's perpetual activity consists of two divine functions, namely his creative role to give life (ζῳοποιέω, v. 21) and his kingly role to judge (κρίνω, v. 22). Just like his Father, Jesus as the Son is capable of giving life (vv. 21.25)[171] and has the authority to judge (vv. 22.27.30).[172] Since the Son has a

---

(Deut 32,36; Ps 43,1; for more texts or references concerning God's judgement on individual accountability and the judgment of the dead in the Old Testament and the apocryphal literature, see R. H. Hiers, "Day of Judgement", *ABD*, II, 80). Philo explains the resting of God on the seventh day mentioned in Gen 2,3 as follows, "For God never ceases from making something or other; but, as it is the property of fire to burn, and of snow to chill, so also it is the property of God to be creating. And much more so, in proportion as he himself is to all other beings the author of their working. Therefore, the expression, 'he caused to rest,' is very appropriately employed here, not 'he rested.' For he makes things to rest which appear to be producing others, but which in reality do not effect anything; but he himself never ceases from creating" (*Leg. All.*, 1.5–6; Yonge, *The Works of Philo*, 47). Cf. Dodd, *Interpretation*, 320–323; Brown, *John*, I, 216–219.

[169] Dodd, *Interpretation*, 325.

[170] See C. H. Dodd, *More New Testament Studies* (Manchester 1968), 30–40; idem, *Historical Tradition*, 386, n. 2; Barrett, *John*, 259.

[171] The two healing miracles narrated in 4,46–5,6 are examples of the life-giving activity of Jesus. Jesus heals the official's son who is at the point of death with his life-giving word from a distance (4,50–53; cf. 1,4). He also heals with his word (5,8) the paralytic, who is having almost "a dead life" (cf. 5,5).

[172] Brown points out that the salvific judgment in the Old Testament is a prerogative of Yahweh. Hence, the Son's power to judge will make people honour him and recognize his exclusive relationship with the Father. Brown also believes that vv. 26–30 form another

share in the Father's life (v. 26) and judgment (v. 22), the Son will be honoured as the Father is honoured (v. 23). The Father is heard in the Son because the Son is sent by the Father and is, thus, his representative (v. 24).[173] Since the Son has life in himself like his Father (v. 26), the voice of the Son has the power to raise and judge the dead (vv. 28–30).[174] The identity in function and authority between the Father and the Son is so complete that it is impossible to honour the Father/God while disregarding Jesus.[175] Thus, vv. 19–30 as a whole make the claim that Jesus does what the Father alone can do and confirm his exclusive relationship with the Father.[176]

In vv. 31–40, Jesus lists several witnesses to support the claims that he has made in vv. 17–30.[177] Among various witnesses, the Father's testimony is the most significant and adequate one. It is in Jesus' works that the Father's testimony is manifest. The works that Jesus does verify that the Father has sent him and is in him (v. 36; cf. 10,25.32.37–38; 14,10–11; 15,24). No one has ever heard the Father's voice or seen his form (v. 37; cf. 1,18). But, if someone believes in Jesus, he hears the Father's voice in him (cf. 14,10). If anyone sees Jesus as the Son of God, he has seen the Father (cf. 14,9). Jesus is the Father's voice (φωνή), his Word (1,1–18) and his image (εἶδος; cf. 2 Cor 4,4; Col 1,15; Heb 1,3). Hence, God's word does not remain in those who reject Jesus (v. 38). Since the Scriptures bear witness to Jesus, they do not provide eternal life to those who refuse to believe in Jesus (vv. 39–40).

In vv. 41–47, there is a change of the tone of Jesus' speech. While in vv. 31–40 Jesus is on trial, presenting witnesses as evidence in his defense, in vv. 41–47 "the Jews" are on trial.[178] Since Jesus comes in the Father's name, he is the Father's representative (v. 43; cf. 12,13). The evidence against the Jews are the writings of Moses. Since they bear witness to Jesus (vv. 39.46), one who accepts Moses should also accept and believe in Jesus. Therefore, if they do not believe in Jesus, their accuser before the Father will be Moses himself (v. 45). Thus, chapter 5 establishes that Jesus is the only Son of the Father

---

version of Jesus' speech reported in vv. 19–25, but with different theological emphases. See Brown, *John*, I, 219–221.

[173] The phrase ὁ πέμψας με or αὐτόν occurs 24 times in John's Gospel.

[174] Keener, *John*, I, 654, views, "By claiming that he has life in himself, Jesus seems to make a claim to deity". It also implies that the believers have only a mediated life and do not have life in themselves, and therefore, they cannot pass on their life to others. Cf. Thompson, *The God of the Gospel of John*, 79.

[175] Barrett, *John*, 260.

[176] Vv. 19–30 constitute a unique example of combining the realized eschatological (vv. 19–24) and the final eschatological (vv. 25–30) perspective of the Gospel. See Brown, *John*, I, 220.

[177] We have already spoken of these witnesses on pp. 230–231, 244.

[178] Here Jesus switches from defense attorney to prosecutor citing evidence against the Jews on account of their unbelief in him. See O'Day, *John*, 587.

and that he has an exclusive relationship with the Father, which no one else has.

4.1.1.5 Jesus as the Son of Man with the Father's Seal (6,27)

In chapter 6, Jesus' exclusive relationship with the Father is explicitly stated in vv. 27.46.57.[179] V. 27 is placed within Jesus' dialogue with the crowd.[180] Jesus contrasts the perishable food, which the crowd seeks, with the imperishable food, which the Son of Man will give for their eternal life. It is on this Son of Man that God the Father has set his seal.[181] The verb σφραγίζω can mean "to mark with a seal as a means of identification", "to certify that something is so", "to attest".[182] Considering the aorist ἐσφράγισεν, it is possible to think of a specific point of time when this identification or attestation was done, i.e., at the descent of the Spirit on Jesus (1,32–34).[183] It is God the Father who certifies the authority and the truth of Jesus. While the addition of ὁ πατήρ in apposition to θεός is quite common in the New Testament (e.g., 1 Cor 1,3; 8,6; 15,24; Jas 1,27; 1 Pet 1,2; 2 John 3), the addition of ὁ θεός after the mention of πατήρ is unique in the entire New Testament. Since the Father is the origin of all things, it may imply that Jesus, the Son of Man, has been identified and attested by the Father, that is, by God, the supreme authority.[184]

4.1.1.6 Jesus as the Only One Who Has Seen the Father (6,46)

6,46 is placed within Jesus' dialogue with the Jews in chapter 6. The Jews question Jesus' claim to be the bread from heaven because they are aware only of his human origin (vv. 41–42). In reply, Jesus asserts that no one can come to him unless he is drawn by the Father (v. 44). This activity of the Father is an inner movement. Only those who have heard and learned from the Father can come to Jesus. But no one can hear the Father apart from Jesus (5,37). When one hears Jesus, he is at the same time taught by the Father and learns from the Father. This is a circular movement. In the process of believing in Jesus, the Father's initiative is involved (6,65), but apart from Jesus one cannot know the Father (cf. 12,45; 14,6–10). Therefore, Jesus can claim that except him no one has ever seen the Father (v. 46; cf. 1,18).

---

[179] In all other references to the Father in chapter 6, the emphasis is not on Jesus' relationship with the Father but on the Father's role in the relationship of the believers with Jesus (cf. vv. 32.37.40.44.45.65).

[180] For the structure of chapter 6, see the outline on p. 245.

[181] The title "Son of Man" can be considered as an eschatological title and its use here probably reflects Johannine realized eschatology. See Brown, *John*, I, 264.

[182] BDAG, 980.

[183] See Schnackenburg, *John*, II, 38; Barrett, *John*, 287.

[184] Cf. Schnackenburg, *John*, II, 38.

4.1.1.7 Jesus' Relationship with "the Living Father" (6,57)

6,57 is placed in the context of a dispute among the Jews as an answer to their question, "How can this man give us his flesh to eat?" (6,52). In his reply, Jesus explicates that eating the flesh and drinking the blood of the Son of Man is a necessary condition for receiving the gift of eternal life (vv. 53–56). The life that Jesus provides for the believer is the very life of "the living Father" (v. 57). The phrase "the living Father" (ὁ ζῶν πατήρ) joins two similar ideas into one: the living One and the Father who is the source of life.[185] This expression is unique in the entire New Testament, while "the living God" is common in both Old Testament and New Testament. The life-giving aspect of God's activity is illumined by the image of the "Father" taken from the human sphere of paternal relationship.[186] The Father is "living" because he is the source of life and only he has life in himself independent of anyone else (5,26). The life which the Son has in himself is the life of the Father (cf. 1,4; 5,26). The believer has access to the life of the Father only through the Son (5,26; 6,57; 14,19). Thus, having a unique access to the life of the Father, the relationship of the Son with the Father is exclusive.

4.1.1.8 Jesus' Origin and Identity under Question (8,12–59)

John 8,12–59 is set within Jesus' conflict with the Jews in Jerusalem at the time of the feast of Tabernacles (7,14–8,59).[187] The controversy begun in chapter 7 continues, and in 8,12–59 it is focused on the person and authority of Jesus himself, especially on his provenance and identity. The questions of the Jews like, "Where is your Father?" (v. 19) and "Who are you?" (v. 25) and Jesus' answers to them, namely "I am from above" (v. 23) and "When you have lifted up the Son of Man, then you will realize that I Am" (ὅτι ἐγώ εἰμι, v. 28a)[188] are concerned with his origin and identity. While discussing these issues, Jesus' unique relationship with the Father is brought into light. When the validity of his testimony and judgment is questioned (v. 13), Jesus points out his divine origin and identity (vv. 14.23) and the Father's presence with him (vv. 16–19.29). He is not alone. The Father is always with him in his testimony and judgment. He declares what he hears from the Father (vv. 26.38) and teaches what the Father teaches (v. 28b; cf. 12,50). It is his origin and end in the Father and the Father's presence in him which justify his testimony and judgment. In the concluding section of the chapter (vv. 39–59), Jesus' divine origin is contrasted with the evil origin of the Jews, and his

---

[185] Thompson, *The God of the Gospel of John*, 72.

[186] Thompson, "The Living Father", 23.

[187] Regarding the authenticity and role of 7,53–8,11, see the comment on p. 239, n. 69.

[188] The translation of this verse is mine. NRSV has rendered ὅτι ἐγώ εἰμι as "that I am he".

superiority over Abraham is asserted. He is not an agent of the devil as his opponents think (v. 48). He always honours the Father (v. 49) and the Father glorifies him (v. 54).

4.1.1.9 Jesus' Oneness with the Father as Messiah and Son of God (John 10)

There are some passages in chapter 10 which highlight Jesus' exclusive relationship with the Father. In the shepherd discourse (vv. 1–18), it is mentioned that the model for the good shepherd's knowledge of his sheep is the mutual knowledge between the Father and the Son (v. 15). His readiness to die for his sheep is out of his love-relationship with the Father (v. 17) and in total obedience to the Father (v. 18). The dialogue in vv. 22–39 is set within the context of the feast of Dedication in Jerusalem (vv. 22–23). While vv. 22–31 are concerned with Jesus' identity as the Messiah, vv. 32–39 deal with his identity as the Son of God. Jesus' messianic identity is to be recognized from his works in which the Father himself bears witness to Jesus (v. 25). The Father and the Son are one. It is a unity of power and operation.[189] It is a functional unity between the Father and the Son in their care for the sheep.[190] The Father and the Son are united in the work that they do, and it is difficult to distinguish Jesus' work from the Father's work.[191] On account of this unity, no one can snatch the sheep from the hand of Jesus and his Father (vv. 28–29).

In vv. 32–39, Jesus' identity as the Son of God is discussed. Jesus defends himself before the Jews who want to stone him, by appealing to his good works from the Father (v. 32). The works that Jesus does at the command and by the power of the Father are the external signs of his oneness with the Father (cf. v. 30). But the Jews want to stone Jesus for his blasphemy, for making himself God (v. 33). In fact, Jesus does not make himself anything; everything that he is stems from the Father.[192] He does not make himself God; he is the Word of God who has become a man (cf. 1,14). Jesus defends his identity by citing Ps 82,6, which states that human beings are addressed by God as "gods" and "sons of the Most High". Jesus argues that if human beings who received the word of God can be called "gods", how much more he deserves to be called the Son of God because he is the one whom the Father has conse-

---

[189] Brown, *John*, I, 407.
[190] Beasley-Murray, *John*, 174.
[191] O'Day, *John*, 677. Keener, *John* I, 825, notices that Jesus' unity with the Father reaffirms his divinity. For Barrett, *John*, 382, "The oneness of the Father and Son is a oneness of love and obedience even while it is a oneness of essence". Schnackenburg, *John*, II, 308, writes, "In the short sentence a vista appears of the metaphysical depths contained in the relationship between Jesus and his Father".
[192] Brown, *John*, I, 408.

crated and sent into the world (vv. 35–36).[193] Whereas the word of God came to human persons in the Old Testament (10,35), Jesus is the Word of God himself (1,1–2.14). Jesus' use of the title "Son of God" is thus a distillation of his portrayal of his relationship with the Father in 5,19–30.[194] The reason for believing in Jesus is the Father's works which Jesus does (vv. 37–38a). They prove his oneness with the Father, which is expressed in the reciprocal formula of intimacy and indwelling in v. 38b (cf. 14,10–11; 17,21). Moreover, Jesus' exclusive relationship and oneness with the Father is presented in a unique manner in 14,7–11.20, using the terminologies of "knowing", "seeing" and "being in".[195]

4.1.1.10 Jesus' Prayer to the Father (11,41–42; 12,27–28; 17,1–26)

John records 3 times Jesus' prayer to the Father. During these three occasions, he addresses God as "Father" in the vocative case. In the Gospel, no one else addresses God as Father. Before the tomb of Lazarus, the first word of his prayer is "Father" (11,41). In fact, Jesus does not ask for anything. It is a prayer of thanksgiving. Jesus is in constant communion with his Father who always hears even the unuttered thoughts of his heart.[196] Jesus' prayer in 11,41–42 is an example of the unique relationship which he has with his Father. In 12,27–28, Jesus' prayer to the Father in the face of the imminent suffering is recorded. He does not want that he escapes from the hour, but that the Father's name may be glorified through his death-resurrection-ascension. The answer from the Father (voice from heaven) is a confirmation of his oneness with the Father for the sake of the crowd (vv. 29–30). Hence, it is again a revelation of his unique relationship with the Father.

Jesus' address to the Father in the farewell discourse (John 17) also reveals his exclusive relationship with the Father. It is the final and the longest prayer of Jesus to the Father. This prayer "in some sort is the ascent of the Son to the Father".[197] It represents the archetypal union of the Son with the Father.[198]

---

[193] It is fitting to regard Jesus as the consecrated one within the setting of the feast of Dedication (10,22) and as such Jesus is the new temple.

[194] O'Day, *John*, 678.

[195] Since we have already analysed these texts, we do not explain them here. The language of oneness with the Father is also found in chapter 17, which is discussed below.

[196] Barrett, *John*, 402. Brown, *John*, I, 436, comments, "If prayer is a form of union with God, then the Johannine Jesus is always praying, for he and the Father are one (10,30)".

[197] Dodd, *Interpretation*, 419.

[198] Dodd, *Interpretation*, 419. Barrett, *John*, 500, remarks, "It is a setting forth of the eternal unity of the Father and the Son in its relation to the incarnation and the temporary (and apparent) separation which the incarnation involved".

We shall examine briefly how the Father-Son relationship is portrayed in this prayer.[199]

Jesus begins the prayer with his address to the Father in the vocative case (v. 1). The Father is addressed by Jesus 6 times in this way (vv. 1.5.11.21.24.25). This invocation clearly shows the Father-Son relationship between Jesus and the Father. Jesus speaks of the arrival of the hour for his own glorification and the glorification of the Father (v. 1). In saying "glorify your Son" instead of "glorify me", Jesus emphasizes his filial relationship with the Father.[200] But he is not seeking his own glory. The purpose of his glorification is the glorification of the Father, which is accomplished when he is lifted up on the cross. It is the Father who has given him the authority over all people (ἐξουσίαν πάσης σαρκός). This authority consists in giving life and doing judgment (cf. 5,21–27).[201] Jesus' mission on earth consists in revealing the Father, and eternal life is knowledge of the Father and the Son. Jesus stands alongside the Father as the object of this knowledge because the Father can be known only through the Son whom he has sent. He has revealed the Father through his words and deeds (cf. 1,18). The work that he has completed is the work of the Father (cf. 4,34). His petition for regaining the pre-existent glory (v. 5; cf. v. 24) implies his pre-existence with the Father, as expounded in the prologue (1,1–2). This pre-existence with the Father is the basis for his exclusive relationship with the Father and his exclusive claims.

Even though Jesus never explicitly says that he reveals the Father's name, his absolute ἐγώ εἰμι-sayings may point out the revelation of the divine name (v. 6a; cf. 8,24.58; 13,19). In evaluating positively the response of the disciples to his revelation, Jesus underscores his relationship with the Father indicating that he has come from the Father and has been sent by the Father (vv. 6–8; cf.16,30). Jesus prays for the protection of his disciples because they belong to the Father (vv. 9–19). The disciples are the Father's gift to Jesus. Jesus' claim "All mine are yours, and yours are mine" (v. 10; cf. 16,15) is an outcome of his unique and exclusive relationship with the Father.[202] The model for the unity of the future disciples is the unity between the Father and the Son (vv. 20–26): "they may be one, as we are one" (v. 22). The disciples participate in the union of the Father and the Son through their union with

---

[199] A broader structure for John 17 is given on p. 252.

[200] M. P. Hera, *Christology and Discipleship in John 17* (WUNT II 342; Tübingen 2013), 127–128.

[201] We have already mentioned that the expression ἐξουσίαν πάσης σαρκός is a Semitism/Hebraism, implying "authority over all people". Schnackenburg, *John*, III, 171, comments that this expression has to be understood as a plenary power, which is capable of deciding about life and death and of bringing about salvation or judgement.

[202] Carson, *The Farewell Discourse*, 188, writes, "Any mere mortal can pray to God, 'All I have is yours, but no mere mortal can pray, 'All you have is mine'".

Jesus.[203] In short, we may say that the underlying theme of Jesus' prayer is unity, and the nature of unity, for which Jesus prays, rests on the unity and the exclusive relationship of the Son with the Father.[204]

4.1.1.11 The Father as the Provenance and Destination of Jesus' Journey

John uses very frequently the language of journey to point out Jesus' provenance and destination. For this purpose, the terminology of "coming" and "going" is consistently used throughout the Gospel.[205] Both verbs emphasize Jesus' divine provenance and destination.[206] He is portrayed as the one who has "come from the Father" (16,28; 17,8) into the world (1,9; 3,19; 9,39; 12,46–47; 18,37) and is to "go to the Father" (13,1; 14,12.28; 16,10.17.28; 20,17). In his direct speech to his Father, he mentions, "I came from you" (17,8) and "I am coming to you" (17,11.13). Besides, there are other sayings which relate to his divine origin (5,43; 7,26b–29; 8,14b). That Jesus "comes from the Father" and "goes to the Father" establishes his divine origin, which no other human being in the Gospel enjoys, and as such it inevitably accentuates Jesus' exclusive relationship with the Father.

4.1.1.12 Jesus' Relationship with the Father in Various Ways

Throughout the Gospel Jesus is characterized as the one whom the Father has sent (5,23.24.36–39; 6,44.57; 8,16.18; 10,36; 11,42; 12,49; 14,24; 17,3.8.18.21.23.25; 20,21).[207] In relationship to the "Father", Jesus is often called "the Son" (3,35–36; 5,19–23.26; 6,40; 8,36; 14,13; 17,1). When Jesus speaks, his words are the words of the Father (8,28.38; 12,49–50; 14,24; 15,15; 17,8.14). His deeds are always in accordance with the will of the Father (14,31; 15,10). There always exists mutual love between them (3,35; 14,31; 15,9; 17,23–24.26). He reveals (γνωρίζω) what he has learnt from the Father (15,15; 17,26). He is never alone; the Father is always with him (8,16; 16,32).

---

[203] The frequent use of the conjunction καθώς in this chapter (vv. 11.14.16.18.21.22.23) shows that John presents Jesus' relationship with the Father as a model for the disciples.

[204] Cf. Hera, *Christology and Discipleship*, 24.

[205] The motif of journey in the Gospel is already discussed. See pp. 94–115.

[206] See Köstenberger, *The Missions of Jesus,* 121.

[207] On many occasions, the subject who sends is not mentioned (4,34; 5,30; 7,16.18.28–29.33; 8,26.29; 9,4; 12,44–45; 13,20; 15,21; 16,5). From the context, it is clear that the subject is the Father or God. The motif of sending is already discussed on pp. 100–101.

4.1.2 Jesus' Relationship with "God" (θεός)

The term θεός occurs 81 times in John's Gospel.[208] Among these occurrences, only 52 of them refer to the Godhead as a divine person. In all other occurrences, θεός is used as a genitive modifier as in Son of God, Lamb of God, children of God, kingdom of God, gift of God, etc. John almost interchangeably uses the terms "Father" and "God" in the Gospel.[209] In the prologue, Jesus as the pre-existent Son, who is called ὁ λόγος, is said to be with God before the creation of the world (1,1–2). 1,18 clearly states Jesus' unique and exclusive relationship with God, "No one has ever seen God. It is God the only Son, who is close to the Father's heart, who has made him known".[210] In relationship to "God", he is often called "the Son of God" (1,34.49; 5,25; 10,36; 11,4.27; 19,7; 20,31), "the Son" (3,17), "the only Son" (3,16) and "the only Son of God" (3,18). He is the "Holy One of God" (ὁ ἅγιος τοῦ θεοῦ 6,69) who has "come from God" (3,2; 8,42; 9,33; 13,3; 16,27.30). He is sent by God (3,17; 3,34; 6,29; 8,42) and is to "go and ascend to God" (13,3; 20,17). God is always with him (3,2). His teaching is from God (7,17), and he speaks the truth that he has heard from God (8,40). Thus, Jesus' relationship with "God" is not something different from his relationship with the "Father" since for Jesus God and the Father are one and the same. These two ways of presentation are like the two sides of the same coin. In short, from this examination of John's usage of θεός and πατήρ, we may say that Jesus' relationship with "God" is as exclusive as his relationship with "the Father".

4.2 Believers' Relationship with the Father/God

Even though the Father motif in the Gospel is mainly expressed in terms of the Father-Jesus relationship, there are also many passages where attention is paid to the Father/God-believers relationship. We shall make initially an overview of the use of πατήρ and θεός in relation to the believers and then in

---

[208] In this calculation, the two occurrences of the plural θεοί in 10,34–35 are not included.

[209] In his terminology, John maintains some sort of reservation with regard to the usage of "Father" and "God". E.g., the evangelist speaks of "children of God" (1,12; 11,52) but never "children of the Father"; of the "wrath of God" (3,36) but never "wrath of the Father". We hear of the "house of the Father" (2,16; 14,2) but never the "house of God"; the "will of the Father" (6,40) but never the "will of God"; the "hand of the Father" (10,29) but never the "hand of God". The believers are "born of God" (1,14), not "of the Father". It is only after Jesus' resurrection that the Father of Jesus becomes the Father of the disciples (20,17). However, Jesus is called "the only Son" of the Father/God (1,14; 3,16.18). "Father" is the subject of eighteen verbs which never appear with "God" as the subject, while "God" appears with only one verb (λαλέω) which is not used with "Father". Cf. Meyer, "Father", 264.

[210] We have already examined above the significance of this verse.

4.2.1 In Terms of πατήρ

Jesus establishes the relationship between the Father (πατήρ) and the believers in various ways. He inaugurates the hour for the worship of the Father in Spirit and truth by the true worshippers (4,21–24). Honouring the Father is equivalent to honouring the Son (5,23), and hatred to the Son is hatred to the Father (15,23.24). It is the Father who gives the true bread from heaven (6,32). Jesus remains as the single mediator in the relationship between the Father and the believers (14,6) because no one has seen the Father and heard his voice except the Son (5,37; 6,46). The Father also plays a decisive role in facilitating the relationship between Jesus and the believers. It is the Father who gives and draws the believers to Jesus (6,37.44–45.65; 10,29). It is the will of the Father that everyone who believes in the Son will have eternal life (6,40). But the unbelieving Jews, who claim to have God as their Father, in fact do not know the Father (8,19.41–42; 16,3). The Father will honour those who serve Jesus (12,26). The Father is in Jesus. Therefore, to see and to know Jesus is equal to seeing and knowing the Father (10,38; 12,45; 14,7–9). The journey of Jesus is intended to bring all the believers into the Father's house, where there are many dwelling places (14,2–3). The Father is the giver of the Holy Spirit to the believers (14,16.26; cf. 15,26). Those who love Jesus will be loved by the Father (14,21; 16,27) and will be able to experience the dwelling presence of the Father and the Son (14,21.23). The relationship between the Father and the believers is allegorically presented in the imagery of vine and branches, where the Father is the vine dresser (15,1). The Father prunes the branches so that they may bear much fruit and give glory to the Father (15,2–3.8). The Father will give the believers whatever they ask in Jesus' name (15,16; 16,23) and protect them in unity (17,11). It is only after Jesus' resurrection that the disciples are raised up to the status of the children of God and enabled to experience God as their Father (20,17; cf. 1,12).[211]

4.2.2 In Terms of θεός

Those who believe in Jesus are born divinely and become children of God (1,12–13; cf. 20,17). No one has seen God except his Son (1,18). It is only out of love that God sends his own Son into the world to save it (3,16–17). Since God is Spirit, he must be worshipped in Spirit and truth by the true worshippers (4,23–24). In order to fulfil the work of God in human beings, one must believe in the Son whom he has sent (6,28–29). And this belief is initiated by God himself (6,44–45). The Jews' unbelief in Jesus disproves

---

[211] This topic will be discussed at length below.

their claim to be children of God the Father (8,41–42; cf. 8,54). Those who are from God hear the words of God (8,47). Negative situations in human life can become means for God's works to be revealed (9,3). In 9,31, John expresses the relation between God and human beings in accordance with the traditional belief in Judaism. It is expressed through the statement of the blind man about Jesus. According to this traditional Jewish teaching, God does not listen to the sinners but to the pious and to those who do his will. The disciples are asked to believe in God and in Jesus at the moment of their internal turmoil due to Jesus' imminent departure (14,1). The eternal life consists in knowing God and Jesus Christ whom he has sent (17,3). It is only after Jesus' resurrection that the disciples are given the power to become the children of God (20,17; cf. 1,12; 3,3–5; 20,22). As a result of it, they are able to see in the risen Jesus God himself (20,28; cf. 12,45; 14,9) and glorify God in their lives (21,19).

4.2.3 Significance of "No One Comes to the Father except through Me"

The statement "No one comes to the Father except through me" portrays the possibility of attaining a unique relationship between believers and the Father/God through Jesus. We will now analyse this statement and bring out its meaning and significance in the light of the larger context of the Gospel and the overall theological perspective of the evangelist.

4.2.3.1 Significance of "No One" (οὐδείς)

The statement οὐδεὶς ἔρχεται πρὸς τὸν πατέρα εἰ μὴ δι' ἐμοῦ positively means "everyone comes to the Father through Jesus". In this statement, the term οὐδείς has a universal implication. Jesus does not say, οὐδεὶς ἐξ ὑμῶν, but rather οὐδείς referring to everyone. In a sense, οὐδείς includes everyone because the statement "no one *comes* (ἔρχομαι) to the Father" presupposes that "all" are separated from the Father.[212] This statement clearly assumes human estrangement from God.[213] The Gospel presupposes this alienation as a fundamental problem of humanity.[214] No mortal is said to have seen God and can claim a direct knowledge of God (1,18). The Word was in the world and the world came into being through him, yet the world did not know him (1,10). He came to his own, but his own people did not accept him (1,11). He came as light, but people loved darkness rather than light because their deeds were evil (3,19; cf. 8,12; 12,46).

---

[212] Cf. Koester, *Word of Life*, 210. The term οὐδείς occurs in the Gospel 53 times. It is used to refer to human alienation from God in 1,18; 3,13; 6,44.65; 14,6.

[213] See Koester, *Symbolism*, 290–294.

[214] The theme of humanity's alienation from God is already introduced on pp. 116–117.

This alienation from God or the inability to *come* to God is experienced by all, not only by Jesus' enemies but also by his disciples. Jesus says to the temple police who want to arrest him, "You will search for me, but you will not find me; and where I am, you cannot *come*" (ἔρχομαι 7,34). He says to the unbelieving Jews, "I am going away, and you will search for me, but you will die in your sin. Where I am going, you cannot *come*" (ἔρχομαι 8,21). Jesus' words to his disciples, who are his own, are not different from his words to the unbelieving Jews. During the supper, he says to his disciples, "Little children, I am with you only a little longer. You will look for me; and as I said to the Jews so now I say to you, 'Where I am going, you cannot *come*'" (ἔρχομαι 13,33). Thus, both his enemies and friends equally experience their inability to *come* to where Jesus goes.

The individual disciples also experience the fundamental problem of human weakness and ignorance. Peter is presented as a loyal disciple from the beginning of Jesus' ministry (1,41–42). When many of Jesus' followers refuse to follow him because of his "hard teaching" on the bread of life, Peter, representing the twelve, proclaims, "Lord, to whom can we *go* (ἀπέρχομαι)? You have the words of eternal life. We have come to believe and know that you are the Holy One of God" (6,68–69). During Jesus' farewell speech, Peter expresses his ardent desire to follow Jesus immediately, "Lord, why can I not follow you now? I will lay down my life for you" (13,37). Jesus then points out Peter's human fragility, "Will you lay down your life for me? Very truly, I tell you, before the cock crows, you will have denied me three times" (13,38). The passion narratives show us how Jesus' prediction of Peter's denial becomes literally true. Peter denies Jesus three times and refuses to be his disciple (18,17.25–27). He is not much better than the Jews who refuse to be Jesus' disciples when they are interrogated by the blind man, "Do you also want to become his disciples?" (9,27–28).

The special difficulty that affects Thomas during Jesus' farewell speech is incomprehension. Hence, he is compelled to ask, "Lord, we do not know where you are going. How can we know the way?" (14,5). Thomas is thus like the Jewish opponents who manifest their inability to understand Jesus in asking, "Where does this man intend to go that we will not find him? What does he mean by saying, 'You will search for me and you will not find me' and 'Where I am, you cannot come'?" (7,35–36; cf. 8,22). Philip also demonstrates his limitations when he asks Jesus, "Lord, show us the Father, and we will be satisfied" (14,8). He has confessed before that Jesus is the one "about whom Moses in the law and also the prophets wrote" (1,45). He has seen the miracle of feeding five thousand by Jesus (6,5.7). However, he is dissatisfied and has not yet been able to see the Father's presence in Jesus. His question in 14,8 is similar to that of the Pharisees, "Where is your Father?" (8,19). Thus, it can be noticed that it is not only the unbelieving Jewish adversaries but also the inner circle of disciples has not known Jesus and the Father in him. They both experience the same kind of alienation from the Father. This alienation is the plight of the whole humanity. Therefore, Jesus has to assert, "*no one* comes to the Father".

4.2.3.2 Significance of "Come to" (ἔρχομαι πρός)

Firstly, the expression ἔρχομαι πρός refers to reaching a goal. The verb ἔρχομαι is a verb of movement, which highlights the journey language implied in the metaphor "way", ἡ ὁδός in 14,6a. One must "come to" (ἔρχομαι πρός) Jesus and "go" (ἔρχομαι) on "the way" which is Jesus to reach the Father who is the destination of the journey. The statement "no one comes to the Father except through me" presupposes that everyone should first come to Jesus in order to come to the Father. One cannot reach the Father without coming first to Jesus because he is the door to the life of the Father (10,7.9).

Secondly, the expression ἔρχομαι πρός has a deeper meaning in the Gospel, as it has already been mentioned.[215] It is also a synonym for "believe in", πιστεύω εἰς (cf. 5,40; 6,35.37.44–45.65; 7,37–39;10,41). Therefore, it may refer to the significance of belief in Jesus as well. Without belief in Jesus, one cannot believe in the Father. It is notable that John never uses the noun "faith", πίστις in the Gospel. He is rather interested in the verb πιστεύω, which occurs 98 times in the Gospel (against 14x in Mark, 11x in Matthew and 9x in Luke). His preference for the verb πιστεύω to the noun πίστις shows that he is not thinking of faith as an internal disposition but as an active commitment.[216] His use of the verb of action ἔρχομαι πρός as a synonym for πιστεύω εἰς is a proof of his emphasis on the dynamic nature of the concept of belief. Thus, as an expression of belief, ἔρχομαι πρός signifies an acceptance of Jesus and of what he claims to be and an active commitment of one's life to him.[217] The motif of believing is predominant in the immediate context of 14,6 as well. It is introduced in 14,1, resumed in 14,6 through the verbal expression ἔρχομαι πρός and continued until 14,12. It is taken up in 14,7 through the verb γινώσκω, which is also, to a certain extent, interchangeable with πιστεύω.[218]

Believing in Jesus is not an end in itself. Its goal or the result is eternal life (e.g., 3,15.16.36; 6,40.47; 20,31; cf. 1 John 5,13), which is the life of and with the Father. Therefore, to believe means to accept the self-revelation of Jesus and to attach oneself to the unique mediator of salvation in order to

---

[215] See pp. 112.

[216] Brown, *John*, I, 512.

[217] Cf. Brown, *John*, I, 513.

[218] E.g., in 17,8, the verbs γινώσκω and πιστεύω are placed in parallelism. In 14,7.9–10, the verbs γινώσκω and ὁράω are closely related to the notion of belief. The verb ὁράω is used in the Gospel for perceptive sight, which is the beginning stage of faith (1,50–51; 3,11.32; 11,40; 14,7.9; 19,35.37; 20,29).

attain eternal life with the Father.[219] Thus, belief in John has not only a Christological character but also a soteriological one.[220]

4.2.3.3 Significance of "the Father" (ὁ πατήρ)

The destination of the believer's journey on the way which is Jesus is the Father who is the source of life. It should be specially noted that John does not say, "No one comes to God", rather "No one comes to the Father". It does not mean that, for John, "God" and "Father" are two different entities. John interchangeably uses "God" and "Father" and for him both refer undoubtedly to the one and the same reality (see 5,18; 6,27.45–46; 8,41–42.54; 13,3; 16,27; 20,17). God is usually called the Father in the sense of creator, provider or protector in the Old Testament (cf. Deut 32,4–6.18; Hos 11,1–4; Jer 3,19; 31,9; Isa 45,9–13; 63,16; 64,8) and in the New Testament (cf. Matt 5,45.48; 6,1.4.9; Mark 11,25; Luke 6,36; 11,2). But in the Gospel of John, the image of God as the Father for the believers has a deeper theological sense. Becoming a child of the Father has a unique status in the Gospel. John insists that it is as Father that God is to be experienced. The significance of the metaphor "Father" in 14,6b can be appreciated only if sufficient attention is paid to the network of the family imagery beautifully and cleverly employed throughout the entire Gospel.[221] Family imagery is the most essential, inclusive and pervasive imagery used by the evangelist. He conveys his message by means of a refined use of family imagery, which mainly consists of interrelated metaphors like house (home), Father, begetting (birth), life, children, mother and brothers.

a. Family of the Father

In ancient families, birth was a defining social event because it determined the family a person belonged to and also his social stratification.[222] It was also believed that a person's character and personality were given to him via the seed of his father and were then augmented by education and other circumstances.[223] The language of house-home-birth-life and Father-Son-children-brothers offers the basic points of orientation in the development of the family imagery in the Gospel. The logical point of entrance into a family

---

[219] Schnackenburg, *John*, I, 560.

[220] Schnackenburg, *John*, I, 567, says, "Johannine faith has a soteriological as well as a Christological character; the aspects are equally important and closely allied".

[221] Van der Watt, *Family of the King*, 398, remarks that "a complex network of different metaphors are woven together to form the family imagery" in John's Gospel.

[222] J. G. van der Watt, *An Introduction to the Johannine Gospel and Letters* (London 2007), 55.

[223] Van der Watt, *An Introduction*, 55.

is birth in a family. Birth and life presuppose a father and a mother.[224] By being born as a child of God through belief in Jesus (1,12–13) and thus having eternal life, the believer is able to be a member in the family of God the Father (3,1–8).[225] John uses the characteristics of an ordinary family as an analogy to explain what happens to a person who believes in Jesus and becomes part of the family of God.[226] It is the responsibility of an earthly father to feed, care and to protect his children, and on the part of the children, it is their duty to obey their father. Similarly, the heavenly Father feeds and protects his children spiritually, and the children of God should obey the Father's words. The various activities of the Father and the Son such as providing food (bread, basket, eating and drinking in chapter 6), educating the family (5,17–30; 7,15–17), protecting their property as well as the notions of property (such as kingdom in 3,3.5; 18,36, vineyard in 15,1–6, sheep in 10,1–16) establish and broaden the family imagery in the Gospel.[227]

b. Believers as Members of the Father's Family

Some important texts (1,12–13; 3,3–8; 20,17.22.28) which are closely related to the family imagery will be now briefly examined in order to recognize the significance of the Father metaphor in relation to the believers in the Gospel

---

[224] In the ancient Mediterranean world, father was the authoritative head of the family. See van der Watt, *Family of the King*, 166–168. In the family imagery employed by John, God the Father as the creator is the head of the divine family. It does not have a mother who is equally responsible for the act of creation like God the Father. However, John speaks of a mother (μήτηρ) in his Gospel. She is only "the mother of Jesus". There is no place for any other mother in this Gospel besides "the mother of Jesus". The noun μήτηρ is found 11 times. It is used once in the imagery of birth obviously without referring to any person in 3,4. All other 10 occurrences refer to Mary who is anonymously called "the mother of Jesus". Hence, she is the only person who is referred to as "the mother" in the Gospel. She appears at the beginning (2,1–12) and at the end (19,25–27) of Jesus' public life. Her presence at the foot of the cross is noteworthy. John narrates, "When Jesus saw his mother and the disciple whom he loved standing beside her, he said to his mother, 'Woman, here is your son'. Then he said to the disciple, 'Here is your mother'. And from that hour the disciple took her into his own home" (19,26–27). Since this mother and this disciple are not named, there is something unusual about their roles. The beloved disciple's acceptance of Jesus' mother as his own mother may have a symbolic meaning as well. Accordingly, the beloved disciple is the representative of all disciples/believers and "the mother of Jesus" is "the mother of all disciples/believers". Therefore, Mary "the mother of Jesus" should be received into the Johannine family imagery as "the mother".

[225] Van der Watt, *An Introduction*, 57, points out, "Being born into the family of God through faith in Jesus implies a new identity, new social relations and new status. As a child is born into an earthly family, the child of God is born into a heavenly family".

[226] Van der Watt, *An Introduction*, 57.

[227] Van der Watt, *Family of the King*, 399, says, "To a certain extent one can say that this Gospel unfolds as part of the family history of the Father and the Son".

and to appreciate its role in 14,6b. These texts will disclose how those who "come to" Jesus become the children of the Father through the begetting of the Holy Spirit and experience the fatherhood of God.[228]

aa. Believers' Birth as Children of God (1,12–13)

In the prologue, precisely in 1,12–13, John shows the possibility of how people can become the children of God by believing in Jesus and experience the fatherhood of God.[229] The adversative particle δέ in v. 12 contrasts the rejection of the incarnated Word by the world and his own (vv. 10–11) with the acceptance by the believers. "All those who received him" (ὅσοι δὲ ἔλαβον αὐτόν) and "those who believed in his name" (τοῖς πιστεύουσιν εἰς τὸ ὄνομα αὐτοῦ) in v. 12 are mutually related and describe each other. The act of "receiving" (λαμβάνω) refers particularly to the definite acceptance of the self-revelation of Jesus as Christ and the Son of God, and "believing in his name" (πιστεύω εἰς τὸ ὄνομα αὐτου) means a commitment which presupposes a complete acceptance of the self-revelation of Jesus as Christ and the Son of God.[230] Those who believe in Jesus and his revelation are given the ἐξουσία[231] to become "the children of God" (τέκνα θεοῦ; cf 1 John 3,2).[232]

V. 13 explains how those who believe in Jesus become children of God. The negation of three natural factors, namely "blood", "will of the flesh" and "will of man" in the birth of the "children of God" emphasizes the supernatural origin of the "children of God".[233] No human being can reproduce the children of God. They are born not of natural descent but of God himself. According to the Johannine view, those who believe and those who are begot-

---

[228] At the same time, John also speaks of the family of the devil in which the devil is the father (8,44). The believers do not belong to the family of the devil. The difference between the children of God and the children of the devil will also be discussed below.

[229] Verses 11 and 12 are often considered to be the short summaries of the two parts of the Gospel, the book of signs (1,19–12,50) and the book of glory (13,1–20,31). Cf. Brown, *John*, I, 29. For a detailed study of 1,12–13, see Vellanickal, *The Divine Sonship*, 105–152.

[230] Vellanickal, *The Divine Sonship*, 148, 145–146. For Schnackenburg, *John*, I, 263, "believe in his name" means "the acceptance of Jesus to the full extent of his self-revelation". Believing in "his name" may also imply trusting in him as God, especially in the light of the divine name "I Am" that he bears. See Brown, *John*, I, 11; Keener, *John*, I, 399–400.

[231] Vellanickal, *The Divine Sonship*, 150, points out that ἐξουσία means "a real ability to become children of God, which concretely consists in the life of faith".

[232] John reserves the title υἱός only for Jesus, who alone has the full right to what the word signifies.

[233] The plural ἐξ αἱμάτων may refer to the involvement of the blood of male and female in the conception of the child, ἐκ θελήματος σαρκός to the sexual desire and ἐκ θελήματος ἀνδρός to the male sexual potency in the act of procreation.

ten (ἐγεννήθησαν) by God are equivalent (cf. 1 John 5,1).[234] To become a child of God is to be born of God. Through belief in Jesus, one is born into the family of God and is able to experience the fatherhood of God.

If believers in Jesus are to become the children of God, those who oppose Jesus are regarded to be the children of the devil (8,44; cf. 1 John 3,8). The fatherhood of God stands in opposition to the fatherhood of the devil. The criterion for filiation is the principle that children should act like their father. In seeking to kill Jesus and standing against the truth, the opponents of Jesus are doing the work of the devil, thus becoming the children of the devil because the devil is a murderer from the beginning and the father of lies (8,44; cf. 1 John 3,8). The children of the devil cannot believe in Jesus and accept his word (8,43.45–46), whereas the children of God love Jesus and hear the words of God (8,42.47). Jesus has come to liberate the people from the fatherhood of the devil (cf. 8,32.34.36) and to make them the children of God.

bb. Believers' Birth through the Holy Spirit (3,3–10)

Another family imagery, where the birth of the believers into the family of God is detectable, is in 3,3–10.[235] Jesus says to Nicodemus that no one can see/enter[236] the kingdom of God[237] without being born ἄνωθεν.[238] The birth

---

[234] Brown, *John*, I, 11. According to BDAG, 193–194, the meanings of the verb γεννάω are: i. to become the parent of, to beget, ii. to give birth to, to bear, iii. to bring forth, to produce.

[235] For a detailed study of this text, see Vellanickal, *The Divine Sonship*, 163–225. Our attention will be mainly on the significance of vv. 3.5.

[236] The verbs ὁράω and εἰσέρχομαι do not make considerable differences in vv. 3.5. Cf. L. P. Jones, *The Symbol of Water in the Gospel of John* (Sheffield 1997), 70; Newman and Nida, *John*, 79; Barrett, *John*, 207–208.

[237] We may assume that kingdom of God and eternal life can be used alternatively in the Gospel of John. The references to "eternal life/life" in the second part of chapter 3 (vv. 15–16.36) will support this view. Brown, *John*, I, 159, states that "eternal life and the kingdom of God are closely allied concepts for John".

[238] The adverb ἄνωθεν is a double meaning word. It has both local and temporal senses. It can mean here either "from above", implying the source and place of origin or "again, anew", involving a repetition at a subsequent point of time. See BDAG, 92. The misunderstanding shown by Nicodemus may favour the translation "again", but the immediate and the large context will support the translation "from above". The word ἄνωθεν is found in John 5 times (3,3.7.31; 19,11.23). In Jesus' answer to Pilate in 19,11, the reference of ἄνωθεν is clearly to the source, namely God. In 19,23, only a local sense (without reference to the source) is possible. In the other three instances, a local sense implying the source or origin is preferable. The birth of the children of God from God in 1,12–13 may support a local sense in 3,3. A sense of source or origin in 3,7 can be assumed from 3,5–6.8, where the focus is on the source of birth. In 3,31, a local sense, implying the source, is created through the contrast of ἄνωθεν with γῆ. For various arguments in favour of the local sense of ἄνωθεν in 3,3.7, see Vellanickal, *The Divine Sonship*, 172–174. However, these two meanings do not exclude each other. In a certain sense, the birth from above is also a new

from above gives the believer a totally new existence and a new life. Since it comes from above, God the Father is the source of this life (5,26). One can enter the kingdom of the Father only when one is begotten by the heavenly Father.[239] When John explicates in v. 5 that this birth is from water and the Spirit, he emphasizes the role of the Holy Spirit in the process of becoming God's children (cf. Titus 3,4–7).[240]

Being the vehicle of life, the Holy Spirit is the medium of rebirth for the children of God.[241] It is through divine begetting that one becomes a member of the family of God.[242] This begetting through the Spirit is mysterious to humans. We can know only the effects of begetting through the Spirit, but we cannot know when and how the Spirit begets the believers (3,8; cf. Mark 4,26–29; Qoh 11,5). Nicodemus' question in 3,9 "How can these things be?" is answered by Jesus in 3,10–21, where death on the part of Jesus and belief on the part of his followers are pointed out as requirements for the begetting through the Spirit. The new birth gives a new access to God. Jesus is characterized as the one who baptizes with the Holy Spirit (1,33). For John, birth into the family of God is realized when the resurrected Jesus gives the Spirit to his disciples (20,22; cf. 7,37–39).

cc. Realization of the Father's New Family (20,17.22.28)

The new birth of the believers as the children of God through the Holy Spirit, which is foreseen in 1,12–13 and 3,3–8, is realized in John 20. The identity of God as the Father for the disciples (believers) and their identity as God's children and as members of the family of the Father are established in this

---

birth and a rebirth. What is important is that we need to emphasize the source and origin of this new birth. Also see J. A. Trumbower, *Born from Above. The Anthropology of the Gospel of John* (HUT 29; Tübingen 1992), 71–73.

[239] Brown, *John*, I, 138, comments, "Life can come to a man only from his father; eternal life comes from the heavenly Father through the Son whom he has empowered to give life" (cf. 1 John 3,9).

[240] It is possible to see an allusion to baptism in the evangelist's reference to water in 3,5, especially in the context of the discussion on baptism in the same chapter (3,22–23.26). But he does not explain the relation between baptism and the Holy Spirit. For a discussion on the relation between baptism and the Holy Spirit, see Vellanickal, *The Divine Sonship*, 179–190; Brown, *John*, I, 141–144. The context (3,6–8) suggests that in the birth "from water and Spirit" the emphasis should be given to the role of the Spirit. This is especially important when, for the evangelist, water represents the Holy Spirit in 7,37–39. Schnackenburg, *John*, I, 370, opines that "Jesus' words to Nicodemus are not concerned directly with baptism, but with the new creation by the Spirit of God".

[241] Dodd, *The Interpretation*, 224.

[242] Brown, *John*, I, 140, writes, "If natural life is attributable to God's giving spirit to men, so eternal life begins when God gives his Holy Spirit to men. The begetting through Spirit of which v. 5 speaks seems to be a reference to the outpouring of the Spirit through Jesus when he has been lifted up in crucifixion and resurrection".

chapter. Many of Jesus' promises in chapter 14 find their fulfilment in chapter 20.[243] At the theological level, his statement in 14,6 that everyone should "come to the Father" through him finds its fulfilment in the life of the disciples in chapter 20. By giving his disciples the access (way) to the Father, the source of life, through the bestowal of the Spirit of truth, Jesus becomes the way, the truth and the life (14,6a). One who "comes to" Jesus (believes in Jesus), begotten through the Holy Spirit, comes to the Father (14,6b). Let us now see how this realization is portrayed in chapter 20.[244]

God as Believers' Father and Jesus as their Brother (20,17)

Much scholarly ink has flowed over to pinpoint the precise meaning of Jesus' statement to Mary Magdalene and the interrelation between 20,17b and 20,17c.[245] There is some ambiguity in interpreting Jesus' words to Mary Magdalene, Μή μου ἅπτου. Usually, the subjunctive present imperative with μή is used to forbid the continuation or the progress of an action.[246] Hence, μή μου ἅπτου can be literally translated as "stop touching me". In order to maintain this sense, many modern versions and scholars translate it as "Do not hold on to me" or "Do not cling to me".[247] There is no mention that Mary ever touched Jesus. But the use of the present subjunctive imperative gives us the impression that she is already touching him (cf. Matt 28,9).[248] The evan-

---

[243] The promises in chapter 14 are discussed on pp. 156–180. The promises, given in chapter 14 and fulfilled in chapter 20, are the following: the coming of Jesus to his disciples (20,19.26; cf. 14,18–19), the gift of the Holy Spirit (20,22; cf. 14,16–17.26), the eschatological gifts of peace (20,19.21.26; cf. 14,27) and joy (20,20; cf. 14,28).

[244] For our purpose, we will take into account only vv. 17.22.28 and pay attention only to the relevant elements.

[245] For an overview of the difficulties found in the interpretation of this verse, see R. Bieringer, "I am ascending to my Father and your Father, to my God and your God (John 20,17). Resurrection and Ascension in the Gospel of John", *The Resurrection of Jesus in the Gospel of John*, ed. C. R. Koester and R. Bieringer (WUNT 222; Tübingen 2008), 209–221; Brown, *John*, II, 992–994, 1011–1012.

[246] See BDF, 172 (§336); E. de Witt Burton, *Syntax of the Moods and Tenses in the New Testament Greek* (Grand Rapids 1900), 75.

[247] E.g., the English versions like NRSV, NLT, NKJ, NJB, NIV, NAB, etc., the German versions like EÜ, NGÜ, Hfa ("Halte mich nicht fest"), the French versions like BDS, BFC ("Ne me retiens pas") and scholars like Zumstein, *Saint Jean 13–21*, 279; Thyen, *Johannesevangelium*, 763; Wengst, *Johannesevangelium*, II, 281; Schnackenburg, *John*, III, 314; Brown, *John*, II, 992; Moloney, *John*, 524, etc., hold on to the progressive sense of the verb.

[248] For a different interpretation of this present imperative, see Schleritt, *Passionsbericht*, 491–492; Bieringer, "I am ascending to my Father", 222–232. According to Reimund Bieringer, John 20,17 is a Johannine redaction and a correction of Matt 28,9–10 to show that the risen Christ is not someone to be worshipped. He translates μή μου ἅπτου under the influence of the cultic use of ἅπτομαι in the book of Numbers (3,10.28; 17,28) thus,

gelist does not give clear reasons for Jesus' prohibition to Mary Magdalene. However, from the following passage (vv. 18–23), we may assume that there is a sense of urgency in Jesus' words, so that the disciples may be prepared to receive the promises of the ascended/glorified Jesus, especially the gift of the Holy Spirit (vv. 22–23) and may continue Jesus' mission.[249] For John, Jesus' hour of glorification is culminated in the act of imparting the Holy Spirit to the disciples (7,37–39; 20,22) that will make them children of God and God their Father.[250]

From Jesus' words to Mary Magdalene, we can notice a remarkable change in the mode of relationship between Jesus and his disciples and between God and the disciples. This is to be noticed in the expression "my brothers" (οἱ ἀδελφοί μου) and in the statement "I am ascending to my Father and your Father, to my God and your God". Jesus here calls his disciples for the first time "my brothers" in the Gospel.[251] Jesus' ascension to the Father will make it possible for God to become the Father of the disciples and for Jesus to become their brother. The power to call God "the Father" and to

"Do not come near to me the way one approaches the tabernacle". He imagines that both μή μου ἅπτου and the expression "my Father and your Father, my God and your God" serve "to shift the focus away from the risen Christ to God". It is very difficult to accept Bieringer's argument, especially when we take into account Thomas' confession "my Lord and my God" (20,28) about which Bieringer is silent. In fact, there is absolutely no attempt at all on the part of the evangelist to correct Matt 28,9 or to shift the focus away from the risen Christ to God, as Bieringer imagines. On the contrary, as the forthcoming discussions on 20,28 will show (see pp. 287–289; 373, n. 81), the evangelist is trying to reveal that the risen Christ is the locus of God the Father. In reality, Bieringer has built up his whole thesis on an extremely shaky foundation. His whole argument is merely based on a variant reading in 9,38, which supports the omission of "and he worshipped him" (καὶ προσε κύνησεν αὐτῷ). The omission of καὶ προσεκύνησεν αὐτῷ is not accepted by most scholars today and there are more sound reasons for the retention of 9,38 (for various reasons for the retention of 9,38, see p. 371, n. 74). Moreover, in Jesus' reply to Thomas in 20,29, there is not any attempt to reject Thomas' proclamation "my Lord and my God" but only an encouragement and support for such a deeper belief, "Blessed are those who have not seen and yet have come to believe".

[249] For a discussion on the difference between the Johannine and Lukan view of the ascension of Jesus, see A. Benoit, "L'Ascension", *RB* 56 (1949), 161–203.

[250] Dodd, *Interpretation*, 442, points out that "it is not the resurrection as Christ's resumption of heavenly glory that needs to be emphasized, but the resurrection as the renewal of personal relations with the disciples".

[251] It is unlikely here that "my brothers" refer to the physical relatives of Jesus (7,8) as Dodd, *Tradition*, 147, suggests. In v. 18, it is to the disciples that Mary Magdalene goes to proclaim the message given by the risen Jesus. The disciples are called "my brothers" in Matt 28,7. The use of "brothers" in John 21,23 also refers to Jesus' disciples. Moreover, the physical relatives of Jesus are not portrayed positively in their relationship and attitude towards Jesus. This is clear when the evangelist says, "For not even his brothers believed in him" (7,5). Moreover, "brothers" became a familiar title for believers among one another in the early Church (e.g., Acts 10,23; 11,1.12.29; Rom 1,13; 7,1.4; Phil 2,25).

become his children is acknowledged in 1 John 3,1, "See what love the Father has given us, that we should be called children of God; and that is what we are". Being children of God means sharing the same Father with Jesus (20,17).[252] Jesus' ascension to the Father will make possible the imparting of the Holy Spirit, who will beget the believing disciples as God's children.[253] They are now recognized as the members of the family of the Father and Jesus. Jesus' ascension to the Father is in view of a full fellowship of the disciples with the Father.

Realization of Believers' Rebirth through the Holy Spirit (20,22)

In 20,19–23, John presents the glorified Jesus' first appearance to his disciples. The presentation of Jesus as the giver of the Holy Spirit is fully actualized in v. 22. Jesus is sanctifying and sending his disciples to continue his mission as he was sanctified and sent by his Father (v. 21; cf. 10,36; 17,19). Just as Jesus is sanctified for the mission, the disciples are sanctified through the Spirit of truth for the purification and sanctification of the world (v. 23; cf. 17,17.19).

Jesus gives the Holy Spirit to his disciples very dramatically by breathing (ἐμφυσάω) upon them. The verb ἐμφυσάω, which occurs only here in the entire New Testament, is used in Gen 2,7 in the LXX (also see Wis 15,11) for the creation of the human being, "Then the Lord God formed man from the dust of the ground and breathed (ἐνεφύσησεν) into his nostrils the breath of life (πνοὴν ζωῆς); and the man became a living being (ψυχὴν ζῶσαν)". John indicates symbolically that just as in the beginning at the moment of first creation God breathed a living spirit into the human being, so now at the moment of new creation, Jesus breathes his own Holy Spirit into the disciples, giving them eternal life (cf. 1,1–4; also see Ezek 37,3–5).[254] The promise of God becoming the believers' Father and the believers becoming God's children, mentioned in 1,12–13; 3,3–8 and 20,17, becomes a reality through the giving of the Holy Spirit in 20,22. Hence, Jesus' giving of the Holy Spirit to the disciples is a pledge of divine begetting to all future believers represented by the disciples.[255] As a result of this divine begetting through the Spirit, the disciples become Jesus' brothers and are in a position to call Jesus' Father their own Father (cf. 20,17). We can also say that 20,22 is the fulfilment of 7,39, where the believers as such are said to be the recipients of the Holy Spirit. This image of Jesus as the giver of the Holy Spirit, which is introduced in 1,33 (cf. 3,34) and reaches its climax in 20,22, asserts Jesus'

---

[252] Keener, *John*, II, 1191, notices that "my God and your God" is a way of emphasizing a common bond (cf. Jub. 21,25).

[253] Brown, *John*, II, 1016.

[254] Cf. Brown, *John*, II, 1037.

[255] Cf. Brown, *John*, II, 1037.

divinity because in biblical imagery only God can baptize in his Spirit (cf. 1,33; 3,5) or pour out his Spirit (Isa 44,3; 63,11; Ezek 36,27; 37,14; 39,29; Joel 2,28–29; Hag 2,5). The power to forgive sins in v. 23 is also associated with the cleansing and giving new life to those who believe in Jesus (cf. 1 John 1,7–9).[256] The promise of the indwelling of the Spirit in 14,17.23 also finds its fulfilment here.

Recognition of the Father in Jesus (20,28)

Thomas' confession of faith ὁ κύριός μου καὶ ὁ θεός μου is considered to be the supreme Christological pronouncement of John's Gospel.[257] In the previous chapters, various titles were attributed to Jesus like Rabbi, Messiah, Prophet, King of Israel, Son of God and Lord. It is for the first time that the title "God" is given to Jesus in a direct speech in the Gospel.[258] The background for the collocation of κύριος and θεός can be found in the LXX, in which this combination is very frequently used for translating יְהוָה אֱלֹהַי (e.g., Gen 9,26; 24,3; Exod 5,1; 7,16; Num 22,18; Deut 4,4[5]; Josh 14,9). The expression ὁ θεός μου καὶ ὁ κύριός μου occurs in Ps 34,23 in the LXX (Hebrew: Ps 35,23, אֱלֹהַי וַאדֹנָי).[259] Thomas' declaration makes clear that one can address Jesus in the same language in which Israel addressed יְהוָה.[260] Thomas

---

[256] There is a relationship between the giving of God's Spirit and the cleansing from sins or forgiveness of sins in Ezek 36,25–27 (cf. 1QS IV,20ff); 1 Cor 6,11; Acts 2,38. In the life of the Qumran community, there is an association between the spirit and the cleansing, "He shall be cleansed from all his sins by the spirit of holiness uniting him to His truth" (1QS III,8); "He will cleanse him of all wicked deeds with the spirit of holiness; like purifying waters He will shed upon him the spirit of truth (to cleanse him) of all abomination and injustice" (1QS IV,22). See Vermes, *The Complete Dead Sea Scrolls*, 101, 103. In Jub. 1,23–25 it is written, "I will create in them a holy spirit, and I will cleanse them so that they shall not turn away from Me from that day unto eternity... and I will be their Father and they shall be My children. And they all shall be called children of the living God, and every angel and every spirit shall know, yea, they shall know that these are My children, and that I am their Father in uprightness and righteousness, and that I love them". See R. H. Charles, *The Apocrypha and Pseudepigrapha of the Old Testament. Pseudepigrapha* (Oxford 1913), II, 12–13.

[257] In the view of R. E. Brown, "Nothing more profound could be said about Jesus". See Brown, *John*, II, 1047–1048. Back, *Gott als Vater der Jünger*, 188, writes, "Das Christusbekenntnis des Thomas ist daher nicht nur der herausragende Höhepunkt an christologischer Einsicht, sondern auch die Klimax an *theo*logischer Erkenntnis".

[258] Barrett, *John*, 573, thinks that Thomas' pronouncement might have been taken from a liturgical setting. Brown, *John*, II, 1047, insists that "the New Testament use of 'God' for Jesus is not yet truly a dogmatic formulation, but appears in a liturgical or cultic context".

[259] Scholars have also noted that the combination of κύριος and θεός appears in pagan religious literature too. It is represented in the "*Dominus et Deus noster*" affected by the emperor Domitian (A. D. 81–96). See Barrett, *John*, 572–573; Brown, *John*, II, 1047.

[260] Brown, *John*, II, 1047.

is seeing in Jesus the One who has ascended to the Father and is glorified in the Father's presence with the glory that he had before the existence of the world (17,5). He penetrates through the miraculous aspect of the appearance and comprehends what the resurrection-ascension reveals about Jesus.[261] It can be regarded as "a response of praise to the God who has revealed Himself in Jesus".[262] An *inclusio* can be noticed between the opening verse of the Gospel "the Word was God" (1,1) and Thomas' proclamation "my Lord and my God" at the end of the Gospel.[263]

Thomas' pronouncement is the fulfilment of what Jesus has said in the previous chapters, "So that all may honour the Son just as they honour the Father" (5,23a); "When you have lifted up the Son of Man, then you will realize that I Am" (8,28).[264] Rev 4,10–11 describes a vision in which the elders fall down and worship God who sits on the throne exclaiming, "Worthy are you, *our Lord and God* (ὁ κύριος καὶ ὁ θεὸς ἡμῶν), to receive glory and honour and power".[265] While in Revelation the acclamation is for the Father, in John it is for the glorified Son. This implies that Thomas sees the Father in the glorified Jesus. For Thomas, in Jesus God himself comes to him and Jesus is for him God in his majesty, power and love.[266] Through his confession, Thomas proclaims that he has seen and recognized the Father in Jesus.[267] In confessing Jesus as Lord and God, Thomas also understands and acknowledges the truth of Jesus' words to him during the last supper (14,6–7), "I am the way and the truth and the life. No one comes to the Father except through me" and "If you know me, you will also know my Father. And from now onward, you know him and have seen him" (cf. 14,9). It means, to

---

[261] Brown, *John*, II, 1047.

[262] Brown, *John*, II, 1047.

[263] Chapter 21 is often regarded as the epilogue of the Gospel.

[264] This is the translation more close to the Greek text, Ὅταν ὑψώσητε τὸν υἱὸν τοῦ ἀνθρώπου, τότε γνώσεσθε ὅτι ἐγώ εἰμι. The NRSV translation is, "When you have lifted up the Son of Man, then you will realize that I am he".

[265] This translation is mine. The NRSV translation is, "Worthy are you, Lord our God, to receive glory and honour and power".

[266] Schnackenburg, *John*, III, 333, explains the confession of Thomas thus, "It is necessary, in this confession of Jesus' divinity on the lips of Thomas, to guard against both a watering down and a dogmatic fixation... In the evangelist's sense, Thomas' confession makes clear that the faith expected of the Church in Jesus the Son of God (cf. 20,31) implies Jesus' Godhead. He is the only true Son of God, one with the Father not only in what he does but also in being. Because the evangelist is not yet thinking from the point of view of the teaching of the two natures, he combines the Godhead of Jesus with the revelatory and saving function of the Son: he is the *Messiah*, the Son of God, that is, he is the Messiah to the extent that he is the Son of God, and the Son of God, in his messianic ministry. This functional understanding can be found expressed likewise in the personal confession formula: '*My* Lord and *my* God'".

[267] Back, *Gott als Vater der Jünger*, 193.

see Jesus is to see the Father, and Jesus is the way to experience the living Father. Thomas sees God the Father fully revealed in Jesus.[268] This proclamation also recognizes the implications of the evangelist's teachings on the Logos (1,1–2), Jesus' unique use of the absolute ἐγώ εἰμι (cf. 6,20; 8,24.28.58; 13,19; 18,5.6.8) and on his claim "I and the Father are one" (10,30; cf. 10,38; 14,10; 17,11.21).

4.2.3.4 Significance of "Except through Me" (εἰ μὴ δι' ἐμοῦ)

The expression "except through me" (εἰ μὴ δι' ἐμοῦ) assumes the Johannine view of reality which is dualistic.[269] The story of Jesus in the Gospel of John unfolds within a world of contrasts, which is presupposed by the Gospel itself. The contrasts can be grouped into creational contrasts and ethical contrasts. The creational contrasts are constituted by the opposites of divine and human (1,13), spiritual and physical (3,6), heavenly and earthly (3,12), above and below (8,23). The ethical contrasts are formed by the opposites of light and darkness (1,5), children of God (1,12) and children of the devil (8,44), truth (1,17; 8,32.40; 14,6) and lie (8,44), love (3,16) and hate (3,20; 15,18; 17,14), life and death (5,24), good and evil (5,29) and freedom from sin and slavery to sin (8,34–38). The dualistic view of reality explains the limitations of the human beings (3,12). The divine is not directly accessible to the human. Hence, the evangelist says that no one has seen God (1,18). One needs spiritual birth from above to become sensitive to the divine and to appreciate the spiritual events taking place in the person of Jesus (cf. 3,1–10).

This world of contrasts provides the setting for Johannine theology and necessitates the coming of the Son into the world. With the coming of the Logos who is God into the world, the divine reality enters into the sphere of the human reality (1,14). Both the heavenly and the earthly realities intersect in the person of Jesus of Nazareth. In him the two worlds coincide. In him the divine and the human, the spiritual and the physical are merged. What is unknown, invisible and spiritual becomes known, visible and physical through and in Jesus (1,14; cf. 1 John 1,1–4). He makes accessible what is inaccessible to the human beings (cf. 14,7–11). He is the locus and source of the divine qualities among the people of this world because through his per-

---

[268] O'Day, *John*, 852, writes, "It is not Jesus' resurrection appearances per se that reveal this truth, but his resurrection appearances as a sign of his return to God in glory". Scholars have often noticed the dimensions of a new covenant in the resurrection appearances in John 20, especially in Jesus' words to Mary Magdalene, "I am ascending to my Father and your Father, to my God and your God" (v. 17) and in Thomas' confession, "my Lord and my God" (v. 28). See Brown, *John*, II, 1016–1017, 1048.

[269] Van der Watt, *An Introduction*, 30, notices that Johannine dualism is not an exact dualism because the divine and human realities are not of equal importance. The divine qualities are far superior to the earthly qualities.

sonal presence the divine qualities like truth, love, life and light become present in the world.[270] When the Word becomes flesh in Jesus, his personal qualities like life, truth and light are not separated from him. Hence, he identifies himself with light, truth and life in the forms of ἐγώ εἰμι-sayings in the Gospel (8,12; 11,25; 14,6).

The phrase "except through me" (εἰ μὴ δι' ἐμοῦ) in 14,6b is like a window that lets light into a closed room.[271] Hence, Jesus is presented in the Gospel as the light that shines in the darkness (1,5.9; 3,19; 8,12), the door that secures life for those who enter it (10,7.9) and the way that leads to the Father (14,6). The phrase εἰ μὴ δι' ἐμου in itself is a conditional phrase, and it indicates the conditionality and uniqueness of salvation brought about by Jesus. The conditionality and the uniqueness of the salvation offered through Jesus are expressed by the evangelist throughout the Gospel (3,3.5.15.16.36; 6,35.46–47.51.57; 7,37; 8,12.19.51; 12,45; 14,6.7.9; 15,6). The basic condition for this unique salvation is belief in Jesus and its outcome is union with the Father.

4.3 Conclusion

When scholars examine John 14,6, often they pay undue attention to the phrase "except through me", but do not pay sufficient attention to "the Father". The notion of "Father" in John 14,6b has deeper theological significance and implications. Behind the statement "No one comes to the Father except through me", there lies the story of Jesus' exclusive relationship with his Father and the possible outcome of that relationship for the believers. For Jesus, God is his Father. John almost interchangeably uses "Father" and "God". Both terms identify the source from which Jesus has come into the world and the goal to which he goes or ascends.[272] John emphasizes the unique character of the relationship between the Son and the Father in a way that makes it difficult to talk about God as the Father apart from talking about Jesus as the Son.[273] We may say that the obverse of the uniqueness of Jesus' filial relationship to God is the uniqueness of God's paternal relationship to Jesus.[274] God is distinctly and uniquely the Father of Jesus. The Father may have many children, but he has only one Son.

---

[270] Van der Watt, *An Introduction*, 33.

[271] Cf. Koester, *Symbolism*, 292.

[272] Cf. Meyer, "Father", 264.

[273] Cf. Thompson, *The God of the Gospel of John*, 71. Hence, Meyer, "Father", 255, remarks, "The unity of Father and Son, a prominent motif in the evangelist's Christology, seems to preclude any talk about God apart from the Son, or at least to render highly problematic any venture to devote a separate chapter on Johannine theology to 'the Father'".

[274] Thompson, *The God of the Gospel of John*, 71.

The actions of God as the Father are distinctly and peculiarly concentrated toward and through his Son Jesus, and what the Father does and gives, he does and gives it through his Son.[275] The Father is the vindicator and authorizer of Jesus' words and deeds. He is the origin of what Jesus says and does. The Father has given life only to his Son (5,26; cf. 1,4), and the Son becomes the exclusive heir of the Father's life.

The basis for Jesus' exclusive claims in the Gospel is his unity with the Father. Hence, the arguments for his absolute and exclusive claims are ultimately the arguments for his unity with the Father. His exclusive relationship with the Father gives him the authority to judge, to give life, to mediate knowledge of the Father, to reveal him and to be the only way to the Father. The unique and exclusive relationship between Jesus and his Father goes back to the pre-existence of Jesus. He is with the Father, close to his heart before the beginning of creation (1,1.18; 17,24). He is the only one who has seen the Father (6,46). Hence, he has a special, exclusive and intimate knowledge of the Father (7,28–29; 8,19.42). The formulas of immanence (8,42; 10,38; 14,10–11.20; 17,21–23) and the expressions of unity (10,30; 17,11.21.23) also highlight the unique relationship of Jesus with the Father. As a result of his unique status, he can claim, "No one comes to the Father except through me". It is worth noticing that the most frequent occurrence of the term πατήρ is found in chapter 14 (23x). In all these instances, it refers to Jesus' Father and it is in the context of Jesus' exclusive relationship with the Father that the exclusivism in 14,6 is to be interpreted and understood.

Jesus' statement in 14,6b implies not only Jesus' exclusive relationship with the Father but also the believers' relationship with the Father accessible through Jesus. The possible relationship of the believers with the Father through Jesus is to be understood in the context of the family imagery used in the Gospel, where the metaphor "father" plays a crucial role. Our analysis of 14,6b in the light of the Gospel theology as a whole has shown how the human family is estranged and separated from God's family and how it can be reunited to God's family through Jesus. According to John's Gospel, the answer to the problem of humanity's estrangement from God is the person of Jesus of Nazareth, the Word that has become flesh (1,14). He is the way and the door for all to become a member of the divine family where God is the Father. Membership in the Father's family requires two conditions, namely belief in Jesus who is the only Son of the Father (1,18; 3,16) and a rebirth through the Holy Spirit (3,3–8). Therefore, everyone should first "come to" Jesus in order to "come to" the Father. One who "comes to" Jesus is at the same time begotten through the Holy Spirit as the child of the Father. The Holy Spirit is the vehicle of rebirth and without him one cannot become a child of the Father.

---

[275] Cf. Thompson, *The God of the Gospel of John*, 69.

The imagery of family enumerated in various parts of the Gospel finds its fulfilment in John 20. This is made possible through the death and resurrection of Jesus. As a result of it, the disciples can call God their own Father and Jesus their own brother (20,17). As the Gospel presupposes, this requires a new birth from above through the Holy Spirit, which happens at the very first appearance of the risen Jesus to his disciples (20,22). Thomas' confession reveals that in the risen Jesus the believer can see and experience the Father (20,28).

All the relationships of the believers with the Father are and should be defined in terms of relationship with Jesus.[276] The exclusivity of the sonship of Jesus actually becomes the means through which believers may receive the life and the freedom that characterize the true "children of God" (1,12).[277] The believers' status as children of God can be attained only through him (cf. 1,12; 20,17). We do not have access to the Father apart from Jesus. The purpose of Jesus' mission is not only to reveal the Father but also to establish an eternal relationship between the Father and the believers, who are his children, by giving eternal life to them. The Father is not known apart from Jesus but through and in relation to Jesus. Belief in Jesus, then, is ultimately belief in the Father. The highest form of belief is the recognition of the Father in his Son (20,28–29; cf. 14,7–11). We can experience God as the Father only through Jesus.

The risen Jesus is the meeting place of not only the Son but also of the Father and the Holy Spirit. He is not only the giver of the Holy Spirit but also the locus of the Father. By giving his disciples the access to the Father, the source of life, through the bestowal of the Spirit of truth, Jesus becomes "the way and the truth and the life" (14,6a). Indeed, John 14,6b is an invitation to believe in Jesus and to experience the fatherhood of God through the begetting of the Holy Spirit.

---

[276] Van der Watt, *An Introduction*, 51.
[277] Thompson, "The Living Father", 29.

Chapter VI

John 14,6 in the Context of "I Am"-Sayings

1. Introductory Remarks

The meaning and significance of John 14,6 is not limited to its immediate and near context. John 14,6 is an ἐγώ εἰμι-saying. Therefore, its meaning and significance are to be understood also in the context of the network of ἐγώ εἰμι-sayings in the Gospel. The use of the ἐγώ εἰμι formula is one of the most important characteristic features of John's Gospel.[1] Therefore, it has attracted much attention in the scholarly world.[2] The phrase ἐγώ εἰμι in all

---

[1] As H. Thyen, "Ich bin das Licht der Welt. Das Ich- und Ich-bin Sagen Jesu im Johannesevangelium", *Jahrbuch für Antike und Christentum 35* (1992), 20, remarks, "Der Autor des Johannesevangeliums hat seinem Werk mit den charakteristischen Ich-Bin-Worten ein unverwechselbares Profil verliehen und damit diese Redeform unvergeßlich gemacht". In the view of Ashton, *Understanding*, 127, ἐγώ εἰμι sayings are "miniature Gospels".

[2] For a detailed study of ἐγώ εἰμι-sayings in John's Gospel from various perspectives, see G. Macaskill, "Name Christology, Divine Aseity, and the I Am Sayings in the Fourth Gospel", *JTI* 12 (2018), 217–241; R. S. Wollenberg, "אני יי רפאך: A Short Note on Ἐγώ Εἰμι Sayings and the Dangers of a Translation Tradition", *NovT* 59 (2017), 20–26; P. N. Anderson, "The Origin and Development of the Johannine Ego Eimi Sayings in Cognitive-Critical Perspective", *JSHJ* 9 (2011), 139–206; S. Petersen, *Brot, Licht und Weinstock. Intertextuelle Analysen johanneischer Ich-bin-Worte* (Leiden 2008); idem, "Die Ich-bin-Worte als Metaphern am Beispiel der Lichtmetaphorik", *Imagery in the Gospel of John*, ed. J. Frey et al. (WUNT 200; Tübingen 2006), 121–138; O. L. Vereşa, "Study of the 'I Am' Phrases in John's Gospel", *Perichoresis* 6 (2008), 109–125; Cebulj, *Ich bin es*; C. H. Williams, *I Am He. The Interpretation of 'Anî Hû in Jewish and Early Christian Literature* (WUNT II 113; Tübingen 2000); Ball, *I Am*; H. Thyen, "Ich-bin Worte", *Reallexikon für Antike und Christentum 17* (1996), 147–213; idem, "Ich bin das Licht der Welt", 19–46; B. Hinrichs, *"Ich bin". Die Konsistenz des Johannes-Evangeliums in der Konzentration auf das Wort Jesu* (SBS 133; Stuttgart 1988); J. -A. Bühner, "The Exegesis of the Johannine 'I-Am' Sayings", *The Interpretation of John*, ed. J. Ashton (Edinburgh 1997), 207–218, originally published in Bühner, *Der Gesandte und sein Weg*, 166–180; A. Hajduk, "'Ego Eimi' bei Jesus und seine Messianität', *Communio Viatorum* 6 (1983), 55-60; Schnackenburg, *John*, II, 79–89; P. B. Harner, *The I am of the Fourth Gospel* (Philadelphia 1970); Brown, *John*, I, 533–538; A. Feuillet, "Les *ego eimi* christologiques du Quartrième Évangile: La Révélation enigmatique de l'être divine de Jésus dans Jean et les synoptiques", *RSR* 54 (1966), 5–22, 213–240; E. Schweizer, *Ego Eimi. Die religionsgeschichtliche Herkunft und theologische Bedeutung der johanneischen*

uses occurs 24 times in John's Gospel (Mark 3x; Matt 5x; Luke 4x). It is attributed to the mouth of Jesus 23 times referring to himself (Mark 2x; Matt 1x; Luke 2x) and once to the blind man (9,9).³ These ἐγώ εἰμι-sayings are to be distinguished from those statements in which Jesus uses the emphatic "I" (e.g., 5,36.43; 6,63; 7,29; 8,21–22.38.42; 9,39; 10,30; 12,46.49-50; 13,33.36, etc.), from the inverted form (ὅπου) εἰμὶ ἐγώ (7,34.36; 12,26; 14,3; 17,24), from the negative form ἐγώ οὐκ εἰμί (1,20; 8,23; 17,14.16; cf. 1,21.27; 3,28; 8,16; 16,32; 18,17.25) and from the use of ἐγώ and εἰμι in various word orders and combinations (9,5; 18,35.37).⁴ We consider ἐγώ εἰμι only in the mouth of Jesus in its bipartite form as the revelatory formula and the predicated ἐγώ εἰμι-sayings as a development of this formula.⁵

Bildreden, zugleich ein Beitrag zur Quellenfrage des vierten Evangeliums (Gottingen ²1965); H. Zimmermann, "Das absolute Ἐγώ εἰμι als die neutestamentliche Offenbarungsformel", *BZ* 4 (1960), 54–69; 266–276; G. Braumann and H. G. Link, "I Am", *NIDNTT*, II, 278–283; E. Stauffer, "Ἐγώ", *TDNT*, II, 342–354; S. Schulz, *Komposition und Herkunft der Johanneischen Reden* (Stuttgart 1960); P. J. Beveridge, "I Am in the Fourth Gospel", *The Expositor* 8 (1923), 418–425.

³ John uses ἐγώ εἰμι in a secular as well as in a revelatory sense. He does not see ἐγώ εἰμι exclusively as a revelatory formula. We should keep in mind that God speaks through human language and human medium. That the blind man speaks ἐγώ εἰμι is not an obstacle to its revelatory usage. The context reveals that in 9,9 ἐγώ εἰμι is used for self-identification. The blind man is compelled to say ἐγώ εἰμι in its everyday usage because of the enquiry in 9,8, "Is this not the man who used to sit and beg?" The predicate can and must be supplied from the question itself, e.g., like this, "I am the man who used to sit and beg". Ball, *I Am*, 22, says, "Neither the context of that saying nor its formulation point to the background, which makes the use of the phrase on Jesus' lips so profound".

⁴ The very fact that John uses the inverted form εἰμὶ ἐγώ is an indication that he does not regard it as a revelatory "formula". The expression ὅπου εἰμὶ ἐγώ refers to the location of Jesus' presence, whatever the meaning of that location may be. The meaning of εἰμὶ ἐγω is to be found in relation to ὅπου, and εἰμὶ ἐγώ has no significance apart from ὅπου. Therefore, ὅπου εἰμὶ ἐγώ does not refer to the identity of Jesus and does not belong to the category of ἐγώ εἰμι-formula. Jesus never utters ἐγώ οὐκ εἰμι, and this form also never appears in the LXX. Indeed, the negative confession of John the Baptist in 1,20 (ἐγώ οὐκ εἰμι) affirms and supports the positive confession by Jesus (ἐγώ εἰμι). The negative proclamation of John the Baptist is only an affirmation of Jesus' messiahship. For an explanation regarding the relationship between John 1,20 and other ἐγώ εἰμι-sayings, especially the one in 4,26, see E. D. Freed, "*Egō Eimi* in John 1,20 and 4,25", *CBQ* 41 (1979), 288–291. In 8,23; 17,14.16, where John is contrasting this world with the world above and explaining in dualistic terms Jesus' origin, there does not occur any revelatory formula.

⁵ Therefore, the "I"-style speeches, the negative form ἐγώ οὐκ εἰμι, the expression ὅπου εἰμὶ ἐγώ and the uses of ἐγώ and εἰμι in various word orders and combinations do not have any significance in our discussion. In the light of the preceding discussions, Laura Tack's view that the Johannine 'I am' is not a homogenised expression is not an adequate argument to deny the revelatory character of "I am". John has not used the "I am" formula in a systematic way with formal homogeneousness as a modern researcher expects. Tack accepts John 8,58 as an absolute "I am"-saying, when she states: "Only John 8,58 can be

2. Classification

In the discussion below, after classifying the various ἐγώ εἰμι-sayings in the Gospel, the possible source of the absolute ἐγώ εἰμι will be examined first. Then, all the ἐγώ εἰμι-sayings without and with images will be taken into account. Special attention will be given to the study of the shepherd discourse. This is due to the following reasons. The ἐγώ εἰμι-sayings in 10,7.9 stand in close relation to the ἐγώ εἰμι-saying in 14,6 and the image of gate has similar functions as the image of way. Moreover, there are altogether four ἐγώ εἰμι-sayings within the shepherd discourse. After examining all the ἐγώ εἰμι-sayings without and with images, the relation of the ἐγώ εἰμι-saying in 14,6 with all other ἐγώ εἰμι-sayings with and without images will be discussed. This study will help us to understand the significance of 14,6 in the context of all ἐγώ εἰμι-sayings in the Gospel.

2. Classification

The ἐγώ εἰμι-sayings in John can be variously classified.[6] They can be broadly divided into two groups: sayings without images (4,26; 6,20;

---

considered an absolute 'I am' word". As long as she cannot deny the absoluteness in 8,58, her interpretation is on a very shaky foundation. Moreover, following Petersen, *Brot, Licht und Weinstock*, 107, Tack has failed to explain the meaning and significance of John 8,59. See Tack, *John 14,6 in Light of Jewish-Christian Dialogue*, 266, 344.

[6] In the light of the ancient Greek and Oriental literature including the Old and New Testaments, Bultmann, *John*, 225, n. 3, classifies ἐγώ εἰμι-sayings into four formulas: i. the presentation formula which answers the question "who are you?" (Gen 17,1; 28,13; Rev 1,17); ii. the qualificatory formula which answers the question "what are you?" (Ezek 28,2.9; Isa 44,6.24; 45,5–7; 48,12); iii. the identification formula in which the speaker identifies himself with another person or object (John 11,25; 14,6); iv. the recognition formula in which ἐγώ is the predicate. Here the essential question is, "Who is the one who is expected, asked for, spoken to?" and its answer is, "I am he" (Isa 41,4; John 6,35.41.48.51; 8,12; 10,7.9.11.14; 15,1.5). Brown, *John*, I, 533–535, distinguishes three types of uses of ἐγώ εἰμι-sayings: i. the absolute use without predicate (8,24.28.58; 13,19); ii. the use where a predicate is understood but not expressed (6,20; 18,5); iii. the use with a predicate nominative (6,35.51; 8,12; 10,7.9.11.14; 11,25; 14,6; 15,1.5). On the borderline of this group, he includes 8,18 and 8,23. Schnackenburg, *John*, II, 79–81, finds four uses of ἐγώ εἰμι-sayings: i. the use of the formula with a metaphor (6,35.41.48.51; 8,12; 10,7.9.11.14; 11,25; 14,6; 15,1.5); ii. the absolute use (6,20; 8,24.28.58; 13,19; 18,5.6.8), here he sees in 6,20 and 18,5.6.8 the double functions of recognition and a unique expression of authority, evident from the epiphany on the lake and the collapse of the soldiers; iii. the passages where the formula does not occur in a pure form but with a nominalized participle (4,26; 8,18) or with a defining preposition (8,23); iv. two passages which have no connection with Jesus' self-identification (9,9; 18,35). Schnackenburg considers the texts under this group (including 1,20) irrelevant to a consideration of Jesus' particular form of expression, but he regards the usage with or without a metaphor (groups i and ii) as very rich and important.

8,18.24.28.58; 13,19; 18,5.6.8) and sayings with images (6,35.41.48.51; 8,12; 10,7.9.11.14; 11,25; 14,6; 15,1.5).[7] According to their grammatical forms, the ἐγώ εἰμι-sayings without images can be further classified into the following three categories:[8]

i. Sayings where ἐγώ εἰμι is immediately followed by a definite article and a present participle (4,26; 8,18).

ii. Grammatically absolute sayings where ἐγώ εἰμι stands alone (6,20; 8,58; 18.5.6.8).

iii. Grammatically absolute sayings which stand in a ὅτι-clause to express future fulfilment (8,24.28; 13,19).

The sayings of the first category (4,26; 8,18) seem to create a formal link between the ἐγώ εἰμι-sayings with images or predicate nominatives and the absolute ἐγώ εἰμι-sayings because in those sayings the participial clause acts grammatically as a predicate.[9]

3. Possible Sources and Background of ἐγώ εἰμι-Sayings[10]

At the very outset, it must be humbly accepted that one cannot know exactly what sources or backgrounds John had in mind when he employed the ἐγώ εἰμι-sayings. What can be suggested are only possibilities or probabilities. Here, one is concerned with the sources and backgrounds of the absolute ἐγώ εἰμι-sayings, which have influence upon the predicated ἐγώ εἰμι-sayings. It is noticed that the predicated ἐγώ εἰμι-sayings are found in ancient Oriental (Jewish and non-Jewish) and Hellenistic literature.[11] But it is very difficult to find in pagan literature parallels for the absolute use of ἐγώ εἰμι, as it is

---

[7] The ἐγώ εἰμι-sayings in 4,26 and 8,18 can be regarded as sayings without images. In 4,26, Jesus' words can be translated as, "I am, the one who speaks to you". The words ὁ λαλῶν σοι do not constitute an image but stand in apposition to ἐγώ εἰμι. In 8,18, the substantive participle ὁ μαρτυρῶν does not have the function of an image or metaphor. The verb μαρτυρέω is used here more literally than metaphorically.

[8] Cf. Ball, *I Am*, 168–169.

[9] Ball, *I Am*, 169.

[10] The difference between "sources" and "backgrounds" consists in the fact that while "sources" have a very specific meaning, "backgrounds" have a more general sense. By the term "sources", we refer to the writings or the vocabularies from which John's use of the absolute ἐγώ εἰμι might have originated. The term "backgrounds" refers more generally to those currents of thought in relation to which his use of ἐγώ εἰμι may be better understood, even if it was not derived from them. Cf. Harner, *The I Am*, 6.

[11] See the works of E. Norden, *Agnostos Theos. Untersuchungen zur Formengeschichte religiöser Rede* (Stuttgart [7]1996); Schweizer, *Ego Eimi*. For various arguments against the view that the Johannine ἐγώ εἰμι-sayings have their background in Hellenistic literature, especially in Gnosticism and Mandaism, see Petersen, *Brot, Licht und Weinstock*, 19–27; Cebulj, *Ich bin es*, 21–35; Ball, *I Am*, 163–166.

3. Possible Sources and Background of ἐγώ εἰμι-Sayings

found in the Gospel of John. The absolute use of ἐγώ εἰμι is not recorded in non-Jewish Greek texts, and it is also absent from the works of Josephus and Philo.[12] The contemporary scholarship prefers to seek the source and background for Johannine ἐγώ εἰμι-sayings in Jewish writings, especially in the Old Testament (Hebrew and LXX).[13] We can notice various models in the Old Testament as the source for the Johannine use of absolute ἐγώ εἰμι. The important ones are the following.

3.1 Exodus 3,14

The first model is God's self-revelation to Moses in Exod 3,14. When Moses enquires God's name, God says to him, אֶהְיֶה אֲשֶׁר אֶהְיֶה ... אֶהְיֶה שְׁלָחַנִי אֲלֵיכֶם ("I Am Who I Am...'I Am' has sent me to you"). In its context, the term אֶהְיֶה, which is the first person singular of the verb הָיָה ("to be") in its qal imperfect form, is understood to be the name of God. This is evident from the following clause אֶהְיֶה שְׁלָחַנִי אֲלֵיכֶם.[14] The LXX translates אֶהְיֶה ... אֶהְיֶה שְׁלָחַנִי אֲלֵיכֶם אֲשֶׁר אֶהְיֶה as ἐγώ εἰμι ὁ ὤν... ὁ ὤν ἀπέσταλκέν με πρὸς ὑμᾶς. The clause ἐγώ εἰμι ὁ ὤν stresses God's existence. It is difficult to say that "I Am" of Exod 3,14 is the direct source for the absolute use of ἐγώ εἰμι in the Gospel of John.[15] It is possible that the use of "I Am" as a divine name in the Hebrew of Exod 3,14 might have influenced the LXX translators of Deutero-Isaiah in

---

[12] The only exception is Philo's citation of the LXX Deut 32,39a in *De Posteritate Caini*, 167–168. See Williams, *I Am He*, 11–12. Zimmermann, "Das absolute Ἐγώ εἰμι", 55–60, also asserts that the absolute use of ἐγώ εἰμι is never noticeable in Hellenistic and mandaistic literature. After an examination of various Hellenistic texts, Harner, *The I Am*, 29, also concludes that we cannot look to the Hellenistic religious milieu as the source for the absolute use of ἐγώ εἰμι in John's Gospel.

[13] This trend is maintained even in comparatively later studies. E.g., Petersen, *Brot, Licht und Weinstock*; idem, "Die Ich-bin-Worte", 121–138; Williams, *I Am He*; Cebulj, *Ich bin es*; Ball, *I Am*; Thyen, "Ich-bin Worte", 147–214; idem, "Ich bin das Licht der Welt", 19–46. Ball, *I Am*, 20, suggests the following three points in support of the view that all ἐγώ εἰμι-sayings (attributed to Jesus) in the Gospel of John derive their meaning from the Old Testament and Judaism: i. Old Testament and Jewish concepts are explicitly alluded to in the context of ἐγώ εἰμι; ii. scholarship has become more and more conscious of the Jewish nature of the Gospel; iii. literary studies reveal that the predicateless and predicated ἐγώ εἰμι-sayings are to be interrelated in order to suggest a similar conceptual background.

[14] "I Am" of Exod 3,14 is considered to be a theological definition or etymology of God's name. See Harner, *The I Am*, 17. For an overview of the literary-critical, etymological and exegetical issues regarding Exod 3,14, see R. de Vaux, "The Revelation of the Divine Name YHWH", *Proclamation and Presence. Old Testament Essays in Honour of Gwynne Henton Davies*, ed. J. I. Durham and J. R. Porter (London 1970), 48–75.

[15] However, we cannot fully rule out an indirect influence of Exod 3,14 upon Johannine usage. Schnackenburg, *John*, II, 84, believes that Exod 3,14 is clearly behind the words of Jesus in John 8,58. In the view of N. Walker, אֲנִי הוּא is a deliberate echo of the use of אֶהְיֶה in Exod 3,14. See N. Walker, "Concerning *Hû'* and *'Ani Hû'* ", *ZAW* 74 (1962), 206.

their translation of אֲנִי הוּא as ἐγώ εἰμι.[16] About the influence of אֲנִי הוּא/ἐγώ εἰμι in Deutero-Isaiah upon the absolute use of ἐγώ εἰμι in John, we will discuss below.

3.2 אֲנִי הוּא and אֲנִי יְהוָה

The second model as source for the Johannine absolute use of ἐγώ εἰμι is the formula אֲנִי יְהוָה, which is considered to be a revelatory formula of the Old Testament.[17] The אֲנִי יְהוָה-sayings in various combinations[18] are found predominantly in Exod 6,2–6, the Decalogue (Exod 20/Deut 5), the Holiness Code (Lev 17–26), Ezekiel and Deutero-Isaiah. The formula אֲנִי יְהוָה occurs 132 times in the Old Testament and refers firstly to Yahweh's power and strength, secondly to his holiness and finally to his fidelity and mercy.[19] The formula is used mainly in the Old Testament with four functions:[20] i. as a revelatory formula in its strict sense – to state what and who God is (e.g., Gen 28,13; Exod 6,2.29; Ezek 20,5; Ps 81,11); ii. to confirm and to assure the authority of a divine saying (Exod 6,6.8; 12,12; 20,1–5; Lev 17–26; Num 3,13); iii. as the content and the object of knowledge, often accompanied with the verb יָדַע (Exod 6,7; 7,5; Deut 29,5; Jer 24,7; Ezek 6,7.13; 7,9); iv. to emphasize the uniqueness and exclusiveness of Yahweh. It is often found in the form of אֲנִי יְהוָה וְאֵין עוֹד, "I am the Lord, and there is no other" (Isa 45,5.6.18.21; cf. 45,22; 46,9; Hos 13,4; Joel 2,27).

---

[16] Harner, *The I Am*, 17. In spite of the various differences, there are significant points of contact between אֶהְיֶה אֲשֶׁר אֶהְיֶה and אֲנִי הוּא. An important point is the emphasis on the active and continuing presence of Yahweh. While אֶהְיֶה is to be understood within the context of God's promise of deliverance from Egypt (Exod 3,8.10.12.17), אֲנִי הוּא serves as the basis of Yahweh's claim to be the deliverer of his people from Babylon. See Williams, *I Am He*, 52–54.

[17] A. A. Diesel argues that "I am Yahweh"-sayings form the keyword of the monotheistic concept of God in the Old Testament. See A. A. Diesel, *Ich bin Yahwe. Der Aufstieg der Ich-bin-Jahwe-Aussage zum Schlüsselwort des alttestamentlichen Monotheismus* (WMANT 110; Neukirchen-Vluyn 2006). In the view of W. Zimmerli, *Gottes Offenbarung. Gesammelte Aufsätze zum Alten Testament* (TB 19; Munich 1963), 14, אֲנִי יְהוָה is a self-presentation formula (Selbstvorstellungsformel). But, in some contexts, it is also understood to be an exclusivity formula (Absolutheits-/Einzigkeits-/Ausschließlichkeitsformel). See D. Michel, *Studien zur Überlieferungsgeschichte alttestamentlicher Texte*, ed. A. Wagner (TB 93; Gütersloh 1997), 1–12; F. X. Sedlmeier, *Das Buch Ezechiel. Kapitel 1–24* (NSK.AT 21,1; Stuttgart 2002), I, 20, 308. For a history of interpretation of אֲנִי יְהוָה, see Diesel, *Ich bin Yahwe*, 13–36.

[18] For the various combinations of אֲנִי יְהוָה and their distribution in the whole Old Testament, see A. Murtonen, *A Philological and Literary Treatise on the Old Testament Divine Names* (Helsinki 1952); Diesel, *Ich bin Yahwe*, 7, 10–11.

[19] Murtonen, *A Philological and Literary Treatise*, 82, 89.

[20] See Zimmermann, "Das absolute Ἐγώ εἰμι", 61–66.

3. Possible Sources and Background of ἐγώ εἰμι-Sayings

The expression אֲנִי יְהוָה is variously translated in the LXX, e.g., κύριος (Ezek 20,5a), ἐγώ κύριος (Gen 28,13; Exod 6,2.29), ἐγώ εἰμι κύριος (Exod 7,5). What is striking is its rendering as ἐγώ εἰμι in Isa 45,18. This rendering is regularly maintained for the formula אֲנִי הוּא, which functions as a representative of אֲנִי יְהוָה, especially in Deutero-Isaiah (also in Deut 32,39). That אֲנִי הוּא represents אֲנִי יְהוָה becomes clear when we compare Isa 43,10 with Isa 45,18, where in the context of Yahweh's exclusivism and uniqueness both forms are translated as ἐγώ εἰμι. The אֲנִי הוּא can thus be regarded as an abbreviated form of אֲנִי יְהוָה and its other variant forms.[21] Many times אֲנִי הוּא appears in Deutero-Isaiah in the same context where אֲנִי יְהוָה or its variant form is used: 41,4; 43,10–11; 43,13–15; 46,4–9; cf. 51,12–15. In 41,4 and 48,12, אֲנִי יְהוָה and אֲנִי הוּא are immediately followed by the same designation of Yahweh, i.e., "the first" (רִאשׁוֹן) and "the last" (אַחֲרוֹן). Like אֲנִי הוּא, אֲנִי יְהוָה is also uttered by Yahweh when he speaks of his unique and exclusive existence as the Godhead (41,4; 42,8; 43,11; 45,5.6.18), as the Lord of history and the redeemer of Israel (42,6; 43,15; 45,3; 49,23.26) and as the creator of the world (44,24; 45,7). This implies that the LXX translators considered both formulas אֲנִי יְהוָה and אֲנִי הוּא as equivalent. It does not mean that ἐγώ εἰμι is always used as a sacred formula or as an absolute formula in the LXX.[22] We can say that the absolute ἐγώ εἰμι in the LXX of Deutero-Isaiah functions as a bridge between אֲנִי הוּא, which is a representative of אֲנִי יְהוָה, and the Johannine absolute ἐγώ εἰμι.[23] Therefore, the absolute ἐγώ εἰμι in the mouth of the Johannine Jesus can be regarded as a revelatory formula that has its origin and continuity from the Old Testament itself.

The significance of אֲנִי הוּא has well been accepted in the Johannine studies as the major key to interpret the absolute use of ἐγώ εἰμι in the Gospel.[24] The

---

[21] Cf. Harner, *The I Am*, 14–15.

[22] Here one has to be aware of the criticism of Schweizer, *Ego Eimi*, 22–24. However, it is not necessary, as Schweizer thinks, that ἐγώ εἰμι should be reserved only to God in order to consider its revelatory character and that the translators of the LXX should have used a different rendering for the revelatory formulas in order to distinguish it from the profane ἐγώ εἰμι. It seems that Schweizer thinks too rigidly. Here we have to keep in mind, as Zimmermann, "Das absolute Ἐγώ εἰμι", 266, points out, that the revelatory aspect of the formulas is more emphasized and used in its strict sense in the later Jewish writings than in the Old Testament itself.

[23] Zimmermann, "Das absolute Ἐγώ εἰμι", 270, writes, "Das absolute ἐγώ εἰμι im Munde Jesu ist die alttestamentliche Offenbarungsformel. Das bedeutet formal gesehen: von אֲנִי יְהוָה, wie die alttestamentliche Offenbarungsformel im hebräischen Text lautet, geht der Weg über אֲנִי הוּא, das an manchen Stellen als Ersatz für אֲנִי יְהוָה auftreten kann, zu dem absoluten ἐγώ εἰμι der LXX, das als Brücke für das ἐγώ εἰμι des NT zu gelten hat".

[24] The earliest attestations in critical studies are found in 1726 by F. A. Lampe, *Commentarius in Evangelium Joannis* (Amsterdam 1726) and after a centuary by J. C. K. Hofmann, *Der Schriftbeweis. Ein theologischer Versuch* (Nördingen 1857–1859). Some of the important proponents of this view in modern and current scholarship are Williams, *I Am*

expression אֲנִי הוּא is predominantly encountered in Deutero-Isaiah. In its bipartite form it is uttered only by Yahweh (Deut 32,39; Isa 41,4; 43,10.13; 46,4; 48,12). On three occasions it is immediately attached to a participle (Isa 43,25; 51,12; 52,6).[25] Only once it is attached to a finite verb, where the speaker is David (1 Chr 21,17). What is striking is that אֲנִי הוּא is uttered only by Yahweh in Deutero-Isaiah and that the LXX regularly translates אֲנִי הוּא as ἐγώ εἰμι.[26] It should be noted that הוּא (along with divine names) is used in many contexts to contrast Yahweh's existence with the non-existence of other gods or to emphasize his exclusive existence (e.g., 1 Kgs 8,60; 18,39; Deut 4,35.39; 7,9; 10,17; Josh 2,11; Pss 24,10; 100,3; 2 Chr 33,13). Therefore, אֲנִי הוּא is a reference to the unique and exclusive divinity of Yahweh.

There is a strong case to believe that אֲנִי הוּא in Deutero-Isaiah is an important possible source for the absolute use of ἐγώ εἰμι in John.[27] The אֲנִי הוּא is uttered by Yahweh alone and not by anyone else.[28] The first three occur-

---

He; Ball, *I Am*; Thyen, "Ich-bin Worte", 174–176; idem, "Ich bin das Licht der Welt", 24–32; Harner, *The I Am*; Schnackenburg, *John*, II, 79–89; Brown, *John*, I, 533–538; Zimmermann, "Das absolute Ἐγώ εἰμι"; J. Richter, *'Anî Hû und Ego Eimi. Die Offenbarungsformel 'Ich bin es' im Alten und Neuen Testament* (Dissertation, Erlangen 1956); E. Stauffer, *Jesus: Gestalt und Geschichte* (Bern 1957); idem, "Ἐγώ", 344; Dodd, *Interpretation*, 350. There are many who have taken this view as a standard position without entering into a detailed examination. E.g., R. Zimmermann, *Christologie der Bilder im Johannesevangelium. Die Christopoetik des vierten Evangeliums unter besonderer Berücksichtigung von Joh 10* (WUNT 171; Tübingen 2004), 125–126; Scott, *Sophia and the Johannine Jesus*, 149.

[25] It should be noted that in Isa 43,25 and 51,12 a longer, emphatic variant אָנֹכִי אָנֹכִי הוּא is employed.

[26] However, one should be aware of the complexity in the LXX translation. The LXX translates אֲנִי הוּא as ἐγώ εἰμι in Isa 41,4; 43,10 and 46,4. In Isa 52,6, אֲנִי הוּא is translated as ἐγώ εἰμι αὐτός. The longer variant אָנֹכִי אָנֹכִי הוּא is rendered ἐγώ εἰμι ἐγώ εἰμι in 43,25 and 51,12. It is specially notable that in Isa 45,18 אֲנִי יְהוָה is rendered as ἐγώ εἰμι. In Isa 46,4, ἐγώ εἰμι occurs twice, possibly due to a variant Hebrew reading. The אֲנִי הוּא of Isa 43,13; 48,12 is not translated in the LXX. While the Hebrew text has אֲנִי alone, it is rendered as ἐγώ εἰμι in Isa 47,8.10; Zeph 2,15, where the subjects are the cities of Babylon and Nineveh respectively. Cf. Harner, *The I Am*, 6–7. There is a view that the translators of the LXX in the later period of Biblical Hebrew (cf. Qoh 1,17; 2,23; 4,8), especially in the third and second centuries BCE, understood הוּא as performing the function of a copula. Cf. Williams, *I Am He*, 57; Harner, *The I Am*, 7. Walker, "Concerning *Hû'* ", 206, supports the view of regarding הוּא as a copula by arguing, "In view of the Aramaic and Syriac form הֲוָא 'be', one may assume that in early Hebrew a like form הֲוָא existed, of which the present participle would be הֹוֶא, 'being', 'existing'. As 'a being' it would signify 'he', but as an adjective 'existing', and after pronouns the present tense of 'be'".

[27] For a detailed discussion on various reasons for preferring אֲנִי הוּא of Deutero-Isaiah as the possible source for Johannine use of ἐγώ εἰμι, see Harner, *The I Am*, 7–15.

[28] It should be noted that when Babylon claims in Isa 47,8.10, "I am, and there is no one besides me", the author of Deutero-Isaiah regards it as a sign of presumptuous pride and an attempt to claim equality with Yahweh. He is actually contrasting the אֲנִי of Babylon with

3. Possible Sources and Background of ἐγώ εἰμι-Sayings

rences of אֲנִי הוּא (Isa 41,4; 43,10.13) within the context of two trial scenes between Yahweh and the other gods of the world (Isa 41,1–4; 43,8–13) express vehemently the exclusive monotheism. For Deutero-Isaiah, Yahweh is the only God and besides him there is no other god (44,6.8; 45,5.6.18.21–22; 46,9).[29] The gods of the world are nothing (אַיִן) before Yahweh and their work is also nothing (אֶפַע). Yahweh is the only Saviour of Israel (Isa 41,14; 43,14; 44,6.24; 47,4; 48,17; 49,7.26; 54,5.8). It is אָנֹכִי אָנֹכִי הוּא who blots out and forgives their sins (43,25) and consoles them (51,12). The phrase אֲנִי הוּא signifies not only a statement of Yahweh's exclusive and eternal existence but also his promise of salvation to Israel (46,4). We find Yahweh's assurance of salvation in the form of two salvation oracles in 41,8–13 and 41,14–16. The designation is also used to point out that Yahweh is the creator of the world (48,12–13; cf. 51,12–13). Yahweh utters אֲנִי הוּא in the context of Israel's despair and lament. Through the statement אֲנִי הוּא he is calling Israel to be his witness and to believe (אמן/πιστεύω) in him (43,10), to listen (שׁמע/ἀκούω) to him (46,3; 48,12) and is challenging them to respond to him in faith (51,1–12; 52,1–6). The יְשׁוּעָה that Yahweh promises is not only for Israel but for all the world (49,6; 52,10).

In the Jewish literature of the later period of ancient Judaism (200 BCE–100 CE),[30] we find the use of terms like אֲנִי, הוּא, and אֲנִי וְהוּא, which are considered as surrogates for Yahweh and variants of אֲנִי הוּא in the Old Testa-

---

the אֲנִי הוּא of Yahweh. He attributes only הוּא to Babylon and does not attribute אֲנִי הוּא to anyone other than Yahweh.

[29] It is possible to assume that the uniqueness and exclusiveness of Yahweh in Deutero-Isaiah are inspired by Deut 32,39. See Williams, *I Am He*, 42–50.

[30] For a good discussion on the use of divine names in relation to אֲנִי הוּא in the Jewish literature of later ancient Judaism, see Williams, *I Am He*, 55–213; Harner, *The I Am*, 17–26. The work of Catrin H. Williams is mainly intended to consider the meaning and status of אֲנִי הוּא in the poetry of Deutero-Isaiah, to carry out a thorough investigation of the interpretation of אֲנִי הוּא in the ancient Jewish traditions and to use the implications of those interpretaions for the study of ἐγώ εἰμι uttered by Jesus in Mark and John. She has tried to trace the development in the application of אֲנִי הוּא in ancient Jewish traditions with the help of a substantial amount of material assembled from targumic and rabbinic texts. It is good to pay attention to some of her findings, which are relevant for our study of the source and background of absolute use of ἐγώ εἰμι. Williams (p. 178) points out that the midrashic traditions "interpret the Deutero-Isaianic usage of אֲנִי הוּא, either implicitly or explicitly, as God's own pronouncement of his sovereignty. This reveals a clear continuity with the application of the expression אֲנִי הוּא in its original Deutero-Isaianic context, and it also parallels the rabbinic interpretation of the solemn self-declaration אֲנִי אֲנִי הוּא in Deut 32,39". Williams (p. 196) also notices that the midrashic traditions "attest the citation of Deut 32,39 and analogous Deutero-Isaianic declarations as decisive proof-texts in which אֲנִי הוּא [אֲנִי] is viewed as a self-contained expression with no referent identifiable from its immediate context".

ment.³¹ These terms may have their own influence in providing a broader Jewish background for the Johannine use of absolute ἐγώ εἰμι. In short, it can be said that the Jewish literature outside the Hebrew Bible as a whole supports (or at least is not against) finding in the Deutero-Isaianic use of אני הוא and in its LXX counterpart the possible source behind the Johannine use of absolute ἐγώ εἰμι. Even though the majority of scholars prefers the influence of Deutero-Isaiah upon the Johannine absolute use of ἐγώ εἰμι-sayings, there are some who seek to find the influence of Wisdom literature. Their views will be briefly discussed now.

3.3 "I"-Style Speeches in Wisdom Literature

The third model suggested as the source for Johannine absolute ἐγώ εἰμι-sayings is the "I"-style speeches in the Wisdom literature, particularly in Proverbs and Sirach.³² In comparison with other revelatory formulas in the rest of the Old Testament, they have very less revelatory character because of the lack of special revelation from God during the period of their formation.³³ In fact, there is no suitable parallel for the "I"-style speeches in the rest of the Old Testament. We should, therefore, notice the difference between the "I"-style speeches in Proverbs/Sirach and the revelatory formulas in the rest of the Old Testament. In the Old Testament, the revelatory formulas like אני יהוה and אני הוא are different from the "I"-style speeches because they make a claim for revelation in history and for the divine will, but the "I"-style speeches in Proverbs and Sirach are rather self-descriptive in a reflective,

---

³¹ Harner, *The I Am*, 18–22. Williams, *I Am He*, 213, proposes that "the distinctive usage of אני הוא in Deut 32,39 and the poetry of Deutero-Isaiah may have been a significant factor in the development of the use of הוא as a designation for God during the Second Temple period, and that this development contributed, in turn, to the formulation of יהו[ה] אני as an interpretation of יי אנא". The phrase יי אנא is said to have been pronounced as יהו[ה] אֲנִי or possibly as אֲנִי הוּא. See *m.Sukk* 4:5; cf. Williams, *I Am He*, 206–207. Harner, *The I Am*, 22–23, indicates that there is some evidence to show that אני הוא was used liturgically during worship in the Jerusalem temple because the Levites are said to have sung the song of Moses (Deut 32) on the day of Sabbath of the feast of Tabernacles.

³² See K. Kundzins, *Charakter und Ursprung der johanneischen Reden* (Acta Universitatis Latviensis; Series Theologica 1.4; Riga 1939), 185–293. Some authors who are attracted to the "I"-style speeches in Wisdom literature for the study of the metaphorical (predicated) ἐγώ εἰμι-sayings are Petersen, *Brot, Licht und Weinstock*; idem, "Die Ich-bin-Worte", 121–138; Cebulj, *Ich bin es*; Scott, *Sophia and the Johannine Jesus*, 116–131.

³³ H. Zimmermann makes a distinction between "I"-form and "I"-style speeches and points out that the "I"-style speeches are used in the Old Testament only in Proverbs and Sirach. He remarks, "So kann auch die Offenbarungsformel dieser Stilart nicht zugeordnet werden, obwohl auf einen ersten Blick manches darauf schließen lassen könnte; vielmehr ist es so, dass die Offenbarungsformel da zurückweicht, bzw. ganz schwindet, wo der Ich-Stil sich in den Vordergrund drängt". See Zimmermann, "Das absolute Ἐγώ εἰμι", 65–66.

theological style.³⁴ There is not a single occurrence of ἐγώ εἰμι in Proverbs, Wisdom, Sirach and Qoheleth, and there is not a single absolute ἐγώ εἰμι-saying in the entire Wisdom literature. Therefore, the Wisdom literature cannot be regarded as the source or background for the Johannine absolute use of ἐγώ εἰμι.³⁵

3.4 Synoptic Tradition³⁶ and Johannine ἐγώ εἰμι

In the Synoptic Gospels, Jesus is presented as using ἐγώ εἰμι with an explicit predicate only in Matthew 24,5. There are eight occurrences of predicateless ἐγώ εἰμι-sayings in the Synoptic Gospels. Except two (Matt 26,22.25), where a predicate from the context (one who will betray Jesus) is clearly understood, all are attributed to Jesus.³⁷ They are found on three occasions: Jesus' reference to false prophets (Mark 13,6; Luke 21,8; cf. Matt 24,5), Jesus' reply during the trial (Mark 14,62; Luke 22,70) and Jesus' walking on the waters (Mark 6,50; Matt 14,27). In the first two instances, it is possible to supply a predicate from the context.³⁸ In the third instance, at a first glance the ἐγώ εἰμι seems to be a formula for self-identification. But the context of Jesus' walking over the waters provides a revelatory character to ἐγώ εἰμι. The ἐγώ εἰμι here functions as the vehicle, which enables him to reveal his identity as the one who exercises God's power to walk on the sea.³⁹ In the Old Testament, Yahweh alone has sovereign control over the waters (Job 9,8; 38,16; Hab 3,15; Sir 24,5–6; Pss 74,12–14; 77,16–20). In Deutero-Isaiah, Yahweh's utterance of אֲנִי הוּא/ἐγώ εἰμι in 43,10.13.25; 51,12 is also associated with his

---

³⁴ Cf. R. E. Murphy, *Wisdom Literature: Job, Proverbs, Ruth, Canticles, Ecclesiastes and Esther* (FOTL 13; Grand Rapids 1981), 51.

³⁵ Scott, *Sophia and the Johannine Jesus*, 148–149, who made a detailed analysis of the influence of Wisdom/Sophia in the Gospel of John, acknowledges that ἐγώ εἰμι is used in an absolute form in 4,26; 6,20; 8,24.28.58; 13,19; 18,5.6.8 and asserts without hesitation, "Undoubtedly John's adoption of the ἐγώ εἰμι formula *must* owe something to the Old Testament tradition of the divine name, firstly in Exod 3,14, but more explicitly in Deutero-Isaiah". However, we need not disregard the possible influence of Wisdom upon the Johannine use of various images in the predicated form of ἐγώ εἰμι-sayings. Cf. Scott, *Sophia and the Johannine Jesus*, 116–131.

³⁶ For a detailed study of the ἐγώ εἰμι in the Synoptic tradition, see Anderson, "The Origin and Development of the Johannine Ego Eimi Sayings", 139–206; Williams, *I Am He*, 214–254; Harner, *The I Am*, 30–36.

³⁷ We do not take into account here the ἐγώ εἰμι-sayings of the risen Jesus in Luke 24,36, witnessed only by some manuscripts and also ἐγώ εἰμι αὐτός in Luke 24,39. The sayings attributed to the risen Jesus are also found in Acts 9,5; 22,8; 26,15; Rev 1,17; 2,23; 22,16.

³⁸ We may assume that Matthew and Luke show little interest in the absolute use of ἐγώ εἰμι. It is Mark or the tradition that he uses that shows some interest in the absolute ἐγώ εἰμι.

³⁹ Williams, *I Am He*, 252.

sovereignty over the creation, natural powers and waters (Isa 43,2.16–17; 51,10). A reading of the Synoptic tradition makes it clear that the ἐγώ εἰμι-formula is not a pure Johannine invention.[40] John has used an existing tradition (Synoptic or other) where he found the absolute ἐγώ εἰμι and has given it much emphasis in the light of the Old Testament revelatory formula, especially אֲנִי הוּא/ἐγώ εἰμι in Deutero-Isaiah.[41]

4. Ἐγώ εἰμι without Images

In our classification of ἐγώ εἰμι-sayings, we have already mentioned that ἐγώ εἰμι in 4,26; 6,20; 8,18.24.28.58; 13,19; 18,5.6.8 is without images. Except 4,26 and 8,18, in all other instances ἐγώ εἰμι is grammatically absolute because in these instances ἐγώ εἰμι stands independently without a predicate. We may distinguish between two uses of ἐγώ εἰμι, everyday use and absolute use, even if ἐγώ εἰμι is grammatically absolute. If a predicate can be supplied from the context, then ἐγώ εἰμι has an everyday use. But if a predicate noun or pronoun cannot be supplied from the context, we should regard the usage in an absolute sense. In some instances, a double usage is also possible. In our investigation into the possible sources and background for the absolute ἐγώ εἰμι in John, we have reaffirmed that the revelatory formula אֲנִי הוּא/ἐγώ εἰμι in Deutero-Isaiah is a valid source behind the formulation of Johannine absolute ἐγώ εἰμι-sayings. We shall now examine briefly how John has used the ἐγώ εἰμι-sayings without images (the absolute ἐγώ εἰμι-sayings) and the significance of his usage in the light of the revelatory formula אֲנִי הוּא/ἐγώ εἰμι in Deutero-Isaiah.

---

[40] Williams, *I Am He*, 216, views that since all three accounts of Jesus' walking on the water record the same words, ἐγώ εἰμι, μὴ φοβεῖσθε, there is the possibility of a core tradition, even though in Mark ἐγώ εἰμι is preceded by θαρσεῖτε. G. L. Parsenios, "Defining and Debating Divine Identity in Mark and John: The Influence of Classical Language and Literature", *John's Transformation of Mark*, ed. E-M. Becker et al. (London 2021), 67–76, argues that the Gospel of John has fully developed the use of ἐγώ εἰμι, which was introduced by Mark in a basic fashion. With a focus on the plausible historical origin, development, and presentation of the Johannine "I am"-sayings as informed by the Synoptic traditions, Anderson, "The Origin and Development of the Johannine Ego Eimi Sayings", 139–206, has pointed out a good deal of similarity between the absolute "I am" sayings in John and the Synoptics and between the Johannine "I am"- metaphors and imagery used by the Synoptic Jesus.

[41] Brown, *John*, I, 538, comments, "Rather than creating from nothing, Johannine theology may have capitalized on a valid theme of the early tradition".

4.1 Ἐγώ εἰμι Addressed to the Samaritan Woman (4,26)

Jesus' utterance of ἐγώ εἰμι in 4,26 is the first and also the only occurrence of the expression communicated to an individual. It has a two-level narrative strategy or a double function.[42] At a first glance, it is clear that Jesus identifies himself as the Messiah because it is possible to supply the predicate Μεσσίας from the context (4,25). But the question is why Jesus does not say ἐγώ εἰμι ὁ Μεσσίας instead of ἐγώ εἰμι, ὁ λαλῶν σοι. Jesus' words are not an answer to a question as to be found in 9,8–9. The clause ὁ λαλῶν σοι is not really a predicate as it appears. It stands in apposition to the subject ἐγώ and can be separated from ἐγώ εἰμι.[43] At a deeper level, Jesus' words ἐγώ εἰμι, ὁ λαλῶν σοι are reminiscent of ἐγώ εἰμι αὐτὸς ὁ λαλῶν (אֲנִי־הוּא הַמְדַבֵּר) in Isaiah 52,6.[44] In this respect, John presents Jesus as the one who speaks like Yahweh. In the Gospel, Jesus is presented as the Word who is God, and his words are identified with those of God/his Father (1,1; 3,34; 8,28; 14,10.24; 17,8). Thus, the formula ἐγώ εἰμι in 4,26 seems to function as a link between Jesus' words and Yahweh's words in Isa 52,6 and points out his claim to be the unique revelatory and salvific presence of God.[45]

Yet other important links can be detected between John 4,25–26 and Isa 43,9–10 and between John 4,42 and Isa 43,11. Jesus' utterance of ἐγώ εἰμι in 4,26 is preceded by the Samaritan woman's belief that the Messiah will reveal (ἀναγγέλλω) all things (4,25). Yahweh's utterance of ἐγώ εἰμι in Isa 43,10 is preceded by rhetorical questions, which imply that only Yahweh is able to reveal (ἀναγγέλλω) what is to come before it actually happens (43,9; cf. 43,12; 46,10; 48,3.5).[46] When Jesus says, ἐγώ εἰμι, ὁ λαλῶν σοι, he im-

---

[42] Cf. G. R. O'Day, *Revelation in the Fourth Gospel. Narrative Mode and Theological Claim* (Philadelphia 1986), 49–92.

[43] Cf. Harner, *The I Am*, 46; William, *I Am He*, 265.

[44] See Harner, *The I Am*, 46–47; Ball, *I Am*, 179; Young, "A Study of the Relation of Isaiah", 224.

[45] After examining the parallel relationship between Deutero-Isaianic and Johannine passages, Williams, *I Am He*, 265, asserts, "The identification of thematic links between John 4,25–26 and the LXX Isaiah in terms of their vocabulary of revelation and salvation indicates that there is a strong case for arguing that the Fourth Evangelist is deliberately playing on the two-level meaning of ἐγώ εἰμι when Jesus pronounces these words for the first time during his ministry". O'Day, *Revelation*, 72, regards ἐγώ εἰμι in 4,26 as an absolute occurrence totally independent of Μεσσίας, one which enables Jesus to identify himself as God's revealer, the sent one of God. For various reasons and arguments for reading 4,26 in the absolute sense and for the discussion about the relation between this verse and Isaiah 52,6, see E. Stauffer, *Jesus and His Story* (London 1960), 152; Williams, *I Am He*, 257–266; Harner, *The I Am*, 46–47; Ball, *I Am*, 179–181; F. J. Moloney, *Belief in the Word. Reading John 1–4* (Minneapolis 1993), 155–156.

[46] The term ἀναγγέλλω is characteristic of Isaiah. The largest number of occurrences of ἀναγγέλλω in the LXX is found in Isaiah (57x). The verb is used to designate a very significant function of God in contrast to false gods and false prophets of foreign nations. God

plicitly acknowledges that he is the revealer of "all things" (ἅπαντα) as the Samaritan woman expects (v. 25). This is confirmed through the witness of the woman before the Samaritans that he has told her "all things" (πάντα) that she had done (vv. 29.39). Another parallelism can be noticed in the same context between Yahweh's role as the only Saviour (Isa 43,11) and Jesus' role as the Saviour of the world (John 4,42). Yahweh wants to convince the exiles of his claim to exclusive divinity by demonstrating his salvific acts in the past (Isa 41,4; 43,12; 51,10) as the basis for his future manifestation as their Saviour (Isa 41,14; 43,3.13; 46,4).[47] He declares, ἐγὼ ὁ θεός καὶ οὐκ ἔστιν πάρεξ ἐμοῦ σῴζων, "I am God; and beside me there is no Saviour" (Isa 43,11). In the Gospel, Jesus is declared to be the Saviour of the world by the Samaritans (John 4,42). If John believes that Yahweh is "the only Saviour/the only one who can save" (וְאֵין מִבַּלְעָדַי מוֹשִׁיעַ/οὐκ ἔστιν πάρεξ ἐμοῦ σῴζων) and that Jesus is the "Saviour of the world" (ὁ σωτὴρ τοῦ κόσμου), we should then conclude that John is identifying Jesus functionally with Yahweh.[48] In short, when we look at John 4,26 and its context in the light of the revelatory formula ἐγώ εἰμι in Isa 43,10; 52,6, we have to admit that John is referring to the divinity in Jesus.[49]

4.2 Ἐγώ εἰμι Addressed to the Disciples on the Waters (6,20)

In 6,20, Jesus reveals himself to his frightened disciples on the Sea of Galilee saying, Ἐγώ εἰμι, μὴ φοβεῖσθε (cf. Mark 6,50; Matt 14,27). At a first glance, the ἐγώ εἰμι is a formula of identification or recognition, making known to the disciples that it is he whom they know. At the same time, their mode of formulation, the Old Testament background and the miraculous atmosphere point to a deeper meaning of God's presence and salvific activity.[50] In the Old

---

challenges the pagan idols to demonstrate their reality and power by announcing events that are to come before they actually occur. See Young, "A Study of the Relation of Isaiah", 224.

[47] Williams, *I Am He*, 263.

[48] The expression "the Saviour of the world" like "only Saviour" can involve an element of exclusivism if we admit that there cannot be two Saviours of the world at a time, just as there cannot be two Gods at a time.

[49] Scholars have already seen the reference to Jesus' divinity in the ἐγώ εἰμι-saying in John 4,26 even without a reference to the texts in Deutero-Isaiah. E.g., Brown, *John*, I, 172, says, "It is not impossible that this use is intended in the style of divinity". Beasley-Murray, *John*, 62, comments, "For the Evangelist, however, the formula has the overtone of the absolute being of God". Schnackenburg, *John*, I, remarks, "'The Messiah' can be easily supplied from the context. But in the mind of the evangelist, it must already suggest the absolute terms in which Jesus reveals his divine being". Also see Ball, *I Am*, 180; O'Day, *John*, 568.

[50] The revelatory character of Jesus' walking over the sea and of his words is already acknowledged by scholars. E.g., G. R. O'Day, "John 6,15–21: Jesus Walking on Water as Narrative Embodiment of Johannine Christology", *Critical Readings of John 6*, ed. R. A.

Testament, the command "Do not fear" (μὴ φοβεῖσθε) is often associated with the assurance or the presence of God.[51] There are also instances in which God's command not to fear is accompanied by ἐγώ εἰμι (e.g., Gen 26,24; 46,3; Jer 1,8.17; 46,28 [LXX 26,28]; 42,11 [LXX 49,11]).

In Isa 43,1, the command not to fear is immediately followed by the notion of God's deliverance of Israel, μὴ φοβοῦ ὅτι ἐλυτρωσάμην σε. God promises that when they pass through the waters, he will be with them (43,2, καὶ ἐὰν διαβαίνῃς δι' ὕδατος μετὰ σοῦ εἰμι). In v. 3, God is presented as their Saviour, ἐγὼ κύριος ὁ θεός σου ὁ ἅγιος Ισραηλ ὁ σῴζων σε. The similarity between John 6,20 and Isa 43,5 is very noteworthy in such a context: Ἐγώ εἰμι, μὴ φοβεῖσθε (John 6,20); μὴ φοβοῦ ὅτι μετὰ σοῦ εἰμι (Isa 43,5; cf. 41,10). A few verses after this promise, there is a significant ἐγω εἰμι utterance in 43,10, which has great impact on John 8 (cf. MT Isa 43,13). The ἐγώ εἰμι in 6,20, however, also reflects the influence of Isa 51,12. It is like the God of Israel, their Saviour, that Jesus comes to the disciples on the waters showing his capacity to dominate the chaotic sea and to save those in distress and fear (John 6,18–19; cf. Mark 6,48; Matt 14,24) with the command "Do not fear".[52] In short, the Old Testament background to Jesus' utterance ἐγώ

Culpepper (BIS 22; Leiden 1997), 149–159; J. P. Heil, *Jesus Walking on the Sea. Meaning and Gospel Functions of Matt 14,22–33; Mark 6,45–52 and John 6,15b–21* (AB 87; Rome 1981); D. A. Lee, *The Symbolic Narratives of the Fourth Gospel. The Interplay of Form and Meaning* (JSNTSS 95; Sheffield 1994), 134; Williams, *I Am He*, 214–228; Ball, *I Am*, 181–185; Richter *'Anî Hû und Ego Eimi*, 64; Stauffer, *Jesus and His Story*, 137; Schnackenburg, *John*, II, 27, 80; Brown, *John*, I, 255–256, 533–534; Dodd, *Interpretation*, 345, etc. O'Day, "Jesus Walking on Water", 155, says, "The phrase, ἐγώ εἰμι, which was found in the tradition and which is appropriate as an identification formula in its Matthean and Markan contexts, is transformed and given its special Johannine meaning in John 6,20. The ἐγώ εἰμι is a revelatory formula here, not a formula of simple identification. The disciples in John do not need to be told that it is Jesus who walks on the water; they already know that. Rather, they need revealed to them the meaning of what they see: how is it possible that Jesus walks across the water. This revelation is at the heart of Jesus' words in 6,20".

[51] The verb φοβέω is preceded by the negative particle μή 88 times in the LXX to form a negative command. Of the 66 occurrences in the Old Testament (Deutero-Canonical/apocryphal books not included), 36 appear in the mouth of God or of an angel, and in a further 12 instances, the reason given not to fear is the presence of God. See Ball, *I Am*, 181–182.

[52] Nevertheless, it is to be noted that John does not emphasize the aspect of rescue in his narrative like other evangelists. He does not say that "the disciples are struggling against an adverse wind" (cf. 6,18) and that "the wind ceases when Jesus enters the boat" (cf. 6,21) as it is found in the Synoptic Gospels (Mark 6,48.51; Matt 14,24.32). Here the reader should not pay attention to what might have happened in the story in the light of the Synoptic tradition, but to John's way of presenting that story. Hence, O'Day, "Jesus Walking on Water", 153, remarks, "The Johannine story of Jesus walking on water is a story of theophany, not rescue. It is a story of the revelation of the divine in Jesus".

εἰμι, μὴ φοβεῖσθε provides a theological explanation for his ability to walk on the sea because no human being can walk on the waters.

4.3 Ἐγώ εἰμι *Addressed to the Jews (8,18.24.28.58)*

The ἐγώ εἰμι-sayings in chapter 8 are placed within the context of Jesus' conflict with the Jews in Jerusalem at the time of the feast of Tabernacles (7,14-8,59). The saying in 8,18 is formally similar to 4,26.[53] In this verse, Jesus describes himself as the one who witnesses about himself. It is possible to see a relation between this verse and the contents in Isa 43,9–10, especially in the LXX.[54] The analogous judicial (trial) context of Deutero-Isaianic and Johannine passages is quite remarkable here.[55] The setting of the confrontation between Jesus and the Jews is reminiscent of the opposition between Yahweh and the foreign nations and their gods as well as the trial speech in Isa 43,8–13 (cf. 41,1–4; 44,6–8; Deut 32,37–42), in which both parties confront each other in the presence of witnesses who are gathered to establish the identity of the supreme God.[56]

Jesus' claim to be the light of the world prompts the Jews to question the validity of his witness (8,12–13). Their accusation against Jesus is that his witness is not true (οὐκ ἔστιν ἀληθής). This is reminiscent of Isa 43,9 where Yahweh calls upon the nations to bring witnesses who will verify the claims made on behalf of their gods and declare, "It is true" (ἀληθής). Jesus argues that his witness is true (ἀληθής) because he knows where he has come from and where he goes (8,14). He defends the validity of his witness by claiming that the Father who sent him (ὁ πέμψας με) bears witness to him (8,18; cf.

---

[53] But there is a difference in function because unlike ὁ λαλῶν σοι in 4,26, the clause ὁ μαρτυρῶν περὶ ἐμαυτοῦ in 8,18 does not have an appositive role.

[54] Scholars have already noticed similarities between Isa 42–43 and John 8. E.g., J. C. Coetzee, "Jesus' Revelation in the *Ego Eimi* Sayings in John 8 and 9", *A South African Perspective on the New Testament*, ed. J. H. Petzer and P. J. Hartin (Leiden 1988), 171, makes a comparison between John 8–9 and Isa 42–43 and asserts that "Jesus' absolute *Ego Eimi* utterances in John 8 deliberately refer to the prophecies of Isaiah 42–43". Blenkinsopp, *Isaiah 40–55*, 224, points out that a messianic allusion underlies the LXX text of Isa 43,10 and recognizes linguistic and thematic links between this text and the scene of the baptism of Jesus (Mark 1,9–11; Matt 3,17; Luke 3,21–22) and the ἐγώ εἰμι uttered by the Jesus of the Fourth Gospel. Also see Hamilton, "The Influence of Isaiah", 155–156; Hanson, *The Prophetic Gospel*, 119–122; Thyen, "Ich bin das Licht der Welt", 24–25; Williams, *I Am He*, 266–283; Ball, *I Am*, 185–198; Harner, *The I Am*, 39–45.

[55] The analogous setting of trial has already been recognized by scholars. E.g., see A. T. Lincoln, "Trials, Plots and Narrative of the Fourth Gospel", *JSNT* 56 (1994), 3–30; A. A. Trites, *The New Testament Concept of Witness* (SNTSMS 31; Cambridge 1977); J. Blank, *Krisis. Untersuchungen zur johanneischen Christologie und Eschatologie* (Freiburg 1964).

[56] Cf. Williams, *I Am He*, 271–272.

5,27).⁵⁷ It is notable that in Isa 43,10, along with his chosen servant, Yahweh too is a witness.⁵⁸ In fact, the context of Isa 43,8–13 points out a far more profound theological statement than one of judicial verification because the issue at stake is the identity of the true God.⁵⁹ Therefore, Isa 43,10 declares, "Be my witnesses; I too am a witness, says the Lord God, and the servant whom I have chosen so that you may know and believe and understand that I am" (γένεσθέ μοι μάρτυρες κἀγὼ μάρτυς λέγει κύριος ὁ θεός καὶ ὁ παῖς ὃν ἐξελεξάμην ἵνα γνῶτε καὶ πιστεύσητε καὶ συνῆτε ὅτι ἐγώ εἰμι).⁶⁰ Similarly, the issue at stake in John 8 is indeed the true identity of Jesus (8,25, ἔλεγον οὖν αὐτῷ, Σὺ τίς εἶ;), which is further explained in 8,24.28.58 in the form of ἐγώ εἰμι.

In vv. 24.28, no antecedent can be supplied for Jesus' utterance of ἐγώ εἰμι.⁶¹ In both verses, ἐγώ εἰμι is presented as the object of belief (v. 24) and knowledge (v. 28). It is commonly acknowledged that אֲנִי הוּא lies at the heart of Jesus' pronouncements in vv. 24.28.⁶² Jesus' utterance of ἐγώ εἰμι here is reminiscent of the ἐγώ εἰμι in LXX Isa 43,10, ἵνα γνῶτε καὶ πιστεύσητε καὶ συνῆτε ὅτι ἐγώ εἰμι.⁶³ Just as in John 8,24.28, the ἐγώ εἰμι in Isa 43,10 is the object of belief (πιστεύω) and knowledge (γινώσκω).⁶⁴ Important clues

---

[57] Williams, *I Am He*, 272, n. 59, believes that ἐγώ εἰμι ὁ μαρτυρῶν περὶ ἐμαυτοῦ in v. 18 may well form a deliberate expansion of ἐγώ εἰμι (cf. LXX Isa 43,25; 51,12; 52,6), otherwise it would take the form ἐγώ μαρτυρῶ. Cf. J.-P., Charlier, "L'exégèse johannique d'un précepte légal: Jean 8,17", *RB* 67 (1960), 513.

[58] Ball, *I Am*, 186, argues that when Jesus claims to be the witness, he seems to take on the role of the servant of the Lord who is called to be a light to the nations (cf. Isa 42,6; John 8,12).

[59] Williams, *I Am He*, 272.

[60] This translation is according to A. Pietersma and B. G. Wright (ed.), *A New English Translation of the Septuagint* (Oxford 2007), 857.

[61] Beasley-Murray, *John*, 125, describes John 8,24 as the most obscure sentence in the Gospel.

[62] For more scholarly views, see the literature given above on p. 308, n. 54.

[63] It is Yahweh's exclusive claim to be the only God and the only Saviour of Israel in the immediately following clauses (Isa 43,10c–11; cf. v. 13) that determines the meaning and significance of ἐγώ εἰμι (אֲנִי הוּא). Yahweh is the only Saviour because he is the only God. The Johannine Jesus seems to take up the words which, in the context of Isaiah, express the exclusive claim of Yahweh to be the Saviour of Israel. According to John, Jesus is given the exclusive soteriological function which, in Isaiah, is reserved for Yahweh alone (cf. John 3,17; 4,42; 10,9).

[64] Ball, *I Am*, 191–192, admits, along with Isa 43,10, the possibility of an influence of the recognition formula "to know that I am Yahweh" in the Old Testament on John 8,28 and thinks that the expression "to know that I am he" in Isa 43,10 is synonymous with the recognition formula "to know that I am Yahweh" in Deutero-Isaiah (Isa 45,3.6.7; 49,23.26; cf. Exod 6,7; 10,2; Ezek 25,7). Cf. C. Westermann, *Isaiah 40–66. A Commentary* (Philadelphia 1969), 123; W. Zimmerli, "Knowledge of God According to the Book of Ezekiel", *I Am Yahweh*, ed. W. Brueggemann (Atlanta 1982), 39–63.

to understand the significance of ἐγώ εἰμι in 8,24.28 are given by the following verses after each utterance of ἐγώ εἰμι, where Jesus speaks about his relationship with the Father (vv. 26–27; 28b–29).[65] Jesus' declaration in v. 24 warns his audience that they will die in their sins unless they believe that he reveals the Father and fulfils his salvific plans. It also points out that belief in him will lead to the forgiveness of their sins (cf. Isa 43,24–25) and to the bestowal of eternal life.[66] The lifting up of Jesus, which will manifest his unity with the Father (vv. 28–29), is to lead to the recognition that his ἐγώ εἰμι-saying discloses his unique identity as the manifestation of God in the world and as the revealer of divine glory in the hour of glorification (cf. 13,19; 18,5–8).[67] Therefore, Jesus' unity with the Father is the basis for his claim, ὅτι ἐγώ εἰμι.

The predicateless ἐγώ εἰμι in 8,58 is used in an absolute sense since there is no possibility of providing a predicate from the context. Jesus does not say, πρὶν 'Αβραὰμ γενέσθαι ἐγενόμην (before Abraham was, I was/existed), rather πρὶν 'Αβραὰμ γενέσθαι ἐγώ εἰμί (before Abraham was, I am). Hence, there is a contrast between Abraham's "coming into existence" (γίνομαι) and Jesus' eternal "being" (εἰμί). Jesus claims not only his existence before Abraham but also his eternal presence. Jesus' claim is his answer to the Jews' questions in v. 53 (cf. 4,12), which are concerned about his identity.

We have already observed some links between vv. 18.24.28 and Isa 43,10. Again it is possible to notice a conceptual and verbal relation between Isa 43,10 and John 8,58:

---

[65] John 8 highlights Jesus' oneness with the Father in the acts of witness (vv. 13–14.17–18) and judgement (vv. 15–16). In Deutero-Isaiah, God is not only a witness (43,10–13; cf. 41,2–4; 45,21) but also a judge in the trial proceedings (43,14–17; cf. 41,21; 45,20). The judgement given by Yahweh in these trial speeches is that he alone is the all-powerful God, and its aim is to convince the exiles that it is he who secures deliverance for Israel, which involves, at the same time, the downfall of Babylon (43,14; cf. 41,1–5). A judicial setting is used by Deutero-Isaiah as a literary vehicle, which will lead to the admission of Yahweh's sovereign power. Jesus' discourse in 8,12–59 demonstrates that his testimony, in fact, becomes judgement. This judgement presupposes an "either-or" situation for the choice is between light or darkness (v. 12), knowledge or ignorance (v. 19), life or death (vv. 21.24.51), the world above or the world below (v. 23), freedom or bondage (vv. 32.36) and descent from Abraham or the devil (v. 44). The discourse emphasizes Jesus' role as the agent of salvation and also demonstrates that rejection of Jesus will lead to condemnation. The primary focus of Jesus' ἐγώ εἰμι-utterances in vv. 24.28 is his role as the one who secures salvation, and the response to Jesus' claim provokes self-judgement. See Williams, *I Am He*, 273–274.

[66] Williams, *I Am He*, 275.

[67] John's interpretation of Isaiah's vision in the temple (Isa 6,1–5) as a vision of the glory of the pre-existent Christ (John 12,41) has already been discussed. See pp. 216–219.

Isa 43,10 ... καὶ συνῆτε ὅτι ἐγώ εἰμι ἔμπροσθέν μου οὐκ ἐγένετο ἄλλος θεὸς ...

John 8,58 πρὶν Ἀβραὰμ γενέσθαι ἐγώ εἰμί.

There is a parallel relation between ἐγένετο and γενέσθαι as well as between ἔμπροσθέν and πρίν. There is a contrast between γίνομαι (past tense) and εἰμί (present tense) in both Isa 43,10 and John 8,58. Isaiah contrasts Yahweh's eternal existence with the non-existence of the gods of the nations. John contrasts the eternal existence of Jesus as the Son with the temporal existence of Abraham. Just as no other god existed before Yahweh, so also Abraham did not exist before Jesus. The eternal existence of Yahweh is also suggested in Isa 43,13, גַּם־מִיּוֹם אֲנִי הוּא (LXX, ἔτι ἀπ' ἀρχῆς). The mention of the name of Abraham in the Targum of Isa 43,12 is also noteworthy, "I declared to Abraham your father what was about to come".[68] This future knowledge of Abraham may explain Jesus' utterance in John 8,56, "Your father Abraham rejoiced that he would see my day; he saw it and was glad". If John knew the Targum of Isaiah, this would again strengthen the relationship between Isa 43 and John 8. The interpretation of ἐγώ εἰμι in v. 58 in terms of Jesus' eternal existence may support the view of regarding Johannine Jesus as the one who bears the divine name (cf. Exod 3,14).[69] The reaction of the Jews to stone Jesus suggests that his utterance is regarded to be blasphemous (v. 59; cf. 10,30–31; Lev 24,16).[70]

4.4 Ἐγώ εἰμι before the Betrayal (13,19)

The ἐγώ εἰμι in 13,19 is used absolutely. It is presented as an object of belief as in 8,24. It is also connected to the death and resurrection of Jesus like the ἐγώ εἰμι in 8,28. The meaning of the verse is explained in the following verse (v. 20). To believe in Jesus is to believe in the Father who sent him. When Jesus is glorified through death and resurrection, the disciples will believe in the true identity of Jesus and his unity with the Father. John 13,19

---

[68] J. F. Stenning, *The Targum of Isaiah* (Oxford 1953), 144. Cf. Ball, *I Am*, 196–197.

[69] Williams thinks that the interpretation of ἐγώ εἰμι exclusively in terms of eternal divine existence does not convey the full force of the expression in 8,58. She points out that it is conceivable that Jesus' utterance of ἐγώ εἰμι (אֲנִי הוּא) in 8,58 could have been interpreted as a divine name. See Williams, *I Am He*, 275–283; Beutler, *Das Johannesevangelium*, 282; K. Wengst, *Das Johannesevangelium* (ThKNT 4,1; Stuttgart ²2004), I, 360; Brown, *John*, I, 533–538.

[70] It should be specially noted that the motifs of Jesus' claim to be equal to God or to be the Son of God and the Jews' attempt to stone and kill him go hand in hand in the Gospel (5,17–18; 8,58–59; 10,30–31.33; cf. 19,7). The failure of Petersen, *Brot, Licht und Weinstock*, 107 and M. Davies, *Rhetoric and Reference in the Fourth Gospel* (JSNTSS 69; Sheffield 1992), 86, at interpreting 8,58 is that they totally neglect or avoid the meaning and significance of 8,59.

is also reminiscent of the ἐγώ εἰμι in Isa 43,10. A parallel relation between John 13,18–19 and Isa 43,10 is noticeable:[71]

John 13,18–19 ἐγὼ οἶδα τίνας ἐξελεξάμην ... ἵνα πιστεύσητε ὅταν γένηται ὅτι ἐγώ εἰμι.

Isa 43,10 κἀγὼ μάρτυς λέγει κύριος ὁ θεός καὶ ὁ παῖς ὃν ἐξελεξάμην ἵνα γνῶτε καὶ πιστεύσητε καὶ συνῆτε ὅτι ἐγώ εἰμι.

In John 13, Jesus is the Lord (κύριος) and his disciples are the servants chosen by him (ἐξελεξάμην).[72] In Isa 43,10, Yahweh is the Lord (κύριος) and Israel is his servant, whom he has chosen (ἐξελεξάμην).[73] The ἐγώ εἰμι in 13,19 is uttered in the context of Jesus' prediction of Judas' betrayal (13,18–30). We may see a relation between Jesus' ability to predict future events and Yahweh's predictive powers in Deutero-Isaiah. Within the context of trial speeches, Yahweh challenges the pagan gods to demonstrate their predictive powers, "Who among them declared this, and foretold to us the former things?" (Isa 43,9).[74] This is immediately followed by the utterance of הוא אני/ἐγώ εἰμι in Isa 43,10.[75] The focus on Yahweh's ability to predict the future highlights his exclusive divinity and sovereignty in Deutero-Isaiah. When Jesus announces that his prediction of the betrayal will lead the disciples to believe his claim ὅτι ἐγώ εἰμι, it is an assertion of his divine authority and sovereignty (cf. John 13,3). The use of ἐγώ εἰμι also stresses his unity with the Father, the one who sent him (cf. 13,20).

4.5 Ἐγώ εἰμι *Addressed to Jesus' Enemies (18,5.6.8)*

The ἐγώ εἰμι in 18,5.6.8 has a double meaning. In one sense, it functions as a means of self-identification. Jesus tells the soldiers who want to arrest him that he is the person whom they seek by saying, ἐγώ εἰμι.[76] But those who

---

[71] Cf. Ball, *I Am*, 199.

[72] The noun κύριος occurs 8 times in chapter 13 and 5 times in 13,6–16. If the disciple can be called δοῦλος (v. 16), Israel is known as παῖς (Isa 43,10).

[73] Ball, *I Am*, 200, remarks that Jesus takes the role of the Lord that parallels that of Yahweh in Isa 43,10.

[74] The foreign gods are not capable of prediction, but Yahweh is. Hence, he says, "The former things I declared long ago, they went out from my mouth and I made them known; then suddenly I did them and they came to pass" (Isa 48,3; cf. 42,9; 45,21; 46,10; 48,5).

[75] Williams, *I Am He*, 285, n. 97, points out that the phraseology adopted in John 13,19 (πρὸ τοῦ γενέσθαι) resembles LXX Isa 44,7 (πρὸ τοῦ ἐλθεῖν) and 46,10 (πρὶν αὐτὰ γενέσθαι).

[76] There are variant readings in 18,5. While manuscripts like א A C L W Θ Ψ, etc., insert ὁ Ἰησοῦς (א omits ὁ) after λέγει αὐτοῖς, Codex Vaticanus (B) adds Ἰησοῦς after ἐγώ εἰμι. Scribes used to contract Ἰησοῦς as ισ. Hence, there is a possibility for an accidental omission of the words ὁ Ἰησοῦς through an oversight in transcription, if they stood originally either after αὐτοῖς or before εἱστήκει (which is in many manuscripts written ἱστήκει). But the temptation to identify the speaker in this situation and the differing position of (ὁ) Ἰησοῦς before or after ἐγώ εἰμι favour the *lectio brevior*. Cf. Metzger, *Textual*

think that this is merely a statement of identification miss the core sense of the Johannine formulation. The ἐγώ εἰμι is uttered as part of Jesus' self-revelation. In the scene of arrest, John presents Jesus as the one who reveals himself without the initiative or interrogation of his opponents. It is Jesus himself who comes forward and asks his enemies, "Whom are you looking for?" (18,4). His opponents do not ask him, "Are you Jesus of Nazareth?" and Jesus does not pronounce ἐγώ εἰμι as an answer to any of their questions, rather it is he himself who takes the initiative to reveal himself.[77]

The reaction of drawing back and falling down on the ground on the part of his opponents and the repetition of ἐγώ εἰμι in vv. 6.8 show that at a deeper level Jesus' utterance has an absolute sense implying his divine identity and authority. No reasons are given for the strange reaction of his opponents.[78] The absolute use of ἐγώ εἰμι in v. 5 is evident from the fact that it is repeated in v. 6 in the form of an indeclinable citation (ὡς οὖν εἶπεν αὐτοῖς, Ἐγώ εἰμι) rather than in the form of indirect speech. This highlights the significance of ἐγώ εἰμι, which functions as a vehicle of self-manifestation and divine revelation by Jesus. Falling down on the ground is a response to divine revelation in the Bible (e.g., Ezek 1,28; 44,4; Dan 8,18; 10,9; Acts 9,4; 22,7; 26,14; Rev 1,17; 19,10; 22,8; cf. 3 En. 1,7).[79] Hence, the strange response of the opponents can be regarded as an involuntary response to the divine revelation by Jesus.

Commentary, 215. There are also other sound reasons to reject these variant readings. The words ὁ Ἰησοῦς can be understood as belonging to λέγει αὐτοῖς because there are numerous parallels for the expression λέγει αὐτοῖς ὁ Ἰησοῦς in the Gospel of John. When the formula ἐγώ εἰμι is repeated in vv. 6.8, it stands independently in all manuscripts. Moreover, as we have already seen, there are other occasions in the Gospel on which Jesus uses the formula ἐγώ εἰμι absolutely and as a means of self-identification (cf. 4,26; 6,20).

[77] In the case of the blind man (9,9), it is the people who take the initiative and ask him, "Is this not the man who used to sit and beg?" (9,8), and the blind man is compelled to answer, ἐγώ εἰμι.

[78] Harner, *The I Am*, 45, remarks that an attitude of fear and reverence is the only fitting response to Jesus' ἐγώ εἰμι in 18,5. Those (e.g., Petersen, *Brot, Licht und Weinstock*, 99; Davies, *Rhetoric*, 83) who regard ἐγώ εἰμι here only as a means of identification neglect or avoid often the full significance of the reaction on the part of Jesus' opponents in 18,6.

[79] In Rev 1,17, the falling down as though dead at the feet of the Son of Man is associated with an ἐγώ εἰμι-saying by him, Μὴ φοβοῦ· ἐγώ εἰμι ὁ πρῶτος καὶ ὁ ἔσχατος, "Do not be afraid; I am the first and the last". There is a legend attributed to Artapanus, a Jewish writer of Egyptian provenance who lived around the second centuary BCE, but is preserved only by Eusebius (*Praeparatio Evangelica*, IX. xxvii. 22–26) and partly by Clement of Alexandria (*Stromata*, I. xxiii). According to it, when Moses uttered the name of God, the Pharaoh fell down on the ground speechless. See R. G. Bury, "Two Notes on the Fourth Gospel", *ExpTim* 24 (1912–1913), 232–233; Brown, *John*, II, 818; Williams, *I Am He*, 291–293. We cannot convincingly connect this story with the Johannine account, but it may shed some light on the strange event of falling down on the ground by the enemies at the pronouncement of ἐγώ εἰμι by Jesus.

It is to be noted that Jesus' utterance of ἐγώ εἰμι in 18,5 is closely related to his previous utterance in 13,19. His prediction of betrayal by Judas is realized in 18,5 when the evangelist says, "Judas, who betrayed him, was standing with them". The fact that the evangelist immediately after this comment mentions the drawing back and the falling down of the opponents may suggest that Judas was one of those who fell down to the ground. The disciples who are witnesses to Judas' betrayal and to the strange response of the opponents are now supposed to know and believe the true identity of Jesus, even though it is only after his resurrection that they realize fully his identity. Thus, Jesus' prophecy in 13,19 is realized in 18,5.

In Deutero-Isaiah, Yahweh's prophecies, unlike those of foreign gods, always come to fulfilment (43,9; cf. 42,9; 45,21; 46,10; 48,3.5). The trial between Yahweh and the foreign nations (Isa 43,9) and the utterance of ἐγώ εἰμι (Isa 43,10) are followed by the description of Yahweh's exclusive sovereignty and the triumph over his enemies (Isa 43,11–17; cf. Deut 32,35). In Isa 43,17, the enemies of Yahweh are made to lie down, "they cannot rise, they are extinguished, quenched like a wick". By exposing the powerlessness of his opponents, Yahweh shows that he is the sole Saviour of Israel.[80] John also hints at the notion that Jesus is the Saviour during the scene of arresting. The second utterance of ἐγώ εἰμι in 18,8 is connected with the protection of the disciples, "So if you are looking for me, let these men go". Their physical release fulfils his claim to be the good shepherd, who lays down his life for the protection and life of his sheep (10,10–14.28). The fulfilment of Jesus' prediction "I did not lose a single one of those whom you gave me" (18,9; cf. 6,39; 17,12) is in the context identified with the physical salvation of his disciples, but their eternal salvation is likewise understood by this prediction. Thus, through the three-fold repetition of ἐγώ εἰμι and the astonishing reaction of the captors, the evangelist portrays on the one hand the sovereignty and triumph of Jesus in his complete control over his enemies and on the other hand the powerlessness and defeat of his enemies. Moreover, his power to protect his disciples corresponds to his power to be the Saviour.

5. Ἐγώ εἰμι with Images

In the case of the ἐγώ εἰμι-sayings with images, John takes several images and concepts (bread, light, door, shepherd, resurrection, life, way, truth, vine) many of which are often used in the Old Testament. John applies them to

---

[80] The powerlessness of the pagan idols is closely linked to the Kidron valley in some traditions in the Hebrew Scriptures. The altars and the images of Baal and Asherah were burned outside Jerusalem and their dust was thrown into the Kidron brook according to 2 Kgs 23,4.6.12 (2 Chr 15,16; 29,16). Cf. Williams, *I Am He*, 295, n. 127.

Jesus and thus shows that Jesus is both the fulfilment and embodiment of these Old Testament images.[81] As a whole, these sayings have a common structure.[82] Many of them have two parts: i. a self-presentation (ἐγώ εἰμι) together with an image word with the definite article; ii. a soteriological statement which may contain any of the following elements – an invitation, a call to decide, a promise of salvation or a challenge (threat) to the unbelievers (6,35.51; 8,12; 10,9; 11,25; 14,6; 15,5).[83]

5.1 Jesus as the Bread of Life (6,35.41.48.51)

Jesus is identified with the image of bread (ἄρτος) 4 times by means of an ἐγώ εἰμι-formula in chapter 6 (6,35.41.48.51).[84] The ἐγώ εἰμι-formula and the image of bread serve to maintain the unity of chapter 6.[85] The image of bread in the first part of the chapter (vv. 5.7.9.11) and the formula ἐγώ εἰμι in the second part (v. 20) are combined to form the predicated ἐγώ εἰμι-sayings in the third part of the chapter 6 (vv. 35.41.48.51).[86] Jesus' ἐγώ εἰμι on the waters continues to sound in this revelatory discourse about himself as the bread of life (vv. 35.48) and as the (living) bread that came down from heaven (vv. 41.51).[87]

Jesus' discourse on the bread of life is often considered to be an exposition of the miracle of multiplication of loaves (vv. 1–15) and a sermon on the

---

[81] The possible Old Testament background of these images will be discussed when each saying is individually dealt with. The notion of resurrection is found only in Deutero-Canonical books. From a form-critical point of view, Bühner, "The Exegesis of the Johannine 'I-Am' Sayings", 207–218, considers "I am"-sayings with predicates as self-introduction of a messenger. See the criticism against Bühner on p. 103, n. 349. Wollenberg, "A Short Note on Ἐγώ Εἰμι Sayings", 20–26, has pointed out that the Johannine "I am"-sayings with predicate nominatives parallel with an extensive collection of verses in the Hebrew Bible, in which God uses the phrase "I am" with predicate nominatives.

[82] See H. Becker, *Die Reden des Johannesevangeliums und der Stil der gnostischen Offenbarungsrede* (FRLANT 68; Göttingen 1956), 54, 56; Schulz, *Komposition*, 87.

[83] Instead of the polemic term "threat" often used by authors, it is better to prefer the term "challenge". The sayings in 6,41.48; 10,7.11.14; 15,1 do not have elements of invitation or promise or challenge. An element of challenge is noticeable only in 14,6 (cf. 8,24).

[84] In 6,41, the words are not uttered by Jesus, but the evangelist cites the previously spoken words of Jesus (vv. 35.38).

[85] For various factors that maintain the unity of John 6, see Crossan, "It is Written", 3–21. Cf. Stare, *Durch ihn leben*.

[86] Cf. Ball, *I Am*, 70.

[87] In the view of O'Day, "Jesus Walking on Water", 158, the ἐγώ εἰμι of 6,20 provides the theological basis for Jesus' subsequent ἐγώ εἰμι-sayings in 6,35.41.48.51. Heil, *Walking on the Sea*, 169, points out that Peter's confession "you are the Holy One of God" (6,69) is the climactic response which concludes the paradigmatic series of revelatory words introduced by the ἐγώ εἰμι formula.

manna in Exodus.[88] Jesus' claim to be the true bread from heaven, however, may allude not only to a particular passage, but also may include all that would be implied in the Old Testament concept of bread from heaven.[89] It means that John 6 may take up not only specific passages that refer to bread but also ideas associated with the concept of bread.[90] The idea of manna can be seen as a type which points to Jesus' role among humanity.[91] The supplement "of life" attached to "the bread" can be seen as a Johannine formulation due to the lack of Old Testament parallels for "the bread of life".[92] The theme of life (ζωή), which plays a decisive role in the chapter (vv. 27.33.35.40.47.48.51.54.58.63), is linked to ἐγώ εἰμι-sayings (vv. 35.48.51). The repetition of ἐγώ εἰμι stresses the dominance of Jesus in the discourse because everything is focused on him, and this dominance creates offence among his audience (vv. 41.42.60).[93] But his dominance goes hand in hand with his obedience to the Father (vv. 38–40). The crowd's misunderstanding (vv. 26–31) and their murmur (v. 41) become the basis for Jesus' discourse on the bread of life and further explanation. Although we cannot say that it is the words ἐγώ εἰμι alone which provoke the division among Jesus' audience, it is the revelatory claim, of which ἐγώ εἰμι forms an essential part, that causes offence.[94]

---

[88] P. Borgen, *Bread from Heaven. An Exegetical Study of the Concept of Manna in the Gospel of John and the Writings of Philo* (NovTSup 10; Leiden 1965), 33–43, thinks that vv. 32–58 is a homily on Exod 16,4. Accordingly, the first part of the quotation cited in v. 31, "he gave them bread from heaven", is paraphrased and discussed in vv. 32–48 and the last word "to eat" is then paraphrased and interpreted in vv. 49–58. Schnackenburg, *John*, II, 11, admits the possibility that the evangelist knew a primitive Christian exegesis of manna, perhaps from Easter liturgy and thinks that he has given the whole composition a shape of his own, using the methods of the Jewish midrash. Cf. Brown, *John*, I, 277–278.

[89] Ball, *I Am*, 213. Freed, *Old Testament Quotations*, 12, views that there is no single passage from the Old Testament that totally agrees with the citation in v. 31 and suggests that John had in mind Exod 16,4 and Ps 78,24 and was probably familiar with both Hebrew and Greek texts. He also notices the similarities in Exod 16,35; Num 11,6–9; Deut 8,3; Josh 5,12; Prov 9,5.

[90] Ball, *I Am*, 213.

[91] D. M. Ball writes, "The bread from heaven is a *type* which points to Jesus' role as the one who satisfies 'true' hunger by giving life to those who come to him (v. 51)". See Ball, *I Am*, 213–214.

[92] Cf. Borgen, *Bread from Heaven*, 73; Ball, *I Am*, 210. Schnackenburg, *John*, II, 43–44, notices parallels in the Babylonian Adapa myth and in the apocryphal *Joseph and Aseneth* and suggests that John might have come to the expression in his own way but from the same conceptual world.

[93] Crossan, "It is Written", 11, thinks that it is not very surprising that the "I" of Jesus should dominate the discourse after the supreme and unqualified revelation of ἐγώ εἰμι in 6,20. It should be noted that only Jesus uses "I" within the discourse.

[94] Ball, *I Am*, 76.

Jesus' claim to be the bread of life has all the force of his claim to divine authority (cf. 6,20) because only God can provide the bread which is capable of imparting divine and imperishable life.[95] Jesus declares that the origin of the bread of life is from God (v. 33). Belief is required to receive the life that Jesus promises (vv. 35–36.40.64.69). With ἐγώ εἰμι Jesus claims that the authentic sign which the crowd seeks is fulfilled in him (v. 35).[96] Jesus' presentation of himself as "the bread of life" is followed by a demand in the form of a conditional statement and a soteriological promise (vv. 35b.51b). The participial clause ὁ ἐρχόμενος πρὸς ἐμὲ is interpreted by another participial clause ὁ πιστεύων εἰς ἐμὲ (v. 35). Therefore, "coming to Jesus" means "believing in him" (cf. 7,37).

The metaphors of hunger and thirst (v. 35; cf. 7,37) may refer to the whole conceptual background of the food of manna and water from the rock in Exodus (16,31.35; 17,6; cf. Deut 8,15; Isa 32,2; 48,21; Neh 9,15) and to the language of Wisdom literature (Prov 9,5; Sir 24,21; 51,24). In view of the Old Testament symbolism of food or bread for divine word and wisdom (Isa 40,10–11; Amos 8,11–13; Sir 15,3; 24,21; Prov 9,5), it is possible to assume that the bread of life may refer to the divine revelation given by and in Jesus. Jesus is, therefore, the divine teacher who has come to nourish with his wisdom.[97] In v. 51, there are not only the echoes of the Eucharistic words of institution but also the echoes of Jesus' incarnation and death (cf. 1 Cor 11,26). It is Jesus' death that makes the Eucharistic participation in his flesh possible.[98]

5.2 Jesus as the Light of the World (8,12)

The setting for Jesus' declaration in 8,12 is the context of the feast of Tabernacles in Jerusalem (7,2.10.14.28.37).[99] His claim to be the light of the world

---

[95] Cf. Schnackenburg, *John*, II, 43.

[96] Ball, *I Am*, 207.

[97] According to Brown, *John*, I, 274, vv. 35–50 primarily refer to the divine revelation in Jesus, but he notices in them a secondary Eucharistic reference. He views that the juxtaposition of hunger and thirst in v. 35 seems to be strange in a discourse on bread, which never mentions water. He argues that it makes more sense if there is also a reference to the Eucharist, which involves flesh and blood and is both to be eaten and drunk.

[98] Brown, *John*, I, 291. For a Eucharistic interpretation of 6,51–58, see pp. 246–248.

[99] The feast of Tabernacles or Booths (7,2) is a week-long celebration which recalls the wandering of Israel for forty years in the desert after the departure from Egypt under the leadership of Moses. The dwelling of the Israelites in booths gave the rationale for this feast (Deut 16,13–15; Lev 23,34–36.39–43; Num 29,12–38). Historical evolution of this feast is obvious in these accounts, and it is the Books of Maccabees (1 Macc 4,36–59; 2 Macc 1,9.18; 10,5–7) and the non-biblical Jewish literature which speak of this feast in association with the light ceremony. See Marottikaparambil, *Jesus the Light of the World*, 48–137.

is an answer to the demand of his brothers, "Show yourself to the world", in 7,4. It is most probably in the historical setting of the light ceremony in the temple during the feast of Tabernacles, which commemorates the pillar of fire in the wilderness (Exod 13,21; cf. Pss 78,14; 105,39; Neh 9,12.19), that Jesus declares that he is the light not only of Jerusalem but of the whole world.[100] The underlying theme of 8,12–59 is the identity and origin of Jesus (cf. vv. 25.53).[101] Jesus' debate with the Jews begins with an ἐγώ εἰμι-saying (v. 12) and ends with another ἐγώ εἰμι-saying (v. 58). Both form an *inclusio* and this *inclusio* may suggest that the various forms of ἐγώ εἰμι-sayings are meant to be considered in relation to one another.

The term φῶς, which appears 23 times in chapters 1–12, never occurs in the second part of the Gospel (13–21). This may be to present Jesus' entrance into the world and his ministry in terms of the radiation of his light. Obviously, the genitive in τὸ φῶς τοῦ κόσμου is objective implying light for the world.[102] The expression τὸ φῶς τοῦ κόσμου, which is similar to τὸ φῶς τῶν ἀνθρώπων in 1,4, may allude to the prophecies in Isaiah concerning universal salvation (9,1–2; 42,6; 49,6; 51,4; cf. Luke 2,32). In Isa 42,1, the identity of the servant is assumed to be the people of Israel. Yahweh has chosen them to bring justice/judgement (מִשְׁפָּט/κρίσις) to the nations. In doing this, they will become light to the nations (42,6). Their role as the light of the nations reveals the exclusivity of Yahweh's divinity (42,8; cf. 43,10).[103] Israel is to become a light to the nations by opening their eyes which are blind (42,7). Israel's role as light to the nations is fulfilled in Jesus when he claims to be the light of the world and opens the eyes of the blind man (John 9,5–7).[104]

---

[100] Mishnah speaks of the ritual of lighting four golden candlesticks in the court of the women in the temple. Each of them had four golden bowls on top, which were reached by ladders. The candlesticks were lighted with the wicks, which were out of the worn-out undergarments and girdles of the priests. It is said that there was not a courtyard in Jerusalem which was not lit up from the light of *bet hashshoebah* (*m.Sukk.* 5:2–3). Cf. J. Neusner, *The Mishnah. A New Translation* (New Haven 1988), 289. Marottikaparambil, *Jesus the Light of the World*, 12, views that Jesus fulfils in himself the meaning of the light ceremony of Sukkot by his declaration in 8,12 since the light ceremony was a representation of the feast itself.

[101] Barrett, *John*, 333, rightly entitles the section 8,12–59 as "Who is Jesus?"

[102] In Matt 5,14, the disciples are said to be the light of the world. This need not contradict John 8,12 because the disciples are the light of the world only in as much as they reflect Jesus. Cf. Brown, *John*, I, 340. The term κόσμος is used in 8,12 neutrally. It is not the sphere of unbelief and enmity (1,10; 7,7), but the place where God's offer of salvation through Jesus is made available (3,16–17).

[103] In Isa 43, the judgement is brought to the nations through the chosen servant's witness to Yahweh. Cf. Ball, *I Am*, 216.

[104] Ball, *I Am*, 220, points out that Israel's role as a light to the nations is a type for the role of Jesus. Since Jesus is considered to arise from Galilee (7,52), his claim to be the

Jesus verifies his claim to be the light of the world in chapter 8 by healing (by giving physical light of this world to) the blind man in chapter 9.

The verb ἀκολουθέω is a term of discipleship in John (1,37.43; 12,26; 13,36–37) as in the Synoptic Gospels (Mark 2,14; 8,34; 10,28; Matt 4,20; Luke 5,27; 18,28). For John, discipleship is a matter of belief in Jesus, which is required of every one for his or her salvation. The expression "walking in darkness" refers to a life without goal and orientation because he who walks in darkness does not know where he goes (12,35). In the Old Testament, "walking in darkness" may also refer to a wicked life and "walking in light" to a righteous life (Prov 4,18–19). The promise of "the light of life" implies that the saying in v. 12b is similar to the basic formula in the Gospel, "He who believes in him may have eternal life" (3,16; cf. 6,35.51.58; 8,51–52; 11,26). The notions of the Lord as "light" (Ps 27,1; Bar 5,9) and "the light of life" (Ps 56,13; Job 33,30) are noticeable in the Old Testament. The image of life-giving light may primarily refer to Jesus' revelation as in the case of the images of water and bread, which are also life-giving.[105] John presents the Logos as the light of everyone (1,9). Hence, Jesus has come into the world as its light so that those who believe in him may not remain in darkness (12,46). Those who believe in him are called sons of light (12,36). The revelation through Jesus provides the believers with eternal life.

5.3 Jesus as the Gate and the Good Shepherd (10,7.9.11.14)

The shepherd discourse[106] in John 10 has become for many scholars a "hard nut to crack".[107] It poses many exegetical problems for the interpreter.[108] Its

---

light of the world fulfils Isa 9,1–2 and God's plan for universal salvation. His coming into the world is intended to provide light to those who live in darkness.

[105] Brown, *John*, I, 344. A possible background for Jesus' use of light as a symbol of revelation can be found in Wisdom literature (Wis 7,26).

[106] The current discussion does not intend a detailed study of the shepherd discourse but only an examination of the meaning of the ἐγώ εἰμι-sayings in 10,7.9.11.14. The ἐγώ εἰμι-sayings with the image of gate in 10,7.9 have more similarity to the ἐγώ εἰμι-saying with the image of way in 14,6. Hence, we may consider 10,7.9 as parallel texts to 14,6 and give more attention to the ἐγώ εἰμι-sayings in 10,7.9. Since all four ἐγώ εἰμι-sayings within 10,1–18 are interrelated, the whole shepherd discourse is taken into account. For a detailed study of the shepherd discourse, see K. M. Lewis, *Rereading the "Shepherd Discourse". Restoring the Integrity of John 9,39–10,21* (Studies in Biblical Literature 113; New York 2008); Zimmermann, *Christologie der Bilder*, 241–404; Theobald, *Herrenworte*, 277–304, 353–393; J. H. Neyrey, "The Noble Shepherd in John 10: Cultural and Rhetorical Background", *JBL* 120 (2001), 267–291; Van der Watt, *Family of the King*, 54–92; B. Kowalski, *Die Hirtenrede (Joh 10,1–18) im Kontext des Johannesevangeliums* (SBB 31; Stuttgart 1996); J. Beutler and R. T. Fortna (ed.), *The Shepherd Discourse of John 10 and Its Context* (Cambridge 1991); R. Kysar, "Johannine Metaphor – Meaning and Function: A Literary Case Study of John 10,1–18", *The Fourth Gospel from a Literary Perspective*, ed. R. A. Culpepper and F. F. Segovia (Semeia 53; Atlanta 1991), 81–111; P.-R.

beginning, order, genre (the meaning of παροιμία), sources, inner structure, internal relationship, in part its wording, its relation to the context, its meaning and purpose are matters of contention. At present, there is a general scholarly consensus that the present verse sequence has a purposeful arrangement, that chapters 9 and 10 are closely related and that the evangelist draws on the world of ideas of the Hebrew Bible.[109]

5.3.1 Context of the Shepherd Discourse

5.3.1.1 Macro Context

John 10 cannot be interpreted in isolation. It finds itself in an important section of the Gospel, i.e., chapters 5–10 in which the great debates and disputes occur.[110] The concentration of these chapters is on Jesus' conflict with the Jews, a theme which interlocks them. Attempts to arrest or kill Jesus permeate these chapters (5,16.18; 7,19.20.25.32.44; 8,20.59; 10,31–33.39). Some of the themes found in previous chapters are also repeated in chapter 10, namely the division among the Pharisees and the Jews (9,16; 10,19–21) and "picking up stones to throw at Jesus" (8,59; 10,31). The fact that the Jews want to arrest Jesus again, but he escapes from their hands (10,39) is an indication of

---

Tragan, *La Parabole du "Pasteur" et ses Explications: Jean 10,1–18. La Genèse, les Milieux littéraires* (StAns 67; Rome 1980); A. J. Simonis, *Die Hirtenrede im Johannesevangelium. Versuch einer Analyse von Johannes 10,1–18 nach Entstehung, Hintergrund und Inhalt* (AnBib 29; Rome 1967); O. Kiefer, *Die Hirtenrede. Analyse und Deutung von Joh 10,1–18* (SBS 23; Stuttgart 1967); Reinhartz, *The Word in the World*, 48–98; J. P. Martin, "John 10,1–10", *Interpretation* 32 (1978), 171–175; S. L. de Villiers, "The Shepherd and His Flock", *The Christ of John. Essays on the Christology of the Fourth Gospel*, ed. A. B. du Toit (Potchefstroom 1971), 89–103; J. D. M. Derrett, "The Good Shepherd: St. John's Use of Jewish Halakah und Haggadah", *ST* 27 (1973), 25–50; P. W. Meyer, "A Note on John 10,1–18", *JBL* 75 (1956), 232–235; J. Quasten, "The Parable of the Good Shepherd: John 10,1–21", *CBQ* 10 (1948), 1–12, 151–169.

[107] J. Beutler, "Der alttestamentlich-jüdische Hintergrund der Hirtenrede in Johannes 10", *The Shepherd Discourse of John 10 and Its Context*, ed. J. Beutler and R. T. Fortna (Cambridge 1991), 18, remarks that "Neben dem Prolog ist die Hirtenrede Jesu wohl immer noch der umstrittenste Text des Johannesevangeliums".

[108] For an overview and an examination of various exegetical problems involved in the interpretation of the shepherd discourse, see Lewis, *Rereading*, 1–32; Kowalski, *Die Hirtenrede*, 5–91; U. Busse, "Open Questions on John 10", *The Shepherd Discourse of John 10 and Its Context*, ed. J. Beutler and R. T. Fortna (Cambridge 1991), 6–17.

[109] See J. Beutler and R. T. Fortna, "Introduction", *The Shepherd Discourse of John 10 and Its Context*, ed. J. Beutler and R. T. Fortna (Cambridge 1991), 3.

[110] J. A. du Rand, "A Syntactical and Narratological Reading of John 10 in Coherence with Chapter 9", *The Shepherd Discourse of John 10 and Its Context*, ed. J. Beutler and R. T. Fortna (Cambridge 1991), 94, observes that from a syntactical point of view chapters 9–10 should be considered as the co-text of John 10 and from a narratological perspective, chapters 5–10.

the motif of the non-arrival of Jesus' hour, which is a frequent motif in the previous chapters (7,30; 8,20; cf. 2,4; 7,6.8). The miracles of Jesus in chapters 5, 6 and 9 lead to Jesus' conflict with the Jews and prepare the basis for his lengthy discourses following the miracles. It is in the context of the conflict between Jesus and the Jews in chapters 5–10 that the shepherd discourse (10,1–18) can be better understood.[111]

5.3.1.2 Micro Context

The immediate context for the shepherd discourse is Jesus' healing of the man born blind and the consequent confrontation of Jesus with the Jews. John 10,1 does not show a new beginning by indicating a change in time, place and audience for the discourse. It rather starts with a characteristic Johannine ἀμὴν ἀμήν saying. In some instances, these sayings are introduced directly by the quotation formula "he said to/answered them" (1,51; 3,3.5; 5,19; 6,26.32.53; 8,34.58; 10,7; 13,21) and in other instances they are not preceded by a quotation formula (3,11; 5,24.25; 6,47; 8,51; 10,1; 12,24; 13,16.20.38; 14,12; 16,20.23; 21,18). Thus, 10,1, without any introductory quotation formula, is formally a continuation of Jesus' dialogue with the Pharisees begun in 9,40–41.[112] The nearest antecedent for ἐκεῖνοι in 10,6, denoting the uncomprehending audience, is the Pharisees (9,40). It is in this manner that the pervasively polemical overtones of the discourse should be understood.[113]

The evangelist's comment, "They did not understand what he was saying to them", in 10,6 is a reference to the "blind" Pharisees in 9,40–41, which ties

---

[111] Chapter 10 has strong links not only with the previous chapters but also with the following ones. In 11,8–10, there is a reference to the attempts to stone Jesus, previously mentioned in 10,31. Likewise, the motifs of arresting Jesus (10,39; 11,57), doing signs (10,41; 11,47) and believing in Jesus (10,42; 11,48) connect both chapters closely. Chapter 10 also includes many allusions to the Johannine Passion account. E.g., Jesus' public teaching in the temple (10,22–30; 18,20–21), the accusation of blasphemy (10,33; 19,7), the motif of authority (ἐξουσία 10,18; 19,10–11), Jesus' protection of his followers (10,28; 18,8–9) and hearing Jesus' voice (τῆς φωνῆς αὐτοῦ ἀκούει 10,3–5.27; ἀκούει μου τῆς φωνῆς 18,37).

[112] It is as a reaction to Jesus' statement in 9,39 that the Pharisees enter into conversation with Jesus. Therefore, 9,39 can be regarded as a part of this dialogue. The relationship of John 10 with 9,40–41 is so close that H. Thyen suggests that chapter 10 should begin at 9,40. See H. Thyen "Johannes 10 im Kontext des vierten Evangeliums", *The Shepherd Discourse of John 10 and Its Context*, ed. J. Beutler and R. T. Fortna (Cambridge 1991), 123. Barrett, *John*, 367, finds no break between chapters 9 and 10 and views that the passage 10,1–21 is rather a comment on chapter 9 than a continuation of it. O'Day, *John*, 666, thinks that the shepherd discourse is Jesus' reflection on what has happened with the blind man and the Pharisees/Jews in chapter 9.

[113] Kowalski, *Die Hirtenrede*, 152–282, sees in the shepherd discourse a "two-level drama": a drama at the level of the narrative (the situation at the time of Jesus) and a drama at the level of the meta-narrative (the situation at the time of the Johannine community).

the discourse together with the previous scene in chapter 9. The shepherd discourse is also well tied to the following context of chapter 10 through the motif of Father-Son relationship, with which the shepherd discourse ends (10,17–18). The motif of Father-Son relationship is continued in 10,25b–30 and 10,34–38. It is evident that the figurative language ends in 10,16. However, what firmly connects 10,17–18 with the discourse is one of the distinguishing features of the good shepherd, namely that he lays down his life for the sheep (τὴν ψυχὴν αὐτοῦ τίθησιν 10,11.15.17) in union with the Father. Thus, we may assume that John 10 is well rooted in its immediate and wider context. Hence, any version of rearrangement becomes unnecessary and the present order of the chapter should be maintained.[114] In short, in 10,1 there is a change in the theme, but the context does not change.

5.3.2 Structure

John 10 can be divided into three sections with subdivisions, vv. 1–21, vv. 22–39 and vv. 40–42. Verses 1–21 consist of a shepherd discourse (vv. 1–18) and the notice of a σχίσμα among the Jews (vv. 19–21). A general tendency among the scholars and commentators is to divide the shepherd discourse (10,1–18) into a παροιμία (10,1–6) and the interpretation/explanation of the παροιμία (10,7–18).[115] This view is based on the comment of the evangelist in 10,6 that the audience did not understand the παροιμία which Jesus was saying to them. Hence, 10,1–5/6 is seen to be the παροιμία and 10,7–18 its explanation. But this understanding has its own limitations. The figurative language of 10,1–5 continues in 10,7–18 as well. There is no one-to-one correspondence between the παροιμία in vv. 1–5 and Jesus' words in vv. 7–18. The same images of 10,1–5 appear again in 10,7–18 like sheepfold (10,16), gate (10,7.9), sheep (10,7.11–13.15–16), shepherd (10,11.14.16) and thieves and bandits (10,8). Some new images like hireling and wolf (10,12) and pasture (10,9) come on the scene in the second part, while some old figures like

---

[114] The schism caused by Jesus' words in 10,19 has made some scholars think that 10,19–21 is a suitable conclusion to 9,39–41, especially because 10,21 refers back to the healing of the blind man. According to this view, 10,22–29 is considered to be the introduction to the new section/chapter, since 10,22–23 provides a new temporal and spatial setting. Then, 10,1–18 would follow 10,22–29. Thus, the order recommended by Bernard and others for chapter 10 is vv. 19–29; vv. 1–18; vv. 30–42 (see Bernard, *John*, II, 341). But there is no textual evidence for this suggestion. The schism of 10,19–21 may imply a broader group such as it is referred to in 9,16 and may not fit the unbelieving Pharisees of 9,40–41. Moreover, the position of 10,26–29 is unlikely since it may presuppose the παροιμία of 10,1–5.

[115] The SNTS seminar on the Shepherd Discourse in 1985–1986 reached a major consensus concerning the overall structure of the Shepherd Discourse, especially with regard to the character of vv. 7–10 and vv. 11–18 as interpretations of the παροιμία in vv. 1–5. See Beutler and Fortna, "Introduction", 3. Also see Brown, *John*, I, 390–393.

stranger (10,5) and gatekeeper (10,3) disappear. The misunderstanding or lack of understanding of the audience begun in 9,39–41 continues through the discourse until 10,19–21 owing to Jesus' figurative language. The παροιμία in 10,6 refers to the figurative language, which is also hinted at in 9,40; 10,19 and 10,21 through the repetition of the demonstrative pronoun οὗτος:
9,40 Ἤκουσαν ἐκ τῶν Φαρισαίων ταῦτα οἱ ...
10,6 Ταύτην τὴν παροιμίαν εἶπεν αὐτοῖς ὁ Ἰησοῦς ...
10,19 Σχίσμα πάλιν ἐγένετο ἐν τοῖς Ἰουδαίοις διὰ τοὺς λόγους τούτους.
10,21 Ταῦτα τὰ ῥήματα οὐκ ἔστιν δαιμονιζομένου·
Moreover, the parable-interpretation model tends to read the ἐγώ εἰμι-sayings in isolation from the use of the figurative language in other discourses and the ἐγώ εἰμι-sayings in John (e.g., 6,35; 8,12; 15,1).[116] Hence, it is difficult to call 10,7–18 an interpretation or explanation of 10,1–5.[117]

The two narratives of 9,39–41 and 10,19–21 frame the shepherd discourse (10,1–18) through the motif of blindness, which forms an *inclusio*.[118] They may be regarded as the introductory and concluding frames of the shepherd discourse. Moreover, the motif of incomprehension of the audience in 9,40; 10,6 and 10,19–20 ties these three units (9,39–41; 10,1–18; 10,19–21) together. In 10,22–23, there is a new temporal (feast of Dedication) and spatial (the portico of Solomon of the Jerusalem temple) setting different from that of 9,39–10,21 (cf. 7,2.10.14.37). Our focus here is exclusively on the discourse proper (10,1–18).

The discourse (10,1–18) can be divided into three sub-units: vv. 1–6; 7–10; 11–18. In vv. 1–6, there is a παροιμία, which describes the events in a sheep pen. V. 6 is a comment by the evangelist. Jesus takes two images belonging to the sheepfold and identifies himself with them in vv. 7–18. In vv. 7–10, Jesus identifies himself with the image of a gate and in vv. 11–18 with the

---

[116] Cf. O'Day, *John*, 668.

[117] Karoline M. Lewis rejects "the parable-explanation" model for the interpretation of the shepherd discourse and argues for a "rereading" of the shepherd discourse, which aims to restore the integrity of John 9,39–10,21. She thinks that the shepherd discourse is a continuation of the events in John 9 and views that 9,1–10,21 has the pattern of "sign-dialogue-discourse" as seen in chapters 5 and 6. Her strategy of "rereading" is based on the work of literary theorists like Matei Calinescu and Marcel Cornis-Pope. It focuses on literary features that enact rereading (repetition, ambiguity, secrecy and textual concealment, orality, synonyms, new terminology) in order to highlight the intra-textual nature and imaginative impact of the narrative. See Lewis, *Rereading the Shepherd Discourse*, 33–176. For a critical evaluation of Lewis' work, see B. Kowalski, review of K. M. Lewis, *Rereading the "Shepherd Discourse". Restoring the Integrity of John 9,39–10,21* (Studies in Biblical Literature 113; New York 2008), *RBL* 8 (2009), 40–43.

[118] It is to be noted that the substantive τυφλός in 9,41 and 10,21 is in the plural. They do not necessarily refer to the blind man but to the "blind" Jewish leaders. O'Day, *John*, 661, thinks that 9,39–41 has a double function, as a conclusion to the controversy about the healing of the blind man and as an introduction to the discourse in 10,1–18.

image of a shepherd. He attaches these two images to ἐγώ εἰμι-sayings, which function as the keys to understand the whole discourse. The ἐγώ εἰμι-sayings are intended to illuminate the παροιμία because of the lack of understanding on the part of the hearers.[119] Without these ἐγώ εἰμι-sayings, the discourse would remain ambiguous. Hence, the whole discourse has to be understood in relationship to Jesus' identification with the gate and with the shepherd. In vv. 7–10, Jesus calls himself the gate and all other images within vv. 7–10 gain their significance in relation to the image of the gate. In vv. 11–18, Jesus calls himself the good shepherd, and all other images within vv. 11–18 receive their value in relation to this image of the good shepherd. Vv. 17–18 are connected to the shepherd image because one of the important features of the shepherd is that he lays down (τίθημι) his life for the sheep (vv. 11.15.17.18[2x]). Thus, we may give the following structure for the shepherd discourse in 10,1–18:

vv. 1–6   The Παροιμία
vv. 7–10   Jesus as the Gate
vv. 11–18   Jesus as the Good Shepherd

5.3.3 Interpretation

The evangelist operates within the framework of the possibilities of the broader world of sheep farming, which is a coherent factor of the whole shepherd discourse.[120] Hence, the entire world of sheep farming is potentially open to be applied metaphorically and not only a single or particular expression within this world, as in vv. 1–5.[121] As a result, the evangelist can choose, adapt and develop the images according to his need and purpose. He uses the imagery of sheep farming in a quite free and open way, changing, adapting, even ignoring some of its elements whenever he feels that it is necessary for the communication of the message because his main interest lies in the message and not in the form.[122]

In vv. 7–18, the evangelist is still staying within the limits of the broad imagery of sheep farming and there is no effort from his part to explain the παροιμία (vv. 1–5) allegorically.[123] Therefore, the differences and the inconsistencies between vv. 1–5 and vv. 7–18 should be explained from a communicative and functional perspective.[124] Throughout the discourse, the method

---

[119] Cf. Kowalski, *Die Hirtenrede*, 117.

[120] Van der Watt, *Family of the King*, 81.

[121] Van der Watt, *Family of the King*, 81.

[122] Van der Watt, *Family of the King*, 77, n. 254.

[123] Van der Watt, *Family of the King*, 80. Van der Watt, *Family of the King*, 82, warns, "Strict mechanical allegorical application will functionally place the emphasis on the wrong aspect of the image".

[124] See van der Watt, *Family of the King*, 81.

of contrast is employed to compare the Jewish leadership with Jesus himself. Hence, both negative and positive characters appear. The wicked Jewish leadership, which is the prototype of negative qualities, is represented by thief, robber, stranger and hireling, while Jesus, who is the prototype of all positive qualities, is represented by gate and good shepherd. The various ἐγώ εἰμι-sayings emphasize that Jesus is a common denominator in the different images which are oriented paradigmatically to the goal of eternal life.[125]

5.3.3.1 The παροιμία[126] (vv. 1–6)

Vv. 1–5 introduce an imagery of sheep farming by depicting the events that take place in a sheep pen.[127] On account of the polemical overtones, the discourse begins not with the prototype but with the antitype, the thief and the robber (v. 1). Vv. 1–3a describe the contrast between the shepherd and his opponents with regard to their entry into the sheepfold. While the thief (κλέπτης) and the robber (λῃστής) climb into the sheepfold stealthily (v. 1), the shepherd (ποιμήν) enters by the gate, which is opened to him by the gate keeper (vv. 2–3a). V. 3b–c mentions the activity of the shepherd in the sheepfold after his entry into the sheepfold by the gate. The shepherd calls the sheep by name and leads them out of the fold (v. 3bc). In vv. 4–5, there is again a contrast between the shepherd and his opponents with regard to the pasturing of the sheep after the exit of the sheep from the sheepfold. The sheep follow the shepherd and know his voice (v. 4), but they will not follow strangers and do not know their voice (v. 5). Thus, the following structure can be given to the verses in 1–5:[128]

A. Contrast between the shepherd and the thief/the bandit with regard to the entry into the fold (vv. 1–3a)
    B. The shepherd's activity in the fold (v. 3b–c)
A¹. Contrast between the shepherd and the stranger with regard to pasturing the sheep (vv. 4–5)

The two references to the contrast between the shepherd and his opponents in vv. 1–3a and vv. 4–5 frame the narration of the shepherd's activity in the sheepfold in v. 3b–c.[129] Functionally, the thief, the bandit and the stranger

---

[125] Van der Watt, *Family of the King*, 81–82.
[126] In order to maintain the enigmatic element of this word, we prefer to use the Greek word throughout.
[127] For a discussion on sheep farming in the ancient Mediterranean world and its relation to the metaphorical language in John 10, see Zimmermann, *Christologie der Bilder*, 290–302; Van der Watt, *Family of the King*, 57–58.
[128] Cf. Reinhartz, *The Word in the World*, 49.
[129] Kiefer, *Die Hirtenrede*, 12; Reinhartz, *The Word in the World*, 49.

have the same role.¹³⁰ Thus, the main elements of the παροιμία are the three characters (shepherd, opponents and sheep) and the sheepfold where they interact. The elements of gate and gatekeeper do not function independently and have their value only in relationship to the sheepfold, serving to control the entry into the sheepfold by legitimating the identity of the shepherd.¹³¹ The main themes of vv. 1–5 are, therefore, the contrast between the shepherd and his opponents (thief, bandit and stranger) and the exclusive relationship between the shepherd and the sheep.

The ἀμήν ἀμήν-saying never begins a new discourse in John's Gospel, but is used to highlight an important point or to change the direction of the discussion. The ἀμήν ἀμήν-saying in v. 1 indicates that the shepherd discourse represents a reflection of the events narrated in the previous chapter. The "blind" Jewish leaders (9,40–41) cast the blind man out of the community (9,34; cf. 9,22) instead of taking care of him. Now Jesus, the true and good shepherd, has found him (εὑρών 9,35; cf. εὑρών in Luke 15,5) and brings him back to God's fold. This background helps us to understand better the contrast between the shepherd and his opponents and the exclusive relationship between the shepherd and his sheep.

After narrating the pastoral image of the sheepfold, the evangelist comments that the audience did not understand the παροιμία Jesus was saying (v. 6).¹³² The issues surrounding the genre of the shepherd discourse are centred on the meaning of the term παροιμία.¹³³ The lexical meanings of παροιμία are a pithy saying, proverb, saw, maxim, a brief communication containing truths designed for initiates, veiled saying, figure of speech.¹³⁴ The term παροιμία occurs elsewhere only in John 16,25.29, where "speaking figuratively" is

---

¹³⁰ See Quasten, "The Parable of the Good Shepherd", 7; Reinhartz, *The Word in the World*, 49.

¹³¹ Reinhartz, *The Word in the World*, 49.

¹³² Brown, *John*, I, 393, thinks that the failure to understand in v. 6 is an unwillingness to respond to the challenge of the παροιμία.

¹³³ For a discussion of the question whether John's παροιμία can be interpreted as a parable (Gleichnis), see M. Stare, "Gibt es Gleichnisse im Johannesevangelium?", *Hermeneutik der Gleichnisse Jesu. Methodische Neuansätze zum Verstehen urchristlicher Parabeltexte*, ed. R. Zimmermann (Tübingen 2008), 320–364. Stare, "Gleichnisse", 363–364, thinks that John's παροιμίαι belong to the network of John's figurative language, and she remarks, "sie sind eine Art der Verkündigung des johanneischen Jesus, mit der er seine Adressaten und auch die Leser/innen des Johannesevangeliums zu einem tieferen Verständnis seiner Person und durch sie zum Vater führt". For a form-critical approach to the shepherd discourse, see Kowalski, *Die Hirtenrede*, 92–151. See also Zimmermann, *Christologie der Bilder*, 277–288, for an overview of various form-critical approaches to the shepherd discourse and various views of παροιμία. In fact, Zimmermann, *Christologie der Bilder*, 288–289, speaks of a "Verzicht auf Gattungszuordnung und eigene Vorgehensweise" in his approach to the interpretation of John 10.

¹³⁴ BDAG, 779–780.

contrasted with "speaking plainly" (cf. 10,24) and also in 2 Pet 2,22, where it is used in the sense of a proverb. The word is absent from the Synoptics, where the roughly equivalent expression παραβολή is found, but παραβολή is not used in John.[135] Παροιμία differs from the Synoptic parable in that there is no connected story. Most people call it an allegory, but in an allegory the same person can scarcely be represented by two figures, as here Jesus is both shepherd and gate. In the LXX, both παροιμία and παραβολή are used to translate the broad Hebrew expression מָשָׁל, which covers almost all types of figurative speech.[136] Παροιμία and παραβολή occur side by side in a few instances (e.g., Sir 39,3; 47,17) and do not differ significantly in meaning. Παροιμία can be called a figurative speech or an imagery.[137] The name we give it matters little, but in our interpretation, we must bear in mind that it does not fit neatly into any of our usual categories.[138]

As we mentioned earlier, those who fail to understand Jesus' figure of speech are likely the Pharisees since the nearest antecedent for the pronoun αὐτοῖς/ἐκεῖνοι in v. 6 is the Pharisees in 9,40. The placement of the discourse after chapter 9 gives us the clues to determine its meaning. The sheepfold may refer to the Jewish community. The contrast between the shepherd and his opponents in vv. 1–5 can be seen in parallel to the contrast between Jesus and the Pharisees in chapters 9–10. The intimate relationship between the shepherd and the sheep may represent the relationship between Jesus and the blind man in chapter 9.

Basically, the παροιμία describes the conflict between belief and unbelief in Jesus. In 9,39, Jesus declares that he came into this world for judgment on those who believe and do not believe. Those who are physically blind will gain sight because they believe in Jesus (9,38), and those who are physically able to see will become spiritually blind and remain in sin because they do not believe in Jesus (9,39–41). Therefore, the blind Jewish leaders, who are

---

[135] Reinhartz, *The Word in the World*, 71, points out that if the passage is a parable, the interpreter must make a judgement as to which elements contribute to its meaning and which are simply ornamental or incidental.

[136] Newman and Nida, *John*, 325; Brown, *John*, I, 385.

[137] Van der Watt, *Family of the King*, 18, defines imagery as "the (total and coherent) account or mental picture of objects, with corresponding actions and relations, associatively (and thematically) belonging together". The ἐγώ εἰμι-sayings as metaphorical expressions control the direction of the application of the imagery. Van der Watt, *Family of the King*, 91, reminds us that the imagery in vv. 1–5 is not developed and discussed in its minutest detail in the rest of the chapter. Therefore, he warns that the παροιμία in vv. 1–5 should not be interpreted on a detailed level, but special attention should be given to the important themes that are mentioned.

[138] Morris, *John*, 445. For further reading on παροιμία, see K. E. Dewey, "Paroimiai in the Gospel of John", *Gnomic Wisdom*, ed. J. D. Crossan (Semeia 17; Chico 1980), 81–99.

the false shepherds, are contrasted with Jesus, the good shepherd, and are unworthy to shepherd the flock of God.

The notion of belief is expressed through the phrase "hear his voice" (τῆς φωνῆς αὐτοῦ ἀκούειν). The sheep listen to his voice (vv. 3.4.27), but the refusal of the Jews to hear his voice and believe in his words (v. 25) keeps them outside the folk of Jesus. The story of the blind man in chapter 9 already depicts this refusal of the Pharisees to believe in Jesus. Hence, they repeatedly inquire about the restoration of the blind man's sight (vv. 15.17.24.26). The blind man wonders at their stubbornness and refusal to believe, "I have told you already, and you would not listen. Why do you want to hear it again?" (v. 27). On the other hand, the blind man is willing to hear Jesus' voice and to believe in him. When Jesus says to him, "Go, wash in the pool of Siloam", he obeys Jesus' command. He goes and washes and comes back, being able to see (9,7). Just as the shepherd leads the sheep from the sheepfold, Jesus leads the blind man from his blindness to sight, from darkness to light (9,4–7). In short, the meaning of the παροιμία resides as much in "the reason for its use – its effect as in its content".[139]

5.3.3.2 Jesus as the Gate[140] (vv. 7–10)

The narrative in 10,1–5 is resumed selectively and expanded in vv. 7–18.[141] There is a selective usage of the images. The discourse in vv. 7–18 is centred on two applications of the images of sheep farming, namely Jesus as the gate and Jesus as the good shepherd. In vv. 7–10, Jesus applies metaphorically to himself the image of the gate (θύρα)[142] using two ἐγώ εἰμι-sayings, which highlight his soteriological mission over against his opponents. The genitive

---

[139] Lewis, *Rereading the Shepherd Discourse*, 4. Cf. Dewey, "Paroimiai", 83.

[140] The term θύρα has the meanings of "door", "a passage for entering a structure", "entrance" and "gate". In the context of a house, θύρα is usually translated as "door" (20,19.26). But the rendering of "gate" seems better in 10,7.9 in the context of αὐλή (10,1.16), which is often understood to be "an area open to the sky, frequently surrounded by buildings and in some cases partially by walls", "enclosed open space", "courtyard", "a dwelling complex". See BDAG, 150, 462. A few manuscripts like P[75] and various Coptic manuscripts replace ἡ θύρα with ὁ ποιμὴν in v. 7. But the majority of the scholars today consider ἐγώ εἰμι ἡ θύρα τῶν προβάτων as the original reading because this seems to be the *lectio difficilior*. See Metzger, *Textual Commentary*, 195; Brunson, *Psalm 118*, 333; Thyen, *Johannesevangelium*, 481; Beutler, "Der alttestamentlich-jüdische Hintergrund", 20; Theobald, *Herrenworte*, 278; Kiefer, *Die Hirtenrede*, 16; Kowalski, *Die Hirtenrede*, 44; Brown, *John*, I, 386; Schnackenburg, *John*, II, 288; Beasley-Murray, *John*, 164; Barrett, *John*, 370–371; J. Jeremias, "θύρα", *TDNT*, III, 179, etc.

[141] Van der Watt, *Family of the King*, 90.

[142] The term θύρα appears in John 7 times. It is found 4 times within the shepherd discourse (10,1.2.7.9) and 3 times within the passion-resurrection narratives (18,16; 20,19.26). Lewis, *Rereading*, 156, points out that Jesus' ability to enter the closed doors and to come to his disciples in 20,19.26 makes sense because he is the door.

of ἡ θύρα τῶν προβάτων is better to be understood as subjective genitive, meaning "the gate for the sheep" because it is the sheep who pass through the gate in the immediate context (cf. v. 9). But if the gate in v. 7 functions the same way as in vv. 1–2, then one has to explain why v. 9 deviates from this pattern.[143]

Jesus' identification as the gate is revealed by means of contrast. When Jesus says, "All who came before me are thieves and bandits; but the sheep did not listen to them" (v. 8), he suggests that his opponents could not become for the sheep the gate that leads to the pasture of life (v. 9), but brought the sheep only to destruction and death (v. 10).[144] As part of the climatic description of Jesus' opponents, the function of the nouns κλέπται and λῃσταί is to accentuate the adversity of his opponents.[145] There is some sort of tension between vv. 1–5 and vv. 7–18 because Jesus is identified both as the gate and the shepherd.[146] This would imply that the evangelist does not feel himself bound by the formal structure of the παροιμία, but adjusts it to fit the message he wants to convey.[147] It is not an issue for him that the image of

---

[143] Cf. Brunson, *Psalm 118*, 342. However, the distinction between "gate for the sheep" and "gate to the sheep" is not so necessary because usually both the shepherd and the sheep pass through the same gate. R. Zimmermann accepts both possibilities and thinks that the evangelist has consciously kept open both possibilities through his metaphorical language. Zimmermann, *Christologie der Bilder*, 315, remarks, "Als Zugang des Hirten kann sie die Tür *zu den Schafen* bedeuten, als Eingang bzw. Ausgang der Herde kann sie ebenso als Tür *für die Schafe* aufgefasst werden". However, when we take into account the soteriology of the passage, especially the explicitly expressed soteriological implications of all ἐγώ εἰμι-sayings with predicative nominatives and the evangelist's characteristic Christocentric treatment of a theme taken from the Gospel tradition (Matt 7,13–14; Luke 13,23–24; cf. John 14,6) about entering (εἰσέρχομαι) the gate (πύλη/θύρα) to life (ζωή)/salvation (σώζω), we must admit that the concern of the evangelist is not about the entrance of the shepherd but of the sheep through the gate. He is interested here in the salvation and life of the sheep and not in the legitimacy of the shepherd.

[144] In the view of Morris, *John*, 451, the verb εἰσίν in v. 8 shows that the emphasis is on his own day when Jesus speaks of thieves and robbers. Barrett, *John*, 371, thinks that the thieves and robbers of v. 8 are the same as those of v. 1.

[145] Van der Watt, *Family of the King*, 70 (also n. 227).

[146] But such apparent tensions are also notable in other parts of the Gospel. E.g., in 6,35 Jesus is the bread of life, but in 6,51 he is the giver of this bread. Jesus claims that he speaks truth in 8,45–46, but in 14,6 he says that he himself is the truth. Westcott, *John*, 151, would say that "in relation to the fold, Christ is the door; in relation to the flock, he is the good shepherd". St. John Chrysostom in his homily (59) on John 10,2–4 says, "when he brings us to the Father he calls himself a Door, when he takes care of us, a Shepherd". See P. Schaff (ed.), *A Select Library of the Nicene and Post-Nicene Fathers of the Christian Church. Chrysostom: Homilies on the Gospel of Saint John and Epistle to the Hebrews* (First Series; Edinburgh 1889), XIV, 214. For Barrett, *John*, 370–371, the unexpected claim of Jesus as the gate in 10,7 shows that what follows is "not simply an interpretation but a development of the parable in characteristic Johannine style".

[147] Van der Watt, *Family of the King*, 72–73.

gate used in 10,7–9 does not represent an exact parallel to the one used in vv. 1–3.[148]

The repetition of the gate metaphor in v. 9, however, suggests the seriousness of the evangelist in the use of this metaphor. The qualities of the gate are now transferred to Jesus. Hence, the people have to enter (εἰσέρχομαι) through (διά) him to achieve salvation.[149] The phrase δι' ἐμοῦ expresses the specific relationship between Jesus and the believers and the exclusiveness of salvation (cf. 14,6b).[150] Jesus is the only One through whom authentic salvation is made possible. The reference to the pasture is related to the motif of life.[151] The sheep need pasture for the sustenance of life. Jesus' self-identification as the gate is, therefore, chiefly oriented to the life of the sheep. Finding pasture and finding salvation are semantically synonymous. The term ἀπόλλυμι is used in the Gospel to refer to the opposite of salvation (cf. 3,16). The three terms κλέπτω, θύω and ἀπόλλυμι (v. 10) are accumulated to create an atmosphere of destruction, functioning as a climatic description.[152]

The promise of finding pasture recalls the pastoral imagery of Ps 23,2; Isa 49,9; Ezek 34,14, where "pasture" is associated with Israel's eschatological deliverance and blessings. However, the image of gate is not found in the Old Testament pastoral symbolism. Hence, the source or the background[153] for John's use of gate is to be sought outside the Old Testament pastoral symbolism. The immediate source for the sayings on gate in John is likely to be the Synoptic tradition (Matt 7,13–14; Luke 13,23–24) or a tradition similar to it.[154] The notions of gate to "life" (ζωή), "entering" (εἰσέρχομαι) and "saving"

---

[148] Van der Watt, *Family of the King*, 73. A. C. Brunson notices that the pericope on the gate (vv. 7–10) borrows the language from the παροιμία but not necessarily the meaning and function. In fact, as he reminds, "A number of problems noted by the commentators are easily resolved or at least significantly eased, if one expects less coherence and strict correlation between 10,1–5 and 10,7–10". See Brunson, *Psalm 118*, 324.

[149] On the provision of access to God through Jesus, see John 14,6; Rom 5,2; Eph 2,18; Heb 10,20; Rev 3,7 (cf. Isa 22,22).

[150] Jeremias, "θύρα", 180, says, "The absolute claim of Jesus to be the only Mediator, to the exclusion of all other mediation, is emphasized by the emphatic, preceding δι' ἐμοῦ (10,9)". Bernard, *John*, II, 355, believes that the form ἐάν τις expresses the universality of the implied appeal (cf. 7,17). Anyone can enter by this gate. In the view of K. Erlemann, "Selbstpräsentation Jesu in den synoptischen Gleichnissen", *Metaphorik und Christologie*, ed. J. Frey et al. (TBT 120; Berlin 2003), 37–52, the Christology of the Johannine παροιμία aims at emphasizing the exclusiveness of the salvific significance of Jesus.

[151] Newman and Nida, *John*, 327, link pasture to the fullness of life.

[152] Van der Watt, *Family of the King*, 75. The threefold repetition of parallel expressions such as "steal and kill and destroy" is a characteristic device denoting emphasis in biblical literature. See Matt 7,7; John 14,6; 1 Thess 1,3; 5,23.

[153] As it is mentioned earlier, a distinction is to be made between source and background. See p. 296, n. 10.

[154] Cf. Theobald, *Herrenworte*, 301–303; M. Sabbe, "John 10 and Its Relationship to the Synoptic Gospels", *The Shepherd Discourse of John 10 and Its Context*, ed. J. Beutler and

(σῴζω) are present in both contexts of John and the Synoptic tradition.[155] However, since there are also notable differences between the two, we may assume that John has transformed the tradition into Christological statements using the ἐγώ εἰμι-formulas under the influence of the messianic interpretation of Ps 118, precisely Ps 118,20. A great number of scholars suggest that Ps 118,20 serves as the background for the gate sayings in John 10,7.9.[156] Psalm 118 is the most frequently quoted psalm in the New Testament.[157] John

---

R. T. Fortna (Cambridge 1991), 90–91; J. Painter, "Tradition, History and Interpretation in John 10", *The Shepherd Discourse of John 10 and Its Context*, ed. J. Beutler and R. T. Fortna (Cambridge 1991), 61–62; F. Hahn, "Die Hirtenrede in Joh 10", *Theologia Crucis, Signum Crucis* Festschrift Erich Dinkler, ed. C. Andresen and G. Klein (Tübingen 1979), 190–191. While Matthew uses πύλη, Luke's term is θύρα which is employed by John as well. Since these terms are interchangeably used in the New Testament, their difference does not have much significance. See the explanation below on p. 332, n. 159.

[155] The saying in Matt 7,13–14 is immediately followed by a saying on false prophets, who come in sheep's clothing but inwardly are ravenous wolves (7,15). It stands in parallel with John 10,12–13.

[156] E.g., Brunson, *Psalm 118*, 317–350; Schnelle, *Johannes*, 197; Ball, *I Am*, 317; P. Stuhlmacher, *Biblische Theologie des Neuen Testaments* (Göttingen 1999), II, 230; Reinhartz, *The Word in the World*, 81; O'Day, *John*, 669; Beutler, "Der alttestamentlich-jüdische Hintergrund", 31; Beasley-Murray, *John*, 169; Simonis, *Die Hirtenrede*, 251; Brown, *John*, I, 394; J. V. Arenas, "Yo soy la puerta (John 10,7.9). Trasfondo y sentido de la imagen cristológica de la puerta", *Carmelus* 37 (1990), 77; T. Kambeitz, "I Am the Door", *Bible Today* 27 (1989), 111; E. Fascher, "Ich bin die Tür: Eine Studie zu Joh 10,1–18", *DTh* 9 (1942), 43, 49. Theobald, *Herrenworte*, 300, considers Ps 118,20 and Jesus' sayings in Luke 13,24/Matt 7,13–14 as the two possible sources for the gate metaphor in John 10,9. Regarding the influence of Ps 118,20, he remarks, "Der Spruch ist aus einer schriftgelehrten Beschäftigung mit Ps 118 erwachsen; dessen christologisch gedeuteter v. 20 bot ihm die Matrix". Schnackenburg, *John*; II, 290, thinks that the gnostic material for the door-motif is much richer, but also believes that "the choice of door as symbol of the Saviour could have ties with the Messianic interpretation of Ps 118 (117)". At the end of 1st centaury CE, St. Clement of Rome (1 Clem 48,2–4) cites Ps 118,20 when he speaks of the gate (πύλη) of righteousness in Christ, "For this is the gate of righteousness which opens on to life, as it is written, 'Open me the gates of righteousness, that I may enter into them and praise the Lord; this is the gate of the Lord, the righteous shall enter in by it'. So then of the many gates which are opened, that which is in righteousness is the one in Christ, in which are blessed all who enter and make straight their way in holiness and righteousness, accomplishing all things without disorder". See K. Lake (tr.), *The Apostolic Fathers* (LCL 24; London 1912), I, 91–93.

[157] Jesus is said to have cited in the Synoptic Gospels from Ps 118,22, "The stone that the builders rejected has become the chief cornerstone" (see Mark 12,10; Matt 21,42; Luke 20,17). All the Gospels relate Jesus' entry into Jerusalem with Ps 118,26, "Blessed is the one who comes in the name of the Lord" (see Mark 11,9; Matt 21,9; Luke 19,38; John 12,13). The monograph of Andrew C. Brunson (*Psalm 118 in the Gospel of John*) is a full-length study about the importance of Ps 118 in the Gospel of John. For a good discussion on the significance of this psalm in the New Testament, specifically in the life of Jesus, see Brunson, *Psalm 118*, 1–7.

explicitly quotes this psalm (118,25–26) in 12,13 and there are also allusions to this psalm in 8,56 (118,24), 10,24 (118,10–12) and in 11,41–42 (118,5.21.28c).[158] The fact that John uses θύρα instead of the πύλη in the LXX (Ps 117,20) does not pose a serious difficulty.[159] At any rate, the combination of θύρα with εἰσέρχομαι in John 10,9 and of πύλη with εἰσέρχομαι in Ps 117,20 is striking. John uses ἔρχομαι to contrast the purpose of Jesus with that of his opponents in 10,10. Thus, in 10,10 an antagonism is made between the false "coming ones" and the true "coming One", who stands in parallel to the "coming One" in Ps 118,26.[160] The shepherd discourse is spatially set in Jerusalem, most probably in the temple area (8,59; 10,23) and temporally at the feast of Tabernacles (7,2.14.37; cf. 10,22) in which Ps 118 plays an important liturgical role.[161] There is a view that "the gates of righteousness" and "the gate of/to Yahweh" in Ps 118,19–20 refer to the eastern gate of the Jerusalem temple, through which the believers enter the temple during the procession at the feast of Tabernacles.[162] Most of the LXX combinations of εἰσέρχομαι with either θύρα or πύλη have to do with entering the gates of the temple.[163] Therefore, the combination of εἰσέρχομαι and ἐξέρχομαι with θύρα in 10,9 would evoke a temple context. The use of the term αὐλή, which is a *terminus technicus* for the courtyard of the temple, is rather surprising for the

---

[158] Cf. Brunson, *Psalm 118*, 2–3.

[159] The Hebrew שַׁעַר is rendered by both θύρα and πύλη in the LXX (e.g., Ezek 46,12). Both terms in the New Testament are sometimes interchangeable, especially when they refer to the same gate (e.g., θύρα in Acts 3,2; 21,30 but πύλη in 3,10; πύλη in Matt 7,13–14 but θύρα in Luke 13,24–25). Even though θύρα and πύλη are found frequently in the LXX, John never uses πύλη. It is likely that John uses the more popular θύρα for the Hebrew שַׁעַר. Moreover, if πύλη is used most often to refer to the gates of a city, the temple or the entrance of the tabernacle court, the semantic range of θύρα is wider, referring frequently to the entrance of a room, house, sepulchre or a prison cell. This difference in the semantic range would probably account for the difference between Matthew's πύλη and Luke's θύρα. It should be noticed that Luke uses θύρα in the context of a house (13,25), whereas Matthew uses πύλη in the context of a road, which is most likely associated with a city. John, then, might have preferred θύρα, which would fit better for the gate of a sheepfold. See BDAG, 462, 897; Cf. Brunson, *Psalm 118*, 328–329.

[160] For a survey of the meaning and function of the "coming One" motif in John and its relationship to Ps 118, see Brunson, *Psalm 118*, 240–264.

[161] For a detailed study regarding the setting of Ps 118, see Brunson, *Psalm 118*, 22–101.

[162] See *m.Sukk.* 5:4; Cf. J. Morgenstern, "The Gates of Righteousness", *HUCA* 6 (1929), 10; Brunson, *Psalm 118*, 335–336.

[163] Brunson, *Psalm 118*, 337.

sheepfold.[164] Hence, there is also a view that αὐλή (10,1.16) may allude to the temple court.[165]

The evangelist believes that in Jesus all the primary institutions and symbols of Judaism find their fulfilment. In Jesus' declarations to be the gate, the motif of the replacement of the temple gate can be noticed.[166] His body is already identified as the temple (2,18–22), and he himself is the locus of true worship (4,19–26). The Hebrew text of Ps 118,20 describes the gate as "the gate to Yahweh" (הַשַּׁעַר לַיהוָה), whereas the LXX (117,20) calls it "the gate of the Lord" (ἡ πύλη τοῦ κυρίου). In both texts, especially in the Hebrew, the gate is the means of access to Yahweh. Jesus' claim to be the gate establishes his mediation in providing access to the Father and communion with him. This view agrees well with that of 14,6b, "No one comes to the Father except through me".

It should be noticed that Jesus is not just the means of salvation and life for the sheep. He himself is the salvation and the life (11,25; 14,6). When he claims to be the gate, it implies not only the means but also the end. In biblical categories, the gate of the city or of the temple can imply the city or the temple itself (e.g., see Pss 87,1–2; 122,2; Ezek 26,2; Jer 14,2; 15,7; Isa 3,26). Thus, in accordance with the principle of *pars pro toto*, the gate can stand for the whole temple.[167] In Ps 118,20, those who enter the gate of/to Yahweh are those who enter the temple. In the Gospel of John, Jesus is not only the gate but also the temple (2,19–21). On the one hand, being the gate, he provides for his believers the access to Yahweh, but on the other hand, being the temple, he himself is the location of Yahweh. In him the believers meet Yahweh. He is the place, where the sheep find salvation.[168] The life that Jesus gives is of an eschatological kind, the attainment of that sphere where the Godhead dwells.[169] Hence, it is life in fullness and superabundance (10,10).

---

[164] Cf. Stare, "Gleichnisse", 349; Zimmermann, *Christologie der Bilder*, 295; B. Kowalski, "Ruf in die Nachfolge (Vom Hirt und den Schafen) Joh 10,1–5", *Kompendium der Gleichnisse Jesu*, ed. R. Zimmermann (Munich 2007), 768–780.

[165] See B. Kowalski, "Ruf in die Nachfolge", 778; Simonis, *Die Hirtenrede*, 125; Reinhartz, *The Word in the World*, 67; Brunson, *Psalm 118*, 339, n. 89. The "bringing out" (ἐκβάλλω) of the sheep by the shepherd in 10,4 is reminiscent of the "driving out" (ἐκβάλλω) of the sheep from the temple by Jesus in 2,15.

[166] See Brunson, *Psalm 118*, 338.

[167] Cf. Simonis, *Die Hirtenrede*, 206.

[168] In the words of Simonis, *Die Hirtenrede*, 206, "Forthin ist Jesus der neue Sammelpunkt des Heils, die neue αὐλή statt der alten, die abgedankt hat. So liegt in v. 7 eine neue Entwicklung beschlossen, eine Entfaltung in Richtung auf den neuen Heilsort, der Jesus ist. Die in der Paroimia anfänglich materielle Lokalisierung des Heils der Schafe findet ihre Vertretung jetzt in Jesus".

[169] Schnackenburg, *John*, II, 293.

5.3.3.3 Jesus as the Good Shepherd (vv. 11–18)

The idea of pasture connects Jesus' activity as the gate (vv. 7–10) with his activity as the good shepherd (vv. 11–18). The image of Jesus as the shepherd, implicitly suggested in vv. 1–5, is explicitly stated in vv. 11–18. The goodness of the shepherd consists in his readiness to die for the well-being of the sheep. The statement "The good shepherd lays down his life for the sheep" (v. 11; cf. v. 15b) is based specifically upon the crucifixion as a known historical event and implies a voluntary acceptance of death by Jesus.[170] Vv. 12–13 should be understood in the light and service of the metaphor in v. 11.[171] The positive image of the good shepherd (vv. 11.14–15) is contrasted with the negative image of the hireling (μισθωτός) in vv. 12–13. The hireling will desert the sheep and flee at the moment of danger because for him his own life and safety are more important than the life and safety of the sheep. The mutual knowledge between the shepherd and the sheep (vv. 14–15) is not of a cognitive quality but a category of relationship. The focus of v. 16 is most probably the gentile mission.[172]

Jesus is the good shepherd not simply because of his relationship to the sheep, but also because of his relationship with the Father.[173] Vv. 17–18 set Jesus' death in the context of his relationship with the Father. They explain how and why Jesus would lay down his life for the sheep and relate his death to his power of resurrection. Different from other Easter tradition, here is an emphasis on Jesus' own power to raise himself from the dead. His death is an expression of his obedience to the Father, but it is inseparable from the resurrection.

John's use of shepherd image is steeped in the Old Testament sheep-shepherd imagery, but he develops it to suit his Christological purpose.[174] The conceptual parallels between Ezek 34 and the shepherd-sheep imagery in John 10 are generally well-recognized.[175] Ezek 34 portrays the image of God as the good shepherd. He cares for the sheep, rescues them, feeds them and tends the weak, the injured and the lost (34,11–16). The image of the false shepherd is contrasted by the image of God as the caring shepherd (vv. 11–16.25–30; cf. Isa 40,11). John's presentation of Jesus as the shepherd suggests that he is the good shepherd promised in Ezekiel. The hireling, the

---

[170] Cf. Barrett, *John*, 374–375; Morris, *John*, 453.

[171] Van der Watt, *Family of the King*, 82.

[172] The significance of this verse will be discussed later. See pp. 384–385.

[173] O'Day, *John*, 670.

[174] For a discussion on the symbol of the shepherd in ancient Oriental (Jewish and non-Jewish) and Greek-Christian literature outside John's Gospel and on the background of the shepherd language in John 10, see Zimmermann, *Christologie der Bilder*, 317–342.

[175] Other Old Testament passages which may have influenced the vocabulary in John 10 are Num 27,17; Jer 23,1–16. The image of Israel as God's sheep is also found in Pss 74,1; 77,20; 78,52; Isa 49,9; 63,11; Jer 13,17; 31,10; Zech 9,16; 10,3.

thieves and robbers in John 10 are paralleled by the false shepherds in Ezek 34,1–7.

In Ezek 34, God promises that he will be the shepherd of Israel (v. 15) and at the same time he will establish his servant David as their shepherd (vv. 23–24). The Davidic Messiah is spoken of as a shepherd in Ps 78,70–72; Mic 5,3 as well. In John, Jesus fulfils the role of God and his servant David as a shepherd by the ἐγώ εἰμι-sayings in 10,11.14. The shepherd role of God and his servant David in Ezekiel is paralleled by Jesus' role as the shepherd and his close relationship and union with the Father as the Son.[176] It should be noted that the relationship between God and his servant David in Ezek 34 is so close that God speaks of only one shepherd. This fact of a single shepherd is emphasized in the Bible only in Ezekiel and in John (10,16.30).[177] The notion of one shepherd is found in Ezek 34,23; 37,24 (cf. Jer 23,3; Ps 23; the notion of one flock in Mic 2,12). Likewise, the notion of salvation (σῴζω) noticeable in Ezek 34,22 is also pointed out in John 10,9. The oneness of Jesus with his Father is similar to the oneness of David the shepherd with God in Ezek 34.[178] In spite of the similarities between John's and Ezekiel's sheep-shepherd imagery, John's conception of shepherd goes beyond any Old Testament pastoral symbolism and is, therefore, unique.[179]

5.3.4 Conclusion

In 10,1–5, an imagery relating to sheep farming is discernible. In 10,7–18, the presented imagery is used to represent the divine reality of Jesus using the ἐγώ εἰμι-sayings (10,7.9.11.14). The role of the ἐγώ εἰμι-formulas is to apply two key images of the παροιμία to Jesus. Hence, there are two ways of viewing him, as the gate and as the good shepherd. Both images have to do with salvation, which consists in the attainment of life. The main concern of the evangelist is not the explanation of the παροιμία in detail, but the Christological application of these two images in a contrasting manner. Hence, the

---

[176] Ball, *I Am*, 225–226.

[177] Reim, *Hintergrund des Johannesevangeliums,* 184; Ball, *I Am*, 226.

[178] In the view of Ball, "Whether Jesus is to be identified with God through his claim to be the shepherd or with his servant David is of little importance, for they both perform the same task. This is true to such an extent that Jesus can claim 'I and the Father are one'". See Ball, *I Am*, 226.

[179] The shepherd's readiness to die for his sheep is not clearly found in the Old Testament. By referring to the shepherd's willingness to lay down his life for the sheep, the evangelist goes beyond the imagery of the shepherd in Ezekiel. Likewise, the mutual knowledge between the shepherd and the sheep (10,14) is also typically Johannine. There is a view that the idea of the shepherd being willing to die for his sheep in John stems from Isa 53,6–9, where the iniquity of the sheep is taken away by the servant of the Lord. However, if Isa 53 is in mind, it has been thoroughly transformed in the light of Jesus' passion and death. See Ball, *I Am*, 230, n. 6.

negative features and figures, too, appear. The negative characters are illustrated in order to highlight the good qualities of Jesus as the gate and as the good shepherd.

As the gate to/of Yahweh (cf. Ps 118,20), he gives access to life and as the good shepherd, he leads the believer to eternal life. He is the gate to life because he himself is life (11,25; 14,6), and he is the shepherd who leads the sheep to life because he lays down his life for the sheep (10,11.14–15). Jesus is able to perform his functions as the gate and the good shepherd due to his oneness with the Father (cf. 10,17–18.30). His claim to be the gate underscores the exclusiveness of salvation offered by him because the sheepfold has only one gate. There is a tendency to highlight Jesus' image as the shepherd at the expense of his Christological image as the gate.[180] In fact, it is his self-revelation as the gate that gives the shepherd discourse its Christological edge and a unique character of salvation.

5.4 Jesus as the Resurrection and the Life[181] (11,25–26)

The ἐγώ εἰμι-saying in 11,25 occurs in the context of Jesus' dialogue with Martha (11,17–27). It is in response to Martha's belief in the final resurrection (v. 24) that Jesus makes the claim to be the resurrection and the life. The raising of Lazarus would be no more than a spectacular miracle without Jesus' claim to be the resurrection and the life.[182] The context of Lazarus' resurrection deepens the meaning of Jesus' claim to be the resurrection and the life.[183] We cannot find a direct quotation from the Old Testament behind v. 25, but Jesus here applies to himself a current expectation, which has its basis in the Old Testament. The idea of resurrection is found in Dan 12,1–2 and 2 Macc 7,9.14; Wis 3,1–4 (cf. Mark 12,18–27; Luke 14,14; Acts 23,6–8; 24,15.21; 1 Cor 15,42; Phil 3,11). Martha's faith in the eschatological resurrection in 11,24 is probably based on the prophetic words of Dan 12,2.

---

[180] O'Day, *John*, 672, says, "When the shepherd image is emphasized in isolation from the gate image, the picture of Jesus in John 10 becomes too easy to appropriate and loses its Christological edge. When the gate imagery is dropped, the Christological focus of the shepherd imagery can become anthropocentric".

[181] Some manuscripts omit the words καὶ ἡ ζωή. But they can be retained in the text on the basis of considerations of the age, weight and diversification of witnesses that include καὶ ἡ ζωή. The omission can also be viewed as accidental, or it might be due to the fact that 11,24 mentions only the resurrection. Cf. Metzger, *Textual Commentary*, 199. Moreover, the notion of life is implicit in vv. 25b–26.

[182] Ball, *I Am*, 103. O'Day, *John*, 689, rightly says, "Jesus' words in vv. 25–26 are the critical theological lens for interpreting the raising of Lazarus and, indeed, for understanding the Fourth Gospel's eschatological categories".

[183] The resurrection of Lazarus is a fulfilment of the prediction in 5,28–29 in a symbolical sense because the resurrection to which 5,28–29 refers is the general resurrection on the last day (cf. 6,40.44.54). See Dodd, *Interpretation*, 366.

Jesus' declaration takes up Martha's words, reinterprets and applies them to himself by means of the ἐγώ εἰμι-formula.[184] He transforms Martha's future expectation into a present reality, which is fulfilled in himself.[185] The terms ἀνάστασις and ζωή can be understood as correlative with the statements in verses 25b and 26a respectively.[186] That means Jesus is the resurrection because those who believe in him, even though they die physically, will live spiritually. He is the life because everyone who lives and believes in him will never die spiritually. In other words, Jesus' identification with the resurrection means that physical death has no power over the believers, and their future is determined by their belief in Jesus (cf. 5,28–29; 6,39–40.44.54).[187] His identification with the life means that he is capable of giving the believers eternal life that survives physical death (cf. 3,16.36; 5,24; 6,47; 10,28; 17,2).[188] Eternal life is the relationship with God that begins in the present through belief in Jesus and endures beyond physical death, issuing into the final and future resurrection.[189] By claiming to be both resurrection and life, Jesus affirms his sovereignty over the present and future lives of believers.[190]

Belief in Jesus is a necessary condition for the gift of life. The participial clause ὁ πιστεύων εἰς ἐμέ functions as a hinge relating v. 25b with v. 26a. The focus of v. 25b is the effect that belief in Jesus has on the believer's death, and the focus of v. 26a is the effect it has on the believer's life.[191] In the Old Testament, God is the only giver of life (Gen 2,7; Deut 4,4; Pss 16,11; 21,5; 36,10) and God alone can give life to the dead. By raising Lazarus, Jesus reveals his unity with God who sent him (11,42; cf. 5,21). The unity proclaimed by Jesus in the prayer between himself and the Father (11,41–42) corresponds to the self-identification of Jesus with life.[192] Jesus'

---

[184] Ball, *I Am*, 248.

[185] Ball, *I Am*, 248.

[186] Cf. Dodd, *Interpretation*, 365.

[187] O'Day, *John*, 688–689.

[188] In the view of O'Day, *John*, 689, Jesus makes a Christological claim in v. 25a that redefines traditional Jewish eschatological expectations and he reveals the soteriological implications of that claim in v. 26a.

[189] Koester, *Symbolism*, 120.

[190] O'Day, *John*, 688. The notions of resurrection and life are joined in 6,40.44.54, which emphasize the final resurrection. We can also notice that while 5,24–25 refer to realized eschatology, 5,28–29 refer to the final eschatology.

[191] O'Day, *John*, 688.

[192] R. Zimmermann, "The Narrative Hermeneutics in John 11. Learning with Lazarus How to Understand Death, Life and Resurrection", *The Resurrection of Jesus in the Gospel of John*, ed. C. R. Koester and R. Bieringer (WUNT 222; Tübingen 2008), 90.

power to raise Lazarus and his claim to be the resurrection and the life are based on the fact that he has been sent by the Father (11,42).[193]

Martha's confession in 11,27, "Yes, Lord, I believe that you are the Messiah, the Son of God, the one coming into the world", is a messianic confession in the full Christian sense and a summary of the identity of Jesus (cf. 20,31). The title "Messiah" shows that Jewish expectations are fulfilled in Jesus, and the title "Son of God" indicates that Jesus' messiahship surpasses the Jewish expectations because of his exclusive union with God/the Father.[194] The title "the one coming into the world" echoes the Johannine designation of Jesus as "the one who comes into the world" (1,9–11; 3,31; 6,51; 7,29; 8,23).

5.5 Jesus as the Vine (15,1.5)

The final ἐγώ εἰμι-sayings with images in the Gospel appear in 15,1.5.[195] There is a confusion regarding the genre of 15,1–8 on account of its figurative language.[196] We may call it a "metaphorical network", where substitutional and interactional metaphors function together to form a larger imagery.[197] Jesus' self-identification as the vine is presented in v. 1 in the context of his relationship with the Father and in v. 5 in the context of his relationship with the disciples. For the first time, ἐγώ εἰμι-sayings are immediately joined through the co-ordinate conjunction καί to other characters than Jesus, like the Father as the vinedresser (v. 1) and the disciples as the branches (v. 5). Jesus is the true vine because he comes from the Father, the only true God (cf. 17,3). The mention of the Father in v. 1 qualifies the vine as something

---

[193] Ball, *I Am*, 104. Zimmermann, "The Narrative Hermeneutics", 77, remarks that the long "warm-up" to the miraculous action at the end of John 11 makes the reader think that this is more than just a miracle story.

[194] Cf. Schnackenburg, *John*, II, 332.

[195] The clause ταῦτα λελάληκα ὑμῖν in 15,11 can be regarded as a division marker (cf. 14,25; 16,1.4.33). Consequently, the discourse on vine and branches and its significance (vv. 1–17) can be divided into two units, vv. 1–11 and vv. 12–17. While the first part emphasizes the importance of bearing fruit, the second part explains the meaning of bearing fruit. The metaphorical language is dominant only in vv. 1–8.

[196] Its genre has been variously identified by the scholars, e.g., as parable (Gleichnis), image, imagery, Bildrede, allegory, figure, symbolic speech, *mashal*, metaphor, etc. For a brief overview of various approaches taken by the scholars, see van der Watt, *Family of the King*, 29.

[197] For a discussion on the metaphorical network in 15,1–8, see van der Watt, *Family of the King*, 123–134. Cf. Petersen, *Brot, Licht und Weinstock*, 289–292; J. Zumstein, "Bildsprache und Relektüre am Beispiel von Joh 15,1–17", *Imagery in the Gospel of John*, ed. J. Frey et al. (WUNT 200; Tübingen 2006), 140–143. Van der Watt, *Family of the King*, 30, points out that the metaphorical nature of 15,1–8 is evident from the very first sentence, namely "I am the vine", because of the incongruence between the person "I" and the plant "vine".

belonging to the heavenly order.[198] The action of the Father is like the one who prunes the branches (v. 2), so that the disciples may bear fruits and glorify the Father (v. 8). The gardener, the vine and the branches are three necessary factors for the production of fruits. The ἐγώ εἰμι-sayings in vv. 1.5 place Jesus as the middle ground between the Father and the disciples.[199]

The characterization of Jesus as the vine and the disciples as the branches (v. 5) expresses the disciples' dependence on Jesus. V. 5c–d restates the claim in v. 4. The emphasis on "bear fruit" (vv. 2.4.5.8.16) and "abide in me" (vv. 4–7.9) points out the intimate relationship between Jesus and the disciples. Jesus is the *exclusive* source of fruitfulness for the disciples because *apart from him* they can do nothing (vv. 4–5). The demand to abide in Jesus implicitly means that Jesus is the giver and sustainer of life for the disciples. Just as the branches receive life from the vine, the disciples must receive life from Jesus. Only those who live in communion with Christ can produce the fruits of the Christian call. The organic union of the branches with the vine and so with one another provides a striking image for the idea of the mutual indwelling of Christ and his disciples, which is made possible only through the principle (fruit) of love (vv. 9–17).[200]

In the current research, two models are presented as the possible background for the metaphorical language in 15,1–17.[201] They are the day-to-day experience from the agricultural life of the society[202] and various texts from the Old Testament.[203] It is possible to assume that both factors have influenced the evangelist. Certainly, John's metaphorical language is rooted in the Old Testament imagery of vine, vineyard and gardener. It is, however, not borrowed from a particular passage, but originates from an entire impression, which is the outcome of a large number of statements and connected ideas.[204] Therefore, we cannot pinpoint a single passage from the Old Testament as the exclusive source of influence, but rather a collection of them as the background material for the metaphorical language in 15,1–8.

Ps 80 (LXX 79) is a good place to begin with, where Israel and God are depicted to be the vine and the gardener respectively.[205] Another possible

---

[198] Brown, *John*, II, 659.

[199] Cf. O'Day, *John*, 757.

[200] Dodd, *Interpretation*, 412.

[201] Zumstein, "Bildsprache", 153.

[202] For a brief orientation on vine farming in antiquity, see van der Watt, *Family of the King*, 26–29.

[203] For a detailed study of the Old Testament parallels to the discourse in John 15, see R. Borig, *Der wahre Weinstock. Untersuchungen zu Joh 15,1–10* (StANT 16; Munich 1967), 79–93; Ball, *I Am*, 241–248.

[204] Ball, *I Am*, 248.

[205] For Dodd, *Interpretation*, 411 and Carson, *John*, 513, this psalm is the primary background for John 15,1–8.

passage is the song of the vineyard in Isa 5,1–7, in which the house of Israel is the vineyard of the Lord and, by implication, the Lord is the gardener.[206] In Isaiah the fruitfulness of the vine is contrasted with the production of bad fruits, whereas John contrasts fruitfulness with fruitlessness. Yet another text that might have supplied the material for the language in John 15,1–8 is Jer 2,21, where Israel is the vine and the Lord is the gardener (also see Isa 27,2–6; Ezek 15,2–6; 17,5–10; 19,10–14; cf. Mark 12,1–9). Thus, we have to admit that Jesus' claim in John 15,1.5 alludes to many Old Testament passages, and it is the typological nature of vine that John emphasizes. The metaphor of vine has also a collective reference. It can refer not only to the stalk but also to the whole plant with its branches. Since, for John, the Christian believers are the genuine Israelites (cf. 1,47), the vine as a symbol of Jesus and the believers is, in a certain sense, the symbol of the new Israel.[207]

6. John 14,6 in Relation to Other ἐγώ εἰμι-Sayings

6.1 John 14,6 in Relation to Absolute ἐγώ εἰμι-Sayings

6.1.1 John 14,6 as a Revelatory Statement

We have already seen that absolute ἐγώ εἰμι is a revelatory formula in Deutero-Isaiah and in John. The Johannine Jesus is presented in the manner in which Yahweh speaks in Deutero-Isaiah.[208] Since John uses the title κύριος for Jesus (20,28), it is possible to think that John considers ἐγώ εἰμι in the mouth of Jesus as the divine name given to Jesus.[209] The sacredness of ἐγώ

---

[206] The distinction between vine in John and vineyard in Isaiah need not be taken so seriously. In the manuscripts of Old Latin, Old Syriac, Ethiopic, Tatian and some Fathers, ἄμπελος renders "vineyard" in John 15,1. R. E. Brown thinks that in the popular Greek attested in the papyri, ἄμπελος sometimes takes on the meaning of ἀμπελών. He also suggests that the expression "thrown away" in v. 6 would fit the image of a vineyard better than that of a vine where we might expect "fallen off". See Brown, *John*, II, 660–661; J. H. Moulton and G. Milligan, *The Vocabulary of the Greek Testament Illustrated from the Papyri and other Non-Literary Sources* (London 1914–1929), 27; Ball, *I Am*, 245, n. 2.

[207] Brown, *John*, II, 670. R. E. Brown thinks that John's notion of vine and branches may originate from a combination of the imagery of Israel as the vine and the imagery of wisdom as a life-giving tree or vine (Sir 24,17–21). He also notices a secondary Eucharistic symbolism in 15,1–8. See Brown, *John*, II, 672–674.

[208] Schnackenburg, *John*, II, 83, rightly remarks, "The One who presents himself as the God of the fathers, who chose Israel, the one who brings about the salvation of his people, is unique, unique in his holiness, righteousness and loyalty, and therefore proves himself to be the true God, and it is for this reason that he must make an exclusive claim. All these elements are included in the revelatory formula and come into prominence according to circumstances. The same is true of the way the Johannine Jesus uses the formula".

[209] Brown, *John*, I, 537.

εἰμι is not in the phrase itself but in the person who utters it. "By saying 'I am' Jesus not only identifies who he is but indicates how he reveals God's power and presence".[210] The absolute use of ἐγώ εἰμι in John is the basis for his use of ἐγώ εἰμι with images.[211] Hence, all ἐγώ εἰμι-sayings with images should be interpreted in the light of the absolute ἐγώ εἰμι-sayings in the Gospel. It is worth noticing that in chapter 6 the absolute ἐγώ εἰμι (6,20) functions as the basis for other ἐγώ εἰμι-sayings with images (6,35.41.48.51). The basis for Jesus' claim to be the light of the world (8,12) is his power to use the absolute ἐγώ εἰμι, which occurs in chapter 8 frequently (8,24.28.58). An *inclusio* may be noticed between 8,12 and 8,58. The ἐγώ εἰμι-saying in 14,6 is presented in the context of Jesus' farewell meal with the disciples and his farewell speech in chapters 13–14. Jesus' use of the absolute ἐγώ εἰμι in 13,19 in the context of his journey to the Father provides the basis for his use of ἐγώ εἰμι with the images way, truth and life in 14,6. Since the images of way, truth and life are attached to the revelatory formula ἐγώ εἰμι, Jesus' claim in 14,6 can be understood as a revelatory statement.[212]

6.1.2 Ἐγώ εἰμι as Expression of Jesus' Oneness with the Father

In Deutero-Isaiah, the formula אֲנִי הוּא/ἐγώ εἰμι is a code word of absolute monotheism.[213] It is used to assert the belief that Yahweh alone is God. Deutero-Isaiah supplied John with a solemn expression that was eminently suitable for expressing the unity of the Father and the Son and had at the same time a strong connotation of monotheism.[214] We can say that John reflects on the phrase אֲנִי הוּא/ἐγώ εἰμι in Deutero-Isaiah and uses the absolute ἐγώ εἰμι in order to communicate his belief that the Son is one with the Father, and yet God remains and continues to be one.[215] When Jesus speaks the absolute ἐγώ εἰμι, he reveals not only himself but also his Father. Hence, we can say that "das ἐγώ εἰμι ist die Offenbarung des Vaters, aber in seinen Namen ist Jesus eingeschlossen: ἐγώ εἰμι = der Vater und Jesus".[216] Ἐγώ εἰμι means ἐγώ καὶ ὁ πέμψας με πατήρ (8,16). "Im Sein Jesu ist das des Vaters eingeschlossen. Theo-Logie ist Christo-Logie... Im 'Ich bin' sind Jesus und Gott

---

[210] Koester, "Jesus as the Way", 130.
[211] Brown, *John*, I, 537.
[212] The other ἐγώ εἰμι-sayings with images (10,7.9.11.14; 11,25; 15,1.5) can be correspondingly interpreted as revelatory statements even though absolute ἐγώ εἰμι does not occur in their near context.
[213] Richter, *'Anî Hû und Ego Eimi*, 42, says, "Diese 'Formel' bildet also gewissermaßen das Herzstück von Deuterojesajas Theologie. Sie wird ein 'Kennwort' seines absoluten Monotheismus".
[214] Harner, *I Am*, 57.
[215] Harner, *I Am*, 57.
[216] Zimmermann, "Das absolute Ἐγώ εἰμι", 271.

vereinigt".²¹⁷ Therefore, the statement "no one comes to the Father except through me" reveals not only the exclusiveness of salvation through Jesus but also his unique and exclusive relationship with the Father. This is a relationship of oneness. It is clearly expressed in 14,7–11. Thus, we can say that the statement "no one comes to the Father except through me" is an explanation of the absolute ἐγώ εἰμι, which is an expression of Jesus' oneness with the Father.²¹⁸

6.2 In Relation to ἐγώ εἰμι-Sayings with Images

6.2.1 Relation with the Context

Jesus' identification with a particular image is closely associated with the context in which Jesus speaks. In chapter 6 Jesus speaks about the bread of life and applies this image to himself in the context of the approaching Passover (6,4) and the multiplication of bread (6,5–13.26–27). It is in the context of the feast of light (7,2.10.14.37) that he applies the image of light to himself (8,12). In chapter 10 in the context of the shepherd discourse, two images from pastoral life, gate and shepherd, are applied to him. In chapter 11 in the context of raising Lazarus from the dead, Jesus claims to be the resurrection and the life (11,25). Even though 14,31b may cause some disjunction, there is connection between Jesus' claim to be the vine in 15,1.5 and his speech on the theme of union of the disciples with himself and the Father in chapter 14 (14,20,23). The imagery of vine and branches is also closely related to the theme of abiding in chapter 15. As in the case of these ἐγώ εἰμι-sayings with images, there is a relation between Jesus' claim in 14,6 and its immediate and near context. Jesus speaks about his imminent departure in John 13–14 and it is in the context of his journey that Jesus claims to be the way. The images of truth and life, which play an important role in the Gospel, are added to the image of way to give it a complete sense, as it is found in other biblical and Jewish literature.

6.2.2 Significance of Soteriology

While the absolute ἐγώ εἰμι-sayings are more concerned with Jesus' identity, the ἐγώ εἰμι-sayings with images are more concerned with his mission, i.e., the salvation of the world. The saving character of Jesus' mission is visible and impressive in all images and concepts: bread, light, gate, shepherd, resurrection, life, way, truth and vine. It can be noticed that all these images and concepts are tied up with soteriological statements, which consist of demands

---

²¹⁷ Hinrichs, *Ich bin es*, 60–61, 65.

²¹⁸ Schnackenburg, *John*, II, 88, writes, "As the Son who exists and acts in the closest association with the Father, he must make the full and exclusive claim to be the only access to the Father (14,6)".

and promises. The soteriological statements demand a strong relationship with Jesus: "come to Jesus and believe in him" (6,35), "eat the bread that Jesus gives" (6,51), "follow Jesus" (8,12), "enter through Jesus" (10,9), "believe in Jesus" (11,25) and "abide in Jesus" (15,5). The promises are expressed variously: "will never be hungry and thirsty" (6,35), "will live forever" (6,51), "will have light of life" (8,12), "will be saved" (10,9), "lays down his life for the sheep" (10,11), "will live and will never die" (11,25–26), "bear much fruit" (15,5). These expressions point out the outcome of Jesus' coming into the world. In the case of 14,6, the images of way, truth and life are also tied up with a soteriological statement, "No one comes to the Father except through me". This statement includes a demand and a promise. The phrase "except through me" refers to the demand that everyone should come to Jesus or believe in Jesus. The promise is that everyone who comes through Jesus "comes to the Father".

6.2.3 Relation between Gate and Way

Jesus' claims to be the gate and the way are literally located in the context of two discourses, the shepherd discourse and the farewell discourse. Both gate and way are presented in association with movement or journey. In the shepherd discourse, there are frequent references to the movement of the thief/bandit, the shepherd, the sheep, the wolf, the hireling and Jesus.[219] In the farewell discourse as well, the verbs of movement frequently appear.[220] In many respects, gate and way have similar functions.[221] Both are intended for movement and journey. If the gate is for the purpose of coming in and going out, the way is also for going and coming.[222] The sheep come in and go out through the gate to the pasture. In the same way, the disciples have to come to the Father who is the source of life through Jesus, the way. Both gate and way connect figuratively two spheres, human and divine, profane and sacred, below and above. "Die Tür ist Sinnbild des Übergangs zwischen zwei

---

[219] The verbs of movement for various characters in the shepherd discourse are the following: thief/bandit – εἰσέρχομαι, ἀναβαίνω (10,1), ἔρχομαι (10,8.10); shepherd – εἰσέρχομαι (10,2), ἐξάγω (10,3), ἐκβάλλω, πορεύομαι (10,4); sheep – ἀκολουθέω (10,4.5), φεύγω (10,5), twice εἰσέρχομαι (10,9), ἐξέρχομαι (10,9); wolf – ἔρχομαι (10,12); hireling – ἀφίημι (10,12), φεύγω (10,12); Jesus – ἔρχομαι (10,10), ἄγω (10,16).

[220] We have already seen how the journey motif controls chapters 13–14. See pp. 107–111.

[221] Schnackenburg, *John*, II, 292, views that "the door-word approximates closest of all to the way-word" (14,6).

[222] Becker, *Das Bild des Weges*, 17, says that ὁδός was used to indicate the entrance and the exit of a building.

Bereichen, zwischen Diesseits und Jenseits, profanem und heiligem Bereich".[223]

There is also an element of exclusiveness associated with gate and way.[224] The phrase "through me" (δι' ἐμοῦ) in 10,9 stands parallel to "through me" (δι' ἐμοῦ) in 14,6.[225] The sheepfold which is described in John 10 has only one gate.[226] In the same way, there is no other way to come to the Father than Jesus. Both gate and way are related to the theme of life. One who enters through the gate, who is Jesus, is saved and receives life (10,9–10). "Being saved" is synonymous with "having eternal life" in the Gospel (e.g., 3,16–17). In 14,6 as well, the life, which corresponds to the Father, stands at the end of the paratactic construction "the way and the truth and the life", showing the destination of the way. From the perspective of Johannine theology, we may say that Jesus is the gate and the way to (of) the Father who is the source of life.[227] Both gate and way have a universal appeal. Both are kept

---

[223] T. Popp, "Die Tür ist offen (Die Tür) Joh 10,7–10", *Kompendium der Gleichnisse Jesu*, ed. R. Zimmermann (Munich 2007), 784.

[224] Therefore, while evaluating the form of the ἐγώ εἰμι-sayings in 10,9 and 14,6, Theobald, *Herrenworte*, 288–289, remarks, "Sieht man sie als isolierte Sprüche, dann gewinnt man aufgrund ihrer Formgebung den Eindruck, dass das Gewicht ihrer Aussage weniger auf ihren Verheißungen ruht, gerettet zu werden bzw. zum Vater zu gelangen, als vielmehr auf der Einschärfung der Exklusivität des Heilswegs Jesus Christus".

[225] The Synoptic Gospels speak of entering through "the narrow gate" (Matt 7,13–14; Luke 13,24). About the gate in John 10,9, Theobald, *Herrenworte*, 303, comments, "Die Enge der Türe besteht jetzt darin, dass sie sich allein in Christus und sonst nirgendwo öffnet".

[226] In the second centuary *Shepherd of Hermas* (Similitude IX, xii, 5–6), the Son of God is identified with the only gate (πύλη), through which those who are to be saved enter into the kingdom of God, "'If then you are not able to enter into the city except through the gate which it has, so,' said he, 'a man cannot otherwise enter into the kingdom of God, except through the name of his Son, who was beloved by him. Do you see,' said he, 'the crowd which is building the tower?' 'Yes, Sir,' said I, 'I see it.' 'They,' said he, 'are all glorious angels; by these then the Lord has been walled round. But the gate is the Son of God, this is the only entrance to the Lord. No man can enter into him otherwise, than through his Son'". See K. Lake (tr.), *The Apostolic Fathers* (LCL 25; London 1912), II, 251.

[227] See Popp, "Die Tür ist offen", 787. St. Ignatius of Antioch, who is considered to have been martyred in Rome in the tenth year of Trajan, i.e., 108 CE, in his letter to the Philadelphians (9,1) identifies Jesus as the θύρα τοῦ πατρός, the door/gate of the Father, "The priests likewise are noble, but the High Priest who has been entrusted with the Holy of Holies is greater, and only to him have the secret things of God been entrusted. He is the door of the Father through which enter Abraham and Isaac and Jacob and the Prophets and the Apostles and the Church". See K. Lake (tr.), *The Apostolic Fathers* (LCL 24; London 1912), I, 249. "The door of/to the Father", about which St. Ignatius speaks, reminds us of "the door of the Lord" in Ps 118,20. Brown, *John*, I, 394, assumes that Ignatius knew John's Gospel and that he is referring to John 10,7–10. See Theobald, *Herrenworte*, 296–299, for a discussion about the relationship between John and St. Ignatius regarding their sayings on the gate.

open to all. There is neither compulsion nor restriction. Both provide freedom of movement for entry and exit.[228] As the gate, Jesus is the way to life and as the shepherd, he leads the way to life.[229] Jesus is the gate to life because he himself is life (11,25;14,6), and he leads the way to life because he lays down his life for the sheep (10,11.14–15).[230]

6.2.4 Significance of Truth

The ἐγώ εἰμι-saying in 14,6 also contains the image of truth. It is, however, not the sole instance where ἐγώ εἰμι stands in relation to truth. The ἐγώ εἰμι in 4,26 is uttered in the context (4,23–26) of the need of worshipping God/the Father "in Spirit and truth" (ἐν πνεύματι καὶ ἀληθείᾳ). In Jesus are fulfilled not only all messianic expectations but also the worship of God in Spirit and truth because he himself is the truth and he can speak ἐγώ εἰμι in the style of divinity (4,26).[231] The theme of truth (ἀλήθεια) is also found in the ἐγώ εἰμι-sayings in 6,32 in the image "the true bread from heaven" (ὁ ἄρτος ἐκ τοῦ οὐρανοῦ ὁ ἀληθινός) and in 15,1 in the image "the true vine" (ἡ ἄμπελος ἡ ἀληθινή). The placement of the adjective ἀληθινός after the nouns for emphasis is striking. The ἐγώ εἰμι-saying in 8,18 is closely related to the theme of the truth of Jesus' judgement and testimony (8,16–17).[232] Since Jesus embodies truth in his own person (14,6), his judgment and testimony are true (8,16–17). The adjective ἀληθινός here indicates exclusivity in the sense of "the only real", as compared with putative or would-be.[233] In 14,6, the definite article before ἀλήθεια suggests that Jesus alone is the truth.[234] Thus, the claim that Jesus is the truth is the basis and the climax of all truth claims in the Gospel.

6.2.5 Significance of Life

All ἐγώ εἰμι-saying with images are directly or indirectly connected with the theme of life. It is directly found in "the bread of life" (6,35), "the light of life" (8,12b), "the resurrection and the life" (11,25) and "the way and the

---

[228] Keener, *John*, II, 811, says, "Coming and going probably represent a Semitic way of expressing freedom of movement".

[229] O'Day, *John*, 672.

[230] O'Day, *John*, 672. Regarding the relation between way and door/gate, Theobald, *Herrenworte*, 292, says, "Wer auf den Bahnen eines (im Unterschied zum Tür-Motiv) relativ breiten jüdisch-hellenistischen Traditionsstroms Christus den Weg nennen konnte, dem stellte sich auch seine Prädikation mit dem Bildwort der (Himmels-) Tür leicht ein".

[231] Also see the discussion on pp. 305–306.

[232] The adjectives ἀληθινός and ἀληθής appear in 8,17–18.

[233] Brown, *John*, I, 500.

[234] The significance of exclusivism in the ἐγώ εἰμι-sayings is further discussed below. See pp. 347–348.

truth and the life" (14,6). In 6,35.48.51, ζωή/ζῶ qualifies the image of bread. In 10,9, the image of gate is directly associated with the theme of "being saved" (σωθήσεται), which is synonymous with "having life" (ζωὴν ἔχωσιν) in 10,10. In 10,11, there is a reference to the laying down of "the physical life" (ψυχή) by the good shepherd for his sheep, which is intended ultimately to give ζωή, the life in abundance (10,10). The verb ζάω also occurs twice in 11,25–26. Except 15,1.5, all other ἐγώ εἰμι-sayings with images have relation to the theme of life explicitly in their context. Even though the terms "life" and "live" do not occur in the context of 15,1.5, the theme of life is pictorially present through the imagery of vine and branches, which bear much fruit. The ἐγώ εἰμι-sayings in 15,1.5 show that the disciples can have life and bear much fruit only if they remain one with Jesus, just as the branches will be able to have life and bear much fruit only if they remain close to the vine (15,4–5).

These various images and metaphors attached to the ἐγώ εἰμι-sayings are simply variations of the single theme that Jesus has come so that human beings may have life (10,10).[235] Jesus identifies twice with life, in 11,25 and 14,6. He never identifies with any other concept twice.[236] In both instances, life is placed at the end showing its importance as the final destination. Thus, all ἐγώ εἰμι-sayings with images are somehow related to the theme of life, highlighting its significance in the Gospel.[237] The table below lists the ἐγώ εἰμι-sayings which are closely related to life.

John	Ἐγώ εἰμι-Sayings with Images Related to Life
6,35	Ἐγώ εἰμι ὁ ἄρτος τῆς ζωῆς· ὁ ἐρχόμενος πρὸς ἐμὲ οὐ μὴ πεινάσῃ, καὶ ὁ πιστεύων εἰς ἐμὲ οὐ μὴ διψήσει πώποτε.
6,48	Ἐγώ εἰμι ὁ ἄρτος τῆς ζωῆς.
6,51	Ἐγώ εἰμι ὁ ἄρτος ὁ ζῶν ὁ ἐκ τοῦ οὐρανοῦ καταβάς· ἐάν τις φάγῃ ἐκ τούτου τοῦ ἄρτου ζήσει εἰς τὸν αἰῶνα, καὶ ὁ ἄρτος δὲ ὃν ἐγὼ δώσω ἡ σάρξ μού ἐστιν ὑπὲρ τῆς τοῦ κόσμου ζωῆς.
8,12	Ἐγώ εἰμι τὸ φῶς τοῦ κόσμου· ὁ ἀκολουθῶν ἐμοὶ οὐ μὴ περιπατήσῃ ἐν τῇ σκοτίᾳ, ἀλλ' ἕξει τὸ φῶς τῆς ζωῆς.

---

[235] Zimmermann, "Das absolute Ἐγώ εἰμι", 272, writes, "Alle diese Begriffe, die letztlich auf den einen, nämlich den Begriff des Lebens, zurückgeführt werden können, weisen auf ihn hin, der das Leben in sich selbst hat (5,26), der das Leben ist (11,25; 14,6), und der das Leben in Fülle zu schenken vermag (vgl. 10,10)".

[236] Stare, *Durch ihn Leben*, 271, says, "Die Ich-bin-Worte Jesu offenbaren das Wesen seiner Person vor allem als ζωή. Jesus verkörpert das Leben, die Gabe Gottes, in seiner Person".

[237] Cebulj, *Ich bin es*, 291, concludes the findings of his research like this, "Mit der Wendung ἐγώ εἰμι sagt Jesus aus, was er für den joh Kreis sein will und wie dieser ihn verstehen soll: Für diejenigen, die am Bekenntnis zu Jesus festhalten ist Jesus Brot, Licht, Tür, Hirt, Weg, Weinstock und Auferstehung, mit einem Wort: Leben".

10,9–10	Ἐγώ εἰμι ἡ θύρα· δι' ἐμοῦ ἐάν τις εἰσέλθῃ σωθήσεται καὶ εἰσελεύσεται καὶ ἐξελεύσεται καὶ νομὴν εὑρήσει. ὁ κλέπτης οὐκ ἔρχεται εἰ μὴ ἵνα κλέψῃ καὶ θύσῃ καὶ ἀπολέσῃ· ἐγὼ ἦλθον ἵνα <u>ζωὴν</u> ἔχωσιν καὶ περισσὸν ἔχωσιν.
11,25–26	Ἐγώ εἰμι ἡ ἀνάστασις καὶ <u>ἡ ζωή</u>· ὁ πιστεύων εἰς ἐμὲ κἂν ἀποθάνῃ ζήσεται, καὶ πᾶς <u>ὁ ζῶν</u> καὶ πιστεύων εἰς ἐμὲ οὐ μὴ ἀποθάνῃ εἰς τὸν αἰῶνα·
14,6	Ἐγώ εἰμι ἡ ὁδὸς καὶ ἡ ἀλήθεια καὶ <u>ἡ ζωή</u>· οὐδεὶς ἔρχεται πρὸς τὸν πατέρα εἰ μὴ δι' ἐμοῦ.

6.2.6. Significance of Exclusivism and Uniqueness

John uses concrete metaphors (bread, light, way, shepherd, gate, vine) and abstract/conceptual metaphors (resurrection, truth and life) in the predicated ἐγώ εἰμι-sayings. The choice of these metaphors signifies that "alles, wonach Menschen sich jemals sehnen, alles, was für sie lebensnotwendig ist, das ist Jesus, er allein und er in ausschließlichem Sinn".[238] Every ἐγώ εἰμι-saying with image has the tone of exclusivism and absolutism. To express this exclusivism and absolutism, every metaphor has a definite article before it. A predicate noun in Greek usually does not have a definite article.[239] If it is used, it means that "the predicate is identical with the subject rather [with] a general class of which the subject is a particular example".[240] Hence, the statement in 14,6a can mean conversely that the way and the truth and the life is Jesus and there is no other. Thus, there is an emphasis on the identity and interchangeability of the subject and predicate.[241] The same can be said in the case of every other ἐγώ εἰμι-saying with image. Therefore, the light of the world or the gate or the shepherd or the bread of life or the resurrection or the vine is Jesus, and there is no other. To show his uniqueness some metaphors are qualified with adjectives, "true bread" (6,32), "living bread" (6,51), "good shepherd" (10,12.14), "true vine" (15,1).

The prediction in 10,16 implies that for John there is only "one" (εἷς) shepherd as there is only one way to the Father (14,6). There is also an element of exclusivism attached to the ἐγώ εἰμι-saying in 15,5 when Jesus claims, "Apart from me, you can do nothing" (χωρὶς ἐμοῦ οὐ δύνασθε ποιεῖν οὐδέν). In a certain way, the exclusivism of this claim is equivalent to that of 14,6b, "No one comes to the Father except through me". It should be noted that Jesus' address to his disciples in 15,5 immediately changes from second

---

[238] Richter, 'Anî Hû und Ego Eimi, 63.

[239] BDF, 143 (§273), states, "Predicate nouns, as a rule, are anarthrous. Nevertheless, the article is inserted if the predicate noun is presented as something well known or as that which alone merits the designation (the only thing to be considered)".

[240] Harner, The I Am, 50. In the view of Schnackenburg, John, II, 84, the definite article before the metaphors gives them sharpness and exclusiveness.

[241] Harner, The I Am, 50.

person plural (implied in δύνασθε) to the indefinite pronoun τὶς in 15,6a, "Whoever does not abide in me is thrown away like a branch and withers". The referent of τὶς can be not only the Christian believers but anyone who yearns for salvation. This fact is differently and much more clearly expressed in 14,6b, "No one comes to the Father except through me".

6.2.7 Significance of Inclusivism and Universality

There are elements of inclusivism and universality associated with the ἐγώ εἰμι-sayings attached to images. The bread that Jesus gives is for the life of the whole world and the expression ἐάν τις φάγῃ suggests the universality of the appeal (6,51). Similarly, the genitive "of the world" attached to the image of light expresses the universal appeal of Jesus' claim (8,12). The image of gate has also an inclusive dimension. Anyone can enter by this gate. In 10,9, the form δι' ἐμοῦ ἐάν τις εἰσέλθῃ comes first for emphasis and expresses the universality of the implied appeal (cf. 7,17). It is open to all and welcomes everyone who enters it.[242] The only requirement is a willingness to enter. There is neither a compulsion to enter nor a forced exclusion. The emphasis is not upon who is unauthorized to enter but on who is authorized.[243] Therefore, the gate with which Jesus identifies himself is an open gate.[244] It is important to note that Jesus does not say that he lays down his life for *his* sheep but for *the* sheep (v. 15).[245] He is the shepherd of all the sheep (10,16). Since Jesus is the resurrection and the life, "everyone" (πᾶς) who lives and believes in Jesus will never die (11,25–26). Because Jesus is the vine (15,5), everyone is asked to abide in Jesus. Otherwise, "everyone who does not abide" (ἐὰν μή τις μένῃ) in him will wither away (15,6). The substantive οὐδείς in 14,6 has a universal appeal because it includes everyone.[246] Hence, Jesus is the way for all. Thus, elements of inclusivism and universality are noticeable either in all images themselves or in the explanation about them.[247]

---

[242] Jesus' mission among the Samaritans, who are excluded from the flock of Israel (John 4), is a concrete sign of this universality and openness.

[243] Brunson, *Psalm 118*, 344.

[244] J. P. Martin, "John 10,1–10", *Interpretation* 32 (1978), 172–173, says, "By his death and resurrection Jesus has become the door to an open community and the door of an open community".

[245] Simonis, *Die Hirtenrede*, 207, points out, "Die Schafe, deren Tür Jesus ist, sind darum in v. 7 nicht mehr zu verstehen als die Seinen im Gegensatz zu den Schafen im allgemeinen; nein, sobald das messianische Ich ausgesprochen ist, erweitert sich die Heilsperspektive für jeden, da hier die Grenzen der historischen Bedingtheit von Jesu Leben durchbrochen werden".

[246] The significance of "no one" (οὐδείς) in 14,6 is already explained. See pp. 276–278.

[247] The theme of universal salvation in John is discussed below in detail. See pp. 381–386.

6.2.8 Images and Their/Jesus' Relationship with the Father

Many of the predicated ἐγώ εἰμι-sayings and the images attached to them stand in close relationship with the Father. It is the Father who gives the true bread (6,32). This bread is called "the bread of God" (ὁ ἄρτος τοῦ θεοῦ) because its origin is from heaven (6,33). Even though the image of light in 8,12 is not directly associated with the Father, Jesus' claim to be the light of the world prompts the Pharisees to question the authenticity of this claim. In his answer, Jesus points out his unique relationship with the Father. It is the Father who judges together with him (8,16) and gives testimony to him (8,18). The image of the shepherd in 10,14–15 is found in direct relation with the Father. The model for the knowledge between the shepherd and his sheep (10,14) is the mutual knowledge between Jesus and his Father (10,15). In 15,1, the image of the vine stands in direct relation with the Father. While Jesus is the vine, the Father is the vinedresser. It is only in 15,1 that an ἐγώ εἰμι-saying with image is further developed with a predication about the Father. The mention of the Father here helps to understand that Jesus is the vine of the divine order. In 14,6 as well, the image of way stands in close relation with the Father because the way leads the believer to the Father.

7. Conclusion

The ἐγώ εἰμι-sayings provide yet another important context for interpreting and understanding the meaning of John 14,6. A survey of the occurrences of the phrase ἐγώ εἰμι in all instances and the manner of its application show that it is consciously used by the evangelist because of its theological significance. The presence of ἐγώ εἰμι-formulas in the Gospel is pervasive. They extend between Jesus' declaration as the Messiah before the Samaritan woman (4,26) and his utterance before his opponents in the garden (18,5.8) that creates an astounding response from them (18,6). They are not limited to any particular setting or audience. They occur with or without predicate in his conversations with the public as well as in his private conversations with the disciples. They are used in his discourses (6,35.41.48.51; 10,7.9.11.14; 14,6; 15,1.5), debates with his opponents (8,12.18.24.28.58), private teaching (4,26; 11,25; 13,19) or even as a declaration (6,20; 18,5–8). Their use with images is sometimes associated with a sign (6,35.41.48.51; 10,7–14; 11,25) or sometimes without a sign (8,12; 14,6; 15,1.5).

The above discussion has shown how the absolute ἐγώ εἰμι-sayings, which are attributed to the Johannine Jesus, derive their meaning and significance from the Old Testament. Deutero-Isaiah is the most probable source of the Johannine use of absolute ἐγώ εἰμι. If John knew the Synoptic tradition, its influence (cf. Mark 6,50) cannot be ruled out. We can notice some kind of similarities between the usages of grammatically absolute ἐγώ εἰμι in the Gospel and the absolute ἐγώ εἰμι in Deutero-Isaiah. It is like Yahweh in Deutero-Isaiah that Jesus utters the absolute ἐγώ εἰμι in the Gospel. This is very evident in John 8. The Johannine Jesus is presented as the one in whom Isaiah's promise of salvation is fulfilled.

The Old Testament also provides the conceptual background for understanding all ἐγώ εἰμι-sayings with images. The images like bread, light, gate, shepherd, resurrection, way and vine draw inspiration from the Old Testament, and in the application of these images to Jesus, the evangelist finds their salvific fulfilment in Jesus. Like the image of way, the image of light stands in close relation to Deutero-Isaiah. If the absolute ἐγώ εἰμι-sayings emphasize Jesus' identity, ἐγώ εἰμι-sayings with images focus on his identity in relation to his role for others.[248] The sayings with images begin at the level of Christology but move on to the theme of soteriology and discipleship. Jesus is the fulfilment of all that has been asserted by these images throughout the Gospel.[249]

The use of ἐγώ εἰμι in chapters 6 and 8 suggests that there is a deliberate interaction between the different forms of ἐγώ εἰμι-sayings in the Gospel.[250] A complete understanding of 14,6 necessarily requires an understanding of all ἐγώ εἰμι-sayings in the Gospel. The character of ἐγώ εἰμι as a revelatory formula reveals that 14,6 is to be understood as a revelatory statement. The absolute use of ἐγώ εἰμι provides the basis for the use of ἐγώ εἰμι with images. Absolute ἐγώ εἰμι is an expression of Jesus' oneness with the Father, which is explicitly stated in 14,6b and in the following verses (vv. 7–11). Hence, the claim "No one comes to the Father except through me" is an explanation of the absolute use of ἐγώ εἰμι.

All ἐγώ εἰμι-sayings with images have a common character by which we need to interpret John 14,6. Like all other ἐγώ εἰμι-sayings with images, 14,6 is closely related to the context. The theme of Jesus' journey in the context corresponds well with the image of way. Like all other ἐγώ εἰμι-sayings with images, 14,6 contains a soteriological statement with a focus on life. The images of way and gate have similar functions. Jesus' identification with the truth is the climax of all his claims about truth in the Gospel. The notion of exclusivism and uniqueness of salvation through Jesus on the one hand and the notion of inclusivism and universality on the other hand are present in all ἐγώ εἰμι-sayings with images in various ways. The mention of the Father is found in other ἐγώ εἰμι-sayings with images as well. In short, the various

---

[248] Schnackenburg, *John*, II, 80, says, "All the images, in other words, are interpreted as referring to the significance of Jesus Christ for believers". In the view of Brown, *John*, II, 534, "The predicate is not an essential definition or description of Jesus in himself; it is more a description of what he is in relation to man".

[249] Ball, *I Am*, 205.

[250] Cf. Ball, *I Am*, 147.

features of 14,6 are present in other ἐγώ εἰμι-sayings with images. Thus, John 14,6 belongs to the network of other ἐγώ εἰμι-sayings in the Gospel, and it should be interpreted in relation to them.[251]

---

[251] Wilckens, *Das Evangelium nach Johannes*, 223, says, "Man kann in 14,6 eine Zusammenfassung aller Ich-bin-Worte sehen".

Chapter VII

John 14,6 in Its Historical Context

The focus of this discussion is not to propose a historical context for the origin and development of the Gospel, which is beyond the scope of this study, but to examine whether the exclusivism of John 14,6 is caused by the historical context of expulsion from the synagogue, to check whether John 14,6 has a polemic character, especially an anti-Judaistic and sectarian tendency, and finally to suggest a possible historical context for the emergence of the exclusivism in John 14,6.[1]

1. Is the Exclusivism of John 14,6 Caused by the Expulsion from the Synagogue?

In the view of James H. Charlesworth, John 14,6 is an embarrassment and a misrepresentation of the fundamental message of Jesus.[2] As the title of Charlesworth's article suggests, his main argument is that the exclusivism of 14,6b is caused by a social setting different from that of Jesus. The social setting different from that of Jesus here refers to the expulsion of the believers in Jesus from the synagogue, which is argued to have happened in the later period of the first centuary. In other words, the exclusive claim "no one

---

[1] The view that the exclusivism of John 14,6 is caused by expulsion from the synagogue can be found in Charlesworth, "Exclusivism", 493–513. D. Rensberger, "Sectarianism and Theological Interpretation in John", *What Is John? Literary and Social Readings of the Fourth Gospel*, ed. F. F. Segovia (Atlanta 1998), II 146–148, believes that Johannine Christology emerged from everyday life struggles of the Johannine Christian community and regards Johannine Christology as a sectarian Christology. R. H. Gundry, *Jesus the Word According to John the Sectarian. A Paleofundamentalist Manifesto for Contemporary Evangelicalism, Especially Its Elites, in North America* (Grand Rapids 2002), also maintains a sectarian view of the Gospel. For a criticism of this work, see P. N. Anderson, review of R. H. Gundry, *Jesus the Word According to John the Sectarian. A Paleofundamentalist Manifesto for Contemporary Evangelicalism, Especially Its Elites, in North America* (Grand Rapids 2002), *The Princeton Seminary Bulletin* 26 (2005), 245–248. Tack, *John 14,6 in Light of Jewish-Christian Dialogue*, 412, also considers John 14,6 partly as a response to "an external threat" on the part of the Jews.

[2] Charlesworth, "Exclusivism", 493.

1. Is the Exclusivism of John 14,6 Caused by the Expulsion from the Synagogue? 353

comes to the Father except through me" (14,6b) was formed or added later as a reaction to the expulsion from the synagogue.[3]

If Charlesworth's article is scrutinized, some contradictions can be noticed. This is evident when he states, "The obvious reason for expulsion was exclusivistic theology and Christology. Messianology or Christology was tolerated within Judaism, but what would be abhorrent is the claim that Jesus was God's Messiah and that the crucified one was to be equated with God". This can also mean that the exclusive claims like "no one comes to the Father except through me" existed before the expulsion from the synagogue and caused the expulsion or separation from the Jewish community. Charlesworth here contradicts the intended argument of his article that the exclusivism of 14,6b was caused by "expulsion from the synagogue" (a social setting different from that of Jesus). When Charlesworth remarks, "Exclusivistic Christology causes divisiveness and it shapes the later layers of the Gospel of John. A prime example is 14,6b",[4] he fails to recognize that 14,6b is already an essential part of the exclusivistic Christology, which caused division and expulsion.

Charlesworth's view that the exclusivism of John 14,6 is caused by expulsion from the synagogue is given the impetus by J. L. Martyn's groundbreaking work, *History and Theology in the Fourth Gospel*. In Martyn's reconstruction of the *Sitz-im-Leben* of the Gospel of John, he attributes much of its content not to the life of Jesus but rather to the life of the Johannine community.[5] For him, the Gospel of John is a drama being acted out on a two-level stage, on one level presenting the story of Jesus and on the other a story of the Johannine community. He argues that the ἀποσυνάγωγος passages (9,22; 12,42; 16,2) do not depict the events that took place during Jesus' life but refer to the expulsion from the synagogue, experienced decades later by the Johannine community.[6] In his view, the Twelfth Benediction of the Eighteen Benedictions, *Birkat haMinim*, which formed part of the Jewish liturgy, was re-rewritten about 85 CE in order to expel the Jewish Christians as heretics. Hence, Martyn places the expulsion mentioned in the Gospel between 85 CE and 115 CE, with an inclination toward the earlier part of this period and

---

[3] In the view of Charlesworth, "Exclusivism", 497–499, John 14,6b is an interpolation. It is already shown on pp. 185–193 that Charlesworth's arguments for a redactional approach are baseless.

[4] Charlesworth, "Exclusivism", 502.

[5] See J. L. Martyn, *History and Theology in the Fourth Gospel* (Louisville ³2003), 35–143.

[6] Therefore, Martyn thinks that "in the two-level drama of John 9, the man born blind plays not only the part of a Jew in Jerusalem healed by Jesus of Nazareth, but also the part of the Jews known to John who have become members of the separated church because of their messianic faith and because of the awesome Benediction". See Martyn, *History and Theology*, 66.

thinks that the Gospel was written as an account of the struggle of the Johannine community with the Jewish synagogue that expelled it.[7]

Even though Martyn's hypothesis is still influential, his arguments regarding the *Birkat haMinim* have been severely attacked.[8] The relationship between what happened to the blind man in John 9 and what happened to Jewish Christians in the Diaspora at that time is not yet clear. Even though the expulsion from the synagogue is anachronistic in John 9, Martyn's two-level reading strategy has serious limitations, which have already been pointed out by scholars.[9] This strategy has no basis in the literary genre of the Gospel of

---

[7] Martyn, *History and Theology*, 60–61, 65–66.

[8] See R. Kimelman, "Birkat haMinim and the Lack of Evidence for an Anti-Christian Jewish Prayer in Late Antiquity", *Jewish and Christian Self-Definition. Aspects of Judaism in the Graeco-Roman Period*, ed. E. P. Sanders et al. (London 1981), II, 226–244; E. E. Urbach, "Self-Isolation or Self-Affirmation in Judaism in the First Three Centuries: Theory and Practice", *Jewish and Christian Self-Definition. Aspects of Judaism in the Graeco-Roman Period*, ed. E. P. Sanders et al. (London 1981), II, 269–298; S. A. Finkel, "Yavneh's Liturgy and Early Christianity", *JES* 18 (1981), 231–250; S. T. Katz, "Issues in the Separation of Judaism and Christianity after 70 CE: A Reconsideration", *JBL* 103 (1984), 43–76; M. Hasitschka, "Sozialgeschichtliche Anmerkungen zum Johannesevangelium", *PzB* 1 (1992), 59–67; B. Visotzky, "Methodological Considerations in the Study of John's Interaction with First-Centuary Judaism", *Life in Abundance. Studies of John's Gospel in Tribute to Raymond E. Brown*, ed. J. R. Donahue (Collegeville 2005), 91–107; R. Hakola, *Identity Matters. John, the Jews and Jewishness* (NovTSup 118; Leiden 2005), 45–55; idem, *Cursing the Christians? A History of the Birkat haMinim* (Oxford 2012), 26–33; idem, *Reconsidering Johannine Christianity. A Social Identity Approach* (New York 2015), 1–42. Martyn, *History and Theology*, 63, n. 78, thinks, "That Christians are *included* among those who are cursed in the Benediction is placed almost beyond question by the term '*Notzrim*'(Nazarenes)". But Y. Y. Teppler, *Birkat haMinim. Jews and Christians in Conflict in the Ancient World* (Texts and Studies in Ancient Judaism 120; Tübingen 2007), 360, states, "The appearance of the term *Notzrim* is relatively late, and does not pre-date the third or fourth century". C. J. Setzer, *Jewish Responses to Early Christians. History and Polemics, 30–150 C.E.* (Minneapolis 1994), 91, questions the link between *Birkat haMinim* and the expulsion of Christians from the synagogue portrayed by the Johannine author. According to E. W. Klink III, "The Overrealized Expulsion in the Gospel of John", *John, Jesus and History. Aspects of Historicity in the Fourth Gospel*, ed. P. N. Anderson et al. (Atlanta 2009), II, 180, the term *minim* originated and functioned before 70 CE, well before the time scholars assume the Gospel of John was written, in the earlier part of the Christian movement and performed an important function in the midst of the intra-Jewish conflict between various "groups" and was flexible enough to be able to refer to a diverse number of groups like Sadducees, Samaritans and Christians.

[9] E.g., A. Reinhartz, "'Jews' and Jews in the Fourth Gospel", *Anti-Judaism and the Fourth Gospel. Papers of the Leuven Colloquium, 2000*, ed. R. Bieringer et al. (Assen 2001), 352, states, "While the two-level reading as proposed by Martyn provides an avenue for imagining a history that is lost to us, we should also remember that the earliest audience would have seen this Gospel as a story of Jesus' life and may not have been troubled by or knowledgeable about its anachronism as we are". W. M. Wright, *Rhetoric and Theology. Figural Reading of John 9* (BZNW 165; Berlin 2009), argues that Martyn's two-

1. Is the Exclusivism of John 14,6 Caused by the Expulsion from the Synagogue? 355

John.[10] The Gospel shows a strong sense of the pastness of the story of Jesus, located temporarily and geographically in its own time and space and often refers explicitly to the difference between the periods before and after the death and resurrection of Jesus (e.g., 2,22; 7,39; 12,16; 13,7).[11] When the evangelist speaks of the content and purpose of the Gospel, he does it in terms of reference to the history of Jesus (20,30–31; 21,24–25) and not to the history of the Johannine community.[12]

Moreover, the two-level reading strategy is not at all easy to practise because the Gospel's narrative cannot be read sequentially as a story about the Johannine community, and the reader can hope to know the sequence of events and theological developments in the history of community only by placing various parts of the Gospel in the temporal order of composition.[13] This reading strategy cannot be applied to every part of the narrative, and every character in the Gospel cannot plausibly represent some group in the community's history and context (e.g., Judas, Pilate, the five thousand).[14] There are narratives in the Gospel where Martyn's two-level reading strategy will not work out at all, e.g., 11,1–44 and 12,11.[15] In 11,1–44, Mary and Martha, who are believers and friends of Jesus, do not seem to be expelled from the Jewish community but are rather comforted by fellow Jews (11,19). In 12,11, the desertion of the believing Jews from the Jewish community is not related to an official Jewish policy of expulsion but implies an act of free will by the Jews themselves.

---

level reading strategy is not a historical reconstruction but a kind of allegorical or figural reading. See also J. Bernier, *Aposynagōgos and the Historical Jesus in John. Rethinking the Historicity of the Johannine Expulsion Passages* (Leiden 2013); E. W. Klink III, "Expulsion from the Synagogue? Rethinking a Johannine Anachronism", *Tyndale Bulletin* 59 (2008), 99–118.

[10] Therefore, R. Bauckham, *The Testimony of the Beloved Disciple. Narrative, History and Theology in the Gospel of John* (Grand Rapids 2007), 117, remarks, "It is genre that generally guides readers as to the reading strategy appropriate for a particular text. What generic category would give its readers to understand that they should read the history of their own community encoded in the story of an historical individual?" This question is relevant in the light of the recent studies on the genre of the Gospels, which argue that contemporaries would have recognized all four canonical Gospels as a specific form of the Greco-Roman biography. Cf. R. A. Burridge, *What Are the Gospels? A Comparison with Greco-Roman Biography* (Grand Rapids ²2004).

[11] Bauckham, *The Testimony*, 117.

[12] Bauckham, *The Testimony*, 117. A. Reinhartz, "The Johannine Community and Its Jewish Neighbours: A Reappraisal", *What Is John? Literary and Social Readings of the Fourth Gospel*, ed. F. F. Segovia (Atlanta 1998), II, 137 says, "The Gospel reflects the complex social situation of the Johannine community but not the specific historical circumstances which gave rise to that situation".

[13] Bauckham, *The Testimony*, 117.

[14] Bauckham, *The Testimony*, 117.

[15] See Reinhartz, "'Jews' and Jews in the Fourth Gospel", 352.

Different from Jesus' negative experiences of the synagogue in the Synoptic Gospels (Mark 3,1–6; 6,1–6; Matt 12,9–14; 13,54–58; Luke 4,16–30; 13,10–17), in the Gospel of John the synagogue is not a place of Jesus' conflict with Jewish authorities, but rather the temple (2,13–21; 5,14–16; 7,14–53; 8,20–59; 10,23–39; 11,56–57). It is to be noted that nouns referring to "the temple" (ἱερόν, ναός) occur altogether 14 times throughout the Gospel (ἱερόν: 2,14–15; 5,14; 7,14.28; 8,2.20.59; 10,23; 11,56; 18,20; ναός: 2,19–21), whereas the noun συναγωγή occurs only twice (6,59; 18,20). John's use of the narrative spatial-markers like synagogue, house and temple does not trace the separation of John's community from the synagogue, as often supposed.[16] Hence, A. Reinhartz warns that "the expulsion theory should not be taken as axiomatic, no matter how useful it may be homiletically or exegetically".[17]

Even though Martyn's hypothesis is still impressive, it is difficult to argue that the exclusivism of John 14,6 is caused by expulsion from the synagogue. On the contrary, it is the exclusive claims like John 14,6 that caused the expulsion from the synagogues.[18] Surprisingly, D. M. Smith in the very postscript of the third edition of J. L. Martyn's *History and Theology in the Fourth Gospel* (2003) disagrees with Martyn's placement of expulsion from the synagogue before the introduction of high Christology and admits along with R. Brown and J. Ashton that the exclusive claims in the Gospel preceded and precipitated expulsion from the synagogue.[19] R. E. Brown too, in his

---

[16] See J. M. Lieu, "Temple and Synagogue in John", *NTS* 45 (1999), 51; idem, "Anti-Judaism in the Fourth Gospel. Explanation and Hermeneutics", *Anti-Judaism and the Fourth Gospel. Papers of the Leuven Colloquium, 2000*, ed. R. Bieringer et al. (Assen 2001), 134. In the view of M. Davies, *Rhetoric and Reference*, 303, "The Gospel does not give the impression that it is formed out of real disputes between Jews and Christians".

[17] A. Reinhartz, "Building Skyscrapers on Toothpicks: The Literary-Critical Challenge to Historical Criticism", *Anatomies of Narrative Criticism. The Past, Present and Futures of the Fourth Gospel as Literature*, ed. T. Thatcher and S. D. Moore (Atlanta 2008), 76. For further criticism of Martyn's hypothesis as a whole, see E. W. Klink III, "The Overrealized Expulsion", 175–184. R. Kysar, *Voyage with John. Charting the Fourth Gospel* (Waco 2005), 237–246; Keener, *John*, I, 208–214; A. Reinhartz, *Befriending the Beloved Disciple. A Jewish Reading of the Gospel of John* (New York 2001), 37–53; Carson, *John*, 361–372.

[18] M. Hengel, *The Johannine Question* (London 1989), 114–115, interprets the ἀπὸ συνάγωγος passages in John as referring to the time of Paul and Stephen.

[19] See D. M. Smith, "Postscript for Third Edition of Martyn, *History and Theology in the Fourth Gospel*" in Martyn, *History and Theology*, 21. J. Frey, "Das Bild der Juden im Johannesevangelium und die Geschichte der johanneischen Gemeinde", *Israel und seine Heilstraditionen im Johannesevangelium. Festgabe für Johannes Beutler SJ zum 70. Geburtstag*, ed. M. Labahn et al. (Paderborn 2004), 51, states, "Der Gegenstand des Streits ist die hohe Christologie des vierten Evangeliums". C. S. Keener points out that much of the Christology in the Gospel of John is pre-Johannine. According to him, persecution is the consequence of high Christology, especially the view of Jesus as deity. See Keener,

monumental work *The Community of the Beloved Disciple*, admits that high Christology existed before the expulsion from the synagogue.[20] Since this scholarly opinion seems more probably to be true, we can come to the conclusion that the exclusive claim in John 14,6 was not a reaction to the expulsion from the synagogue and that the exclusivism which was existing before led to expulsion from the synagogue. This conclusion will be further supported by the discussions below, where a possible historical context will be suggested for the emergence of the exclusive claim in 14,6.

2. Is John 14,6 an Anti-Judaistic and a Sectarian View?

There is a tendency to regard the exclusive claim in John 14,6 as anti-Judaistic.[21] We need to look at the historical and literary contexts to make a judgment on this issue. Since we believe that exclusivism existed before expulsion from the synagogue, it is possible to argue from the viewpoint of the historical context that 14,6 is not an anti-Judaistic text. Now let us see whether the literary context of 14,6 suggests an anti-Judaistic perspective.

During Jesus' public ministry (1,29–12,50) and his passion (18–19), the opponents of Jesus are Jews including Pharisees, the high priests, etc. But in the farewell discourse (13–17), the situation drastically changes. The Jews disappear totally from the scene.[22] Jesus is alone with his disciples (13,1–5),

---

John, I, 202 (also n. 304). Hengel, *Johannine Question*, 123–124, relates high Christology to the primitive church.

[20] R. E. Brown, *The Community of the Beloved Disciple. The Life, Loves and Hates of an Individual Church in New Testament Times* (New York 1979), 43–47.

[21] E.g., Charlesworth, "Exclusivism", 493, writes, "This verse states that Jesus is the one and only way to God. Such an exclusivistic claim has been at the centre of the use of the Gospel of John to initiate or to inflame hatred of Jews".

[22] The term Ἰουδαῖος occurs only once in the entire farewell discourse (13,33) in a statement by Jesus, "Little children, I am with you only a little longer. You will look for me; and as I said to the Jews so now I say to you, where I am going, you cannot come". This verse does not suggest any anti-Judaistic motivation. In reality, it points out the fact that the disciples are not superior to the Jews. The condition of the disciples is the same as that of the Jews. That is why Jesus reminds his disciples that he will be betrayed (13,21–30) and denied (13,38) by his own disciples. Both the Jews and the disciples are not able to go with Jesus in his hour. Therefore, the reference to 'the Jews' in John 13,33 need not be seen as anti-Judaistic in nature, as Tack, *John 14,6 in Light of Jewish-Christian Dialogue*, 23, thinks. S. Motyer, "Bridging the Gap: How might the Fourth Gospel help us cope with the legacy of Christianity's exclusive claim over against Judaism?", *The Gospel of John and Christian Theology*, ed. R. Bauckham and C. Mosser (Grand Rapids 2008), 158, remarks that the disciples in the farewell discourse "speak not as a privileged group of confidants, but as excluded inquirers voicing puzzled questions exactly like those of some of Jesus' interlocutors earlier in the narrative".

and he is addressing them alone. It is the time of his farewell speech. The concern of Jesus is to console and encourage the disheartened disciples. John 14,6 is uttered not in the context of a situation of conflict with the Jews, as in chapters 5–10, but as a reply to the question of ignorant Thomas (14,5).

While the opposing Jews disappear totally in the farewell discourse, there emerges another antagonist in the form of "the world" (κόσμος).[23] In the first part of the farewell speech (13,31–14,31), the term κόσμος occurs 6 times (14,17.19.22.27.30–31). This change of the antagonist implies that the revelation in the post-Easter dimension is conceived of at a cosmic and universal level.[24] The concern of the evangelist is no longer to show the fate of Israel but the relation of the world to God and to his revelation in Jesus. The hostility is no more thought on the level of Israel but in a cosmic fashion, and "anti-Jewish polemic is absent from this reflection".[25]

In the post-Easter period, the revelation of Christ will continue through the Paraclete, whom the world cannot accept (14,17). The theme of hatred of the world continues in the remaining part of the farewell discourse (15–17). In 16,2, the exclusion from the synagogue is presented as a special and concrete instance of the hatred of the world, but the synagogue is not explicitly mentioned, criticized or disqualified.[26] Thus, one can definitely say that there is not any anti-Judaistic element behind the exclusive claim in 14,6 from the perspective of the literary context of the text, especially in the context of the first part of the farewell speech in 13,31–14,31.

Having thus freed John 14,6 from the accusation of anti-Judaism in the light of the historical and literary contexts, it seems good to look at the so-called anti-Judaism in the rest of the Gospel. Even though this study is not concerned with the anti-Judaism in the rest of the Gospel of John, a few observations can be made here. Anti-Judaism is often detected at three levels:

---

[23] The term κόσμος appears 78 times in the Gospel of John. It occurs 40 times within the farewell discourse (13–17): 2x in chapter 13, 6x in chapter 14, 14x in chapters 15–16 and 18x in chapter 17.

[24] J. Zumstein, "The Farewell Discourses (John 13,31–16,33) and the Problem of Anti-Judaism", *Anti-Judaism and the Fourth Gospel. Papers of the Leuven Colloquium, 2000*, ed. R. Bieringer et al. (Assen 2001), 464.

[25] Jean Zumstein rightly states, "At the time the Johannine school is faced with the challenge of formulating the Christological faith for the time after Easter, it does so, in the first farewell discourse, independently of any polemic against Judaism". See Zumstein, "The Farewell Discourses", 465.

[26] Zumstein, "The Farewell Discourses", 469. The idea that belief in Jesus leads or will lead to conflict with the synagogues or to persecution by the Jews is a common topic in the New Testament (Matt 10,17.23.34; Mark 13,9; Luke 12,11; 21,12; cf. Luke 6,22). It is concretely expressed in the Book of Acts, e.g., Acts 6,8–8,3.

the text, the author and the interpreter.[27] Apparently, there is anti-Jewish language in the Gospel. But it is not the focus and emphasis of the author of the Gospel.[28] In the conflict situations, the focus of the author is on the identity of Jesus and not on anti-Jewish polemic. It is the misuse of the text and the wrong emphasis that have created anti-Judaistic propaganda down through the centuries until the modern period. Therefore, there is a great responsibility at the level of the interpreter.

The most important thing one needs to take into account when one deals with the anti-Judaistic language of the Gospel is that the real enemy of Jesus according to John is not the Jews, but sin and the devil. But this aspect is neglected in the modern discussions on anti-Judaism of the Gospel of John. It is not Jewishness that makes one a child of the devil but his sinfulness (8,44; 1 John 3,8–10). In this sense, anyone can be called or become a child of the devil, not the Jews alone. When Jesus calls the Jews sons of the devil, their sinfulness consists in two things: murder and lying (8,44). The Jews who oppose Jesus are called sons of the devil because they possess these two characteristic features of the devil. Hence, they seek to kill Jesus and do not accept the truth like the devil (8,40–46).

The evangelist intends that the Jews who stand in opposition to Jesus are wrong and that they need re-thinking about themselves and the identity of Jesus.[29] The anti-Jewish language of the first part of the Gospel can be understood positively in the light of the conflict between Jesus and the world in the farewell discourse. The Jews who oppose Jesus are only representatives of the opposing "world".[30] The Jews' reaction to Jesus, both positive and negative, is a symbol of the world's reaction to him.[31] At the end of Jesus' public ministry, the evangelist indicates that the disbelief and rejection of the Jews

---

[27] See R. Bieringer et al., "Wrestling with Johannine Anti-Judaism: A Hermeneutical Framework for the Analysis of the Current Debate", *Anti-Judaism and the Fourth Gospel. Papers of the Leuven Colloquium, 2000*, ed. R. Bieringer et al. (Assen 2001), 5–17.

[28] There is also a view that "what may look to us like anti-Judaism today, did not sound the same at the time of the composition of the Gospels". See H. Hoet, "'Abraham is our Father' (John 8,39). The Gospel of John and Jewish-Christian Dialogue", *Anti-Judaism and the Fourth Gospel. Papers of the Leuven Colloquium, 2000*, ed. R. Bieringer et al. (Assen 2001), 189.

[29] In the view of J. D. G. Dunn, "The Embarrassment of History: Reflections on the Problem of Anti-Judaism in the Fourth Gospel", *Anti-Judaism and the Fourth Gospel. Papers of the Leuven Colloquium, 2000*, ed. R. Bieringer et al. (Assen 2001), 59, "John's language is more the language of intra-Jewish polemic than of anti-Jewish polemic. He seeks by it to warn fellow Jews not to follow what was emerging as the dominant view of 'the Jews'". Hamid-Khani, *Revelation and Concealment of Christ*, 210, remarks, "John's polemic stance is not against all Jews but against Jewish authorities".

[30] Hasitschka, "Anmerkungen", 67, states, "Die Juden sind Typos und Sinnbild für die Menschheit insgesamt".

[31] Hasitschka, "Anmerkungen", 66.

360   *Chapter VII: John 14,6 in Its Historical Context*

are part and parcel of the salvific plan of God, which is to be fulfilled through his suffering Servant (12,37–41).[32] Thus, the evangelist believes that even the negativity from the part of the Jews is meaningful and necessary for the revelation of Jesus' glory.

Naturally, the belief in the divine identity of Christ is a stumbling block to the relationship between the believers in Christ and the Jewish community, and it causes the Jewish Christians to move away from their parent religion. Thus, the motivating force behind the exclusivism is not anti-Judaism but the conviction of the evangelist about the divine identity of Christ.[33] In the view of Bultmann, the claim of Jesus is absolute and exclusive because of the "intolerance of the revelation".[34] The intention of the evangelist is not anti-Judaism, but the inculcation of exclusive faith in Jesus as the Saviour. Since the evangelist believes in the divine identity of Christ, he cannot think of two or more Saviours because his Scripture will not allow it. Hence, it is Scripture that exerts more influence on the evangelist in his presentation of Jesus in the Gospel than the anti-Judaistic agenda.[35] According to his Scripture, there is "only one God and only one Saviour" (Isa 43,11; 45,21; Hos 13,4).[36] There-

---

[32] It should be mentioned here that the Scripture plays a role in the general portrait of the Jews in the Gospel. The Jews as religiously disobedient and rebellious people in the Gospel are very much like the Israelites in the book of Deuteronomy. They murmur against Jesus (e.g., John 6,41) just as the Israelites murmured against Moses. Cf. Davies, *Rhetoric and Reference*, 303–304.

[33] Reinhartz, "'Jews' and Jews in the Fourth Gospel", 354, says, "The Gospel's anti-Judaism is a by-product of the evangelist's strong convictions regarding the identity and salvific role of Jesus". Ball, *I Am*, 274, expresses the same, "The exclusive polemical aspect of the 'I am' sayings is often the necessary by-product of John's proclamation of Jesus as the fulfilment of the Jewish scriptures and is not the main emphasis of the evangelist".

[34] Bultmann, *John*, 378, states, "Jesus' ἐγώ εἰμι ...always means that there is only *one* who can lead man to salvation, only *one* Revealer. There are not various possible answers to man's quest for salvation, but only one. A decision must be made. This is the basis of the *intolerance of revelation*". The emphasis in italics is original.

[35] Cf. Davies, *Rhetoric and Reference*, 304. We have already examined how the evangelist's Scripture has shaped the exclusivism of John 14,6 when we discussed the literary background of 14,6b. See pp. 209–212.

[36] The presentation of Jesus as "God and Saviour" in juxtaposition can be found in the New Testament itself. Titus 2,13, says, "...while we wait for the blessed hope and the manifestation of the glory of our great God and Saviour, Jesus Christ". M. J. Harris, *Jesus as God. The New Testament Use of Theos in Reference to Jesus* (Grand Rapids 1992), 173–185, has scrutinized and found that in Titus 2,13 it is highly probable that Jesus Christ is called "our great God and Saviour", a verdict shared with varying degrees of assurance by almost all grammarians, lexicographers, many commentators and many writers on New Testament theology or Christology. 2 Peter 1,1 says, "Simeon Peter, a servant and apostle of Jesus Christ, to those who have received a faith as precious as ours through the righteousness of our God and Saviour Jesus Christ". Harris, *Jesus as God*, 229–238, has, with

fore, it is Christological monotheism, i.e., John's belief in Jesus' identity as "God and Saviour" on account of his oneness with the Father (cf. 1,1–2; 10,30; 14,7–11; 20,28) that determines the exclusivism of 14,6 and not anti-Judaism.

One of the hermeneutical siblings of the expulsion hypothesis is the sectarian interpretation of the Gospel and its Christology. But recent studies have challenged such an interpretation.[37] The view that the Johannine community

---

the support of the great majority of commentators with varying degrees of assurance and by most grammarians and authors of general works on Christology or 2 Peter, concluded that it is inescapable that in 2 Peter 1,1 the title ὁ θεός ἡμῶν καὶ σωτήρ is applied to Jesus Christ.

[37] The work of Hakola, *Reconsidering*, displays a full-scale application of the social identity approach to the Johannine writings. Hakola examines the assumption that the Gospel and the Epistles of John reflect the situation of an introverted early Christian group. He claims that dualistic polarities appearing in these texts should not be taken as evidence of social isolation but as attempts to construct a secure social identity. The author proposes that we should not regard different branches of early Christianity as localized and closed groups but as imagined communities that envision distinct early Christian identities, and argues that the Johannine tradition, already in its initial stages, was diverse. Previously, Hakola, *Identity Matters*, suggested that John's presentation of the Jews cannot be interpreted as a reaction to the violent policy of John's opponents and argued that John's portrayal of Jewishness is much more ambivalent than is often claimed today. D. A. Lamb, *Text, Context and the Johannine Community. A Sociolinguistic Analysis of the Johannine Writings* (LNTS 477; London 2014), 145–210, adopts a new approach to the social context of the Johannine writings by drawing on modern sociolinguistic theory, particularly on register analysis. His analysis of the Gospel and the Epistles of John does not support the idea of a close-knit sectarian group. He proposes that a better indication of the Gospel's "context of situation" is to be found in its narrative asides. He compares selected narrative asides with the Johannine Epistles. He notices that the interpersonal relationship between the author and the readers is formal and there is no affective involvement or shared knowledge in the case of the Gospel. But there is some shared knowledge or affective involvement in the case of the Epistles. He believes that the audience of the Gospel is broad and hard to define precisely. E. W. Klink III, *The Sheep of the Fold. The Audience and Origin of the Gospel of John* (SNTSMS 141; Cambridge 2007), 64–87, also argues against a sectarian interpretation of the Gospel and points out (p. 250) that the Gospel does not depict itself and its audience as standing against or outside of the rest of the Christian movement. He suggests (p. 246) that the *Sitz im Leben* of the Gospel should be understood within a more complex model of community, a model that functions broadly in the early Christian movement and tradition. K. S. Fuglseth, *Johannine Sectarianism in Perspective. A Sociological, Historical and Comparative Analysis of Temple and Social Relationships in the Gospel of John, Philo and Qumran* (NovTSup 119; Leiden 2005), too, challenges the sectarian interpretation of the Gospel and remarks in the conclusion (p. 374), "The 'sectarian' way of characterising the background of the Gospel of John that points towards a totally exclusive and segregated community cannot be upheld... Both the temple relationship and the relationship to 'others', like the Samaritans and alleged Greeks and Romans, are indications in the Gospel of a different social nature than the 'sectarian'".

was a sectarian and a closed group is fading today.[38] There is a tendency to interpret the Gospel's exclusive claims and its high Christology as a reflection of the traumatic experience of the Johannine community.[39] But such a reading goes against the positive attitude of the apostles towards rejection and persecution, e.g., in Acts 5,40–41 (cf. Matt 5,10–12). The "driving out" (ἐκβάλλω ἔξω) of the blind man (cf. John 9,34–35) from the Jewish community need not be interpreted as a very traumatic experience of the Johannine Christians because the Gospel also (6,37b; cf. 10,28–29) assures a better security in Jesus, "Anyone who comes to me I will never 'drive away' (ἐκβάλλω ἔξω)".[40] Three points can be suggested for the rejection of the theory that John's Gospel directly reflects a traumatic experience of the Johannine community: i. the lack of external evidence for a formal expulsion; ii. the overlooking of other models within the Gospel of the relationship between Jesus' followers and the synagogue; iii. the lack of evidence that the intended audi-

---

[38] R. Sheridan, "Johannine Sectarianism: A Category Now Defunct?", *The Origins of John's Gospel*, ed. S. E. Porter and H. T. Ong (Leiden 2016), 142–166, demonstrates that the term "sect" is problematic when applied to John's Gospel, not only because it is anachronistic but also because it is defined so variously in the sociological literature. In the light of current studies, J. Beutler, "Von der johanneischen Gemeinde zum Relecture-Modell", *ThPh* 90 (2015), 17, concludes that the hypothesis of a Johannine community, separated from the original Christian community with a different existence cannot be maintained today. D. Kim, "Was Johannine Christianity Sectarian?" *Fire in My Soul. Essays on Pauline Soteriology and the Gospels in Honor of Seyoon Kim*, ed. S. B. Choi et al. (Eugene 2014), 202–211, shows that Johannine Christianity was sectarian neither in a sociological sense nor in a theological sense. T. L. Brodie, *The Quest for the Origin of John's Gospel. A Source-Oriented Approach* (New York 1993), 151, remarks, "...many of the sectarian attitudes attributed to the hypothetical Johannine community are based on a misreading of the gospel – on a separating of John from the Synoptics, on a bypassing of the gospel's theology, and on a projection of polemic". Scholars have even expressed doubt about the notion of Johannine community which is separated from mainstream Christianity. P. N. Anderson, "The Community that Raymond Brown Left Behind: Reflections on the Johannine Dialectical Situation", *Communities in Dispute. Current Scholarship on the Johannine Epistles*, ed. R. A. Culpepper and P. N. Anderson (Atlanta 2014), 61, says, "The idea that the Johannine situation was always a 'community' is flawed; it enjoyed some time as such in Asia Minor or elsewhere, but it might not have been an individuated community during its Palestinian phase (30–70 CE), and it clearly developed into multiple communities in its later Asia Minor phase (85–100 CE) as suggested by the Epistles". For a critical review of the notion of Johannine community, see R. Kysar, "The Whence and Whither of Johannine Community", *Life in Abundance. Studies of John's Gospel in Tribute to Raymond E. Brown*, ed. J. R. Donahue (Collegeville 2005), 65–81.

[39] E.g., Cebulj, *Ich bin es*, 81–114, 229–234, regards the absolute claims in the Gospel like 14,6 as expressions of "stigma management".

[40] Hasitschka, "Anmerkungen", 65, rightly remarks, "Sollte für die Jünger Jesu die befürchtete Isolierung von der Synagoge Wirklichkeit werden, so haben sie zugleich die Gewissheit, dass sie sich in einer neuen und geheimnisvollen Zugehörigkeit zu Jesus befinden, von der sie niemand trennen kann".

ence read the Gospel as a story of their particular historical experience.[41] More importantly, the Gospel's emphasis on universal salvation should prevent a sectarian interpretation of it and its exclusive claims.[42] The words of H. Thyen are worth mentioning here. According to him, the claim in 14,6 is "nicht zufälliger Ausdruck der historisch bedingten Aporie einer bedrängten Gemeinde, sondern notwendiger Ausdruck der Gewißheit des Glaubens".[43]

3. Possible Historical Context for the Exclusive Claim in John 14,6

3.1 An Appeal to the Context of Acts 4,12

What could be the possible historical and social context for the exclusive claim in John 14,6? A better possibility to answer this question is to examine how and when the exclusive Christological and soteriological claims began in the life of the first Christians. Here we may observe the beliefs and practices of the apostles themselves and their exclusive claims about Jesus. The best parallel New Testament evidence with an exclusive claim is Acts 4,12, "There is salvation in no one else, for there is no other name under heaven given among mortals by which we must be saved". This text with its historical-social context may perhaps provide a pattern or model to understand the exclusivism of John 14,6 in its historical context, in the life of the Johannine Christians. It should be specially noted that in Acts 4,12 the exclusive claim of salvation is bound with "the name of Jesus", which is implied in the context (4,11). Acts 4,12 is part of Peter's bold speech before the Jewish council (4,5–12) in the context of an interrogation by them (4,1–22). The reason for the interrogation of the apostles by the council is the healing of a crippled beggar "in the name of Jesus" (3,1–10). This is clear from 4,7 that it is the healing act "in the name of Jesus Christ of Nazareth" (3,6) rather than the speech of Peter together with John (3,11–26) that provokes the authorities to arrest them. That is why the authorities are very curious and concerned to

---

[41] See Reinhartz, "The Johannine Community", 137.

[42] John's focus on universal salvation will be discussed later. See pp. 381–386. Saeed Hamid-Khani argues, "Emphatic missionary theology in the Fourth Gospel diametrically opposes the opinion of those who depict John's Gospel simply as a sectarian writing... It is highly questionable that a document in which there is so much emphasis upon the outreach of God in the world could be legitimately characterised as the writing of a sect...Neither Johannine Christianity, nor its gospel, nor the language of the Gospel, can be in any meaningful way characterised as sectarian since the theological tenets of the Gospel negate the validity of the sectarian hypothesis". See Hamid-Khani, *Revelation and Concealment of Christ*, 214, 217, 219.

[43] Thyen, *Johannesevangelium*, 626.

know "by which power" (ἐν ποίᾳ δυνάμει) and "in whose name" (ἐν ποίῳ ὀνόματι) the apostles did the miracle (4,7). Peter makes clear that the crippled man is "healed/saved" (σῴζω) "in the name of Jesus Christ of Nazareth" (4,9–10). A further link between the exclusive claim in 4,12 and the narrative in chapter 3 is the fact that the crippled man is not merely mentioned (4,9), but is physically present in the midst of the Jewish council (4,10.14) when Peter speaks in 4,12.

Peter cites Ps 118,22 in his defence before the religious authorities. Jesus became "the rejected stone" through his crucifixion but is made "the cornerstone" through his resurrection (cf. Acts 4,10).[44] It means that there is a pointed contrast between man's treatment of Jesus and God's treatment of him. Peter's speech before the council ends with a bold statement that there is salvation in no one else, except "in the name of Jesus" (4,12). "Salvation" (σωτηρία) is a key term in the theology of Acts (cf. 7,25; 13,26.47; 16,17). In 4,12, it is bound exclusively with "the name of Jesus". "The name of Jesus" becomes a means by which the saving power of Jesus is invoked and applied.[45] Luke insists on the universality of salvation "in the name of Jesus" for all human beings. Just as the crippled man is healed/saved "in the name Jesus" (3,6), everyone on earth can be saved "in the name of Jesus" (4,12).[46] Jesus Christ is the only source and ground of salvation available for humanity and there is no other saving name anywhere.[47] In the Old Testament, the God of Israel is the only Saviour (Isa 43,11; 45,21; Hos 13,4). Now Peter claims this role for Jesus Christ.

The "name of Jesus" is a predominant motif throughout the book of Acts. It occurs very frequently (about 31 times), especially in the ministry of apostles' preaching, baptizing and healing (e.g., 2,21.38; 3,6.16; 4,7.10.12.17.18.30; 5,28.40–41; 8,12.16; 10,48; 19,5, etc.). Invoking the name of Jesus has a great significance in Acts, and it deserves our special attention.[48] The apostles are presented as invoking "the name of Jesus" in

---

[44] The "crucifixion" and "resurrection" of 4,10 stand in parallel relationship with "rejection" and "becoming cornerstone" of 4,11.

[45] C. K. Barrett, *A Critical and Exegetical Commentary on the Acts of the Apostles I–XIV* (ICC; London 1994), I, 232.

[46] In 4,12, the relative pronoun with preposition ἐν ᾧ ("in which" or "by which") refers to the name of Jesus.

[47] Barrett, *Acts*, I, 232.

[48] There are some instances in the Jewish literature where angels are venerated. But veneration of angels should not be seen as worship of angels. After a careful study of angel veneration in early Judaism, L. T. Stuckenbruck, *Angel Veneration and Christology. A Study in Early Judaism and in the Christology of the Apocalypse of John* (WUNT II 70; Tübingen 1995), 203, asserts, "Angel veneration is not conceived as a substitute for the worship of God. Indeed, most often the venerative language is followed by an explanation which emphasizes the supremacy of God". R. Bauckham, "Devotion to Jesus Christ in Earliest Christianity: An Appraisal and Discussion of the Work of Larry Hurtado", *Mark,*

healing the crippled beggar (3,6). Invoking the name of Jesus in 3,6 may imply that Jesus is the object of prayer.[49] Since the Jewish council recognizes something unique and special with "the name of Jesus" and its "power" (4,7.13–16), they warn the apostles not to speak or teach any more "in the name of Jesus" (4,17–18).[50] But the apostles are convinced that the right response and obedience to God demanded of them is their veneration of the name of Jesus (cf. Acts 4,19–20).[51] Paul (Saul) takes action against the first Christians because they "invoked (ἐπικαλέω) the name of Jesus" (Acts 9,14.21). The term ἐπικαλέω in the Old Testament also has cultic significance and is used frequently to refer to the worship of God (e.g., Gen 4,26; 12,8; 13,4; 21,33; 26,25; 2 Sam 6,2; 1 Kgs 18,24; LXX Ps 115,4; cf. Acts 2,21; 22,16; Rom 10,13).[52] "To call upon Jesus" in prayer was evidently a defining

---

Manuscripts and Monotheism. Essays in Honour of Larry W. Hurtado, ed. C. Keith and D. T. Roth (London 2015), 176–200, argues that petitions addressed to angels are not found in the literature of second Temple period Judaism, and there is also no evidence for organized worship of angels. M. F. Bird, "Of Gods, Angels and Men", *How God became Jesus. The Real Origins of Belief in Jesus' Divine Nature – A Response to Bart Ehrman*, ed. M. F. Bird (Grand Rapids 2014), 40, remarks, "The various intermediary figures known in ancient sources, whether angelic or human, do not make monotheism malleable, because such figures shared neither in God's exclusive worship nor in God's unique identity, whereas Jesus certainly did".

[49] That Jesus becomes the object of prayer is evident in Stephen's, the first Christian martyr's prayer to him, "Lord Jesus, receive my spirit" (Acts 7,59). It should be noted that before he prays, he "invokes" (ἐπικαλέω) the Lord. Prayer addressed to Jesus can also be found in Acts 1,24; 13,2; 2 Cor 12,8–9. Personal prayer to Jesus is taken for granted in 1 Thess 3,11–13; 5,28; 2 Thess 2,16–17; 3,5.16.18; Rom 16,20b; 1 Cor 16,23; Gal 6,18; Phil 4,23; Phlm 25; 1 Tim 1,12; 2 Tim 1,16–18; 4,22. Healing and exorcism in Jesus' name are mentioned in Jas 5,13–15; Acts 3,6; 16,18.

[50] The Greek preposition ἐπί is equivalent in meaning to ἐν. Hence, the expression ἐπὶ τῷ ὀνόματι τοῦ Ἰησοῦ (4,17–18) is rendered by translators mostly as "in the name of Jesus". See B. M., Newman and E. A. Nida, *A Handbook on the Acts of the Apostles* (New York 1972), 101. The apostles are warned not just to speak and teach about the name of Jesus, but also not to speak "in the name of Jesus". This is evident from the question of the authorities, Ἐν ποίᾳ δυνάμει ἢ ἐν ποίῳ ὀνόματι ἐποιήσατε τοῦτο ὑμεῖς; (4,7) and from the arrest reported in the next chapter. In chapter 5, even though the authorities accuse the apostles of filling Jerusalem with their teaching about Jesus (5,28), the context reveals that the main reason for the arrest is jealousy because of the apostles' miracles which are supposed to have been done "in the name of Jesus" (5,12–16). In other words, it is not just the teaching about Jesus that disturbs the authorities but the signs and wonders done "in the name of Jesus". Also see 9,27–28; 16,18; 19,13; 22,16.

[51] L. W. Hurtado, *God in New Testament Theology* (Nashville 2010), 64, points out that the "remarkable devotion to Jesus is treated in the New Testament not as optional, but as mandatory, as obedience to God".

[52] Hurtado, *God in New Testament*, 63–64. It should be noted that Acts 2,21 cites LXX Joel 2,32 (3,5 in Hebrew), which promises salvation to all who "call upon the name of the Lord (Yahweh)". In Acts 2,21, the reference is probably to the cultic invocation of Jesus,

and distinguishing feature of earliest Christian worship (cf. 1 Thess 3,11–13; 1 Cor 1,2).⁵³ Acts 9,14.21 make clear that the reason for the persecution of the first Christians from the part of the Jewish authorities was the cultic veneration of "the name of Jesus".⁵⁴

There is an inseparable relation between the veneration of "the name of Jesus" and the exclusive claim, "There is *no other name* under heaven given among mortals by which we must be saved" (Acts 4,12). It is because of the fact that Peter heals the sick man, invoking "the name of Jesus" (Acts 3,6) and thus "saves" him (cf. σῴζω in 4,9), he can make the exclusive claim in the very presence of the healed/saved beggar that there is "no other name" to be "saved" (σῴζω, 4,12). Therefore, we can assume that the exclusive claim in Acts 4,12 about "the name of Jesus" presupposes the veneration or cultic use of "the name of Jesus" in the near (3,6) and larger context (7,59; 9,14.21; 16,18; 19,13; 22,16) of the book of Acts. The exclusivism of Acts 4,12 can be regarded as an utterance of the worshipping community. Immediately after the release of the apostles, the believers are said to gather together in prayer (4,23–31) in which the cultic veneration of "the name of Jesus" in healing (4,30) is explicitly expressed. Thus, we can infer that in Acts 4,12 it is the cultic veneration of Jesus that provides the historical and social context for the exclusive claim that there is no salvation in anyone else except in Jesus and there is no name under heaven other than "the name of Jesus" to be saved. This inference is corroborated by the fact that worship of God for the Jews of the second Temple period involves exclusivism. The inseparable relation between worship and exclusivism will be discussed below.

3.2 Relation between Worship and Exclusivism

The pervasive concern of the Jews during the second Temple period for the uniqueness of their God was the exclusive worship of one God and no other.⁵⁵

---

who has now been made "Lord" (2,36) and whose name is efficacious for exclusive salvation (4,12). Phil 2,9–11, which extols the veneration of the name of Jesus, is also worth mentioning here. Cf. L. W. Hurtado, *How on Earth Did Jesus Become a God? Historical Questions about Earliest Devotion to Jesus* (Grand Rapids 2005), 161; Bauckham, *Jesus and the God of Israel*, 129.

⁵³ J. D. G. Dunn, *Did the First Christians Worship Jesus? New Testament Evidence* (London 2010), 36.

⁵⁴ In the light of the New Testament evidence, Hurtado, *How on Earth*, 152–178, demonstrates how the cultic veneration of Jesus has led to conflict between Jewish followers of Jesus and Jewish religious authorities.

⁵⁵ Bauckham, *Jesus and the God of Israel*, 11; L. W. Hurtado, "What Do You Mean by 'First-Centuary Jewish Monotheism'", *Society of Biblical Literature 1993 Seminar Papers*, ed. E. H. Lovering (Atlanta 1993), 348–368. R. Bauckham, "Jesus, Worship of ", *ABD*, III, 816, states, "Judaism was unique among the religions of the Roman world in demanding the *exclusive* worship of its God. It is not too much to say that Jewish monotheism was

3. Possible Historical Context for the Exclusive Claim in John 14,6

For them worship of God was the recognition of the unique incomparability of the one God and a response to God's self-revelation as the sole creator and ruler of all.[56] It is in the light of the worship practices of the first Christians that their exclusive Christological and soteriological claims should be understood. Larry Hurtado asserts:

> The devotional practice of early Christians is the crucial context for assessing the meaning of their verbal expressions of beliefs about Christ... In any account of early Christianity that seeks to take account of the historical context, therefore, the devotional practices and scruples of Christians should be central. In its ancient Roman context, two features in particular characterized and distinguished early Christian worship. First, it was exclusivist, with disdain for the worship of the many deities of the Roman environment, and, secondly, it involved devotion offered exclusively to the God of the Bible and to Christ.[57]

The supposition that the exaltation of Christ to the status of an object of prayer and worship is the historical and social context for the exclusive claims by the first Christians is more strengthened when we examine the apocryphal acts of the apostles, where the worship of Christ is presented in terms of exclusive claims about him.[58] Even though the narratives in the apocryphal

---

defined by its adherence to the first and second commandments". The emphasis in italics is original. The close association of exclusivism with worship can be noticed in the Jewish literature of the inter-testamental period. E.g., Jub. 12,19; 20,7–9; Sib. Or. 1,15–18

[56] Bauckham, *Jesus and the God of Israel*, 12. Hurtado, *God in New Testament*, 28, states, "The 'monotheism' of ancient Christians and Jews was not primarily or typically expressed as a denial of the existence of any heavenly (or even divine) being other than the one God. Instead, their emphasis was that only the one God was the rightful recipient of worship, whether from them or from anyone else. That is, they believed that the one God held a universal right to exclusive worship and that the religious devotion offered to any other deity was an offence against the one God – 'idolatry'".

[57] L. Hurtado, *At the Origins of Christian Worship. The Context and Character of Earliest Christian Devotion* (Grand Rapids 2000), 2–3. Idem, *God in New Testament*, 30, also states, "The uniqueness of the New Testament 'God' was to be matched by an exclusivity in the devotional behaviour of believers".

[58] There are plenty of examples of which only a few are given here. Acts of Paul (PHeid p.6): "...and I also believe, my brethren, that there is no other God save Jesus Christ, the son of the Blessed, to whom is glory forever. Amen". Acts of Peter 21: "So Peter praised the Lord and said, 'You alone are the Lord God, to praise whom we need many lips able to thank you for your mercy'". Acts of Peter 39: "We now ask undefiled Jesus for that which you promised to give us; we praise you, we thank you, we confess you in glorifying you, though we are weak, because you alone are God and no other, to whom be glory now and forever, Amen". Acts of John 42: "And the people of the Ephesians cried, 'There is only one God, that of John, only one God who has compassion for us; for you alone are God; now we have become converted, since we saw your miraculous deeds. Have mercy upon us, God, according to your will, and deliver us from our great error'". Acts of John 43: "And John stretched out his hands and prayed with uplifted soul to the Lord, 'Glory be to you, my Jesus, the only God of truth, who procure your servants in manifold ways'!". Acts of John 44: "We know that the God of John is the only one, and henceforth we worship

writings are often unreliable and sometimes deviate from the New Testament, they shed light on the historical and social context in which they originated.[59] Worship of Christ along with exclusive claims about him by the first Christians is also polemically depicted in the anti-Christian writings of pagan writers. E.g., Celsus, a second centuary Greek philosopher and an opponent of Christianity writes, *"They worship only this Son of Man, on the pretext that he is really a great god*. And they say further that he is mightier than the lord of the almighty God. It was from this that they took their notion of not serving two masters, trying to ensure that [Jesus] would be preserved *as the god and lord of the cult, unrivalled by any other"*.[60] Another second centuary writer, Lucian of Samosata in his *The Death of Peregrine*, 11–13, remarks:

> They took him for a God, accepted his laws, and declared him their president. The Christians, you know, worship a man to this day – the distinguished personage who introduced their novel rites, and was crucified on that account... You see, these misguided creatures start with the general conviction that they are immortal for all time, which explains the contempt of death and voluntary self-devotion which are so common among them; and then it was impressed on them by their original lawgiver that they are all brothers, from the moment that they are converted, and *deny the gods of Greece, and worship the crucified sage*, and live after his laws.[61]

The Alexamenos Graffito (ca. 193–238 CE), one of the most well-known pieces of graffiti from the Roman world, reflects a popular non-Christian misunderstanding of Christian worship. In it, we can see a donkey-headed man crucified on a cross and another man standing below the cross, his right

---

him, since we have obtained mercy from him". Acts of John 77: "We praise, glorify, and honour you and thank you for your great goodness and long-suffering holy Jesus, for you alone are God and none else; you, against whose power all devices can do nothing now and in all eternity! Amen". Acts of John 85: "We thank you that you are in need of a saved human nature. We thank you that you gave this sure faith, that you alone are God, now and forever". Acts of Thomas 25: "And the apostle, seized with joy, said, 'I give thanks to you, Lord Jesus, that you have revealed your truth in these men. For you alone are the God of truth and not another; and you are he who knows all things that are unknown to many'". The English translation of these texts is according to J. K. Elliott, *The Apocryphal New Testament. A Collection of Apocryphal Christian Literature in an English Translation* (Oxford 1993).

[59] Regarding the historical value of the apocryphal acts of the apostles, F. Bovon and E. Junod, "Reading the Apocryphal Acts of the Apostles", *Apocryphal Acts of Apostles*, ed. D. R. MacDonald (Semeia 38; Decatur 1986), 163 state, "Through the medium of dramatic or funny narrations, prodigies, praiseworthy or reproachful behaviour, conversions, speeches, dialogues, and prayers they give prominence to religious convictions, moral values, cultic and ritual practices as well as to social conceptions linked to the milieu from which they sprang".

[60] See Celsus, *On the True Doctrine. A Discourse Against the Christians*, tr. R. J. Hoffmann (Oxford 1987), 116–117. The emphasis in italics is by me.

[61] As translated by H. W. Fowler and F. G. Fowler, *The Works of Lucian of Samosata* (Oxford 1905), IV, 82–83. The emphasis in italics is by me.

3. Possible Historical Context for the Exclusive Claim in John 14,6

arm outstretched toward the crucified figure. Together with this portrayal, there is a Greek inscription that says, 'Ἀλεξάμενος σέβετε θεόν ("Alexamenos worships God/god").[62] This caricature brings into light the prevailing hostility between the Roman empire and the Christian believers and seems to be a mockery of the exclusive worship of Christ. The first centuary Christians refused to worship the emperor or the traditional Roman state gods, and they were severely persecuted and killed on account of their exclusive monotheistic worship.[63] However, they were more concerned to proclaim Jesus' significance and to express their devotion to him than to give explanations of how they came to the convictions that prompted them to do so.[64]

3.3 Worship in the Gospel of John

It is in the light of the historical and social context, which portrays the worship practices of the first Christians, that we need to understand the exclusive claim in John 14,6. Hence, it is important to examine whether the Gospel of John presupposes that Jesus is the object of worship in the historical context of the Gospel.[65] Early Christian worship had primarily a verbal character and was not tied to particular places, but it could be practiced virtually everywhere.[66] The devotional practices which seem to characterize early Christian worship were hymns, prayer through or in the name of Jesus and even to Jesus, calling upon the name of Jesus, creeds, confessions of Christ, doxologies, prophecy, sermons, Scripture reading, sacred rituals like Eucharist and

---

[62] See J. B. Tschen-Emmons, *Artifacts from Ancient Rome* (Santa Barbara 2014), 14–19.

[63] Cf. Bauckham, "Jesus, Worship of", 817.

[64] Cf. Hurtado, *How one Earth*, 198–199.

[65] An adequate understanding of the meaning of worship seems to be required. A too narrow understanding of worship is a wrong approach to understand worship in the Bible. H. Hagan, "Worship", *The Collegeville Pastoral Dictionary of Biblical Theology*, ed. C. Stuhlmueller (Bangalore 1996), 1103–1104, says, "Worship is essentially those actions and words of human beings that define and acknowledge and re-establish their relationship to God". The theme of worship in the Gospel of John has been recently examined by scholars in various ways. E.g., J. P. Heil distinguishes three dimensions of worship in John, namely confessional worship, sacramental worship and ethical worship. See J. P. Heil, *The Gospel of John: Worship for Divine Life Eternal* (Cambridge 2015), 1–2. K. Troost-Cramer, *Jesus as Means and Locus of Worship in the Fourth Gospel. Sacrifice and Worship Space in John* (Eugene 2017), argues that John presents Jesus' resurrected body as the correct locus of sacrificial worship in the absence of a temple in which believers in Jesus could offer proper worship to the God of Israel. Also see Neyrey, *The Gospel of John*, 377–411; idem, "Worship in the Fourth Gospel", 107–117; J. J. Kanagaraj, "Worship, Sacrifices and Mission: Themes Interlocked in John", *Indian Journal of Theology* 40 (1998) 16–39.

[66] D. E. Aune, "Worship, Early Christian", *ABD*, VI, 973.

baptism.⁶⁷ Many of these elements of worship like hymns, prayer to Jesus, prayer in the name of Jesus, confessions of Christ, possible allusions to sacred rituals like baptism and Eucharist, etc., are clearly discernible in the Gospel of John.

Even though the prologue (1,1–18) cannot be explicitly identified as a hymn, the possibility of detecting a redacted earlier hymn still remains.⁶⁸ If an earlier Christian hymn is discernible, that may suggest the use of the hymn in the context of early Christian worship.⁶⁹ There are, furthermore, clear allusions to baptism and Eucharist in 3,19 (cf. 13,9–10; 19,34) and 6,51–58 respectively, which may reflect the cultic practices of early Christians.⁷⁰ The theme of worship is dominant in John 4. Of 11 occurrences of the verb προσκυνέω in the Gospel, 9 of them occur in John 4. Since Jesus is the new locus of worship (2,21) and the truth (14,6), true worship (4,20–24) must be fulfilled in and through him.⁷¹ John 5,23 may imply that Jesus is the object of

---

⁶⁷ Aune, "Worship, Early Christian", 973–989; Hurtado, *God in New Testament*, 52. Idem, *One God, One Lord. Early Christian Devotion and Ancient Jewish Monotheism* (Edinburgh ²1998), 100, suggests six features of the religious devotion of early Christianity that indicate a significant variation in the Jewish monotheistic tradition: i. hymnic practices, ii. prayer and related practices, iii. use of the name of Christ, iv. the Lord's Supper, v. confession of faith in Jesus, and vi. prophetic pronouncements of the risen Christ. Dunn, *Did the First Christians*, 30, points out that the practice of worship at the time of Jesus included prayer, hymns, sacred place and sacrifice. On the various practices of early Christian worship, see A. B. McGowan, *Ancient Christian Worship. Early Church Practices in Social, Historical, and Theological Perspective* (Grand Rapids 2014).

⁶⁸ There is no scholarly consensus regarding the literary form of the Johannine prologue. If John uses an earlier hymn, he may be adapting it to fit the rest of the Gospel better, especially by adding the materials about John the Baptist. A great number of scholars today contend that the Prologue was built around a previously existing Logos-hymn. See J. Ashton, "Really a Prologue?", *The Prologue of the Gospel of John. Its Literary, Theological, and Philosophical Contexts. Papers read at the Colloquium Ioanneum 2013*, ed. J. G. van der Watt et al. (WUNT 359; Tübingen 2016), 27–44; Keener, *John*, I, 334–337; Schnackenburg, *John*, I, 225–226; O'Day, *John*, 518; Moloney, *John*, 34; W. Schmithals, "Der Prolog des Johannesevangeliums", *ZNW* 70 (1979), 16–43; Thyen, *Johannesevangelium*, 62; T. H. Tobin, "The Prologue of John and Hellenistic Jewish Speculation", *CBQ* 52 (1990), 252–269. Brown, *John*, I, 23–24, thinks that "the prologue is a description of the history of salvation in a hymnic form". Heil, *The Gospel of John*, 4, views that the hymnic prologue in 1,1–18 sets a preliminary tone of communal worship for the rest of the narrative.

⁶⁹ L. Thompson, "Hymns in Early Christian Worship", *ATR* 55 (1973), 471, points out that among the various ways that the Christ could be described, the hymn-form was distinctive through its power to make Christ present to the church at worship.

⁷⁰ See p. 283, n. 240 for reference to the significance of baptism and pp. 246–248, 317 for references to the significance of the Eucharist in the Gospel.

⁷¹ Barrett, *John*, 68, states, "The basis of John's thought is that true worship can exist only in and through Jesus, and that worship in and through him is true worship. Conse-

3. Possible Historical Context for the Exclusive Claim in John 14,6

worship along with the Father since the Son's activity is an exact replication of the Father's (5,19–23).[72] In Jewish writings "divinity is always defined by the prerogative and power to give life" (cf. Philo, *Embassy to Gaius*, 118).[73] Since the Son has life in himself like the Father (5,26) and can give life to anyone he wishes (5,21), he is worthy of worship along with the Father. There is explicit reference to the worship of Jesus in 9,38.[74] This reference

---

quently, it is correct to say that, wherever Jesus is, there worship in Spirit and truth is possible".

[72] Bauckham, *Jesus and the God of Israel*, 180; Hurtado, *Lord Jesus Christ*, 363–364. Hurtado, *God in New Testament*, 46, remarks, "Jesus is so central to the understanding of 'God' in the New Testament that one cannot speak adequately of this God without explicit reference to Jesus. Likewise, one cannot adequately worship 'God' without including Jesus explicitly as a divinely authorized recipient of worship". D. Lee, "In the Spirit of Truth: Worship and Prayer in the Gospel of John and the Early Fathers", *Vigiliae Christianae* 58 (2004), 297, asserts, "Worship and prayer are to be offered *through* Jesus but also, since he is the visible manifestation of God, *to* him". The emphasis in italics is original.

[73] Thompson, *The God of the Gospel of John*, 225.

[74] Some manuscripts omit 9,38–39a, but most manuscripts and scholars support the retention of 9,38–39a. The view that 9,38–39a is a later liturgical addition is not accepted today. There are more reasons based on internal evidence to retain 9,38–39a than to omit it. The v. 38 is placed within the small pericope of 9,35–38. This pericope presents the final encounter between the blind man and Jesus. In v. 39, the focus is on judgment upon the Pharisees. There is a clear logic and thought flow within 9,35–38. In v. 35, Jesus asks the blind man whether he believes in the Son of Man. In v. 36, the blind wants to know who the Son of Man is before he believes in him. In v. 37, Jesus makes it clear to him that the one who speaks with him is the Son of Man. Then, in v. 38 the blind man admits his readiness to believe in the Son of Man and worships him. In fact, v. 38 is a conclusion of 9,35–38 because the real reply to Jesus' question in v. 35 is given only in v. 38. Hence, v. 35 is written in view of v. 38. Jesus' answer in 9,39b is based on the positive reply of the blind man in v. 38, "Lord, I believe". Thus, v. 38 is the climax of the whole story of the blind man and without his confession of faith, Jesus' question in v. 35 remains unanswered and the purpose of the healing story remains unfulfilled. The "seeing" of the blind in v. 39 corresponds with the "believing" of the blind man in v. 38. It seems possible that 9,38–39a are omitted in order to unify the teaching of Jesus in v. 37 and v. 39. An accidental error on the part of the scribes cannot be fully disregarded because v. 37 and v. 39 begin in the same way. The vocabulary in vv. 38–39 is purely Johannine. The rare verb φημί, used in v. 38, is found in 1,23 and 18,29. There are many vocabularies in the Gospel which occur rarely. It does not mean that they are non-Johannine. Moreover, the omission in 9,38–39a can be better understood in the light of the variant reading in 9,35, where some important manuscripts read υἱὸς τοῦ θεοῦ in place of υἱὸς τοῦ ἀνθρώπου. It appears that even scribes (cf. P[75], ℵ*, W) experienced difficulties in combining the title υἱὸς τοῦ ἀνθρώπου with the verb προσκυνέω. Above all, in the perspective of the Synoptic Gospels as well, Jesus is an object of worship (Matt 2,2.8.11; 8,2; 9,18; 14,33; 15,25; 20,20; 28,9.17; Mark 5,6; Luke 24,52; cf. Matt 21,15–16; John 20,28; Phil 2,9–11; Rev 4,10; 5,14). In the light of these arguments, the view that vv. 38–39a are a later addition can, therefore, be rejected. See also Metzger, *Textual Commentary*, 195; M. Steegen, "To Worship the Johannine Son of Man. John 9,38 as Refocusing on the Father", *Bib* 91 (2010), 534–554; Moloney, *John*,

fits well in the context of John's high Christology (1,1.18; 20,28; cf. Rev 4,10; 5,14).

It is also important to notice the theme of prayer in the immediate context of 14,6. In 14,13–14, Jesus says, "I will do whatever you *ask in my name*, so that the Father may be glorified in the Son. If you *ask me* anything *in my name*, I will do it".[75] Larry Hurtado points out that John's use of the expression "in my name" (ἐν τῷ ὀνόματί μου) in making petitions in 14,13–14; 15,16; 16,23–24.26 should be seen distinctively from its use in the rest of the Gospel with an emphasis on the efficacy of invoking Jesus' name in prayer.[76] He suggests that the expression "in my name" has a special significance because "we simply have no analogy for prayers being offered 'through' or 'in the name of' some other figure, certainly not in the second temple Jewish tradition".[77] Whatever may be the meaning one gives to the expression "in my name" (ἐν τῷ ὀνόματί μου), what is important is that in 14,14 Jesus is regarded as the object of prayer.[78]

---

299. Keener, *John*, I, 795, comments on 9,38 thus, "In its broader Johannine context (cf. 4,20–24; 12,20–21), including John's Christology (cf. 1,1.18; 20,28), it fits the Johannine portrait of Jesus' deity and invites John's own audience to worship Jesus".

[75] We have already shown that the variant readings in 14,14 can be neglected. See p. 150–151.

[76] Hurtado, *Lord Jesus Christ*, 390. Hurtado further states, "These passages show Jesus' name being explicitly invoked as *a feature of the prayer practice promoted and observed in Johannine circles*. That is, in these references we have a glimpse of the actual devotional customs advocated and followed by Johannine Christians. This ritual use of Jesus' name has no known parallel in the Jewish tradition of the time, and it amounts to 'Jesus' being treated in devotional practice as itself carrying and representing divine efficacy and significance". The emphasis in italics is original. See Hurtado, *Lord Jesus Christ*, 391. Coutts, *The Divine Name*, 188, remarks, "John had every motivation to present reverence for Jesus and the cultic use of his name as an expression of fidelity to the divine name".

[77] Hurtado also adds, "To my knowledge, there is no parallel devotional practice in the wider pagan religious environment either". See Hurtado, *God in New Testament*, 62. In the view of Coutts, *The Divine Name*, 186, "The emphasis in John's Gospel on Jesus' name as the locus of belief and eternal life and as the means of efficacious prayer is not a Johannine innovation, but reflects well-established Christian devotional practice".

[78] Various meanings are given to the expression, "in my name" (ἐν τῷ ὀνόματί μου) in John's Gospel. E.g., "with the invocation of my name" (Barrett, *John*, 460), "in union with me" [Brown, *John*, II, 633–636; F. G. Untergaßmaier, *Im Namen Jesu. Der Namensbegriff im Johannesevangelium. Eine exegetisch-religiogeschichtliche Studie zu den johanneischen Namensaussagen* (FzB 13; Stuttgart 1973), 108–112, 158–162], "as my representative" (Schnackenburg, *John*, III, 73; Keener, *John*, II, 949). Dunn, *Did the First Christians*, 33, comments, "Requests to the Father in Jesus' name are of a piece with requests to Jesus himself". "In my name" in John 14,13–14 may have the sense of calling upon the name of Jesus as well since "in my name" is here associated with "greater works" (14,12), which include miracles in the name of Jesus. Jesus has promised the disciples that they can do miracles "in his name" (ἐν τῷ ὀνόματί μου) in Mark 16,17. In many respects, there is a close affinity between the promises in Mark 16,17 and John 14,12. In Mark, the

3. Possible Historical Context for the Exclusive Claim in John 14,6 373

Prayers are offered usually to a deity, who is also worthy of organized and communal worship. It should be noted that John does not use the common New Testament terms for prayer like προσεύχομαι, προσευχή, δέομαι and δέησις. But he frequently uses the verb αἰτέω to refer to petitionary prayer (14,13–14; 15.7.16; 16,23–24.26). The verb αἰτέω is used in the farewell discourse only to refer to prayer. The prayer of adoration, penitence, confession, petition and of intercession was at the heart of worship at the time of Jesus.[79] Hence, Jesus' intercessory prayer in chapter 17 may reflect the worship practices of early Christians.[80] Thomas' confession "my Lord and my God" (20,28; cf. 6,69) may be taken not simply as a statement about the identity of the risen Christ but rather as an acknowledgment and confession of him in keeping with religious or cultic practice.[81] Moreover, the Gospel's repudiation of temple, Sabbath and other religious feasts implies the cultic practices of the Johannine Christians in and through Jesus. Thus, from this brief examination, it is possible to assume that the Gospel presupposes a historical and social context in which Christ was regarded as an object of worship. The exclusivism in John 14,6 is rooted in Jewish monotheism and exclusivism because, for the Jews, devotion to God as an object of prayer and

---

verse is placed in the post-resurrection setting. In John 14,12 also, the presupposed setting for the fulfilment of the promise is post-resurrection period. There is correspondence between the miraculous signs in Mark and works in John because works in John also include miracles (e.g., 7,3). In both verses, signs and works are promised to those who "believe" in Jesus. In Mark, the signs are to be performed in Jesus' name. In John 14,12, works are immediately associated with asking in Jesus' name (14,13–14). In John, the greater works by the believers are possible because Jesus goes to the Father. In Mark as well, Jesus' ascension to the Father is in view. Immediately after promising the miraculous signs (16,17–18), Jesus is taken up to heaven and seated at the right hand of God (16,19). Coutts, *The Divine Name*, 86, n. 60, Lagrange, *Saint Jean*, 379 and W. Heitmüller, *Im Namen Jesu. Eine sprach-u. religionsgeschichtliche Untersuchung zum Neuen Testament, speziell zur altchristlichen Taufe* (Göttingen 1903), 264–265, recognize in John 14,13–14 the sense of prayer by invoking the name of Jesus. According to O. Cullmann, *Early Christian Worship* (London 1953), 114, "'Prayer in Christ's name' is equivalent to the 'worship in Spirit and in truth' to which Jesus referred in the talk with the woman of Samaria".

[79] Dunn, *Did the First Christians*, 30.

[80] Schnackenburg, *John*, III, 200–201, has already recognized a cultic setting for Jesus' prayer in John 17. Jerome H. Neyrey regards the farewell discourse as a model of worship. See his cultural interpretation of John 14–17 and the comments on it on pp. 126–127.

[81] Thompson, *The God of the Gospel of John*, 222. Carson, *The Farewell Discourse*, 34, states, "In a moment of high drama, Thomas worships the resurrected Jesus in terms rightly applicable to God alone: 'my Lord and my God'". A. J. Köstenberger, "The Destruction of the Second Temple and the Composition of the Fourth Gospel", *Challenging Perspectives on the Gospel of John*, ed. J. Lierman (WUNT II 219; Tübingen 2006), 105, views, "Thomas' confession climaxes the entire Gospel, making the decisive point that the only proper response to the Fourth Gospel's revelation that Jesus is the fulfilment of Jewish religious symbolism is that of worship".

374 Chapter VII: John 14,6 in Its Historical Context

worship made every other religion idolatrous and worthy only of reprobation.[82] Hence, we may assume that the historical and social context in which the cultic devotion to Jesus as divine arose is also the historical context for the exclusive Christological claim in John 14,6, as in Acts 4,12.[83]

3.4 Possibility for an Early High Christology

Now some complementary observations should be made regarding the question of when the "high Christology" of the New Testament in general emerged.[84] A non-biblical evidence that Christ was venerated as an object of

---

[82] Cf. R. A. Culpepper, "Anti-Judaism in the Fourth Gospel as a Theological Problem for Christian Interpreters", *Anti-Judaism and the Fourth Gospel. Papers of the Leuven Colloquium, 2000*, ed. R. Bieringer et al. (Assen 2001), 81. D. E. Aune, *The Cultic Setting of Realized Eschatology in Early Christianity* (NovTSup 28; Leiden 1972), 76, points out that the depiction of the Johannine Jesus includes "the current experience of the living Jesus as the mediator of salvific benefits and the object of cultic worship within the Johannine community".

[83] In the view of Aune, *The Cultic Setting*, 63, "The essential elements of the theology of the Fourth Gospel generally, and the eschatology of the Gospel in particular, were developed within the context of the worship, preaching and teaching of what we may ambiguously designate as the 'Johannine community'". M. M. Thompson, "Reflections on Worship in the Gospel of John", *Princeton Seminary Bulletin* 19 (1998), 262, states, "John's community was in conflict with the 'Jews' not simply because of *what* it *believed*, but because of the *way* in which its *beliefs* were mirrored in its *practices*". The emphasis in italics is original.

[84] By "high Christology" is meant here a Christology that includes Jesus as an object of divine worship. The topic of early high Christology with a focus on the worship of Christ by first Christians is well highlighted in current New Testament studies by the works of scholars like Larry W. Hurtado, Martin Hengel, Richard Bauckham, William Horbury, C. Fletcher-Louis, etc. For a detailed study of this topic, see L. W. Hurtado, *Honoring the Son. Jesus in Earliest Christian Devotional Practice* (Bellingham 2018); idem, *Ancient Jewish Monotheism and Early Christian Jesus-Devotion. The Context and Character of Christological Faith* (Waco 2017); idem, *One God, One Lord*; idem, *At the Origins*; idem, *Lord Jesus Christ*; idem, *How on Earth*; M. Hengel, *Between Jesus and Paul. Studies in the Earliest History of Christianity* (Eugene 2003); idem, *Studies in Early Christology* (Edinburgh 1995); Bauckham, "Devotion to Jesus Christ", 176–200; idem, *Jesus and the God of Israel*; idem, "The Worship of Jesus in Apocalyptic Christianity", *NTS* 27 (1981), 322–341; W. Horbury, *Jewish Messianism and the Cult of Christ* (London 1998); C. Fletcher-Louis, *Jesus Monotheism. Christological Origins: The Emerging Consensus and Beyond* (Eugene 2015), I; C. C. Newmann et al. (ed.), *The Jewish Roots of Christological Monotheism. Papers from the St. Andrews Conference on the Historical Origins of the Worship of Jesus* (Supplements to the Journal for the Study of Judaism 63; Leiden 1999). Larry W. Hurtado, who died in 2019, even co-founded with Alan Segal a club of scholars called, "The Early High Christology Club" (EHCC). EHCC is, in fact, a jocular self-designation coined by a group of scholars of various backgrounds with research interests in earliest Christianity, who emphasize that an exalted place of Jesus in belief and devotional practice (including corporate worship) is evident in the earliest Christian sources and likely

3. Possible Historical Context for the Exclusive Claim in John 14,6

worship by the first Christians in the first centuary can be found in the writing of Pliny the Younger who was a special imperial legate in the Roman province of Bithynia. Pliny wrote to the emperor Trajan around 112 CE that Christians had confessed under questioning:

> They maintained, however, that all that their guilt or error involved was that they were accustomed to assemble "at dawn on a fixed day, to sing a hymn antiphonally to Christ as God" (ante lucem convenire carmenque Christo, quasi deo, dicere secum invicem), and to bind themselves by an oath, not for the commission of some crime, but to avoid acts of theft, brigandage, and adultery, not to break their word, and not to withhold money deposited with them when asked for it. When these rites were completed, it was their custom to depart, and then to assemble again to take food, which was however common and harmless.[85]

The singing of hymns to Christ as to God was a formative influence on the development of the worship of Jesus.[86] Pliny's testimony to early Christian faith and worship is all the more reliable and important because it comes obviously from a non-believer, especially from a hostile source. In his letter to Polycarp, St. Ignatius of Antioch (died ca. 108 CE) wrote:

> I bid you farewell always in our God Jesus Christ; may you remain in him in the unity and care of God. I greet Alce, a name very dear to me. Farewell in the Lord (*To Polycarp*, 8,3).[87]

These words from an extra-biblical source also express the prevailing devotional attitude to Jesus as God among early Christians. In 2005 archaeologists unearthed at the Meggido prison in northern Israel the remains of an ancient Church building used for Eucharist, datable to the third centuary, may be as early as ca. 230 CE. The building had four mosaic panels and on one of them is an inscription that reads, "The God-loving Akeptous has offered the table

---

goes back to the first circles of Jesus' followers from shortly after his crucifixion. This group included late scholars like Alan Segal, Martin Hengel and Larry Hurtado. It includes now scholars like Richard Bauckham, Jörg Frey, Pheme Perkins, Donald Juel, David Capes, Charles Gieschen, Marianne Meye Thompson, Loren Stuckenbruck, April DeConick, Karl-Wilhelm Niebuhr, etc.

[85] Pliny, *Epistle*, 10,96.7. As translated by P. G. Walsh, *Pliny the Younger. Complete Letters* (Oxford World's Classics; Oxford 2006), 278–279. In this letter, Pliny the Younger also speaks of those Christians who under the pressure of punishment abandoned their faith in Christ some 20 years ago. See Pliny, *Epistle*, 10,96.6. In consideration with the time of the letter, this is an indication that the cultic veneration of Christ was prevalent in the first centuary itself.

[86] See M. Daly-Denton, "Singing Hymns to Christ as to a God (Cf. Pliny, *Ep.* X, 96)", *The Jewish Roots of Christological Monotheism. Papers from the St. Andrews Conference on the Historical Origins of the Worship of Jesus*, ed. C. C. Newmann et al. (Supplements to the Journal for the Study of Judaism 63; Leiden 1999) 277–292.

[87] Lake, *The Apostolic Fathers*, I, 277. There are repeated references to Jesus Christ as God in the letters of St. Ignatius. E.g., *Eph.* 7,2; 18,2; 19,3; *Rom.* 3,3; 6,3; *Trall.* 7,1.

to God Jesus Christ as a memorial".[88] This inscription is yet another extra-biblical proof against the view that Jesus was not regarded as God before the reign of Constantine.

The earliest New Testament writings, which approximately date from 50–60 CE, already presuppose cultic devotion to Jesus as a familiar and defining feature of Christian circles (e.g., Rom 10,9–14; 1 Cor 1,2; 2 Cor 12,8–9; Phil 2,10–11).[89] On the basis of New Testament writings, Larry Hurtado suggests that the phenomenon of cultic devotion to Jesus emerged not at slow stages, but was a quick phenomenon like a volcanic eruption.[90] In the view of Martin Hengel, the Christological development from Jesus to Paul took place within about eighteen years and he asserts very boldly and confidently, "In essentials more happened in Christology within these few years than in the whole subsequent seven hundred years of church history".[91] The early Christians experienced that Jesus was exalted to heavenly glory and legitimated by God himself as an object of their worship (Matt 28,9.17; Luke 24,52; Phil 2,6–11; Rev 5,6–14; cf. Matt 2,2.8.11).[92]

---

[88] See E. Adams, "The Ancient Church at Megiddo: The Discovery and an Assessment of its Significance", *ExpTim* 120 (2008), 62–69.

[89] Cf. Hurtado, *How on Earth*, 25.

[90] Hurtado, *How on Earth*, 25. Hengel, *Between Jesus and Paul*, 31, states, "The time between the death of Jesus and the fully developed Christology which we find in the earliest Christian documents, the letters of Paul is so short that the development which takes place within it can only be called amazing". Martin Hengel points out that the time available for the Christological development leading up to Paul was very short. The earliest letter (1 Thess) was written probably at the beginning of 50 CE, at a time when Paul began his activity in Corinth and the last letter, to the Romans, was written presumably in the winter of 56/57 CE. It is not possible to detect any development in the basic Christological views in his letters. Moreover, Paul presupposes that the Christological titles, formulae and concepts he uses are already known to the communities. That means that the Christology of his writings goes back to the content of his mission preaching when he founded these communities. Hengel views that all essential features of Paul's Christology were already fully developed towards the end of the 40s. Hengel places Jesus' death on Friday, 14th Nisan (7th April) 30 CE and Paul's conversion, with the help of Gal 1,18; 2,1, between 32 CE and 34 CE. See Hengel, *Between Jesus and Paul*, 31. Hurtado, *How on Earth*, 35, 205, thinks that "between the emergence of a Jewish movement in Jesus' name almost immediately after Jesus' crucifixion and Paul's conversion (perhaps within a year or two, and certainly no more than a few years), devotion to Jesus was already a prominent feature of the movement", a notable religious innovation within the second Temple Jewish religion.

[91] Hengel, *Between Jesus and Paul*, 39–40. Hurtado, *How on Earth*, 37, also points out that "the really crucial period for the origin of remarkable beliefs about Jesus' significance is the first four or five years of the early Christian movement". Cf. Hengel, *Between Jesus and Paul*, 44.

[92] Hurtado, *One God, One Lord*, 124. J. D. G. Dunn, *Christology in the Making. An Inquiry into the Origins of the Doctrine of the Incarnation* (London ²1989), 254, states "The single most striking feature of earliest Christology is the impact of the resurrection of Jesus". However, Dunn, *Did the First Christians,* expresses some reservations or qualifica-

On the basis of evidence of extra-biblical sources and the New Testament, it is thus possible to believe that high Christology in terms of worship of Christ emerged at a very early stage of Christianity.[93] Along with the majority view, we may suppose that some concepts of the high Christology of the Gospel of John arose at a later period of the first centuary. However, ascribing high Christology that consists of divine worship of Christ to a period during or after the reign of emperor Constantine is not admissible. It is divine worship of Christ begun at an early stage of Christianity that gave rise to the historical context for the exclusive claims like John 14,6.

4. Conclusion

In the light of the above given discussion, it is clear that the exclusivism of John 14,6 is not caused by expulsion from the synagogue. On the contrary, it is cultic veneration of Christ and the consequent exclusive claims that caused the expulsion from the synagogue.[94] Therefore, an anti-Judaistic and a sectarian interpretation of John 14,6 should be discouraged. The Gospel may presuppose an inevitable separation of the Jewish Christians from the Jewish community, which is integral to the community's self-understanding.[95] The expulsion passages may perhaps refer to a situation after the life of Jesus, but it is not necessary to believe that the Gospel was written as a response to the expulsion.[96] The limitations of J. L. Martyn's hypothesis show that his hypothesis should not be regarded as a solid foundation for the building up of skyscrapers of imaginative theories and interpretations.

---

tions regarding the worship of Jesus by the first Christians. But he does not deny the fact that the first Christians worshipped Jesus. In the very introduction of this book itself (p. 2), he openly admits, "Of course, the first Christians worshipped Jesus".

[93] It is beyond the scope of this study to enter into a detailed examination of this topic. For further study, see the literature given on p. 374, n. 84. How the worship of Christ was incorporated into Jewish monotheism by the first Christians is a matter of ongoing debate and discussion and not the focus of this study. The concern here is only to point out that there existed a cult of Christ in the first centuary, already at an early stage of Christian history, which paved the way for the exclusive claims like John 14,6.

[94] Thompson, *The God of the Gospel of John*, 191, also believes that the tension between the synagogue community and the Johannine community developed because a relatively exalted view of Jesus was coupled with the practice of worshipping him.

[95] Cf. Reinhartz, "The Johannine Community", 135.

[96] Kathleen Troost-Cramer and Andreas J. Köstenberger argue that the Gospel of John was composed in response to the aftermath of the Jerusalem temple's destruction in 70 CE. Kathleen does not attribute John's high Christology to a late composition date and proposes that the Gospel of John emerged in a sudden flash with the necessity of finding a new expression and mode of worship. See Troost-Cramer, *Jesus as Means and Locus of Worship*, 147–148; Köstenberger, "The Destruction of the Second Temple", 69–108.

The emergence of worship of Jesus is "the most significant step of all in the history of the origins of Christianity".[97] The historical and social context for exclusive claims in earliest Christianity is the cultic veneration of Christ because exclusivism is regarded as an essential part of the Jewish monotheistic worship during the second Temple period. This study suggests that the historical context of the exclusive claim in Acts 4,12 is a model for understanding the historical and social context of the exclusive claim in John 14,6. According to this model, it is the cultic veneration of Christ that paved the way for the exclusive claim in John 14,6. Along with the cultic veneration of Christ, the study and interpretation of the Old Testament have played an important role. The author's awareness of Christ's divine identity and his monotheistic perception of "one God and one Saviour" in Deutero-Isaiah (43,11; 45,21) are likely the motivating forces behind the exclusive claim.[98] Moreover, it is unlikely that the Johannine exclusive claim in 14,6 is isolated from the exclusive claims of mainstream Christianity. The exclusive claims in Acts 4,12 and 1 Tim 2,5 suggest that the exclusivism in John 14,6 should not be seen as a Johannine invention and an isolated view in the New Testament. Synoptic parallels (Matt 11,27; Luke 10,22) show that some form of exclusivism can already be traced back to the early Jesus tradition.

---

[97] J. Weiss, *The History of Primitive Christianity*, tr. F. Friends; ed. F. C. Grant (London 1937), I, 37. Aune, *The Cultic Setting*, 5, states, "Perhaps the single most important historical development within the early church was the rise of the cultic worship of the exalted Jesus within the primitive Palestinian church".

[98] The influence of Deutero-Isaiah on John 14,6 and on its context has already been discussed. See pp. 197–225. Moreover, it is also already shown how the ἐγώ εἰμι-sayings in John have been influenced by Deutero-Isaiah. See pp. 298–302, 305–314, 318–319. Gollwitzer, "Außer Christus", 182, asserts, "Die Exklusivität im Alten Testament meint die strikte Gebundenheit Israels an diese eine Offenbarungsgeschichte; ebenso ist im Neuen Testament die strikte Gebundenheit der Kirche an diese eine Geschichte des in Israel sich offenbarenden Gottes mit Jesus Christus (= des Vaters mit dem Sohne) gemeint. In der neutestamentlichen Exklusivität ist also die alttestamentlich-jüdische mit einbegriffen und bejaht". In the view of Hurtado, *Lord Jesus Christ*, 3, the intense devotion to Jesus, which includes reverencing him as divine, was offered and articulated characteristically within a firm stance of exclusivist monotheism, particularly in the circles of early Christians that anticipated and helped to establish the mainstream Christianity.

Chapter VIII

John 14,6 in the Context of Today's Religious Pluralism

When one thinks of the exclusivism of the Gospel of John or, to a greater extent, that of Christianity itself, what may come to his/her mind is John 14,6. For many, John 14,6 is the summary and climax of the exclusive claim of the Gospel about Jesus. Today we live in a religiously pluralistic world. Hence, it is very important to discuss the question of how we should interpret the Christological exclusivism of John 14,6 in the context of a religiously pluralistic culture.[1] Exegetes and interpreters are often disturbed and frightened by the exclusivism of John 14,6. This is mainly due to an imbalanced approach to the exclusivism of the Gospel. The Gospel of John teaches not only the exclusivism of salvation but also more importantly its universalism. Therefore, it is inevitable to pay due attention to the universal scope of salvation in the Gospel and balance its exclusivism with its universalism.[2] In the following discussion, we will survey briefly the universal scope of salvation in John. After that, in order to show that exclusivism and universalism in the

---

[1] Culpepper, "The Gospel of John as a Document of Faith", 112, thinks that challenges to the Gospel of John in the modern pluralistic culture are not primarily historical or theological but ethical. He raises the following three ethical concerns: i. is the Gospel of John anti-Jewish? ii. does the Gospel have anything to say to the marginalized and the oppressed? iii. how should we interpret the theological exclusivism of the Gospel in a pluralistic culture? Among these three concerns, the first (partly) and the last are relevant to the present study. Even though the focus of this study is not on the issue of anti-Judaism, it has already examined whether John 14,6 is anti-Jewish and has suggested some attitudes and precautions to deal with the issue of anti-Judaism in the rest of the Gospel. Now, it is time to deal with the issue of interpreting the exclusivism of John 14,6 in the context of today's religiously pluralistic culture.

[2] Although Culpepper is pessimistic about the Gospel's approach to Judaism, he admits, "Indeed, the Gospel holds forth the hope of universal salvation, at least in a general sense". See Culpepper, "Anti-Judaism in the Fourth Gospel", 84. J. Nissen, *The Gospel of John and the Religious Quest. Historical and Contemporary Perspectives* (Eugene 2013), 171, points out, "John's Gospel is one of the best examples in the Bible of the uniqueness *and* universality of Christ". The emphasis in italics is original.

New Testament go hand in hand, the juxtaposition of exclusivism and universalism in Acts 4,12 and 1 Tim 2,3–5 will be briefly examined.[3]

The Gospel of John does not give any direct guidelines on how to deal with the issues involved in today's world of religious pluralism, as modern interpreters and readers would desire and expect. It should be kept in mind that the Gospel had its origin and existence in the community of the faithful. Hence, we need to turn to the community of the faithful, the Church, for insights to confront with the modern problems of religious pluralism.[4] Accordingly, attention will be paid to the interpretative traditions of the Church, mainly here to the teachings of the Catholic Church, in approaching today's religious pluralism.

---

[3] Since the exclusivism in Acts 4,12 is already examined (see pp. 363–366), the focus will be on the universal scope of salvation in it.

[4] The problem of exclusivism of John 14,6 cannot be *fully* settled within the boundaries of biblical exegesis. The failure of Laura Tack's work is that she has tried to solve the problems of exclusivism in John 14,6 within the frontiers of biblical exegesis. This has led her to accuse the Johannine Jesus and the evangelist and to make conclusions which are misleading and unacceptable. See Tack, *John 14,6 in Light of Jewish-Christian Dialogue*, 355–356, 364, 423–424, 440. It is beyond the scope of this study to discuss the issues of inter-religious dialogues, which come under the discipline of systematic and pastoral theology. The teachings of the Church, supported by systematic and pastoral theologians, can shed much light on the issue of inter-religious dialogues. One should take into account what S. C. Barton, "Johannine Dualism and Contemporary Pluralism", *The Gospel of John and Christian Theology*, ed. R. Bauckham and C. Mosser (Grand Rapids 2008), 17, rightly points out, "Given that the Gospel of John is part of the fourfold Gospel of the Christian canon, a canon that has shaped and been shaped by the church down the centuries, then it would be folly not to seek insight from the interpretative traditions of the church as embodied in its worship, prayer, and teaching". At this juncture, it is worth quoting what the document of the Second Vatican Council, *Dei Verbum* (*DV*) 12, says, "Since Holy Scripture must be read and interpreted in the sacred spirit in which it was written, no less serious attention must be given to the content and unity of the whole of Scripture if the meaning of the sacred texts is to be correctly worked out. The living tradition of the whole Church must be taken into account along with the harmony which exists between elements of the faith".

1. Universal Salvation in John[5]

1.1 Universalism in John 14,6 and in its Immediate Context

It is already pointed out that even in the very exclusivism of John 14,6 there are elements of inclusivism and universalism.[6] The exclusive claim "no one comes to the Father except through me" has a universal implication. It presupposes the problem of human alienation and estrangement from God. Everyone in himself is separated from God. The negative substantive οὐδείς, in fact, includes everyone in human incapability to approach God. Jesus does not say οὐδεὶς ἐξ ὑμῶν, rather οὐδείς referring to every human being on earth. It has already been mentioned that even the disciples of Jesus are not better than his opponents in the fundamental problem of approaching God as the Father (7,33–36; 8,21–22; 13,33.36–38; cf. 20,17). Jesus' statement is, therefore, addressed not only to the unbelievers but also to believers. It includes the whole humanity, Christians and non-Christians alike.

John 14,6 is an invitation to all to join the family of God the Father as his children through Christ.[7] The emphasis on the image of "the Father" for God in 14,6 is worth noticing. It represents love, care and protection. John invites everyone to experience God as a loving Father, becoming his loving children. The images of "Father" (14,6) and "house" (14,2) have a universal appeal since they are part of the life of every human being, irrespective of his/her religion. The house with "many dwelling places" (14,2) may suggest the universal and spacious character of salvation. In the "Father's house" (14,2) there is "enough room for all".

1.2 Universalism in the Broad Context

The universal scope of salvation is more emphasized in the Gospel of John than in the Synoptic Gospels.[8] Let us take a view on the important elements of the universal salvation in John.

---

[5] Jesus' universal salvific mission in John is well complemented and supported by that in the Synoptic Gospels. For an overview of Jesus' universal salvific mission in the Synoptic Gospels, see G. O'Collins, *Salvation for All. God's Other Peoples* (Oxford 2008), 79–120, 142–175.

[6] See the discussion on pp. 276–278.

[7] The discussion below on the teachings of the Church will show that even non-Christians can be saved through Christ on account of his universal presence.

[8] Cf. M. Hasitschka, "...'damit die Welt glaubt' (Joh 17,21): Lebenspraxis der Kirche als universales Zeichen. Johanneische Perspektiven", *Kirche als universales Zeichen. In Memoriam Raymund Schwager SJ*, ed. R. Siebenrock and W. Sandler (Beiträge zur mimetischen Theorie 19; Wien 2005), 415.

1.2.1 Significance of "the World" (κόσμος)

The term "world" (κόσμος) plays an important role in John with regards to universal salvation. Its significance becomes clear when we notice that the most frequent use of κόσμος in the New Testament is found in John. It appears 78 times in John alone.[9] The Johannine uses of the term "world" can be, for practical purpose, grouped into three categories: i. world as a creation, the physical universe; ii. mankind; iii. the realm where evil and darkness are active (the system which is at enmity with God). Thus, the term "world" (κόσμος) has three senses in the Gospel – neutral, positive and negative, in almost exactly equal proportions.[10] A neutral sense may be detected in 1,10b; 9,32; 17,5.24; 21,25. The world as creation is created through the Logos (1,10b). In its positive sense, the world is the object of God's unconditional love and Jesus' salvific mission (1,9; 3,16–17; 8,12; 11,27; 18,37, etc.). In its negative sense, the world is an evil realm and it is at enmity with God (7,7; 8,23; 12,31; 15,18–19; 16,11, etc.).

In the first part of the Gospel, the world is predominantly an object of God's benevolence and salvific mission, whereas in the second part the negative dimension of the world is highlighted. In 1,9 John states, "The true light, which enlightens everyone, was coming into the world".[11] The God of the Gospel of John is a God who loves the whole world so much that he gives his

---

[9] The term κόσμος occurs 186 times in the entire New Testament. It is not so frequently used in the Synoptic Gospels where it appears only 15 times altogether (Matt 9x; Mark 3x; Luke 3x). The second most frequent use is found in 1 John (23x).

[10] The comment of W. A. Meeks is misleading and partly wrong when he says, "Faith in Jesus, in the Fourth Gospel, means a removal from the 'world', because it means transfer to a community which has totalistic and exclusive claims". See W. A. Meeks, "The Man from Heaven in Johannine Sectarianism", *JBL* 91 (1972), 70–71. Meeks neglects the neutral and positive uses of the term "world" in the Gospel. He does not recognize the fact that the world came into being through the Logos (1,10) and that it is the object of God's love and Jesus' mission. A believer in Jesus does not belong to the negative (evil) realm of the world, but he can still live in the world and love it as God loves it (3,16).

[11] This verse has had a great influence in shaping Christianity's approach to other religions. Its influence can be noticed even in the documents of the Second Vatican Council when Catholic Church teaches the universal salvific presence of Christ as the Logos and as the risen Lord (see the discussion under "Catholic Church's Approach to other Religions"). For a detailed study on universal salvation through Christ in other religions, see G. O'Collins, *A Christology of Religions* (New York 2018); idem, *Rethinking Fundamental Theology. Toward a New Fundamental Theology* (Oxford 2011), 292–321; idem, *Christology. A Biblical, Historical and Systematic Study of Jesus* (Oxford ²2009), 315–358; idem, *Salvation for All*; idem, *Jesus Our Redeemer. A Christian Approach to Salvation* (Oxford 2007), 218–237. Some interpreters and theologians use the notion of "cosmic Christ". E.g., Culpepper, "The Gospel of John as a Document of Faith", 123–124; J. Moltmann, *The Way of Jesus Christ* (London 1990), 274–312. Since this phrase can lead to confusion, the notion of "the universal presence of Christ" is preferable.

only Son for its salvation (3,16; cf. 1 John 4,9). He sends his Son into the world to save it from perishing (3,17; 10,36; 12,47; 17,18).[12] The various images and titles that John attributes to Jesus indeed highlight the universal significance of Jesus' salvific role. Jesus is the Lamb of God who takes away the sin of the world (1,29),[13] the light of the world (8,12; 9,5; 12,46; cf. 3,19), the Saviour of the world (4,42), the prophet who is to come into the world (6,14), the bread that gives life to the world (6,33.51), the Christ and the Son of God who is to come into the world (11,27) and the one who has come into the world to witness to the truth (18,37). Thus, in terms of Jesus' earthly mission, John emphasizes Jesus' universal salvific mission and differs from the Synoptic Gospels according to which Jesus is sent only to Israel (Matt 15,24; Luke 4,43; cf. Matt 10,5–6).

Jesus' mission in Samaria, beyond the boundaries of Judaism, has a unique significance because of its universal appeal (4,1–42). It reveals John's openness to peoples of other faiths and religions. It also indicates that no one, of whatever race, culture or religion, is to be excluded in the Johannine theology of revelation and salvation.[14] John 3,17 is being acted out in the narrative of Jesus' mission in Samaria (cf. 12,47).[15] John affirms Jesus' universal saving role in the expression "Saviour of the world" (4,42).[16] Its occurrence is especially notable because it occurs only once in the rest of the whole New Testament (1 John 4,14). The Samaritans are presented as acknowledging Jesus' universality as the Saviour. Salvation may come from the Jews (4,22). But, as the Saviour of the world, Jesus does not belong to one group of people or a certain place but exercises a saving sovereignty over the whole world (cf. 17,2; 18,37).

Jesus is the bread of life that gives life to the world through his incarnation, death and resurrection (6,33.51). It should be noted that the expression ἡ τοῦ κόσμου ζωή has no parallel in the entire New Testament. The Mosaic manna provided nourishment for Israel, but the true bread from heaven gives life to the whole world. Since the bread of life comes from heaven, the domain of divine life, it has the power to give divine life not only to Israel but

---

[12] There is an emphasis to present the judgement in 3,18 in terms of realized eschatology. It means that the judgment against the non-believers in 3,18 is to be understood in the context of Jesus' earthly ministry, depending on how the people respond to him (9,39; cf. 12,31). See Keener, *John*, I, 571.

[13] The use of the singular, "sin" (ἁμαρτία) in 1,29 emphasizes the world's collective alienation and estrangement from God, not just individual sins.

[14] Moloney, *John*, 148.

[15] Moloney, *John*, 148.

[16] Schnackenburg, *John*, I, 457, points out that the title "Saviour" (σωτήρ) was transferred from Yahweh to Jesus by the Christian community (cf. Luke 1,47; 2,11; Acts 5,31; 13,23; Phil 3,20, etc.).

also to the whole world.[17] Jesus is also presented as "the light of/into the world" 3 times (8,12; 9,5; 12,46). If the Isaianic texts (Isa 9,1–2; 42,6; 49,6; 51,4; 60,3) provide the Old Testament background for the Johannine texts, John may be emphasizing the universal salvific role of Jesus as the light of the world.[18]

At the same time, the realm of evil and darkness is at work in the world. Hence, the world in John is not simply a place where people live but also comprises a sinful mankind which turns away from God.[19] The world hates Jesus (7,7) and his followers (15,18–19; 16,33) because neither Jesus (8,23; 17,14) nor his followers (15,19; 17,16) belong to it. Jesus has, however, power over the ruler of the world (12,31; 14,30; 16,11). In Johannine thought, the world is not evil in itself, but rather evilly oriented and dominated.[20] In spite of the evil realm of the world, Jesus is committed to continue his saving mission in the world through his disciples (17,18). The death of the Son on the cross is the supreme manifestation of God's love for the whole world. Thus, it is the whole sinful humanity that becomes the object of God's love and mercy.

1.2.2 One Flock and One Shepherd (10,16)

John emphasizes Jesus' universal mission of salvation clearly in 10,16, "I have other sheep that do not belong to this fold. I must bring them also, and they will listen to my voice. So there will be one flock, one shepherd".[21] It is to be noted that even "the other sheep" already belong to Jesus. Hence, he can say, "I *have* other sheep" (ἄλλα πρόβατα ἔχω). The statement κἀκεῖνα δεῖ με ἀγαγεῖν suggests the necessity of God's universal salvation. It is also worth noticing that Jesus says that "there would be one flock" (μία ποίμνη), not "one fold" (μία αὐλή). In one flock, there can be many folds. The idea that one shepherd will lead one people of God has a rich tradition in the Old Testament (cf. Mic 5,3–5; Jer 3,15; 23,4–6; Ezek 34,23–24). It is through his

---

[17] Schnackenburg, *John*, II, 43.
[18] See the comments on John 8,12 on pp. 317–319. Cf. Thyen, *Johannesevangelium*, 421. J. Beutler, "Ich bin das Licht der Welt. Jesus und das Heil der Welt nach dem Johannesevangelium", *Bibel und Kirche* 69 (2014), 217, believes that the Gospel of John belongs to the mainstream of Christianity like the other three Gospels and offers salvation for the whole world.
[19] Schnackenburg, *John*, I, 399.
[20] Brown, *John*, I, 509.
[21] The most common scholarly view is that "the other sheep" in this verse refers to the Gentiles. Cf. A. Köstenberger, "Jesus the Good Shepherd Who Will also Bring Other Sheep (John 10,16): The Old Testament Background of a Familiar Metaphor", *BBR* 12 (2002), 67–96; Thyen, *Johannesevangelium*, 490–491; Keener, *John*, I, 819; Schnelle, *Johannes*, 199; Moloney, *John*, 305; Schnackenburg, *John*, II, 299–300; Brown, *John*, I, 396; Barrett, *John*, 376; Carson, *John*, 388; Morris, *John*, 455–456, etc.

death that Jesus will bring the Gentile folk to his flock (cf. 11,52; 12,20–36). The unity among the flock is not a natural unity, but one brought about by the activity of the Shepherd.[22] The strong future tense (γενήσονται) indicates that John 10,16 can be regarded as a prophecy.[23]

1.2.3 Gathering God's Children (11,51–52)

The evangelist's comment on Caiaphas' prophecy about the true meaning of Jesus' death in 11,49–52 is likely to include an element of the universal significance of his death. It may immediately refer to the eschatological hope of gathering together all dispersed tribes of Israel (cf. Isa 43,5–6; 49,5; Jer 23,2–5; 31,10; Ezek 34,12; 37,21).[24] But his eschatological vision may also include the gathering of all God's children with an orientation towards the future, in which all those who believe in Jesus will become God's children (cf. 1,12).[25] It seems that the status of believers as "children of God" in 11,52 is taken for granted by the evangelist.[26] Jesus' death is not only for the Jewish nation but also for the estranged and scattered children of God, who will be brought together and made one (cf. 10,16).

1.2.4 Salvation for the Gentiles (12,20–23.32; 19,19–20)

The arrival of the Greeks "to see"[27] Jesus in 12,20 confirms that Jesus' death will result in the gathering of the Jews and the Gentiles alike (cf. 11,52).[28]

---

[22] Morris, *John*, 456.

[23] Schnackenburg, *John*, II, 300.

[24] There are also references in the Old Testament to the gathering of the Gentiles to Zion (Isa 2,3; 56,7; 60,6; 66,23; Mic 4,1–3; Zech 14,16).

[25] J. A. Dennis, *Jesus' Death and the Gathering of True Israel. The Johannine Appropriation of Restoration Theology in the Light of John 11,47–52* (WUNT II 217; Tübingen 2006), 302, recognizes the Old Testament/Jewish ideas of the inclusion of the Gentiles in the eschatological day of restoration and admits (p. 310), "Although the primary purpose of 1,12 and 11,52 is to reveal Jesus' messianic mission to Israel, there is, nevertheless, a certain universal significance inherent in the eschatological designation, 'children of God'".

[26] Schnackenburg, *John*, II, 350.

[27] In Johannine theological context, "to see" may also mean "to believe in" (12,45; 14,9). It is an expression associated with discipleship (cf. 1,39.46).

[28] The Greeks ("Ελληνες) mentioned here (cf. 7,35) are to be distinguished from the Greek-speaking Jews ('Ελληνισταί; cf. Acts 6,1; 9,29; 11,20). It is possible that they are Gentile proselytes or God-fearers (cf. Luke 7,5; Acts 10,2.22; 13,16.26) since they come to worship God at the Jewish feast. Their approach first to Philipp and Philip's movement to Andrew are worth noticing. Andrew and Philip are the first disciples to receive a direct invitation from Jesus. These are the only two disciples among Jesus' twelve disciples, having Greek names. Their provenance is, as the evangelist presents, from Bethsaida in Galilee (cf. 1,44; 12,21), which was permeated by Hellenism and bordered on pagan areas (cf. Matt 4,15). According to tradition, Philip and Andrew are believed to have worked

The Pharisees unknowingly prophesy the coming of the Gentiles to Jesus when they say that the world is indeed going after him (12,19). The Gentile conversion proleptically begins with the coming of the Greeks (12,20–23). Jesus' reply to Philip and Andrew is apparently not an answer to the Greeks but a theological interpretation of the significance of their visit. Until the arrival of the Greeks, Jesus or the evangelist used to say that his (Jesus') hour has not yet come (2,4; 7,30; 8,20). Now Jesus can say, "The hour has come for the Son of Man to be glorified" (12,23). These words imply that Jesus must be glorified through death and resurrection in order to bring salvation to the Greeks (cf. 11,52; 12,24). The role of the visit of the Greeks is that it marks the imminent conversion of the Gentile world as a result of Jesus' glorification. The "bearing of much fruit" in 12,24 is a reference to the fruitful mission of the apostles, including the Gentile conversion, as a result of Jesus' death and resurrection.

Jesus' death is the moment of driving out the ruler of the world (12,31). When Jesus is lifted up, he will draw all people to himself, to the sphere of divine life (12,32), because the power of the ruler of the world will be then blocked (cf. 14,30) and the people will be freed from the realm of darkness and death. Jesus' death will bring many sheep from various folds into one flock (cf. 10,16; 11,52) and thus result in the offer of universal salvation. The inscription on the cross in three languages of Hebrew, Latin and Greek signifies the universality of his rule and the universal significance of Jesus' death (19,19–20; cf. 12,32). Moreover, the use of πᾶς in 3,26; 6,37; 8,2; 11,48 may imply the universal scope of Jesus' mission and salvation.[29]

2. Juxtaposition of Exclusivism and Universalism in Acts 4,12; 1 Tim 2,3–5

It is already shown that exclusivism and universal salvation are present in John 14,6, in its immediate context and in the large context of the Gospel. This pattern of juxtaposition of exclusivism and universalism is not something unique in the Gospel of John, but is also prevalent in the rest of the

---

among the Gentiles. Cf. Keener, *John*, I, 480–482; Schnackenburg, *John*, II, 381–382; Barrett, *John*, 421–422.

[29] While narrating the miraculous catch of fish by the disciples, John records that there were 153 fishes (21,11). There is ambiguity regarding the significance of the number 153. If one concedes Jerome's interpretation, this number refers to all species of fish in the sea and thus to the universal scope of Jesus' salvific mission. The "untorn net" may symbolize the unity of the Church, which consists of all believers from all races and nations of the earth. This view is in harmony with the meaning of the kingdom of heaven, which is compared to a net that catches "all kinds of fish" in Matt 13,47. Cf. Brown, *John*, II, 1097–1098.

New Testament. Acts 4,12 and 1 Tim 2,3–5 are clear examples. Thus, the Gospel of John is in harmony with the theological outlook of the rest of the New Testament. The exclusivism of Acts 4,12 has already been examined.[30] The phrase "under heaven" (ὑπὸ τὸν οὐρανόν) in Acts 4,12 refers to the universal aspect of salvation. Luke holds on to the universal scope of salvation when he insists that everyone on earth can be saved "in the name of Jesus" just like the crippled man who is "saved" (Acts 4,9) "in the name of Jesus".

It is remarkable that the exclusivism of 1 Tim 2,5 is also inseparably bound with God's plan of universal salvation (1 Tim 2,3–4). The literal context of 1 Tim 2,3–5 is, as the letter claims, Paul's instructions to Timothy concerning prayer (2,1–7).[31] The emphasis of 2,1–7 is God's desire to save every human being through Christ (cf. 1 Tim 4,10; Titus 2,11; 3,2.8). Since God is concerned with the salvation of all, there is an insistence on prayer for every human being (1 Tim 2,1). This intercessory prayer should also include kings and all those who are in authority, so that they may allow the Christian community to live in peace and may come to the knowledge of the truth (vv. 2–4).[32] V. 5 asserts very clearly without any element of doubt that there is only one God and only one mediator between God and humankind.[33] If God is one and also the Saviour, he must be concerned with the salvation of all peoples, not just with one particular community or a nation. Christ is the only mediator between God and mankind because of his testimony through his sacrificial death as a ransom for all (v. 6; cf. Mark 10,45; Matt 20,28; 2 Tim 1,8). He alone can establish peace between God and the sinners, and he is the only mediator of the new covenant (Heb 8,6; 9,15; 12,24). Paul is a herald and teacher of this message of God's salvation through Christ (2,7). Thus, Acts 4,12 and 1 Tim 2,3–5 impressively highlight the exclusive salvation through Christ as well as the universality of Christ's salvific work as the only mediator between God and mankind. And they parallel the exclusive claim and the universal scope of salvation in the Gospel of John.

---

[30] See pp. 363–366.

[31] 1 Tim is considered as a deutero-Pauline letter. However, according to the information given in the letter, 1 Tim is addressed by Paul to Timothy who is in Ephesus to represent the apostle there (1 Tim 1,3). The structure of 1 Tim 2,1–7 can be given as follows: vv. 1–2 command to pray for all, especially for all in authority; vv. 3–4 God's will to save all; vv. 5–6 stress on one God and one mediator; v. 7 Paul's appointment as the apostle and teacher of the Gentiles.

[32] The insistence on prayer for kings and authorities is notable. Ephesus was at that time well-known for the cult of the goddess Artemis (cf. Acts 19,21–41). Along with the worship of Artemis, the imperial cult was also a dominant religious-political fixture in Ephesus. Christians, however, like Jews did not participate in these forms of worship. Hence, a peaceful co-existence with the political authority was a need of the time.

[33] The repetition of the word "one" in εἷς θεός, εἷς καὶ μεσίτης suggests the close relationship of Christ with God.

3. The Catholic Church's Approach to Other Religions

The documents of the Second Vatican Council provide the basis for the Catholic Church's current approach to other religions.[34] "The Constitution on the Church in the Modern World", *Gaudium et Spes (GS)*, emphasizes the unity of humanity, pointing out that all human beings are created in the image of God *(GS* 12; 29; 34; 68*)*. "The Decree on the Mission Activity of the Church", *Ad Gentes Divinitus (AGD)* 3 states that the universal plan of God for the salvation of the human race is carried out secretly in the soul of human beings *(*cf. *AGD 7).*[35] Christ is the revealer for all people and the light of all nations, one who enlightens all peoples *(LG* 1; 16*)*. He is the head of the entire human race and the source of salvation for the whole world *(Sacrosanctum Concilium* 83; *LG* 16–17*)*. Christ is now at work in the hearts of human beings through the energy of his Holy Spirit arousing in them an eschatological desire and strengthening it *(GS* 38*).*[36] Whatever good or truth is found among them is given by him who enlightens everyone (cf. John 1,9), so

---

[34] Unless otherwise indicated, the English translation of all Church documents used here is according to Libreria Editrice Vaticana, available at http://www.vatican.va. Besides, A. Flannery (tr.), *Vatican Council II: The Conciliar and Postconciliar Documents* (Collegeville 2014) is also consulted. Since the full names of all documents are given in their first occurrence, their abbreviations are not included in the list of abbreviations.

[35] *AGD* 11 speaks of "the seeds of the Word which lie hidden" among peoples of other religions. According to "the Constitution on the Church", *Lumen Gentium (LG)* 16, "those also can attain to salvation who through no fault of their own do not know the Gospel of Christ or His Church, yet sincerely seek God and moved by grace strive by their deeds to do His will as it is known to them through the dictates of conscience". *GS* 16 explains the role of conscience as follows, "For man has in his heart a law written by God; to obey it is the very dignity of man; according to it he will be judged. Conscience is the most secret core and sanctuary of a man. There he is alone with God, Whose voice echoes in his depths. In a wonderful manner conscience reveals that law which is fulfilled by love of God and neighbour". J. Ratzinger, "The Dignity of the Human Person", *Commentary on the Documents of Vatican II*, ed. H. Vorgrimler (New York 1969), V, 136, comments on *GS* 16 thus, "Conscience is presented as the meeting-point and common ground of Christians and non-Christians and consequently as the real hinge on which dialogue turns. Fidelity to conscience unites Christians and non-Christians and enables them to work together to solve the moral tasks of mankind, just as it compels them both to humble and open inquiry into truth". G. O'Collins, *The Second Vatican Council on Other Religions* (Oxford 2013), 131, comments, "It is through the voice of conscience that all human beings, whatever their religious convictions, can hear and follow the universal law of God".

[36] O'Collins, *Salvation for All*, 219, points out that the risen Christ "is absent from nobody, but he interacts differently with everybody". For a discussion on the universal presence of Christ and the Holy Spirit for the salvation of God's other peoples, see O'Collins, *A Christology of Religions*; idem, *Rethinking Fundamental Theology*, 292–321; idem, *Christology. A Biblical, Historical and Systematic Study of Jesus*, 334–358; idem, *Salvation for All*, 207–229.

that they may finally have life *(LG 16)*.[37] *LG* 48 calls the Church "the universal sacrament of salvation", however, the Council admits that the kingdom of God extends beyond the Church *(LG* 5; *9)*.[38] Church encourages, in accordance with 1 Tim 2,1–7, intercessory prayer for the salvation of the entire world *(SC* 53; 83*)* and dialogue and collaboration with other religions and international associations *(AGD* 12; 16; 34; 41; cf. *Gravissimum Educationis* 11*)*.

The Church in its "Declaration on the Relationship of the Church to Non-Christian Religions", *Nostra Aetate (NA)*, teaches universal salvation for all peoples irrespective of race, religion and culture. *NA* 1 acknowledges mankind as a community which is created by one God (Acts 17,26) and believes that his providence, goodness and his saving design extend to all humankind (Wis 8,1; Acts 14,17; Rom 2,6–7; 1 Tim 2,4).[39] It is worth quoting a remarkable passage on other religions from *NA* 2:

The Catholic Church rejects nothing that is true and holy in these religions. She regards with sincere reverence those ways of conduct and of life, those precepts and teachings which, though differing in many aspects from the ones she holds and sets forth, nonethe-

---

[37] *AGD* 7–8 reaffirms that there is no salvation outside Christ (Acts 4,12; cf. *GS* 10) and that Christ is the way and the truth (John 14,6).

[38] According to *SC* 2, through the celebration of the liturgy, the Church becomes to those who are outside "a sign lifted up among the nations (Isa 11,12) under which the scattered children of God may be gathered together (John 11,52), until there is one sheepfold and one shepherd" (John 10,16). *AGD* 9 speaks of the positive effects of missionary activities, especially through the preaching of the Word of God and the celebration of the sacraments, particularly the Eucharist. They heal, uplift and perfect whatever is good, "sown in the hearts and minds of men, or in the rites and cultures peculiar to various peoples for the glory of God". It regards "whatever truth and grace" found among the nations "as a sort of secret presence of God".

[39] The reference made by the document to the biblical texts is to be specially noted. Acts 17,26 speaks of the common origin of the humanity as God's creation. Wis 8,1 personifies the divine activity through the figure of Lady Wisdom and expresses satisfactorily the universal scope of divine providence. O'Collins, *Salvation for All*, 233, states, "'Where there is wisdom', we should say, 'there is Christ *(ubi sapientia, ibi Christus)*'. To deny to others and their religions any true knowledge of God and mediation of salvation would be to belittle the scope of Christ's activity as universal Wisdom". In accordance with John 1,9, we may say that it is as universal Wisdom that Christ enlightens everyone. Acts 14,17 is spoken by the apostles Barnabas and Paul to the worshippers of Zeus and Hermes in Lystra who regard them to be gods who have come down in the human form. The apostles recognize that God through the testimony of nature shows his concern for all people everywhere irrespective of their religious beliefs. Rom 2,6–7 refers to God's righteous and impartial judgement according to each one's deeds, whether he is a Jew or a Gentile (cf. 2,1–11). In today's multi-religious context, Paul's words can be applied to people of all religious faiths. God judges everyone according to his deeds, not according to his religion. As it is already shown, 1 Tim 2,4 speaks of God's desire of saving everyone and bringing him to the knowledge of truth.

less often reflect a ray of that Truth which enlightens all men. Indeed, she proclaims, and ever must proclaim Christ "the way, the truth, and the life" (John 14,6), in whom men may find the fullness of religious life, in whom God has reconciled all things to Himself (2 Cor 5,18–19).[40]

It is to be specially noted that in this passage the Catholic Church gives due attention to two key texts from the Gospel of John (1,9; 14,6) when it speaks of Christian revelation and salvation in relationship to other religions. The Church is open to accept whatever is "true and holy" in all other religions, however different they may be. The source of the "true and holy" in all other religions is Christ because he is the truth (14,6), whose rays of light others may enjoy (8,12), and the Logos, who enlightens all human beings (1,9). The Church does not waver to assert that Christ is the way, the truth and the life and the meeting point for reconciliation between God and humanity *(cf. NA 2)*. It is only in him that the fullness of revelation and salvation is to be found *(cf. NA 2; Acts 4,12; 1 Tim 2,5)*. At the same time, the Church encourages respect for all religions and universal fraternity. In this regard, it is worth mentioning that *NA* 4 takes special effort to deal with the issue of anti-Judaism, which is still a heated topic in Johannine studies:

True, the Jewish authorities and those who followed their lead pressed for the death of Christ (John 19,6); still, what happened in His passion cannot be charged against all the Jews, without distinction, then alive, nor against the Jews of today. Although the Church is the new people of God, the Jews should not be presented as rejected or accursed by God, as if this followed from the Holy Scriptures. All should see to it, then, that in catechetical work or in the preaching of the word of God they do not teach anything that does not conform to the truth of the Gospel and the spirit of Christ.

Nostra Aetate concludes with an emphasis on God's universal fatherhood and the principle of love. In this small document the term "Father" occurs 4 times *(NA* 2; 5*)*. It highlights the recognition of God as a Father *(cf. NA 2)* and teaches that people's relationship with God the Father truly depends on how they relate with their fellow beings, who are their brothers and sisters because "those who do not love, do not know God" (1 John 4,8; cf. *NA* 5). *Nostra Aetate*'s emphasis on God's fatherhood goes well in harmony with John's insistence on experiencing God as Father, who represents love and concern.

In the encyclical letter *Redemptor Hominis*, issued in 1979, Pope John Paul II points out that the non-Christian religions are various reflections of the one truth, "seeds of the Word", which all are directed to the single goal of the quest for God, even though the routes taken by each may differ (*RH* 11). It is worth noticing that the Pope teaches that Christ, the Son of God, by his incarnation in a certain way united himself with each human being, and he pre-

---

[40] Even though this passage is written with reference to Hinduism and Buddhism, it can be applied to all non-Christian religions. For a discussion on Catholic-Muslim and Catholic-Jewish relations after Vatican II, see O'Collins, *A Christology of Religions*.

sents Christ as the redeemer of the whole world *(RH* 8; cf. *GS* 22*)*. The Pope emphasizes that the Holy Spirit also works outside the visible confines of the Mystical Body *(RH 6)*.[41] In the Message to the People of Asia during his visit in Asian countries, given at Manila on 21st February 1981, Pope John Paul II admonishes all Christians to be committed to the dialogue with the believers of all religions, so that mutual understanding may grow, moral values may be strengthened and God may be praised in all creation (n. 4–5).[42] In his Letter to the Bishops in Asia for the plenary assembly of the Federation of the Asian Bishops' Conferences in 1990, the Pope makes clear, "The fact that the followers of other religions can receive God's grace and be saved by Christ apart from the ordinary means which he has established does not thereby cancel the call to faith and baptism which God wills for all people" (n. 4; cf. *AGD* 7).[43] Hence, it is wrong to think that the Church is only one way of salvation among many and to assert that her mission to the followers of other religions should be nothing more than to help them be better followers of those religions (n. 4).[44] Her mission is to bear witness to Christ and to be a leaven of love and goodness in the affairs of the world until Christ returns in glory (n. 5).[45]

In the encyclical letter *Redemptoris Missio*, issued on 7th December 1990, John Paul II admonishes that those engaged in inter-religious dialogue should be consistent with their own religious traditions and convictions and be open to understanding those of the other party without pretence or close-mindedness, but with truth, humility and frankness, knowing that dialogue can enrich each other *(RM* 56*)*.[46] In a document on inter-religious dialogue, jointly published by the Pontifical Council for Inter-Religious Dialogue and the Congregation for the Evangelisation of Peoples on 19th May 1991, the Church reminds that inter-religious dialogue is a mutual challenge.[47] The

---

[41] This point, already taught by the Second Vatican Council *(LG* 16; *GS* 22; *AGD* 15*)*, is repeated in the document entitled "The Attitude of the Church toward the Followers of other Religions: Reflections and Orientations on Dialogue and Mission" (n. 24), published by the Secretariat for Non-Christians in 1984. See J. Neuner and J. Dupuis (ed.), *The Christian Faith in the Doctrinal Documents of the Catholic Church* (Bangalore 72001), 445.

[42] Neuner and Dupuis, *The Christian Faith*, 443–444. During the first visit to India, Pope John Paul II expressed his appreciation for the spiritual values enshrined in the Indian religious traditions and stressed the importance of inter-religious dialogue in his address to the leaders of other religions on 5th February 1986 in Madras (Chennai).

[43] Neuner and Dupuis, *The Christian Faith*, 452.

[44] Neuner and Dupuis, *The Christian Faith*, 452.

[45] Neuner and Dupuis, *The Christian Faith*, 452.

[46] Neuner and Dupuis, *The Christian Faith*, 454.

[47] The joint document explains this mutual challenge thus, "While entering with an open mind into dialogue with the followers of other religious traditions, Christians may have also to challenge them in a peaceful spirit with regard to the content of their belief.

document teaches that all men and women who are saved share, though differently, in the same mystery of salvation in Jesus Christ through the Holy Spirit (n. 29).[48] The mystery of salvation reaches out to all members of other religions, in a way known to God, through the invisible action of the Spirit of Christ (n. 29).[49] Even though the members of other religions do not recognize or acknowledge Jesus Christ as their Saviour, they receive salvation in Jesus Christ concretely in the sincere practice of what is good in their own religious traditions and by obeying the dictates of their conscience (n. 29).[50]

In the document *We Remember. A Reflection on the Shoah*, issued on 16th March 1998 by the Commission for Religious Relations with the Jews, the Catholic Church expresses deep regret over the evils committed by the members of the Church who were involved in the Nazi persecution of the Jews and is resolved to build a new future, in which there will be no more anti-Judaism among Christians and anti-Christian sentiments among the Jews but a shared mutual respect.[51] Pope John Paul II made a landmark in the approach of the Catholic Church to other religions by devoting more attention to inter-religious dialogue and by expressing more fraternal gestures with other religious followers than any other Pope who preceded him.[52] The declaration *Dominus Iesus (DI)* on "the unicity and salvific universality of Jesus Christ and the Church" by the Congregation for the Doctrine of the Faith, which was issued in 2000, continues the line of thought of NA and maintains a high regard for what is true and holy in other religions *(DI 2)*. DI 2 proclaims universal salvation through Christ as follows:

But Christians too must allow themselves to be questioned. Notwithstanding the fullness of God's revelation in Jesus Christ, the way Christians sometimes understand their religion and practice, it may be in need of purification" (n. 32). See Neuner and Dupuis, *The Christian Faith*, 456.

[48] Neuner and Dupuis, *The Christian Faith*, 455.

[49] Neuner and Dupuis, *The Christian Faith*, 455.

[50] Neuner and Dupuis, *The Christian Faith*, 455.

[51] Cf. Neuner and Dupuis, *The Christian Faith*, 458–460.

[52] In October 1986, Pope John Paul II boldly broke new ground by going off to Assisi with the Dalai Lama and other leaders or representatives of the world's religions to pray for peace. On 19th August 1985, at the invitation of King Hassan II of Morocco, he spoke in Casablanca to over 100,000 young Muslims on the religious and moral values common to Islam and Christianity. On 13th April 1986, John Paul II visited the main synagogue in Rome. He was probably the first Pope to enter and pray in a synagogue since the early days of Christianity. On 7th April 1994, the Pope hosted a Holocaust memorial concert in the Vatican. On 6th May 2001, on a visit to Syria, the Pope prayed in a mosque in Damascus and so became the first Pope ever to visit and pray in a mosque. Cf. O'Collins, *The Second Vatican Council*, 167–180. Pope Francis as well visited the Roman synagogue on 16th January 2016. For more information about the personal involvement of recent Popes in interfaith relationships, see M. L. Fitzgerald, "Vatican II and Interfaith Dialogue", *Interfaith Dialogue: Global Perspectives*, ed. E. K-F. Chia (New York 2016), 12–14.

The Church's proclamation of Jesus Christ, 'the way, the truth, and the life' (John 14,6), today also makes use of the practice of inter-religious dialogue. Such dialogue certainly does not replace, but rather accompanies the *missio ad gentes*, directed toward that 'mystery of unity', from which 'it follows that all men and women who are saved share, though differently, in the same mystery of salvation in Jesus Christ through his Spirit'.[53]

This document challenges the religious relativistic attitudes of the faithful towards Christian revelation *(DI 4)* and makes it clear: "In fact, it must be firmly believed that, in the mystery of Jesus Christ, the Incarnate Son of God, who is "the way, the truth, and the life" (Jn 14:6), the full revelation of divine truth is given" *(DI 5)*; "the full and complete revelation of the salvific mystery of God is given in Jesus Christ" *(DI 7)*.[54] In the apostolic exhortation *Evangelii Gaudium*, issued on 24th November 2013, Pope Francis repeats the prevalent teachings of the Church, "Non-Christians, by God's gracious initiative, when they are faithful to their own consciences, can live 'justified by the grace of God and thus be associated to the paschal mystery of Jesus Christ'" *(EG 254)*. He too insists, "Interreligious dialogue is a necessary condition for peace in the world, and so it is a duty for Christians as well as other religious communities" *(EG 250)*.[55] In his Apostolic Constitution *Praedicate Evangelium (PE, 149,1)*, issued on 19th March, 2022, Pope Francis maintains an openness to all religions and encourages a true search for God among the believers of all religions. At the same time, he does not waver to proclaim, "we believe firmly in Jesus as the sole Redeemer of the world" (*Querida Amazonia*, 107).

---

[53] The encyclical letter *Fides et Ratio (FR 2)* on "the relationship between faith and reason", which was released in 1998, states the role of the Church as follows, "From the moment when, through the Paschal Mystery, she received the gift of the ultimate truth about human life, the Church has made her pilgrim way along the paths of the world to proclaim that Jesus Christ is "the way, and the truth, and the life" (John 14,6)".

[54] At the same time, *DI* recognizes the mysterious presence of Christ in other religions: "the sacred books of other religions, which in actual fact direct and nourish the existence of their followers, receive from the mystery of Christ the elements of goodness and grace which they contain" *(DI 8)*.

[55] The encyclical letter *Fratelli Tutti (FT)*, issued in 2020, promotes dialogue among believers of different religions: "The different religions, starting from the recognition of the value of every human person as a creature called to be a son or daughter of God, offer a precious contribution for the construction of fraternity and for the defense of justice in society. Dialogue between people of different religions is not done solely out of diplomacy, courtesy or tolerance. As the Bishops of India have taught, 'the goal of dialogue is to establish friendship, peace, harmony and to share moral and spiritual values and experiences in a spirit of truth and love'" *(FT 271)*.

4. Conclusion

From its earliest to its latest books, the New Testament does not waver in acknowledging Christ as the one Saviour for all people.[56] Hence, the interpreters of the New Testament have to be cautious of a naïve embrace of religious pluralism as the determining context for responsible interpretation.[57] Pluralism is only an ideological strategy for the sake of maintaining unity in a situation of cultural and religious diversity.[58] Inter-religious dialogue and positive approach to other religions do not mean forgetting one's own roots and the foundation of one's own faith. Diversities in religions can be respected and even unity can be maintained without abandoning one's own self-identity. Today, the Catholic Church keeps in its attitude to other religions a very balanced approach, which is sincere to the message of the New Testament as well as sensitive to today's religiously pluralistic world. The example set by the Catholic Church can serve as a model for the other Christians to follow.

The exclusive claim of John 14,6 is not a footnote to the Gospel of John but the very Gospel itself. According to John, Jesus is the only way to God, the only way to the Father. This is because John very strongly believes in and emphasizes the divine identity of Christ. It is his belief and conviction, in accordance with his Scripture (cf. Isa 43,11), that make him assert that Jesus is the only way to the Father. This is an irrefutable truth of the Gospel. But this irrefutable truth does not necessarily imply that all believers of other religions are doomed and not saved. We need to balance the exclusivism of the Gospel with its equal emphasis on universal salvation, as shown above. This is what the Catholic Church advocates through the documents of the Second Vatican Council and the teachings of recent Popes. It is to be noted that the documents like *NA, DI* do not cite the clause "no one comes to the Father except through me" when they cite John 14,6. Probably, it is to avoid the misunderstanding that the followers of other religions are not saved if they do not believe in Jesus.

What the Christians need to highlight today in their approach to other religions is not the exclusiveness of salvation, but the universality of salvation, i.e., that Jesus Christ is the Saviour of all the world (4,42) and that all are included in the salvific plan of God through Christ. John 14,6 does not teach or propagate fundamentalism. "No one comes to the Father except through me" does not mean that all those who do not believe in Jesus are damned, but only that all are saved through Christ and that he is the Saviour of the whole

---

[56] It is often modern interpreters who waver in this regard. See O'Collins, *Salvation for All*, 165. Cf. Neuner and Dupuis, *The Christian Faith*, 446–448.

[57] Cf. Barton, "Johannine Dualism", 5.

[58] Barton, "Johannine Dualism", 17.

mankind.[59] God's love for mankind and his plan of salvation in Christ embrace every human being through the working of the Holy Spirit in a manner unknown to us.[60] By practising what is good in their own religious traditions and by obeying the dictates of their conscience, the followers of other religions can be saved through Christ because Christ is salvifically present in every human being and he is the light that enlightens everyone to do good through his Holy Spirit. God wants that everyone should be saved. Therefore, the Christians have the duty to pray and work for the salvation of all people (1 Tim 2,1–7) and should not give up the hope of the Gospel that there shall be one flock and one shepherd (John 10,16).

---

[59] K. R. MacGregor, *A Historical and Theological Investigation of John's Gospel* (Cham 2020), 193, views, "While by no means demanding inclusivism or even favoring inclusivism over particularism, John 14,6 is nonetheless consistent with the notion that persons in non-Christian religions today can receive salvation, which unbeknownst to them occurs through the person of Jesus".

[60] Dettwiler, *Die Gegenwart des Erhöhten*, 168, asserts, "Die vom christlichen Glauben behauptete Absolutheit der Wahrheit in Christus kann nur die Absolutheit der göttliche Liebe sein. Diese allerdings ist ihrem Wesen nach, wenn auch nicht relativ, so doch höchst relational. Sie ist ausschließliches Bezogenseins auf den verlorenen und doch schon durch diese Liebe geretteten Menschen".

General Conclusion

The conclusions given at the end of every chapter may give the reader a complete picture of the findings of this monograph. Some important findings and observations of this study and their theological implications are presented here.

1. Some Insights from Classical Greek Literature

The most important way-lexeme in classical Greek literature is ὁδός. In classical Greek literature, as a metaphor way has mainly moral and philosophical meanings. In the moral sense, it refers to human conduct which can be good or bad. In the context of the pursuit for philosophical knowledge, it may refer to a method or a system of enquiry. In this regard, as in the Bible, way is seen as a means to reach a goal or a destination without which the notion of way in itself is incomplete. In Greek philosophy, there is a tendency to consider truth as a goal in itself and the Greek thinkers are concerned with the way of knowing the truth. In opposition to Greek thought, in the Gospel of John truth is never regarded as a goal in itself but only as a means.

Some points of comparison can be suggested between Greek thought and Johannine thought. E.g., Parmenides speaks of two ways of enquiry: "it is" (ἔστιν), which is accompanied by truth, and "it is not" (οὐκ ἔστιν), which is an untrustworthy way.[1] He contrasts them with each other. The first one is the way of truth and the second is the way of error or opinion. The first is real and the other is illusory. John also contrasts the way of Jesus with the way of the devil. Jesus speaks truth and is the truth (John 8,45–46; 14,6),[2] whereas the devil speaks lies and is the father of lies; he does not stand in the way of truth and there is no truth in him (8,44). Taking into account Jesus' eternal existence in the Gospel, one can say that Jesus is always "it is" (ἔστιν).[3] He is

---

[1] Parmenides, *On Nature*, 2,1–5.

[2] In the Synoptic Gospels (Mark 12,14; Matt 22,16; Luke 20,21), Jesus is considered to be the one who is "true" (ἀληθής) and who teaches "the way of God upon/in truth" (ἐπ' ἀληθείας τὴν ὁδὸν τοῦ θεου/τὴν ὁδὸν τοῦ θεοῦ ἐν ἀληθείᾳ).

[3] The way of "it is" is uncreated, indestructible, complete, immovable and without end. See Parmenides, *On Nature*, 8,1–4.

ever "I am" (ἐγώ εἰμι) without change (8,24.28.58; 13,19; 18,5–6.8; cf. Heb 7,24–25; 13,8).[4]

Heraclitus says, "The way up and down is one and the same".[5] These words can be applied to the Johannine Jesus, whatever may be their meaning in their original context. He is the way up and the way down for the angels of God to ascend and to descend (1,51). He is the only one who has ascended into heaven and similarly he alone has descended from heaven (3,13). In Jesus, the way up and the way down meet together. As the way up, he leads the believers to the Father (14,2–6), and as the way down, he brings the Father and the Spirit to the believers (14,16–23).

2. Jesus as the Way in the Light of the Old Testament Salvation History

John's hermeneutical strategy is Scriptural hermeneutics. Hence, his concern is to reread his Scripture and to show, often not through direct quotations but through allusions and echoes, how the salvific images of his Scripture are fulfilled in Jesus. Way is one of the most important salvific images in the Old Testament. The whole salvation history planned by God in the past and for the future in the Old Testament can be described as "the way". Usually, commentators and interpreters understand the meaning of way in John 14,6 within a limited scope. But John's presentation of Jesus as the way should be understood in the broader context of the use of the way/journey motif not only in the Gospel but also in the whole Old Testament. This is mainly because John attaches special significance to the term way and also to the verbs of journey. He uses only one way-lexeme in the entire Gospel, namely ὁδός. He uses ὁδός exclusively to cite Isa 40,3 in 1,23 and to present Jesus as the way in 14,4–6. He does not use it like the Synoptic evangelists who use it frequently in a literal sense. For John, way is exclusively a salvific term and it is applicable only to Jesus. Therefore, he cannot use this term in any other manner. For him, there are not many ways but only one way which is Jesus. Hence, he does not cite "the paths of our God" from Isa 40,3 as the Synoptics do (Matt 3,3; Mark 1,3; Luke 3,4). He derives this salvific significance of the

---

[4] Parmenides aligns truth with being that does not change. For him, to be wise is to know what does not change. Philosophy, as the love of wisdom, is a godlike search for what is "uncreated and indestructible", what is "complete, immovable, and without end". However, most people do not seek unchanging truth. They do not love wisdom but folly; they have opinions without knowledge; they embrace falsehood and the lie. See L. Zuidervaart, "Philosophy, Truth, and the Wisdom of Love", *Christian Scholar's Review* 48 (2018), 31–43.

[5] Heraclitus, *Fragments*, 60.

way motif from an understanding of its usage in the whole Old Testament. John seems to have in his horizon the complete picture of the way in the Old Testament salvation history when he calls Jesus the way. In the light of the salvation history of the Old Testament, the following two points can be highlighted: i. Jesus opens and is the way to the tree of life, ii. Jesus leads the new exodus.

2.1 Jesus as the Way to the Tree of Life

The concept of way can elucidate the whole story of salvation in the Bible. The various nuances of the meaning of way in the Bible clearly reveal a progression of thought.[6] The Bible begins with the story of humanity's estrangement from God (cf. Gen 3,24) and ends with the positive message of humanity's reconciliation with God through Jesus (cf. Rev 22,14). When John presents Jesus as the way to the Father, he means that God's promise of salvation is fulfilled in Jesus. The first occurrence of "way" (דֶּרֶךְ/ὁδός) in the Bible is found in Gen 3,24 in the context of humanity's separation and alienation from God. The serpent deceives Adam and Eve, and they are sent out from the garden of Eden on account of their sin. As a result, "the way to the tree of life" is blocked and they are denied access to the tree of life in the garden.

The human way becomes all the more corrupt (Gen 6,12). It is in the context of the increasing sinfulness of humanity that the notion of "the way of the Lord" occurs for the first time in the Bible (Gen 18,19). In his salvific plan, God selects Abraham and promises to make him the father of a nation (Gen 12,1–3) that will live according to "the way of the Lord" (Gen 18,19). His love and fidelity to the people of Israel are concretely manifested when they are redeemed from Egypt. The Lord himself "goes" in front of them in a pillar of cloud and fire by day and night "to lead them along the way" (Exod 13,21; cf. 14,19). He makes a covenant with them so that they may walk in his "way" (Deut 5,33; 8,6; Jer 7,23) by keeping his commandments. However, the Israelites constantly fail to walk in "the way of the Lord".

Therefore, the Lord promises to establish a new and an everlasting covenant by giving them "one heart and one way" and by leading them like a shepherd (Jer 32,39–40; Isa 40,11; cf. Ezek 34,11–16). The Lord himself will come to save his people and will establish "the way of holiness" for his "redeemed" "to walk" (Isa 35,4.8–9). In Deutero-Isaiah, the way is closely related to the coming or leading of the Lord in the future (Isa 40,1–11; 42,1–9; 49,7–12). The Lord's coming requires "the preparation of the way". The prophetic voice on the notion of way in the Old Testament occurs lastly when Mal 3,1 restates Isaianic "preparation of the way of the Lord" for the Lord's

---

[6] Gros, *Je suis la route*, 32.

coming (cf. Isa 40,3). Like all other evangelists, John cites Isa 40,3, which was also regarded in high esteem by the Qumran community with reference to eschatological salvation. But John indicates in the manner he cites Isa 40,3 (cf. 1,23; 14,2–6) that "the preparation of the way" can be done only by Jesus. Immediately after introducing the theme of "the way of the Lord" (John 1,23; cf. Gen 18,19; Isa 40,3; Mal 3,1), John speaks of the need of removing the obstacle of the sin of the world (John 1,29). In fact, both situations of Mal 3,1 (cf. Isa 40,3) and Gen 3,24, namely the need for the way of the Lord and the obstacle/blockage of sin, are present in the very first chapter of the Gospel itself (1,23.29).

"The preparation of the way of the Lord" in Deutero-Isaiah necessarily involves the removal of the obstacles (Isa 40,3–4; 57,14; 62,10).[7] Whereas the Synoptic Gospels emphasize the moral aspect in the removal of the obstacles for "the preparation of the way" (Mark 1,4–5; Matt 3,7–10; Luke 3,7–14), for John, the removal of the obstacles necessarily and mainly involves the overthrow of the rulership and power of the ruler of the world/the devil over human hearts, so that they may be liberated from the slavery of sin (cf. 1,29; 8,34–36) and God may dwell in them (14,17.20.23). That is why John refers to the devil or Satan (cf. Gen 3,1–7; Rev 12,9) or the ruler of the world (14,30) and his interference in the heart of Judas Iscariot in the near context (13,2.27; cf. 6,70–71) when he speaks of Jesus' "preparation" (14,2–3) and presents Jesus as "the way" (14,4–6).[8] John 13–14 is framed by the theme of conflict over power between Jesus and the devil/ruler of the world (13,2; 14,30). Since Jesus is the cosmic saviour (4,42) and his journey is a cosmic journey, his journey involves inevitably a cosmic conflict – the battle with the ruler of this world who blocks the way to God. Jesus came into this world to remove this block (cf. 1 John 3,8b) and to open the way to the Father and thus to provide access to God for all people (cf. Heb 10,19–20).

The ruler of the world has no power over Jesus (14,30) and his overthrow is already prophesied by Jesus (12,31; cf. 16,11). The fall and the powerlessness of the ruler of the world is dramatically foreseen and represented when John narrates the fall to the ground of Judas Iscariot, who is ruled by "the devil/Satan" in his heart (13,2.27; cf. 6,70–71), along with the soldiers, at the utterance of "I am" (ἐγώ εἰμι) by Jesus (18,5–6). Through his journey of death and resurrection, Jesus prepares the way to the Father by overthrowing the devil's rule over human hearts and by enabling God's rule and dwelling in

---

[7] "The removal of obstacle from people's way" in Isa 57,14 may refer to the removal of sins of the people, mentioned in the immediate context (57,3–13). See pp. 51–52 for comments on Isa 40,3–4 and p. 54 for comments on Isa 57,14.

[8] In the Book of Revelation too, the defeat and destruction of Satan are envisaged (Rev 20) before the believers are given access to the tree of life in the heavenly Jerusalem (Rev 22,14).

them.⁹ Consequently, the Spirit, the Father and the Son can make their dwelling within them (14,17.20.23; cf. 20,22). Thus, the hour of Jesus is the hour of preparation of the way to the Father by overthrowing the ruler of this world.

We can assume that John presupposes humanity's alienation from God as a result of the sin of Adam and Eve, which blocks "the way to the tree of life" (Gen 3,24). According to John, sin causes the estrangement of humanity from God (9,31; cf. 3,19–20) and Jesus is the lamb of God who takes away "the sin of the world" (1,29; cf. 8,34.36; 1 John 3,5). The expression "the way to the tree of life" in Gen 3,24 may imply the way to the source of life. Since for John the Father is the ultimate source of life (5,26) and Jesus is the way to the Father (14,6; cf. Eph 2,18), it can be argued that Jesus opens "the way to the tree of life" and he himself is "the way to the tree of life" (cf. Rev 22,14). Jesus has the Father's life in himself (John 5,26) and is the mediator of this life for the believers (6,57; 14,19). Therefore, he can claim himself to be not only the way but also the life for the believers (11,25; 14,6).

2.2 Jesus as the Leader of the New Exodus

One of the major themes of Deutero-Isaiah is the new exodus in which Yahweh will finally act to save his people. It is even regarded as the overarching theme of Isa 40–55.[10] The main strands of the new exodus motif are return from exile, defeat of Israel's enemies and return of Yahweh.[11] These characteristic features are also discernible in John 13–14 at a spiritual, eschatological and cosmic level.[12]

The exile refers to a condition of someone being sent or kept away from his/her homeland. Adam and Eve were sent out from the garden of Eden and kept away from the tree of life. They lost their original and unique relationship with God due to their sin under the influence of the serpent, the evil one. The purpose of Jesus' mission is to bring back the estranged humanity to the family of God. Exile is a situation of slavery. For John, the real slavery is the slavery to sin, the servitude to demonic power and the true return from exile

---

[9] That Jesus through his death destroys the devil and delivers his believers is explicitly stated in Heb 2,14–15: "Since, therefore, the children share flesh and blood, he himself likewise shared the same things, so that through death he might destroy the one who has the power of death, that is, the devil, and free those who all their lives were held in slavery by the fear of death".

[10] Lim, *The Way of the Lord*, 47.

[11] Brunson, *Psalm 118*, 155.

[12] In John 13, there are features like Passover (13,1) and new commandment (13,34), which evoke the exodus tradition. For a study of the new exodus motif in the Gospel of John, see P. S. Coxon, *Exploring the New Exodus in John. A Biblical Theological Investigation of John. Chapters 5–10* (Eugene 2014); Brunson, *Psalm 118*, 153–179; Gros, *Je suis la route*, 100–107.

is liberation from sin through Jesus (8,34–36.44; cf. 9,41; 1 John 3,8). It is sin that keeps the children of Abraham in slavery (8,34–38). Jesus as the Son has a permanent place in the Father's house, but the slave who is subject to sin has no permanent place there (8,35). Jesus has come to remove the sin of the world (1,29). He has come to save the people from the slavery of sin and to lead them back to the Father's house, back to their original relationship with God. Therefore, Jesus says, "If the Son makes you free, you will be free indeed" (8,36). Jesus' return to the Father's house is intended to free all from the slavery of sin and to bring all to the Father's house (14,2–3). In Jesus' return to the Father, it is really all mankind who returns to God (cf. Rom 6,1–11; Eph 2,6).[13]

Israel's exodus or return from exile necessarily involves the defeat of Israel's enemies: Egyptians (Exodus 14) and Babylonians (Isa 47,11; Dan 5,30–31). Through the formation of those who are "his own" (13,1.18), Jesus forms a new Israel. The membership in the new Israel is based not on bloodline or race but on belief in Jesus (1,12–13) and rebirth through the Holy Spirit (3,5). The enemies of the new Israel are not the gentile nations but Satan/the devil and his agents. The fundamental enemy of the disciples is the same enemy of Jesus who works through Judas Iscariot to betray Jesus (13,2.27; cf. 6,70). He is the ruler of this world who is powerless before Jesus and will be condemned and thrown out (12,31; 14,30; 16,11). The victory of Jesus over the world (16,33) is ultimately the victory of the disciples who form the new Israel.

During the exile, the expectation that Yahweh would return to Jerusalem and dwell among his people was high.[14] The return of Yahweh to Jerusalem/Zion/the temple is an essential feature of eschatological salvation (Isa 40,9–10). For John, the temple in Jerusalem is intended to be the Father's house (2,16), but it will be replaced through Jesus' death and resurrection with a new temple (2,19). Its culmination is in the world to come when the believers will be able to dwell in the Father's house with Jesus (14,2–3). However, John also envisages the possibility that in this world itself God can make his dwelling in the believers as a result of Jesus' death and resurrection (14,17.23). The way for God to come to the believers and the way for the believers to come to God meet in Jesus. The way that Jesus prepares through his death and resurrection is not just one-way but two-way intended for an up and down journey (cf. 1,51).

In the first and the second exodus, it is the Lord himself who makes the way in the sea (Exod 14,29; Isa 43,16–17; Wis 14,3) and in the desert (Isa

---

[13] Gros, *Je suis la route*, 102.

[14] The prophets, especially the post-exilic prophets, looked forward to the coming of Yahweh and the deliverance of his people (e.g., Isa 40,1–5.9–11; 42,13–16; 51,4–5.11–12; 52,7–12; 54,1–8).

43,19). According to John, it is Jesus himself who prepares (John 14,2–3) and leads/is the way (ἡ ὁδός, 14,4–6) for the new exodus (ἔξοδος), which is eschatological in character.

3. Significance of Journey Language

Way and journey are inseparable concepts. Apart from the purpose of a journey, way has no meaning and significance. The Gospel of John presupposes that life is a journey. The evangelist presents the life of Jesus in terms of a journey. The story of Johannine Jesus is a story of his journey from the Father to this world, from this world to the Father and finally with the Father to the believers. Jesus' being the way is inseparable from his going the way.

Unlike the Synoptic Gospels, John attaches a pre-eminent role to the figurative sense of the verbs of journey. The spatial language of journey has various functions. It discloses his view of the universe which is dualistic. His universe is divided into heavenly and earthly realities, above and below. God belongs to the world above and the human beings to the world below. Human beings have to go up in order to reach God, and God has to come down in order to bring himself to the level of the human beings. The spatial language of journey is also intended to highlight Jesus' heavenly and divine origin and destination. By establishing Jesus' heavenly and divine origin and destination, John asserts that Christians do not believe in a deified man, but in one whose rightful place is in heaven.[15] The language of journey also implies a distance between the traveller and his destination. The evangelist frequently uses the language of journey (e.g., "coming", "going", "ascending", "descending") to demonstrate the distance between the above and the below, the distance between God and human beings, the estrangement between God and mankind. Jesus removes this distance through his passion, death, resurrection and ascension. In him the distance between God and human beings disappears because in him the way and the destination, the Son and the Father converge.[16]

The theme of Jesus as the way to the Father is explicitly stated only in 14,6. But the Gospel as a whole, especially John 13–14, answers the question of how Jesus becomes the exclusive way to the Father, using the journey motif. The motif of Jesus' cosmic journey controls John 13–14 from the be-

---

[15] J. F. McGrath, "Going up and Coming down in Johannine Legitimation", *Neot* 31 (1997), 115.

[16] Nötscher, *Gotteswege*, 7, expresses his wish in the introduction to this book, "Es wäre ein biblisches Ideal, daß die Wege Gottes und die Wege der Menschen dieselben sind, daß sie gleichlaufen oder wenigstens keinen Gegensatz bilden". We may say that in Jesus God's way and the human way become one.

ginning till the end. It is in the context of his imminent journey to the Father that John's presentation of Jesus as the exclusive way to the Father in 14,6 is to be understood. Jesus, who comes from the Father into this world and goes from this world to the Father and again comes to the disciples in order to dwell with and within them, alone can claim to be the way to the Father. The exclusive claim of 14,6b is not an isolated case in the Gospel. It is differently expressed even in the journey language of 3,13 and 6,68 (cf. 3,26).

The disciples of Jesus are asked to follow Jesus because he himself is the way. However, they cannot go with him now but only afterwards. The journey of the disciples depends on Jesus' prior journey and his "preparation of a place" for them. Jesus goes first (13,33.36; 14,3) to the Father's house because he is from there. After Jesus' physical departure, the believers are not abandoned. They also have the abiding presence of the Spirit, the Son and the Father (14,16–17.23). Journey needs a way, a guide and a destination. In the future, the belief in Jesus will be their *way* and the Spirit of *truth* will be their guide on the way (16,13) to the destination of the Father's *life*.

There is a closer affinity between the salvific dimension of journey language in the Old Testament and Jesus' salvific journey in the Gospel of John. When John narrates Jesus' salvific journey, he is likely to see in it the fulfilment of the Old Testament promises of God's salvific coming. Since exile, God's coming is hoped for in a more concrete fashion to bring salvation. This line of thought, which is kept alive in the Pseudepigraphic writings and within the Qumran community, may have influenced the Johannine journey language.

The New Testament identifies ὁ ἐρχόμενος ("the One who comes"/"the coming One") of Ps 117,26 in the LXX as Jesus Christ. The expression ὁ ἐρχόμενος is applied to Jesus 7 times in the Gospel of John. The future coming of God in the Old Testament is intended to judge and to save. John associates these two functions with the purpose of Jesus' coming (to judge: 5,22.27.30; to save: 3,17; 10,9; 12,47; cf. 8,15–16). The ἦλθον-sayings of Jesus may reveal that in Jesus the coming of the expected Saviour is realized. In the coming of Jesus, it is the coming of Yahweh himself that the evangelist sees.

When John speaks of Jesus' cosmic journey, he may be aware of the God of Israel who "comes down" to save his people, "goes ahead" of them "to lead them along the way" and "brings" them from the land of slavery to the promised land. At the spiritual level, this is what Jesus does in the Gospel of John. Jesus "comes down" from above/the Father into this world to save it from the slavery of sin and "goes ahead" and prepares the way to "lead" all to the Father. It is by going the way of death-resurrection that Jesus prepares the way to the Father, "leads" the believers to the Father's house and thus becomes the way to the Father. In short, it is possible to assume that John sees in Jesus the image of a God who comes down from above to save his people and to lead them along the way to the promised land of the Father's house. Hence, we may assume that the salvific journey language in the Old Testament forms the basic literary background for the Johannine salvific journey language.

4. Influence of Isaiah upon John 14,6 and Its Context

This study uses the text of the Gospel itself to determine the possible literary background for the designation of Jesus as the way as well as for the exclusive claim in John 14,6b and its surrounding context. John calls Jesus the way because he finds in Jesus the fulfilment of the future salvation promised through the prophets. Deutero-Isaiah frequently speaks of the way of the Lord and the Lord's imminent coming. The two Isaianic citations which John has used in the Gospel (1,23; 12,38–41) have some kind of influence upon John 14,6 and its context.

For John's presentation of Jesus as the way, the underlying text of inspiration seems to be Isa 40,3 cited in 1,23. John's reserved and peculiar use of the verb ἑτοιμάζω and the noun ὁδός can make us think that he interprets Isa 40,3 christologically and eschatologically in 14,2–6. The immediate shift from the motif of "preparation" (14,2–3) to the motif of "way" (14,4–6), especially to "Jesus'/the Lord's way" (14,4), may remind the careful reader of the Isaianic exhortation "prepare the way of the Lord" (Isa 40,3). It is by preparing a place in the Father's house through his death-resurrection and the overthrow of the rulership of the devil that Jesus prepares the way for the people to come to the Father. The background for the exclusive claim in John 14,6b at literary level is to be sought in the context of Isa 40,3 itself, where the near context is concerned with the incomparability and uniqueness of Yahweh (40,12–31) and the broader context with the exclusive monotheistic claims of Yahweh (Isa 40–55). Previous studies have not sufficiently emphasized and demonstrated the role of Isaiah, especially Isa 40,3 and its context, behind the formulation of John 14,6 and its surrounding context.[17] The present study can satisfactorily explain the literary background for the exclusivism in 14,6, which former approaches could not do.

The 'iceberg' of Isaiah's influence stretches forward from the 'tip' in John 12,38–41 towards John 13–14. It is like the Isaianic Suffering Servant (Isa 53) that Jesus washes the feet of his disciples. The evangelist's focus on the motifs of "understanding" (νοέω) and "seeing" (ὁράω) in 12,40 corresponds

---

[17] Even though Ball, *I Am*, 233–240, speaks of the relation between Isa 40,3 and John 14,6, he is not steady in his position. Hence, he makes allusions to so many way passages in Isa 42,16; 43,19; 48,17; 57,15; 62,10; Mal 2,8; 3,1, and moreover, he is totally silent about the background of John 14,6b.

with his focus on the motifs of "knowing" (γινώσκω) and "seeing" (ὁράω) in 14,7.[18] John's view of the unity between Yahweh and his Servant, based on Isaiah's vision (12,41), seems to function as a model for his understanding of the unity between the Father and Jesus (14,7–14). There is correspondence between the simultaneous vision of Christ's glory and God's glory by Isaiah (12,41) and the simultaneous vision of the Father and Jesus by the disciples (14,7–9; cf. 20,28). The combination of "words" and "works" of Jesus in relation to an appeal to "believe" in 14,10 corresponds well with the combination of "message" and "arm of the Lord" along with the motif of "believing" in 12,38 (cf. Isa 53,1).[19] The sequence of thought in 14,10b–c, i.e., the immediate shift from "words" to "works", has confounded scholars. If we make a recourse to Isa 53,1 cited in John 12,38, we can find the reason for the anomalous shift from "words" to "works" in 14,10b–c. Moreover, John 14,10a is a question just as Isa 53,1/John 12,38 is a question. In short, we may assume that the Isaianic citation in 12,38–41 has shaped John's thought and language in 14,7–14.

5. Convergence of Preparer of the Way and the Way in Jesus

It is something peculiar in the Gospel of John that in Jesus the giver and the gift, the doer and the deed converge. He gives and does what he is. Jesus gives light (I ,5.9), which is demonstrated in the healing of the man born blind in chapter 9. At the same time, he is the light (1,9; 8,12; 9,5). He gives life (5,21; 6,33; 10,28; 17,2) and is the life (11,25; 14,6). He raises the believers from the dead (6,39–40.44.54) and is the resurrection (11,25). That he is the resurrection is demonstrated in his act of raising Lazarus (11,1–44; cf. 12,1.9.17) and also in other signs (4,46–54; 5,1–9). Jesus speaks the truth (8,40.45–46; 16,7) and is the truth (14,6). He speaks God's word or words (3,34; 14,10.24; 17,8.14) and he is God's Word (1,1.14). John uses the same model when he presents Jesus as the way to the Father. Jesus is the way because he goes the way. He alone is the way to the Father because he alone comes from the Father (16,28; 17,8; cf. 8,42; 13,3; 16,27.30), goes the way to the Father (13,1; 16,28; 17,11.13) and will come again to the believers (14,3.18.23.28; 21,22–23).

According to Isa 43,16.19, it is the Lord himself who makes the way. The way that Jesus goes is prepared by himself through his journey of incarnation, death, resurrection and ascension. The basis for his being the way is his going the way. This is literally true in the case of Johannine Jesus. Among the Gos-

---

[18] The verb γινώσκω is a synonym of νοέω.

[19] "Message and arm of the Lord" refer in the context to "the words and works" of Jesus.

pels, only John records that Jesus carried the cross by himself and "went out" to Golgotha to be crucified and to die (19,17).[20] He alone can prepare a place in the Father's house (14,2–3). Indeed, by preparing a place in the Father's house he is preparing the way to the Father. Jesus' going to the Father is also to bring along with him the Father and the Spirit to the believers (cf. 14,16–23). Hence, Jesus is not only the way to the Father but also the way to the believers for the Father and the Spirit. In other words, he is, on the one hand, "the way of the Lord" (John 1,23; cf. Isa 40,3) for God to come to the people and, on the other hand, he is "the way for the people" (John 14,6; cf. Isa 57,14; 62,10) to come to God. It is by going the way to the Father that Jesus prepares and becomes the way to the Father. Thus, the preparer of the way and the way converge in Jesus.

6. Argument in Favour of "Competition Hypothesis"

It is a concern of the evangelist to emphasize the superiority of Jesus over John the Baptist in various matters (1,6–9.15.19–34; 3,25–30; 4,1; 5,36; 10,41). This concern may be detected in the matter of the preparation of the way too. It can be pointed out in two ways. Firstly, the evangelist presents John the Baptist only as the voice in the desert and denies him the role of preparer of the way (1,23). Secondly, he ascribes the role of preparation to Jesus (14,2–3) and presents him as the way (14,4–6). This observation is yet another argument in favour of "the competition hypothesis" with regard to the relationship between the disciples of John the Baptist and the disciples of Jesus. Perhaps this may be only a healthy and friendly competition for the evangelist and need not be necessarily regarded as a rivalry between two parties.[21]

7. Discipleship as Following the Method (μέθοδος) of Jesus

According to John, discipleship is a journey. On the one hand, it is "coming to" Jesus and, on the other hand, it is going "the way" (ὁδός) of Jesus. The purpose of coming to Jesus is to come to the Father (14,6b). Journey needs a way. Jesus himself is the way for the disciples. Jesus has gone ahead and prepared the way to the Father. The disciples have to follow him. Discipleship is following "the method" (μέθοδος) of Jesus, i.e, following "after the

---

[20] The use of the verb ἔρχομαι for the appearance of the risen Jesus is unique to the Gospel of John (20,19.24.26; cf. 21,13).

[21] Wink, *John the Baptist*, 103, points out, "Nowhere does he regard John as an enemy, nor does he attack his sect or even censure it for its unbelief".

way" (μεθ' ὁδόν) of Jesus. Even in Jesus' physical absence, the disciples are not orphaned. The Father, the Son and the Spirit will make their dwelling with them. Their guide on the way is the Holy Spirit, the Spirit of truth (cf. 16,13). Believing in Jesus will enable them to keep his commandments and to love one another as he loved them. Jesus' claim in 14,6 is placed between two commands, the command to believe (14,1) and the command to to love (14,15). In fact, these commands dominate the surrounding context of 14,6. It is by following the way of believing (14,1–14) and loving (14,15–24; cf. 13,34–35) that one becomes a disciple of Jesus.

8. Relation of Way with Truth and Life

The occurrence of the way along with truth and life in 14,6 really confounds many scholars. They forget the fact that way has an independent significance in the context apart from truth and life and are often entangled in a fruitless search for a particular text where these three terms occur. It should be noted that before John speaks of "the way and the truth and the life" in v. 6, he has already spoken of the way in vv. 4–5 and that truth and life appear like intruders in v. 6. Hence, the significance of way is to be examined independently of truth and life.

To understand the relevance of truth and life, which are added to the way, we need to be aware of the association of the way/journey motif with truth and life, found in the Bible and other Jewish literature. Behind this association, there lies an imagery of a way leading to life under the guidance of truth. While truth is regarded as a means or a medium like a guide, life is regularly seen as a goal. The Gospel of John itself bears testimony to this fact. An analysis of the motifs of truth and life in the Gospel convincingly shows that for the evangelist truth is not a goal in itself. Truth is only a mode or a means or an agent of salvation (e.g., 4,23–24; 8,32; 17,17.19). It is the event of revelation in Jesus. But it is a plain fact that life is regularly regarded as the very goal and destination throughout the Gospel (e.g., 3,15.16; 5,40; 6,40; 10,10; 17,2; 20,31). In a few instances, life is found in association with the journey motif and is presented as the destination of the human journey (5,24.40; 6,68; 8,12). If truth is essentially the revelation of salvation fulfilled in Jesus, life is the end result of the revelation brought out by Jesus.

The metaphor of way is incomplete without any reference to a destination. Truth as a means or a medium like a guide and life as the final destination or goal give a complete sense to the metaphor of way. Moreover, the presentation of Jesus as the way is not adequate to express fully the Johannine vision of Jesus' identity. Hence, the first καί in 14,6 should be interpreted not epexegetically but in an ascensive sense. It means that Jesus is not just the way alone, he is even the truth and the life. That Jesus is the way to life corresponds well with the view that Jesus is the way to the Father because for John only the Father is the original source of life (5,26; 6,57). The position of truth in the middle and life at the end is not accidental in 14,6 but well planned by the evangelist. This word order reveals the fact that Jesus is the way which, under the guidance of truth, leads the believer to the life of the Father (cf. Rev 22,14).

9. Triadic Pattern and Trinitarian Significance

It seems that the evangelist has a keen interest in the triadic pattern. This is very evident in the larger context of John 14,6.[22] A pattern of three in various ways is discernible in the near context of 14,6. Peter is warned that he will deny Jesus "three times" (τρίς, 13,38). The text of 14,6 is placed within the context of the cosmic conflict between Jesus, the Holy One (6,69), and the devil, the evil one (17,15). In the near context, there are three specific names for the evil one: devil (13,2), Satan (13,27) and ruler of the world (14,30). It is three times that the name of Judas Iscariot, who is the betrayer of Jesus and the agent of the evil one, is mentioned in the near context to indicate his role and function (13,2.26.29). In opposition to the evil one, the three persons of the Holy Trinity, namely the Father (vv. 2.6–13.16.20–21.23–24,26.28.31; cf. 13,1.3), the Son (v. 13) and the Spirit (vv. 16–17.26) are explicitly mentioned in John 14. There are three names for the third person of the Trinity, namely παράκλητος (14,16.26), τὸ πνεῦμα τῆς ἀληθείας (14,17) and τὸ πνεῦμα τὸ ἅγιον (14,26). In John 14, there is also reference to the coming of the three persons of the Trinity to the believers: the coming of the Son (vv. 3.18.23), the coming of the Spirit (vv. 16–17.26) and the coming of the Father (v. 23).

A triadic pattern is present in 14,6 as well. It is noteworthy that 14,6 is the only ἐγώ εἰμι-saying in the Gospel with three predicate nominatives: the way, the truth and the life. These three terms are also related to the functions of the three persons of the Trinity in a distinct manner. The way is a concrete metaphor, while truth and life are abstract metaphors. Way is visible, but truth and life are invisible. The way corresponds well with the function of the Son, the Word (ὁ λόγος) who has become flesh in the historical person of Jesus of Nazareth (1,14). One can see the way and touch it and experience the

---

[22] E.g., the wedding at Cana takes place on "the third day", τῇ ἡμέρᾳ τῇ τρίτῃ (2,1). The evangelist records three appearances of the risen Jesus and remarks, "This was now 'the third time' (τρίτον) that Jesus appeared to the disciples after he was raised from the dead" (21,14). It is three times that Peter is asked to confess his love for his Lord. The evangelist takes an effort to highlight it, "He said to him 'the third time' (τὸ τρίτον), 'Simon, son of John, do you love me?' Peter felt hurt because Jesus said to him 'the third time' (τὸ τρίτον), 'Do you love me?'" (21,17).

journey along with it. The Son is visible, audible and touchable in the person of Jesus (e.g., 1,14; cf. 1 John 1,1). But the Father and the Spirit are invisible (1,18; 5,37; 6,46; 14,17), just as truth and life are invisible.

In the Gospel, truth and life are related in a distinct manner to the functions of the Spirit and the Father respectively. The Spirit is called "the Spirit of truth", τὸ πνεῦμα τῆς ἀληθείας (14,17; 15,26; 16,13; 1 John 4,6).[23] The title "the Spirit of truth" is a soteriological title and a functional label for the Holy Spirit.[24] His main function is associated with "the truth" revealed in Jesus.[25] His presence with and within the believers is intended "to teach" (διδάσκω)[26] them and to remind them of "the truth" revealed in Jesus (14,26) and to guide (ὁδηγέω) them into all "truth" about Jesus (16,13).

For the evangelist, life is the basic feature of the Father because the Father is the ultimate source of life (5,26). The expression ὁ ζῶν πατήρ in 6,57 implies that the Father is the ultimate giver of life, the creator. He has life in the absolute sense, without depending on anyone. The Son has life because of the Father, κἀγὼ ζῶ διὰ τὸν πατέρα (6,57). We cannot separate the affirmation that God is the Father from the affirmation that God is the source of life. The life of the Father has been given to human beings through the Son (14,19; cf. 1 John 4,9). It is to be noted that immediately after mentioning the motif of life (ζῶ) in 14,19, Jesus speaks of his Father (14,20–24), his existence/life in the Father and the believers' existence/life in him (14,20) and of the coming of the Father to the believers (14,23). Thus, truth and life in John are respectively related to the functions of the Spirit and the Father as well. In Jesus there is the presence of the Father (e.g., 8,19; 14,7–9; 20,28) and the Spirit (1,32–33; 16,7; 20,22). One cannot have any knowledge of the Father and the Spirit apart from the Son. As the way, Jesus is the access point for the believers to the Father and the Spirit. In short, in and through Jesus the believers have the access to the three persons of the Trinity. Therefore, he can

---

[23] To say that Spirit is "of truth" means that Spirit conveys God's truth as revealed in Jesus. Cf. Koester, *The Word of Life*, 148. 1 John 5,6 says, "The Spirit is the truth" (τὸ πνεῦμά ἐστιν ἡ ἀλήθεια).

[24] Cf. C. Bennema, *The Power of Saving Wisdom. An Investigation of Spirit and Wisdom in Relation to the Soteriology of the Fourth Gospel* (WUNT II 148; Tübingen 2002), 227.

[25] De la Potterie, "The Truth in Saint John", 73, states, "In Johannine theology the function of the Spirit is carried out mainly in relation to the truth of Christ and consists in arousing faith in Christ".

[26] The verb διδάσκω is practically a verb of revelation in John. See I. de la Potterie, "The Paraclete", *Bible Bhashyam* 2 (1976), 127. However, the Holy Spirit will not bring independent revelation but interprets Jesus' revelation. He will continue the revelatory life-giving work of Jesus by drawing out the significance of the historical revelation in Jesus. See Bennema, *The Power of Saving Wisdom*, 231.

utter the statement formulated with a triadic pattern, "I am the way and the truth and the life".[27]

10. John 14,6 as an Invitation to the Father's Family

The Father metaphor in the Gospel of John is presented either in terms of Jesus' exclusive relationship with his Father or in terms of a promised relationship between the believers and the Father through Jesus. It is in the context of Jesus' exclusive relationship with the Father that the exclusivism in John 14,6 is to be interpreted and understood. Jesus' statement "No one comes to the Father except through me" (14,6b) speaks not only of an exclusive relationship between Jesus and his Father but also of a relationship between the believers and the Father attainable through Jesus.

Often, scholars pay undue attention to the phrase "except through me" but do not pay sufficient attention to the promised relationship between the believers and the Father when they read John 14,6. It should be specially noted that John does not say, "No one comes to God except through me", rather "No one comes to the Father except through me". In this Gospel, God and Father are one and the same. However, John gives special emphasis to experiencing God as the Father through Jesus.

The metaphor "father" plays a crucial role in the family imagery used throughout the Gospel. The analysis of 14,6b in the light of the Gospel theology has shown how the human family is estranged and separated from God's family. This estrangement is due to slavery to sin under the rulership of the devil, who is the ruler of this world. Hence, there is a contrast between the family of God and the family of the devil, between the children of God and the children of the devil. The children of God love Jesus and hear the words of God (8,42.47), whereas the children of the devil cannot believe in Jesus and accept his word (8,43.45–46). The works of the children of the devil reflect the very character of the devil who is a murderer from the beginning and the father of lies (8,44; cf. 1 John 3,8). Jesus has come to liberate the people from the fatherhood and the family of the devil (cf. 8,34.36) and to make them the members of the family of God.

Therefore, according to John's Gospel, the answer to the problem of humanity's estrangement from God is the person of Jesus, the Word that has become flesh (1,14). He is the way and the gate for all to become a member of the divine family, where God is the Father. The membership in the Fa-

---

[27] Also in the light of the relation of truth and life with the role and function of the Father and the Spirit in the Gospel, Tack's view that the Father and the Spirit are sidelined in John 14,6 cannot be accepted. Cf. Tack, *John 14,6 in Light of Jewish-Christian Dialogue*, 341–342, 356, 363, 423, 438.

ther's family requires two conditions, namely belief in Jesus who is the only Son of the Father (1,18; 3,16) and a rebirth through the Holy Spirit (3,3–8). Hence, everyone should first "come to" Jesus in order to come to the Father (14,6b). One who "comes to" (believes in) Jesus is begotten through the Holy Spirit as a child of the Father (cf. 1,12–13; 3,3–8). The Holy Spirit is the vehicle of rebirth, and without him one cannot become a child of the Father.

The new family of the believers is established only after Jesus' death-resurrection because the Holy Spirit can be given only after Jesus' glorification (cf. 7,39). God becomes the Father of the believers and Jesus becomes their brother after Jesus is glorified (20,17). When they receive the Holy Spirit from the risen Jesus at his very first appearance, they receive a new birth and become totally a new creation (20,22; cf. Gen 2,7). They are then able to see in Jesus the Father, their God and their Lord (20,28). Thus, according to John, we can experience God as Father only through Jesus. We do not have access to the Father apart from Jesus. The purpose of Jesus' mission is not only to reveal the Father, but also to establish an eternal relationship between the Father and the believers, who are his children, by giving them eternal life.[28] The Father is not known apart from Jesus but through and in relation to Jesus. It is in terms of relationship with Jesus that all relationships of believers with the Father are and should be defined. Belief in Jesus is ultimately belief in the Father. The highest form of belief is the recognition of the Father in his Son, Jesus (20,28–29). Indeed, John 14,6b is an invitation to become a member in the Father's family and thus to experience the fatherhood of God by believing in Jesus and by being reborn through the Holy Spirit as a child of God the Father.

11. John 14,6 as an ἐγώ εἰμι-Saying

Since John 14,6 is an ἐγώ εἰμι-saying, it should be interpreted in the context of other ἐγώ εἰμι-sayings in the Gospel as well. John presents Jesus as the one in whom Isaiah's promise of salvation is fulfilled. The absolute ἐγώ εἰμι-sayings, which are attributed to the Johannine Jesus, derive their meaning and significance from the Old Testament, especially from Deutero-Isaiah. It is like Yahweh of Deutero-Isaiah that Jesus utters the absolute ἐγώ εἰμι in the Gospel. In Deutero-Isaiah, the formula אֲנִי הוּא/ἐγώ εἰμι is a code word of absolute monotheism.[29] It is used to assert the belief that Yahweh alone is

---

[28] Van der Watt, *An Introduction*, 58, remarks, "Eternal life opens up the opportunity for a person to exist and participate in, and be part of the divine family of God".

[29] Richter, *'Anî Hû und Ego Eimi*, 42, says, "Diese 'Formel' bildet also gewissermaßen das Herzstück von Deuterojesajas Theologie. Sie wird ein 'Kennwort' seines absoluten Monotheismus".

God. Deutero-Isaiah, thus, supplied John with this solemn expression that was eminently suitable for expressing the unity of the Father and the Son and had at the same time a strong connotation of monotheism.[30] We can say that John reflects on the phrase אני הוא/ἐγώ εἰμι in Deutero-Isaiah and uses the absolute ἐγώ εἰμι in order to communicate his belief that the Son is one with the Father and yet God remains and continues to be one.[31] When Jesus speaks the absolute ἐγώ εἰμι, he reveals not only himself but also his Father. Hence, we can say, "Das ἐγώ εἰμι ist die Offenbarung des Vaters, aber in seinen Namen ist Jesus eingeschlossen: ἐγώ εἰμι = der Vater und Jesus".[32] Ἐγώ εἰμι means ἐγώ καὶ ὁ πέμψας με πατήρ (8,16). "Im Sein Jesu ist das des Vaters eingeschlossen. Theo-Logie ist Christo-Logie... Im 'Ich bin' sind Jesus und Gott vereinigt".[33] Therefore, the statement "no one comes to the Father except through me" reveals not only the exclusiveness of salvation through Jesus but also his unique and exclusive relationship with the Father, which is a relationship of oneness clearly expressed in 14,7–11. Thus, we can say that the statement "no one comes to the Father except through me" is an explanation of the absolute ἐγώ εἰμι, which is an expression of Jesus' oneness with the Father. In the light of the absolute ἐγώ εἰμι-sayings in the Gospel, Jesus' claim in 14,6 can be understood as a revelatory statement.

The absolute use of ἐγώ εἰμι in John is the basis for his use of ἐγώ εἰμι with images.[34] Hence, all ἐγώ εἰμι-sayings with images should be interpreted in the light of the absolute ἐγώ εἰμι-sayings in the Gospel. If the absolute ἐγώ εἰμι-sayings emphasize Jesus' identity, the ones with images focus on his identity in relation to his role for others. The ἐγώ εἰμι-sayings with images begin at the level of Christology but move on to the theme of soteriology and discipleship.

The Old Testament again provides the conceptual background for understanding all ἐγώ εἰμι-sayings with images. The Johannine images like bread, light, gate, shepherd, resurrection, way and vine, which are concrete in nature, are related to some Old Testament images and to their fulfilment in Jesus. The ἐγώ εἰμι-sayings with images usually have a common character, with which we need to interpret John 14,6. Like many other ἐγώ εἰμι-sayings with images, in 14,6 Jesus' identification with the images of way, truth and life is immediately followed by a soteriological statement: "no one comes to

---

[30] Harner, *The I Am*, 57.

[31] Harner, *The I Am*, 57. Laura Tack's effort to deny the revelatory and divine character of "I am"-saying is pointless and in vain because John recognizes Jesus' divine identity from the beginning of the Gospel to its end and his divine status is not merely limited to the meaning of a phrase like "I am". Cf. Tack, *John 14,6 in Light of Jewish-Christian Dialogue*, 341–345.

[32] Zimmermann, "Das absolute Ἐγώ εἰμί", 271.

[33] Hinrichs, *Ich bin*, 60–61, 65.

[34] Cf. Brown, *John*, I, 537.

the Father except through me". This statement includes a demand and a promise. The phrase "except through me" implies the demand that everyone should come to Jesus or believe in Jesus. The promise is that everyone who comes through Jesus "comes to the Father". The theme of truth is also present in other ἐγώ εἰμι-sayings (6,32; 15,1; cf. 4,23–26; 8,16–17). In 14,6, the definite article before ἀλήθεια suggests that Jesus alone is the truth. Thus, the claim that Jesus is the truth is the basis and the climax of all claims about truth in the Gospel.

All ἐγώ εἰμι-sayings with images are directly or indirectly connected with the theme of life. Miscellaneous images and metaphors associated with the ἐγώ εἰμι-sayings are simply variations of the single theme that Jesus has come so that people may have life in abundance (10,10). Jesus identifies twice with life in 11,25 and 14,6. In both instances, life is placed at the end showing its theological importance as the final destination. Every ἐγώ εἰμι-saying with image has the tone of exclusivism and absolutism. To express this exclusivism and absolutism, every metaphor has a definite article before it. As there is only one shepherd and one gate, there shall be only one way. The elements of inclusivism and universality are associated with all ἐγώ εἰμι-sayings attached with images. In the case of 14,6, the substantive οὐδείς has a universal appeal because it includes everyone. Hence, Jesus is the way for all. Many of the predicated ἐγώ εἰμι-sayings and the images attached to them stand in close relation with the Father. In 14,6, the image of way stands in close relation with the Father because the way leads the believer to the Father. As all other ἐγώ εἰμι-sayings with images are related to the context, Jesus' claim to be the way in 14,6 is also closely related to the context. Jesus speaks about his imminent departure in John 13–14. It is in the context of his journey that Jesus claims to be the way. Thus, the ἐγώ εἰμι-saying in 14,6 is in many ways closely related to the absolute ἐγώ εἰμι and to other ἐγώ εἰμι-sayings with images in the Gospel.

12. Relation between Gate (10,7.9) and Way (14,6)

Jesus' identification with the way in 14,6 stands in parallel relationship with his identification with the gate in 10,7.9. The images of gate and way are literally located in the context of two discourses: the shepherd discourse and the farewell discourse. Both gate and way receive their conceptual background from the Old Testament (cf. Ps 118,20; Isa 40,3). In various ways, gate and way have similar functions. Both images are presented in association with movement or journey. If the gate is for the purpose of coming in and going out, way is also for going and coming. The sheep come in and go out to the pasture through the gate. Similarly, the believers come to the Father through Jesus, the way.

There is an element of exclusiveness associated with gate and way. The phrase "through me" (δι' ἐμοῦ) in 10,9 is comparable to "through me" (δι' ἐμοῦ) in 14,6. The sheepfold which is described in John 10 has only one gate. Likewise, there is no way other than Jesus to come to the Father. Both gate and way are related to the theme of life. One who enters through the gate, which is Jesus, is saved and receives life (10,9–10). In 14,6 as well, the life which has correspondence with the Father stands at the end of the paratactic construction, showing the destination of the way. From the perspective of Johannine theology, we may say that Jesus is the gate and the way to (of) the Father who is the source of life.

Both gate and way have a universal character because they are kept open to all and allow freedom of movement. In a literal sense, both gate and way are intended to connect two spatial entities. Figuratively, Jesus as both gate and way connects two spheres, divine and human, sacred and profane, above and below, spiritual and physical. The phrase "through me" (δι' ἐμοῦ) in 10,9 and 14,6 also denotes that Jesus is the meeting point between these two spheres. He makes visible and accessible what is invisible and inaccessible.

13. Rejection of Anti-Judaistic Interpretation of John 14,6

This study suggests that the possible historical and social setting for the exclusive claim in John 14,6 is not anti-Judaism as a result of expulsion from the Jewish community or a sectarian view of the Johannine community. An understanding of the Johannine community as sectarian was, to a great extent, triggered by the hypothesis of J. L. Martyn. The limitations of Martyn's hypothesis and the probability of the existence of exclusivism before the expulsion from the synagogue may prohibit an anti-Judaistic and sectarian interpretation of 14,6. The current trend in Johannine studies to reject the sectarian interpretation of the Gospel also helps to liberate 14,6 from an anti-Judaistic and sectarian interpretation. Moreover, the proposal of a cultic setting for exclusive claims may also repel the anti-Judaistic and sectarian interpretation of 14,6. From the viewpoint of grammar, vocabulary, structure, context and theology, there is no doubt regarding the unity and integrity of John 14,6. Therefore, the opinion that 14,6b is a later addition as a result of anti-Judaism cannot be accepted.

From the literary context of the text, especially from its immediate and near context, it is not possible to argue that John 14,6 is anti-Judaistic in nature. Jesus speaks in 14,6 not to his opponents but to his disciples. His real opponents are, in fact, not the Jews but the world and its ruler, the devil. What makes one a son of the devil is not his Jewishness but his sinfulness. The motivating force behind the exclusivism is not anti-Judaism but the conviction of the author about the divine identity of Christ. In other words, the exclusivism is due to the intolerance of the revelation through Christ. The anti-Judaistic tendency of the Gospel as a whole is only a by-product of the evangelist's strong convictions regarding the identity and salvific role of Christ.

This study suggests that the anti-Judaistic language in the Gospel should be interpreted with great responsibility. It is not meant for anti-Judaistic propaganda but for the persuasion of the belief that Jesus is the Christ and the Son of God so that the believer may attain life through him (20,31). The disbelief and rejection by the Jewish authorities are part and parcel of God's salvific plan, which is to be fulfilled through his suffering Servant (12,37–41). The Gospel neither tells nor reflects the story of the psychological trauma of the believers as a result of their expulsion from the synagogue, but tells the story of God who loves the world so much that he sends and gives his only Son in order to save it (3,16–17). Too much dependence on Martyn's hypothesis of two-level drama may lead to wrong and distorted interpretations.

14. Root Cause of Exclusivism in John 14,6

The root cause of exclusivism in John 14,6 can be discerned at theoretical and practical levels. While Christological monotheism paved the way for exclusivism at the theoretical level, cultic veneration of Christ became the determining factor for exclusivism at the practical level.

14.1 Christological Monotheism

Jesus' statement that "no one comes to the Father except through me" is not an expression of *Christomonism* as Laura Tack thinks,[35] but an expression of *Christological monotheism*. Jesus' absolute claim as the only way to the Father is in fact the same as his claim for his oneness with the Father. The basis for Jesus' claim to be the exclusive way in 14,6 is explicitly expressed in the immediate context in the reciprocal formula of immanence, "I am in the Father and the Father is in me" (14,10.11). His unity with the Father is the reason for his claim of exclusive authority over access to the Father. His exercise of authority (14,6–9) is grounded in his position of authority (14,10–11).[36] Jesus' claim as the only way to the Father is based on who he is.

The exclusivism of 14,6 should not be seen as an isolated case of exclusivism in the Gospel. In fact, the whole Gospel from the beginning till the end

---

[35] See Tack, *John 14,6 in Light of Jewish-Christian Dialogue*, 361, 363–364, 423. It seems that Laura Tack has not propely understood the oneness of Jesus with his Father, implied in John 14,6 and immediately explained in the following verses (14,7–11).

[36] Woll, *Johannine Christianity*, 48.

maintains exclusive claims about Christ.[37] They are differently expressed throughout the Gospel, e.g., in terms of Father-Son relationship (1,18; 14,7–11, etc.),[38] in terms of journey language (cf. 3,13; 6,68–69), etc., and well supported by the use of absolute ἐγώ εἰμι, which is an expression of monotheism. It should be noticed that just as no one can come to the Father without the Son, so also no one can come to the Son without the Father (6,44). The readers are to believe in the oneness of Jesus with the Father due to the greater works done by Jesus' disciples (14,12). The greater works of the disciples will prove that Jesus is one with the Father and thus he is the true way to the Father. Moreover, the belief in "one God and one Saviour" based on the Scripture (cf. Isa 43,11) also motivates the evangelist to make exclusive claims about Christ. In short, John 14,6 is an assertion of Christological monotheism.

14.2 Cultic Veneration

Christological monotheism arises from the worship practices of the early Christians. In order to understand the possible historical and social setting behind the exclusivism in 14,6, an appeal is made to examine the setting behind the highly exclusive claim in Acts 4,12. This text, in its historical-social setting, provides us a pattern or a model to understand the exclusivism of John 14,6 in its respective historical context, in the life of the first centuary Christians. It was noted that in Acts 4,12 the exclusive claim to salvation through Jesus is bound with the veneration of "the name of Jesus". Invoking the name of someone (e.g., a deity) for healing is a cultic act. The apostles are presented as invoking "the name of Jesus" for healing the crippled beggar (Acts 3,6). It implies that Jesus is regarded by them as an object of cultic veneration. The view that the cultic veneration of Christ provides the historical and social setting for the exclusive claim in Acts 4,12 is corroborated by the fact that for the Jews of the second Temple period, worship of God involved exclusivism. This perspective is further supported by the apocryphal acts of the apostles, where worship of Christ and exclusive claims about him go hand in hand and by the anti-Christian writings of pagan writers who accuse the Christians of exclusive worship of Christ.

It is important, then, to examine whether the Gospel itself gives any indications that Jesus is already an object of cultic veneration or worship in its historical context. It is possible to detect many devotional practices of early Christian worship in the Gospel of John like hymn, prayer to Jesus, prayer in the name of Jesus, confessions of Christ, possible allusions to sacred rituals

---

[37] There are exclusive claims of Jesus in the Synoptic Gospels as well (cf. Matt 11,27; Luke 10,22).

[38] See the discussion on pp. 262–273.

like baptism and Eucharist, etc.[39] In 9,38, the Gospel itself certifies that Jesus was an object of worship. A model of worship in the form of prayer is detectable in the farewell discourse itself.[40] The motif of prayer is present in every chapter within John 14–17 (14,13–14; 15,7.16; 16,23–24.26; 17,1–26). This may reflect the worship practices of Johannine Christianity. The very immediate context of 14,6, namely 14,13–14 shows that Jesus is regarded as an object of prayer and worship in the Johannine community. Since exclusive worship of a deity and exclusive claims about him are inseparable, one can easily understand that the historical and social setting behind the exclusive claim of John 14,6 is the worship practice of the Johannine community.

Since a majority of scholars ascribe a later origin to the Gospel of John, it is necessary to show when the high Christology, which admitted the worship of Christ as a deity, emerged. There is non-biblical or secular evidence even from a hostile source to show that Christ was worshipped as a deity in the first centaury itself. Much earlier than the evidence from Pliny the Younger, the earliest New Testament writings (AD 50–60) already presupposed cultic devotion to Jesus as a familiar and defining feature of Christian circles. Scholars even suggest that the cultic veneration of Christ as a deity already emerged at an early stage of Christianity. In the light of the worship practices of the early Christians, we can argue that the historical-social setting or the root cause at the practical level for the exclusive claim in John 14,6 is the cultic veneration of Christ in the Johannine community.

15. John 14,6 and Today's Religious Pluralism

This work proposes that interpreters should avoid an imbalanced approach to the exclusivism in John 14,6 in the context of today's religious pluralism. They need to be aware of the fact that the exclusivism in 14,6 and the rest of the Gospel is balanced with the Gospel's equal emphasis on the universal scope of salvation through Christ. The elements of universalism are present even in 14,6 and in its immediate context. The Gospel teaches that God's plan for salvation encloses the whole world in its scope and that Jesus is the Saviour of the whole world (ὁ σωτὴρ τοῦ κόσμου, 4,42). The Gospel still maintains the hope of having one shepherd and one flock and of gathering all God's children through Christ (10,16; 11,52). Exclusivism and universalism go hand in hand in the rest of the New Testament as well (e.g., Acts 4,12; 1 Tim 2,4–5).

---

[39] See the discussion on pp. 369–374.

[40] The cultural interpretation of the farewell discourse by Jerome H. Neyrey has highlighted the form of worship in John 14–17. See pp. 126–127.

John 14,6 is an irrefutable truth of the Gospel. But this does not mean that all those who do not believe in Jesus are doomed. The statement "no one comes to the Father except through me" implies that all are saved through Christ and that he is the Saviour of the whole mankind. John 14,6 is a statement of Christological monotheism. Monotheism creates a genuine bridge between Christians and the followers of other religions. It provides a good platform for inter-religious relationships and dialogue. All who believe in one God need not fight each other in the name of God, but can admire and respect each other. However, inter-religious dialogue and positive approach to other religions do not mean forgetting one's own roots and the foundation of one's own faith. Diversities in religions can be respected and even unity can be maintained without giving up one's own self-identity.

The Gospel does not give direct guidelines to handle the issues of religious pluralism in the modern world. Hence, an appeal to the interpretative traditions of the Church, supported by systematic and pastoral theology, becomes necessary. Today, the Catholic Church keeps a balanced and healthy approach to other religions and thus sets an example for all other Christians to follow. This is clearly evident in the documents of the Second Vatican Council, the Papal teachings and other recent documents. The Church accepts whatever is true and holy in all other religions and encourages universal fraternity and inter-religious dialogue. At the same time, it does not waver to assert that Jesus is the way, the truth and the life and that no one comes to the Father except through him. The Church teaches that every human being is embraced by God's salvific plan in Christ through the working of the Holy Spirit in a manner unknown to us. By doing what is good in their own religious traditions and by obeying the dictates of their conscience, the followers of other religions can be saved through Christ because Christ is salvifically present in every human being, and he is the light that enlightens everyone to do good through his Holy Spirit (1,9; 8,12).

John 14,6 is not an expression of triumphalist Christianity but a necessary expression of certainty of Christian faith. It is not a weapon to proclaim and to propagate fundamentalism or to condemn the followers of other religions but a means to teach the universal love of God, made flesh in the person of Jesus Christ (1,14; 3,16). Jesus reveals through his own life who God is and what God is like. God is conceived by John as an unconditionally loving Father (3,16; cf. 1 John 3,1; 4,8.16), and Jesus is the incarnation of God's love (cf. 1,14; 3,16).[41] The insistence "to love one another as I have loved" (13,34–35) should not be seen as an instruction with a narrowed scope. Every human being who loves his fellow beings as Christ loved/loves is a true dis-

---

[41] J. Dupuis, "The Practice of Agape is the Reality of Salvation", *International Review of Mission* 74 (1985), 477, states, "In Christ, who is God's Son made man, God has united with humankind in an irrevocable bond of love".

ciple of Christ (13,35). Wherever there is Christ-like love, there is Christ. In this sense, the uniqueness of Christ lies in the uniqueness of his love as well.[42]

Often, scholars consider John 14,6 as a problem to be solved. John 14,6 becomes a problem only when it is approached and interpreted without sensitivity to the overall perspective of the Gospel. In fact, John 14,6 is not a problem to be solved but a mystery to be understood. We need to shift the focus from the exclusiveness of salvation to the universality of salvation through Christ and to the fact that Jesus is the Saviour of the whole humanity. Interpreters of John 14,6 need to come out of their narrow-minded vision and broaden their horizons in order to comprehend the universal salvific role of Christ the divine Word who works mysteriously in every human being through his Spirit. In a nutshell, the view that "outside Christ there is no salvation" is ever valid, provided that we immediately add, "there is no outside Christ at all".[43]

---

[42] Schnelle, *Johannes*, 253, views, "Der joh. Absolutheitsgedanke ist nichts anders als eine Variation der Absolutheit der göttlichen Liebe zu den Menschen in Jesus Christus. Der Wahrheitsanspruch Jesu Christi ist die Unbedingtheit der Liebe". Dietzfelbinger, *Johannes*, 45, explains the exclusivism of John 14,6 thus, "Verkörpert und vollzieht sich aber in Jesus das Geschehen, in dem die Liebe Gottes als die Grundmacht der Welt die Geschichte der Menschen in einen neuen Horizont stellt, dann ist damit wesenhaft die Frage verbunden, ob es innerhalb unserer Geschichte ein gleichwertiges Geschehen abseits der Jesusoffenbarung gegeben hat und geben kann. Es bedarf keines Nachweises, daß sowohl das Johannesevangelium als auch das Neue Testament insgesamt die Frage verneint".

[43] Cf. O'Collins, *Jesus Our Redeemer*, 225. Moltmann, *The Way of Jesus Christ*, 276, meaningfully remarks, "We can only think of Christ *inclusively*. Anyone who thinks of Christ *exclusively*, not for other people but against them, has not understood the Reconciler of the world". The emphasis in italics is original.

Bibliography

Aalen, S. "'Truth', a Key Word in St. John's Gospel", *Studia Evangelica*. Ed. F. L. Cross (Berlin 1964), II, 3–24.
Abbott, E. A. *Johannine Grammar* (London 1906).
–, *Johannine Vocabulary. A Comparison of the Words of the Fourth Gospel with Those of the Three* (London 1905).
Abegg Jr., M. G. *The Dead Sea Scrolls Concordance Volume I. The Non-Biblical Texts from Qumran, Parts 1–II* (Leiden 2003).
Adams, E. "The Ancient Church at Megiddo. The Discovery and an Assessment of Its Significance", *ExpTim* 120 (2008), 62–69.
Aeschylus, *Tragoediae: Agamemnon, Eumenides*. Ed. D. Page (OCT; Oxford 1972).
Aitken, J. K. "דֶּרֶךְ", *Semantics of Ancient Hebrew*. Ed. T. Muraoka (Abr-Nahrain Supplement Series 6; Leuven 1998), 11–37.
Akpunonu, P. D. *The Overture of the Book of Consolations (Isaiah 40:1–11)* (New York 2004).
Aland, B. et al. (ed.), *Novum Testamentum Graece* (Stuttgart ^{28}2012).
–, *The Greek New Testament* (Stuttgart ^{5}2014).
Aletti, J.-N. "Jn 13 – Les problèmes de composition et leur importance", *Bib* 87 (2006), 263–272.
Allen, L. C. *Psalms 101–150* (WBC 21; Dallas 2002).
Anderson, P. N. "The Community that Raymond Brown Left Behind: Reflections on the Johannine Dialectical Situation", *Communities in Dispute. Current Scholarship on the Johannine Epistles*. Ed. R. A. Culpepper and P. N. Anderson (Atlanta 2014), 47–93.
–, review of R. H. Gundry, *Jesus the Word According to John the Sectarian. A Paleofundamentalist Manifesto for Contemporary Evangelicalism, Especially Its Elites, in North America* (Grand Rapids 2002), *The Princeton Seminary Bulletin* 26 (2005), 245–248.
–, *The Christology of the Fourth Gospel. Its Unity and Disunity in the Light of John 6* (WUNT II 78; Tübingen 1996).
–, "The Origin and Development of the Johannine Ego Eimi Sayings in Cognitive-Critical Perspective", *JSHJ* 9 (2011), 139–206.
Andreas, O. *Die christologische Erfüllung der Schrift im Johannesevangelium. Eine Untersuchung zur johanneischen Hermeneutik anhand der Schriftzitate* (WUNT II 83; Tübingen 1996).
Appasamy, A. J. *The Johannine Doctrine of Life. A Study of Christian and Indian Thought* (London 1934).
Aquinas, T. *Commentary on the Gospel of John. Chapters 13–21*. Tr. F. Larcher and J. A. Weisheipl (Washington 2010).
Arenas, J. V. "Yo soy la puerta (John 10,7.9). Trasfondo y sentido de la imagen cristológica de la puerta", *Carmelus* 37 (1990), 38–80.

Arens, E. *The ΗΛΘΟΝ-Sayings in the Synoptic Tradition. A Historico-Critical Investigation* (Freiburg 1976).
Ashton, J. "Riddles and Mysteries. The Way, the Truth and the Life", *Jesus in Johannine Tradition*. Ed. R. T. Fortna and T. Thatcher (Louisville 2001), 333–342.
–, *Understanding the Fourth Gospel* (Oxford ²2007).
–, "Really a Prologue?", *The Prologue of the Gospel of John. Its Literary, Theological, and Philosophical Contexts. Papers Read at the Colloquium Ioanneum 2013*. Ed. J. G. van der Watt et al. (WUNT 359; Tübingen 2016), 27–44.
Attridge, H. W. "Genre Bending in the Fourth Gospel", *JBL* 121 (2002), 3–21.
Augenstein, J. *Das Liebesgebot im Johannesevangelium und in den Johannesbriefen* (BWANT 134; Stuttgart 1993).
Aune, D. E. "Worship, Early Christian", *ABD*, VI, 973–989.
–, *Revelation 6–16* (WBC 52B; Dallas 1998).
–, *The Cultic Setting of Realized Eschatology in Early Christianity* (NovTSup 28; Leiden 1972).
Back, F. *Gott als Vater der Jünger im Johannesevangelium* (WUNT II 336; Tübingen 2012).
Baker, D. W. "נהל", *NIDOTTE*, III, 44.
Ball, D. M. *'I Am' in John's Gospel. Literary Function, Background and Theological Implications* (JSNTSS 124; Sheffield 1996).
Balz, H. and Schneider, G. (ed.), *Exegetical Dictionary of the New Testament*. Tr. V. P. Howard and J. W. Thompson (Grand Rapids 1990), I–III.
Bammel, E. "The Farewell Discourse of the Evangelist John and Its Jewish Heritage", *TynB* 44 (1993), 103–116.
Barrett, C. K. *A Critical and Exegetical Commentary on the Acts of the Apostles I–XIV* (ICC; London 1994), I.
–, *The Gospel According to St. John. An Introduction with Commentary and Notes on the Greek Text* (London ²1978).
Bartholomä, P. F. *The Johannine Discourses and the Teaching of Jesus in the Synoptics. A Contribution to the Discussion Concerning the Authenticity of Jesus's Words in the Fourth Gospel* (TANZ 57; Tübingen 2012).
Barton, S. C. "Johannine Dualism and Contemporary Pluralism", *The Gospel of John and Christian Theology*. Ed. R. Bauckham and C. Mosser (Grand Rapids 2008), 3–18.
Bauckham, R. J. *2 Peter, Jude* (WBC 50; Dallas 2002).
–, "Devotion to Jesus Christ in Earliest Christianity: An Appraisal and Discussion of the Work of Larry Hurtado", *Mark, Manuscripts and Monotheism. Essays in Honour of Larry W. Hurtado*. Ed. C. Keith and D. T. Roth (London 2015), 176–200.
–, "Jesus, Worship of ", *ABD*, III, 812–819.
–, *Jesus and the God of Israel. God Crucified and other Studies on the New Testament's Christology of Divine Identity* (Grand Rapids 2008).
–, *The Testimony of the Beloved Disciple: Narrative, History and Theology in the Gospel of John* (Grand Rapids 2007).
–, "The Worship of Jesus in Apocalyptic Christianity", *NTS* 27 (1981), 322–341.
Bauer, W. et al. (ed.), *A Greek-English Lexicon of the New Testament and other Early Christian Literature* (Chicago ³2000).
Bauer, W. *Das Johannesevangelium* (HNT 6; Tübingen ³1933).
Beasley-Murray, G. R. *John* (WBC 36; Dallas ²1999).
Becker, H. *Die Reden des Johannesevangeliums und der Stil der gnostischen Offenbarungsrede* (FRLANT 68; Göttingen 1956).

Becker, J. *Das Evangelium nach Johannes. Kapitel 11–21* (ÖTK 4.2; Gütersloh ³1991).
–, "Die Hoffnung auf ewiges Leben im Johannesevangelium", *ZNW* 91 (2000), 192–211.
Becker, O. *Das Bild des Weges und verwandte Vorstellungen im frühgriechischen Denken* (Berlin 1937).
Beekes, R. *Etymological Dictionary of Greek* (Leiden 2010), I.
Behm, J. "Καρδία", *TDNT*, III, 608–614.
Bennema, C. *The Power of Saving Wisdom. An Investigation of Spirit and Wisdom in Relation to the Soteriology of the Fourth Gospel* (WUNT II 148; Tübingen 2002).
Benoit, A. "L'Ascension", *RB* 56 (1949), 161–203.
Berges, U. F. *Jesaja 40–48* (HThKAT; Freiburg 2008).
–, *The Book of Isaiah. Its Composition and Final Form* (Hebrew Bible Monographs 46; Sheffield 2012).
Bernard, J. H. *A Critical and Exegetical Commentary on the Gospel According to St. John* (ICC; Edinburgh 1928), I–II.
Bernier, J. *Aposynagōgos and the Historical Jesus in John. Rethinking the Historicity of the Johannine Expulsion Passages* (Leiden 2013).
Betz, O. *Offenbarung und Schriftforschung in der Qumransekte* (WUNT 6; Tübingen 1960).
Beuken, W. A. M. *Jesaja Deel IIA* (Nijkerk 1979).
Beutler, J. and Fortna, R. T. "Introduction", *The Shepherd Discourse of John 10 and Its Context*. Ed. J. Beutler and R. T. Fortna (Cambridge 1991), 1–5.
Beutler, J. *Habt keine Angst. Die erste johanneische Abschiedsrede* (SBS 116; Stuttgart 1984).
–, "The Use of 'Scripture' in the Gospel of John", *Exploring the Gospel of John*. Ed. R. A. Culpepper and C. C. Black (Louisville 1996), 147–162.
–, *Do not Be Afraid. The First Farewell Discourse in John's Gospel*. Tr. M. Tait (Frankfurt am Main 2011).
– "Der alttestamentlich-jüdische Hintergrund der Hirtenrede in Johannes 10", *The Shepherd Discourse of John 10 and Its Context*. Ed. J. Beutler and R. T. Fortna (Cambridge 1991), 18–32.
–, "Ich bin das Licht der Welt. Jesus und das Heil der Welt nach dem Johannesevangelium", *Bibel und Kirche* 69 (2014), 217–221.
–, "Jesus on the Way to Galilee. The Movement of the Word in John 1–4", *Melita Theologica* 62 (2012), 7–22.
–, "The Structure of John 6", *Critical Readings of John 6*. Ed. R. A. Culpepper (Leiden 1997), 115–127.
–, "Von der johanneischen Gemeinde zum Relecture-Modell", *ThPh* 90 (2015), 1–18.
–, *Das Johannesevangelium*. Kommentar (Freiburg 2013).
–, *Judaism and the Jews in the Gospel of John* (Subsidia Biblica 30; Rome 2006).
–, *Studien zu den johanneischen Schriften* (SBAB 25; Stuttgart 1998).
Beveridge, P. J. "I Am in the Fourth Gospel", *The Expositor* 8 (1923), 418–425.
Bieringer, R. et al., "Wrestling with Johannine Anti-Judaism: A Hermeneutical Framework for the Analysis of the Current Debate", *Anti-Judaism and the Fourth Gospel. Papers of the Leuven Colloquium, 2000*. Ed. R. Bieringer et al. (Assen 2001), 3–46.
Bieringer, R. "I am Ascending to my Father and your Father, to my God and your God (John 20,17). Resurrection and Ascension in the Gospel of John", *The Resurrection of Jesus in the Gospel of John*. Ed. C. R. Koester and R. Bieringer (WUNT 222; Tübingen 2008), 209–235.

Bird, M. F. "Of Gods, Angels and Men", *How God Became Jesus. The Real Origins of Belief in Jesus' Divine Nature – A Response to Bart Ehrman.* Ed. M. F. Bird (Grand Rapids 2014), 22–40.

Blank, J. *Krisis. Untersuchungen zur johanneischen Christologie und Eschatologie* (Freiburg 1964).

–, "Der Johanneische Wahrheitsbegriff", *BZ* 7 (1963), 163–173.

Blass, F. et al., *A Greek Grammar of the New Testament and Other Early Christian Literature* (Chicago 1961).

Blenkinsopp, J. *Isaiah 40–55. A New Translation with Introduction and Commentary* (AB 19A; New Haven 1974).

–, *Isaiah 56–66. A New Translation with Introduction and Commentary* (AB 19B; New York 2003).

–, *Opening the Sealed Book. Interpretations of the Book of Isaiah in Late Antiquity* (Grand Rapids 2006).

Boismard, M.-E. "Critique textuelle et citations patristiques", *RB* 57 (1950), 388–408.

Borgen, P. *Bread from Heaven. An Exegetical Study of the Concept of Manna in the Gospel of John and the Writings of Philo* (NovTSup 10; Leiden 1965).

Borgen, P. et al., *The Philo Index. A Complete Greek Word Index to the Writings of Philo of Alexandria* (Grand Rapids 2000).

Borgen, P. *The Gospel of John: More Light from Philo, Paul and Archaeology. The Scriptures, Tradition, Exposition, Settings, Meaning* (Supplements To Novum Testamentum 154; Leiden 2014).

Borig, R. *Der wahre Weinstock. Untersuchungen zu Joh 15,1–10* (StANT 16; Munich 1967).

Bovon, F. and Junod, E. "Reading the Apocryphal Acts of the Apostles", *Apocryphal Acts of Apostles*. Ed. D. R. MacDonald (Semeia 38; Decatur, 1986), 161–182.

Braumann, G. and Link, H. G. "I Am", *NIDNTT*, II, 278–283.

Brendsel, D. J. *'Isaiah Saw His Glory'. The Use of Isaiah 52–53 in John 12* (BZNW 208; Berlin 2014).

Briley, T. R. *Isaiah* (The College Press NIV Commentary; Joplin 2004), II.

Brock, S. "The Two Ways and the Palestinian Targum", *A Tribute to Geza Vermes. Essays on Jewish and Christian Literature and History.* Ed. P. R. Davies and R. T. White (JSOTSS 100; Sheffield 1990), 139–152.

Brockington, L. H. "The Greek Translator of Isaiah and his Interest in Δόξα", *VT* 1 (1951), 23–32.

Brodie, T. L. *The Quest for the Origin of John's Gospel. A Source-Oriented Approach* (New York 1993).

Brown, F. et al., *The Brown-Driver-Briggs Hebrew and English Lexicon. With an Appendix Containing the Biblical Aramaic* (Peabody 2005).

Brown, R. E. *The Community of the Beloved Disciple. The Life, Loves and Hates of an Individual Church in New Testament Times* (New York 1979).

–, *The Epistles of John. Translated, with Introduction, Notes, and Commentary* (New Haven 1982).

–, *The Gospel According to John. Introduction, Translation, and Notes* (AB 29–29A; New Haven 1966, 1970), I–II.

Brown, S. *Gift upon Gift. Covenant through Word in the Gospel of John* (Eugene 2010).

Brunson, A. C. *Psalm 118 in the Gospel of John. An Intertextual Study on the New Exodus Pattern in the Theology of John* (WUNT II 158; Tübingen 2003).

Büchsel, F. *Der Begriff der Wahrheit in dem Evangelium und den Briefen des Johannes* (Gütersloh 1911).
Bühner, J. A. "The Exegesis of the Johannine 'I-Am' Sayings", *The Interpretation of John.* Ed. J. Ashton (Edinburgh 1997), 207–218.
–, *Der Gesandte und Sein Weg im 4. Evangelium. Die kultur- und religionsgeschichtlichen Grundlagen der johanneischen Sendungschristologie sowie ihre traditionsgeschichtliche Entwicklung* (WUNT II 2; Tübingen 1977).
Bultmann, R. et al., "ζωή", *TDNT*, II, 832–875.
Bultmann, R. *The Gospel of John. A Commentary.* Tr. G. R. Beasley-Murray et al. (Philadelphia 1971).
Burridge, R. A. *What Are the Gospels? A Comparison with Greco-Roman Biography* (Grand Rapids ²2004).
Bury, R. G. "Two Notes on the Fourth Gospel", *ExpTim* 24 (1912–1913), 232–233.
Busse, U. "Open Questions on John 10", *The Shepherd Discourse of John 10 and Its Context.* Ed. J. Beutler and R. T. Fortna (Cambridge 1991), 6–17.
Buth, R. "*Oun, De, Kai* and Asyndeton in John's Gospel", *Linguistics and New Testament Interpretation.* Ed. D. A. Black et al. (Nashville 1992), 144–161.
Campbell, R. J. *The Concept of Truth in Johannine Writings, Related to Modern Critical Tensions* (Diss. Strasbourg 1970).
Carr, G. L. "עָלָה", *TWOT*, II, 666–670.
Carson, D. A. *The Farewell Discourse and Final Prayer of Jesus. An Exposition of John 14–17* (Grand Rapids 1980).
–, *The Gospel According to John* (Grand Rapids 1991).
Cebulj, C. *Ich bin es. Studien zur Identitätsbildung im Johannesevangelium* (SBB 44; Stuttgart 2000).
Celsus. *On the True Doctrine. A Discourse Against the Christians.* Tr. R. J. Hoffmann (Oxford 1987).
Chantraine, P. *Dictionnaire étymologique de la langue grecque. Histoire des mots* (Paris 1984), II.
Charles, R. H. *The Apocrypha and Pseudepigrapha of the Old Testament. Pseudepigrapha* (Oxford 1913), II.
Charlesworth, J. H. "John the Baptizer and the Dead Sea Scrolls", *The Bible and the Dead Sea Scrolls. The Scrolls and Christian Origins* (Waco 2006), III, 1–35.
–, "The Gospel of John: Exclusivism Caused by a Social Setting Different from that of Jesus (John 11,54 and 14,6)", *Anti-Judaism and the Fourth Gospel. Papers of the Leuven Colloquium, 2000.* Ed. R. Bieringer et al. (Assen 2001), 479–513.
Charlier, J.-P. "L'exégèse johannique d'un précepte légal: Jean 8,17", *RB* 67 (1960), 503–515.
Chenattu, R. *Johannine Discipleship as Covenant Relationship* (Peabody 2006).
Chibici-Revneanu, N. "Variations on Glorification: John 13,31f. and Johannine δόξα Language", *Repetitions and Variations in the Fourth Gospel. Style, Text, Interpretation.* Ed. G. van Belle et al. (Leuven 2009), 511–522.
Childs, B. *Isaiah* (OTL; Louisville 2001).
Clines, D. J. A. (ed.), "דֶּרֶךְ", *The Dictionary of Classical Hebrew* (Sheffield 1995), 464–473.
Coetzee, J. C. "Jesus' Revelation in the *Ego Eimi* Sayings in John 8 and 9", *A South African Perspective on the New Testament.* Ed. J. H. Petzer and P. J. Hartin (Leiden 1988), 170–177.

Colacrai, A., "Gesù Cristo Salvatore e Signore Via Verità e Vita, Secondo Gv 14,6", *Studia Missionalia* 52 (2003), 117–168.

Collins, B. J. (ed.), *The SBL Handbook of Style. For Biblical Studies and Related Disciplines* (Atlanta ²2014).

Coloe, M. L. "Sources in the Shadows: John 13 and the Johannine Community", *New Currents through John. Global Perspective*. Ed. F. Lozada Jr. and T. Thatcher (Resources for Biblical Study 54; Atlanta 2006), 69–82.

Coloe, M. L. and Thatcher, T. (ed.), *John, Qumran, and the Dead Sea Scrolls. Sixty Years of Discovery and Debate* (Atlanta 2011).

Conrad, E. W. *Reading Isaiah* (OBT; Minneapolis 1991).

Conzelmann, H. "φῶς", *TDNT*, IX, 309–358.

Coppes, L. J. "נָהַג I", *TWOT*, II, 558–559.

–, "נהל", *TWOT*, II, 559.

Cordero, N. L. *By Being, It Is. The Thesis of Parmenides* (Las Vegas 2004).

Coutts, J. J. F. *The Divine Name in the Gospel of John. Significance and Impetus* (WUNT II 447; Tübingen 2017).

Coxon, P. S. *Exploring the New Exodus in John. A Biblical Theological Investigation of John. Chapters 5–10* (Eugene 2014).

Crossan, J. D. "It is Written: A Structuralist Analysis of John 6", *Narrative Discourse in Structural Exegesis. John and 1 Thessalonians*. Ed. D. Patte (Semeia 26; Chico 1983), 3–21.

Cullmann, O. *Early Christian Worship*. Tr. A. S. Todd and J. B. Torrance (London 1953).

Culpepper, R. A. "Anti-Judaism in the Fourth Gospel as a Theological Problem for Christian Interpreters", *Anti-Judaism and the Fourth Gospel. Papers of the Leuven Colloquium, 2000*. Ed. R. Bieringer et al. (Assen 2001), 68–91.

–, "Inclusivism and Exclusivism in the Fourth Gospel", *Word, Theology and Community in John*. Ed. J. Painter et al. (St. Louis 2002), 85–108.

–, "The Gospel of John as a Document of Faith in a Pluralistic Culture", *"What is John?" Readers and Readings of the Fourth Gospel*. Ed. F. F. Segovia (Atlanta 1996), 107–127.

–, "The Johannine *Hypodeigma*: A Reading of John 13", *The Fourth Gospel from a Literary Perspective*. Ed. R. A. Culpepper and F. F. Segovia (Semeia 53; Atlanta 1991), 133–152.

–, *Anatomy of the Fourth Gospel. A Study in Literary Design* (Philadelphia 1983).

–, *The Gospel of Luke. Introduction, Commentary and Reflections* (NIB IX; Nashville 1995).

Dahl, N. A. "'A New and Living Way' – the Approach to God according to Hebrews 10,19–25", *Interpretation* 5 (1951), 401–412.

Dahms, J. V. "The Johannine Use of *Monogenes* Reconsidered", *NTS* 29 (1983), 222–232.

Dahood, M. J. "Some Northwest-Semitic Words in Job", *Bib* 38 (1957), 306–320.

–, *Psalms 101–150* (AB 17A; New Haven 1974), III.

–, *Psalms 51–100* (AB 17; New Haven 1974), II.

Daly-Denton, M. "Singing Hymns to Christ as to a God (Cf. Pliny, *Ep*. X, 96)", *The Jewish Roots of Christological Monotheism. Papers from the St. Andrews Conference on the Historical Origins of the Worship of Jesus*. Ed. C. C. Newmann et al. (Supplements to the Journal for the Study of Judaism 63; Leiden 1999) 277–292.

Davidson, R. *The Vitality of Worship. A Commentary on the Book of Psalms* (Grand Rapids 1998).

Davies, M. *Rhetoric and Reference in the Fourth Gospel* (JSNTSS 69; Sheffield 1992).

Davies, W. D. and Allison, D. C. *A Critical and Exegetical Commentary on the Gospel According to Saint Matthew* (ICC; London 2004), I.
Davis, C. J. *The Name and the Way of the Lord* (JSNTSS 129; Sheffield 1996).
De Jonge, M. *Jesus: Stanger from Heaven and Son of God* (Missoula 1977).
De Kruijf, T. C. "The Glory of the Only Son (John 1,14)", *Studies in John*. Ed. M. C. Rientsma et al. (NovTSup 24; Leiden 1970), 111–123.
De la Potterie, I. "Je suis la voie, la vérité et la vie (Jn 14,6)", *NRTh* 88 (1966), 907–942.
–, "La verità in San Giovanni", *RivBib* 11 (1963), 3–24.
–, "The Truth in Saint John", *The Interpretation of John*. Ed. J. Ashton (Edinburgh 1997), 67–82.
–, *La vérité dans Saint Jean. Le Christ et la vérité, L'Ésprit et la vérité* (AnBib 73; Rome 1977), I.
–, *La vérité dans Saint Jean. Le croyant et la vérité* (AnBib 74; Rome 1977), II.
–, "The Paraclete", *Bible Bhashyam* 2 (1976), 120–140.
De Pury, A. et al. (ed.), *Israel Constructs Its History. Deuteronomistic Historiography in Recent Research* (JSOTSS 306; Sheffield 2000).
De Vaux, R. "The Revelation of the Divine Name YHWH", *Proclamation and Presence. Old Testament Essays in Honour of Gwynne Henton Davies*. Ed. J. I. Durham and J. R. Porter (London 1970), 48–75.
De Villiers, S. L. "The Shepherd and His Flock", *The Christ of John. Essays on the Christology of the Fourth Gospel*. Ed. A. B. du Toit (Potchefstroom 1971), 89–103.
De Witt Burton, E. *Syntax of the Moods and Tenses in the New Testament Greek* (Grand Rapids 1900).
Delling, G. "τέλος", *TDNT*, VIII, 49–87.
Dennis, J. A. *Jesus' Death and the Gathering of True Israel. The Johannine Appropriation of Restoration Theology in the Light of John 11,47–52* (WUNT II 217; Tübingen 2006).
Derrett, J. D. M. "The Good Shepherd: St. John's Use of Jewish Halakah und Haggadah", *ST* 27 (1973), 25–50.
Dettwiler, A. *Die Gegenwart des Erhöhten. Eine exegetische Studie zu den johanneischen Abschiedsreden (Joh 13,31–16,33) unter Berücksichtigung ihres Relecture-Charakters* (FRLANT 169; Göttingen 1995).
Dewey, K. E. "Paroimiai in the Gospel of John", *Gnomic Wisdom*. Ed. J. D. Crossan (Semeia 17; Chico 1980), 81–99.
Diesel, A. A. *Ich bin Yahwe. Der Aufstieg der Ich-bin-Jahwe-Aussage zum Schlüsselwort des alttestamentlichen Monotheismus* (WMANT 110; Neukirchen-Vluyn 2006).
Dietzfelbinger, C. "Die größeren Werke (Joh 14,12f)", *NTS* 35 (1989), 27–47.
–, *Das Evangelium nach Johannes. Kapitel 13–21* (Züricher Bibelkommentare NT 4.2; Zurich 2001).
–, *Der Abschied des Kommenden. Eine Auslegung der johanneischen Abschiedsreden* (WUNT 95; Tübingen 1997).
Dodd, C. H. *Historical Tradition in the Fourth Gospel* (Cambridge 1963).
–, *More New Testament Studies* (Manchester 1968).
–, *The Interpretation of the Fourth Gospel* (Cambridge 1968).
Dorsey, D. A. "Another Peculiar Term in the Book of Chronicles: מסלה, 'Highway'?", *JQR* 75 (1985), 385–391.
–, *The Roads and Highways of Ancient Israel* (Baltimore 1991).
Du Rand, J. A., "A Syntactical and Narratological Reading of John 10 in Coherence with Chapter 9", *The Shepherd Discourse of John 10 and Its Context*. Ed. J. Beutler and R. T. Fortna (Cambridge 1991), 94–115.

–, "The Johannine 'Group' and 'Grid': Reading John 13,31–14,31 from Narratological and Sociological Perspectives", *Miracles and Imagery in Luke and John*. Festschrift U. Busse. Ed. J. Verheyden et al. (Leuven 2008), 125–140.

Dunn, J. D. G. "The Embarrassment of History: Reflections on the Problem of Anti-Judaism in the Fourth Gospel", *Anti-Judaism and the Fourth Gospel. Papers of the Leuven Colloquium, 2000*. Ed. R. Bieringer et al. (Assen 2001), 47–67.

–, *Christology in the Making. An Inquiry into the Origins of the Doctrine of the Incarnation* (London ²1989).

–, *Did the First Christians Worship Jesus? New Testament Evidence* (London 2010).

Dupriez, B. M. *A Dictionary of Literary Devices. Gradus A–Z*. Tr. A. W. Halsall (Toronto 1991).

Dupuis, J. "The Practice of Agape is the Reality of Salvation", *International Review of Mission* 74 (1985), 472–477.

Durham, J. I. *Exodus* (WBC 3; Dallas 1987).

Ebel, G. "ὁδός", *NIDNTT*, III, 935–943.

Elledge, C. D. *The Bible and the Dead Sea Scrolls* (SBL Archaeology and Biblical Studies 14; Atlanta 2005).

Elliger, K. and Rudolph, W. (ed.), *Biblia Hebraica Stuttgartensia* (Stuttgart ⁵1997).

Elliott, J. K. *The Apocryphal New Testament. A Collection of Apocryphal Christian Literature in an English Translation* (Oxford 1993).

Erlemann, K. "Sebstpräsentation Jesu in den synoptischen Gleichnissen", *Metaphorik und Christologie*. Ed. J. Frey et al. (TBT 120; Berlin 2003), 37–52.

Ernst, J. *Johannes der Täufer: Interpretation, Geschichte, Wirkungsgeschichte* (BZNW 53; Berlin 1989).

Euripides. *Fragments: Aegeus-Meleager*. Ed. and tr. C. Collard and M. Cropp (LCL 504; Cambridge 2008).

Fascher, E. "Ich bin die Tür: Eine Studie zu Joh 10,1–18", *DTh* 9 (1942), 33–57, 118–133.

Fee, G. D. "John 14,8–17", *Interpretation* 43 (1989), 170–174.

–, "On the Text and Meaning of John 20,30–31", *The Four Gospels*. Festschrift F. Neirynck. Ed. F. van Segbroeck et al. (Leuven 1992), III, 2193–2206.

Fensham, F. C. "I am the Way, the Truth and the Life", *Neot* 2 (1968), 81–88.

Feuillet, A. "Les *Ego Eimi* christologiques du Quatrième Evangile: La Révélation enigmatique de l'être divine de Jésus dans Jean et les Synoptiques", *RSR* 54 (1966), 5–22, 213–240.

Finkel, S. A. "Yavneh's Liturgy and Early Christianity", *JES* 18 (1981), 231–250.

Fischer, G. *Die himmlischen Wohnungen. Untersuchungen zu Joh 14,2f* (Bern 1975).

Fitzgerald, M. L. "Vatican II and Interfaith Dialogue", *Interfaith Dialogue: Global Perspectives*. Ed. E. K-F. Chia (New York 2016), 3–14.

Fitzmyer, J. A. "Jewish Christianity in Acts in Light of the Qumran Scrolls", *Studies in Luke-Acts*. Ed. L. E. Keck and J. L. Martyn (Nashville 1966), 233–257.

–, *First Corinthians. A New Translation with Introduction and Commentary* (AB 32; New Haven 2008).

–, *The Dead Sea Scrolls and Christian Origins* (Grand Rapids 2000).

–, *The Gospel According to Luke. Introduction, Translation, and Notes* (AB 28; New Haven 1974), I.

Flannery, A. (tr.), *Vatican Council II: The Conciliar and Postconciliar Documents* (Collegeville 2014).

Flavius J. *Josephus. With an English translation*. Tr. H. J. Thackeray et al. (LCL; Cambridge 1926–1965), I–IX.

Fleischhauer, T. "Das Bild des Weges in der antiken griechischen Literatur: drei Streiflichter", *Symbolik von Weg und Reise*. Ed. P. Michael (Schriften zur Symbolforschung 8; Bern 1992), 1–17.

Fletcher-Louis, C. *Jesus Monotheism. Christological Origins: The Emerging Consensus and Beyond* (Eugene 2015), I.

Fohrer, G. "σῴζω", *TDNT*, VII, 969–980.

Fowler, H. W. and Fowler, F. G. (tr.), *The Works of Lucian of Samosata* (Oxford 1905), IV.

Fox, M. V. *Proverbs 1–9* (AB 18A; New Haven 1974).

Franke, J. R. "Still the Way, the Truth and the Life", *Christianity Today* 53 (2009), 27–31.

Freed, E. D. "*Egō Eimi* in John 1,20 and 4,25", *CBQ* 41 (1979), 288–291.

–, *Old Testament Quotations in the Gospel of John* (NovTSup 11; Leiden 1965).

–, "Who or What Was before Abraham in John 8,58?", *JSNT* 17 (1983), 52–59.

–, "Ps 42/43 in John's Gospel", *NTS* 29 (1983), 62–73.

Frey, J. "Das Bild der Juden im Johannesevangelium und die Geschichte der johanneischen Gemeinde", *Israel und seine Heilstraditionen im Johannesevangelium*. Festgabe für Johannes Beutler SJ zum 70. Geburtstag. Ed. M. Labahn et al. (Paderborn 2004), 33–53.

–, "The Use of Δόξα in Paul and John as Shaped by the Septuagint", *The Reception of Septuagint Words in Jewish-Hellenistic and Christian Literature*. Ed. E. Bons et al. (WUNT II 367; Tübingen 2014), 85–104.

–, *Die johanneische Eschatologie* (WUNT 117; Tübingen 2000), III.

–, "Between Torah and Stoa: How Could Readers Have Understood the Johannine Logos?", *The Prologue of the Gospel of John. Its Literary, Theological, and Philosophical Contexts. Papers read at the Colloquium Ioanneum 2013*. Ed. J. G. van der Watt (WUNT 359; Tübingen 2016), 189–234.

Frey, J.-B. "Le Concept de Vie dans l'Évangile de St. Jean", *Bib* 1 (1920), 37–58, 211–239.

Fuglseth, K. S. *Johannine Sectarianism in Perspective. A Sociological, Historical and Comparative Analysis of Temple and Social Relationships in the Gospel of John, Philo and Qumran* (NovTSup 119; Leiden 2005).

Gebauer, R. "'Aletheia' im Johannesevangelium", *Theologische Wahrheit und die Postmoderne*. Ed. H. H. Klement (Wuppertal 2000), 233–254.

George, R. B. "Jesus the Way to the Father in John 14,1–14 and African Situation", *Hekima Review* 35 (2006), 33–45.

Gilbert, R. W. *The Meaning of Hodos in John 14,4–6* (Master's Degree Dissertation, Grace Theological Seminary; Winona Lake 1985).

Glancy, J. A. "Torture: Flesh, Truth, and the Fourth Gospel", *BInterp* 13 (2005), 107–136.

Godley, A. (tr.), *Herodotus. An English Translation* (London 1975), I.

Gollwitzer, H. "Außer Christus kein Heil? (Johannes 14,6)", *Anti-Judaismus im Neuen Testament. Exegetische und Systematische Beiträge*. Ed. W. P. Eckert et al. (ACJD 2; Munich 1967), 171–194.

Griffiths, D. R. "Deutero-Isaiah and the Fourth Gospel", *ExpTim* 65 (1954), 355–360.

Gros, A. *Je suis la route. Le thème de la route dans la Bible* (Bruges 1961).

Gubler, M. L. "Ich bin der Weg und die Wahrheit und das Leben (Joh 14,6)", *Diakonia* 24 (1993), 373–382.

Guelich, R. A. *Mark 1–8* (WBC 34A; Dallas 1989).

Gundry, R. H. *Jesus the Word According to John the Sectarian. A Paleofundamentalist Manifesto for Contemporary Evangelicalism, Especially Its Elites, in North America* (Grand Rapids 2002).
Haenchen, E. *A Commentary on the Gospel of John*. Tr. R. W. Funk (Hermeneia; Philadelphia 1984), II.
Hagan, H. "Worship", *The Collegeville Pastoral Dictionary of Biblical Theology*. Ed. C. Stuhlmueller (Bangalore 1996), 1103–1105.
Hahn, F., "Die Hirtenrede in Joh 10", *Theologia Crucis, Signum Crucis*. Festschrift E. Dinkler. Ed. C. Andresen and G. Klein (Tübingen 1979), 185–200.
Hahn, H.-C. and Brown, C. "Light", *NIDNTT*, II, 484–496.
Hajduk, A. "'Ego Eimi' bei Jeus und seine Messianität', *Communio Viatorum* 6 (1983), 55–60.
Hakola, R. *Cursing the Christians? A History of the Birkat haMinim* (Oxford 2012).
–, *Identity Matters. John, the Jews and Jewishness* (NovTSup 118; Leiden 2005).
–, *Reconsidering Johannine Christianity. A Social Identity Approach* (New York 2015).
Hamid-Khani, S. *Revelation and Concealment of Christ: A Theological Inquiry into the Elusive Language of the Fourth Gospel* (WUNT II 120; Tübingen 2000).
Hamilton, J. "The Influence of Isaiah on the Gospel of John", *Perichoresis* 5 (2007), 139–162.
Hanson, A. T. *The Prophetic Gospel. A Study of John and the Old Testament* (Edinburgh 1991).
Harner, P. B. *The I am of the Fourth Gospel* (Philadelphia 1970).
Harris, M. J. *Jesus as God. The New Testament Use of Theos in Reference to Jesus* (Grand Rapids 1992).
Hasitschka, M. and Stare, M. "'...damit sie Leben haben und es in Fülle haben' (Joh 10,10): Der zentrale Heilsbegriff im Johannesevangelium und seine aktuelle Bedeutung", *Gutes Leben - für alle? Theologisch-kritische Perspektiven auf einen aktuellen Sehnsuchtsbegriff*. Ed. A. Findl-Ludescher et al. (Kommunikative Theologie - inter-disziplinär 16; Vienna 2012), 259–271.
Hasitschka, M. *Befreiung von Sünde nach dem Johannesevangelium. Eine bibeltheologische Untersuchung* (Innsbrucker theologische Studien 27; Innsbruck 1989).
–, "...'damit die Welt glaubt' (Joh 17,21): Lebenspraxis der Kirche als universales Zeichen Johanneische Perspektiven", *Kirche als universales Zeichen*. In Memoriam Raymund Schwager SJ. Ed. R. Siebenrock and W. Sandler (Beiträge zur mimetischen Theorie 19; Wien 2005), 415–425.
–, "Die Parakleteworte im Johannesevangelium: Versuch einer Auslegung in synchroner Textbetrachtung", *SNTU* 18 (1993), 97–112.
–, "Sozialgeschichtliche Anmerkungen zum Johannesevangelium", *PzB* 1 (1992), 59–67.
Hatch, E. and Redpath, H. *A Concordance to the Septuagint and the Other Greek Versions of the Old Testament* (Oxford 1897), I–II.
Hauck, F. and Schulz, S. "πορεύομαι", *TDNT*, VI, 566–579.
Hauck, F. "μονή", *TDNT*, IV, 579–588.
Hawkin, D. J. "The Johannine Concept of Truth and Its Implications for a Technological Society", *EvQ* 59 (1987), 3–13.
Hayes, J. H. and Holladay, C. R. *Biblical Exegesis. A Beginner's Handbook* (Louisville ³2007).
Heer, J. *Leben hat Sinn. Christliche Existenz nach dem Johannesevangelium* (Stuttgart 1974).

Heil, J. P. *Jesus Walking on the Sea. Meaning and Gospel Functions of Matt 14,22–33; Mark 6,45–52 and John 6,15b–21* (AnBib 87; Rome 1981).
–, *The Gospel of John: Worship for Divine Life Eternal* (Cambridge 2015).
Heitmüller, W. *Im Namen Jesu. Eine sprach- u. religionsgeschichtliche Untersuchung zum Neuen Testament, speziell zur altchristlichen Taufe* (Göttingen 1903).
Helfmeyer, F. J. "הָלַךְ", *TDOT*, III, 390–403.
Hengel, M. *Between Jesus and Paul. Studies in the Earliest History of Christianity* (Eugene 2003).
–, *Studies in Early Christology* (Edinburgh 1995).
–, *The Johannine Question* (London 1989).
Hera, M. P. *Christology and Discipleship in John 17* (WUNT II 342; Tübingen 2013).
Heraclitus. *Fragments. A Text and Translation.* Tr. T. M. Robinson (Toronto 1987).
Herodotus, *Histories.* Ed. N. G. Wilson (OCT; Oxford 1927).
Hiers, R. H. "Day of Judgement", *ABD*, II, 79–82.
Hill, A. *Malachi. A New Translation with Introduction and Commentary* (AB 25D; New Haven 1998).
Hinrichs, B. *"Ich bin". Die Konsistenz des Johannes-Evangeliums in der Konzentration auf das Wort Jesu* (SBS 133; Stuttgart 1988).
Hoegen-Rohls, C. *Der nachösterliche Johannes: Die Abschiedsreden als hermeneutischer Schlüssel zum vierten Evangelium* (WUNT II 84; Tübingen 1996).
–, "Ewigkeit und Leben. Der biblische Vorstellungskreis III: Johannes", *Das Leben: Historisch-systematische Studien zur Geschichte eines Begriffs: Band 1.* Ed. P. Bahr and S. Schaede (Religion und Aufklärung 17; Tübingen 2009), 129–152.
Hoet, H. "'Abraham is our Father' (John 8,39). The Gospel of John and Jewish-Christian Dialogue", *Anti-Judaism and the Fourth Gospel. Papers of the Leuven Colloquium, 2000.* Ed. R. Bieringer et al. (Assen 2001), 187–201.
Hofmann, J. C. K. *Der Schriftbeweis. Ein theologischer Versuch* (Nördingen 1857–1859).
Holloway, P. A. "Left Behind: Jesus' Consolation of His Disciples in John 13,31–17,26", *ZNW* 96 (2005), 1–34.
Homer, *Iliad.* Ed. D. B. Monro and T. W. Allen (OCT; Oxford 1963), I–II.
–, *Odyssey.* Ed. D. B. Monro and T. W. Allen (OCT; Oxford 1963), III–IV.
Horbury, W. *Jewish Messianism and the Cult of Christ* (London 1998).
Hoskyns, E. C. *The Fourth Gospel* (London 1947).
Hübner, H. "ἀλήθεια", *EDNT*, I, 57–60.
–, "Wahrheit und Wort: Heideggers 'Vom Wesen der Wahrheit' und Wahrheit im Johannes-Evangelium", *Testimony and Interpretation: Early Christology in Its Judeo-Hellenistic Milieu: Studies in Honour of Petr Pokorný.* Ed. J. Mrázek and J. Roskovec (London 2004), 201–222.
Hurtado, L. W. *Honoring the Son. Jesus in Earliest Christian Devotional Practice* (Bellingham 2018).
–, *Ancient Jewish Monotheism and Early Christian Jesus-Devotion. The Context and Character of Christological Faith* (Waco 2017).
–, "What Do You Mean by First-Centuary Jewish Monotheism", *Society of Biblical Literature 1993 Seminar Papers.* Ed. E. H. Lovering (Atlanta 1993), 348–368.
–, *At the Origins of Christian Worship. The Context and Character of Earliest Christian Devotion* (Grand Rapids 2000).
–, *God in New Testament Theology* (Nashville 2010).
–, *How on Earth Did Jesus Become a God? Historical Questions about Earliest Devotion to Jesus* (Grand Rapids 2005).

–, *Lord Jesus Christ. Devotion to Jesus in Earliest Christianity* (Grand Rapids 2003).
–, *One God, One Lord. Early Christian Devotion and Ancient Jewish Monotheism* (Edinburgh ²1998).
Ibuki, Y. *Die Wahrheit im Johannesevangelium* (BBB 39; Bonn 1972).
Jacobs, M. R. and Person Jr., R. F. (ed.), *Israelite Prophecy and the Deuteronomistic History. Portrait, Reality and the Formation of a History* (Ancient Israel and Its Literature 14; Atlanta 2013).
Jenni, E. "יָצָא", *TLOT*, II, 561–566.
–, "בּוֹא", *TLOT*, I, 201–204.
Jeremias, G. *Der Lehrer der Gerechtigkeit. Studien zur Umwelt des Neuen Testaments* (Göttingen 1963).
Jeremias, J. "θύρα", *TDNT*, III, 173–180.
Jerumanis, P.-M. *Réaliser la communion avec Dieu: Croire, vivre et demeurer dans l'évangile selon S. Jean* (Etudes bibiliques 32; Paris 1996).
Johnston, P. S. "Faith in Isaiah", *Interpreting Isaiah. Issues and Approaches*. Ed. D. G. Firth and H. G. M. Williamson (Downers Grove 2009), 104–121.
Jones, L. P. *The Symbol of Water in the Gospel of John* (Sheffield 1997).
Kambeitz, T. "I Am the Door", *Bible Today* 27 (1989), 110–112.
Kanagaraj, J. J. "Worship, Sacrifices and Mission: Themes Interlocked in John", *Indian Journal of Theology* 40 (1998) 16–39.
Katz, S. T. "Issues in the Separation of Judaism and Christianity after 70 CE: A Reconsideration", *JBL* 103 (1984), 43–76.
Kee, H. C. "Knowing the Truth: Epistemology and Community in the Fourth Gospel", *Neotestamentica et Philonica: studies in honor of Peder Borgen*. Ed. D. E. Aune et al. (Leiden 2003), 254–280.
Keener, C. S. *The Gospel of John. A Commentary* (Peabody 2003), I–II.
–, "Historical Tradition in the Fourth Gospel's Depiction of the Baptist", *Jesus Research. The Gospel of John in Historical Inquiry*. Ed. J. H. Charlesworth and J. G. R. Pruszinski (Jewish and Christian Texts in Contexts and Related Studies 26; London 2019), 155–167.
Kellum, L. S. *The Unity of the Farewell Discourse. The Literary Integrity of John 13,31–16,33* (JSNTSS 256; London 2004).
Kennedy, G. A. *New Testament Interpretation through Rhetorical Criticism* (Chapel Hill 1984).
Kiefer, O. *Die Hirtenrede. Analyse und Deutung von Joh 10,1–18* (SBS 23; Stuttgart 1967).
Kilpp, N. *Niederreißen und Aufbauen. Das Verhältnis von Heilsverheißung und Unheilsverkündigung bei Jeremia und im Jeremiabuch* (Biblisch-Theologische Studien 13; Neukirchen-Vluyn 1990).
Kim, D. "Was Johannine Christianity Sectarian?", *Fire in My Soul. Essays on Pauline Soteriology and the Gospels in Honor of Seyoon Kim*. Ed. S. B. Choi et al. (Eugene 2014), 202–211.
Kimelman, R. "Birkat haMinim and the Lack of Evidence for an Anti-Christian Jewish Prayer in Late Antiquity", *Jewish and Christian Self-Definition. Aspects of Judaism in the Graeco-Roman Period*. Ed. E. P. Sanders et al. (London 1981), II, 226–244.
Kirchschläger, P. G. "'Ich bin der Weg, die Wahrheit und das Leben' (Joh 14,6). Der Wahrheitsanspruch des johanneischen Christus und Wahrheit in anderen Religionen", *BLit* 85 (2012), 123–147.

–, "Spannung und Interaktion: Das Begriffsfeld 'Wahrheit'", *Repetitions and Variations in the Fourth Gospel. Style, Text, Interpretation*. Ed. G. Van Belle et al. (Leuven 2009), 213–234.
–, *Nur Ich bin die Wahrheit. Der Absolutheitsanspruch des johanneischen Christus und das Gespräch zwischen den Religionen* (HBS 63; Freiburg 2010).
Klauck, H.-J. *Judas ein Jünger des Herrn* (Quaestiones Disputatae 111; Freiburg 1987).
Klink III, E. W. "Expulsion from the Synagogue? Rethinking a Johannine Anachronism", *Tyndale Bulletin* 59 (2008), 99–118.
–, "The Overrealized Expulsion in the Gospel of John", *John, Jesus and History. Aspects of Historicity in the Fourth Gospel*. Ed. P. N. Anderson et al. (Atlanta 2009), II, 175–184.
–, *The Sheep of the Fold. The Audience and Origin of the Gospel of John* (SNTSMS 141; Cambridge 2007).
Knoppers, G. N. and McConville, J. G. (ed.), *Reconsidering Israel and Judah. Recent Studies on the Deuteronomistic History* (Winona Lake 2000).
Kobel, E. *Dining with John. Communal Meals and Identity Formation in the Fourth Gospel and Its Historical and Cultural Context* (BIS 109; Leiden 2011).
Koch, K. "דֶּרֶךְ", *TDOT*, III, 270–293.
Koester, C. R. "Jesus as the Way to the Father in Johannine Theology (John 14,6)", *Theology and Christology in the Fourth Gospel. Essays by the Members of the SNTS Johannine Writings Seminar*. Ed. G. van Belle et al. (BETL 184; Leuven 2005), 117–133.
–, "Jesus the Way, the Cross and the World According to the Gospel of John", *Word & World* 21 (2001), 360–369.
–, *Symbolism in the Fourth Gospel. Meaning, Mystery, Community* (Minneapolis ²2003).
–, *The Word of Life. A Theology of John's Gospel* (Grand Rapids 2008).
Koester, H. "John 14,1–20: A Meditation", *ExpTim* 73 (1961), 88.
Kohlenberger III, J. R. and Swanson, J. A. *The Hebrew English Concordance to the Old Testament* (Grand Rapids 1998).
Köstenberger, A. J. "The Destruction of the Second Temple and the Composition of the Fourth Gospel", *Challenging Perspectives on the Gospel of John*. Ed. J. Lierman (WUNT II 219; Tübingen 2006), 69–108.
–, "What is Truth? Pilate's Question in its Johannine and Larger Biblical Context", *JETS* 48 (2005), 33–62.
–, *John* (BECNT; Grand Rapids 2004).
–, *The Missions of Jesus and the Disciples According to the Fourth Gospel* (Grand Rapids 1998).
–, "Jesus the Good Shepherd Who Will also Bring Other Sheep (John 10,16): The Old Testament Background of a Familiar Metaphor", *BBR* 12 (2002), 67–96.
Kovacs, J. L. "'Now shall the ruler of this world be driven out': Jesus' Death as Cosmic Battle in John 12,20–36", *JBL* 114 (1995), 227–247.
Kowalski, B. "Ruf in die Nachfolge (Vom Hirt und den Schafen) Joh 10,1–5", *Kompendium der Gleichnisse Jesu*. Ed. R. Zimmermann (Munich 2007), 768–779.
–, *Die Hirtenrede (Joh 10,1–18) im Kontext des Johannesevangeliums* (SBB 31; Stuttgart 1996).
–, review of K. M. Lewis, *Rereading the "Shepherd Discourse". Restoring the Integrity of John 9,39–10,21* (Studies in Biblical Literature 113; New York 2008), *RBL* 8 (2009), 40–43.
–, "Was ist Wahrheit? (Joh 18,38a): Zur literarischen und theologischen Funktion der Pilatusfrage in der Johannespassion", *Im Geist und in der Wahrheit: Studien zum*

Johannesevangelium und zur Offenbarung des Johannes sowie andere Beiträge. Festschrift für Martin Hasitschka SJ zum 65. Geburtstag. Ed. K. Huber and B. Repschinski (Münster 2008), 201–227.

Kühschelm, R. *Verstockung, Gericht und Heil. Exegetische und bibeltheologische Untersuchung zum sogennanten "Dualismus" und "Determinismus" in Joh 12,35–50* (BBB 76; Frankfurt am Main 1990).

Kundsin, K. "Die Wiederkunft Jesu in den Abschiedsreden des Johannesevangeliums", *ZNW* 33 (1934), 210–215.

Kundzins, K. *Charakter und Ursprung der johanneischen Reden* (Acta Universitatis Latviensis; Series Theologica 1.4; Riga 1939).

Kuschke, K. "Die Menschenwege und der Weg Gottes im Alten Testament", *ST* 5 (1951–1952), 106–119.

Kuyper, L. J. "Grace and Truth: An Old Testament Description of God and Its Use in the Johannine Gospel", *Interpretation* 18 (1964), 3–19.

Kysar, R. "Johannine Metaphor – Meaning and Function: A Literary Case Study of John 10,1–18", *The Fourth Gospel from a Literary Perspective*. Ed. R. A. Culpepper and F. F. Segovia (Semeia 53; Atlanta 1991), 81–111.

–, *John's Story of Jesus* (Philadelphia 1984).

–, *Voyage with John. Charting the Fourth Gospel* (Waco 2005).

–, "The Whence and Whither of Johannine Community", *Life in Abundance. Studies of John's Gospel in Tribute to Raymond E. Brown*. Ed. J. R. Donahue (Collegeville 2005), 65–81.

Labahn, M. *Offenbarung in Zeichen und Wort. Untersuchungen zur Vorgeschichte von Joh 6,1–25a und seiner Rezeption in der Brotrede* (WUNT II 117; Tübingen 2000).

Lacomara, A. "Deuteronomy and the Farewell Discourse (John 13,31–16,33)", *CBQ* 36 (1974), 65–84.

Lagrange, M.-J. *Évangile selon Saint Jean* (Paris 1936).

Lake, K. (tr.), *The Apostolic Fathers* (LCL 24–25; London 1912), I–II.

Lamb, D. A. *Text, Context and the Johannine Community. A Sociolinguistic Analysis of the Johannine Writings* (LNTS 477; London 2014).

Lampe, F. A. *Commentarius in Evangelium Joannis* (Amsterdam 1726).

Lang, M. "Johanneische Abschiedsreden und Senecas Konsolationsliteratur. Wie konnte ein Römer Joh 13,31–17,26 lesen?", *Kontexte des Johannesevangeliums. Das vierte Evangelium in religions- und traditionsgeschichtlicher Perspektive*. Ed. J. Frey and U. Schnelle (WUNT 175; Tübingen 2004).

Lasic, H. *Recherches sur la notion de la vie chez S. Jean et les influences sur lui* (Dissertation, Freiburg 1970).

Lee, D. A. *The Symbolic Narratives of the Fourth Gospel. The Interplay of Form and Meaning* (JSNTSS 95; Sheffield 1994).

–, "In the Spirit of Truth: Worship and Prayer in the Gospel of John and the Early Fathers", *Vigiliae Christianae* 58 (2004), 277-297.

Léon-Dufour, X. *Lecture de l'Évangile selon Jean. Les adieux du Seigneur: Chapitres 13–17* (Paris 1993), III.

Levinsohn, S. H. *Discourse Features of New Testament Greek* (Dallas ²2001).

Lewis, K. M. *Rereading the "Shepherd Discourse". Restoring the Integrity of John 9,39–10,21* (Studies in Biblical Literature 113; New York 2008).

Libreria Editrice Vaticana, http://www.vatican.va. [accessed, February 6, 2016].

Liddel, H. G. and Scott, R. *A Greek-English Lexicon*. Revised and Augmented throughout by H. S. Jones; With New Supplement (Oxford 1996).

Lieu, J. M. "Anti-Judaism in the Fourth Gospel. Explanation and Hermeneutics", *Anti-Judaism and the Fourth Gospel. Papers of the Leuven Colloquium, 2000*. Ed. R. Bieringer et al. (Assen 2001), 126–143.
–, "Temple and Synagogue in John", *NTS* 45 (1999), 51–69.
Lim, B. H. *The 'Way of the Lord' in the Book of Isaiah* (Library of Hebrew Bible/Old Testament Studies 522; New York 2010).
Lincoln, A. T. "Trials, Plots and Narrative of the Fourth Gospel", *JSNT* 56 (1994), 3–30.
–, *The Gospel According to Saint John* (London 2005).
–, *Truth on Trial. The Lawsuit Motif in the Fourth Gospel* (Peabody 2000).
Lindars, B. *The Gospel of John* (NCBC; Grand Rapids 1972).
–, *The Theology of the Letter to the Hebrews* (Cambridge 1991).
Lindsay, D. R. "What is Truth? *Alētheia* in the Gospel of John", *ResQ* 35 (1993), 129–145.
Link, H. G. "Life", *NIDNTT*, II, 476–484.
Lisowsky, G. *Konkordanz zum hebräischen Alten Testament* (Stuttgart ³1993).
Louw, J. P. and Nida, E. A. *Greek-English Lexicon of the New Testament Based on Semantic Domains* (New York ²1989), I.
Kilburn, K. (tr.), *Lucian. With an English Translation* (LCL 430; Cambridge 1959), VI.
Lund, Ø. *Way Metaphors and Way Topics in Isaiah 40–55* (WUNT II 28; Tübingen 2007).
Lust, J. et al., *A Greek-English Lexicon of the Septuagint* (Stuttgart 2003).
MacArthur, J. *John 12–21* (MacArthur NT Commentary; Chicago 2008).
MacGregor, K. R. *A Historical and Theological Investigation of John's Gospel* (Cham 2020).
Macaskill, G. "Name Christology, Divine Aseity, and the I Am Sayings in the Fourth Gospel", *JTI* 12 (2018), 217–241.
Mack, B. L. *Logos und Sophia. Untersuchungen zur Weisheitstheologie im hellenistischen Judentum* (SUNT 10; Göttingen 1973).
Mallen, P. *The Reading and Transformation of Isaiah in Luke-Acts* (Library of New Testament Studies 367; London 2008).
Marcus, J. *Mark 1–8. A New Translation with Introduction and Commentary* (AB 27A; New Haven 2000).
–, *John the Baptist in History and Theology* (Columbia 2018).
Marottikaparambil, T. *John 8,12–20: Jesus the Light of the World. A Study of the Johannine Christological Reinterpretation of the Feast of Sukkot* (Dissertation, Pontificia Universitas Urbaniana; Rome 2011).
Marshall, I. H. *The Acts of the Apostles. An Introduction and Commentary* (Leicester 1980).
Martens, E. A. "בוא", *TWOT*, I, 93–95.
Martin, J. P. "John 10,1–10", *Interpretation* 32 (1978), 171–175.
Martínez, F. G. and Tigchelaar, E. J. C. *The Dead Sea Scrolls. Study Edition. Transcriptions* (Leiden 1997–1998), I–II.
–, *The Dead Sea Scrolls. Study Edition. Translations* (Leiden 1999), I.
Martyn, J. L. *History and Theology in the Fourth Gospel* (Louisville ³2003).
Matera, F. J. "On Behalf of Others, Cleansing and Return: Johannine Images for Jesus' Death", *LS* 13 (1988), 161–178.
Mathew, B. *The Johannine Footwashing as the Sign of Perfect Love: An Exegetical Study of John 13,1–20* (WUNT II 464; Tübingen 2018).
Mathys, F. "Gott und Mensch auf dem Weg. Einige Hinweise zur hebräischen Bibel, ausgehend von Jes 55,9", *Symbolik von Weg und Reise*. Ed. P. Michel (Symbolforschung 8; Bern 1992), 19–28.

Mayer, R. "'Ich bin der Weg, die Wahrheit und das Leben'. Ein Versuch über das Johannes Evangelium aus Anlass der neu erwachten Debatte zur Judenmission", *Johannes Aenigmaticus. Studien zum Johannesevangelium für Herbert Leroy.* Ed. S. Schreiber and A. Stimpfle (Regensburg 2000), 183–195.

McCaffrey, J. *The House with Many Rooms. The Temple Theme of John 14,2–3* (AnBib 114; Rome 1988).

McCasland, S. V. "The Way", *JBL* 77 (1958), 222–230.

McGowan, A. B. *Ancient Christian Worship. Early Church Practices in Social, Historical, and Theological Perspective* (Grand Rapids 2014).

McGrath, J. F. "Going up and Coming down in Johannine Legitimation", *Neot* 31 (1997), 107–118.

Meeks, W. A. "The Man from Heaven in Johannine Sectarianism", *JBL* 91 (1972), 44–72.

Menken, M. J. J. "John 6,51c–58: Eucharist or Christology?", *Critical Readings of John 6.* Ed. R. A. Culpepper (Leiden 1997), 183–204.

–, "Observations on the Significance of the Old Testament in the Fourth Gospel", *Neot* 33 (1999), 125–143.

–, "The Quotation from Isa 40,3 in John 1,23", *Bib* 66 (1985), 190–205.

–, *Old Testament Quotations in the Fourth Gospel. Studies in Textual Form* (Kampen 1996).

Merrill, E. H. "הָלַךְ", *NIDOTTE*, I, 1032–1035.

–, "דֶּרֶךְ", *NIDOTTE*, I, 989–993.

–, "נָתִיב", *NIDOTTE*, III, 202–203.

–, *Haggai, Zechariah, Malachi. An Exegetical Commentary* (Chicago 1994).

Metzger, B. M. *A Textual Commentary on the Greek New Testament* (Stuttgart ²1994).

Meyer, P. W. "'Father:' The Presentation of God in the Fourth Gospel", *Exploring the Gospel of John.* Ed. R. A. Culpepper and C. C. Black (Louisville 1996), 255–273.

–, "A Note on John 10,1–18", *JBL* 75 (1956), 232–235.

Michaelis, W. "ὁδός", *TDNT*, V, 78–84.

–, "ὁράω", *TDNT*, V, 315–381.

Michel, D. *Studien zur Überlieferungsgeschichte alttestamentlicher Texte.* Ed. A. Wagner (TB 93; Gütersloh 1997).

Michel, O. "οἰκία", *TDNT*, V, 131–134.

–, "πίστις", *NIDNTT*, I, 593–606.

Minear, P. S. "The Original Functions of John 21", *JBL* 102 (1983), 85–98.

Miranda, J. P. *Der Vater, der mich gesandt hat. Religionsgeschichtliche Untersuchungen zu den johanneischen Sendungsformeln. Zugleich ein Beitrag zur johanneischen Christologie und Ekklesiologie* (Frankfurt am Main 1972).

–, *Die Sendung Jesu im vierten Evangelium. Religions- und theologiegeschichtliche Untersuchungen zu den Sendungsformeln* (SBS 87; Stuttgart 1977).

Moloney, F. J. *Belief in the Word. Reading John 1–4* (Minneapolis 1993).

–, *Glory Not Dishonor. Reading John 13–14* (Minneapolis 1998).

–, *The Gospel of John* (Sacra Pagina 4; Collegeville 1998).

–, "The Gospel of John as Scripture", *CBQ* 67 (2005), 454–468.

Moltmann, J. *The Way of Jesus Christ* (London 1990).

Moon, J. N. *Jeremiah's New Covenant. An Augustinian Reading* (JTISup 3; Winona Lake 2011).

Morgenstern, J. "The Gates of Righteousness", *HUCA* 6 (1929), 1–37.

Morris, L. *The Gospel According to John* (NICNT 4; Grand Rapids 1995).

Motyer, S. "Bridging the Gap: How might the Fourth Gospel help us cope with the Legacy of Christianity's Exclusive Claim over against Judaism?", *The Gospel of John and Christian Theology*. Ed. R. Bauckham and C. Mosser (Grand Rapids 2008), 143–167.

Moule, C. F. D. "Fulfilment-Words in the New Testament: Use and Abuse", *NTS* 14 (1968), 293–320.

Moulton, J. H. and Milligan, G. *The Vocabulary of the Greek Testament Illustrated from the Papyri and other Non-Literary Sources* (London 1914–1929).

Moulton, J. H. and Turner, N. *A Grammar of New Testament Greek Syntax* (London ²1963), III.

Muilenburg, J. *The Way of Israel. Biblical Faith and Ethics* (New York 1961).

Muraoka, T. *A Greek-English Lexicon of the Septuagint* (Louvain 2009).

Murphy, R. E. *Wisdom Literature: Job, Proverbs, Ruth, Canticles, Ecclesiastes and Esther* (FOTL 13; Grand Rapids 1981).

Murtonen, A. *A Philological and Literary Treatise on the Old Testament Divine Names* (Helsinki 1952).

Mussner, F. *Zoe. Die Anschauung vom "Leben" im vierten Evangelium unter Berücksichtigung der Johannesbriefe. Ein Beitrag zur biblischen Theologie* (MThS 1.5; München 1952).

Natividad, Ma. L. C. "I am the Way, the Truth and the Life (John 14,6)", *Asian Perspectives in the Arts and Humanities* 2 (2012), 75–92.

Neef, H-D. "דרך", *Theologisches Wörterbuch zu den Qumrantexten*. Ed. H-J. Fabry and U. Dahmen (Stuttgart 2011), I, 716–725.

Neuner, J. and Dupuis, J. (ed.), *The Christian Faith in the Doctrinal Documents of the Catholic Church* (Bangalore ⁷2001).

Neusner, J. *The Mishnah. A New Translation* (New Haven 1988).

Newman, B. M. and Nida, E. A. *A Handbook on the Acts of the Apostles* (New York 1972).

–, *A Handbook on the Gospel of John* (New York 1980).

Newman, B. M. and Stine, P. C. *A Handbook on the Gospel of Matthew* (New York 1988).

Newman, C. C. et al. (ed.), *The Jewish Roots of Christological Monotheism. Papers from the St. Andrews Conference on the Historical Origins of the Worship of Jesus* (Supplements to the Journal for the Study of Judaism 63; Leiden 1999).

Neyrey, J. H. "The Noble Shepherd in John 10: Cultural and Rhetorical Background", *JBL* 120 (2001), 267–291.

–, "Worship in the Fourth Gospel: A Cultural Interpretation of John 14–17", *BTB* 36 (2006), 107–117.

–, *The Gospel of John in Cultural and Rhetorical Perspective* (Grand Rapids 2009).

Nicholson, G. C. *Death as Departure. The Johannine Descent-Ascent Schema* (SBLDS 63; Chico 1983).

Nida, A. E. *Lexical Semantics of the Greek New Testament* (Atlanta 1992).

Niederwimmer, K. and Attridge, H. W. *The Didache. A Commentary* (Hermeneia; Minneapolis 1998).

Niemand, C. *Die Fußwaschungserzählung des Johannesevangeliums. Untersuchungen zu ihrer Entstehung und Überlieferung im Urchristentum* (StAns 114; Rome 1993).

Nissen, J. *The Gospel of John and the Religious Quest. Historical and Contemporary Perspectives* (Eugene 2013).

Norden, E. *Agnostos Theos. Untersuchungen zur Formengeschichte religiöser Rede* (Stuttgart ⁷1996).

Nötscher, F. *Gotteswege und Menschenwege in der Bibel und in Qumran* (BBB 15; Bonn 1958).

O'Collins, G. *Jesus Our Redeemer. A Christian Approach to Salvation* (Oxford 2007).
–, *Salvation for All. God's Other Peoples* (Oxford 2008).
–, *Christology. A Biblical, Historical and Systematic Study of Jesus* (Oxford ²2009).
–, *Rethinking Fundamental Theology. Toward a New Fundamental Theology* (Oxford 2011).
–, *The Second Vatican Council on Other Religions* (Oxford 2013).
–, *A Christology of Religions* (New York 2018).
O'Day, G. R. "John 6,15–21: Jesus Walking on Water as Narrative Embodiment of Johannine Christology", *Critical Readings of John 6*. Ed. R. A. Culpepper (BIS 22; Leiden 1997), 149–159.
–, *Revelation in the Fourth Gospel. Narrative Mode and Theological Claim* (Philadelphia 1986).
–, *The Gospel of John. Introduction, Commentary and Reflections* (NIB IX; Nashville 1995).
Obermann, A. *Die christologische Erfüllung der Schrift im Johannesevangelium. Eine Untersuchung zur johanneischen Hermeneutik anhand der Schriftzitate* (WUNT II 83; Tübingen 1996).
Okure, T. *The Johannine Approach to Mission. A Contextual Study of John 4,1–42* (WUNT II 31; Tübingen 1988).
Oswalt, J. N. *Isaiah. Chapters 40–66* (NICOT; Grand Rapids 1998).
Painter, J. "Monotheism and Dualism. Reconsidering Predestination in John 12,40", *Transcending Boundaries. Contemporary Readings of the New Testament*. Ed. R. M. Chennattu and M. L. Coloe (Biblioteca Di Scienze Religiose 187; Roma 2005), 119–139.
–, "Tradition, History and Interpretation in John 10", *The Shepherd Discourse of John 10 and Its Context*. Ed. J. Beutler and R. T. Fortna (Cambridge 1991), 53–74.
Pamment, M. "Path and Residence Metaphors in the Fourth Gospel", *Theology* 88 (1985), 118–124.
Pao, D. W. *Acts and the Isaianic New Exodus* (WUNT II 130; Tübingen 2000).
Parrinder, G. "Only One Way? John 14,6", *ExpTim* 107 (1995), 78–79.
Parsenios, G. L. *Departure and Consolation. The Johannine Farewell Discourses in Light of Greco-Roman Literature* (NovTSup 117; Leiden 2005).
–, "Defining and Debating Divine Identity in Mark and John: The Influence of Classical Language and Literature", *John's Transformation of Mark*. Ed. E-M. Becker et al. (London 2021), 67–76.
Pascher, J. *Hē Basilikē Hodos. Der Königsweg zu Wiedergeburt und Vergottung bei Philon von Alexandreia* (Paderborn 1931).
Pathrapankal, J. "Christianity as a Way According to the Acts of the Apostles", *Les Actes des Apôtres. Traditions, Rédaction, Théologie*. Ed. J. Kremer (Leuven 1979), 533–539.
Patterson, R. D. "בלל", *TWOT*, II, 626–627.
Pendrick, G. "Μονογενής", *NTS* 41 (1995), 587–600.
Percy, E. *Untersuchung über den Ursprung der johanneischen Theologie. Zugleich ein Beitrag zur Entstehung des Gnostizismus* (Lund 1939).
Perschbacher, W. J. *New Testament Greek Syntax. An Illustrated Manual* (Chicago 1995).
Person Jr., R. F. *The Deuteronomic School. History, Social Setting and Literature* (Studies in Biblical Literature 2; Atlanta 2002).
Petersen, S. "Die Ich-bin-Worte als Metaphern am Beispiel der Lichtmetaphorik", *Imagery in the Gospel of John*. Ed. J. Frey et al. (WUNT 200; Tübingen 2006), 121–138.

–, *Brot, Licht und Weinstock. Intertextuelle Analysen johanneischer Ich-bin-Worte* (NovTSup 127; Leiden 2008).
Philo, A. *Philo*. Ed. and tr. F. H. Colson and G. H. Whitaker (LCL; London 1949–1963), I–XI.
Pietersma, A. and Wright, B. G. (ed.), *A New English Translation of the Septuagint* (Oxford 2007).
Pindar, *Olympian Odes. Pythian Odes*. Ed. and tr. W. H. Race (LCL 56; Cambridge 1997), I.
Plato, *Euthyphro, Apology, Crito, Phaedo, Phaedrus*. Tr. H. N. Fowler (LCL 36; Cambridge 1914).
–, *Republic*. Ed. and tr. C. Emlyn-Jones and W. Preddy (LCL 237, 276; Cambridge 2013), I–II.
–, *Theaetetus, Sophist*. Tr. H. N. Fowler (LCL 123; Cambridge 1921).
Plummer, A. *A Critical and Exegetical Commentary on the Gospel According to St. Luke* (ICC; London ³1909).
Pope, M. H. *Job. Introduction, Translation and Notes* (AB 15; New Haven 1974).
Popp, T. "Die konsolatorische Kraft der Wiederholung: Liebe, Trauer und Trost in den johanneischen Abschiedsreden", *Repetitions and Variations in the Fourth Gospel. Style, Text, Interpretation*. Ed. G. van Belle et al. (Leuven 2009), 523–588.
–, "Die Tür ist offen (Die Tür) Joh 10,7–10", *Kompendium der Gleichnisse Jesu*. Ed. R. Zimmermann (Munich 2007), 781–787.
Porter, S. E. "Was John the Baptist a Member of the Qumran Community? Once More", *Christian Origins and Hellenistic Judaism. Social and Literary Contexts for the New Testament*. Ed. S. E. Porter and A. W. Pitts (TENT 10; Leiden 2013), II, 283–313.
Preuss, H. D. "בוא", *TDOT*, II, 20–49.
Pribnow, H. *Die johanneische Anschauung vom "Leben"* (Greifswald 1934).
Quasten, J. "The Parable of the Good Shepherd: John 10,1–21", *CBQ* 10 (1948), 1–12, 151–169.
Quell, G. et al., "ἀλήθεια", *TDNT*, I, 232–251.
Rahlfs, A. and Hanhart, R. (ed.), *Septuaginta. Editio altera* (Stuttgart 2006).
Ratner, R. "Derek: Morpho-Syntactical Considerations", *JAOS* 107 (1987), 471–473.
Ratzinger, J. "The Dignity of the Human Person", *Commentary on the Documents of Vatican II*. Ed. H. Vorgrimler (New York 1969), V, 136–140.
Reim, G. *Studien zum alttestamentlichen Hintergrund des Johannesevangeliums* (Cambridge 1974).
Reinhartz, A. (ed.), *God the Father in the Gospel of John* (Semeia 85; Atlanta 1999).
–, "'Jews' and Jews in the Fourth Gospel", *Anti-Judaism and the Fourth Gospel. Papers of the Leuven Colloquium, 2000*. Ed. R. Bieringer et al. (Assen 2001), 341–356.
–, "Building Skyscrapers on Toothpicks: The Literary-Critical Challenge to Historical Criticism", *Anatomies of Narrative Criticism. The Past, Present and Futures of the Fourth Gospel as Literature*. Ed. T. Thatcher and S. D. Moore (Atlanta 2008), 55–76.
–, "The Johannine Community and Its Jewish Neighbours: A Reappraisal", *What Is John? Literary and Social Readings of the Fourth Gospel*. Ed. F. F. Segovia (Atlanta 1998), II, 111–138.
–, *Befriending the Beloved Disciple. A Jewish Reading of the Gospel of John* (New York 2001).
–, *The Word in the World. The Cosmological Tale in the Fourth Gospel* (SBLMS 45; Atlanta 1992).

Rengstorf, K. H. and Justus, B. *A Complete Concordance to Flavius Josephus* (Leiden 1979), III.
Rensberger, D. "Sectarianism and Theological Interpretation in John", *What Is John? Literary and Social Readings of the Fourth Gospel*. Ed. F. F. Segovia (Atlanta 1998), II, 139–156.
Repo, E. *Der Weg als Selbstbezeichnung des Urchristentums. Eine traditionsgeschichtliche und semasiologische Untersuchung* (Helsinki 1964).
Richter, G. *Die Fußwaschung im Johannesevangelium. Geschichte und Deutung* (Regensburg 1967).
Richter, J. *'Anî Hû und Ego Eimi. Die Offenbarungsformel 'Ich bin es' im Alten und Neuen Testament* (Dissertation, Erlangen 1956).
Ridderbos, H. *The Gospel of John. A Theological Commentary*. Tr. J. Vriend (Grand Rapids 1997).
Riesenfeld, H. "Zu den johanneischen *Hina*-Sätzen", *ST* 19 (1965), 213–220.
Rissi, M. "Der Aufbau des Vierten Evangeliums", *NTS* 29 (1983), 48–54.
Robertson, A. T. *A Grammar of the Greek New Testament in the Light of Historical Research* (London ³1919).
Römer, T. *The So-Called Deuteronomistic History. A Sociological, Historical and Literary Introduction* (London 2005).
Sabbe, M. "John 10 and Its Relationship to the Synoptic Gospels", *The Shepherd Discourse of John 10 and Its Context*. Ed. J. Beutler and R. T. Fortna (Cambridge 1991), 75–93.
Sadananda, D. R. *The Johannine Exegesis of God. An Exploration into the Johannine Understanding of God* (BZNW 121; Berlin 2004).
Sauer, G. "הָלַךְ", *TLOT*, I, 365–370.
–, "דֶּרֶךְ", *TLOT*, I, 343–346.
Schaff, P. (ed.), *A Select Bibliography of the Nicene and Post-Nicene Fathers of the Christian Church. St. Augustine: Homilies on the Gospel of John, Homilies on the First Epistle of John, Soliloquies* (First Series; Edinburgh 1887), VII.
–, *A Select Library of the Nicene and Post-Nicene Fathers of the Christian Church. Chrysostom: Homilies on the Gospel of Saint John and Epistle to the Hebrews* (First Series; Edinburgh 1889), XIV.
Schenk, W. "νοέω", *EDNT*, II, 469–470.
Schenke, L. *Johannes. Kommentar* (Düsseldorf 1998).
Schleritt, F. *Der vorjohanneische Passionsbericht. Eine historisch-kritische und theologische Untersuchung zu Joh 2,13–22; 11,47–14,31 und 18,1–20,29* (Berlin 2007).
Schlier, H. "δείκνυμι", *TDNT*, II, 25–30.
Schmithals, W. "Der Prolog des Johannesevangeliums", *ZNW* 70 (1979), 16–43.
–, "γινώσκω", *EDNT*, I, 248–251.
Schnackenburg, R. *The Gospel According to St. John*. Tr. K. Smyth (New York 1968).
–, *The Gospel According to St. John*. Tr. C. Hastings et al. (London 1980), II.
–, *The Gospel According to St. John*. Tr. K. Smyth and G. A. Kon (New York 1982), III.
–, *The Johannine Epistles. A Commentary*. Tr. R. Fuller and I. Fuller (New York 1992).
Schneider, J. "ἔρχομαι", *TDNT*, II, 666–684.
Schneiders, S. M. "Biblical Spirituality", *Int* 56 (2002), 133–142.
Schnelle, U. "Die Abschiedsreden im Johannesevangelium", *ZNW* 80 (1989), 64–79.
–, *Das Evangelium nach Johannes* (ThHKNT 4; Leipzig ³2003).
Scholtissek, K. "Abschied und neue Gegenwart. Exegetische und theologische Reflexionen zur johanneischen Abschiedsrede Joh 13,31–17,26", *EThL* 75 (1999), 332–358.

–, *In ihm Sein und Bleiben. Die Sprache der Immanenz in den johanneischen Schriften* (HBS 21; Freiburg 2000).
Schottroff, L. "ζῶ/ζωή", *EDNT*, II, 105–109.
Schrenck, V. *Die johanneische Anschauung vom "Leben" mit Berücksichtigung ihrer Vorgeschichte* (Leipzig 1898).
Schrenk, G. and Quell, G. "πατήρ", *TDNT*, V, 945–1014.
Schuchard, B. G. *Scripture within Scripture. The Interrelationship of Form and Function in the Explicit Old Testament Citations in the Gospel of John* (SBLDS 133; Atlanta 1992).
Schulz, S. *Komposition und Herkunft der Johanneischen Reden* (Stuttgart 1960).
Schwartz, E. "Aporien im 4. Evangelium I–IV", *Nachrichten von der Königlichen Gesellschaft zu Göttingen* (Berlin 1907–1908), 115–148; 149–188; 342–372; 497–560.
Schweizer, E. *Ego Eimi. Die religionsgeschichtliche Herkunft und theologische Bedeutung der johanneischen Bildreden, zugleich ein Beitrag zur Quellenfrage des vierten Evangeliums* (Gottingen ²1965).
Scott, M. *Sophia and the Johannine Jesus* (JSNTSS 71; Sheffield 1992).
Sedlmeier, F. X. *Das Buch Ezechiel. Kapitel 1–24* (NSK.AT 21,1; Stuttgart 2002), I.
Segovia, F. F. "John", *A Postcolonial Commentary on the New Testament Writings*. Ed. F. F. Segovia and R. S. Sugirtharajah (London 2009), 156–193.
–, "The Journey(s) of the Word of God: A Reading of the Plot of the Fourth Gospel", *The Fourth Gospel from a Literary Perspective*. Ed. R. A. Culpepper and F. F. Segovia (Semeia 53; Atlanta 1991), 23–54.
–, "The Structure, *Tendenz* and *Sitz im Leben* of John 13,31–14,31", *JBL* 104 (1985), 471–493.
–, *The Farewell of the Word. The Johannine Call to Abide* (Minneapolis 1991).
Setzer, C. J. *Jewish Responses to Early Christians. History and Polemics, 30–150 CE* (Minneapolis 1994).
Sheridan, R. "John's Gospel and Modern Genre Theory: The Farewell Discourse (John 13–17) as a Test Case", *ITQ* 75 (2010), 287–299.
–, "Johannine Sectarianism: A Category Now Defunct?", *The Origins of John's Gospel*. Ed. S. E. Porter and H. T. Ong (Leiden 2016), 142–166.
Simoens, Y. *La Gloire d'Aimer. Structures stylistiques et interprétatives dans le discours de la Cène (Jn 13–17)* (AnBib 90; Rome 1981).
–, *Selon Jean* 1. *Une Traduction* (CIET 17; Brussels 1997).
–, *Selon Jean*. 3. *Une interprétation* (CIET 17; Brussels 1997).
Simon, U. E. "Eternal Life in the Fourth Gospel", *Studies in the Fourth Gospel*. Ed. F. L. Cross (London 1957), 97–109.
Simonis, A. J. *Die Hirtenrede im Johannesevangelium. Versuch einer Analyse von Johannes 10,1–18 nach Entstehung, Hintergrund und Inhalt* (AnBib 29; Rome 1967).
Smalley, S. S. "The Sign in John 21", *NTS* 20 (1974), 275–288.
Smilde, E. *Leven in de Johanneische Geschriften* (Kampen 1943).
Smith, D. M. "Postscript for Third Edition of Martyn, *History and Theology in the Fourth Gospel*" in J. L. Martyn, *History and Theology in the Fourth Gospel* (Louisville ³2003), 19–23.
Smith, E. W. (ed.), *Dictionary of Greek and Roman Biography and Mythology* (Boston 1870), III.
Snell, B. *Die Entdeckung des Geistes. Studien zur Entstehung des Europäischen Denkens bei den Griechen* (Göttingen 1993).

Söding, T. "Die Macht der Wahrheit und das Reich der Freiheit: Zur johanneischen Deutung des Pilatus-Prozesses (Joh 18,28–19,16)", *ZTK* 93 (1996), 35–58.
–, "Die Wahrheit des Evangeliums: Anmerkungen zur johanneischen Hermeneutik", *EThL* 77 (2001), 318–355.
Sophocles, *Antigone, The Women of Trachis, Philoctetes, Oedipus at Colonus*. Ed. and tr. H. Lloyd-Jones (LCL 21; Cambridge 1994).
Spicq, C. and Ernest, J. D. "ἀλήθεια", *TLNT*, I, 66–86.
Spicq, C. "ταράσσω", *TLNT*, III, 372–376.
Staley, J. F. "The Structure of John's Prologue: Its Implications for the Gospel's Narrative Structure", *CBQ* 48 (1986), 241–264.
Stare, M. "Ethics of Life in the Gospel of John", *Rethinking the Ethics of John. "Implicit Ethics" in the Johannine Writings*. Ed. J. van der Watt and R. Zimmermann (WUNT 291; Tübingen 2012), 213–228.
–, "Der Lebensbegriff als ethische Norm im Johannesevangelium", *Ethische Normen des frühen Christentums: Gut – Leben – Leib – Tugend*. Ed. F. W. Horn et al. (WUNT 313; Tübingen 2013), 257–279.
–, "Gibt es Gleichnisse im Johannesevangelium?", *Hermeneutik der Gleichnisse Jesu. Methodische Neuansätze zum Verstehen urchristlicher Parabeltexte*. Ed. R. Zimmermann (Tübingen 2008), 320–364.
–, *Durch ihn leben. Die Lebensthematik in Joh 6* (NTA.NF 49; Münster 2004).
Stauffer, E. "Ἐγώ", *TDNT*, II, 342–354.
–, *Jesus and His Story*. Tr. D. M. Barton (London 1960).
–, *Jesus: Gestalt und Geschichte* (Bern 1957).
Steegen, M. "To Worship the Johannine Son of Man. John 9,38 as Refocusing on the Father", *Bib* 91 (2010), 534–554.
Stenning, J. F. *The Targum of Isaiah* (Oxford 1953).
Stibbe, M. "Telling the Father's Story: The Gospel of John as Narrative Theology", *Challenging Perspectives on the Gospel of John*. Ed. J. Lierman (WUNT II 219; Tübingen 2006).
Stowasser, M. *Johannes der Täufer im Vierten Evangelium. Eine Untersuchung zu seiner Bedeutung für die johanneische Gemeinde* (ÖBS 12; Klosterneuburg 1992).
Strack, H. L. and Billerbeck, P. *Kommentar zum Neuen Testament aus Talmud und Midrasch. Das Evangelium nach Markus, Lukas und Johannes und die Apostelgeschichte* (Munich ²1956), II.
Stube, J. C. *A Graeco-Roman Rhetorical Reading of the Farewell Discourse* (Library of New Testament Studies 309; London 2006).
Stuckenbruck, L. T. *Angel Veneration and Christology. A Study in Early Judaism and in the Christology of the Apocalypse of John* (WUNT II 70; Tübingen 1995).
Stuhlmacher, P. *Biblische Theologie des Neuen Testaments* (Göttingen 1999), II.
Stuhlmueller, C. *Creative Redemption in Deutero-Isaiah* (AnBib 43; Rome 1970).
Sturdevant, J. S. *The Adaptable Jesus of the Fourth Gospel: The Pedagogy of the Logos* (Supplements To Novum Testamentum 162; Leiden 2015).
Tack, L. *John 14:6 in Light of Jewish-Christian Dialogue: Sharing Truth on the Way to Life* (WUNT II 557; Tübingen 2021).
–, "Onderweg met de dialogerende Jezus. Enkele hermeneutische richtlijnen bij het Jezuswoord in Joh 14,6", *Tijdschrift voor Theologie* 57 (2017), 116–133.
–, *Weg van de Waarheid? Een historisch-kritisch en hermeneutisch onderzoek van Joh 14,6 in het licht van de joods-christelijke dialoog* (Dissertation, Katholieke Universiteit Leuven 2015).

Talbert, C. H. *The Development of Christology During the First Hundred Years. And Other Essays on Early Christian Christology* (NovTSup 140; Leiden 2011).
Tate, M. E. *Psalms 51–100* (WBC 20; Dallas 1990).
Teppler, Y. Y. *Birkat haMinim. Jews and Christians in Conflict in the Ancient World* (Texts and Studies in Ancient Judaism 120; Tübingen 2007).
Tesh, S. E. and Zorn, W. D. *Psalms* (The College Press NIV Commentary; Joplin 1999), II.
Theobald, M. *Die Fleischwerdung des Logos. Studien zum Verhältnis des Johannesprologs zum Corpus des Evangeliums und zu 1 Joh* (NTA.NF 20; Münster 1988).
–, *Herrenworte im Johannesevangelium* (HBS 34; Freiburg 2002).
Thettayil, B. *In Spirit and Truth. An Exegetical Study of John 4,19–26 and a Theological Investigation of the Replacement Theme in the Fourth Gospel* (Leuven 2007).
Thiselton, A. C. "Truth", *NIDNTT,* III, 889–894.
Thomas, R. W. "The Meaning of the Terms 'Life' and 'Death' in the Fourth Gospel and in Paul", *SJT* 21 (1968), 199–212.
Thompson, L. "Hymns in Early Christian Worship", *ATR* 55 (1973), 458–472.
Thompson, M. M. "'God's Voice You Have Never Heard, God's Form You Have Never Seen': The Characterization of God in the Gospel of John", *Characterization in Biblical Literature*. Ed. A. Berlin and E. S. Malbon (Semeia 63; Atlanta 1993), 177–204.
–, "Eternal Life in the Gospel of John", *ExAud* 5 (1989), 35–55.
–, "Reflections on Worship in the Gospel of John", *Princeton Seminary Bulletin* 19 (1998), 259–278.
–, "The Living Father", *God the Father in the Gospel of John*. Ed. A. Reinhartz (Semeia 85; Atlanta 1999), 19–31.
–, "Thinking about God: Wisdom and Theology in John 6", *Critical Readings of John 6*. Ed. R. A. Culpepper (Leiden 1997), 221–246.
–, *The God of the Gospel of John* (Grand Rapids 2001).
–, *The Promise of the Father. Jesus and God in the New Testament* (Louisville 2000).
Thucydides, *History of the Peloponnesian War*. Tr. C. F. Smith (LCL 108–109; Cambridge 1920), I–II.
Thyen, H. "Aus der Literatur zum Johannesevangelium", *ThR* 42 (1977), 213–261.
–, "Ich bin das Licht der Welt. Das Ich- und Ich-bin Sagen Jesu im Johannesevangelium", *Jahrbuch für Antike und Christentum* 35 (1992), 19–46.
–, "Ich-bin Worte", *Reallexikon für Antike und Christentum* 17 (1996), 147–213.
–, "Johannes 10 im Kontext des vierten Evangeliums", *The Shepherd Discourse of John 10 and Its Context*. Ed. J. Beutler and R. T. Fortna (Cambridge 1991), 116–134.
–, *Das Johannesevangelium* (HNT 6; Tübingen 2005).
–, *Studien zum Corpus Iohanneum* (WUNT 214; Tübingen 2007).
Tidwell, N. "A Road and a Way. A Contribution to the Study of Word-Pairs", *Semitics* 7 (1980), 50–80.
–, "No Highway! The Outline of a Semantic Description of Mesilla", *VT* 45 (1995), 251–269.
Tobin, T. H. "The Prologue of John and Hellenistic Jewish Speculation", *CBQ* 52 (1990), 252–269.
–, "Logos", *ABD*, IV, 348–356.
Tolmie, D. F. "Jesus, Judas and a Morsel: Interpreting a Gesture in John 13,21–30", *Miracles and Imagery in Luke and John*. Festschrift U. Busse. Ed. J. Verheyden et al. (Leuven 2008), 105–124.
–, "The Characterization of God in the Fourth Gospel", *JSNT* 69 (1998), 57–75.

–, *Jesus' Farewell to the Disciples. John 13,1–17,26 in Narratological Perspective* (BIS 12; Leiden 1995).
Tragan, P.-R. *La Parabole du "Pasteur" et ses Explications: Jean 10,1–18. La Genèse, les Milieux littéraires* (StAns 67; Rome 1980).
Trites, A. A. *The New Testament Concept of Witness* (SNTSMS 31; Cambridge 1977).
Troost-Cramer, K. *Jesus as Means and Locus of Worship in the Fourth Gospel. Sacrifice and Worship Space in John* (Eugene 2017).
Trumbower, J. A. *Born from Above. The Anthropology of the Gospel of John* (HUT 29; Tübingen 1992).
Tschen-Emmons, J. B. *Artifacts from Ancient Rome* (Santa Barbara 2014).
Untergaßmaier, F. G. *Im Namen Jesu. Der Namensbegriff im Johannesevangelium. Eine exegetisch-religionsgeschichtliche Studie zu den johanneischen Namensaussagen* (FzB 13; Stuttgart 1973).
Urbach, E. E. "Self-Isolation or Self-Affirmation in Judaism in the First Three Centuries: Theory and Practice", *Jewish and Christian Self-Definition*. Ed. E. P. Sanders et al. (London 1981), II, 269–298.
Van der Watt, J. G. *Family of the King: Dynamics of Metaphor in the Gospel According to John* (BIS 47; Leiden 2000).
–, "Repetition and Functionality in Johannine Research: A General Historical Survey", *Repetitions and Variations in the Fourth Gospel. Style, Text, Interpretation*. Ed. G. van Belle et al. (Leuven 2009), 87–94.
–, "The Good and the Truth in John's Gospel", *Studien zu Matthäus und Johannes/Études sur Matthieu et Jean*. Festschrift J. Zumstein. Ed. A. Dettwiler and U. Poplutz (Zurich 2009), 317–333.
–, "The Use of Ἀιώνιος in the Concept Ζωή Ἀιώνιος in John's Gospel", *NovT* 31 (1989), 217–228.
–, *An Introduction to the Johannine Gospel and Letters* (London 2007).
Van Oudtshoorn, A. "Where Have All the Demons Gone?: The Role and Place of the Devil in the Gospel of John", *Neot* 51 (2017), 65–82.
Vattapparambil, S. *Ist Jesus der wahre Weg zum Heil? Eine Bibeltheologische Analyse von Joh 14,6* (Diplomarbeit, Universität Innsbruck; Innsbruck 1988).
Vellanickal, M. *The Divine Sonship of Christians in the Johannine Writings* (AnBib 72; Rome 1977).
Vereşa, O. L. "Study of the 'I Am' Phrases in John's Gospel", *Perichoresis* 6 (2008), 109–125.
Vermes, G. (tr.), *The Complete Dead Sea Scrolls in English* (London 2004), 101.
Visotzky, B. "Methodological Considerations in the Study of John's Interaction with First-Centuary Judaism", *Life in Abundance. Studies of John's Gospel in Tribute to Raymond E. Brown*. Ed. J. R. Donahue (Collegeville 2005), 91–107.
Vogel, H. "Predigt über Johannes 14,6", *BThZ* 3 (1986), 127–131.
Volf, M. *Exclusion and Embrace. A Theological Exploration of Identity, Otherness, and Reconciliation* (Nashville 1996).
Völkel, M. "ὁδός", *EDNT*, II, 491–493.
Wagner, J. *Auferstehung und Leben. Joh 11,1–12,19 als Spiegel johanneischer Redaktions- und Theologiegeschichte* (Regensburg 1988).
Walker, N. "Concerning *Hû'* and *'Ani Hû'* ", *ZAW* 74 (1962), 205–206.
Wallace, D. B. *Greek Grammar Beyond the Basics. An Exegetical Syntax of the New Testament* (Grand Rapids 1996).
Wallace, H. N. "Tree of Knowledge and Tree of Life", *ABD*, VI, 656–660.

Walsh, P. G. (tr.), *Pliny the Younger. Complete Letters* (Oxford World's Classics; Oxford 2006).
Watts, R. E. "Isaiah in the New Testament", *Interpreting Isaiah. Issues and Approaches*. Ed. D. G. Firth and H. G. M. Williamson (Downers Grove 2009), 213–233.
Webb, W. J. *Returning Home. New Covenant and Second Exodus as the Context for 2 Corinthians 6,14–7,1* (JSNTSS 85; Sheffield 1993).
Weder, H. *Einblicke ins Evangelium. Exegetische Beiträge zur neutestamentlichen Hermeneutik* (Göttingen 1992).
Wehmeier, G. "יָרַד", *TLOT*, II, 883–896.
Weidemann, H.-U. *Der Tod Jesu im Johannesevangelium. Die erste Abschiedsrede als Schlüsseltext für den Passions- und Osterbericht* (BZNW 122; Berlin 2004).
Weiss, J. *The History of Primitive Christianity*. Tr. F. Friends; ed. F. C. Grant (London 1937), I.
Wengst, K. *Das Johannesevangelium* (ThKNT 4,1–2; Stuttgart ²2004, 2001), I–II.
Wenthe, D. O. "The Rich Monotheism of Isaiah as Christological Resource", *CTQ* 71 (2007), 57–70.
Westcott, B. F. *The Gospel According to St. John. Introduction and Notes on the Authorized Version* (Cambridge 1881).
Westermann, C. *Das Buch Jesaja. Kapitel 40–66* (Göttingen 1966).
–, *Isaiah 40–66. A Commentary*. Tr. D. M. G. Stalker (Philadelphia 1969).
Weyde, K. W. *Prophecy and Teaching. Prophetic Authority, Form Problems and the Use of Traditions in the Book of Malachi* (BZAW 288; Berlin 2000).
White, R. E. O. "No One Comes to the Father but by Me", *ExpTim* 113 (2002), 116–117.
Wilckens, U. *Das Evangelium nach Johannes* (Das Neue Testament deutsch; Teilband 4; Göttingen 2000).
Williams, C. H. "Isaiah in John's Gospel", *Isaiah in the New Testament*. Ed. S. Moyise and M. J. J. Menken (London 2005), 101–116.
–, "Seeing the Glory: The Reception of Isaiah's Call-Vision in John 12,41", *Judaism, Jewish Identities and the Gospel Tradition. Essays in Honour of Maurice Casey*. Ed. J. G. Crossley (London 2010), 186–206.
–, "The Testimony of Isaiah and Johannine Christology", *'As Those Who Are Taught'. The Interpretation of Isaiah from the LXX to the SBL*. Ed. C. M. McGinnis and P. K. Tull (Leiden 2006), 107–124.
–, *I Am He. The Interpretation of 'Anî Hû in Jewish and Early Christian Literature* (WUNT II 113; Tübingen 2000).
Wilson, A. I. "Send your Truth: Psalms 42 and 43 as the Background to Jesus' Self-description as 'Truth' in John 14,6", *Neot* 41 (2007), 220–234.
Wink, W. *John the Baptist in the Gospel Tradition* (Cambridge 1968).
Winter, M. *Das Vermächtnis Jesu und die Abschiedsworte der Väter. Gattungsgeschichtliche Untersuchung der Vermächtnisrede im Blick auf Joh 13–17* (Forschungen zur Religion und Literatur des Alten und Neuen Testaments 161; Göttingen 1994).
Wolf, H. "דָּרַךְ", *TWOT*, I, 196–197.
Woll, D. B. *Johannine Christianity in Conflict. Authority, Rank and Succession in the First Farewell Discourse* (SBLDS 60; Chico 1981).
Wollenberg, R. S. "אני יי רפא: A Short Note on Ἐγώ Εἰμι Sayings and the Dangers of a Translation Tradition", *NovT* 59 (2017), 20–26.
Wright, W. M. *Rhetoric and Theology. Figural Reading of John 9* (BZNW 165; Berlin 2009).

Xenophon, *Memorabilia, Oeconomicus, Symposium, Apology*. Tr. E. C. Marchant and O. J. Todd (LCL 168; Cambridge 2013).
Yonge, C. D. *The Works of Philo. Complete and Unabridged* (Peabody 1993).
Young, F. W. "A Study of the Relation of Isaiah to the Fourth Gospel", *ZNW* 46 (1955), 215–233.
Young, R. A. *Intermediate New Testament Greek. A Linguistic and Exegetical Approach* (Nashville 1994).
Zehnder, M. P. *Wegmetaphorik im Alten Testament. Eine semantische Untersuchung der alttestamentlichen und altorientalischen Weg-Lexeme mit besonderer Berücksichtigung ihrer metaphorischen Verwendung* (BZAW 268; Berlin 1999).
Zerwick, M. and Grosvenor, M. *A Grammatical Analysis of the Greek New Testament* (Rome ⁵2010).
Zerwick, M. *Biblical Greek. Illustrated by Examples* (SPIB 114; Rome 1963).
Zimmerli, W. "Knowledge of God according to the Book of Ezekiel", *I Am Yahweh*. Ed. W. Brueggemann (Atlanta 1982), 39–63.
–, *Gottes Offenbarung. Gesammelte Aufsätze zum Alten Testament* (TB 19; Munich 1963).
Zimmermann, H. "Das absolute Ἐγώ εἰμι als die neutestamentliche Offenbarungsformel", *BZ* 4 (1960), 54–69; 266–276.
Zimmermann, J. O. *Die johanneische ἀλήθεια* (Dissertation, Freiburg 1977).
Zimmermann, R. "The Narrative Hermeneutics in John 11. Learning with Lazarus How to Understand Death, Life and Resurrection", *The Resurrection of Jesus in the Gospel of John*. Ed. C. R. Koester and R. Bieringer (WUNT 222; Tübingen 2008), 75–102.
–, *Christologie der Bilder im Johannesevangelium. Die Christopoetik des vierten Evangeliums unter besonderer Berücksichtigung von Joh 10* (WUNT 171; Tübingen 2004).
Zingg, E. *Das Reden von Gott als "Vater" im Johannesevangelium* (HBS 48; Freiburg 2006).
Zuidervaart, L. "Philosophy, Truth, and the Wisdom of Love", *Christian Scholar's Review*, 48 (2018), 31–43.
Zumstein, J. *L'Evangile selon Saint Jean 13–21* (CNT 4b; Geneva 2007).
–, "Bildsprache und Relektüre am Beispiel von Joh 15,1–17", *Imagery in the Gospel of John*. Ed. J. Frey et al. (WUNT 200; Tübingen 2006), 139–156.
–, "Intratextuality and Intertextuality in the Gospel of John", *Anatomies of Narrative Criticism. The Past, Present and Futures of the Fourth Gospel as Literature*. Ed. T. Thatcher and S. D. Moore (Atlanta 2008), 121–135.
–, "The Farewell Discourses (John 13,31–16,33) and the Problem of Anti-Judaism", *Anti-Judaism and the Fourth Gospel. Papers of the Leuven Colloquium, 2000*. Ed. R. Bieringer et al. (Assen 2001), 461–478.
–, *Das Johannesevangelium* (Kritisch-exegetischer Kommentar über das Neue Testament 2; Göttingen 2016).
–, *Kreative Erinnerung. Relecture und Auslegung im Johannesevangelium* (Zurich 1999).

Index of References

Old Testament

Genesis		8,6	61, 398
3,8	59	13,5	46
3,24	45, 71, 72, 116, 207, 398, 399, 400	18,15	97
5,22	60	*Joshua*	
5,24	60	22,1–6	61
6,9	60	23,14	68
6,12	45, 83, 86, 398	24,17	46
6,24	71		
18,19	45, 71, 398	*Judges*	
18,33	59	2,12	63, 76
28,12	66, 100	2,19	63
		2,22	61
Exodus		*1 Samuel*	
3,8	72, 119	2,10	77
3,14	297	2,31	69
13,21	45, 119, 398		
14,29	401	*1 Kings*	
16,4	316	2,3	61
19,9	69	3,14	61
20,20	69	8,36	62
20,24	69	11,33	61, 62
23,20	45, 89	11,38	61
33,13	46		
33,18	166	*2 Kings*	
34,6	229	20,17	69
		21,22	61
Numbers		*Nehemiah*	
20,17–21	86	5,9	63
21,8–9	240		
		Tobit	
Deuteronomy		1,3	206
1,30–33	119	3,2	74
1,31	46	4,5	74
5,33	47, 61, 207, 398		
8,2	119		

Index of References

4,19	74	*Proverbs*	
5,17	73	1,19	57
		8,20	57, 62
Judith		8,22	44
5,8	74	16,17	57
5,18	74	20,28	229
		22,25	57
1 Maccabees			
5,24	73	*Wisdom*	
		3,1–4	336
2 Maccabees		5,6–7	74, 206
7,9	336	10,17	74
7,14	336	12,24	74
		14,3	401
Job			
19,8	56	*Sirach*	
22,14	59	6,26	74
26,5–14	44	14,21–22	74
26,14	44	33,13	73
40,19	44	37,15	74, 206
		48,22	74
Psalms			
15,8–11	90	*Isaiah*	
16,11	70, 207	5,1–7	340
24,5	206	6,1	218, 219, 221
25,10	229	6,10	217
34,23	287	35,4	398
42–43	194	35,8–9	64, 71, 398
42,3	78, 206	35,8	58
61,8	229	40–55	209, 210
67,2	46	40	215
78,70–72	335	40,1–11	51, 213, 398
80	339	40,1–4	84
81,13	62	40,1	213
85,11	206	40,3–5	204
86,15	229	40,3–4	399
101,6	62	40,3	51, 72, 82, 84, 89, 91, 94, 97, 116, 201, 204, 205, 209, 213, 216, 223, 397, 399, 404
103,7	46		
104,3	59		
117,20	332		
117,26	77, 119, 403		
118,19–20	332	40,4	203
118,20	331, 333	40,5	213
118,26	69, 332	40,8	214
119,1	61	40,9–11	205
119,3	61	40,9–10	214, 401
119,35	57	40,9	98
119,101	56	40,11	71, 214, 398
145,17	44	40,12–31	210, 211, 212

40,18	211	31,9	55, 64
40,25	210, 211	32,39	55, 71
41,4	301	32,39–40	398
42,1–9	398		
42,1	318	*Baruch*	
42,16	52, 64	3,13	74
42,24	62	4,13	74
43,1	307		
43,9–10	305, 308	*Ezekiel*	
43,10	301, 306, 309, 310, 312	18,9	63
		21,32	69
43,11	212, 224, 305, 306	34	334
43,13	301, 311	34,1–7	335
43,16–17	401	34,11–16	334
43,19	53, 402	34,22	335
44,6	212	34,23	335
45,5–6	212	37,24–25	64
45,5	298	37,24	335
45,6	298		
45,18	212, 298, 299	*Daniel*	
45,21–22	212	7,13	69, 100
45,21	298	12,1–2	336
46,9	212	12,2	238, 336
47,8	212		
47,10	212	*Hosea*	
48,17	62	14,10	62
49,7–12	398		
49,9	53	*Micah*	
49,11	53	4,2	62
52,6	305, 306	4,5	62
52,13–14	218	5,3	335
52,13	218, 221		
53,1	217, 220, 222, 405	*Nahum*	
53,11	222	1,3	44
57,2	62		
57,14	54, 203, 205, 399	*Zephaniah*	
57,15	218, 219	3,16	98
62,10	54, 203, 205, 399		
63,14	78	*Zechariah*	
		9,9	69, 98
Jeremiah		10,12	62
2,17	46		
5,4	61	*Malachi*	
6,16	50, 57, 62	2,4–6	60
7,23	47, 61, 398	3,1	55, 72, 89, 116, 398
21,8	207		

Old Testament Pseudepigrapha

Assumption of Moses
10.1–4   182

1 Enoch
21.5   227
39.4   159
41.2   159
71.16   159

2 Enoch
61.2   159

4 Ezra
8.52–53   181

Joseph and Aseneth
8.11   159

Jubilees
12.19   367

12.20   179
20.7–9   367

Sibylline Oracles
1.15–18   367

Testament of Abraham
20.14   159

Testament of Joseph
1.1   124

Testament of Reuben
1.2–4   124

Testament of Simeon
1.2   124

Dead Sea Scrolls

CD (Damascus Document)
I,1–II,1   81
1,3   205
I,9   81
I,11   81
I,13–16   81
II,6   81
II,16   81
III,13–16   81, 207
III,15–20   84
III,15   83, 207
III,17   81
III,20   84
VIII,4–5.9   81
VIII,16   81
XI,1   81
XIX,17.21   81
XIX,29   81
XX,18   81
XX,24   81

1QH^a (Thanksgiving Hymns)
VII,22   83
XII,4   83
XII,17–18   81
XII,18–19   83
XII,21   81
XII,24   81
XII,31   83
XIV,6–7   81
XIV,20   81
XIV,21   81
XV,13b–15   83, 207
XV,31–32   83

1QM (War Scroll)
III,10   81

1QS (The Community Rule)
I,13   81
III,3   81

III,8	287		II,1–2	83
III,10	81			
III,20–21	82		*4Q200 (4QTobit^e)*	
III,26–IV,11	82		2,5	81
IV,6	227			
IV,15	82		*4Q212 (4QEnoch^g)*	
IV,20–21	227		1,iv.22	83
IV,20ff	287			
IV,22	287		*4Q223–224 (4QpapJubilees^h)*	
V,11	82		2,ii.6	81
VIII,12–16	205			
VIII,12–16	82		*4Q246 (4QAramaic Apocalypse)*	
VIII,13–16	201		1,ii.5	83
VIII,14	201			
VIII,18.21	82		*4Q256 (4QRule of the Community^b)*	
IX,2.5	81		IX,4	81
IX,17–20	82		XVIII,4	81
IX,17–18.21	205			
IX,20	201		*4Q258 (4QRule of the Community^d)*	
XI,2	82		VIII,4	82
XI,4–5	82, 207			
XI,10–11	82		*4Q259 (4QRule of the Community^e)*	
			III,4–5	82

1Q17 (1QJubilees^a)
4   81

4Q268 (Damascus Document^c)
1,16   81

1Q19 (1QNoah)
1,3   83

4Q270 (Damascus Document^e)
2,ii.20   83, 207

1QIsa^a (Great Isaiah Scroll)
work   84

4Q299 (Mysteries^a)
79,3   83, 207

4Q88 (4QPsalms^f)
VIII,4   83

4Q416 (4QSapiential Work A^b)
2,iii.14   83, 207

4Q158 (4QReworked Pentateuch^a)
1–2,10   81

4Q418 (4QSapiential Work A^a)
9+9a–c.15   83, 207

4Q161–4 (4QIsaiah Pesher^{a-d})
work   84

4Q420–4Q421
(Ways of Righteousness^{a-b})
Work   83

4Q180 (4QAges of Creation)
5–6,3   81

4Q429 (4QHymns^c)
4,i.10   81

4Q184 (4QWiles of the Wicked Woman)
1,9.14.16.17   81

4Q434 (BarkhiNafshi^a)
1,i.11   81

4Q185 (4QSapiential Work)
1–2ii,1–2   207

4Q473 (4QThe Two Ways)
Work   83

4QTanh (The Consolations)
work   84

11Q5 (Psalms Scroll[a])

XXII,10   83

11Q13 (Melchizedek)
II,24   81

11Q19 (Temple Scroll[a])
LII,14   81

New Testament

Matthew	
1,1	23
3,3	72, 397
3,7–10	399
7,13–14	89, 331
7,14	208
7,24–27	89
8,19	90
11,10	89
14,27	303
21,9	77, 98, 119
21,21–22	169
21,32	90
22,16	90, 208, 396
23,39	77, 119
24,5	303
26,22	303
26,25	303
26,31	147
28,9	376
28,17	376

Mark	
1,1	23
1,2–3	89
1,2	89
1,3	72, 89, 397
1,4–8	89
1,4–5	399
5,36	153
6,50	303
8,19	90
9,11–13	89
10,37–40	159

10,52	90
11,9	77, 98, 119
11,22	153
11,23–24	169
12,14	90, 208, 396
13,6	303
14,27	147
14,42	180
14,62	303
16,17	171, 372

Luke	
1,79	90
2,14	90
3,4–6	89
3,4	72, 92, 197, 209, 397
3,7–14	399
9,31	90
9,57	90
13,24	331
13,35	77, 119
16,9	159
19,38	77, 98, 119
20,21	90, 208, 396
22,29–30	158
22,22	160, 204
22,42	180
22,53	180
24,26	90
24,36	303
24,39	303

Index of References

24,52	376	10,16	384–385
		11,25	250
John		11,25–26	336–338
1,1–18	370	11,41–42	271
1,4	239	11,51–52	385
1,9	382	12,15	98
1,12–13	281–282	12,20–23	385–386
1,14	229, 263	12,25	251
1,17	229	12,27–28	271
1,18	263–264	12,32	386
1,23	197–201, 399	12,38–41	216–219
1,29	399	12,50	251
1,51	99	13–17	123–129
3,3–10	282–283	13–14	107–111, 129–184
3,13	100	13	139–147
3,15	240	13,1–30	139–144
3,16	241	13,1	139
3,21	229	13,2–3	140
3,35	264	13,2	399
4,14	242	13,3a	265
4,23–24	230	13,4–5	141
4,26	305–306	13,6–11	141–142
4,36	242	13,12–20	142–143
4,42	383	13,19	311–312
5	243–244, 265–268	13,21–30	143–144
5,23	370–371	13,31–38	144–147
5,33	230–231	13,31–32	145–146
6	245–249	13,33	146
6,20	306–308	13,34–35	146–147
6,27	268	13,36–38	147
6,35–51	315–317	14	147–184, 213–216
6,46	268	14,1–14	147–171
6,57	269	14,1	156–157
8,12–59	269	14,2–6	197–216
8,12	239–240, 317–319	14,2–3	158–163, 200–204, 399
8,18	308–309		
8,24	309–310	14,4–7	190–192
8,28	309–310	14,4–6	163–165
8,32	231	14,6–7	189–190
8,40	231	14,6	1–25, 164–165,
8,44	231–232		185–193, 197–216,
8,45	231		206–212, 232–252,
8,46	231		276–292, 340–351,
9,38	371–372		352–378, 381
10	249–250, 270–271	14,6a	255–260
10,1–18	319–336	14,6b	209–212, 276–290
10,1–6	325–328	14,7–14	221–223
10,7–10	328–333	14,7–11	165–168
10,11–18	334–335	14,12–14	168–171

14,13–14	372	18,26	91
14,15–31	171–180	19,9	91
14,15–24	171–175	19,23	91
14,15	172	22,4	91
14,16–17	172–173	24,14	91
14,17	233	24,22	91
14,18–21	173–174		
14,22–24	174–175	*Romans*	
14,25–31	175–180	2,6–7	389
14,25–26	176–177	5,2	203
14,27	177–178	10,9–14	376
14,28–29	178	12,19	161, 203
14,30–31	178–180	11,33	92
14,30	399		
15,1–5	338–340	*1 Corinthians*	
15,26	233	1,2	376
16,7	231	2,14	173
16,13	233	4,17	92
17,1–26	271–273	12,31	92
17,2–3	252–253		
17,2	265	*1 Timothy*	
17,17	233	2,1–7	389, 395
17,19	233	2,3–5	387
18,5–8	312–314	2,4	389
18,37–38	234–235	2,5	387
19,19–20	386		
20,17	284–286	*Hebrews*	
20,22	286–287	9,8	92
20,28	287–289	10,19–20	92, 94
20,31	253	10,19	93
		10,20	94, 208
Acts			
1,25	160	*James*	
2,21	365	1,8	93
2,25–28	90	5,13–15	365
2,28	208	5,20	93
3,6	365, 366		
4,12	363–366, 374, 378, 386–387, 416–417	*2 Peter*	
		2	93
7,55–60	162	2,2	93
9,2	91	2,15–16	93
9,14	366	2,15	93
9,21	366	2,21	93
13,10	92		
14,16	92	*1 John*	
16,17	91–92, 389	1,1	239
17,26	389	1,6	229
18,25	91		

3,1	286	*Revelation*	
3,8–10	359	1,17	313
3,8	181, 401	1,18	243
3,14	110	4,10–11	288
3,18–19	234	5,6–14	376
4,6	230, 232, 409	7,17	259
5,3	172	12,8	161
5,6	233, 409	12,9	179
5,11	240	15,3	93
5,19	181	16,12	93
		20,2	179
Jude		21,9–22,5	158
11	93	21,22	159
		22,14	181

New Testament Apocrypha

Acts of John		*Acts of Peter*	
42	367	21	367
43	367	39	367
44	367		
77	368	*Acts of Thomas*	
85	368	25	368

Acts of Paul
PHeid p.6   367

Philo of Alexandria

De Abrahamo		95	87
172	87		
204	85	*De congressu eruditionis gratia*	
269	85	10	85
		170	86
De aeternitate mundi			
109	85	*De vita contemplativa*	
		86	85
De agricultura			
104	85	*De decalogo*	
177	85	81	87, 207
De confusione linguarum		*Quod deterius potiori insidari soleat*	
4	87	19	85

21	85	174	87
24	85		
29	87, 207	*De vita Mosis*	
114–118	87, 207	1.86	87
114	87	1.164	87
		1.166	87
Quod Deus sit immutabilis		1.177	85
61	85	1.195	85
142–143	13, 20	1.290	87
142–144	86	2.138	85
142–183	86	2.189	85
159–161	13, 20	2.265	87
180	85, 86		
181–182	87	*De opificio mundi*	
		101	85
De ebrietate		114	85
150	85		
		De plantatione	
De fuga et inventione		37	85, 207
21	85	97–98	85
De gigantibus		*De posteritate Caini*	
55	87	7	85
64	86	31	87
		101–102	86
Quis rerum divinarum heres sit		102	13, 20, 86
149	85	154	85
		167–168	297
De Iosepho			
212	85	*De praemiis et poenis*	
		1.167	87
Legum allegoriae			
1.5–6	266	*Quaestiones et solutiones in Exodum*	
1.57	85	1.10	87, 207
2.85	87, 207	2.40	87, 207
2.98	85		
3.40	87, 207	*De somniis*	
3.253	85	1.3	87
		1.71	87
Legatio ad Gaium		1.179	85, 87
118	371	1.237	85
216	85	1.246	85
		I.256	158
De migratione Abrahami		2.161	85
143	87, 207		
146	86	*De specialibus legibus*	
170–171	87, 207	1.132	85
171	87, 207	1.192	85
173–174	87	1.215	85

1.243	85	4.111	85
1.300	85	4.154	85
1.335	85	4.168	86
3.29	85		
4.108	85		

Josephus Flavius

Antiquitates judaicae (A.J)		16.258	203
2.133	88	17.84	88
2.175	88		
2.338	88	*Bellum judaicum (B.J.)*	
2.339	88	2.212	88
3.86	88	2.551	88
6.34	88	5.402	88
7.31	88		
8.227	88	*Vita*	
8.235	88	108	88
8.330	88	118	88
9.84	88	241	88
12.198	88	253	88
13.290	88		

Rabbinic Literature

Mishnah Sukkah		*Targum Isaiah*	
4:5	302	6:1	217
5:2–3	318		
5:4	332		

Early Christian Literature

Augustine		*Didache*	
Tract. Ev. Jo.		1–6	89
(In Evangelium Johannis tractatus)		1.1	89
68,2	161		
69.2	260	Eusebius	
		Praeparatio Evangelica	
1 Clement		IX.xxvii.22–26	313
7.5	203		
48.2–4	331	Ignatius of Antioch	
		Ephesians	
Clement of Alexandria		7.2	375
Stromata		18.2	375
I.xxiii	313	19.3	375

Philadelphians
9.1 344

Philippians
4.1 247

To Polycarp
8.3 375

Romans
3.3 375
6.3 375
7.3 247

Smyrnaeans
7.1 247

Trallians
7.1 375

John Chrysostom
Homiliae in Joannem
59 329

Justin Martyr
Apologia 1
66 247

Shepherd of Hermas
Similitude
IX.xii.5–6 344

Graeco-Roman Literature

Aeschylus
Agamemnon
80 35

Eumenides
989 35

Celsus
On the True Doctrine
116–117 368

Euripides
Fragments
289 35

Heraclitus
Fragments
60 35, 397

Herodotus
Histories
I.8–10 36
1.11.2 36
1.95.1 35
1.104 35

Hesiod

Works and Days
286–292 36, 85

Homer
Iliad
1.151 35
2.273 35
2.285 35
8.150 35
12.168 34
16.374 34

Odyssey
17.196 34

Lucian of Samosata
Hermotimus
46 38

The Death of Peregrine
11–13 368

Parmenides
On Nature
1.1–30 37
1.5 35
1,10 37

1,20	37	*Theaetetus*	
1,25	37	208b	38
2,1–5	37, 396		
8,1-4	396	*Phaedrus*	
8,1	38	263b	38

Pindar
Olympian Odes
8.13   35

Plato
Apology
Work   124

Phaedo
Work   124
116a   173

Republic
4.435a   38
7.514b   38
7.533b   38
10.600b   35

Sophist
218d   38

Pliny the Younger
Epistle
10.96.6   375
10,96.7   375

Sophocles
Antigone
807   35

Tacitus
Annals
15.62   124

Thucydides
History of the Peloponnesian War
3.64.4   36

Xenophon
Memorabilia
2.1.21–34   36

Index of Modern Authors

Aalen, S., 228
Abbott, E., 157, 264
Abegg Jr., M. G., 80
Adams, E., 376
Aitken, J. K., 40–42
Akpunonu, P. D., 52
Aland, B., XIX
Aletti, J.-N., 131
Allen, L. C., 47
Anderson, P. N., 245, 293, 303–304, 352, 362
Appasamy, A. J., 237
Arenas, J. V., 331
Arens, E., 96–99, 101, 104, 114, 118–119
Ashton, J., 8, 125, 238, 293, 370
Attridge, H. W., 89, 125
Augenstein, J., 134
Aune, D. E., 94, 369–370, 374, 378

Back, F., 131, 134–135, 158, 165, 287–288
Baker, D. W., 66
Ball, D. M., 6–7, 204–205, 258, 293–294, 296–297, 300, 305–309, 311–312, 315–318, 331, 335–340, 350, 360, 404
Bammel, E., 124, 127
Barrett, C. K., 104, 128, 131, 148, 202, 234, 236, 247–248, 255, 266–268, 270–271, 282, 287, 318, 321, 328–329, 334, 364, 370, 372, 384, 386
Bartholomä, P. F., 208
Barton, S. C., 380, 394
Bauckham, R. J., 93, 210–211, 218–219, 225, 355, 364, 366–367, 369, 371, 374
Bauer, W., 149, 154
Beasley-Murray, G. R., 131, 155, 157, 166, 169, 229, 235, 239, 255, 263, 270, 306, 309, 328, 331
Becker, H., 315
Becker, J., 131, 133, 237, 258
Becker, O., 34, 343

Beekes, R., 34
Behm, J., 156
Bennema, C., 409
Benoit, A., 285
Berges, U. F., 51
Bernard, J. H., 136, 149, 169–170, 256–257, 322, 330
Bernier, J., 355
Betz, O., 244
Beuken, W. A. M., 52
Beutler, J., 12, 24, 105, 123, 131, 133–135, 137, 154, 158, 163, 171, 174, 176–177, 179–180, 194, 196, 219, 222, 245, 258, 311, 320, 328, 331, 362, 384
Beveridge, P. J., 294
Bieringer, R., 14, 284–285, 337, 354, 356, 358–359, 374
Billerbeck, P., XX
Bird, M. F., 365
Blank, J., 228, 308
Blass, F., XVIII, 255
Blenkinsopp, J., 54, 201, 205, 256, 308
Boismard, M.-E., 159
Borgen, P., 21, 85, 228, 316
Borig, R., 339
Bovon, F., 368
Braumann, G., 294
Brendsel, D. J., 216–220, 224
Briley, T. R., 202
Brock, S., 117
Brockington, L. H., 214
Brodie, T. L., 362
Brown, C., XIX
Brown, F., XVIII
Brown, R. E., 12, 22, 25, 95, 98–100, 102, 104–105, 114, 127–129, 131, 133–135, 139–143, 145–148, 157, 162, 166–168, 170–175, 177–178, 180–181, 189, 198, 202, 206, 222, 226–230, 232–234, 237–242, 244, 246–250, 252–255, 258, 264–268, 270–271, 278, 281–284, 286–289, 293, 295, 300, 304, 306–307, 311,

313, 316–319, 322, 326–328, 331,
  339–341, 344–345, 350, 354, 356–
  357, 362, 370, 372, 384, 386, 412
Brown, S., 177
Brunson, A. C., 97–98, 119, 328–333,
  348, 400
Büchsel, F., 228
Bühner, J. A., 103, 118, 293, 315
Bultmann, R., 128, 135, 148, 150, 233,
  238, 260, 295, 360
Burridge, R. A., 355
Bury, R. G., 313
Busse, U., 135, 144, 320
Buth, R., 130

Campbell, R. J., 228
Carr, G. L., 65
Carson, D. A., 1, 149, 157, 165, 169–
  170, 272, 339, 356, 373, 384
Cebulj, C., 7–8, 258, 293, 296–297,
  302, 346, 362
Chantraine, P., 34
Charles, R. H., 4, 287, 375
Charlesworth, J. H., 1, 8, 185–188, 191–
  193, 200–201, 352–353, 357
Charlier, J.-P., 309
Chenattu, R., 177
Chibici-Revneanu, N., 145
Childs, B., 54
Clines, D. J. A., 40
Coetzee, J. C., 308
Colacrai, A., 248
Collins, B. J., 81, 85
Coloe, M. L., 131–132, 205, 224
Conrad, E. W., 210
Conzelmann, H., 240
Coppes, L. J., 66–67
Cordero, N. L., 37–38
Coutts, J. J. F., 224, 372–373
Coxon, P. S., 400
Crossan, J. D., 245, 315–316, 327
Cullmann, O., 373
Culpepper, R. A., 5–6, 24, 30, 105,
  131–132, 199, 209, 237, 245, 247,
  261, 307, 319, 362, 374, 379, 382

Dahl, N. A., 92–93
Dahms, J. V., 263
Dahood, M. J., 44, 46

Daly-Denton, M., 375
Davidson, R., 46
Davies, M., 311, 313, 356, 360
Davies, W. D., 89–90
Davis, C. J., 202
De Jonge, M., 129
De Kruijf, T. C., 263
De la Potterie, I., 3–4, 6, 12, 165, 187–
  188, 226–228, 233, 255, 409
De Pury, A., 61
De Vaux, R., 297
De Villiers, S. L., 320
De Witt Burton, E., 284
Delling, G., 139
Dennis, J. A., 385
Derrett, J. D. M., 320
Dettwiler, A., 17, 123, 128, 131, 134–
  136, 149, 165, 169, 227, 395
Dewey, K. E., 327–328
Diesel, A. A., 298
Dietzfelbinger, C., 131, 133, 149, 170,
  202, 260, 419
Dodd, C. H., 21, 170, 226, 228, 230,
  232, 238, 265–266, 271, 283, 285,
  300, 307, 336–337, 339
Dorsey, D. A., 40–42, 56–57
Du Rand, J. A., 135, 184
Dunn, J. D. G., 359, 366, 370, 372–
  373, 376
Dupriez, B. M., 187
Dupuis, J., 25, 391–392, 394, 418
Durham, J. I., 46, 297

Ebel, G., 35, 91, 203
Elledge, C. D., 84
Elliott, J. K., 368
Erlemann, K., 330
Ernest, J. D., 226, 228
Ernst, J., 204

Fascher, E., 331
Fee, G. D., 169, 253
Fensham, F. C., 4–5
Feuillet, A., 293
Finkel, S. A., 354
Fischer, G., 149, 154, 158–159, 164
Fitzgerald, M. L., 392
Fitzmyer, J. A., 90–92, 201
Flannery, A., 388

Fleischhauer, T., 33–34
Fletcher-Louis, C., 374
Fohrer, G., 158
Fortna, R. T., 320, 322
Fowler, F. G., 368
Fowler, H. W., 368
Fox, M. V., 44
Franke, J. R., 11
Freed, E. D., 195, 224, 294, 316
Frey, J., 20–21, 131, 134–135, 161–162, 214, 219, 356, 375
Frey, J.-B., 237
Fuglseth, K. S., 361

Gebauer, R., 228
George, R. B., 25
Gilbert, R. W., 25
Glancy, J. A., 228, 235
Godley, A., 36
Gollwitzer, H., 1, 4, 260, 378
Griffiths, D. R., 224
Gros, A., 3, 40, 70, 398, 400–401
Grosvenor, M., 154
Gubler, M. L., 25
Guelich, R. A., 89
Gundry, R. H., 352

Haenchen, E., 140, 161
Hagan, H., 369
Hahn, F., 331
Hahn, H.-C., 240
Hajduk, A., 293
Hakola, R., 354, 361
Hamid-Khani, S., 27, 359, 363
Hamilton, J., 8, 224, 308
Hanson, A., 224, 308
Harner, P. B., 293, 296–303, 305, 308, 313, 341, 347, 412
Harris, M. J., 360
Hasitschka, M., VII, 117, 172–173, 228, 237, 354, 359, 362, 381
Hatch, E., 73–79, 212
Hauck, F., 76, 159–160
Hawkin, D. J., 228
Hayes, J. H., 26
Heer, J., 237
Heil, J. P., 1, 25, 217, 257, 307, 315, 369–370, 384
Heitmüller, W., 373

Helfmeyer, F. J., 59–63, 76
Hengel, M., 356–357, 374, 376
Hera, M. P., 272–273
Hiers, R. H., 266
Hill, A., 55, 124
Hinrichs, B., 293, 342, 412
Hoegen-Rohls, C., 131, 237
Hoet, H., 359
Hofmann, J. C. K., 299
Holladay, C. R., 26
Holloway, P. A., 123, 125, 136, 162, 174
Horbury, W., 374
Hoskyns, E. C., 253
Hübner, H., 228
Hurtado, L. W., VII, 221–222, 225, 364–367, 369–372, 374, 376, 378

Ibuki, Y., 228

Jacobs, M. R., 61
Jenni, E., XXI, 58, 64, 68
Jeremias, G., 244
Jeremias, J., 328, 330
Jerumanis, P.-M., 237
Johnston, P. S., 213
Jones, L. P., 282
Junod, E., 368
Justus, B., 88

Kambeitz, T., 331
Kanagaraj, J. J., 369
Katz, S. T., 354
Kee, H. C., 228
Keener, C. S., 131, 141, 143, 153, 200, 204, 218, 242, 251, 253, 255, 267, 270, 281, 286, 345, 356, 370, 372, 383–384, 386
Kellum, L. S., 127–128, 131, 134–135, 149, 171
Kennedy, G. A., 124, 128
Kiefer, O., 320, 325, 328
Kilburn, K., 38
Kilpp, N., 55
Kim, D., 362
Kimelman, R., 354
Kirchschläger, P. G., 11–12, 131, 226–227, 229, 232

Index of Modern Authors

Klauck, H.-J., 140
Klink III, E. W., 354–356, 361
Knoppers, G. N., 61
Kobel, E., 248
Koch, K., 40–42, 46, 49, 56–57, 207
Koester, C. R., 10, 27, 179, 276, 290, 337, 341, 409
Koester, H., 181
Kohlenberger III, J. R., 42
Köstenberger, A. J., 22, 100–101, 113, 131, 135, 168, 170, 228, 235–236, 256, 273, 373, 377, 384
Kovacs, J. L., 140, 179–180
Kowalski, B., 227, 319–321, 323–324, 326, 328, 333
Kühschelm, R., VII, 217–218, 251
Kundsin, K., 162
Kundzins, K., 302
Kuschke, K., 40, 71
Kuyper, L. J., 226
Kysar, R., 95, 319, 356, 362

Labahn, M., 245, 356
Lacomara, A., 123
Lagrange, M.-J., 167, 257, 373
Lake, K., 25, 55, 61, 331, 344, 375
Lamb, D. A., 200, 231, 274, 361, 383
Lampe, F. A., 299
Lang, M., 125
Lasic, H., 237
Lee, D. A., 307, 371
Léon-Dufour, X., 163, 194, 255
Levinsohn, S. H., 169
Lewis, K. M., 319–320, 323, 328
Liddel, H. G., XIX
Lieu, J. M., 356
Lim, B. H., 51, 54, 400
Lincoln, A. T., 149, 169–170, 210, 212, 219, 224, 308
Lindars, B., 92, 95, 197, 218
Lindsay, D. R., 228
Link, H. G., 238, 294
Lisowsky, G., 42
Louw, J. P., 107–108
Lund, Ø., 40, 51–54, 238
Lust, J., 73, 75–79

MacArthur, J., 91
Macaskill, G., 293

MacGregor, K. R., 395
Mack, B. L., 87
Mallen, P., 91
Marcus, J., 89, 204
Marottikaparambil, T., 240, 317–318
Marshall, I. H., 91
Martens, E. A., 68
Martin, J. P., 320, 348
Martínez, F. G., 80, 83
Martyn, J. L., 91, 353–356, 377, 414–415
Matera, F. J., 142
Mathew, B., 141
Mathys, F., 40
Mayer, R., 7
McCaffrey, J., 149, 159, 161, 214
McCasland, S. V., 91
McConville, J. G., 61
McGowan, A. B., 370
McGrath, J. F., 402
Meeks, W. A., 382
Menken, M. J. J., 198–199, 217, 221, 223–224, 247
Merrill, E. H., 40–41, 47, 55, 57–58, 63
Metzger, B. M., 148, 150–151, 239, 250, 312, 328, 336, 371
Meyer, P. W., 261–262, 274, 290, 320
Michaelis, W., 2–3, 35–37, 39, 73, 79, 86, 89, 167
Michel, D., 298
Michel, O., 157, 159
Milligan, G., 340
Minear, P. S., 253
Miranda, J. P., 118
Moloney, F. J., 24–25, 131–132, 134–135, 161–163, 166, 249, 255, 284, 305, 370–371, 383–384
Moltmann, J., 382, 419
Moon, J. N., 55
Morgenstern, J., 332
Morris, L., 136, 153, 157, 169, 171, 222, 235, 327, 329, 334, 384–385
Motyer, S., 357
Moule, C. F. D., 201
Moulton, J. H., 153–154, 340
Muilenburg, J., 40, 45, 51
Muraoka, T., 40, 76–78
Murphy, R. E., 303
Murtonen, A., 298

Mussner, F., 237, 254

Natividad, Ma. L. C., 12
Neef, H-D., 80, 83–84
Neuner, J., 391–392, 394
Neusner, J., 318
Newman, B. M., 154, 169, 208, 229, 249, 254, 259, 282, 327, 330, 365
Newman, C. C., 374
Neyrey, J. H., 126–127, 319, 369, 373, 417
Nicholson, G. C., 99
Nida, E. A., 107–108, 143, 154, 169, 229, 249, 254, 259, 282, 327, 330, 365
Niederwimmer, K., 89
Niemand, C., VII, 141
Nissen, J., 379
Norden, E., 296
Nötscher, F., 40–41, 74, 80, 84, 402

O'Collins, G., VII, 381–382, 388–389, 390, 392, 394, 419
O'Day, G. R., 25, 97–101, 128, 131–132, 135–136, 140, 157, 240, 243–244, 247, 249–250, 253, 258, 265, 267, 270–271, 289, 305–307, 315, 321, 323, 331, 334, 336–337, 339, 345, 370
Obermann, A., 223–224
Okure, T., 113
Oswalt, J. N., 52

Painter, J., 224, 331
Pamment, M., 5
Pao, D. W., 91–92, 205, 214
Parrinder, G., 25
Parsenios, G. L., 123, 125, 128, 304
Pascher, J., 86
Pathrapankal, J., 91
Patterson, R. D., 58
Pendrick, G., 263
Percy, E., 238
Perschbacher, W. J., 257
Person Jr., R. F., 61
Petersen, S., 19, 293, 295–297, 302, 311, 313, 338
Pietersma, A., 309

Plummer, A., 90
Pope, M. H., 44, 323, 390–393
Popp, T., 135, 344
Porter, S. E., 201, 297, 362
Preuss, H. D., 68
Pribnow, H., 237, 254

Quasten, J., 320, 326
Quell, G., 226–228, 235, 260

Ratner, R., 40, 42
Ratzinger, J., VIII, 388
Redpath, H., 73–79, 212
Reim, G., 224–225, 335
Reinhartz, A., 95, 261, 320, 325–327, 331, 333, 354–356, 360, 363, 377
Rengstorf, K. H., 88
Rensberger, D., 128, 352
Repo, E., 80, 84, 207
Richter, G., 141
Richter, J., 300, 307, 341, 347, 411
Ridderbos, H., 1
Riesenfeld, H., 253
Rissi, M., 105
Robertson, A. T., 257
Römer, T., 61, 125

Sabbe, M., 330
Sadananda, D. R., 261, 264
Sauer, G., 40, 42, 44, 58, 63
Schaff, P., 161, 260, 329
Schenk, W., 221
Schenke, L., 131, 137
Schleritt, F., 131, 136, 284
Schlier, H., 166
Schmithals, W., 166, 370
Schnackenburg, R., 1, 12, 22, 104, 128, 131, 133–134, 136, 139, 145, 148, 157, 160–162, 165, 167–169, 181, 217–218, 223, 226–229, 231–233, 235–237, 241–242, 244, 246, 248, 250, 253, 255, 263–265, 268, 270, 272, 279, 281, 283–284, 288, 293, 295, 297, 300, 306–307, 316–317, 328, 331, 333, 338, 340, 342–343, 347, 350, 370, 372–373, 383–386
Schneider, G., XVIII
Schneider, J., 77, 96

Schneiders, S. M., 16, 27
Schnelle, U., 125, 131, 135–136, 149, 162, 257, 331, 384, 419
Scholtissek, K., 128, 163, 168, 175
Schottroff, L., 238
Schrenck, V., 237
Schrenk, G., 260
Schuchard, B. G., 198, 223–224
Schulz, S., 76, 294, 315
Schwartz, E., 128
Schweizer, E., 293, 296, 299
Scott, M., 87, 300, 302–303
Scott, R., XIX
Sedlmeier, F. X., 298
Segovia, F. F., 105, 123, 128–129, 131, 133, 135–136, 149
Setzer, C. J., 354
Sheridan, R., 123–126, 362
Simoens, Y., 22, 128, 131, 149
Simon, U. E., 237
Simonis, A. J., 320, 331, 333, 348
Smalley, S. S., 253
Smilde, E., 237
Smith, D. M., 356
Smith, E. W., 36
Snell, B., 34
Söding, T., 228
Spicq, C., 156, 226, 228
Staley, J. F., 105
Stare, M., 237, 245, 248, 315, 326, 333, 346
Stauffer, E., 294, 300, 305, 307
Steegen, M., 371
Stenning, J. F., 311
Stibbe, M., 261
Stine, P. C., 208
Stowasser, M., VII, 200
Strack, H. L., XX
Stube, J. C., 128, 212
Stuckenbruck, L. T., 364, 375
Stuhlmacher, P., 331
Stuhlmueller, C., 211, 369
Sturdevant, J. S., 20
Swanson, J. A., 42, 56, 58, 64–65, 68

Tack, L., 1, 8, 12–26, 131, 134–135, 138, 186, 195, 199, 227, 236, 255, 294, 352, 357, 380, 410, 412, 415
Talbert, C. H., 118

Tate, M. E., 46
Teppler, Y. Y., 354
Tesh, S. E., 47
Thatcher, T., 8, 27, 131, 205, 356
Theobald, M., 8–9, 185, 187–188, 205, 209, 255, 257–258, 263, 319, 328, 330–331, 344–345
Thettayil, B., 230
Thiselton, A. C., 226–229, 231, 235
Thomas, R. W., 237
Thompson, L., 370
Thompson, M. M., 22, 237, 258–259, 261–262, 267, 269, 290–292, 371, 373–375, 377
Thyen, H., 11, 19, 131, 149, 162, 165, 253, 255, 284, 293, 297, 300, 308, 321, 328, 363, 370, 384
Tidwell, N., 40
Tigchelaar, E. J. C., 80, 83
Tobin, T. H., 21, 370
Tolmie, D. F., 128, 131, 135, 144, 261
Tragan, P.-R., 320
Trites, A. A., 308
Troost-Cramer, K., 369, 377
Trumbower, J. A., 283
Tschen-Emmons, J. B., 369
Turner, N., 153–154

Untergaßmaier, F. G., 372
Urbach, E. E., 354

Van der Watt, J. G., 19, 229, 233, 243, 249, 279–280, 289–290, 292, 319, 324–325, 327–330, 334, 338, 411
Van Oudtshoorn, A., 179–180
Vattapparambil, S., 25
Vellanickal, M., 238, 281–283
Vereşa, O. L., 293
Vermes, G., 82–83, 117, 287
Visotzky, B., 354
Vogel, H., 25
Volf, M., 235
Völkel, M., 203

Wagner, J., 237, 298
Walker, N., 297, 300
Wallace, D. B., 154–155, 232
Wallace, H. N., 117

Walsh, P. G., 375
Watts, R. E., 221
Webb, W. J., 55
Weder, H., 245
Wehmeier, G., 66
Weidemann, H.-U., 131, 133, 135
Weiss, J., 378
Wengst, K., 131, 149, 284, 311
Wenthe, D. O., 211
Westcott, B. F., 169, 329
Westermann, C., XXI, 52, 309
Weyde, K. W., 55
White, R. E. O., 9, 117
Wilckens, U., 22, 351
Williams, C. H., 198–200, 217, 219, 223–224, 293, 297–314
Wilson, A. I., 194
Wink, W., 204, 406
Winter, M., 123–124
Wolf, H., 40, 67–68
Woll, D. B., 135, 183–184, 415
Wollenberg, R. S., 293, 315

Wright, B. G., 309
Wright, W. M., 354

Yonge, C. D., 86–87, 266
Young, F. W., 224–225, 305–306
Young, R. A., 154–155, 232, 257

Zehnder, M. P., 40, 42–44, 70
Zerwick, M., 154–155
Zimmerli, W., 298, 309
Zimmermann, H., 294, 297–300, 302, 341, 346, 412
Zimmermann, J. O., 228
Zimmermann, R., 19, 300, 319, 325–326, 329, 333–334, 337–338
Zingg, E., 261
Zorn, W. D., 47
Zuidervaart, L., 397
Zumstein, J., 1, 22, 27, 128, 130–131, 162, 165, 197, 227, 255, 284, 338–339, 358

Index of Subjects

Abraham 45, 71, 86, 218, 241, 270, 310–311, 344, 398
Anti-Judaism/anti-Judaistic 12, 16, 357–363, 377, 379, 390, 392, 414–415

Belief in Jesus 99, 112, 115, 152, 156–157, 167–171, 220, 222, 240–242, 250, 254, 278–282, 311, 327–328, 337–338, 401, 403, 411
Bread of life 100, 245–248, 315–317, 383

Children of God 146, 279–287, 385, 410–411
Christ
– cosmic 5–6, 382
– cultic veneration of/devotion to/worship of 126–127, 284–285, 287, 363–378, 416–417
– glory of 102, 145–146, 178, 204–205, 217–219, 221–222, 224, 263, 272, 288, 360, 367, 376, 405
– uniqueness of 11, 290, 419
– universal 9
– *see also* Jesus
Christology
– exclusive/exclusivistic 6, 17, 289–290, 347–348, 352–357, 363–369, 379, 387
– high 12, 356–357, 362, 372, 374–378
– of divine identity 219, 222
Competition hypothesis 203–204, 406
Cosmic conflict 111, 137, 139–141, 176, 178–181, 399
Covenant 47, 61–64, 70–71, 74, 80–84, 171, 177
– new 55, 64, 71, 289, 387, 398
Cult, *see* Christ (cultic veneration of/devotion to/worship of)

Devil/Ruler of the world/Satan 107–108, 110–111, 130, 137, 139–140, 144, 177–182, 184, 203, 231–232, 265, 282, 359, 384, 386, 396, 399, 401, 404, 408, 410, 414
Discipleship 111–113, 406–407
Door/Gate 54, 99–100, 112, 187, 208, 249, 259, 278, 290–291, 295, 319, 322–336, 343–348, 413–414
– relation between gate/door and way 343–345, 413–414
Dwelling place 148, 158–161, 175, 202, 381

Ego eimi formula/sayings
– classification 295–296
– *ego eimi* with images 314–340
– *ego eimi* without images 304–314
– in relation to John 14,6 340–351, 411–413
– preliminary remarks 293–294
– sources and background 296–304
– structure 192, 315
Eucharist 246–248, 317, 340, 369–370, 417
Exclusivism, *see* Christology (exclusive/exclusivistic)
Expulsion from the synagogue 7, 124, 185, 352–357, 361–362, 377, 414–415

Family of God/the Father 158, 279–292, 381, 400, 410–411
Father's house 15, 102, 117, 119–120, 148, 151, 158–165, 175, 181–184, 190, 202–203, 205, 213–214, 223, 275, 381, 401, 403–404, 406
Flock 46, 52, 54, 66, 328–329, 335, 348, 384–386, 395, 417
Farewell discourse
– backdrop of farewell discourse 139–144
– genre of farewell discourse 123–127
– structure of farewell discourse 129
– structure of John 13–14 129–138
– unity of farewell discourse 127–129

Gentiles 92, 112, 384–387
Glorification 102, 109, 113, 131–134, 137, 139, 144–146, 166, 168, 171, 182, 202, 204–205, 214, 219, 251–252, 272, 285, 310, 386, 411
God the Father 260–292, 381, 390, 400, 410–411
– believers' relationship with the Father 274–292
– Jesus' relationship with the Father 262–274
Greeks 10, 103, 112, 139, 145, 251, 264, 361, 385–386

Holy Spirit/Paraclete/Spirit of truth 96, 99, 101–105, 107, 113, 115, 120, 124–126, 132, 134, 136–137, 162–163, 167, 169–170, 172–178, 180, 183–184, 188, 213–215, 227, 223, 230–234, 236, 240–242, 254, 262, 275, 281–286, 291–292, 358, 388, 391–392, 395, 401, 403, 407, 409, 411, 418–419

Inclusivism 6, 276–278, 348, 350, 364, 379–395, 413, 417–419
Isaiah, the Book of
– influence of 194–226, 298–302, 304–314, 318, 400, 404–405, 411–412
"I"-style speeches 302–303
Inter-religious dialogue/Approach of the Catholic Church 388–395, 417–419

Jesus
– as the preparer of the way 160–161, 198–205, 405–406
– in the name of Jesus 363–366, 369–370, 372–373
– see also Christ
John the Baptist 89–91, 94, 97, 99, 114, 161, 197–201, 203–204, 230–231, 244, 294, 406,
Journey motif
– believers' journey to Jesus 111–113
– coming of God/Saviour to his people 69
– coming of the people to God 69
– going after Yahweh 63–64

– Jesus' cosmic journey 95–105, 107–111, 139–141, 178–180
– Jesus' geographical journey 105–106
– leading of God in the past 60
– leading on the way of future salvation 64
– significance of journey motif 114–115, 118–120, 180–184, 402–404
– turning aside from the way 50
– verbs of journey in the Old Testament 58–72, 75–80
– verbs of journey in the Gospel of John 94–115
– walking in the ways of God 61–63, 74, 81, 83, 86
– walking of God 59
– walking with/before God 60
Judas Iscariot 107–109, 129–132, 138–146, 178–184, 204, 314, 399, 401, 408

Lamb of God 117, 200, 231, 274, 383, 400
Life/eternal life in John 237–255, 266, 269, 315–317, 336–338, 345–347
– belief and life 240–241
– commandment and eternal life 251
– earthly life and eternal life 251
– gate/shepherd and life 249–250
– Jesus as the life 252
– Jesus' authority over life 243–244
– Jesus' words and life 248–249
– knowledge of God/Jesus and eternal life 252–253
– light and life 239–240
– purpose of the gospel and life 253
– reaping for eternal life 242
– resurrection and life 250
– the bread of life 245–248
– the living water and the life 241–242
– witnesses to Jesus and life 244
Light of the world 239–240, 308, 317–319, 341, 347, 349, 383–384
Living water 53, 241–242, 245
Logos 5–6, 13, 20–21, 95, 199, 236, 263, 289, 319, 382, 390
Love in John 139–143, 146–147, 172–176, 182, 184, 241, 264, 275, 282, 381–382, 384, 407, 418–419

– commandment of love 146–147

Monotheism
– Christological 219, 221–222, 224, 341–342, 361, 365–369, 373–378, 411–412, 415–418
Moses 3, 45–46, 65–66, 69, 77, 79, 82, 86–87, 97, 123, 127, 166, 178, 218, 240, 244, 267, 277, 297, 313, 317

New exodus 3, 64, 71, 98, 114, 119, 202, 205, 398, 400–402

Oneness/unity of Jesus with the Father 165–168, 262–274, 341–342, 411–412, 415–416

"Preparing a place" 160–161, 202–204

Qumran community 7, 82, 84, 91, 116, 119, 198, 201, 205, 244, 287, 399, 403

Religious pluralism and John 14,6 379–395, 417–419

Salvation, universal 214, 319, 363, 379–395, 417–418
Samaritans 10, 97, 106, 111, 115, 306, 348, 354, 361, 383
Saviour of the world 106, 112, 115, 212, 306, 383
Sectarianism, rejection of 357–363, 414–415
Shepherd discourse 319–336
– context 320–322
– Jesus as the gate 328–333
– Jesus as the good shepherd 334–335, 384–385
– structure 322–324
– the *paroimia* 325–328
Sin
– sin of Adam and Eve 45, 71-72, 116, 139, 181, 398, 400
– sin of the world 117, 203, 383, 399, 400–401
Soteriology 188, 237–255, 260, 276–291, 329, 342–343, 345–347, 350, 412

Tree of life 45, 71, 72, 116, 117, 181, 207, 398–400
Triadic pattern 184, 408–410
Trinity 171–175, 184, 408–410,
Truth 226–236, 255–260, 345, 407–408
– doing the truth 229
– grace and truth in Jesus Christ 229
– Jesus as the truth 232
– knowing and saying the Truth 231
– sanctification in the truth 233–234
– the Spirit of truth 232–233
– truth and life 231–232
– truth on trial 234–235
– witness to the truth 230–231
– worship in Spirit and truth 230

Unity of John 14,6 185–193
Universalism/universality, *see* inclusivism

Vine 134, 275, 338–340, 342, 346–350

Way 33–120, 163–165, 180–184, 194–209, 255–260, 343–345, 396–408, 413–414
– background of the way in John 14,6 197–206
– background of the way, the truth and the life in John 14,6 206–209
– Christian community as the way 91
– God as the moral administrator of the way 48
– living way 3, 92, 93, 203, 208
– preparation of the way (of the Lord) 51, 54–55, 71–72, 82, 84, 89, 94, 103, 114, 116–117, 139, 146, 161, 177, 182, 197–206, 398–400, 404, 406
– prophetic fulfilment of salvation in Jesus as the way 116–118
– Qumran community as the way 82, 84
– true way 91, 93, 183, 416
– turning aside from the way 50
– two ways 21, 36–39, 49–50, 71, 83–85, 89, 396
– way as a method 37–39, 85
– way as covenant relationship 47–48

- way as God's activity in creation 44–45
- way as God's salvation in the past 45–46
- way as God's salvation in the future 50–55
- way for the people 52, 205, 223, 404, 406
- way in classical Greek literature 33–39, 396–397
- way in Josephus Flavius 88
- way in Philo of Alexandria 85–87
- way in relation to truth and life 255–260, 407–408
- way in the Dead Sea Scrolls 80–84
- way in the Hebrew Bible 40–72
- way in the New Testament 88–94
- way in the Septuagint 72–80
- way of God 5, 12, 74, 81, 83, 90–91, 208, 396
- way of holiness 51, 58, 64, 71, 117, 398
- way of knowledge 37, 74
- way of life 5, 9, 11, 33, 43, 49, 60, 78, 83, 90, 91, 92, 93, 172, 207, 233
- way of peace 90
- way of philosophy 37–38, 86
- way of righteousness 71, 90, 93
- way of salvation 91–92, 391
- way of truth 9, 12, 35, 39, 74, 83, 93, 94, 144, 182, 206, 208, 396
- way of the Lord 6–7, 45, 47–48, 50–52, 54, 56, 61–62, 67, 70–71, 74, 91, 161, 197, 199, 201–202, 205–206, 209, 223, 398–399, 404, 406,
- way of the people 81, 84
- way of wisdom 48–49, 57, 73–74, 86–87
- way to life 94, 207, 255, 345, 407
- way to the tree of life 45, 71–72, 116–117, 398–400

World 95–96, 139–140, 382–384

Worship, *see* Christ (cultic veneration of/devotion to/worship of)